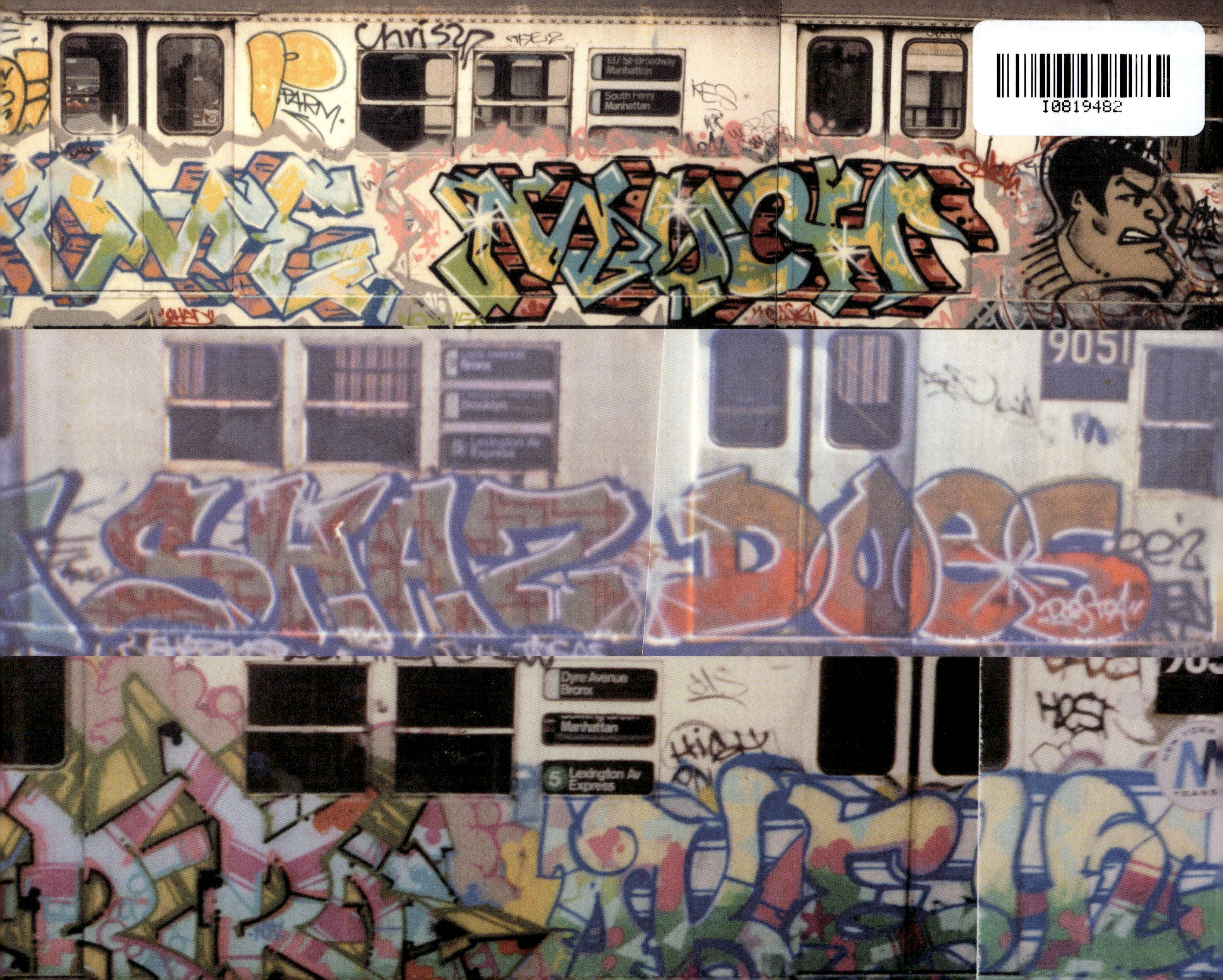

I0819482
137 St-Broadway
Manhattan
South Ferry
Manhattan
9051
Dyre Avenue
Bronx
Manhattan
5 Lexington Av
Express

From the Platform 2

More NYC Subway Graffiti, 1983–1989

Paul Cavalieri
Kenny Cavalieri
FOREWORD BY Henry Chalfant

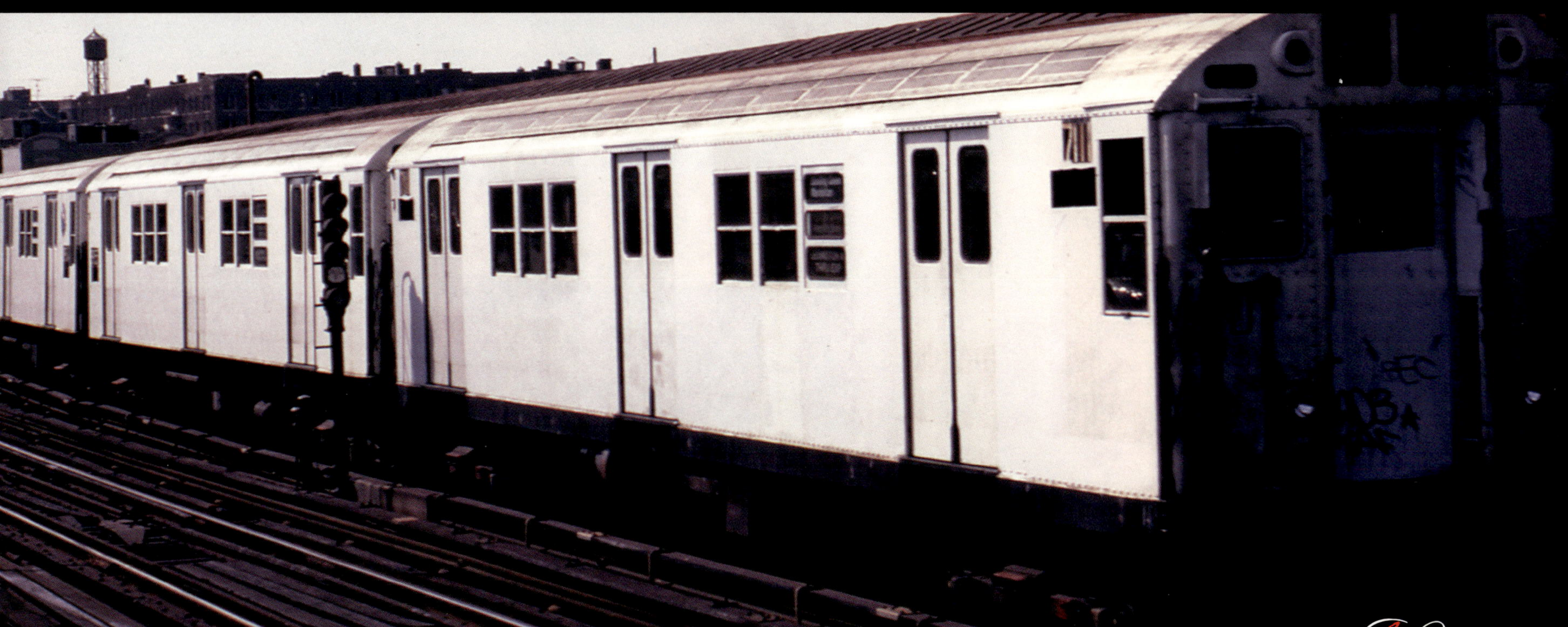

East Tremont Train Station 1983

Schiffer Publishing Ltd
4880 Lower Valley Road • Atglen, PA 19310

OTHER SCHIFFER BOOKS BY THE AUTHOR:
From the Platform: Subway Graffiti, 1983-1989, 978-0-7643-3723-9
Under the Bridge: The East 238th Street Graffiti Hall of Fame, 978-0-7643-4592-0

OTHER SCHIFFER BOOKS ON RELATED SUBJECTS:
Don1, The King from Queens: The Life and Photos of a NYC Transit Graffiti Master, Louie Gasparro, 978-0-7643-4500-5
New York Subways and Stations: 1970-1990, Tod Lange, 978-0-7643-3849-6
New York City Graffiti: The Destiny Children, George McAvoy, 978-0-7643-3720-8

Library of Congress Control Number: 2011920451

Designed by Justin Watkinson
Type set in ITC Avant Garde Gothic Std/Univers LT Std

ISBN: 978-0-7643-5290-4
Printed in China
6 5 4 3

Published by Schiffer Publishing, Ltd.
4880 Lower Valley Road
Atglen, PA 19310
Phone: (610) 593-1777; Fax: (610) 593-2002
E-mail: Info@schifferbooks.com
Web: www.schifferbooks.com

Foreword by Henry Chalfant

Graffiti writing as we think of it today is a fully developed art, accepted by many art institutions as prestigious as the Whitney Museum in New York City and the Tate Modern in London. Graffiti-based paintings are purchased and cherished by art collectors around the world. Graffiti art was born nearly five decades ago on the streets of decaying North American cities, primarily New York City where it all began. The graffiti nickname was an alternative identity for an adolescent venturing out into those streets, a chosen identity with a symbolic power often conjuring up visions of toughness or humor that helped a kid to get along in that tough environment. Tagging grew out of the territorial markings made by rival gang members to establish their boundaries. Out of such rude beginnings, amazing things happened. The innate human impulse to create form and aspire to beauty drove these youths to develop their skills, to become virtuosos of calligraphy and experts at producing attention-grabbing imagery, all contributing to the unforgettable impact of these works of art upon the eye and spirit.

Writing was not only the act of painting or tagging with marker and spray can, a craft developed by young teenagers, it was also a culture of appreciation. Benching was an integral part of the scene. Writers and a whole array of connoisseurs were constantly watching the trains and judging the skills of the painters, whether one piece burned another, and which ones deserved the "masterpiece" designation. At the bench, peers would assess the originality of a passing piece, and trace the derivation of a writer's style, determining from whom he may have bit, and judging the excellence of the hand style or tags. A whole, specialized language grew up around the practice. A painting was "fresh" or "wak," the inexperienced writer was a "toy." A long list of graffiti-related vocabulary included "burner," "throw-up," "married couple," "top-to-bottom," and "bomb." These artists and aficionados had the immense privilege of enjoying the rolling, ever-present array of works of art that were on view, courtesy of the Transit Authority of the city of New York.

I worked diligently to capture as many painted subway cars as I could starting in 1977, finally stopping my trips to the elevated lines in 1984. I slowed down in my efforts to capture every good piece that I could, because I was getting busy doing productions like *Subway Art*, *Spraycan Art*, and *Style Wars*, work which had grown out of my photo documentation. At the same time, for me, taking pictures was no longer as emotionally rewarding as it had been, because of the cross-out wars and the increased buffing activity of the Metropolitan Transportation Authority (MTA). There were still masterpieces running, works by both veteran writers whom I knew, and by new, determined younger writers who were dedicated to lighting up the lines again. Occasionally I would see a beautiful piece running and I would regret not getting out there to catch it. I missed some extraordinary masterpieces by such crews as TATS and such writers as Ghost, Reas, Sento, Poem, Dero, Wane, Web, West, and Poke who were still painting in an increasingly hostile environment. But as fortune would have it, some of the writers themselves had seen the value of preserving these ephemeral objects of art. One of the most engaged and dedicated of these was Paul Cavalieri. Cavs began to drop by my studio in the early eighties and he would show me the photos he had taken. I could see that he had great dedication, and I watched as his work rapidly improved and continued to improve as he acquired more skills and a better camera. He was a graffiti writer and he did pieces on the trains, but he was also becoming part of the culture of appreciation.

At the height of my efforts to catch masterpieces, when I had occasion to speak publicly or to do interviews, I was often asked to explain the motives of writers, to describe their cultural ways, their social organization, their techniques, their rivalries and beefs, and the special places where they preferred to paint. I was always a little uncomfortable, because it had never been my direct personal experience to paint a train, rack paint, or run from the cops. Why should I speak for them, I thought, shouldn't the writers themselves be talking, telling their own stories, documenting their own work? I knew that there was a new trend within the discipline of cultural anthropology to train the people of a newly contacted tribe to portray themselves, to study and to publish a portrait of their own culture, a practice called ethno-science, in reaction to the days when paternalistic westerners wrote their studies tainted with their own cultural biases.This is why I embraced the efforts of writers like Cavs and Key, who, as participant-scholars and photographers, have documented important aspects of the writing culture; especially the years from 1983 to 1989, when the transit authority finally took the last painted train out of service. *From the Platform* is a document of those years. It includes interviews of writers such as Ven, Quik, the late IZ the Wiz, and Ale, who tell the story as writers, but also as photographers and chroniclers of the culture.

I think it's stupid. The idea of having all this barbed wire and fences and protection. Trains are still going to get written on. They invented the White Elephant. It's still got, well, they weren't bombed, but they had little mosquito bites. Call it what you want. They were still written on. They're still not spotless, completely.

–Izthewiz (From *Style Wars* by Tony Silver and Henry Chalfant, Copyright Public Art Films, Inc. 1983)

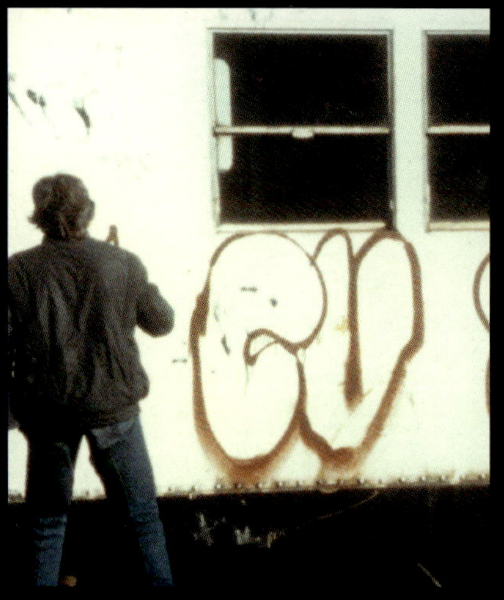

Cav bombing the East 238th Street layup, 1984

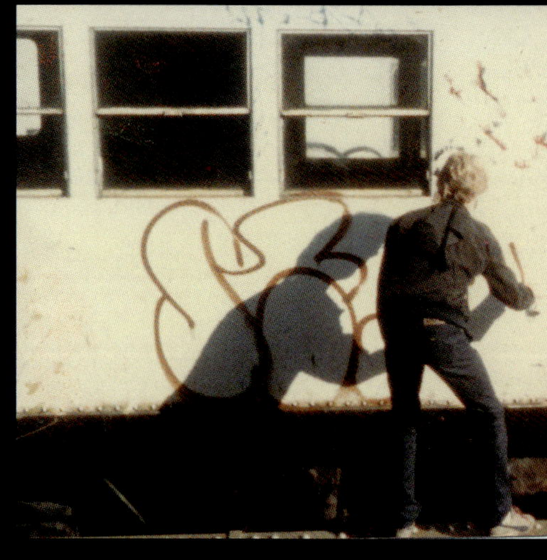

Jent bombing the East 238th Street layup, 1984

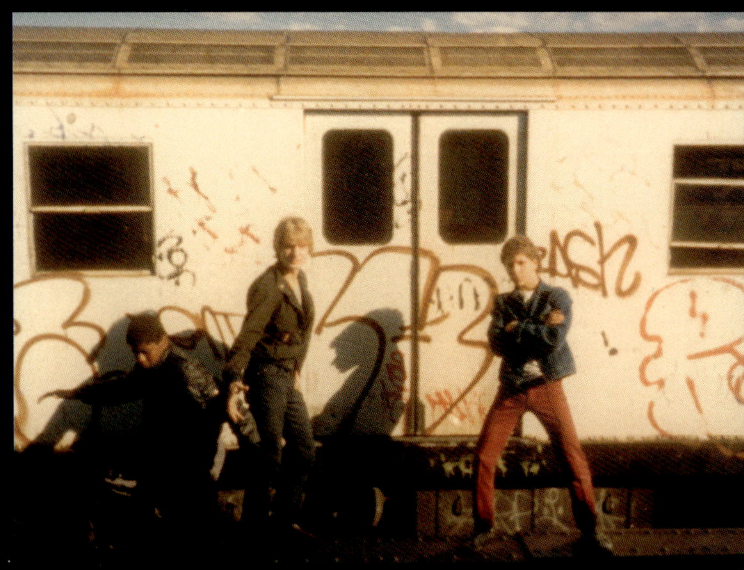

Unknown, Jent, Lash at the East 238th Street layup, 1984

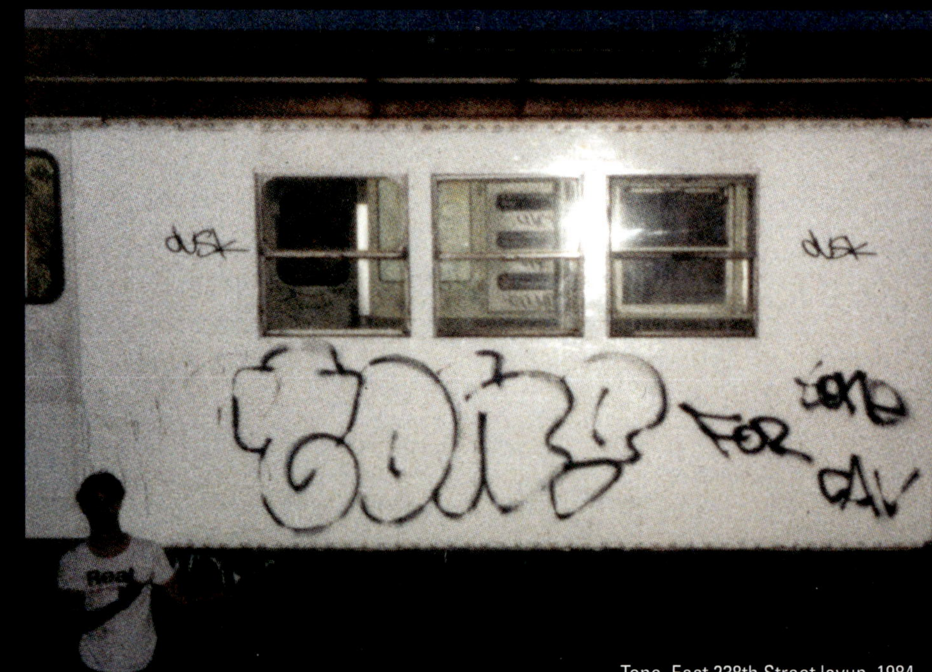

Tone, East 238th Street layup, 1984

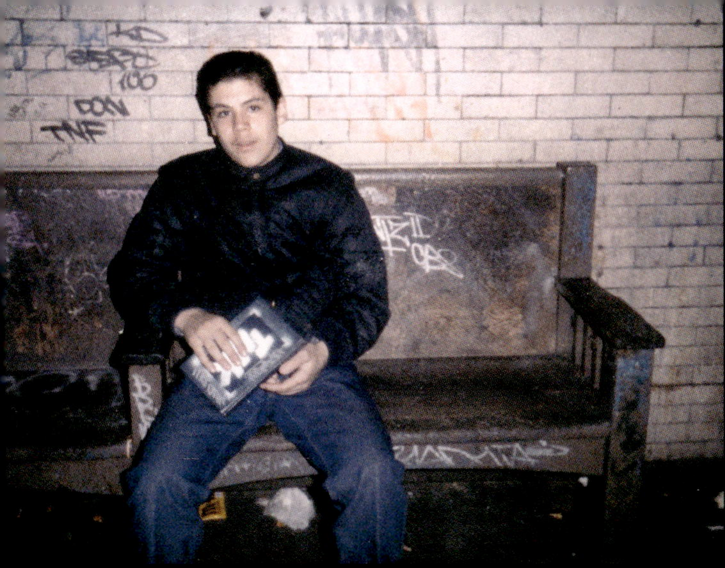

Sept at the Bench, 149th Street, Grand Concourse (Mott Avenue), 1983

Vice is ready to go bombing with his shoe dye, 1984

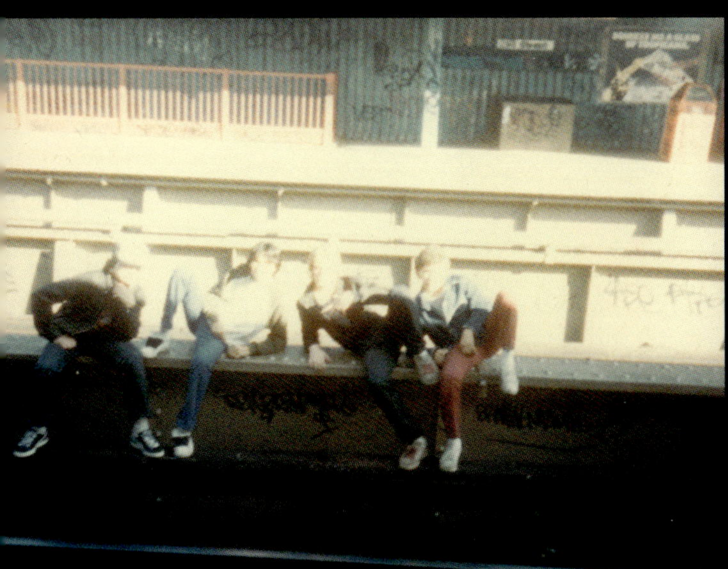

Cay, Mk, Jent, Lash, East 238th Street station (Nereid Avenue) on the 2 line, 1984

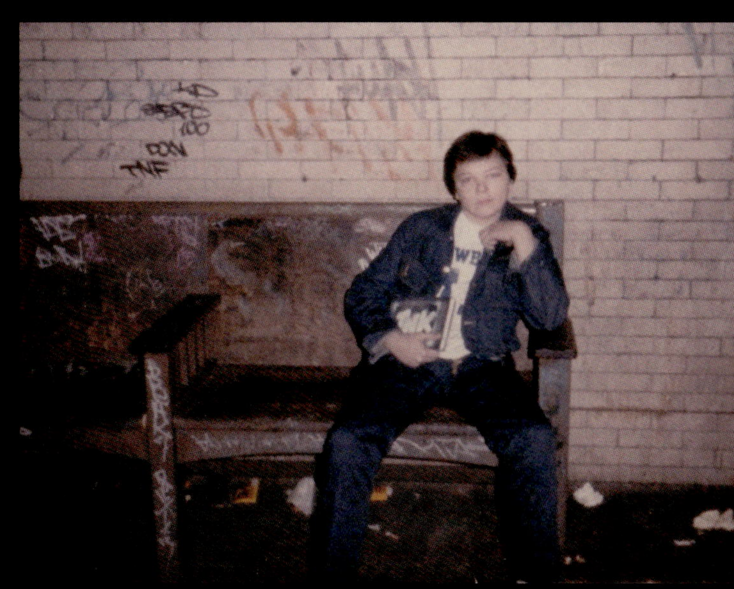

Cay at the Bench 149th street, Grand Concourse (Mott Avenue), 1983

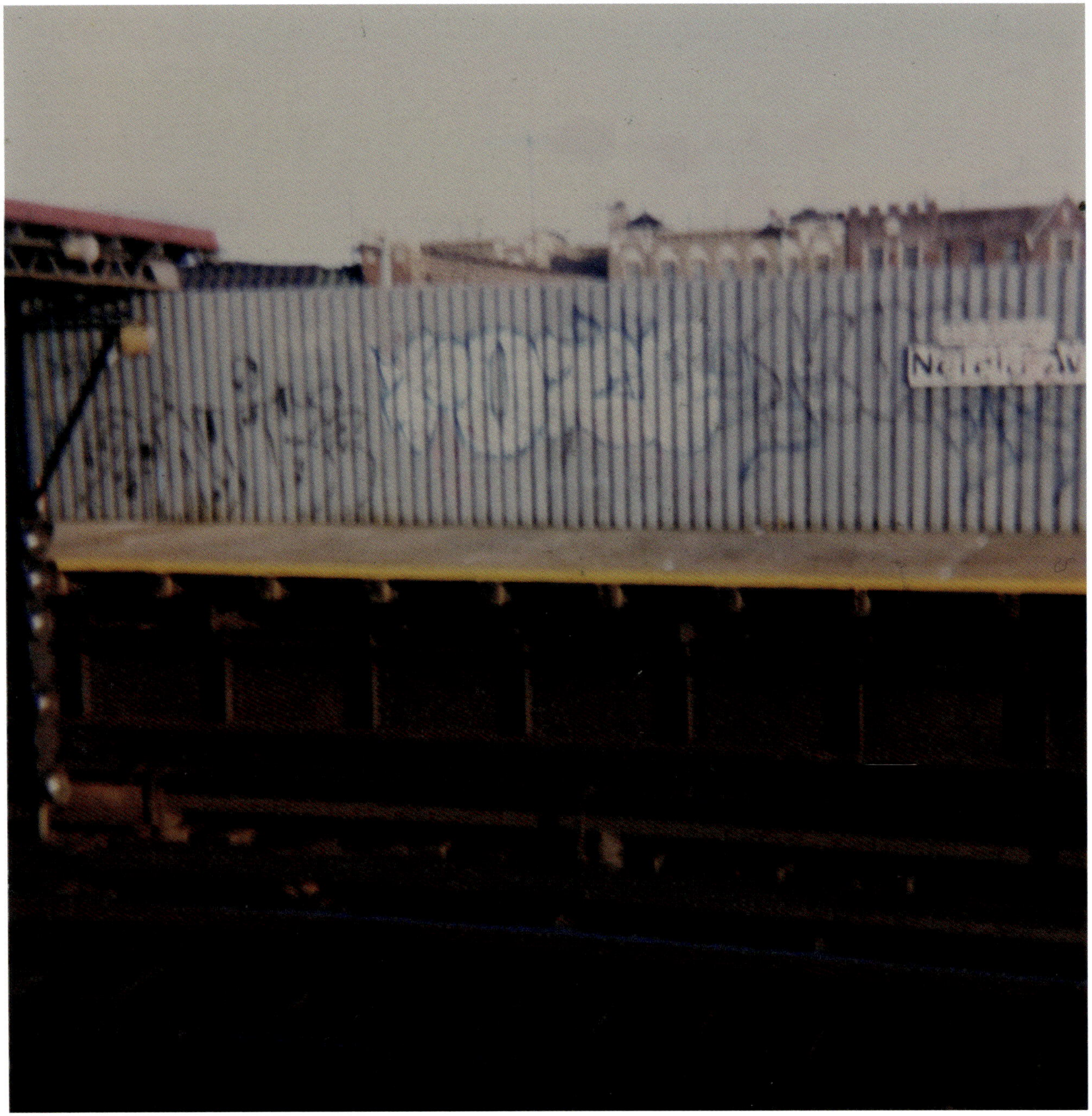

Roze by Mars, 1983

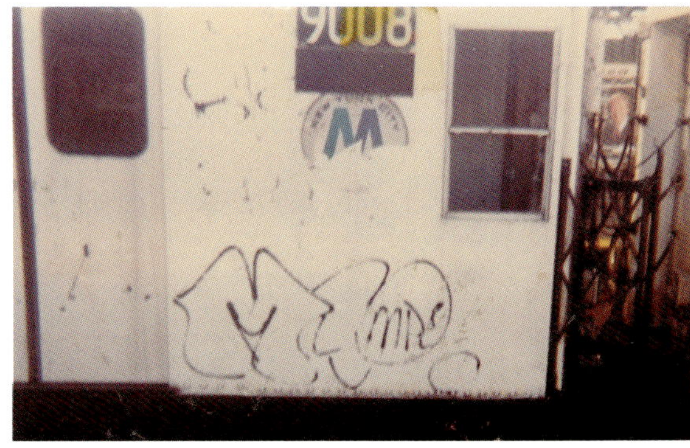

Mars MPC, 1983

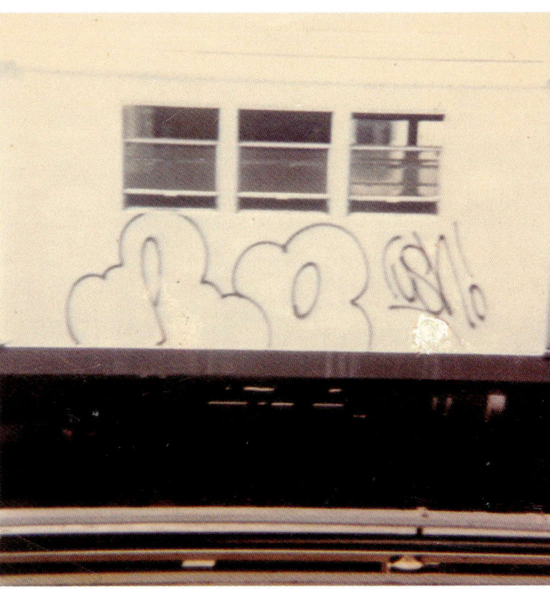

No by Rush MPC, 1983

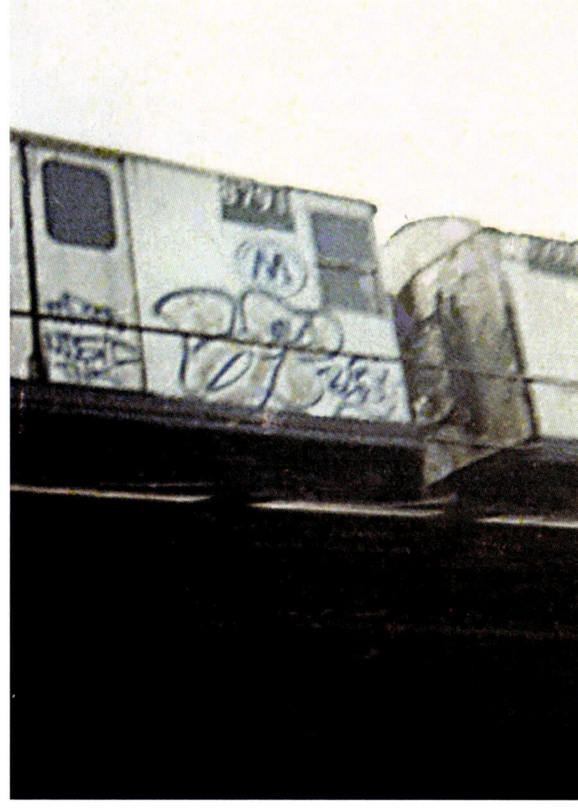

Blist, 1983

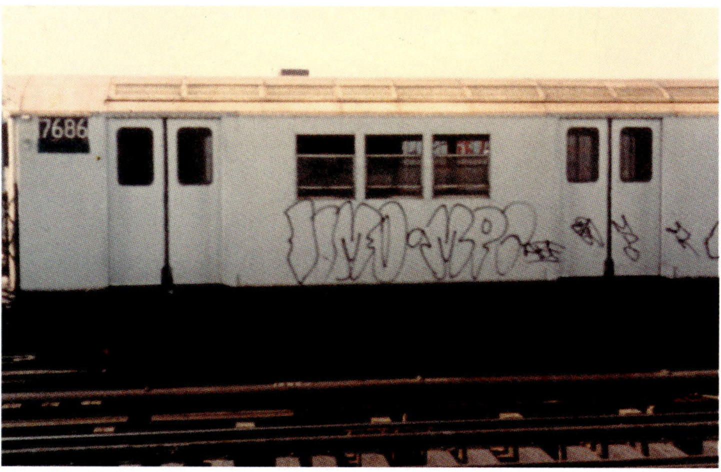

Limo MPC by Gin, 1984

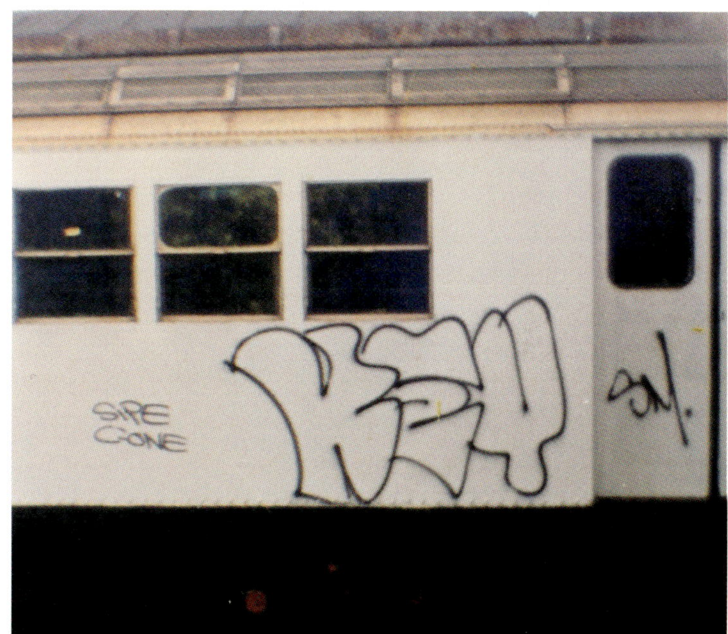

Key, 1984

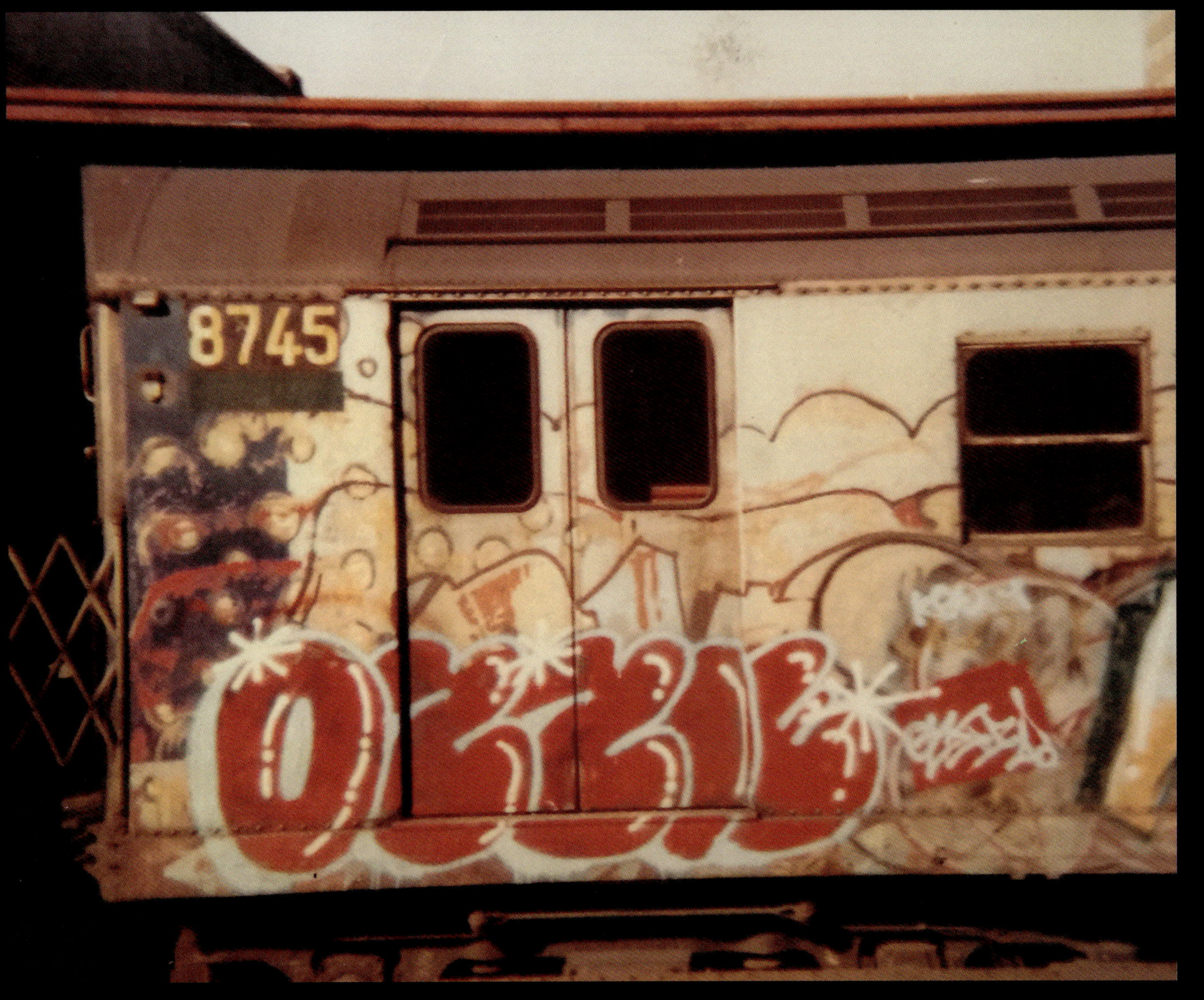

Ozzie, 1982 (Photo courtesy of Ozzie TGF)

This was my first piece, first time in a yard. I can still remember the feel, the sounds, and the smells of the 241st yard. I was hooked . . .

Graff has been a blessing in my life. I have made many lifelong friends, shared many adventures, and understand and respect our underground culture. Peace, love, and unity to all writers.

–Ozzie TGF

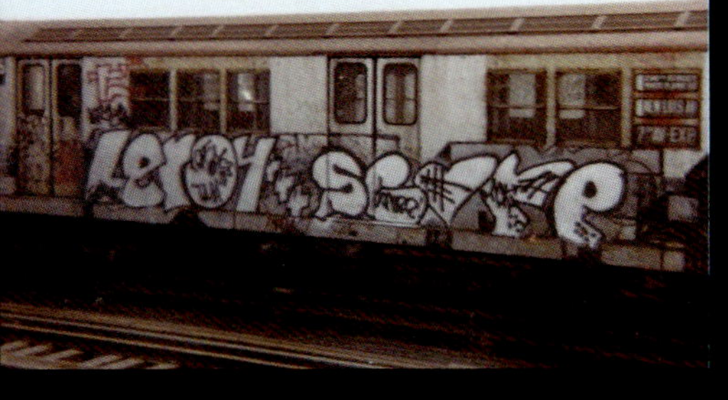

Leroy444, Scorp, 1982

My favorite graff quote is from Lm4, a.k.a. Leroy444: "Graffiti never dies, it just fades away."

–Mr. Edd

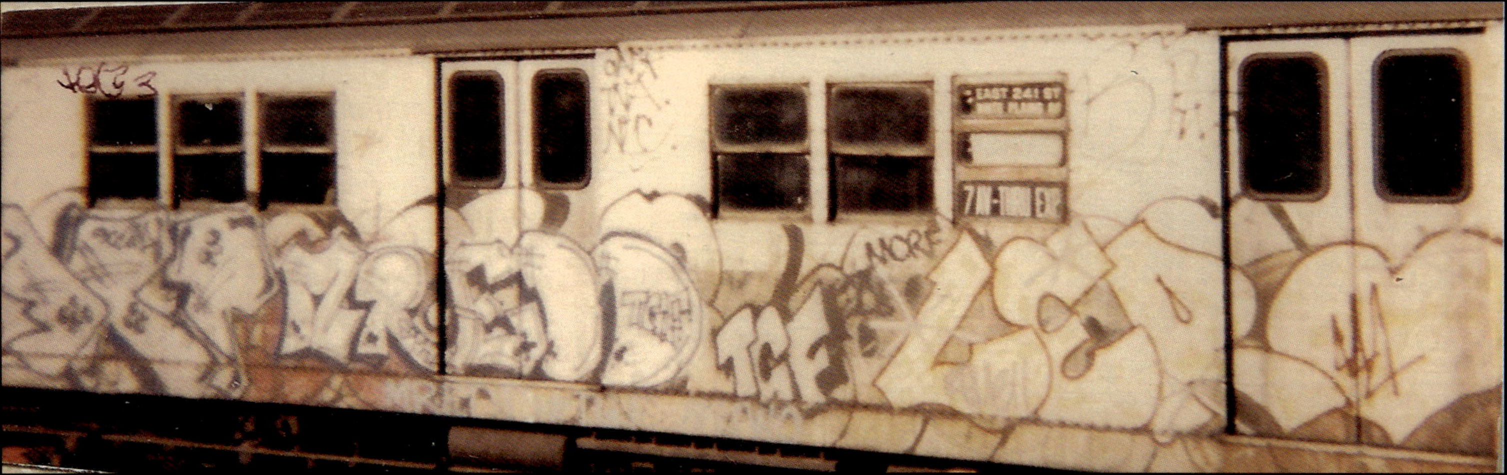

Scorp, Mr. Edd TGF, Leroy444, 1982 (Photo courtesy of TER3)

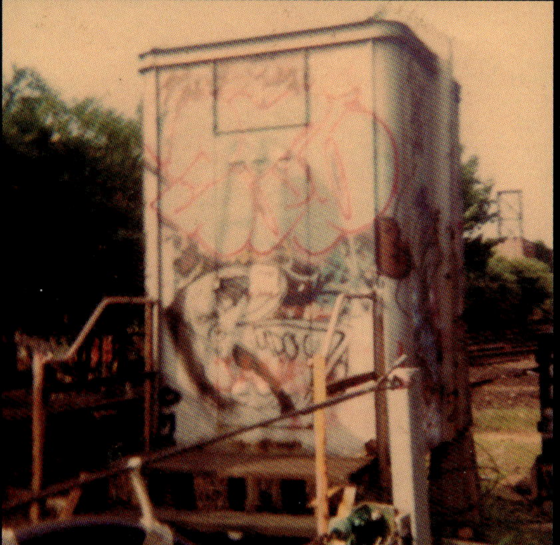
Cap, Rook MPC

We caught this White Elephant (white train) at the stick outs of the Morris Park "Esplanade" (5 line) layups. That is Pove, Janet, and myself. I had skinny caps and did this Cap on the train.

–Cap MPC

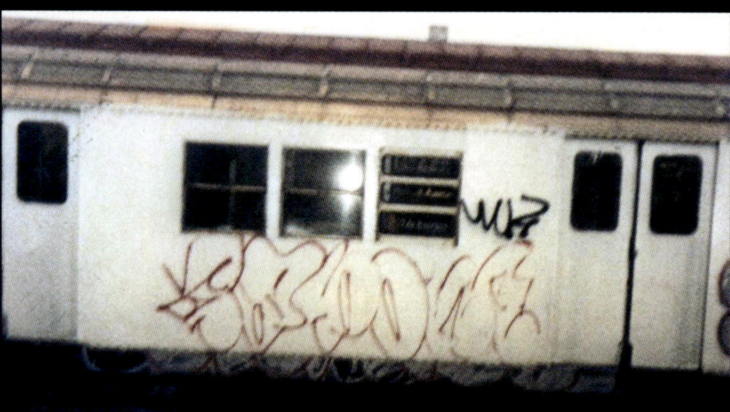
Capone, 1984

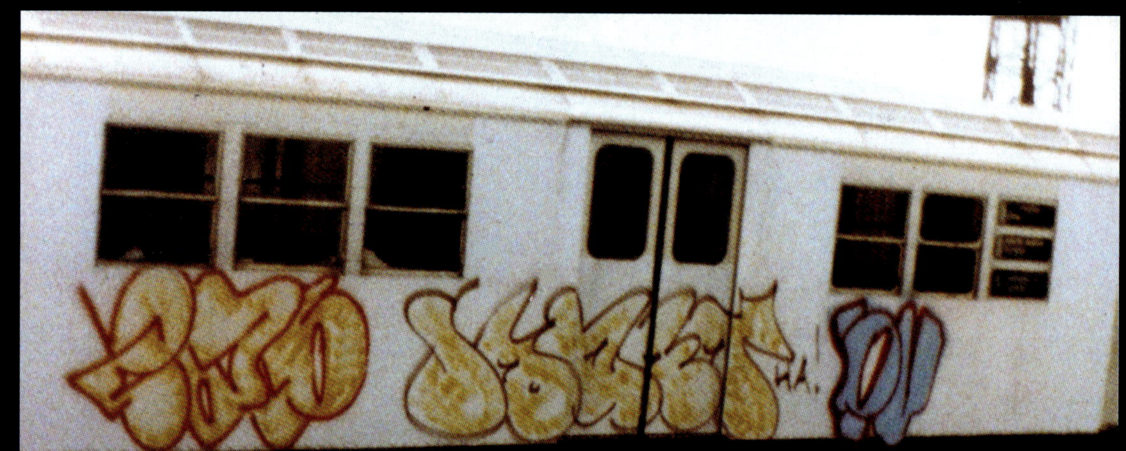
Cap, Janet, Pove, 1984

Myself, Quik, and Sach went to New Lots on a Saturday night. To my surprise the yard was stacked with clean white trains. When you walked in the yard, you could smell the paint off the trains, that's how recently they were painted. I went and scoped out the yard like I usually do before I start bombing to see if it was a setup, which I knew it was! I told Quik and Sach that it was a setup because I used to go to New Lots almost every night. I said, "Let's go hit the Es & Fs in Queens." And they were just mad, saying that I was just saying it was a setup because I was already king of the 2s and 5s. Anyway, we went in the yard, we bombed about four or five lanes. The next thing I knew, DTs with Workbum vests were running through the trains. We grabbed our paint; I opened up the side door of the train. We jumped out, ran down the hill out the yard into Quik's car (a blue Cordoba), and as we were pulling away, there were transit police everywhere and I thought they were gonna pull us over but they didn't. One car followed us for about five blocks and they sped off. Then we went and hit the E and F yard off the Van Wyck Expressway. (1983)

–Min RTW

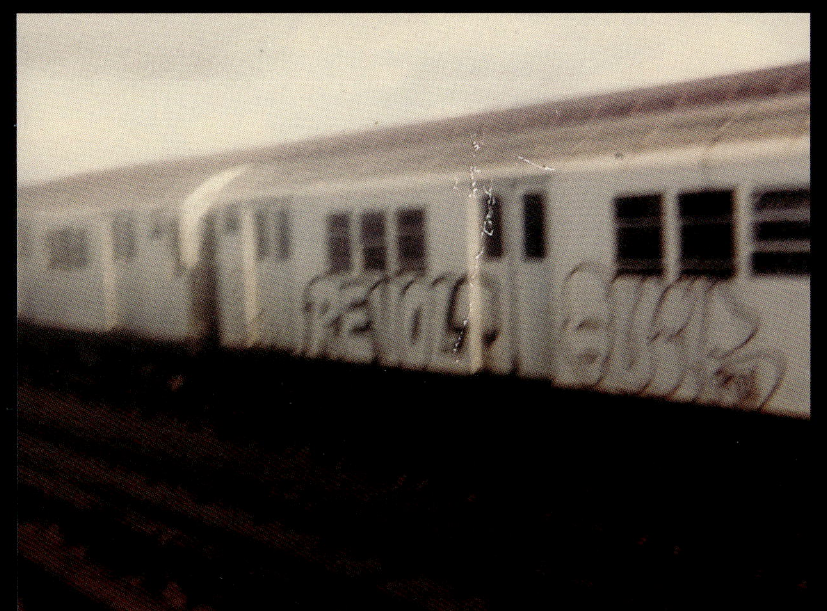

Revolt, Quik RTW, 1983

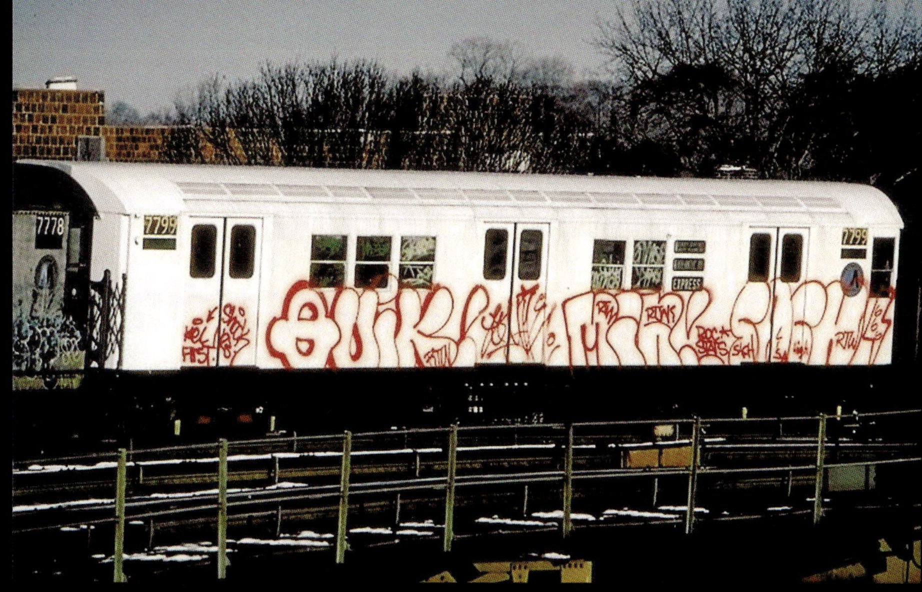

Quik, Min, Sach RTW (Photo courtesy of Martha Cooper)

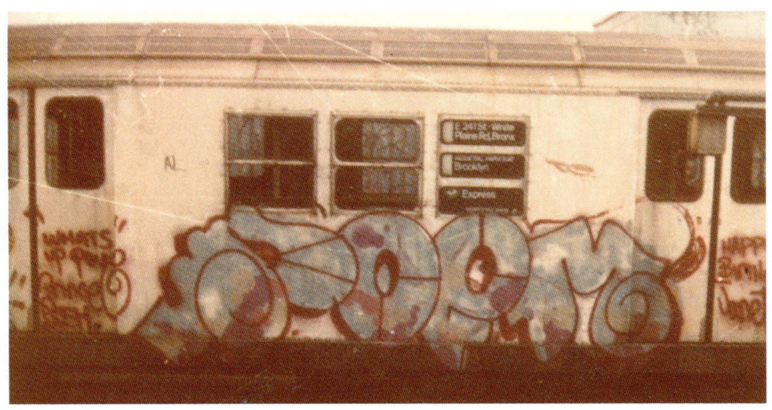

Poem

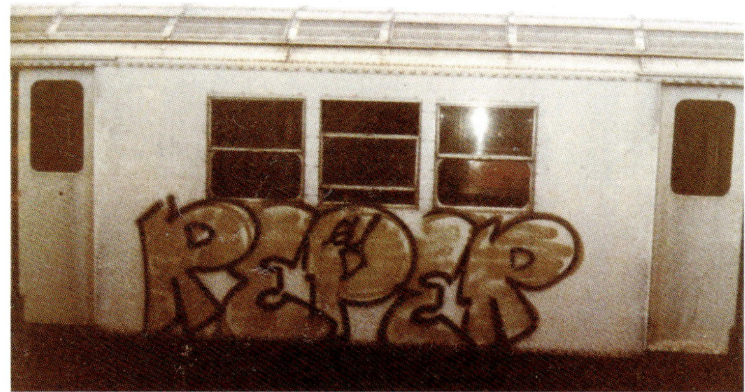

Reper

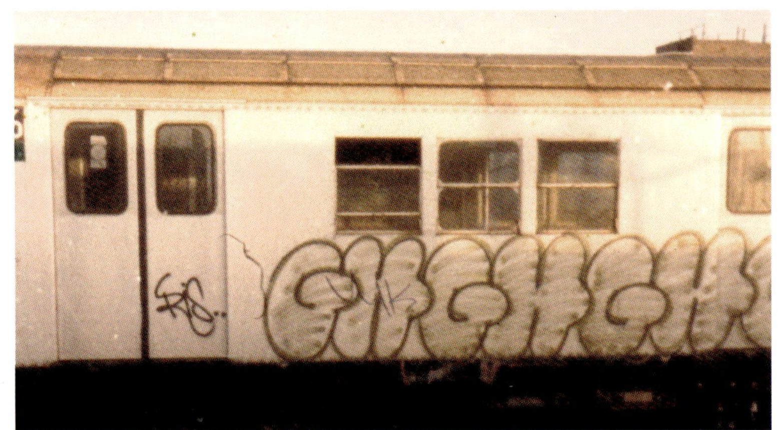

Ghost

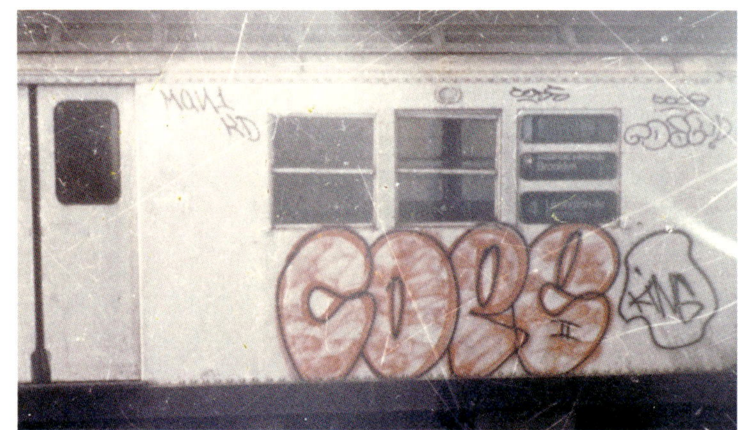

Cope2

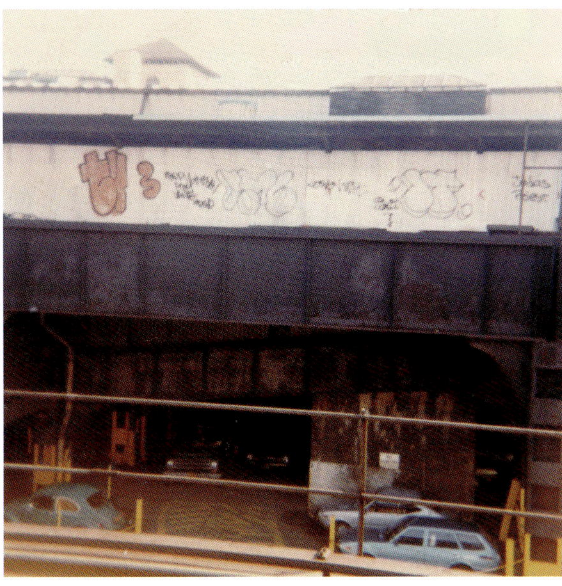

Ty3, Caban, Janet

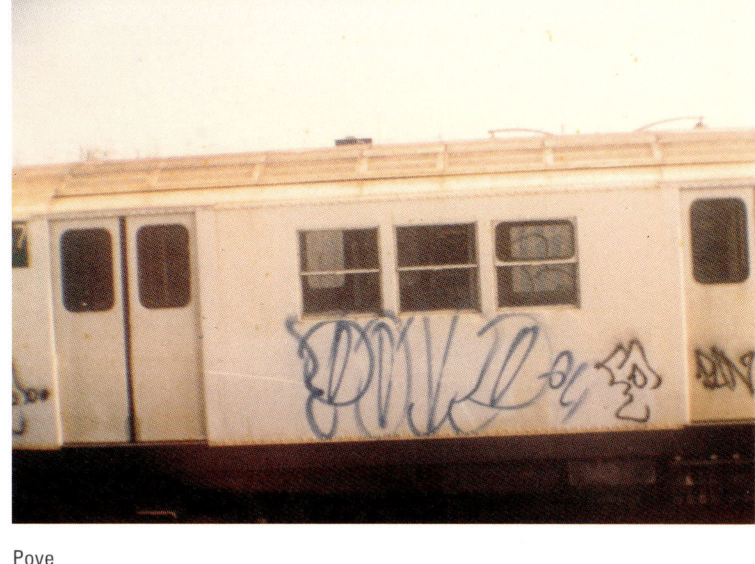

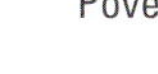

Pove

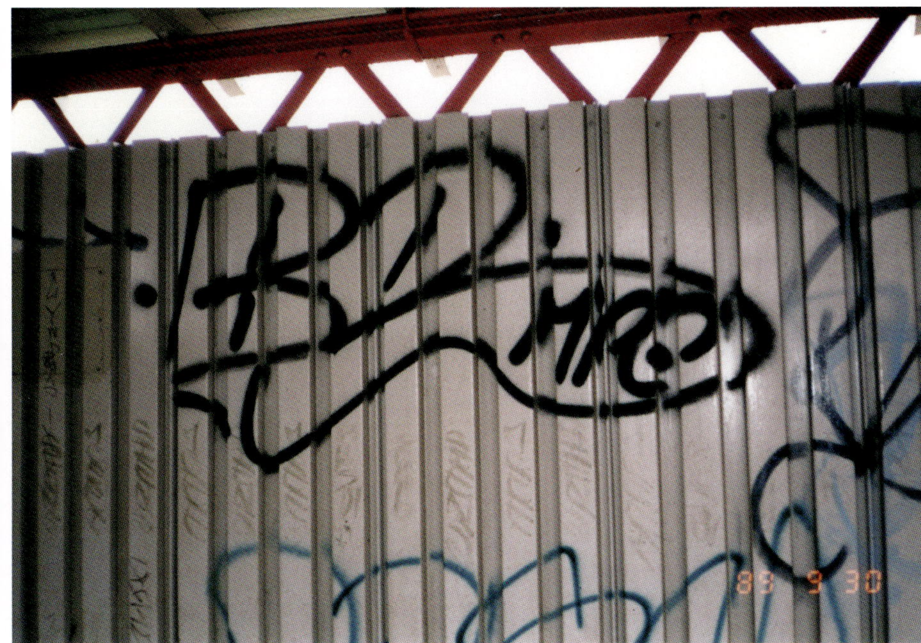

Buste

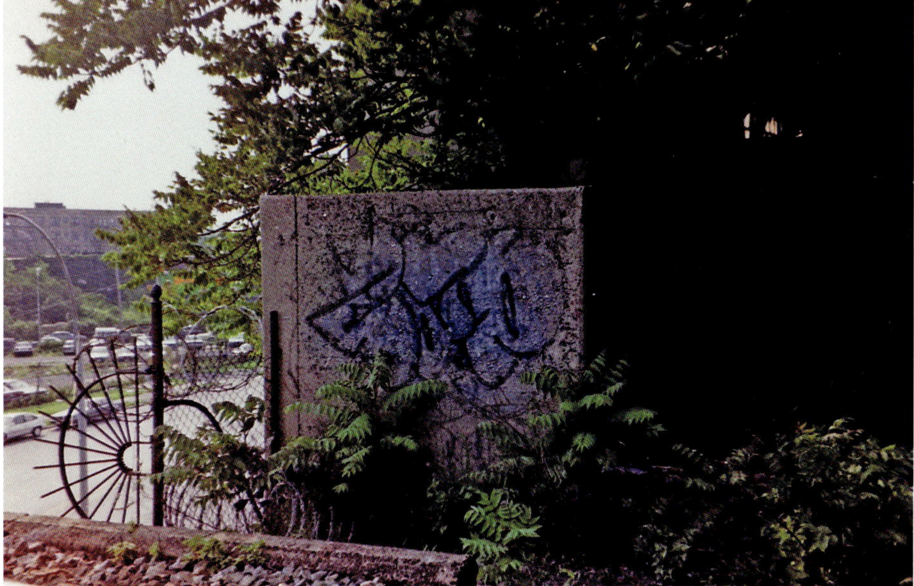

Cap

I came from Yonkers to smash the lines. My home was the 241st Street yard. I did whole cars, pieces, and insides there. I wrote so much that I went over my own name, lol. I came out in the movie *Beat Street* from hitting that yard, I had them on lock. My crew GU (Graffiti Unlimited) was eighty-eight members deep at that time. All races of writers who got up from Westchester and the city, we ran it back then. I would break nights in there solo. I remember seeing Cavs going to school one morning when I was just coming out of there from an all-night mission. I also loved hitting Baychester and Esplanade layups as well as other yards and layups. Esplanade was my favorite layup for day time or night. I had some good times there with Cavs, Janet (RIP), Rook2 MPC (RIP), Dibo GU (RIP), and Buste GU (RIP) just to name a few . . . .

–Pove GU

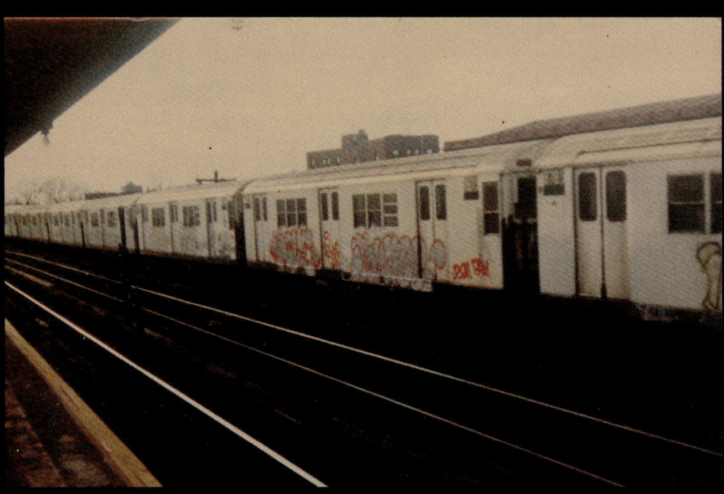

Pove The MOB

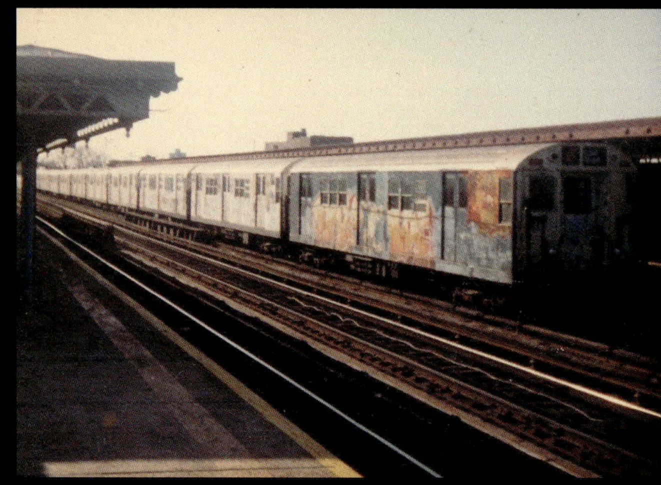

Pove, 1983

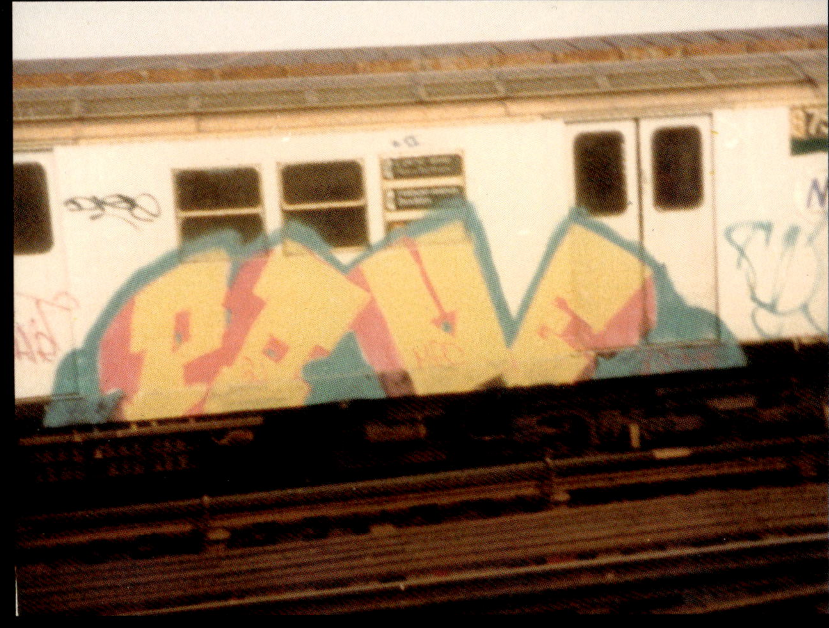
Pove GU, 1984

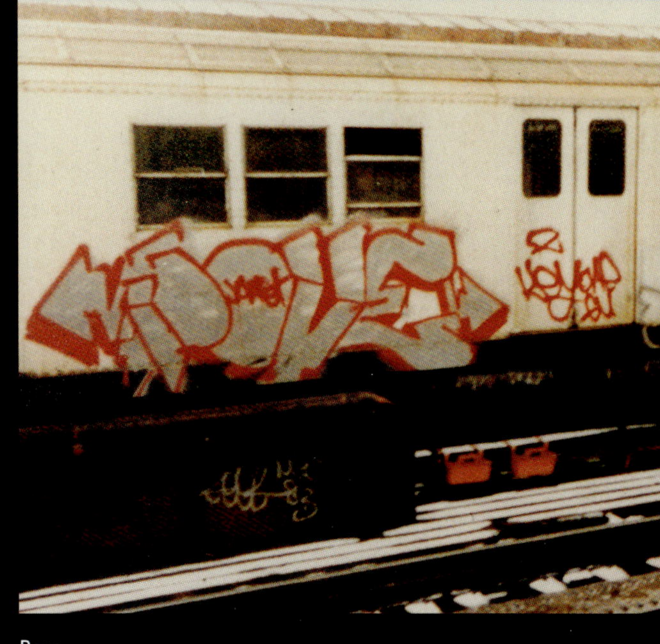
Pove

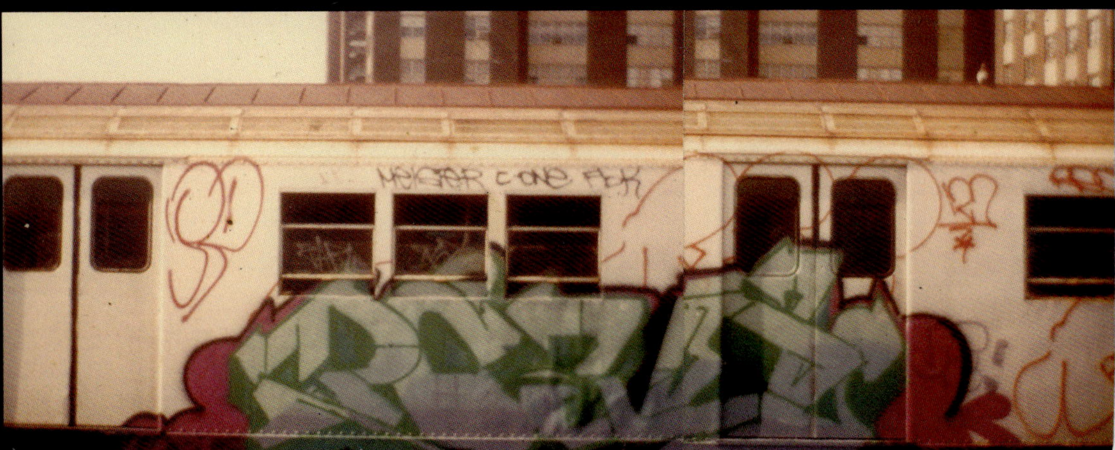
Pove, 1984

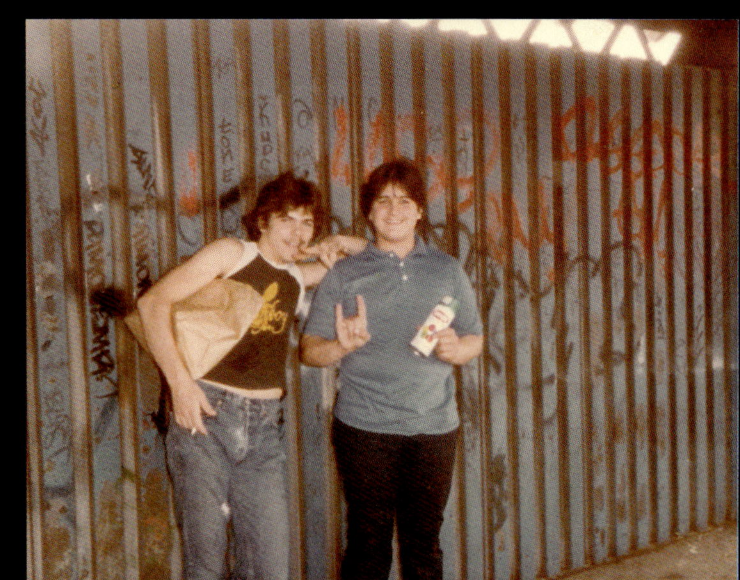

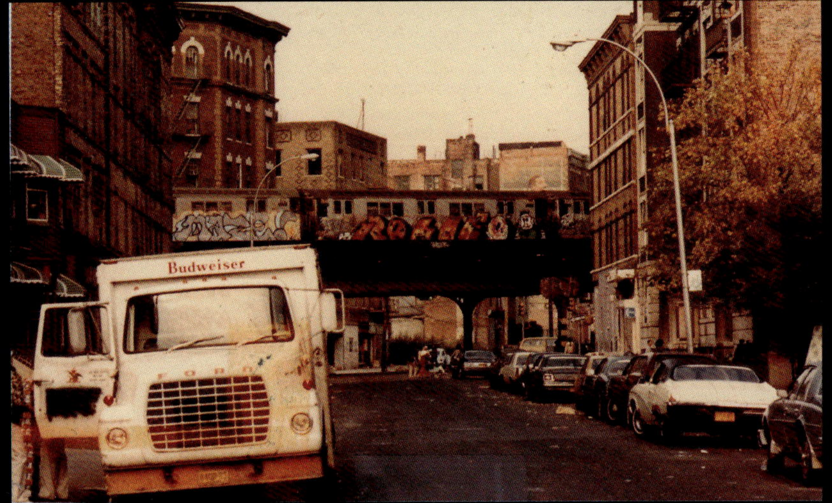

Maze, Rolieo passing at Prospect Avenue, South Bronx, 1981 (Photo courtesy of Rolieo)

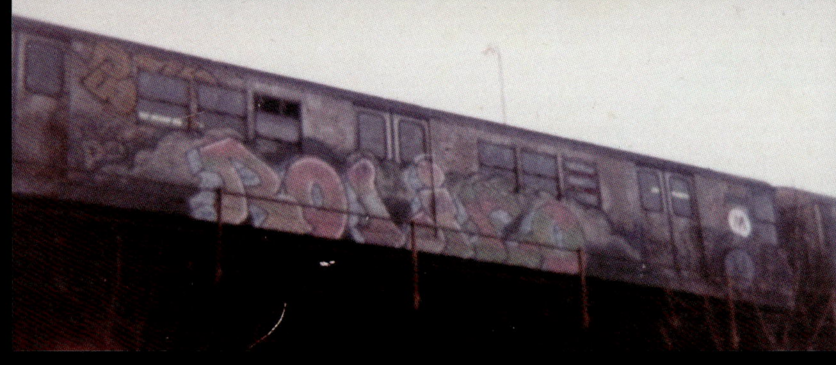

Rolieo 12/1982 (Photo courtesy of Rolieo)

As a teenager growing up in the Bronx I was privileged to see some of the best subway art ever done from 1976 to 1980 and early 1981. At the same time there was the sound of disco blasting from radios, which we called a "box." Of course this was before they added the word "boom" to it. Yes, you had your heavy metal, as well, blasting! At times we would try to outdo others. Sometimes fights broke out. It was crazy! *Saturday Night Fever* came out and it got worse. Just check out the "Demolition Disco Day" video from 1979. To make matters worse, the first rap group to make a record on vinyl was the Sugar Hill Gang. That same year I was making history. I was introduced to graffiti from a kid called Maze. We lived on the same block. He was also Blade's in-law. From there I was introduced to The Crazy 5. All those dudes hung out on my block as well. No doubt Blade and Comet influenced me. Other writers played a role as I slowly got better. There was Lee, Izthewiz, Caz, and Kit17. Later on in 1980 was Seen UA and Pjay, and of course Mitch77. When those guys did their whole cars you could not miss them. If you noticed my pieces all of them were huge. By 1983, I called it quits! The trains were painted white, also by this time I was maturing. I went to a trade school to learn plumbing and that's what I do today! I did try to do some pieces in 1985 but the feeling was not the same. A whole new generation in control.

–Rolieo

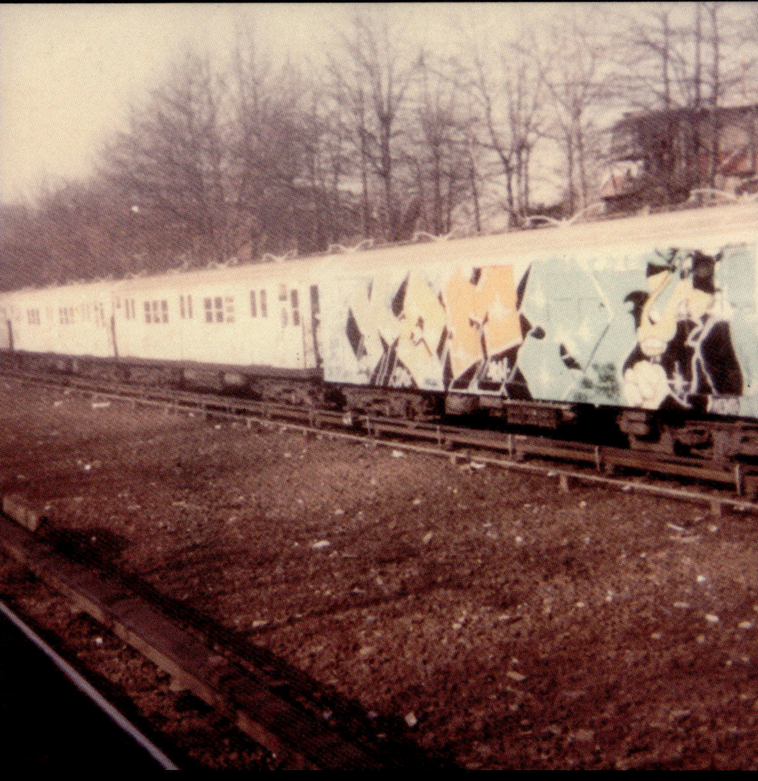

Kemt 58 TCS, 1983 (Photo courtesy of Rolieo)

In 1981, I started a crew called The Crazy Shit (TC5), because that's what we were doing! Of course I wrote The Crazy 5, although I was not an original member but enjoyed the privilege of writing with some of its members. The members of my crew were Kato, Dien, Kemt5, and Beast, then later on Dero.

–Rolieo

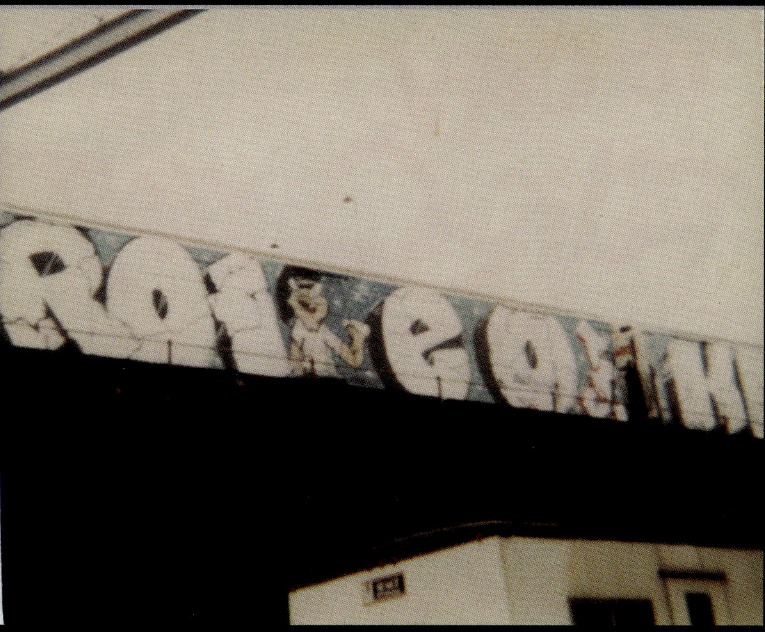

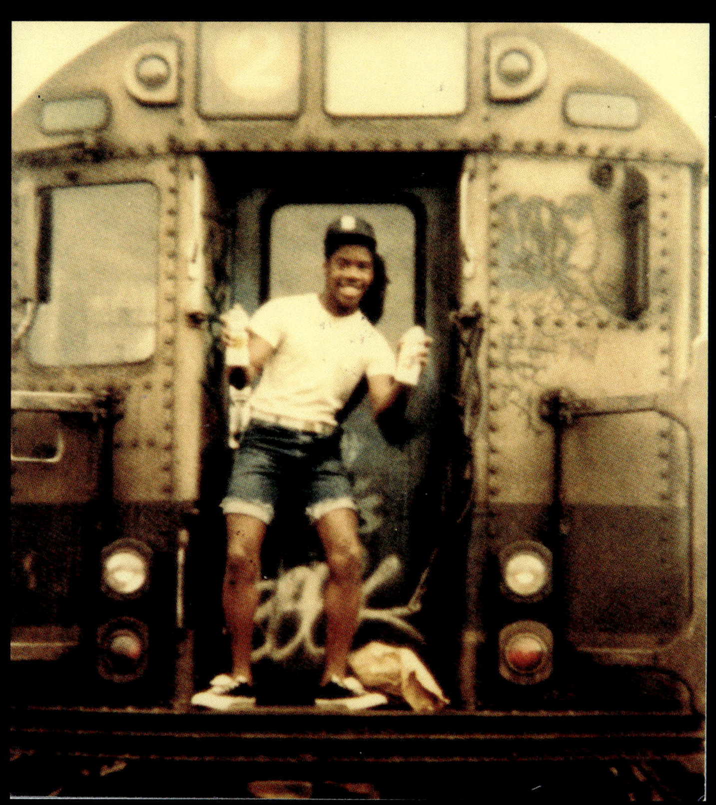

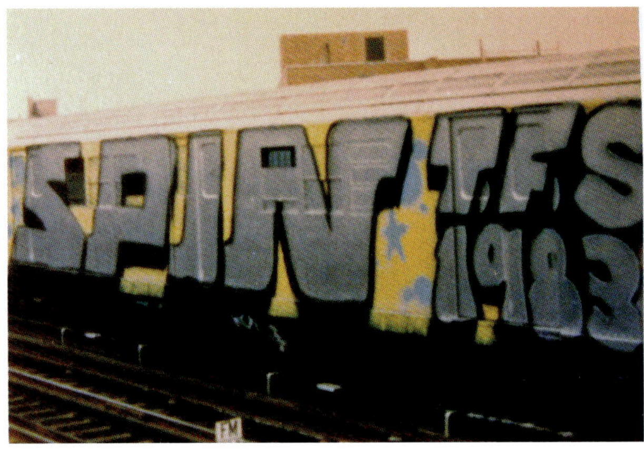

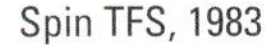
Spin TFS, 1983

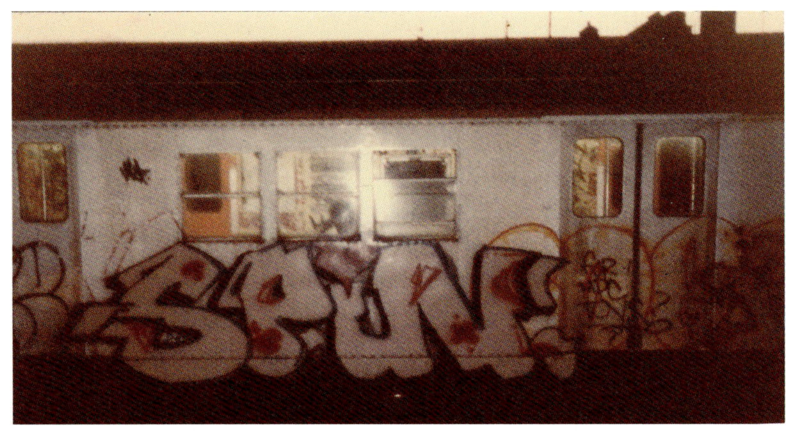

Spin, 1984

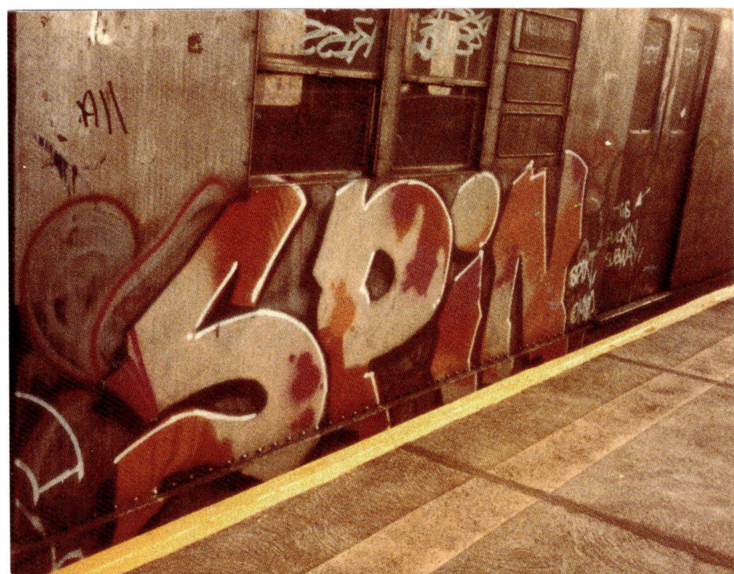

Spin, 1983

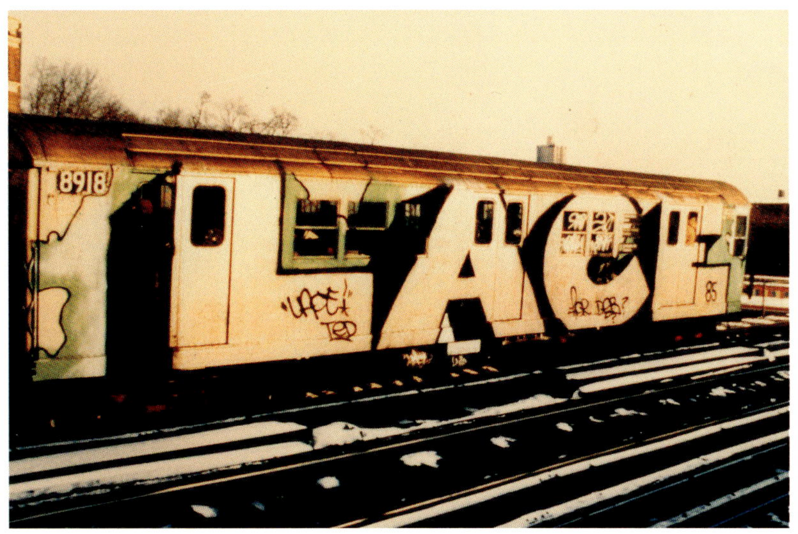

Lace, 1985

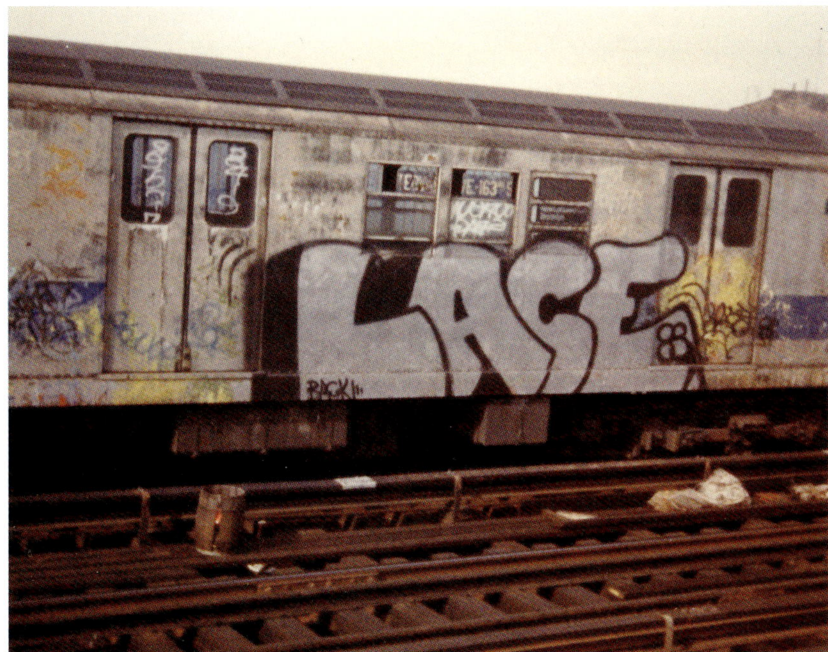

Lace, 1983 (Photo courtesy of LACE 357)

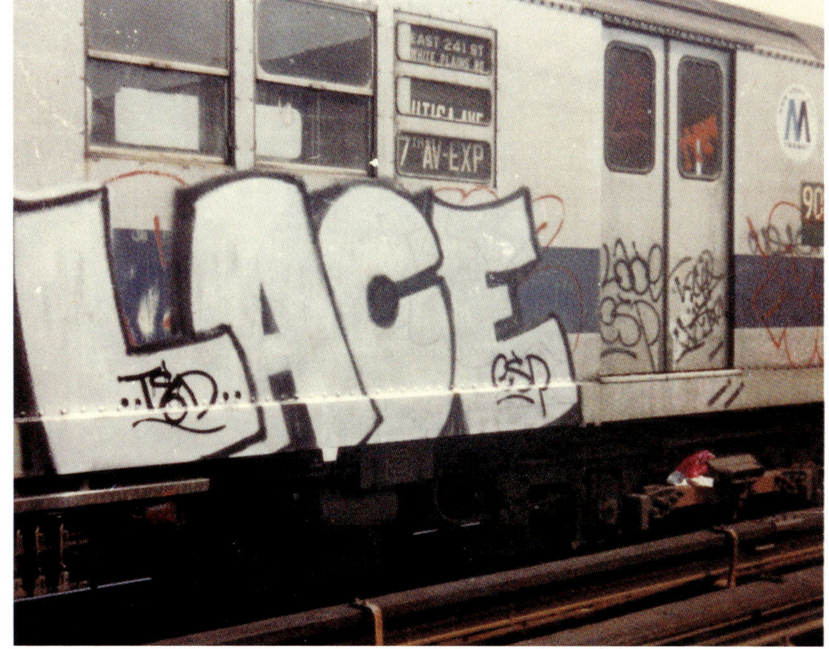

Lace (Photo courtesy of LACE 357)

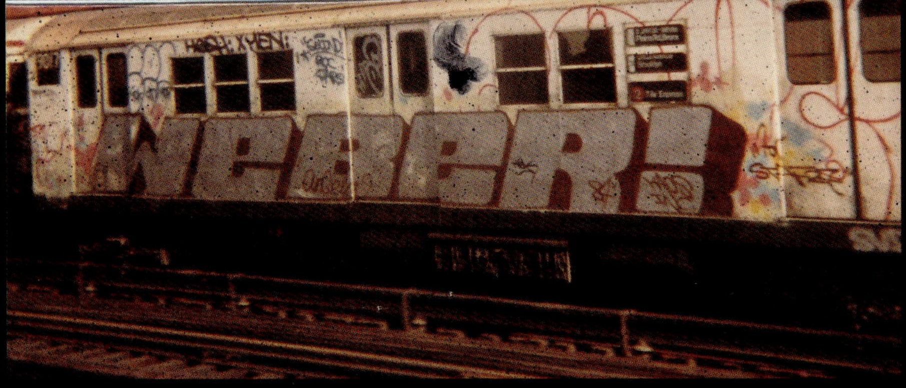

Weber, 1984

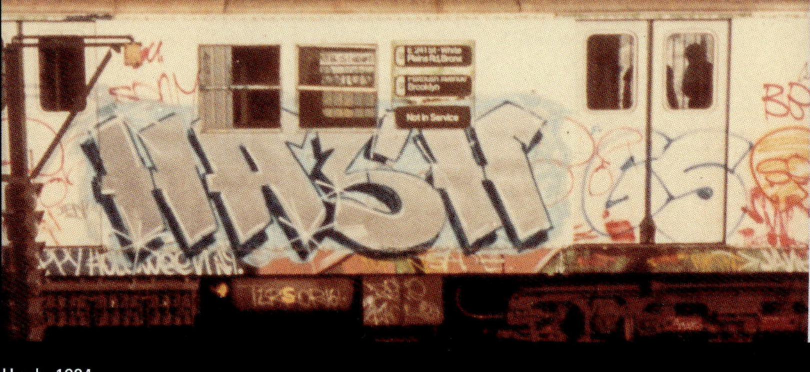

Hash, 1984

We did this in Bergen layup with cheap Whiz-on silvers. That second one I really don't remember. Hash may have done that in Kingston. Depends on who he was with; I'm thinking Tekay (Track2). If so, Kingston for sure.

–Web

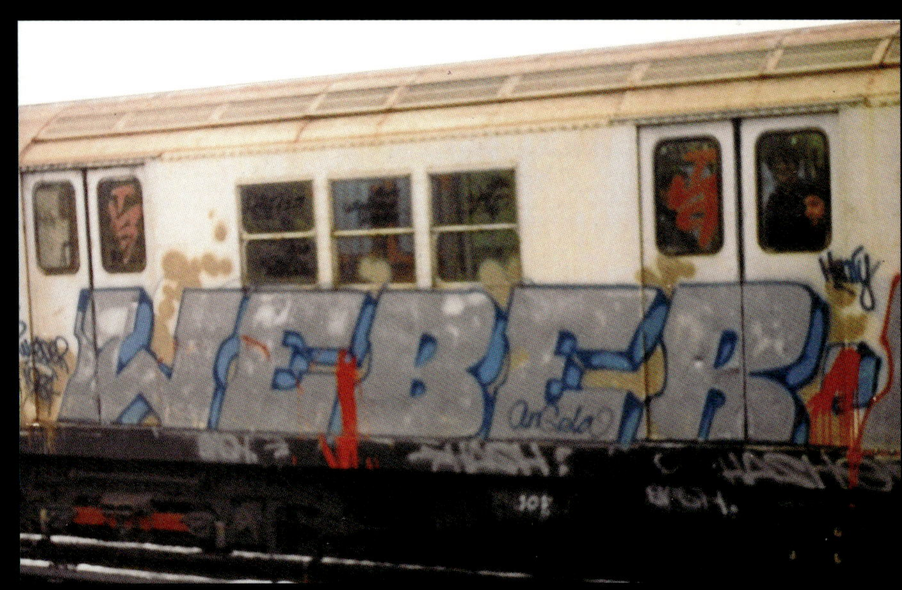

Weber, 1984

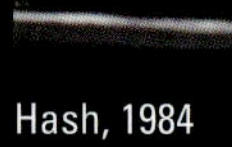

Hash, 1984

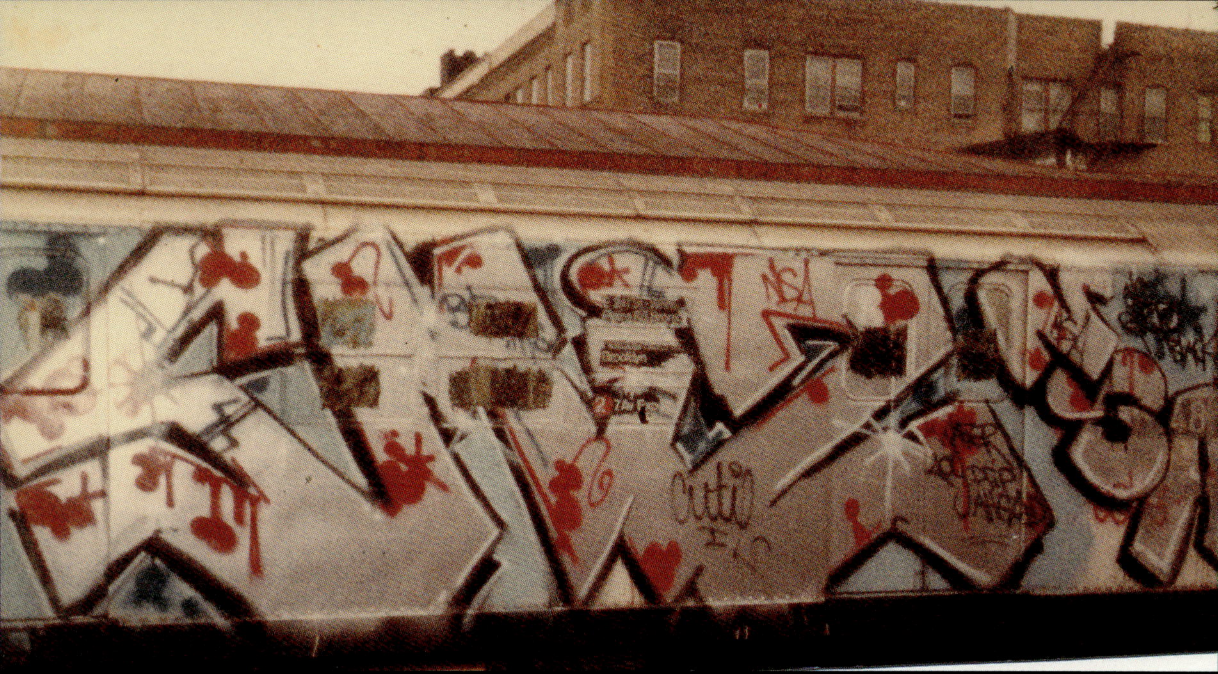

Smiz NSA, 1984

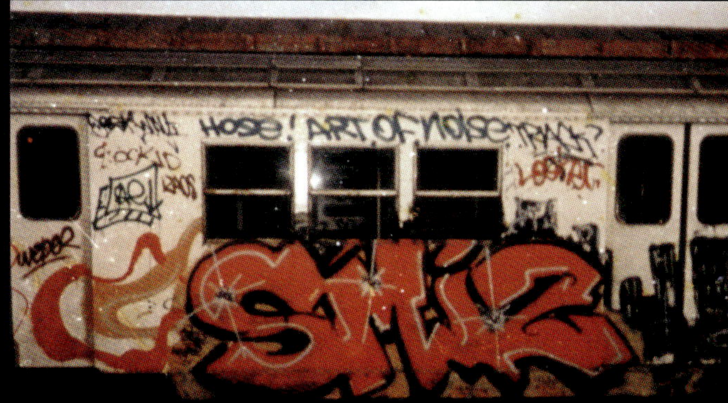

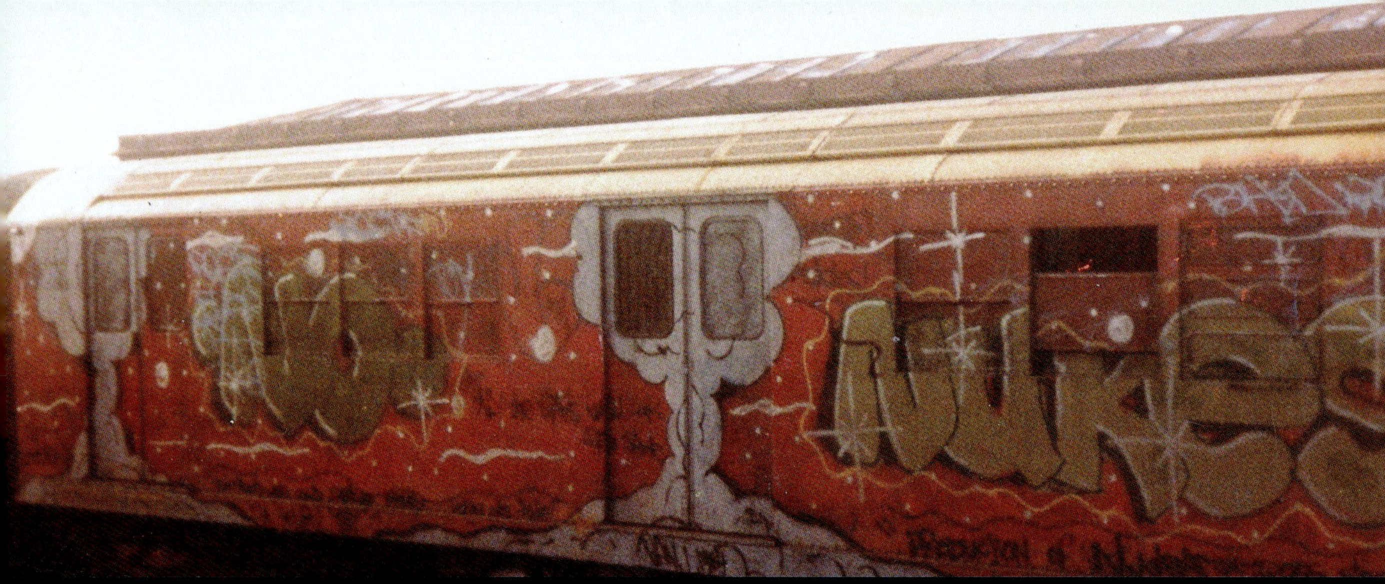

No Nukes by Med, 1984

The *No Nukes* car was the first whole car I ever did. That was when I first started writing. I probably did that in 1984, not the best piece. The letters were kinda like throw-ups but it was the message that was important. It was a time where the tensions between the US and Russia were high and Reagan wasn't having it, and a nuclear war was a real possibility. This train was done at the Dyre Avenue layup on the 5 line. Happened to be walking distance from my house and it was a real quiet spot back then. Lots of whole cars were done there, some never finished because it would pull out on us unexpectedly sometimes. I may need to do another *No Nukes* car now with the way things are going.

–Med

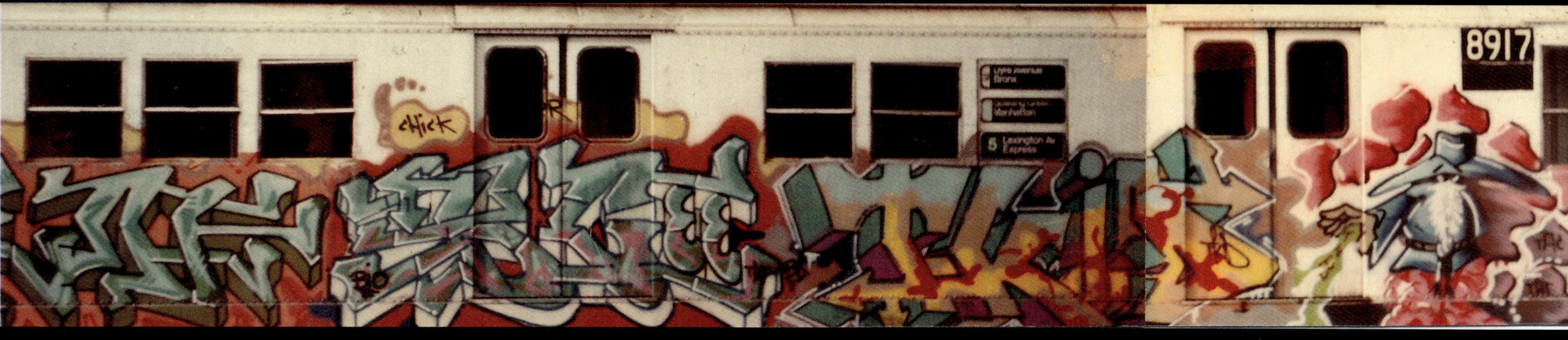

Ken (missing), Bgee, Tkid, 1983

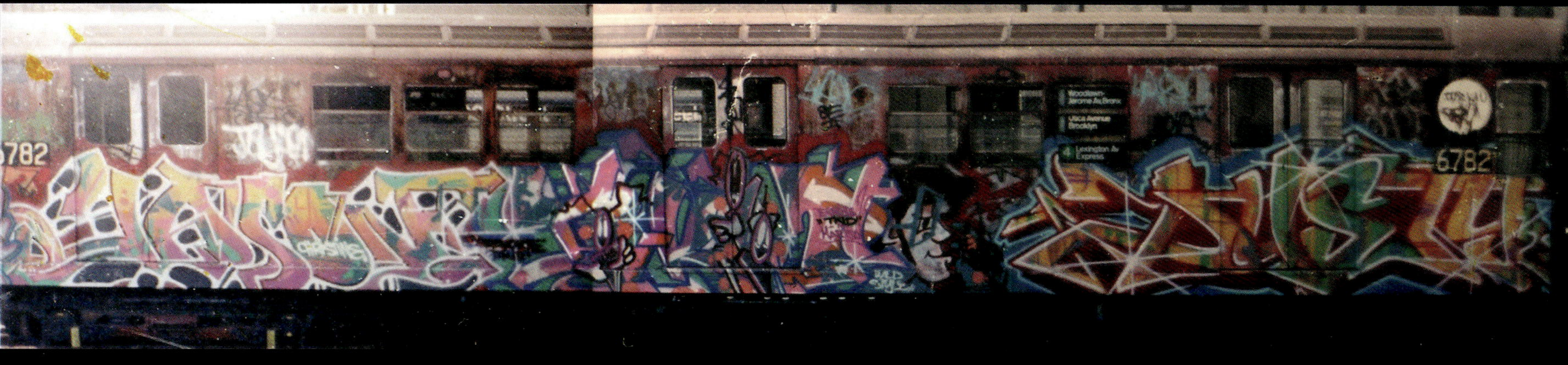

Jason, Tkid, Dusty, 1984

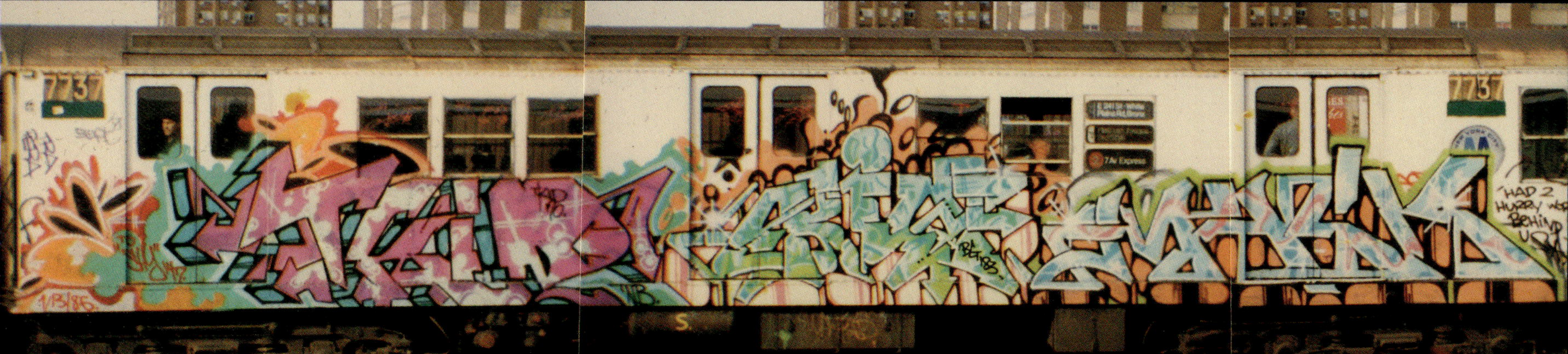

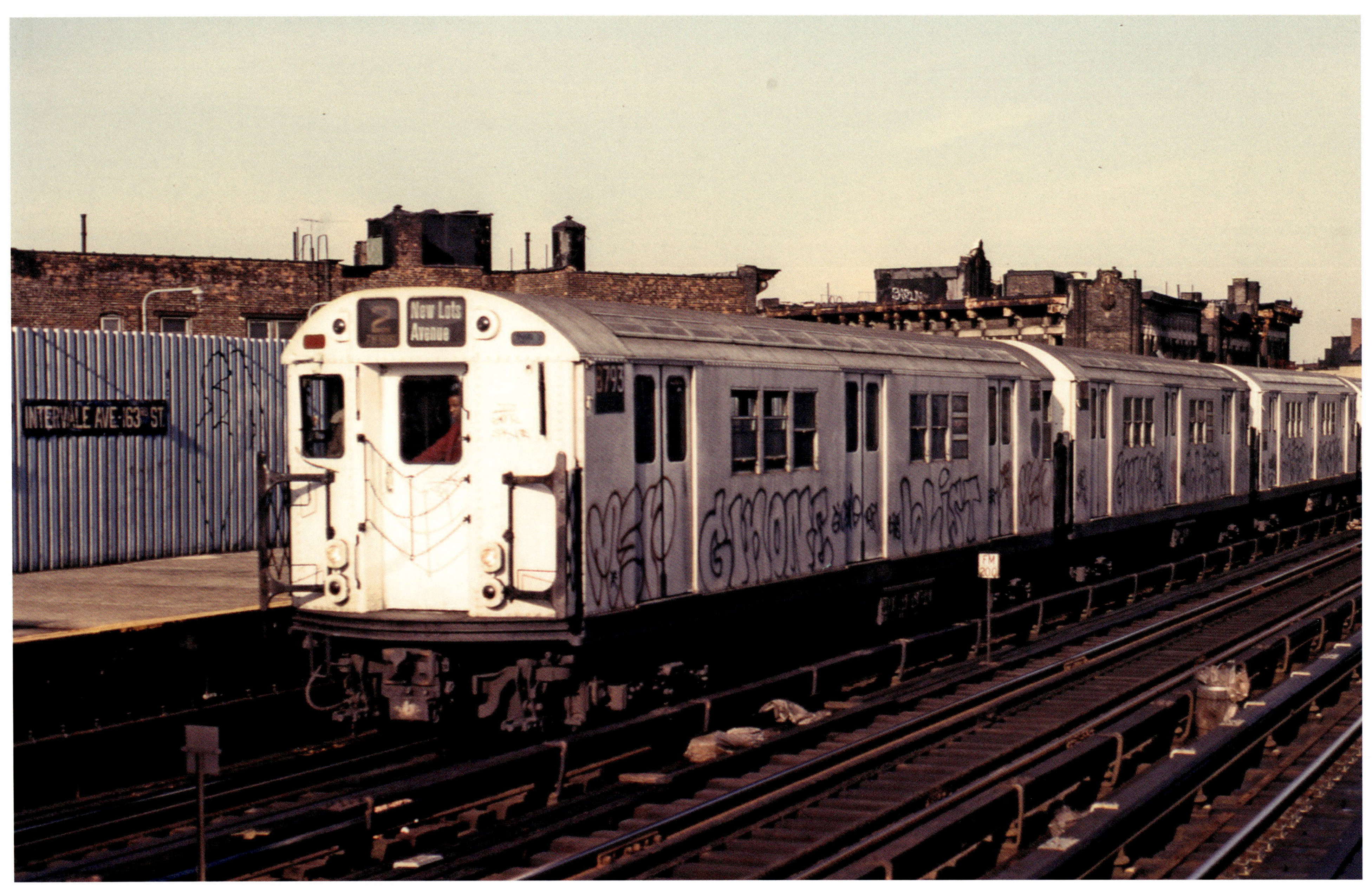

Ginone, Blist, 1983

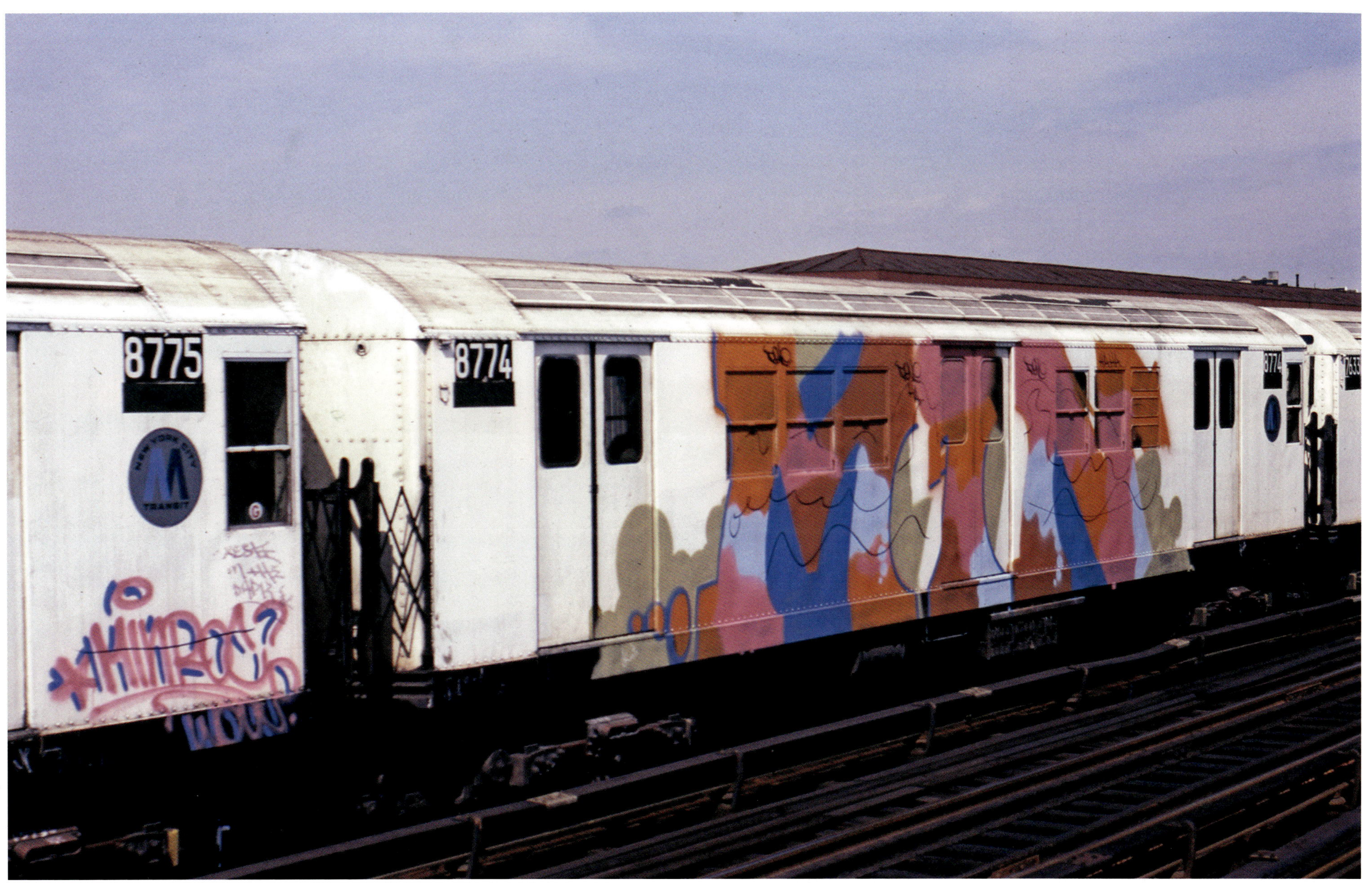

Min RTW, 1983

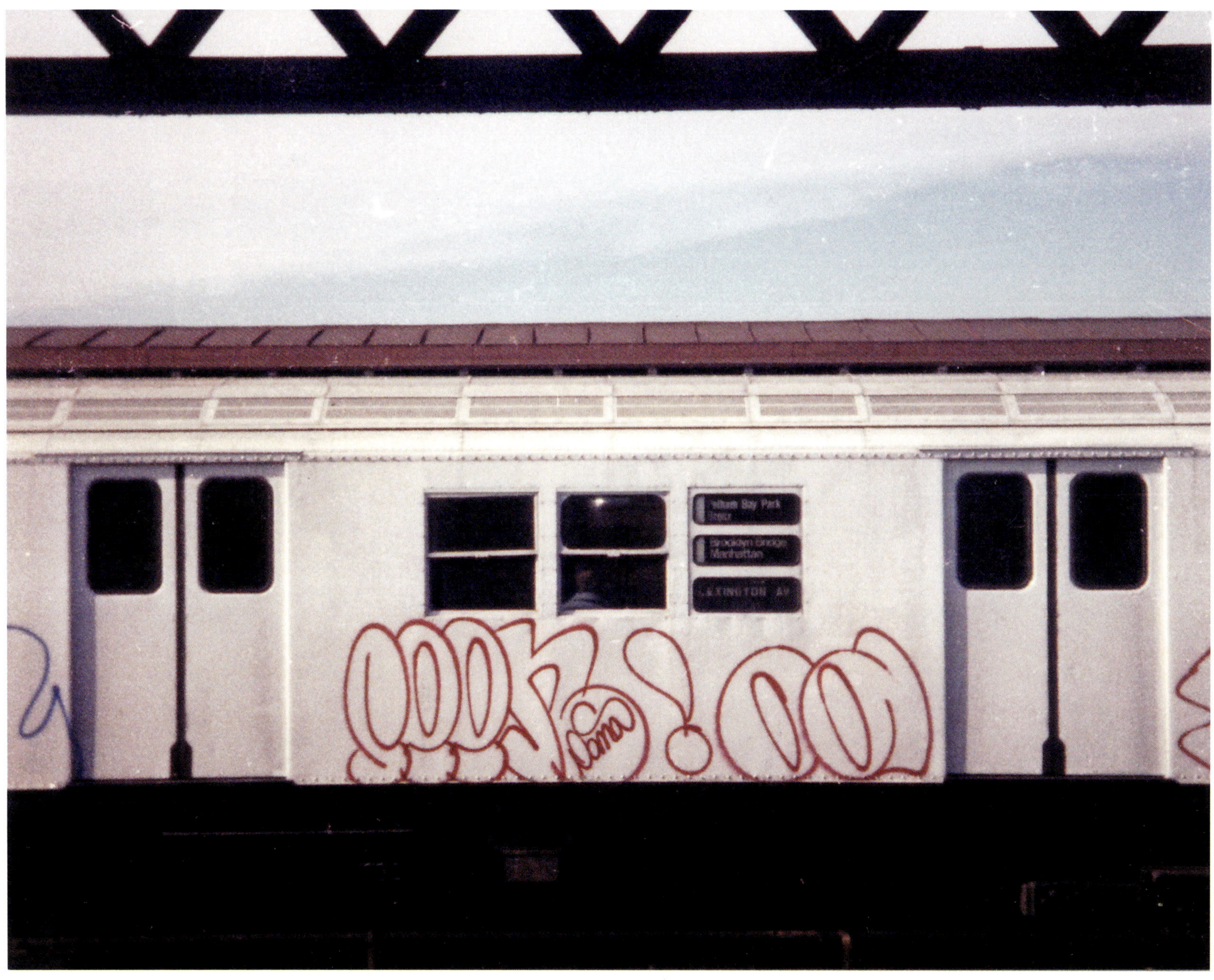

Seen, OD3

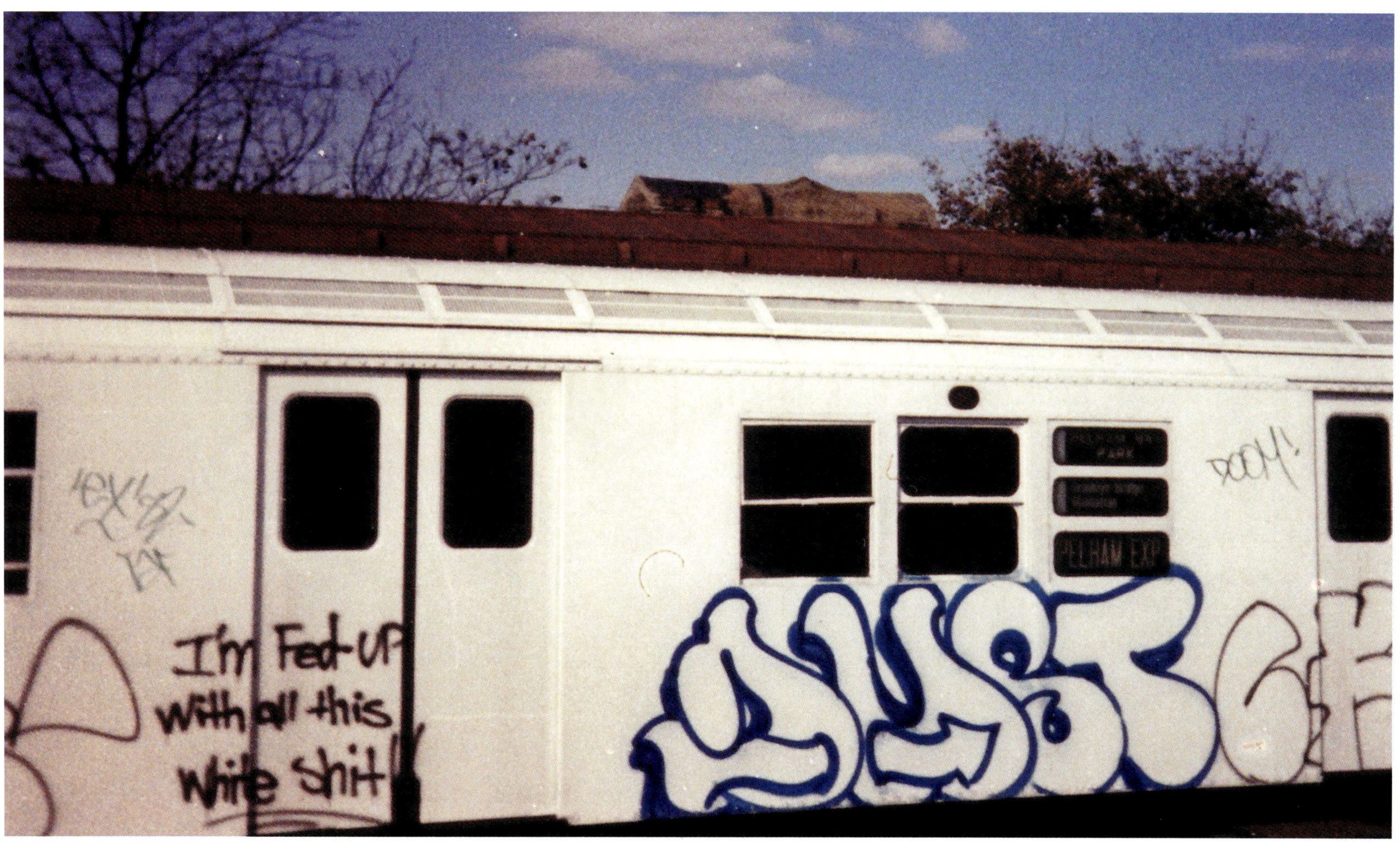

Dust

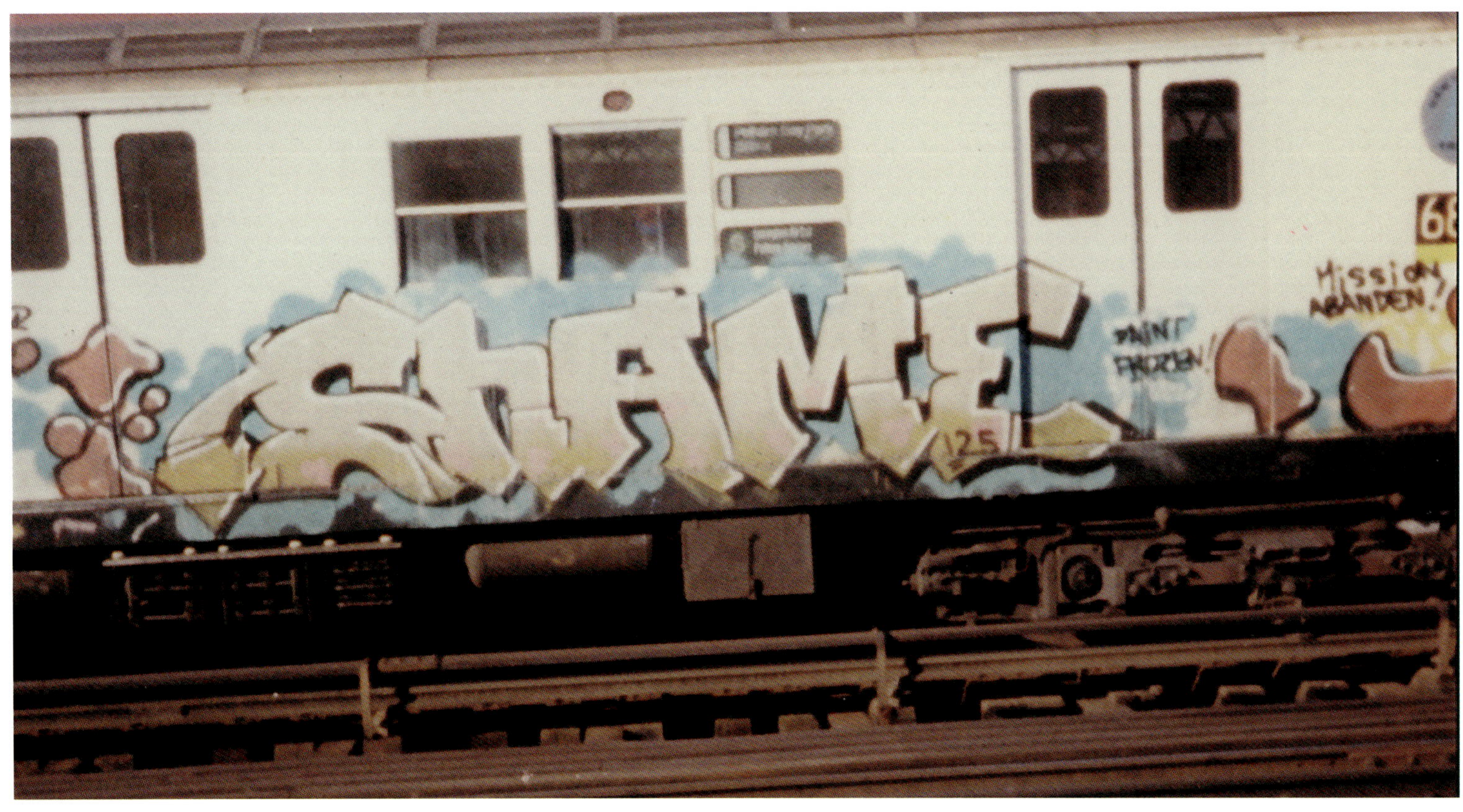

Shame125, 1983

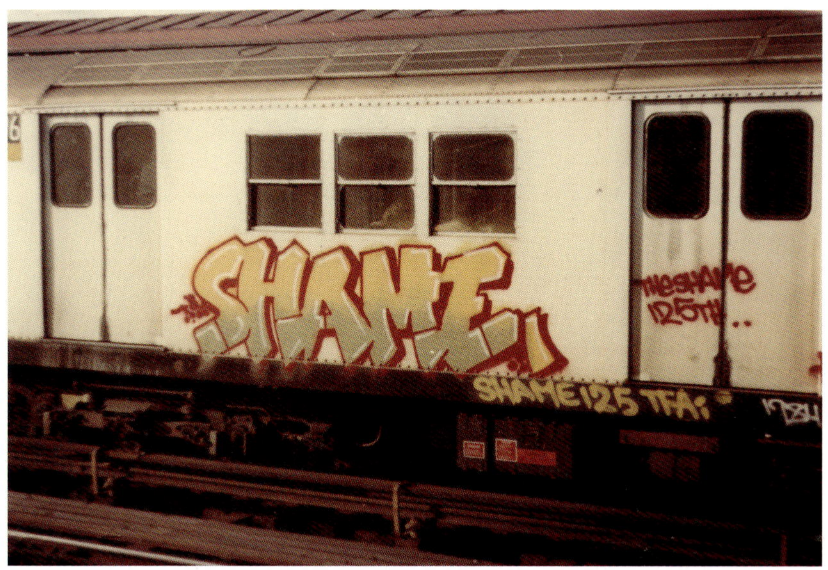

Shame125, 1983 (Photo courtesy of SENTO)

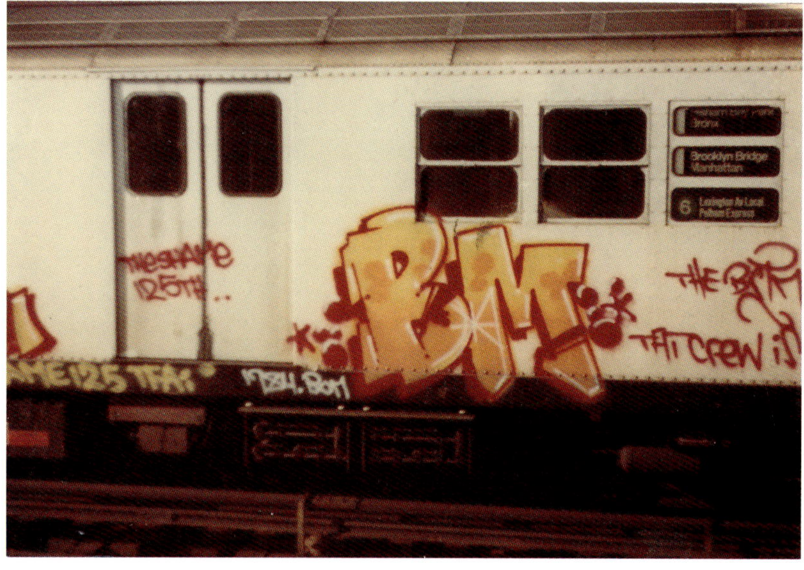

Brim, 1983 (Photo courtesy of SENTO)

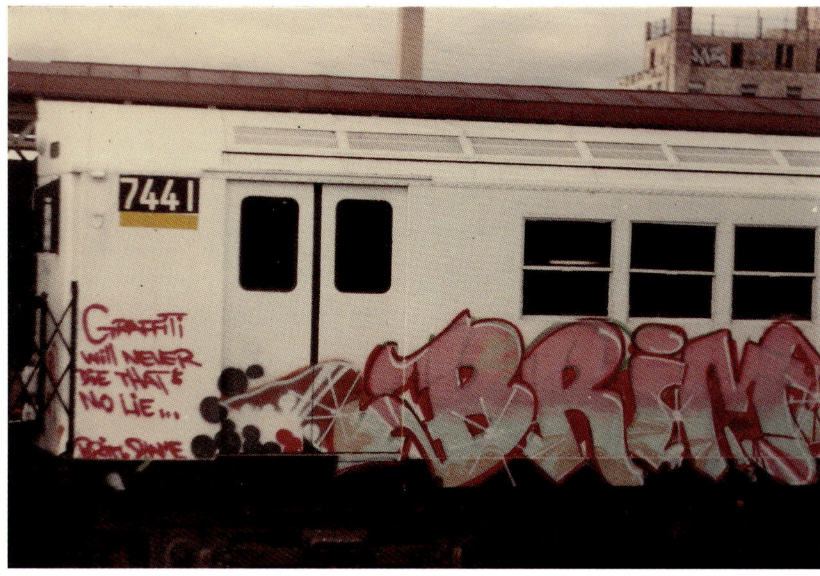

Brim, 1983 (Photo courtesy of SENTO)

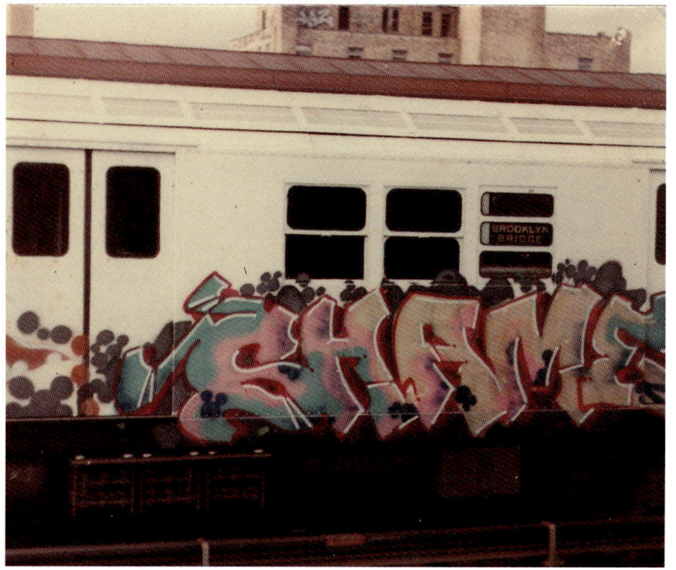

Shame125, 1983 (Photo courtesy of SENTO)

Where it all began . . . my love of graff came way before I even knew what graff was. It started with my love of trains in general. I was fascinated with trains ever since I was four years old. I loved all kinds of trains. The sound, lights, and the smell. I remember my mom dragging me off the 4 train. I just fell out like a starfish on the floor because I did not want to leave the train. By the age of five or six I started noticing images on the sides of the trains, in graphic form. I'd say around 1976, I started seeing pieces accompanied with cartoon characters. I would see it whiz by and at that age, the first thing I gravitated to were the cartoon characters because the train would be going by too fast for me to make out what the piece said. The cartoon characters I was especially able to identify with because I loved cartoons as a kid. The first whole car I saw was all in black, the pieces in the middle was hot pink and at the far end was a top-to-bottom, full body Pink Panther. At the other end was the inspector pointing at the Pink Panther. I later found out that this car was done by Peso131. Totally mind blowing shit to a six-year-old. The second whole car I saw had two top-to-bottom faces of b-boy characters. One on the left with a giant afro and shades and on the other end was a character with a ski hat. Later on I found out that Peso131 did that car as well. So it's safe to say that Peso was my first influence into the game. What hypnotized me to subway graffiti were these key factors: the illustrations, the pieces, and the colors. The fact that it wasn't idle, I only had seconds to take everything in, intrigued me even further. Also the throw-up king "In" TOP crew. I remember the whole car that had about a hundred little "In" pieces on it. It said "In in in in in in," etc. from top to bottom. Later was Ko, Use2, Neil, the mob, I'm talking 1976. By 1977 it was on and popping, I stared more and more at the trains and started seeing work by Team, Max, Fuse, Part, Comet (pre Fed2). By 1978 it was full throttle; Kase2, Kool131, Noc167, and Part were doing beautiful whole cars with characters and all. Along with Chain3 and his Ernie and Burt window-down burner, it destroyed me. I would be on 96th Street with my mother and a 2 train would pull into the station. Out of ten cars, seven of them had something worth looking at. When the 1 line would pull in, out of ten cars maybe three cars had something to look at. Even though they say Broadway was the style line, it wasn't consistent like the 2s and 5s. At the time I was too young to bench trains or take flix. By 1978/79 Fed2 and Leo were holding it down on Broadway with dope cars. 1979 is when I started doing motion tagging, and went to the Ghost Yard for the first time. By 1980 it was Roc stars, TVS, TNB, RTW, and TDS. 1981 and 1982 TFA, TNT, and FBA were going strong! Also, they were my influences. So, when I finally started killing shit on the lines, I always had two audiences in mind, my peers and the public. I implemented characters into the majority of my work because I knew it would wow the public just as it did for me when I was a spectator. My active years on subways were 1979 to 1986. One of my favorite cars was the "Sak and Slin" done in the 1 tunnel. We only had seven cans but I did a nice car with that paint. What's so special to me about this car is halfway through we got chased out by thirty ballbusters. We waited like two hours and went back and finished the car. It ran fresh for one solid week. The second week I seen it running with Ne (Min) and Quik RTW throw-ups on it. Not over the pieces but on the car. Ne partially over my character and Quik over the scroll at the end. I looked at that two ways, it was a diss but in a weird way I saw it as some level of respect to me because the pieces weren't dissed. I guess it was a pecking order (rock, paper, scissors), ha ha. They were well seasoned and established writers. I was still on the come up but they saw my potential and let me live. We are talking 1984, and then by week three the car got buffed. The Ne throw-up was completely gone and the Quik was half buffed. Then later, by 1988, it was spotted in the scrap yard buffed a second time. This time the background was gone on both pieces, but the pieces and characters were still very visible in a ghostly state. The car was completely gutted out, though. Another favorite was the "Sak, Mic, Dae1" window-down done in the Ghost Yard. Then there was the gremlin car with Kc and Rac7. The Sak, Rize Easter car and the Dia, Sak, Rize car was the third car done after I got down with FBA in 1983. On Broadway, I ran mostly with Rize, Kc, Run, Poem, and others like Dae1, Dia, and 2New. Then the cars me and Shame125 and Kc did on the 2s and 5s. By this point we were full throttle. Fun times.

–Sak MBT

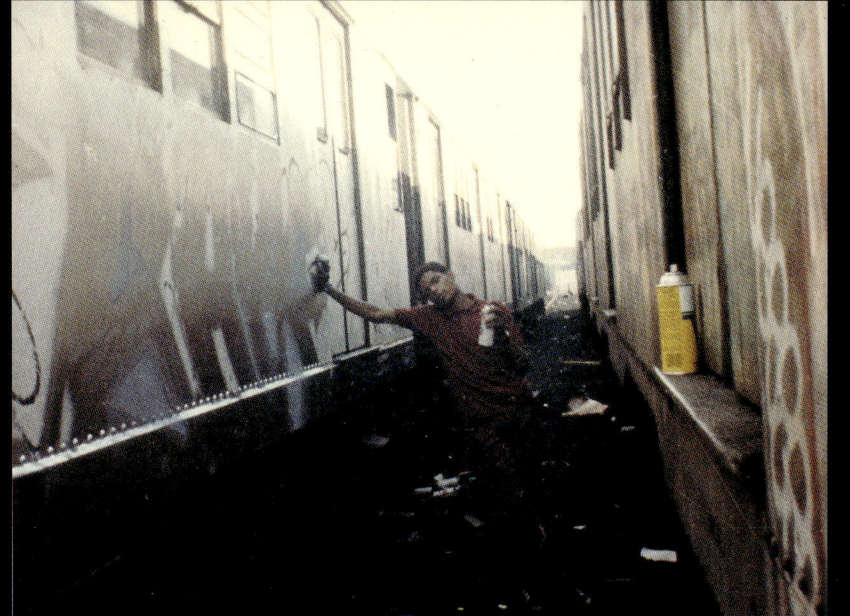

Sak MBT in the Ghost Yard, 1984 (Photo courtesy of Sak MBT)

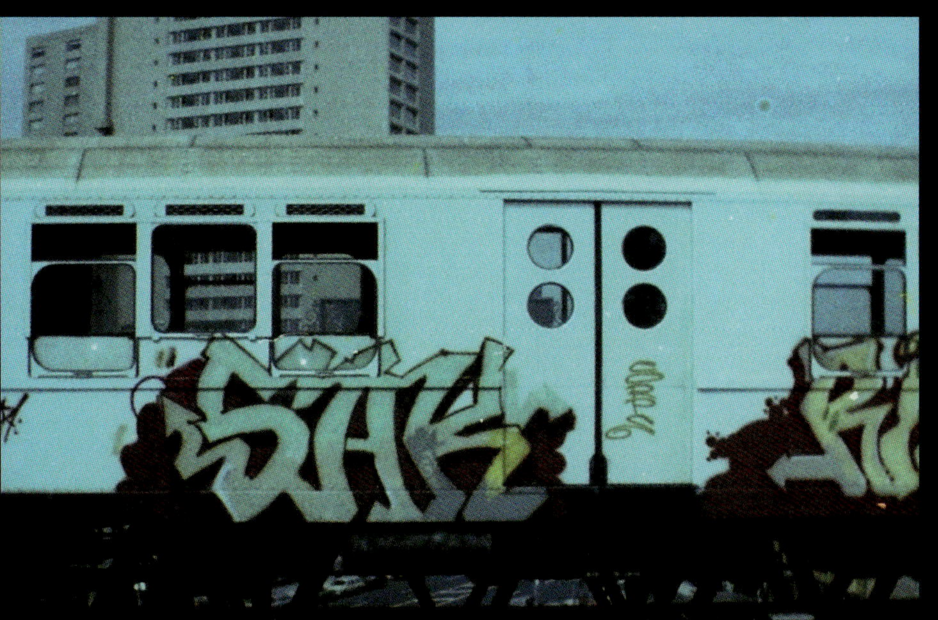

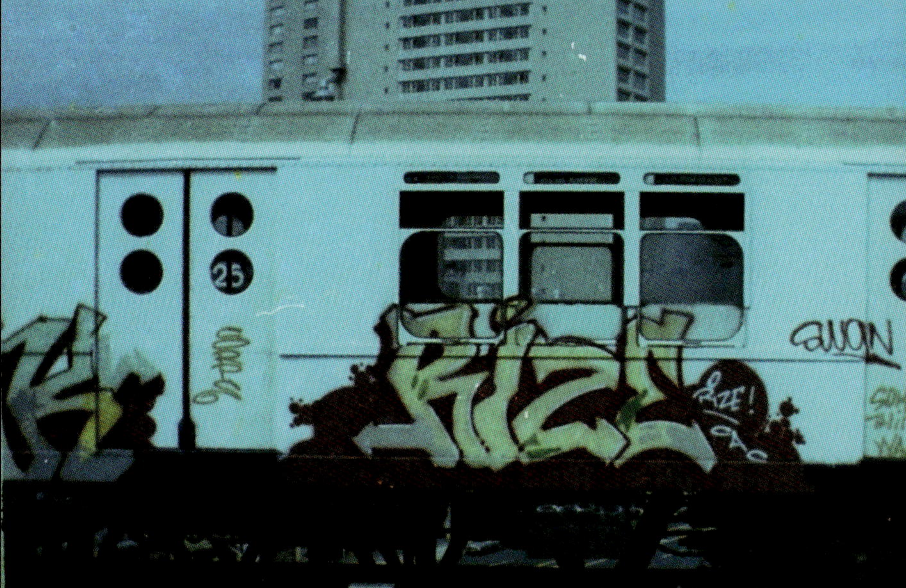

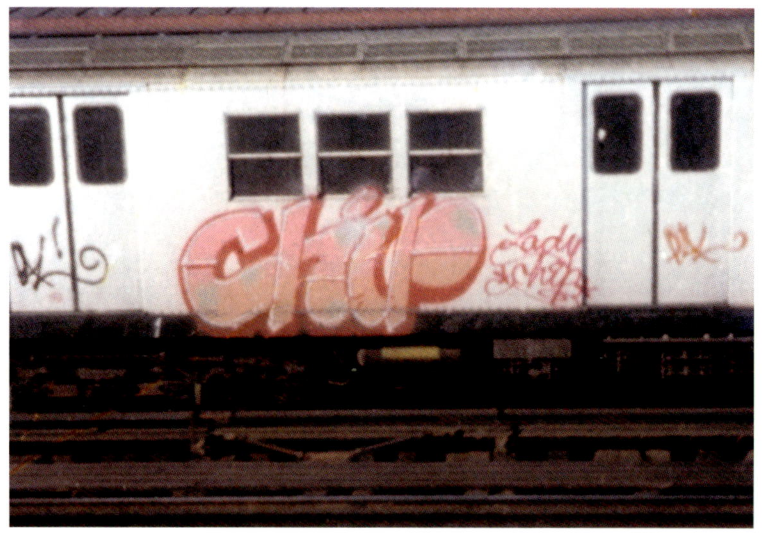

Chip, 1983

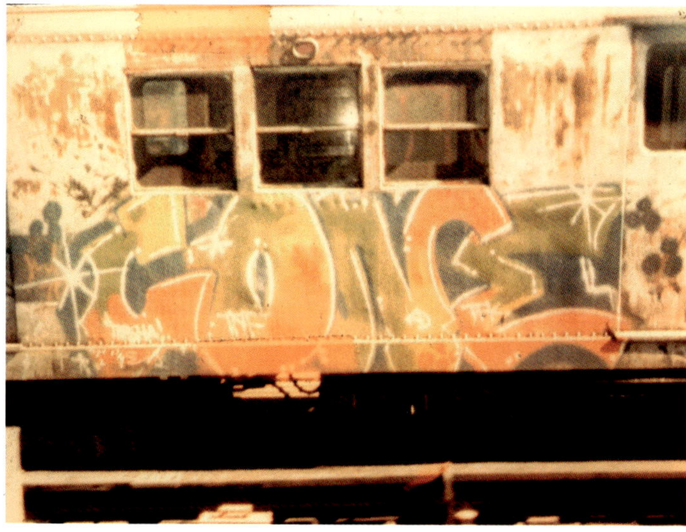

Cone TNF KD, 1983

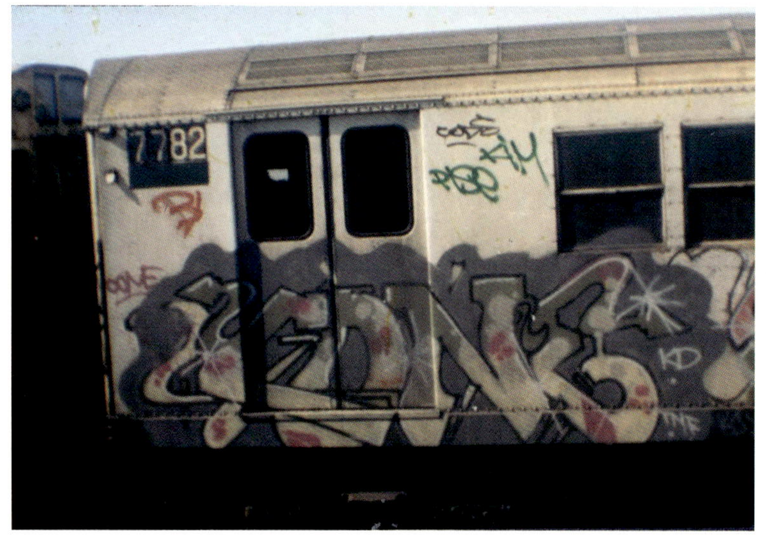

Cone KD TNF, 1984

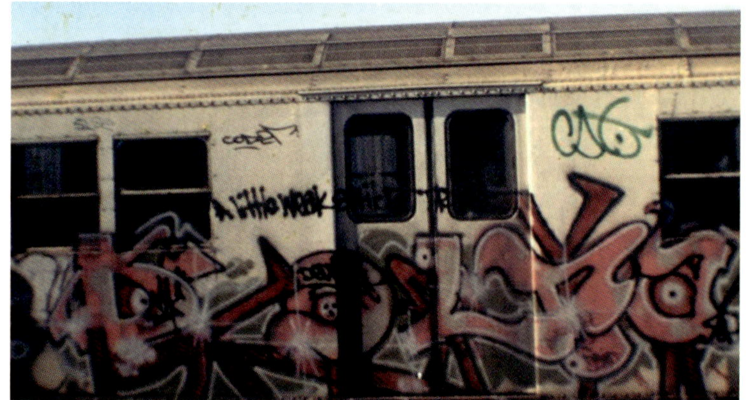

Delta, 1984

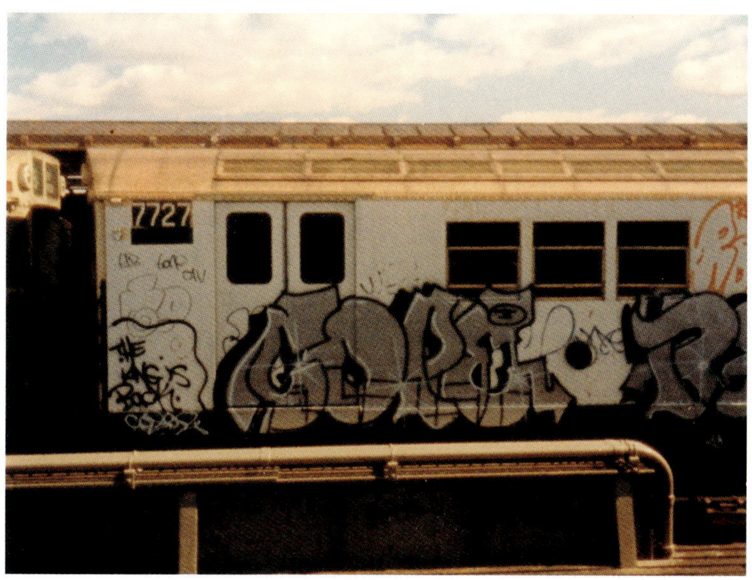

Cope2, 1984

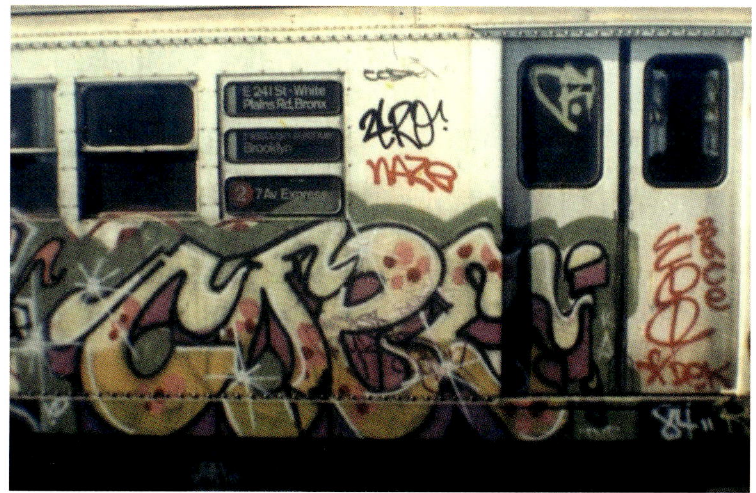

Cope2 KD TNF, 1984

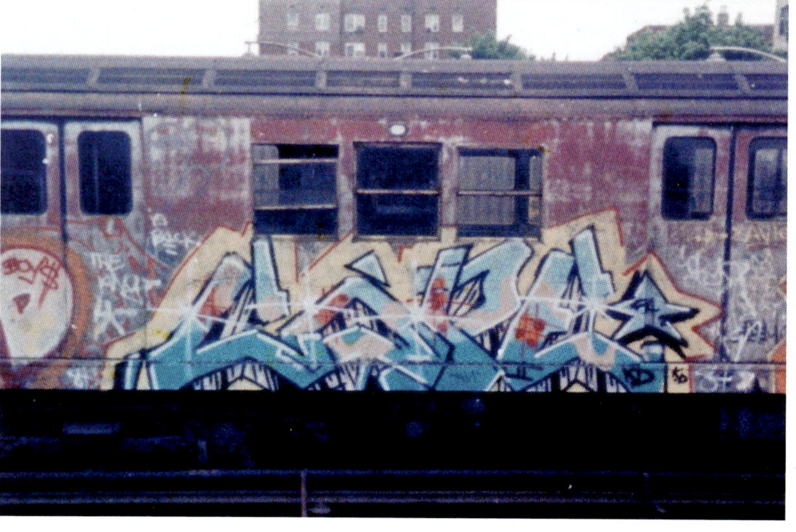

Cope2 KD, 1984

For Your Eyes Only was not actually my last, last whole car, contrary to popular belief, though it was a good candidate by virtue of its name. It was the second wind to another car done in the same place shortly after that was never seen again. This last whole car, for which I still have the original drawing, was called "Lee Lives" and was featured in my last show at the Klagsbrun pop-up gallery in May 2015. This strange phenomenon of what I call "Ghost cars" has happened to me before only twice and I'm sure to many other cats as well. Cars get decommissioned, laid up for repairs and cleaning, and/or assigned to other tasks, i.e., work trains, garbage trains, money trains. Fortunately, images of *Eyes Only* were captured, technically making it my last visionary car on the lines.

–LEE TF5

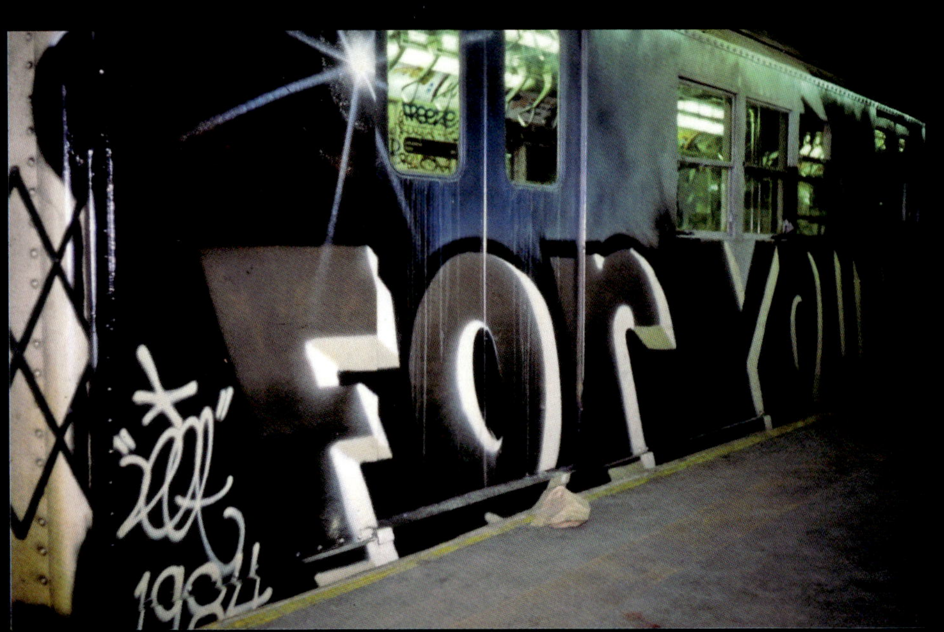

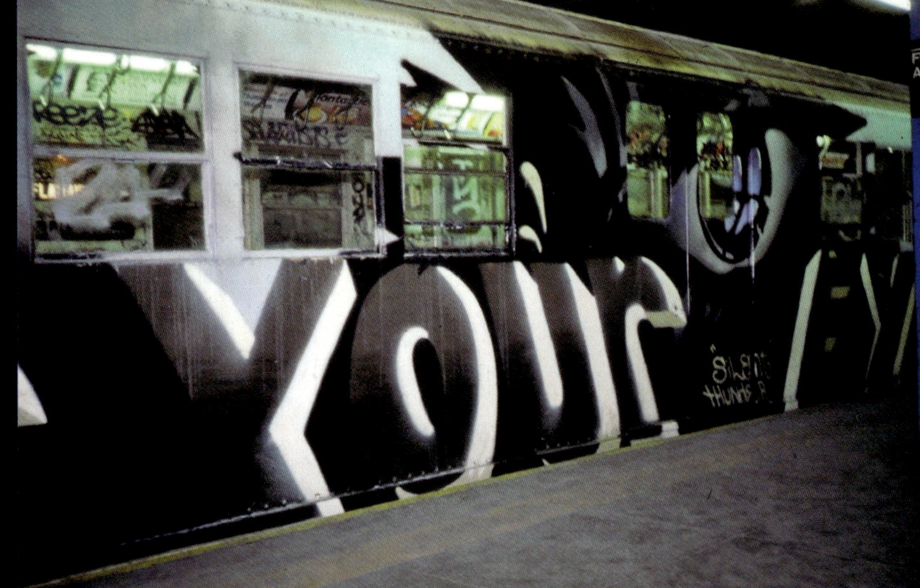

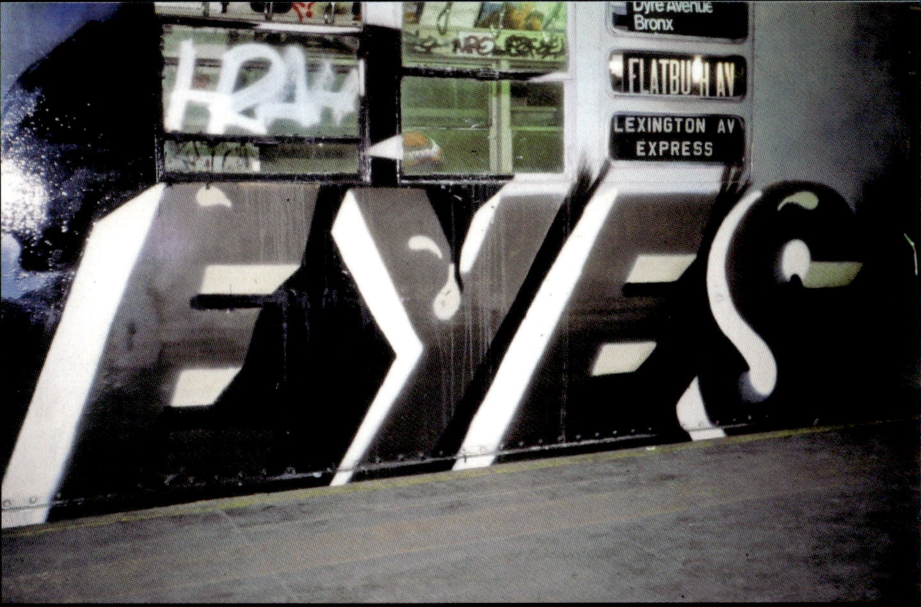

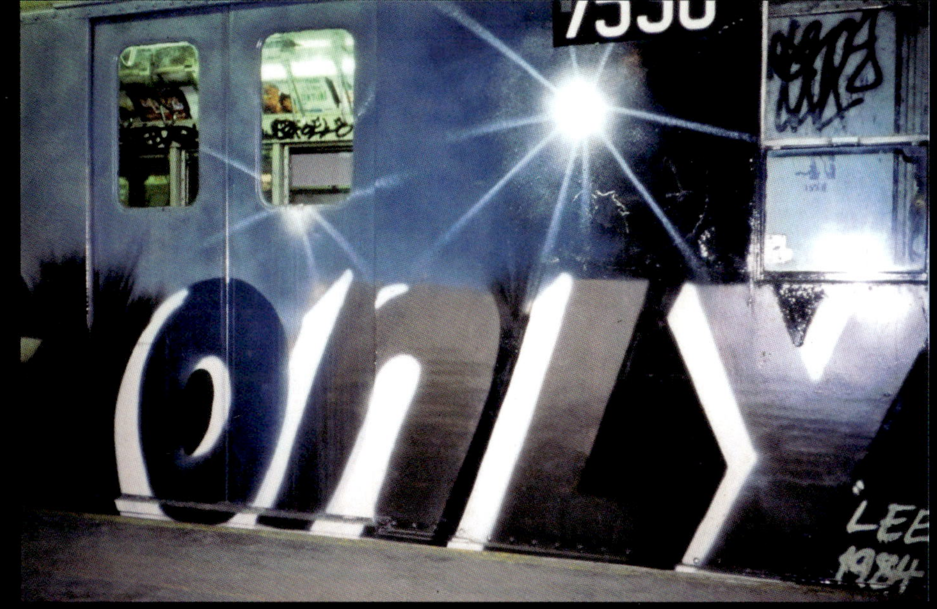

For Your Eyes Only by LEE TF5, 1984

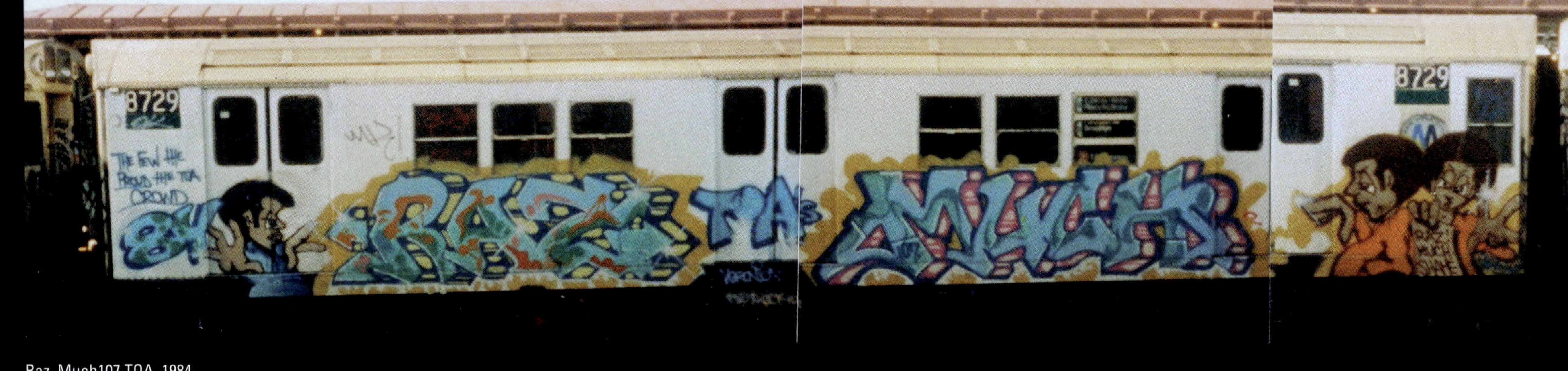

Raz, Much107 TOA, 1984

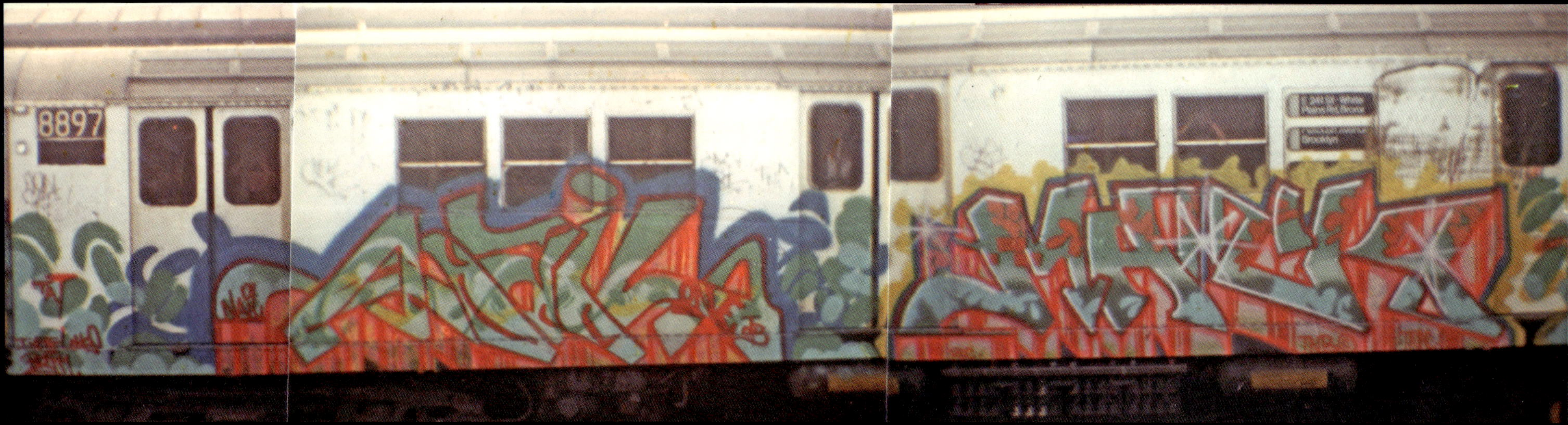

Nail, Mack, 1984

What can I say? I guess one of the best years in graff was my era. The hottest crews were going all in. TATs, FBA, UA, TC5 (The Cool 5), and many more. We made those trains look colorful.

–Raz

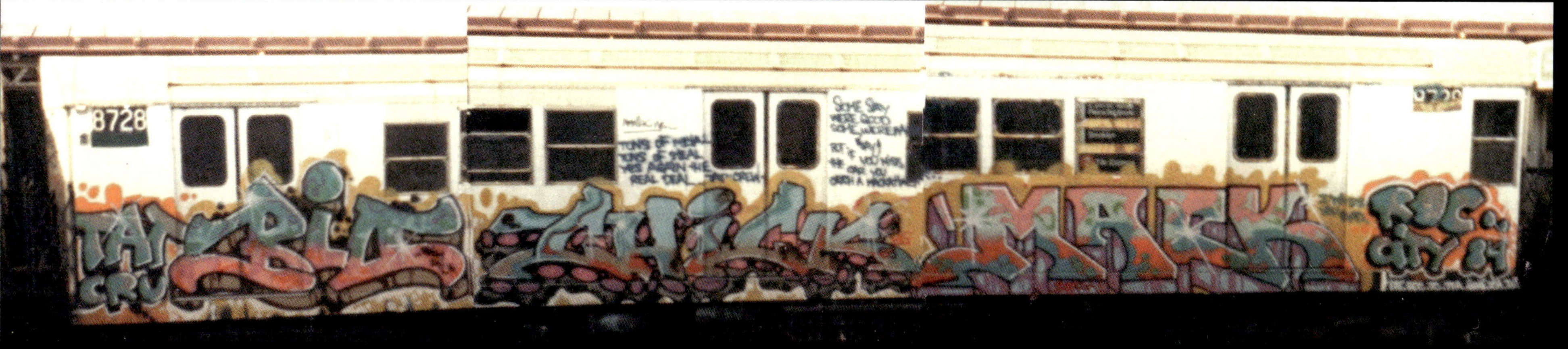

Bio, Chick, Mack TATS CRU, 1984

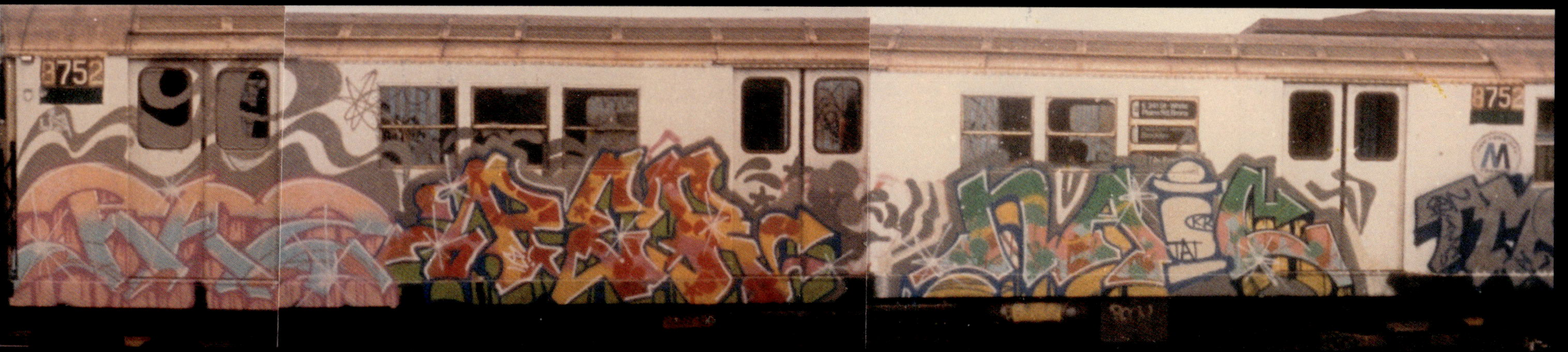

Raz, Per, Nail, 1984

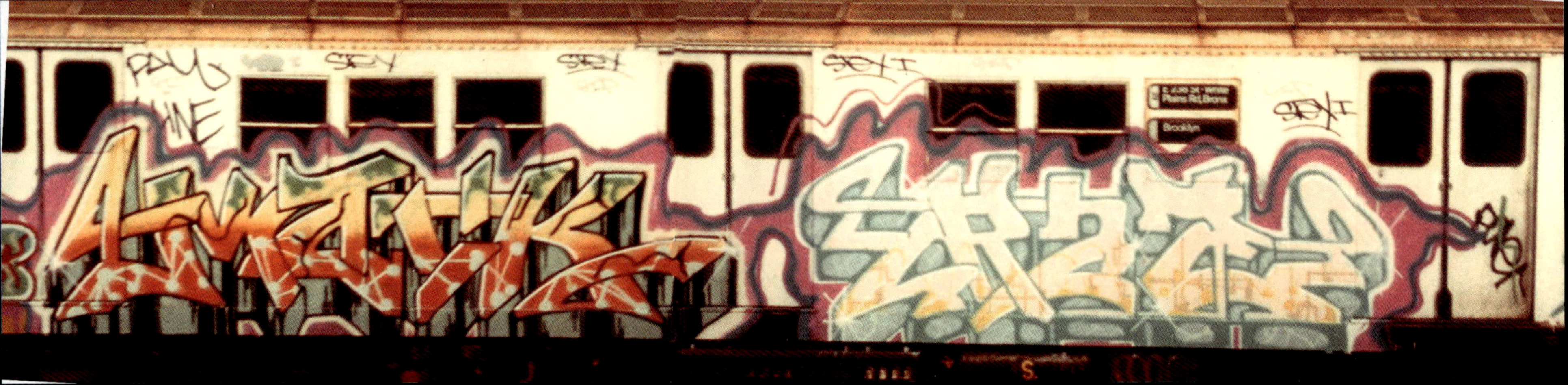

Mack, Raz, 1984

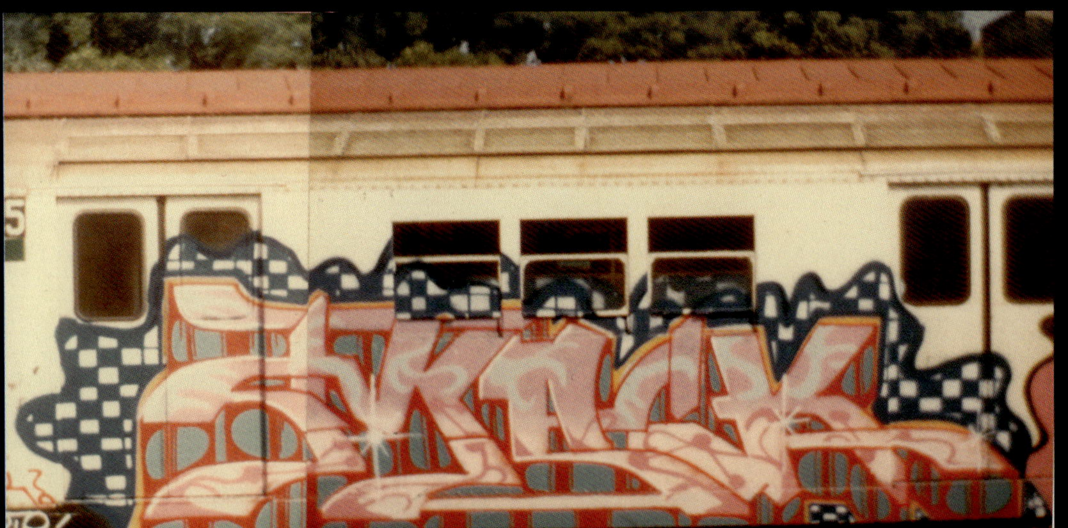

Mack TAT

What's up, Cavs? I hope all is well. I saw your brother, Key, three weeks ago. Always good seeing him. It trips me out because the picture I got of you guys in my mind is two young kids so amped and enthusiastic about taking flicks on the train station. I still think I could go to the train station and bump into ya'll, ha ha. That's life and nothing lasts forever, but we sure had fun back then. The train station was the real Instagram for real graffiti artists. How I miss when graffiti was spontaneous. Today it is too organized and has lost its edge, but I still enjoy it and appreciate it more when it's illegal and on trains.

–Mack TAT

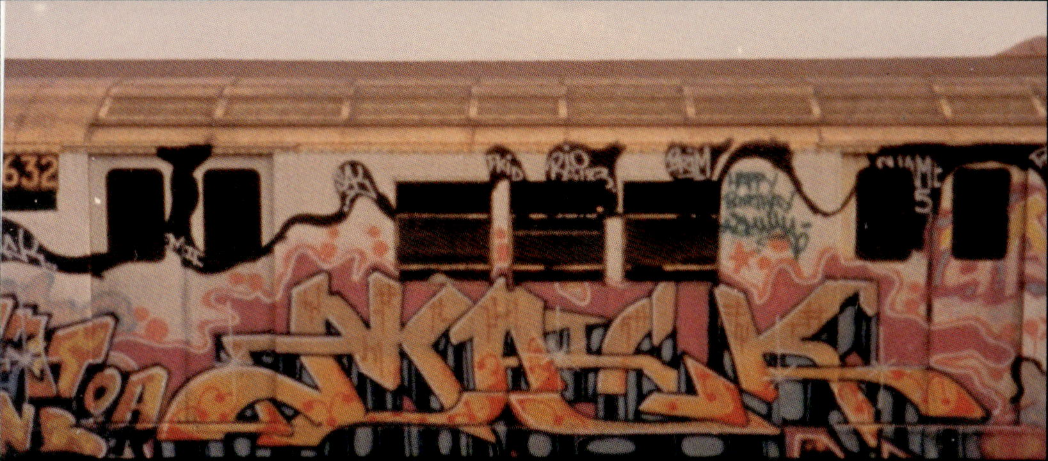

Mack TATOA TNB, 1984

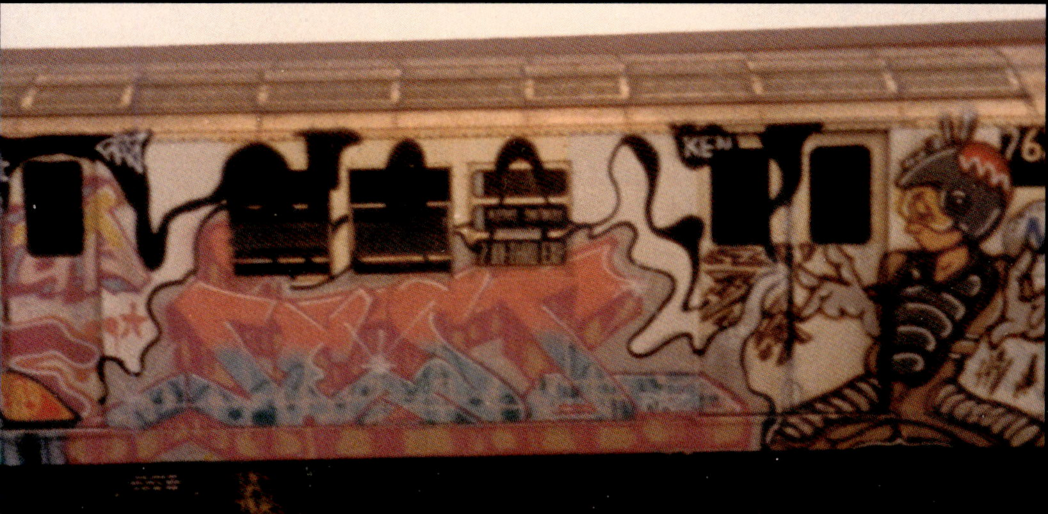

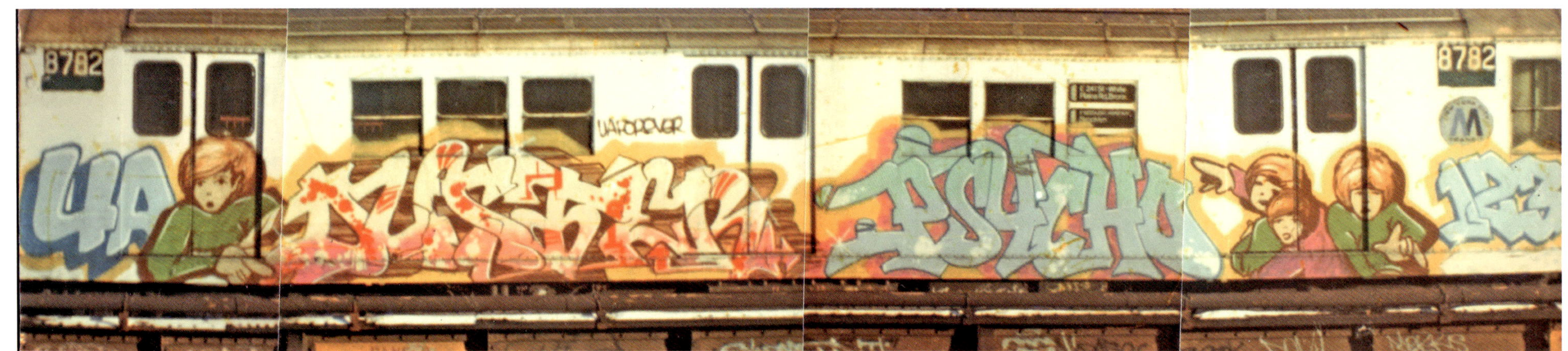

Duster, Psycho123 (Seen UA), 1984

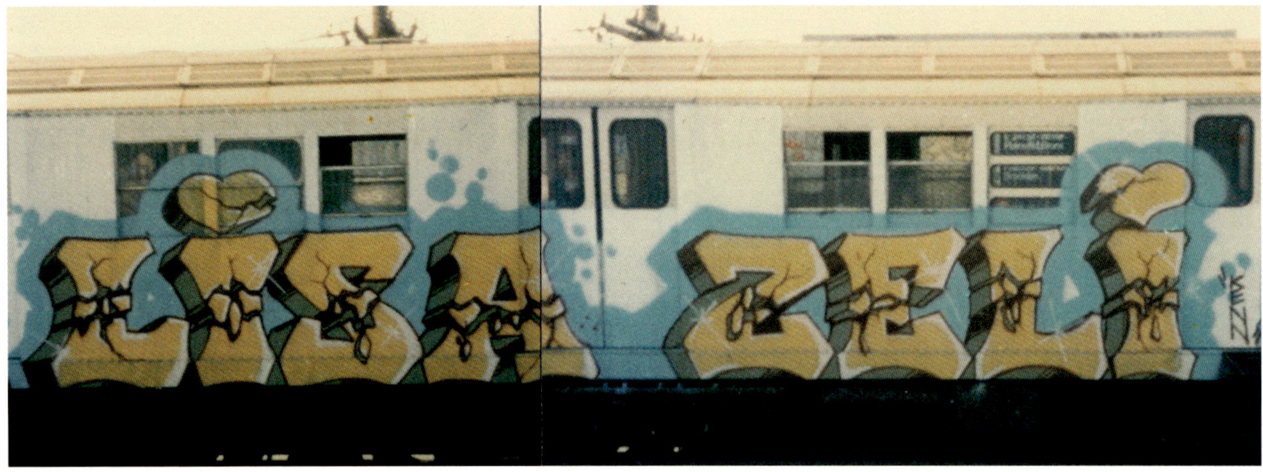

Lisa, Zeli, 1984

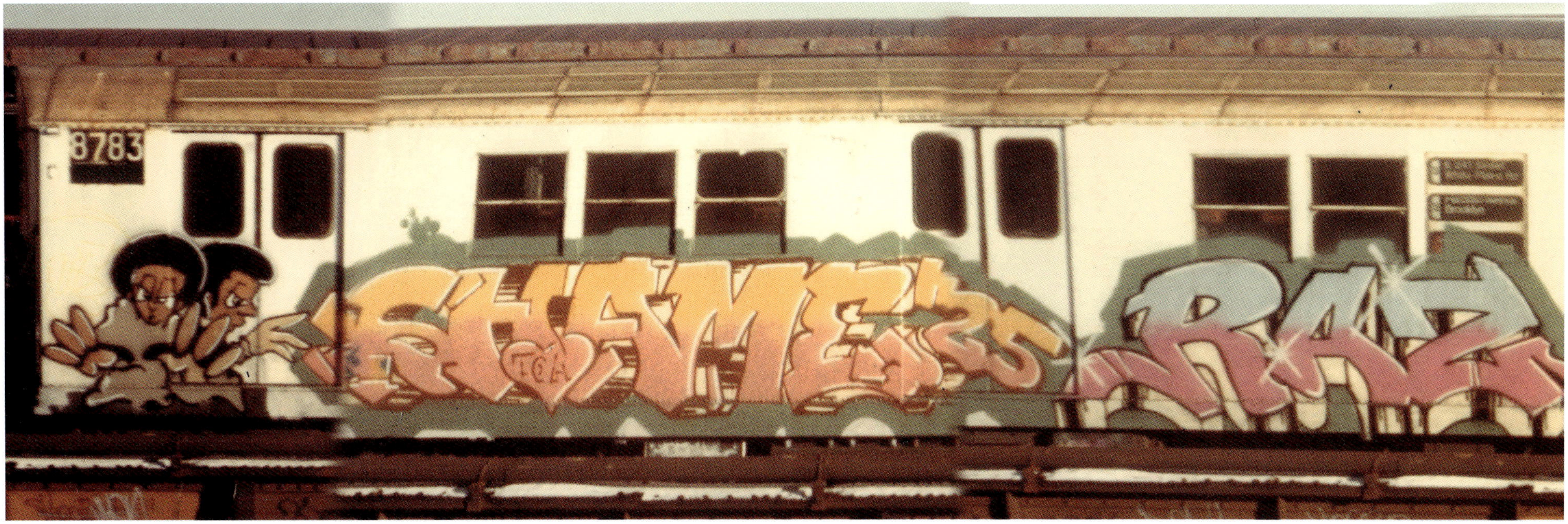

Shame, Raz, 1984

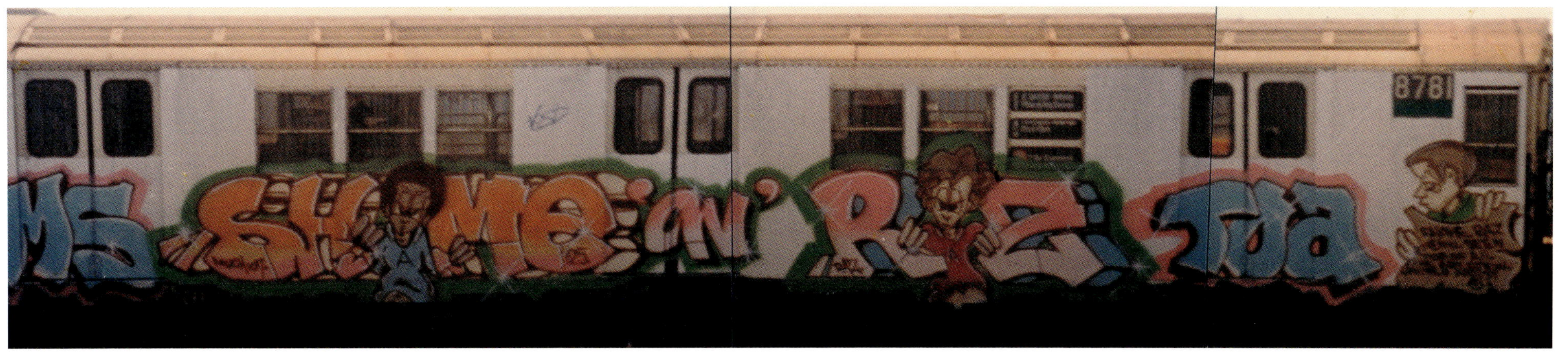

Shame on Raz, 1984

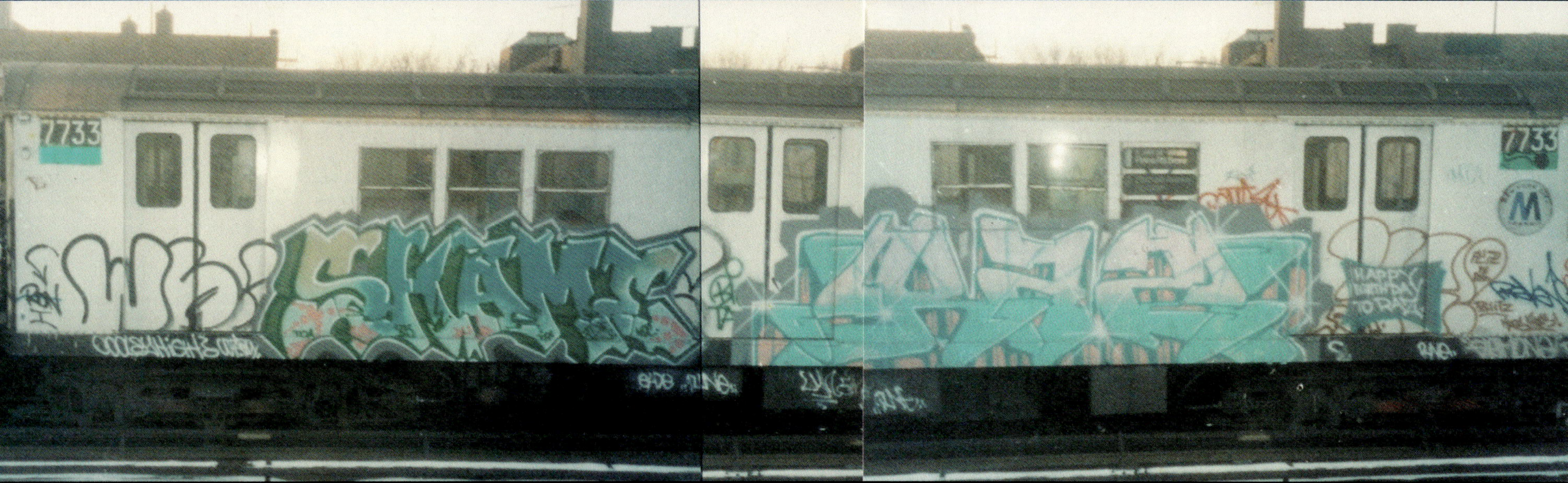

Shame, Raz, 1985

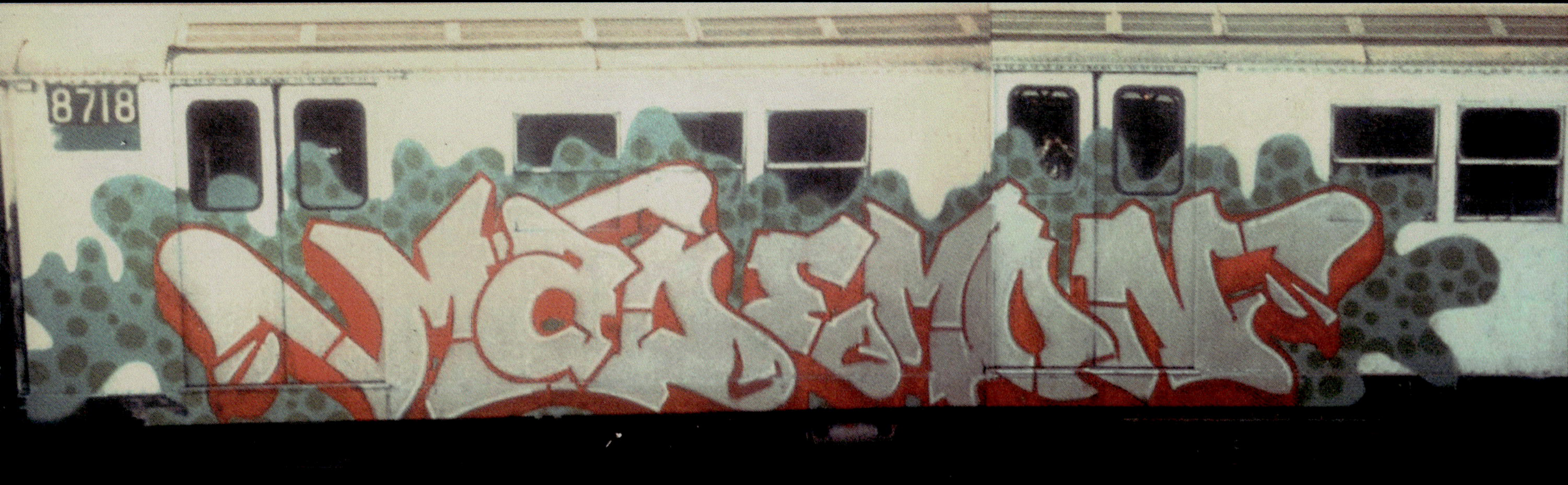

Mademon (Mad, Demon), 1985

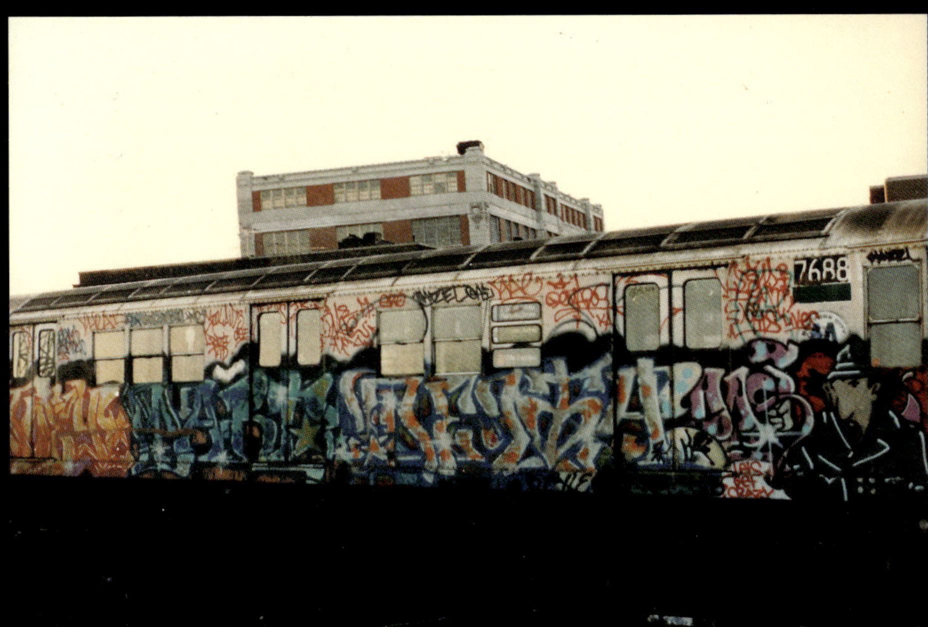

Joey, Part, Delta, 1984

The *Inspector Gadget* car was Delta2's idea. It was pretty much the cartoon at that time. We pulled it off in the Harlem tunnel, which for me was my backyard. I was one of the first to do pieces in there. The car was done in the mid 80s.

–Part TDS

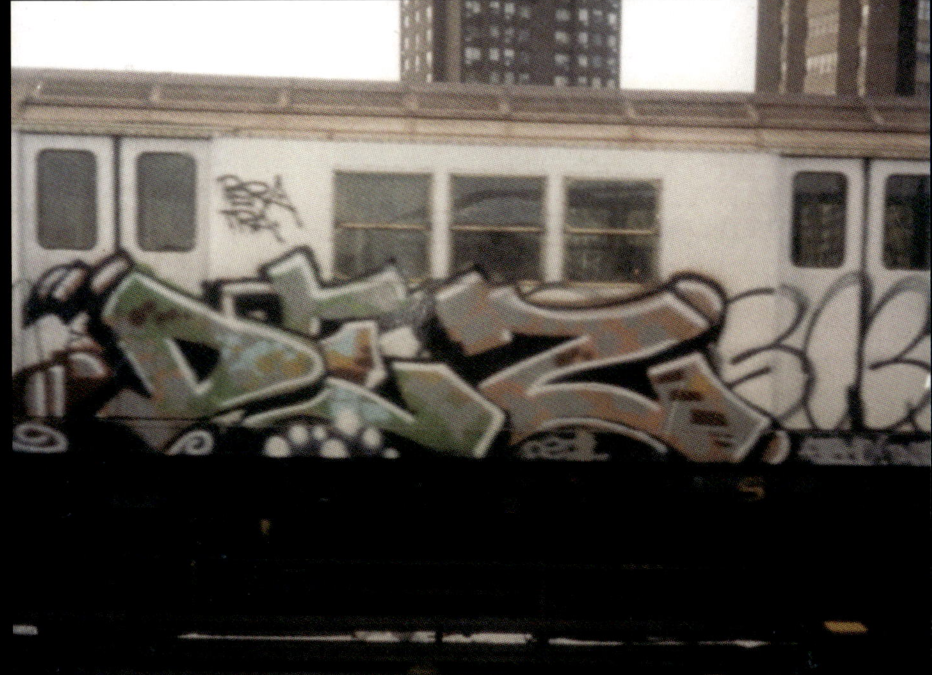

Dez, 1984

This was a basic throw-up I did with left over paint and a fat cap in 1983. I was high as hell and always hated it but other people seemed to like it.

–Dez TFA

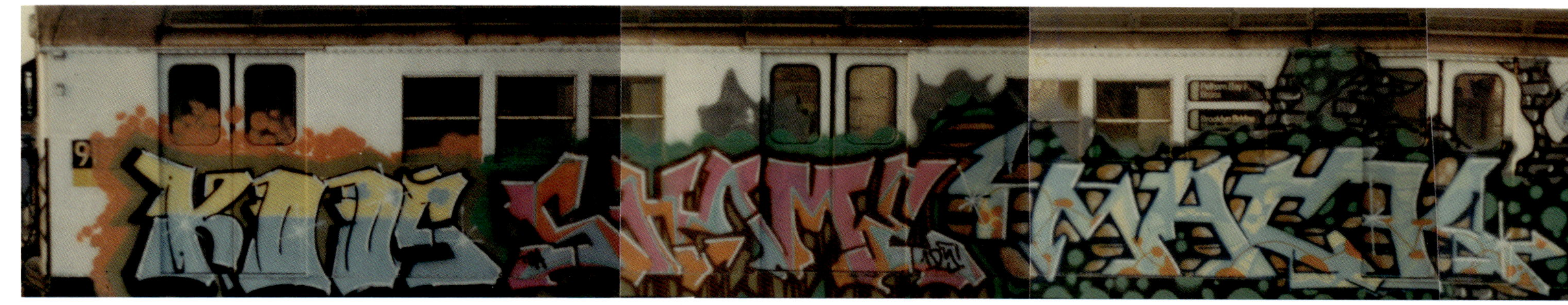

Koos, Shame, Mack, 1984 (Photo courtesy of SENTO)

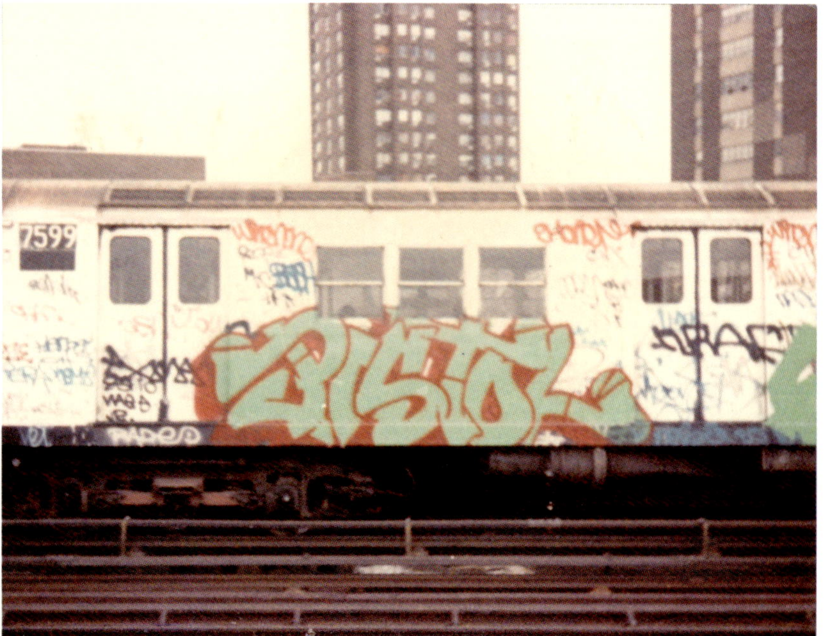

Pistol (Seen UA), 1985

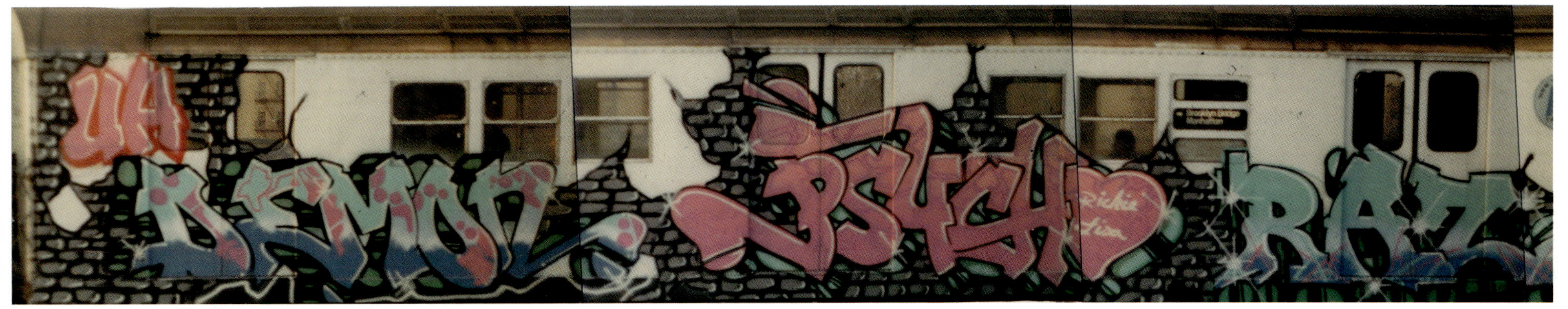

Demon, Psycho123, Raz, 1984 (Photo courtesy of SENTO)

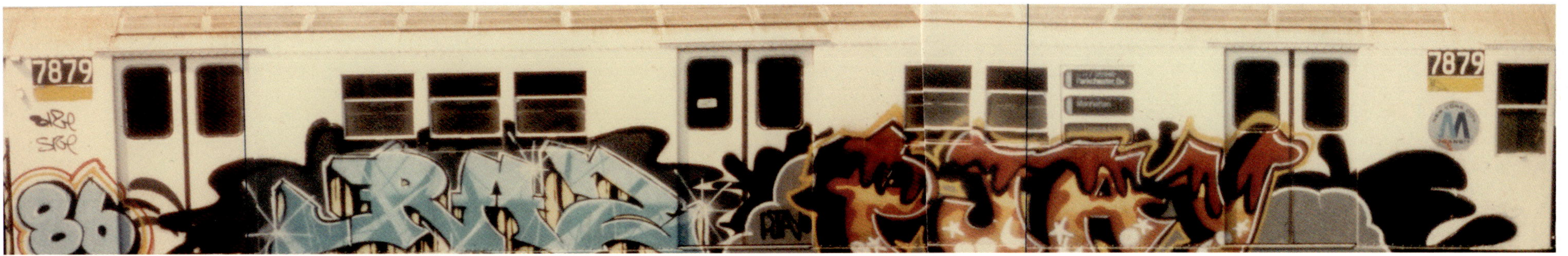

Raz, Pjay, 1986

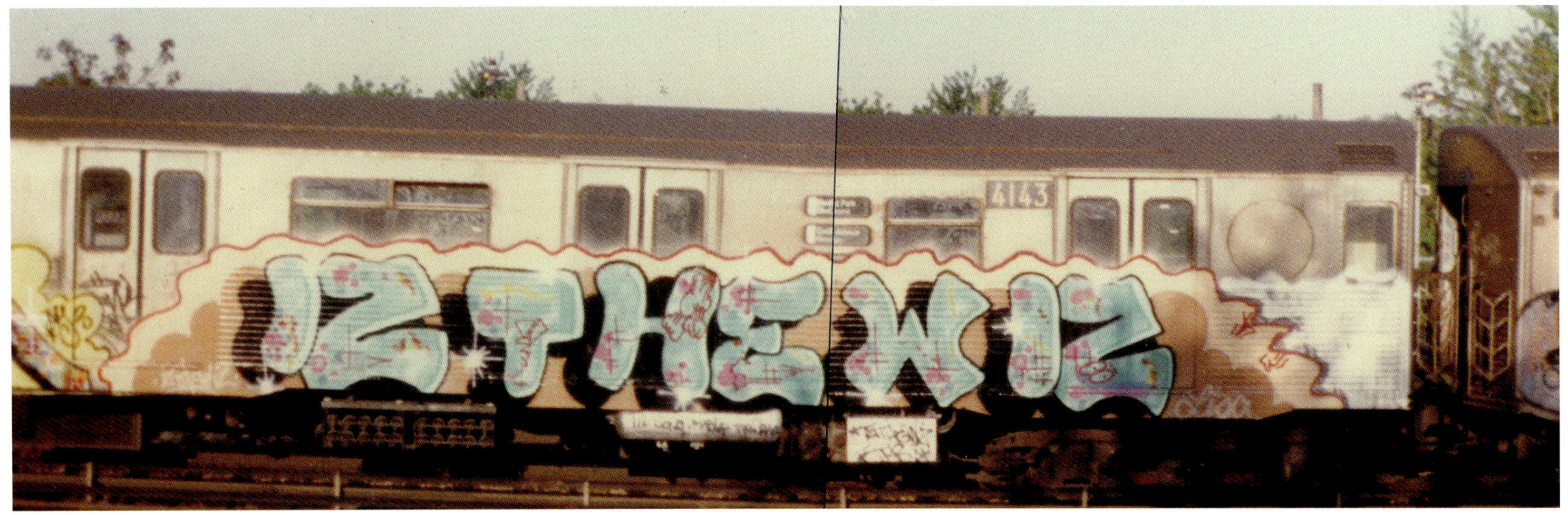

Izthewiz TMB

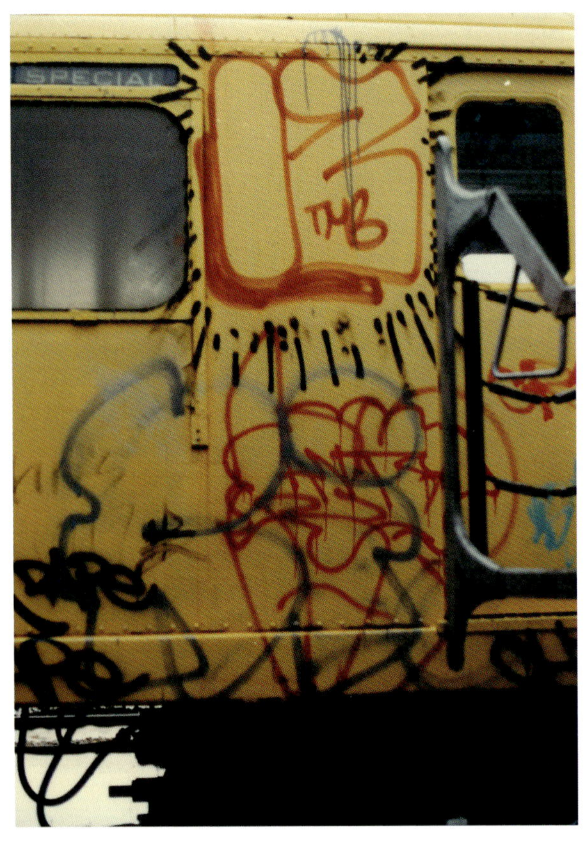

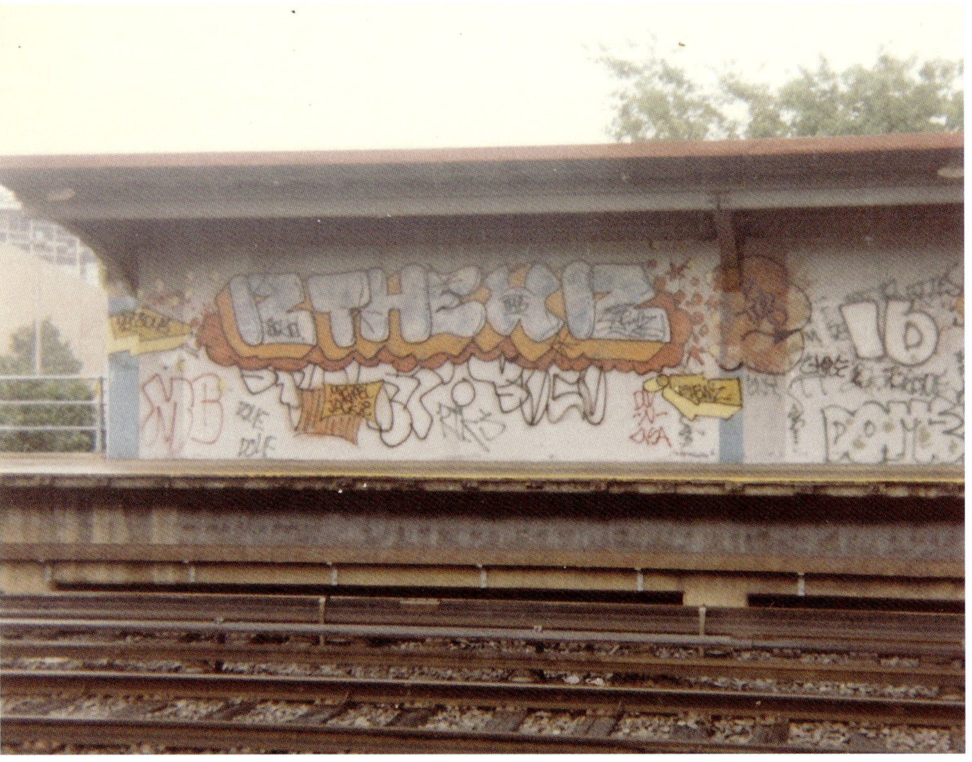

Izthewiz, Aqueduct Train Station

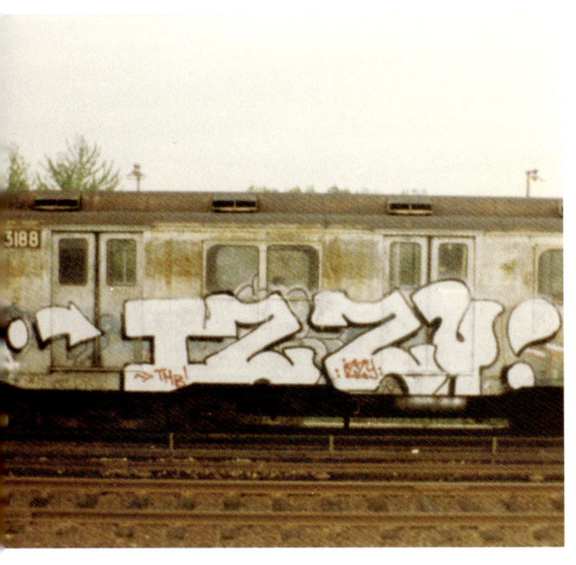

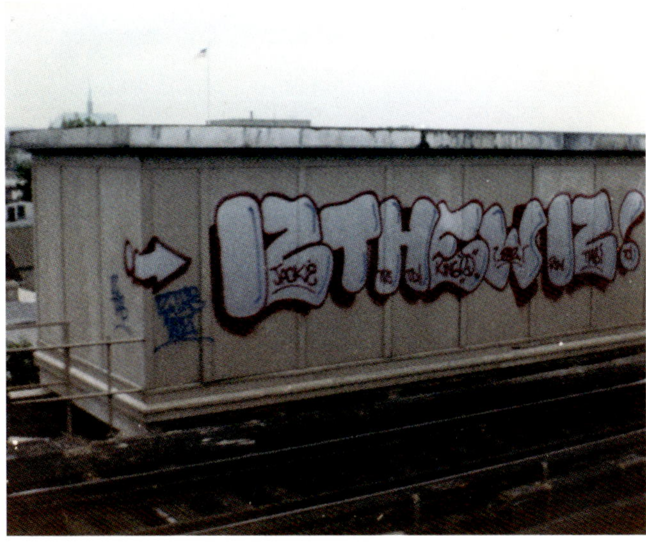

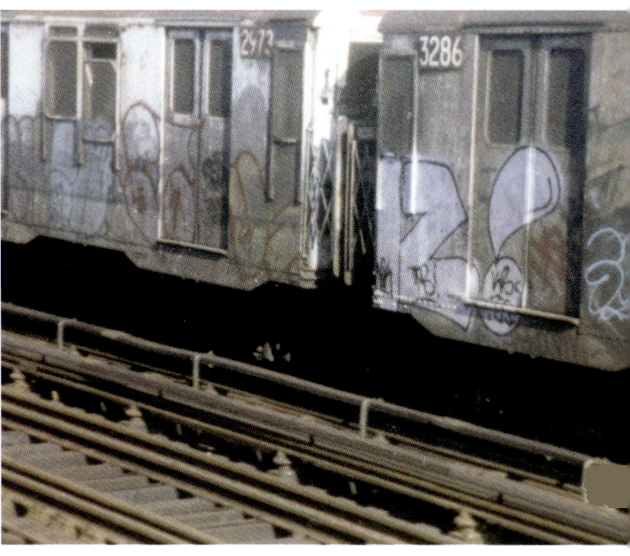

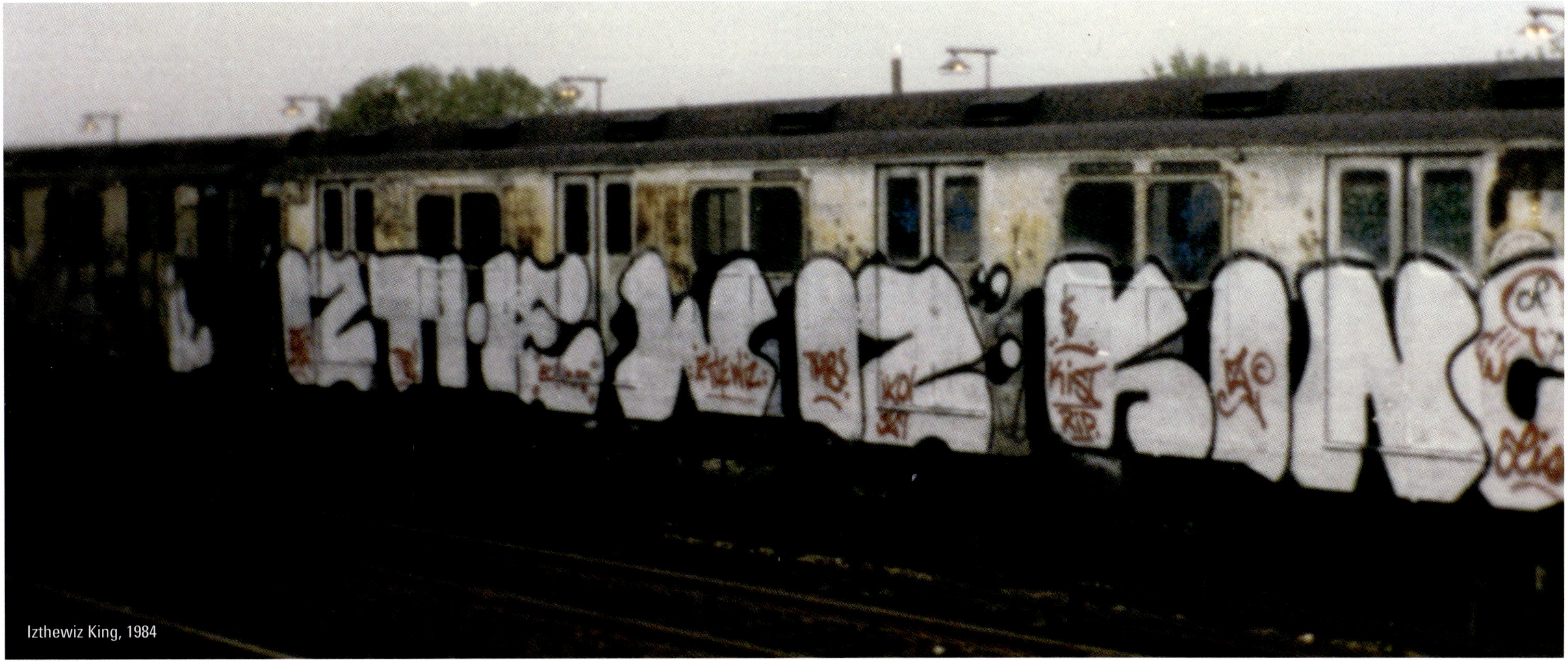

Izthewiz King, 1984

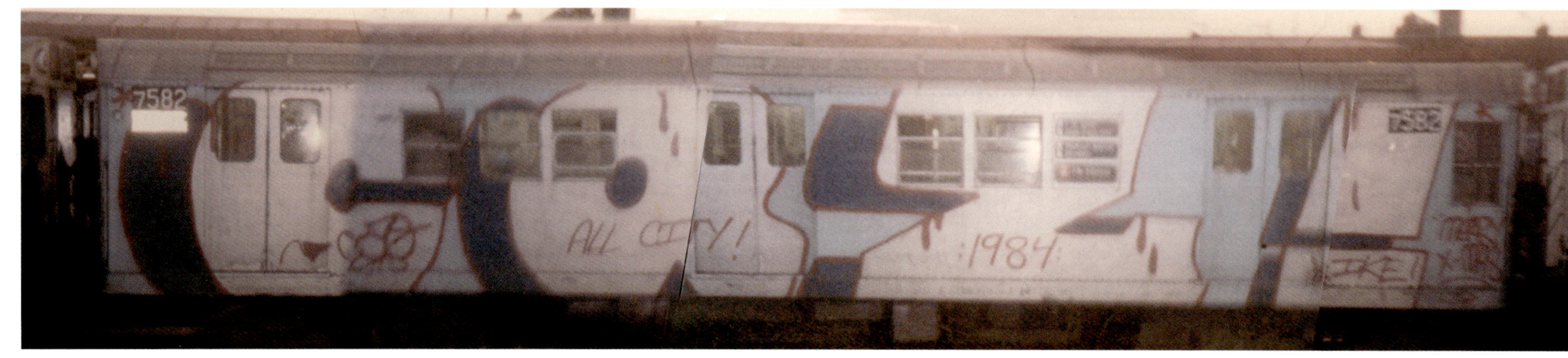

Caz TMB, 1984

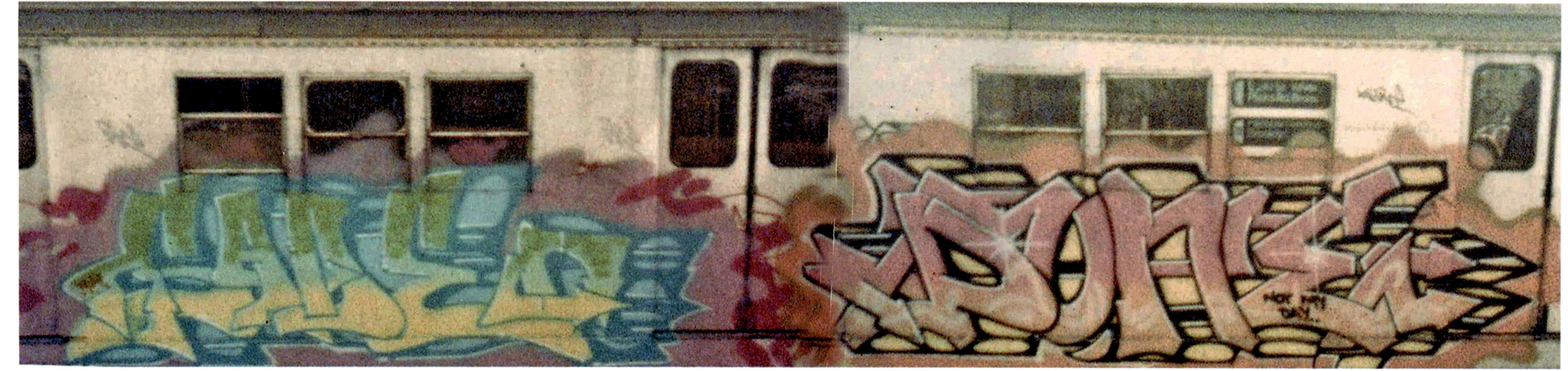

Sade, Dune, 1984

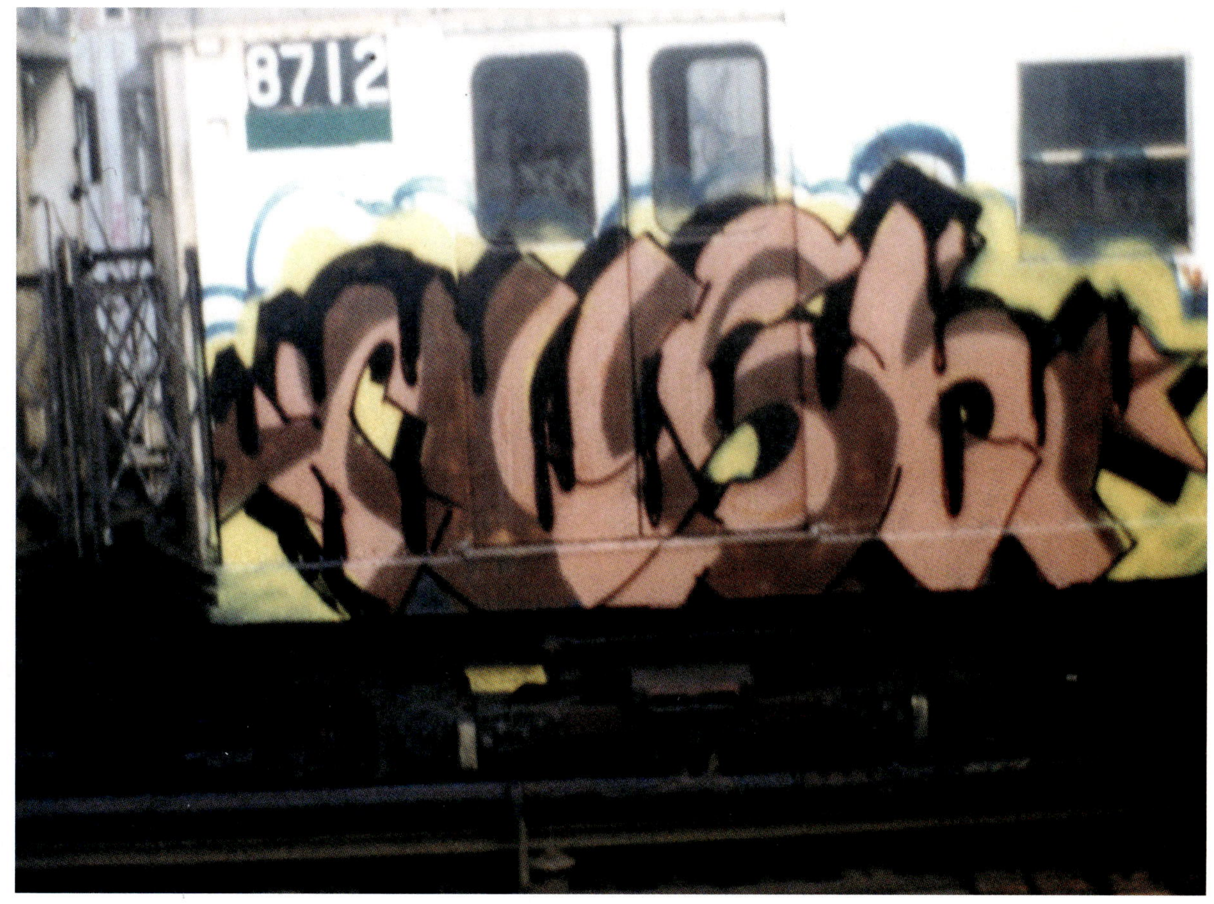

Rush MPC, 1984

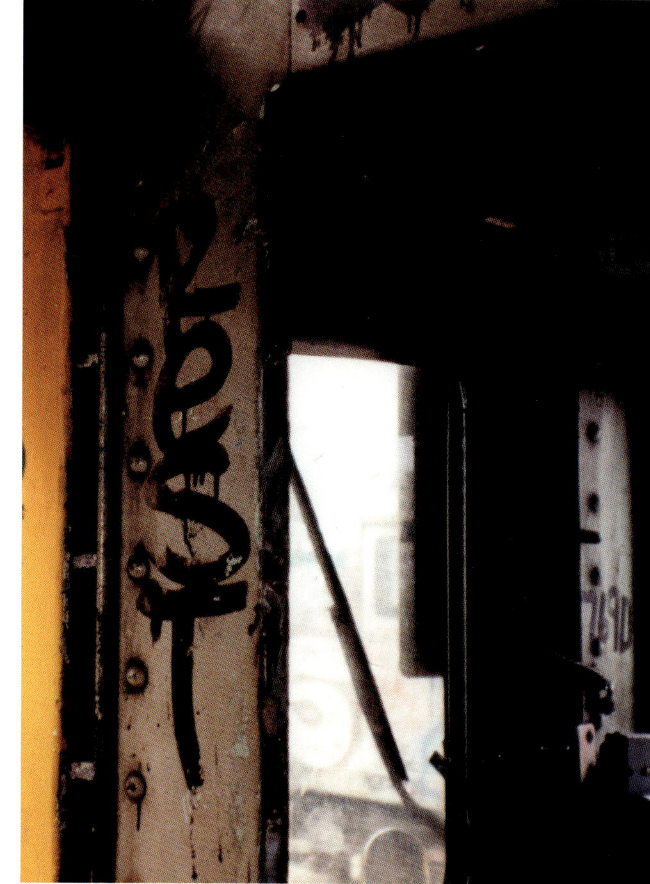

Rest MPC

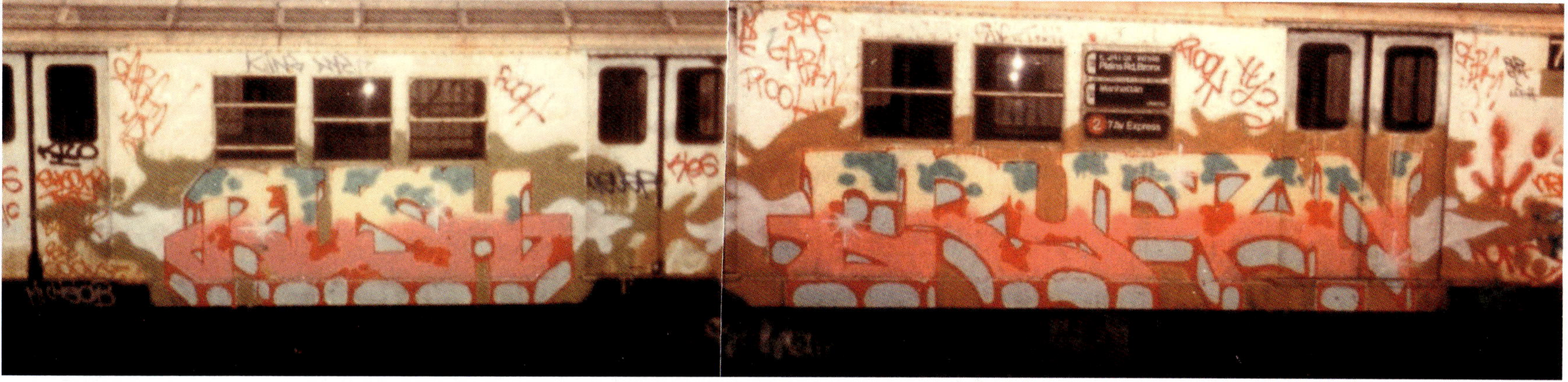

Rush, Crypton, 1984

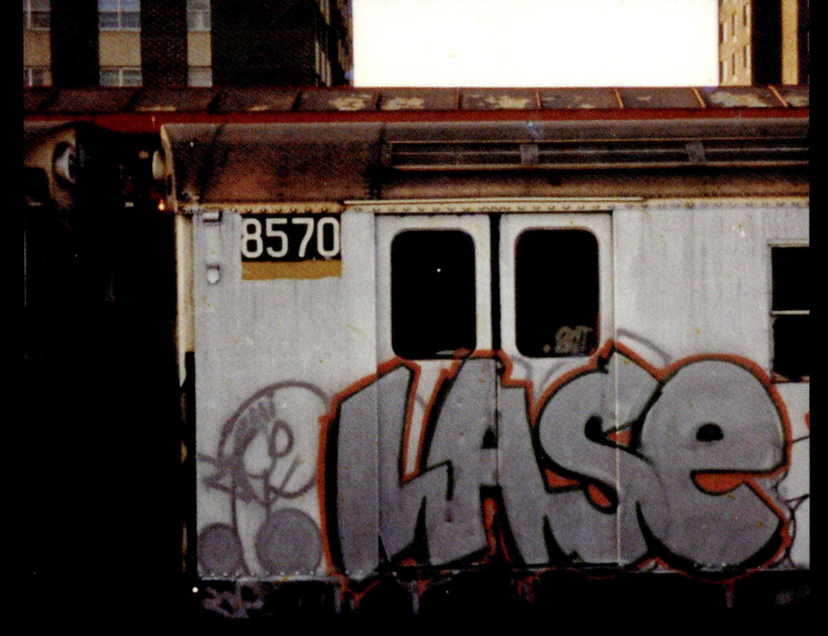

Lase, 1984

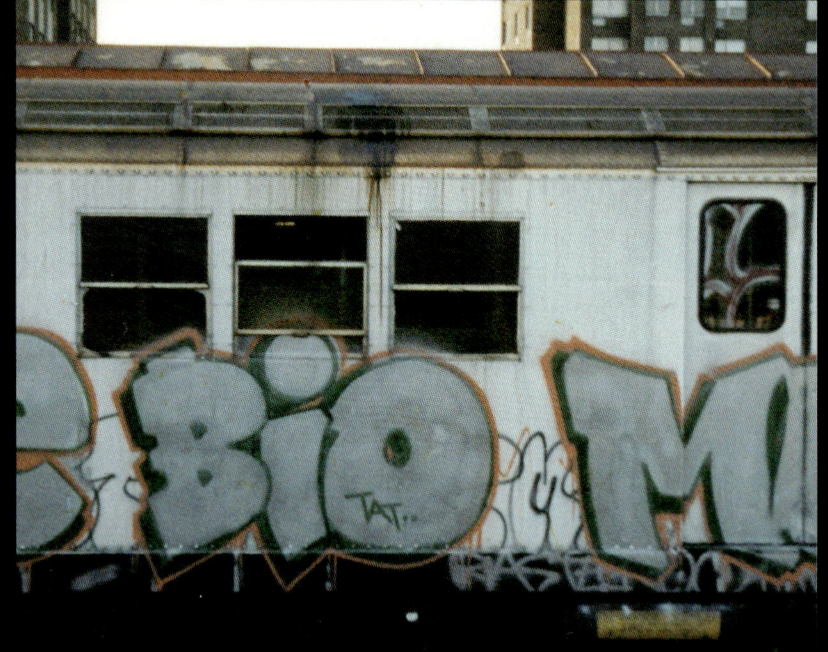

Bio, 1984

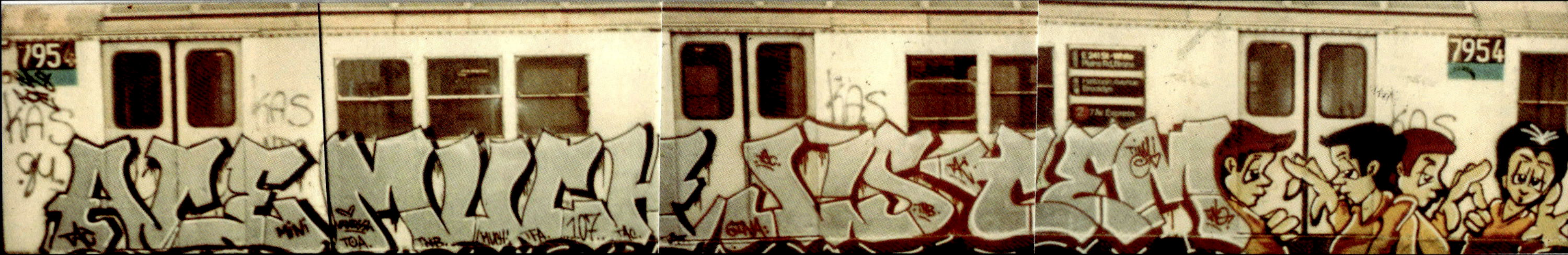

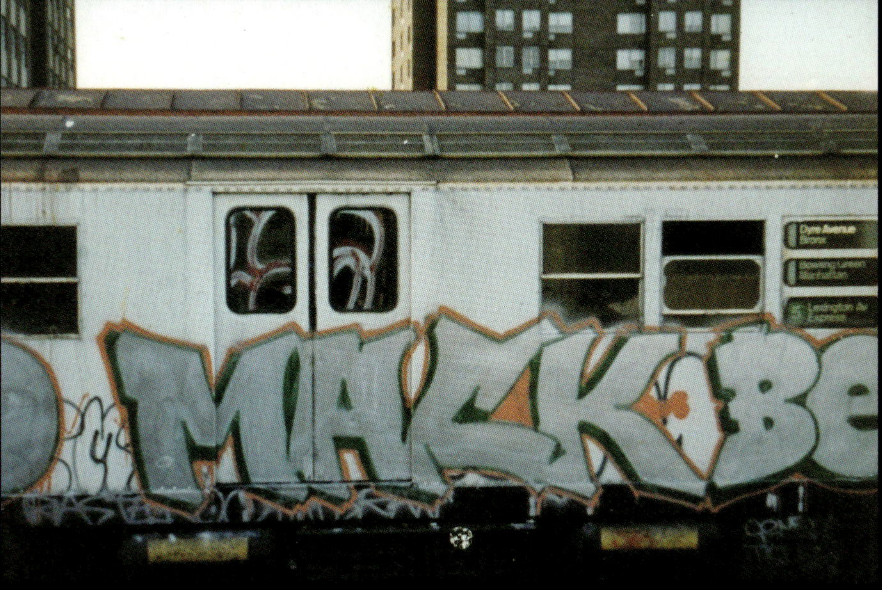

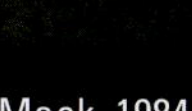

Mack, 1984

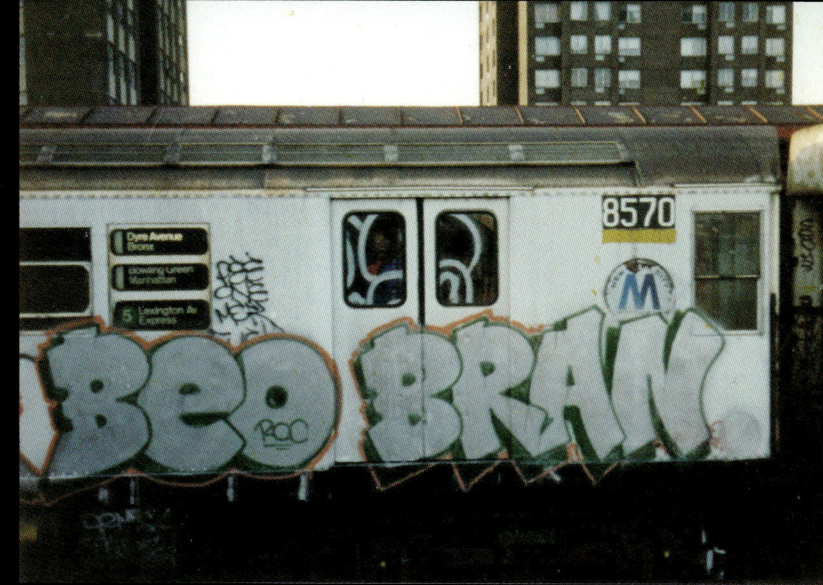

Beo, Bran, 1984

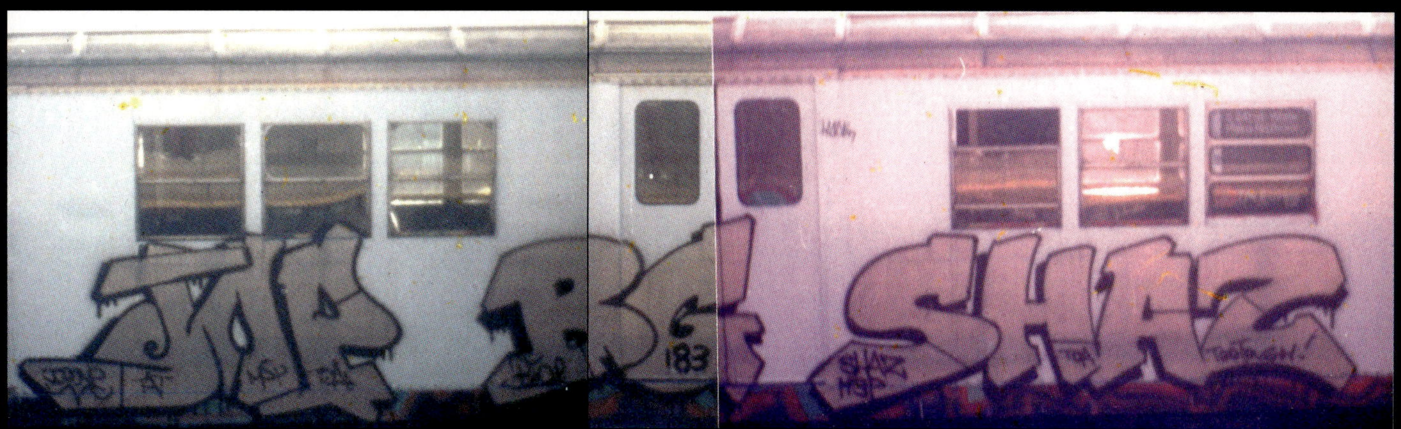

Jop, BG183, Shaz, 1984

A writer from the 80s. It was the best times of my life. I racked spray cans, hopped over the turnstiles, and painted with the best writers. I ran from the police because all I wanted to do was write my name on the subway trains.

–BG183

TATS CRU FOREVER

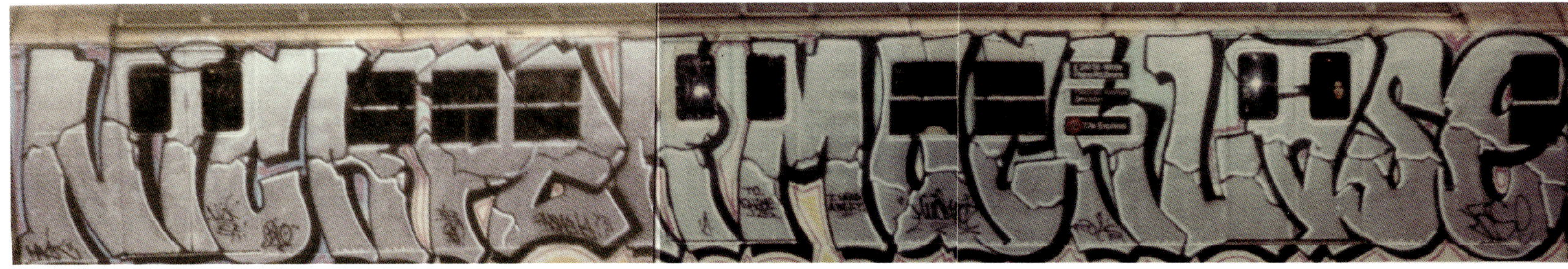

Nick, Per, Much, Lase, 1984

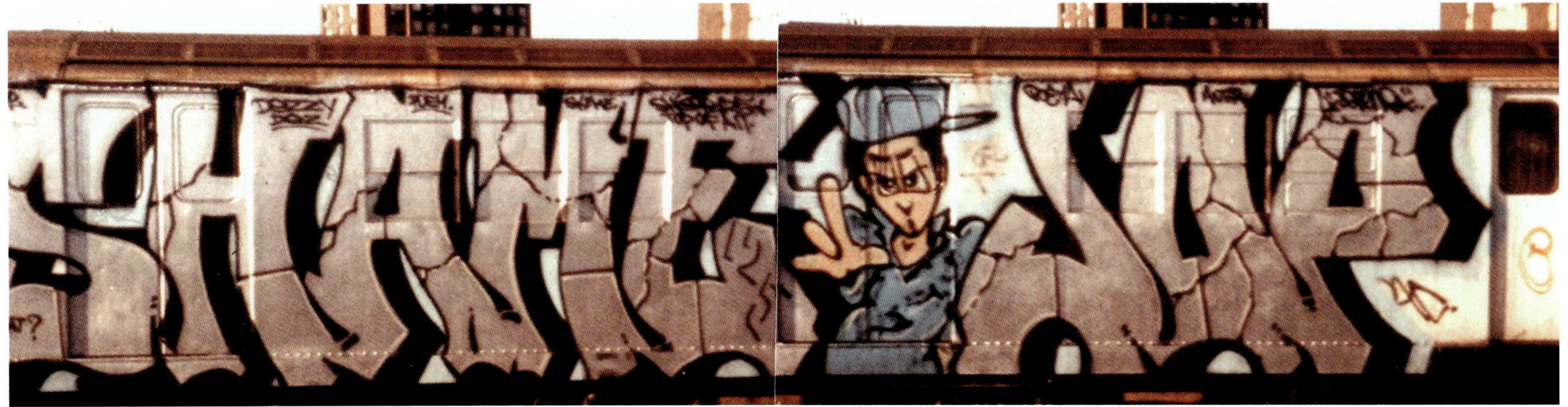

Shame, Jop, 1985

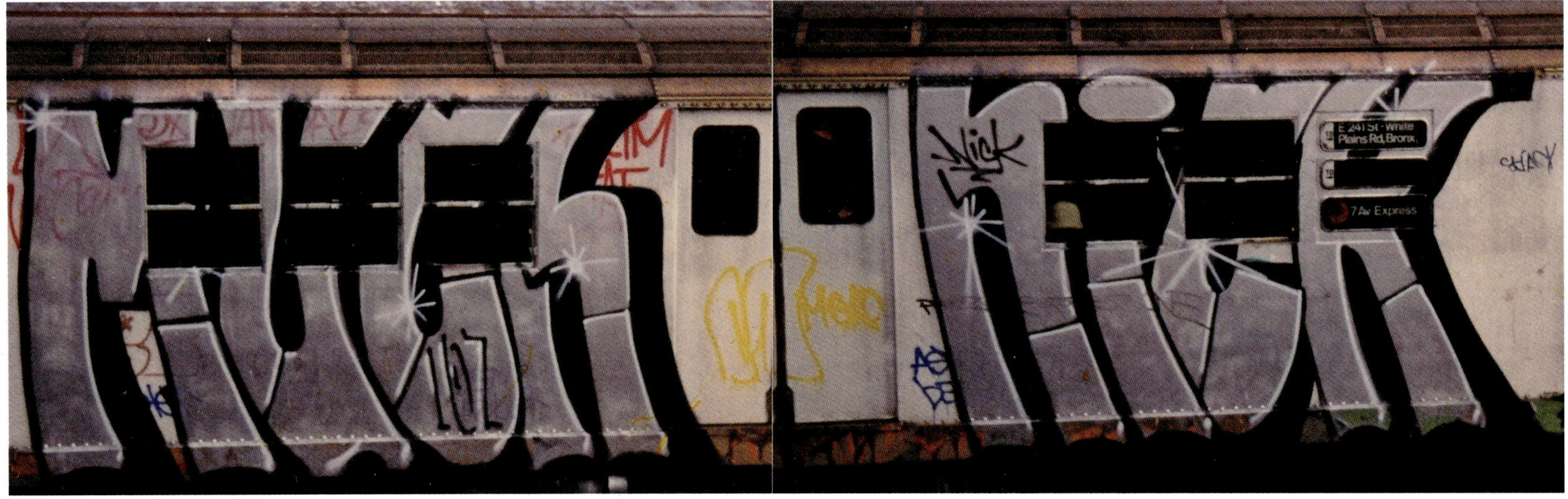

Much, Nick

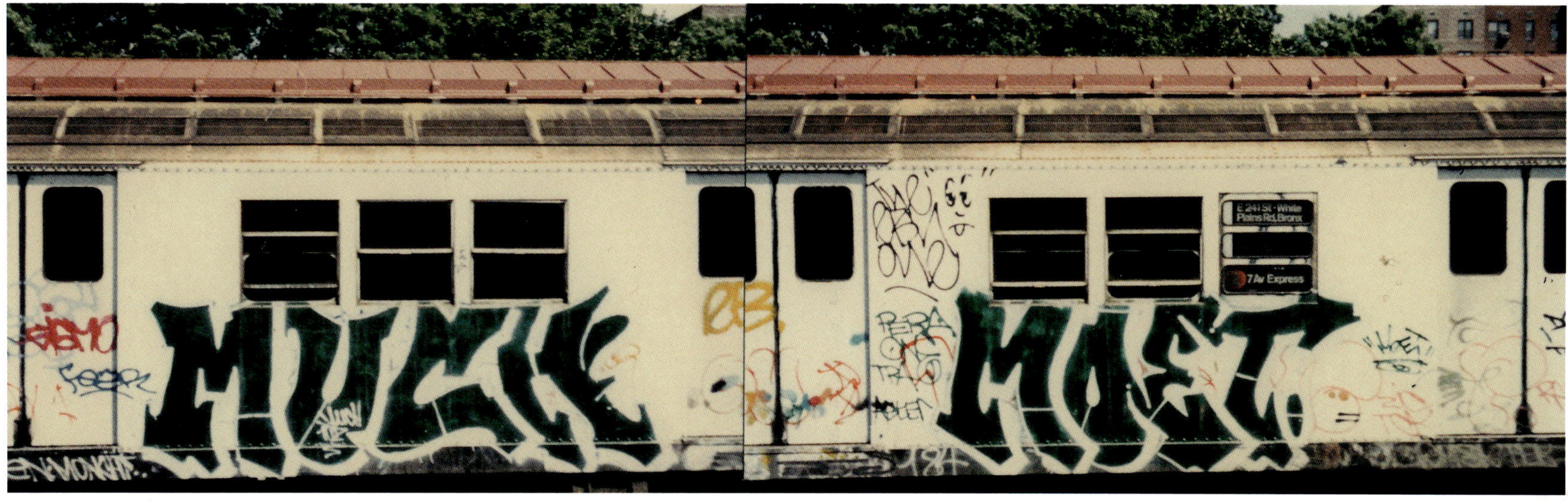

Much, Moet

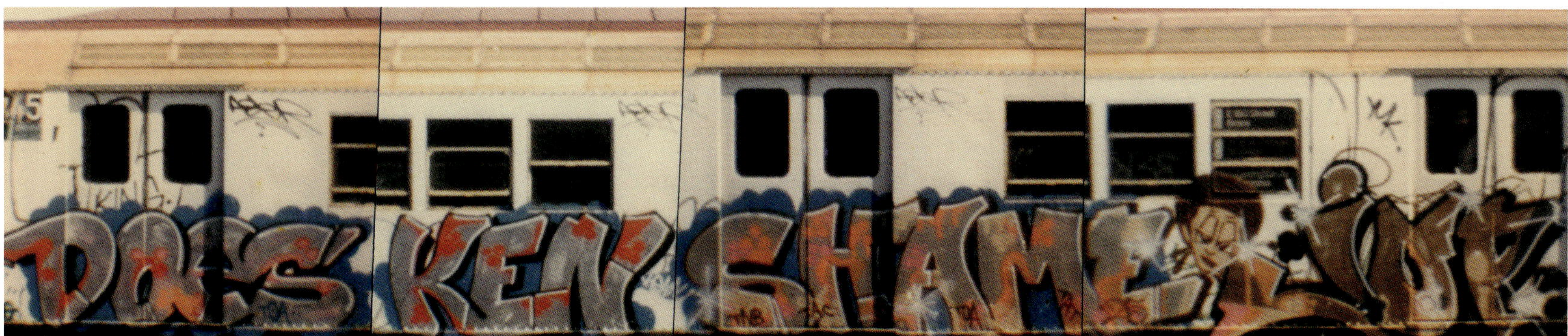

Does, Ken, Shame, Jop

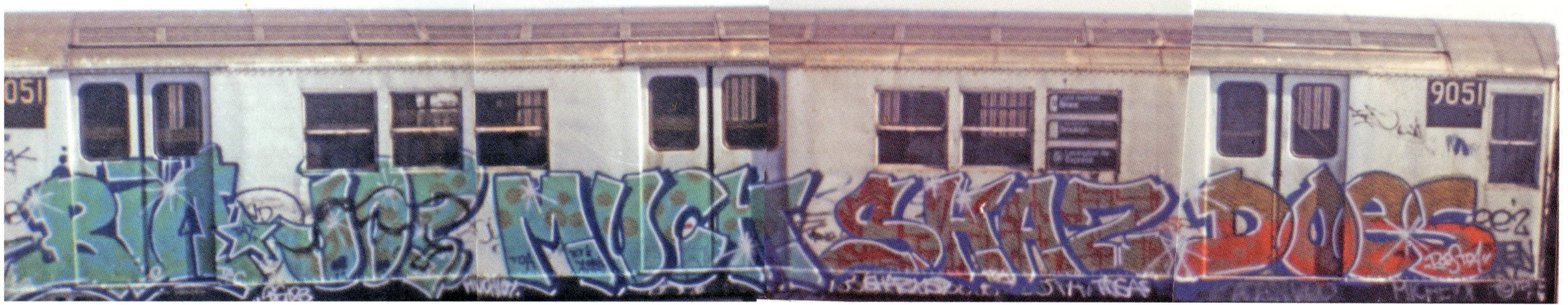

Bio, Jop, Much, Shaz, Does

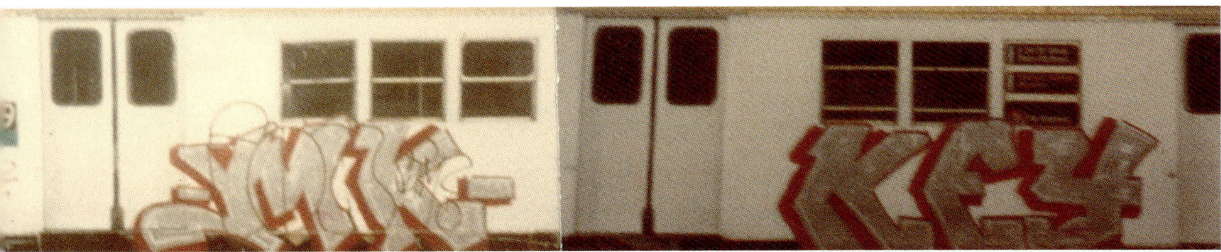

Mk, Key, 1984

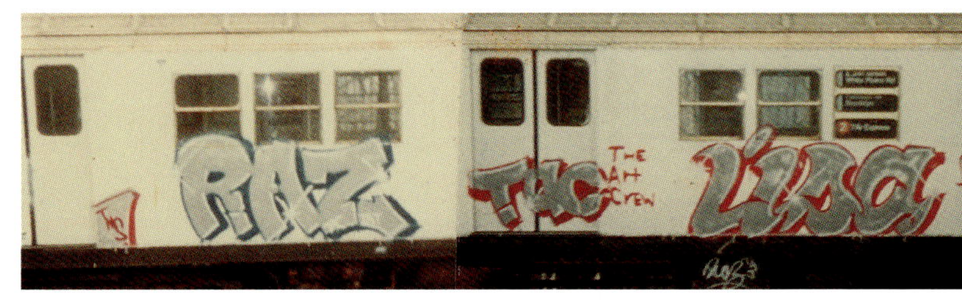

Raz, Lisa

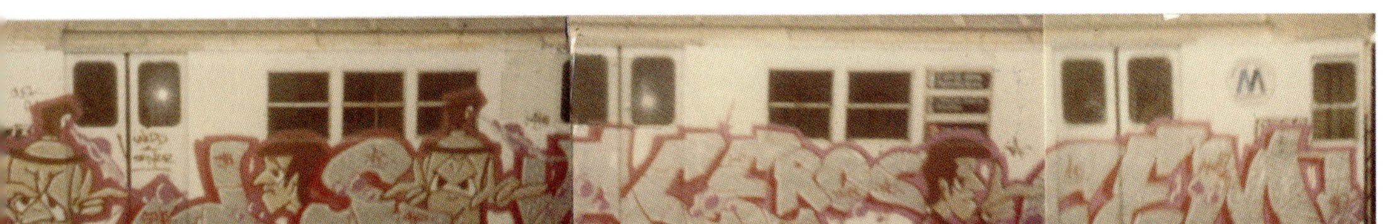

Jis, Aceroc, Cem, 1984

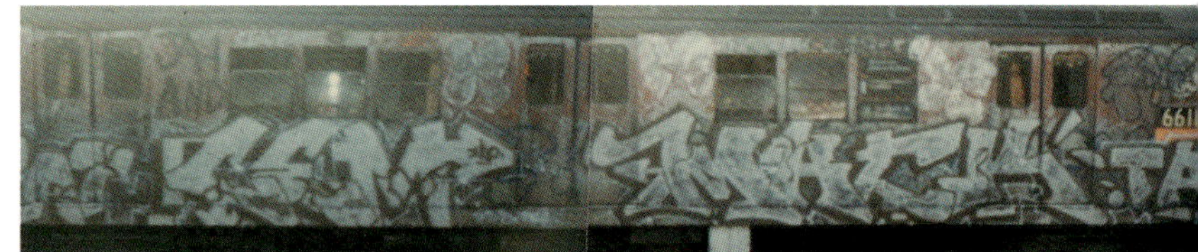

Cem, Mack

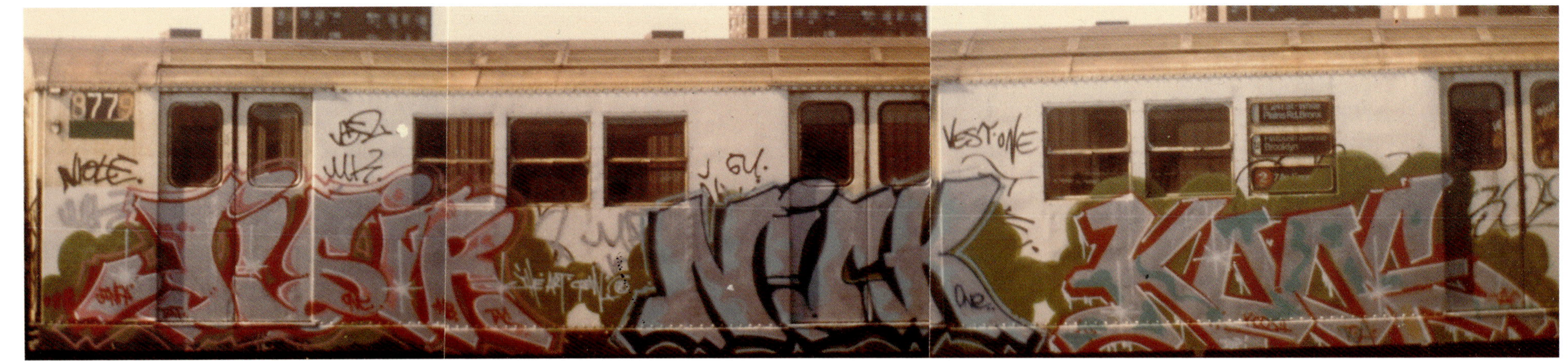

Jisir, Nick, Koos

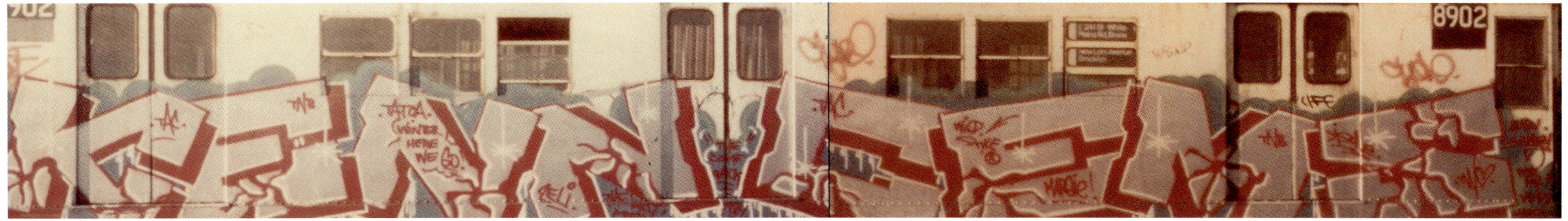

Kenn, Cems

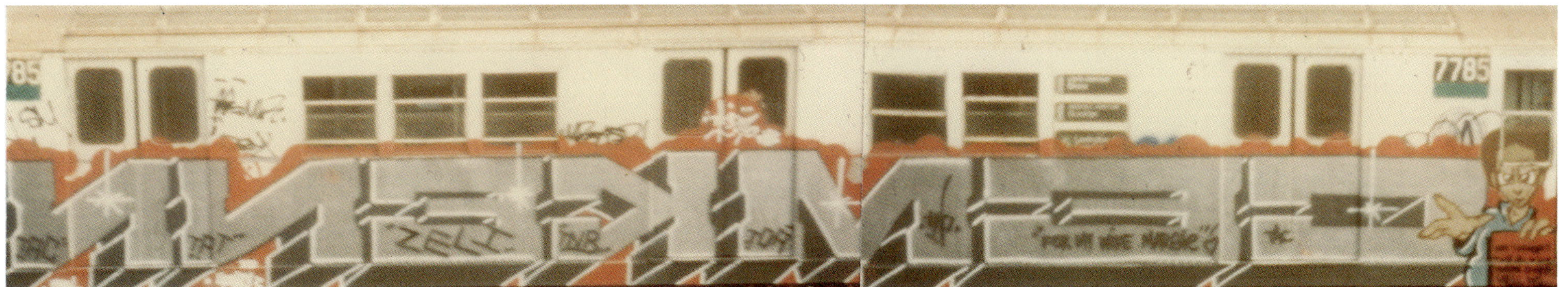

Cem, Kenn (Backwards), 1984

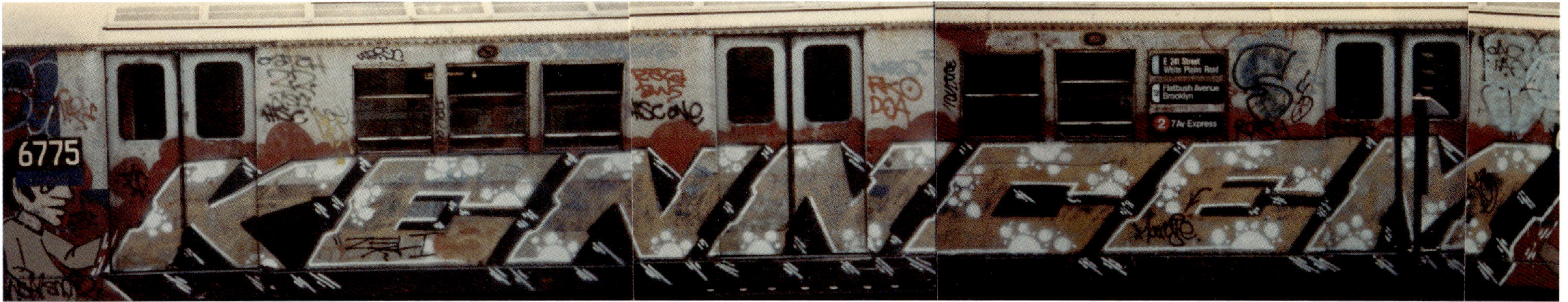

Kenn, Cem

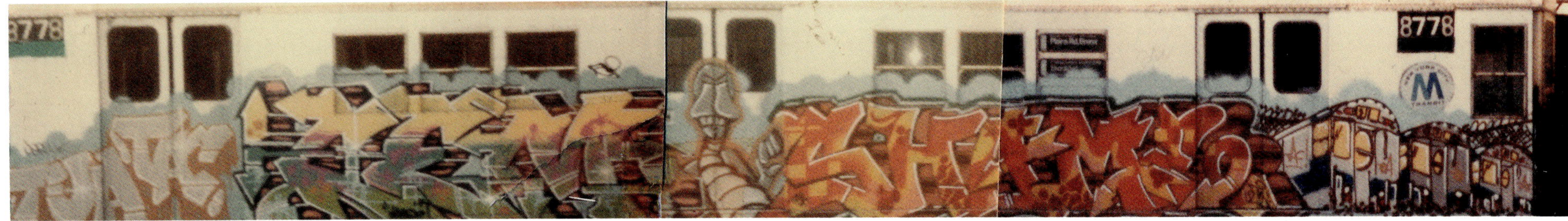

Cem, Shame, 1984

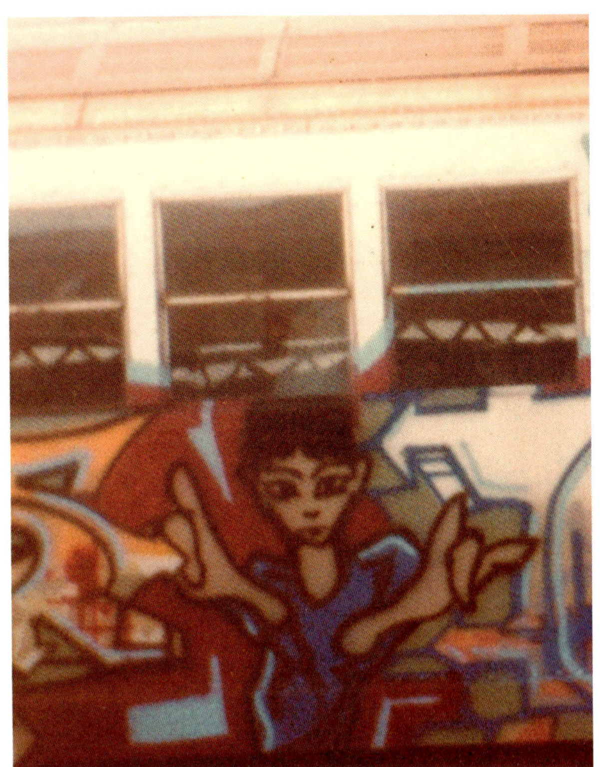

Ken (missing), Cems, Tkid, 1984

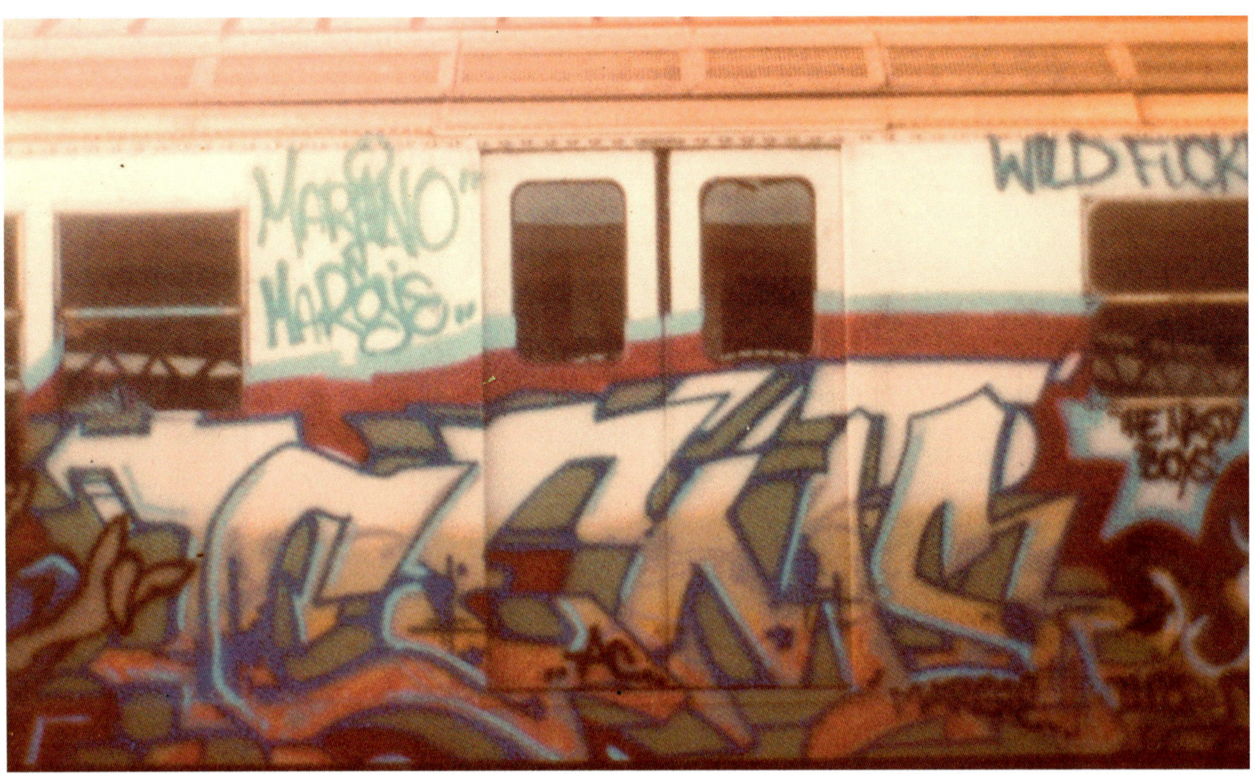

Cems, 1984

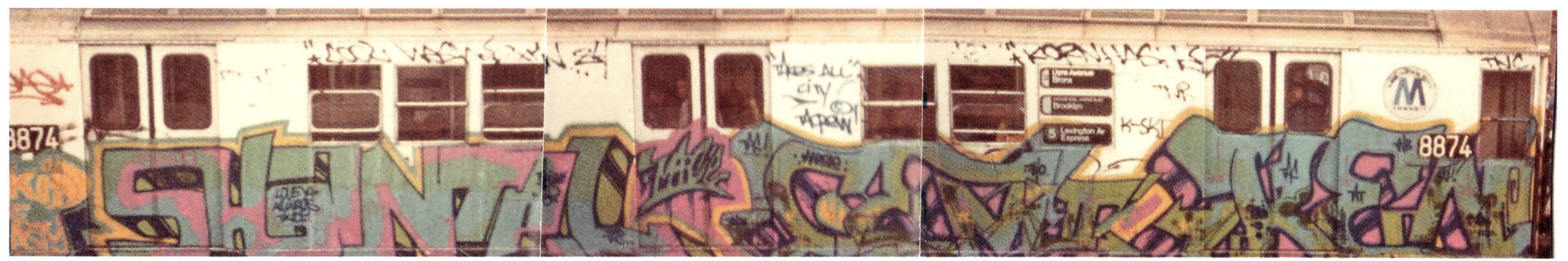

Shantel by Tkid, Cem2, Ken, 1984

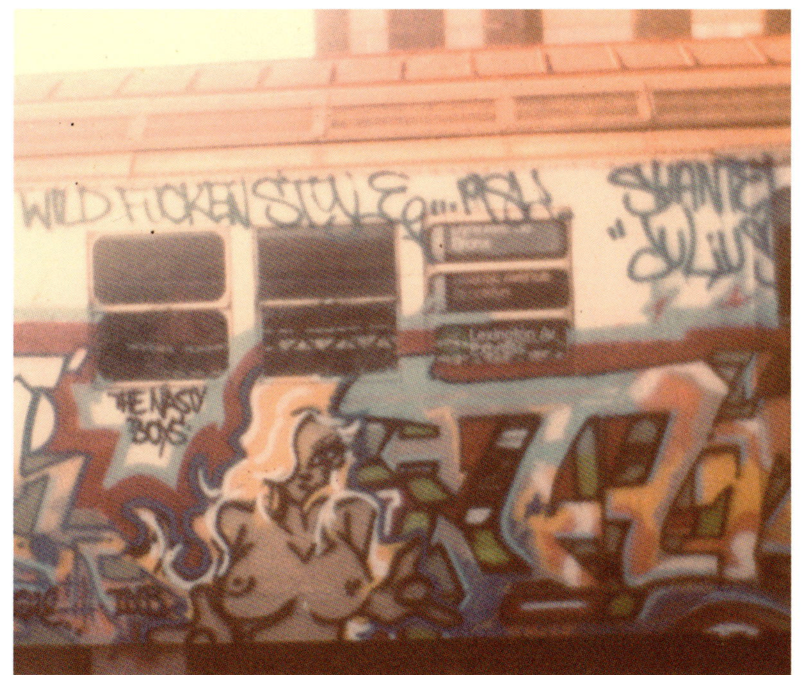

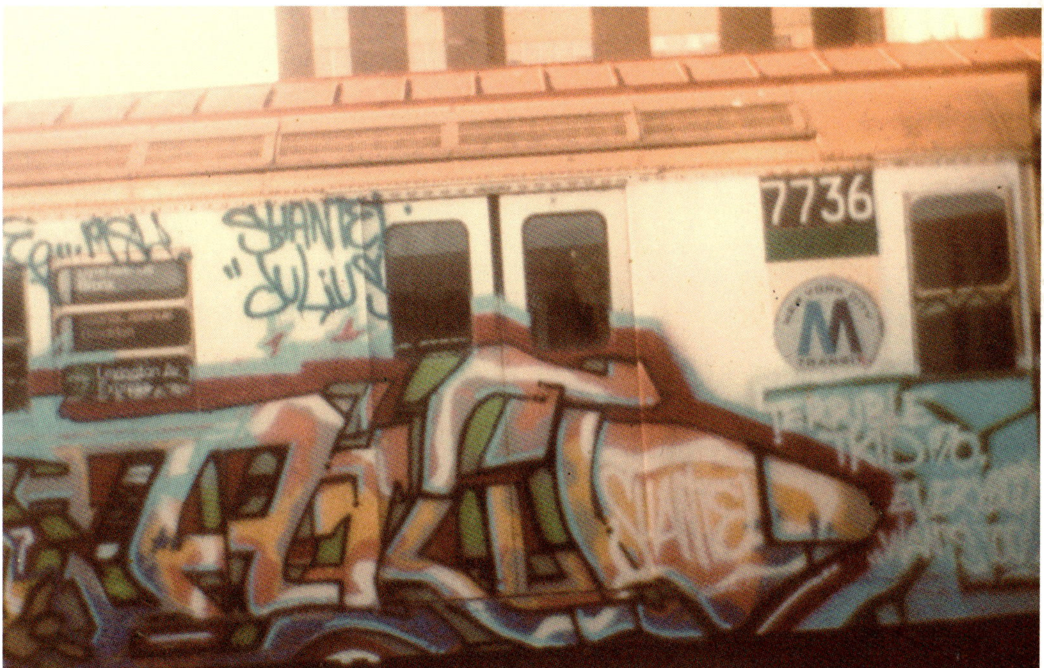

Tkid170, 1984

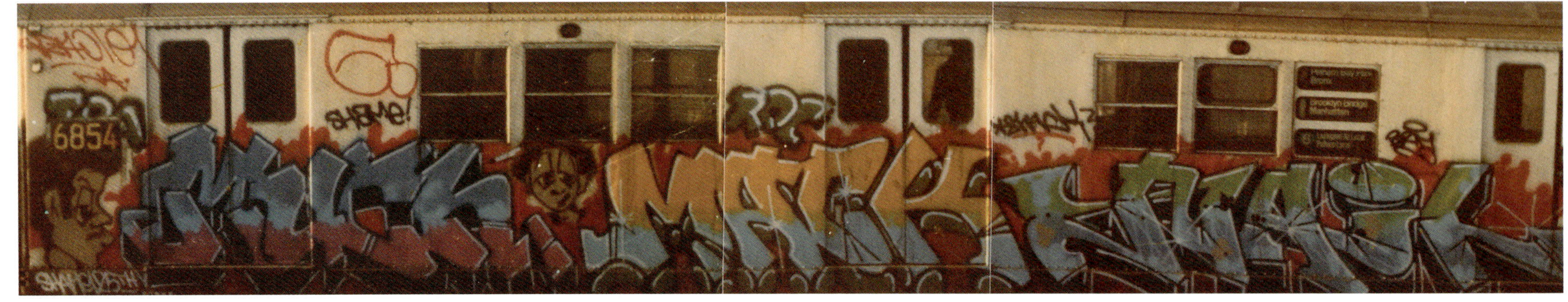

Much, Mack, Nail, 1983

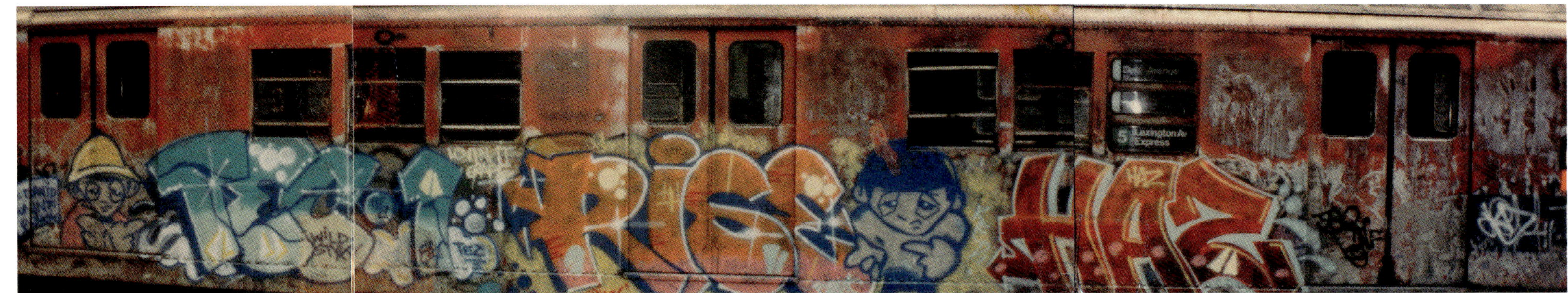

Tec1, Rise, Haz, 1984

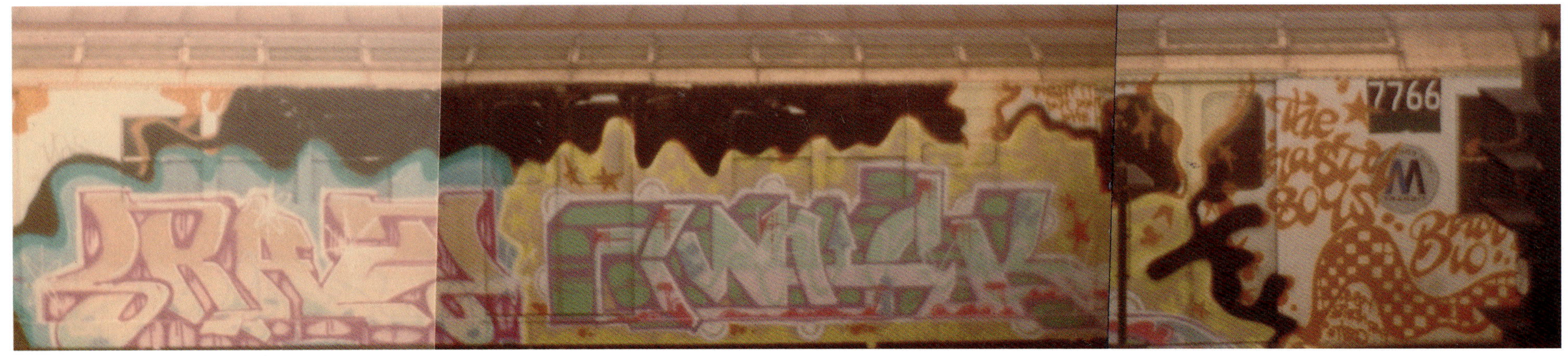

Raz, Mack, 1984

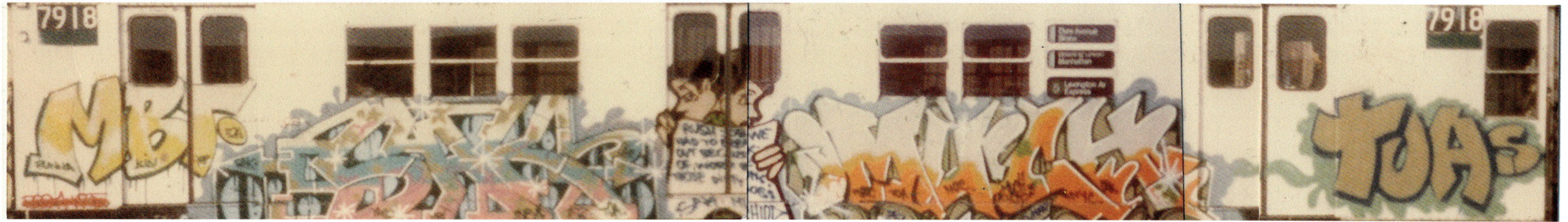

Sak, Much, 1985

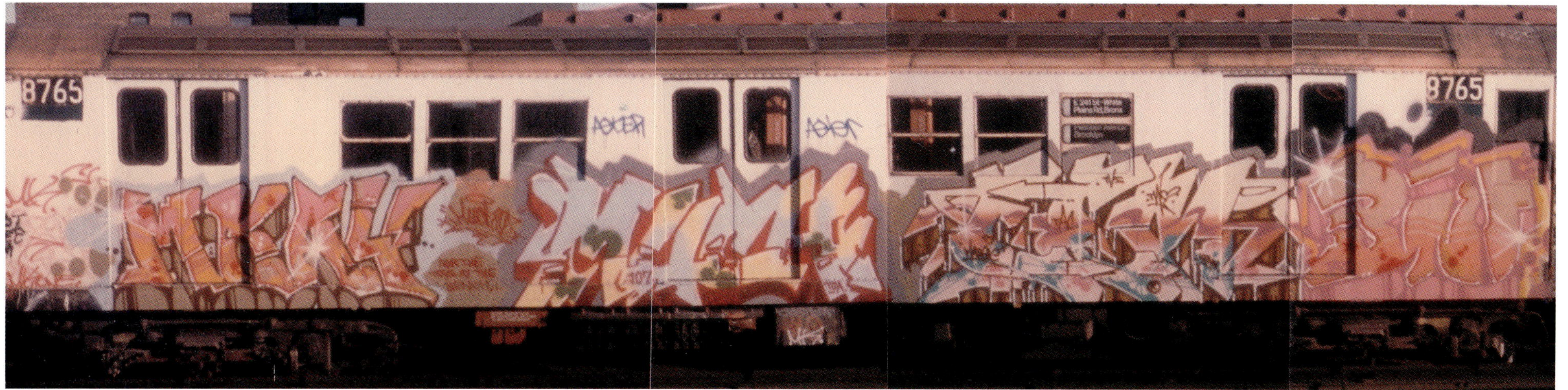

Mkay, Much, Cem, Bio, 1984

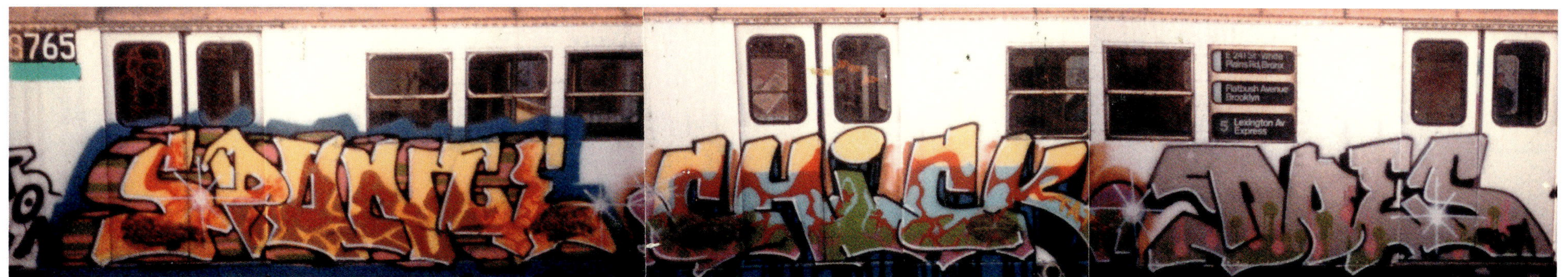

Sponge, Chick, Does, 1984

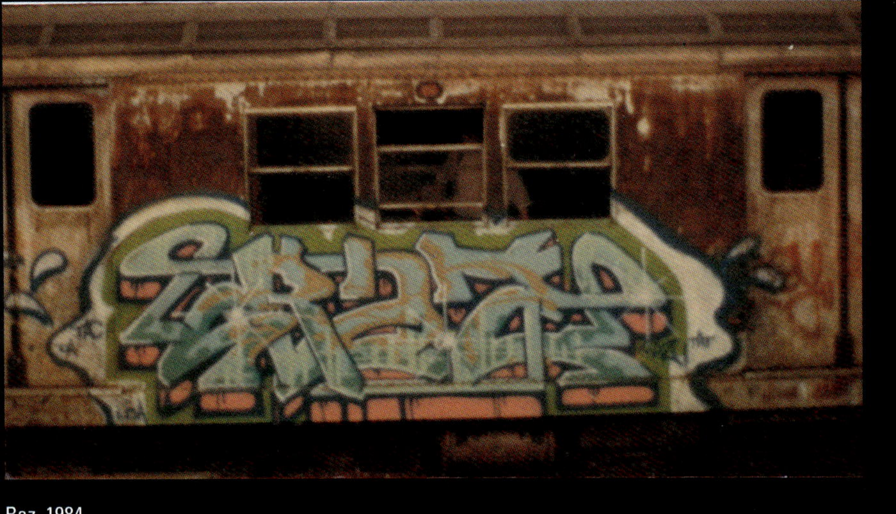

Raz, 1984

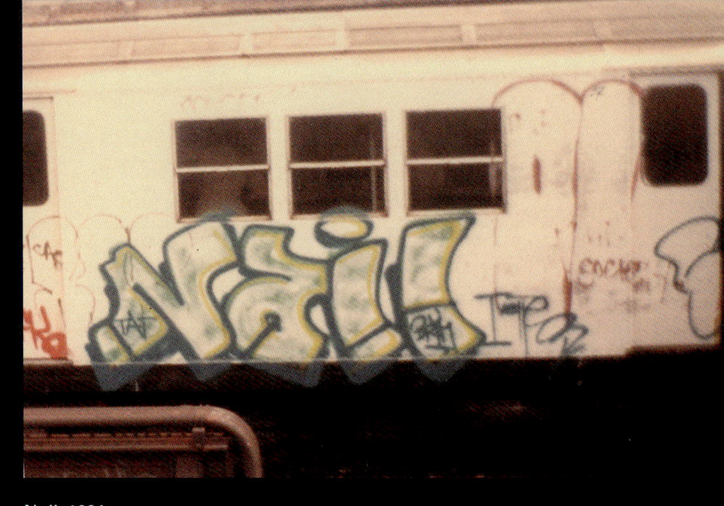

Nail, 1984

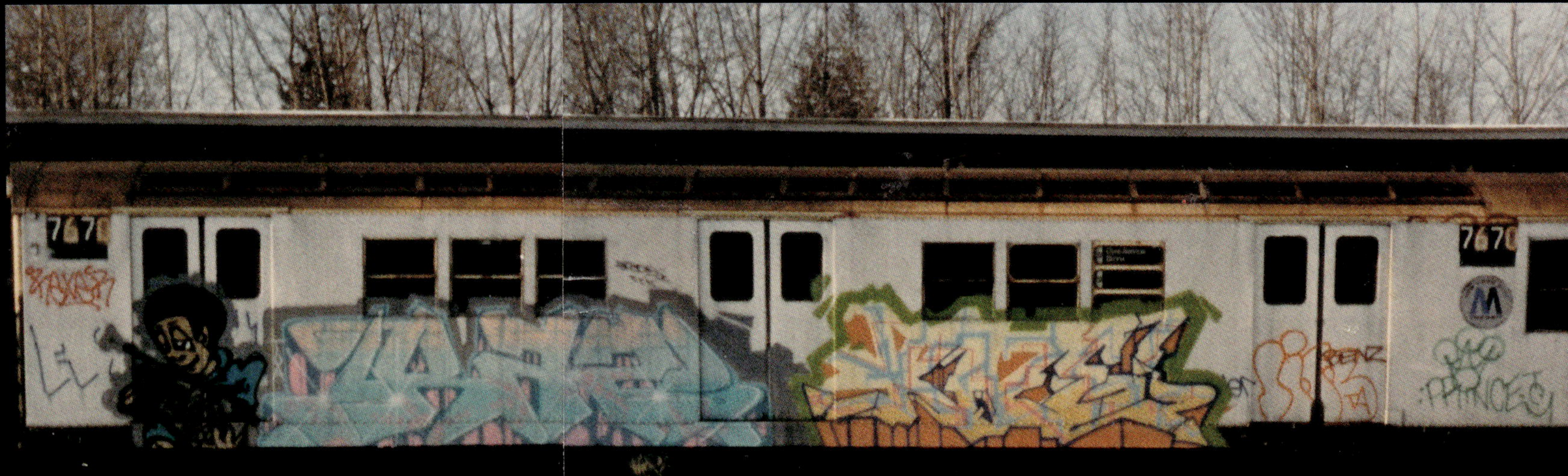

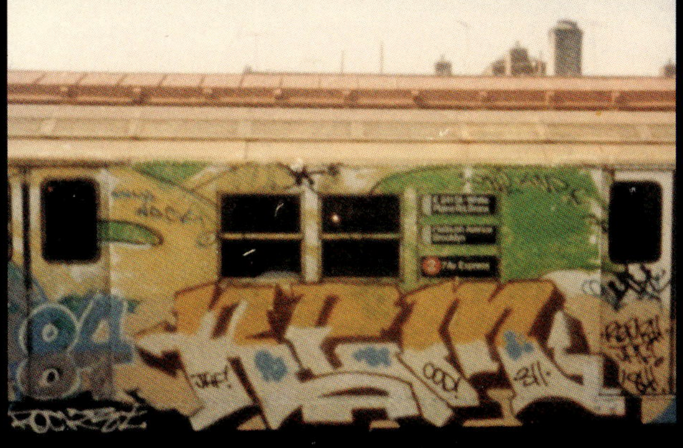

Rem311 JHF, 1984

Stash2, 1984

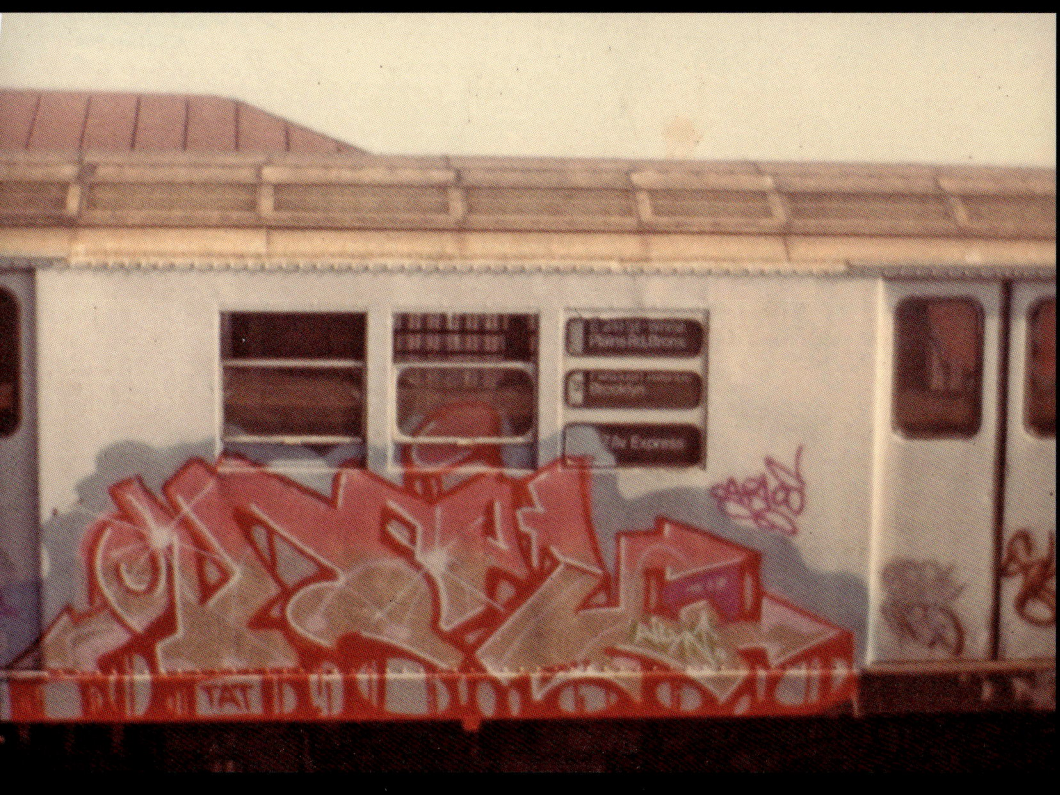

Dil TAT, 1984

Bio, 1984

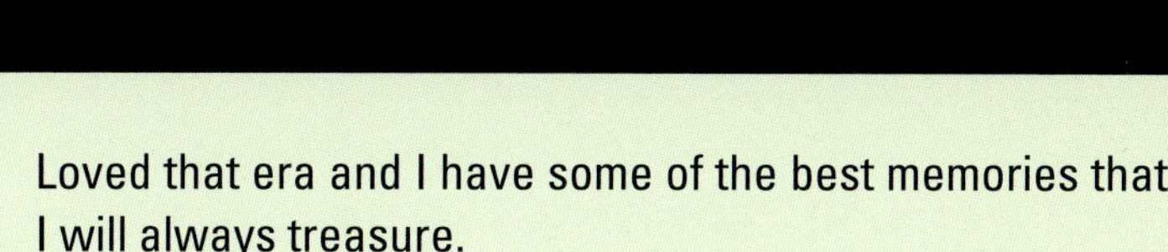

Loved that era and I have some of the best memories that I will always treasure.

–Bio

TATS CRU

Sometime in 1978 I started writing. I wrote on my school desk tops, I wrote in the project hallways where I lived. In theory I was scrawling on the walls, or so my teacher Ms. Mintz thought, she used to scream at me, "Aaron you will never amount to anything if you continue to write on everything." My homework was stylized graffiti. I started to write on trains in 1980—motion tags (tagging on trains when in service). I was greatly inspired by Z-ro; Zephyr; Dondi; and Dez TFA, a.k.a. Spade429, a.k.a. Dj Kay Slay. In the neighborhood I lived in I was writing with the Addicted to Graffiti crew: Page, Estre, Realone, Darkone, Mar2, and Amazon (RIP). Our crew was based in Yorkville, right on the border of Spanish Harlem. In the late 1970s the gangs were dying out and crews were replacing them, but before this transition I rolled with C.B.S. (can't be stopped), Afro Eddie, and Black Eddie to name a few. There was the 94th Street Crew: Abeeo; Javier; Flaco, a.k.a. Nestorius; Red; Sylvino (RIP); Tito (RIP); Carlos (RIP); Elvin; Nesto; Angel; Abe; Suki; and Renee. Our days were spent hanging on the block drinking quarts of Apple Malt Duck, Old English 800, smoking the hardest hard, and watching each other's backs in case the Budweiser gang rolled up on us.

You had the crazy bunch on 122nd, between Lexington and Park Ave. They were many blocks away from our block but we were affiliated. Shaker 179 and Brian, Kryp, and Louie represented for me. I can't forget Marcito (RIP) and my crime partner, Junito. Junito and I went to the same junior high school. We used to cut out of school, smoke a joint after third period lunchtime. We would go rob the kids from New Lincoln around the corner so we could get money to go buy pizza from Ray's up the block, the same pizza parlor where the pizza connection ran their enterprise out of the basement, not that we were aware of it at the time.

The other brothers of the bomb that was making noise was Hoi ESP, Nada ESP, and Lace ESP. The 6 line was the one we took to school every day unless we were on roller skates, then we would hold onto the Second Ave bus to make our way down Second Ave to get to Wagner JHS. By the time I got to high school, Julia Richman, I was looking to affiliate myself with other writers because I wanted to hit the layups. I had seen Delta 2 pieces on the 6 line, along with Brim and Mack pieces, benching trains at 96th Street. I knew Delta 2 lived close by, because his tags were sprinkled around the neighborhood. I had been to the layups once with my boy Real One to hit insides, but we got grabbed coming back from the layups and the cops beat his ass on the platform on 138th Street. He did not want to take the risk anymore, so I needed another partner. I was just getting my dick wet, I was a toy but I had big dreams. I wanted to be king of the line, I wanted my name to ring out like ringalario—one, two, three.

I went to a hundred streets and asked my boy Dar from the real crew if he knew Delta 2 because I was ready to get down James Brown. The real crew was fam, besides Dar, you had his brother Glitter and Lil Pop. I asked Dar where I could find Delta. In the pre-cell-phone-era one had to do reconnaissance to find people. Dar said he thought he hung out at the game room on 101st Street and Madison.

So every day I went there after school and waited to see if I could see him. I would hang out in the game room in the back next to the pool table and the *Missile Command* machine to see if I could meet the brother. I waited every day for an hour or two. On the third day he showed up. When he walked through the door, I knew it was him. I had never seen him before, but when I saw him, I knew it was him. I stepped to him and introduced myself. I told him my plans about being king of the line. He initially shut me down, but I pulled his card. I told him that he was soft, he had been slapped around by his dad and did not want no more drama. In the end we would form an alliance that would last many years to come, along with the serious young bombers crew, Halter, Frener, and Syster. We would make our mark on society . . . a bunch of children started a movement that would go on to be, in my opinion, the only true American art form. We would influence a generation of children from Japan to France to Italy, Spain, Norway, and Denmark to name a few.

Writing on the trains was a full time job, it took all of our time and energy. From this point on everything else was secondary to our mission. We cut school, but not enough to fail. I could be absent twenty-eight days a year and still pass. In the day time I went money racking with G-Man and B.S.119. They put us down with The Ebony Dukes, Smily149 (RIP) was the president. We would venture out to Staten Island, rack paint, toothpaste, aspirin, and sell it to bodegas in the Bronx. It gave us some pocket money to buy some weed, some beer, and a little stimo. And then we'd go hit the layups. All of our cars were done on the elevated train tracks, unless we were meeting up with our homeboy in Brooklyn, Spin, from the T.F.S. crew, to hit the daytime layups in Kingston.

We, for the most part, were creating a stylized alphabet to adorn the subway cars with our own creative dialogue, our interpreted version of the Helvetica alphabet that we were learning in school. But the educational system supported by the board of education was attempting to brainwash us. It was not what we wanted to engage in, our desire was to jump across train tracks to express our inner angst. We were consumed by the chains that bound us, coming from dysfunctional, broken homes. We needed to find an outlet for the fire in our hearts. NO one thought that our focus had any redeemable qualities. The only people who encouraged us and thought that we had any value were people like Henry Chalfant, Martha Cooper, Guillame Gallozzi (RIP), and Joe Laplaca. In spite of the obstacles, we never let our detractors influence us. When we got arrested and had to stand before a judge, we stood tall. When we got jumped by other graffiti writers, win or lose we went toe to toe. There is a tremendous amount of danger that goes with a career in the urban underground: electrocution, rivals dropping dimes, baseball to the temple, spray can to the temple. In the end, our passion and unquenchable desire to get our name up all over would never be extinguished. As we grew older and the laws changed, I moved away from writing on the trains.

There were other outlets for creativity. Making work on canvas became a new avenue of expression. As protagonists of the art world, our alliance with the East Village art movement was taking shape. There was a night life where all the subcultures came together socially: punk, hardcore, performance art. Clubs like Danceteria, Area, Berlin, became the playing field. Instead of running through tunnels, we started running through airports. We became ambassadors of the movement and helped to teach and spread the movement to other states and cities throughout the planet. And with the power of example from Zephyr, the rebels, and Phase2, the evolution of the Helvetica abecedary would expand. I stopped painting trains in 1985 and although I no longer get the adrenaline that accompanies this crime of passion, the visceral and animalistic energy that pumps through the blood of a true b-boy king of line still lives in my heart. Along the way there have been many trials and tribulations, personal spiritual obstacles that block the path of the righteous. But the saga continues, and while many of the old school crew have left the building, some live behind the wall. But the freaks are still at large and when the wood work squeaks, out come the freaks. The King's Arrived, The Rebels continue to rock the blind light.

Roll Call:

Shout out to: Pate BKB, Des, Sash (RIP), Ero (RIP), and Pc kid (RIP). Peace to the Playboys, Kitchen Crips, The Crusaders, Smokey, Aaron, Tank, Jt 108. Shout out to Stretch Armstrong; Stash; Aone (RIP); Ace two; Revolt; Futura; Fab Five Freddy; Frosty Freeze (RIP); Ramellzee (RIP); Case 2, a.k.a. Universal Lord Supreme Justice Allah (RIP); and Gnome.

Peace to the Asiatique Black God Jamel Shabbaz for teaching me the knowledge and Buddy Esquire (RIP). Peace to Murphy's Law, Agnostic Front, Jimmy Gestapo, Vinny Stigma, Cavity Sreeps, Poss, Luster, The Pedantics, Sam, Baba, Ksn, and Eklips. Peace to 16 k; Nail, a.k.a. Salchiche; Ezo; Jr. Sweet (RIP); Lords of Brooklyn; and Kaves. Peace to the Fashion Moda Gallery; Stefan Eins; Patti Astor; Ginevra Griggolo; Tomaso Trini; Duster; Mace T.C.P.; Sting Ray; Vulcan; Popping Taco; Ice-T; Dj Evil E; Fable Wiggles; Storm; Swift; Poet; Rew; Gabin; Solo; Mode2; Lucian; Jonone; Ash; Skki; The Black Picasso, a.k.a. Jay One; Foe TDS (RIP); Speedy (RIP); Mike Ice; Bronx Style Bob; Manny; Fast Break; Float; Frank and Freddy; Checker170; Fuzzone; Kit17; and, of course, Mom Dukes, Benny, Deacon Jones, Moet, Part, and Ban2.

–Sharp

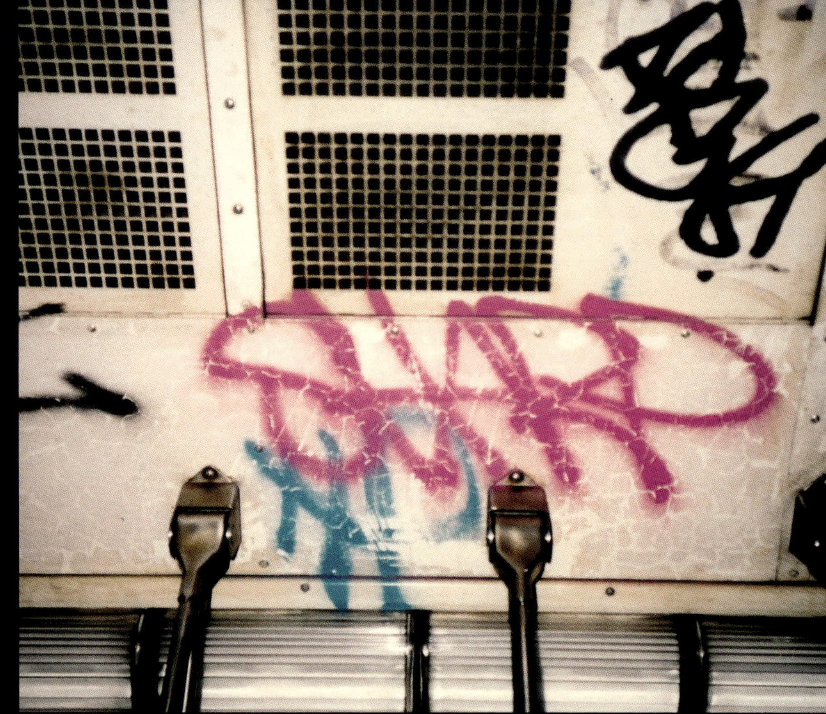

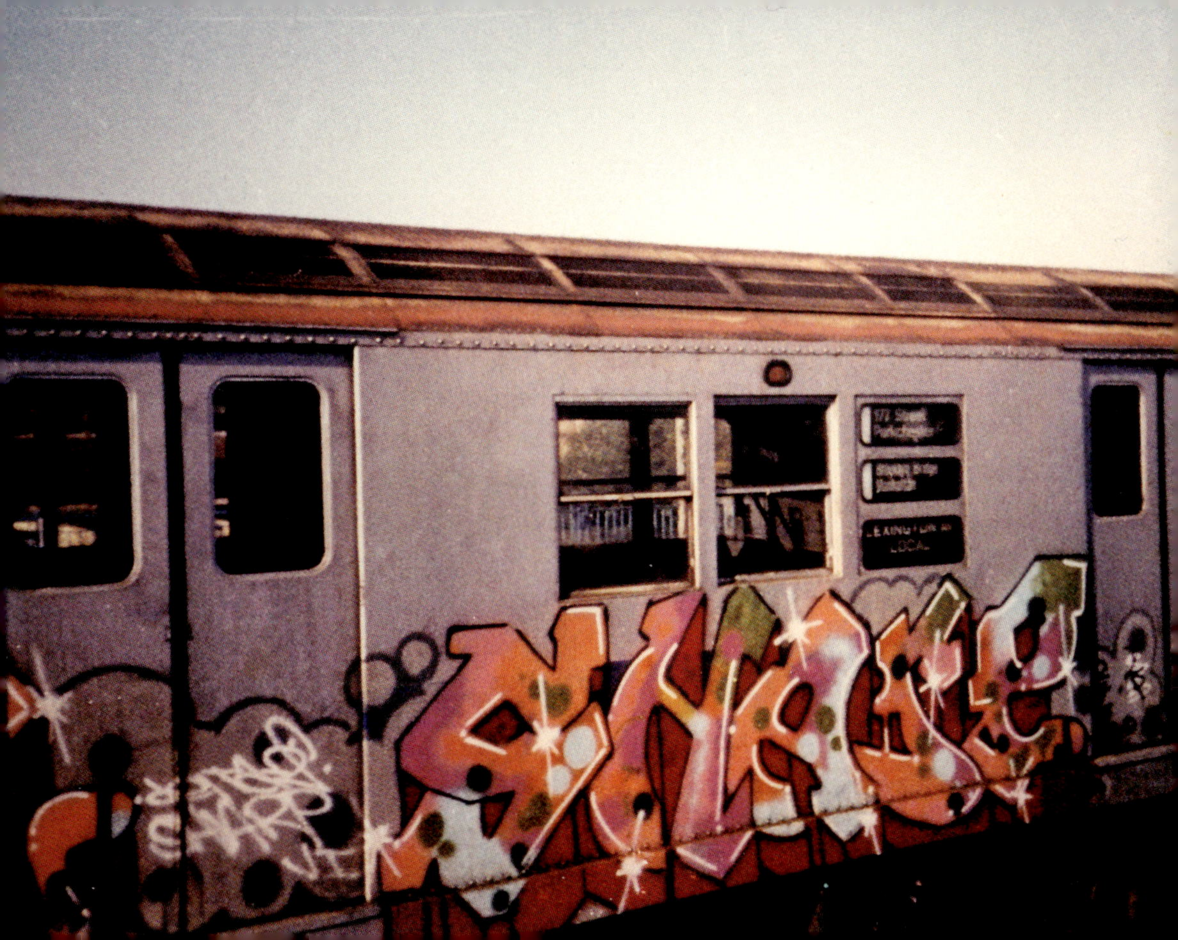

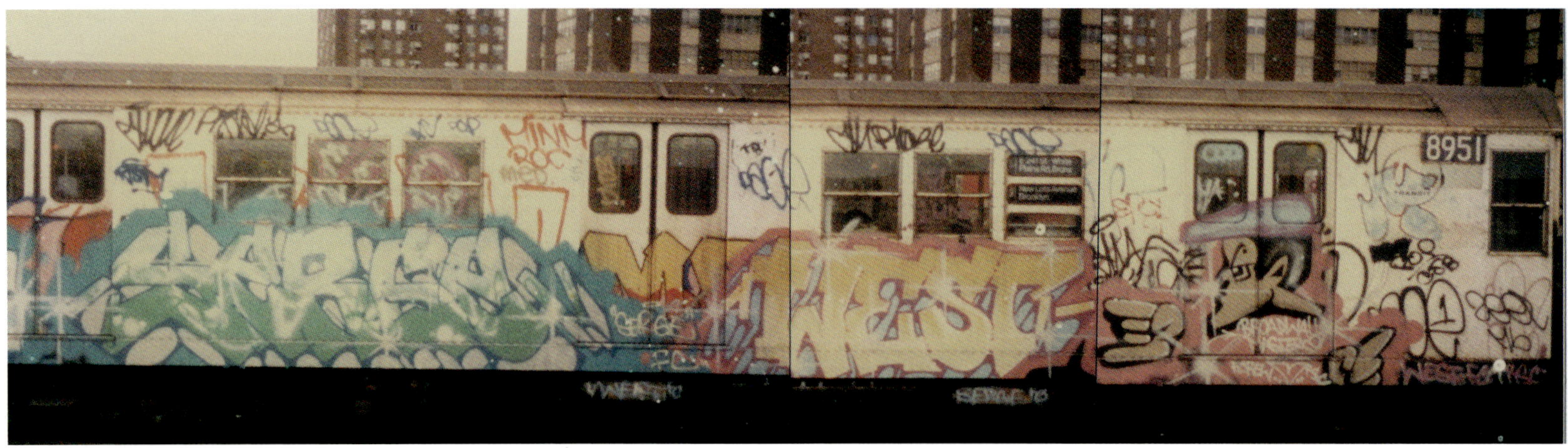

Serge, West FC, 1985

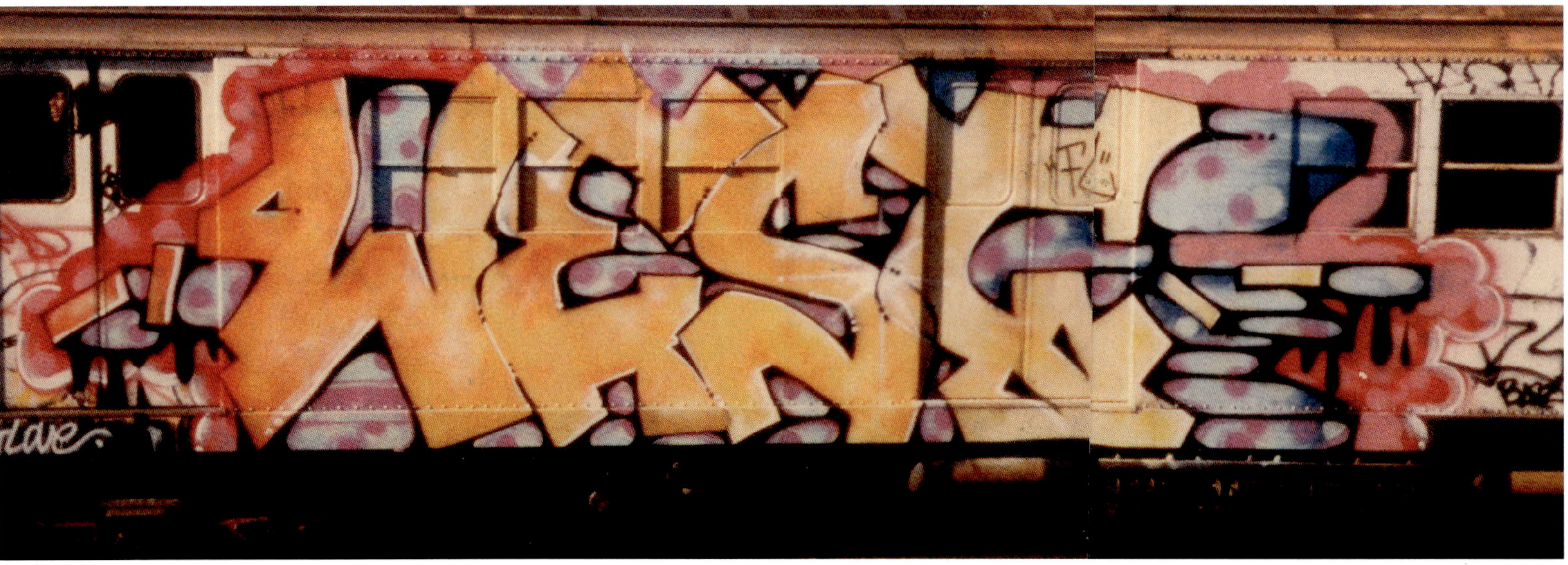

West FC, 1985

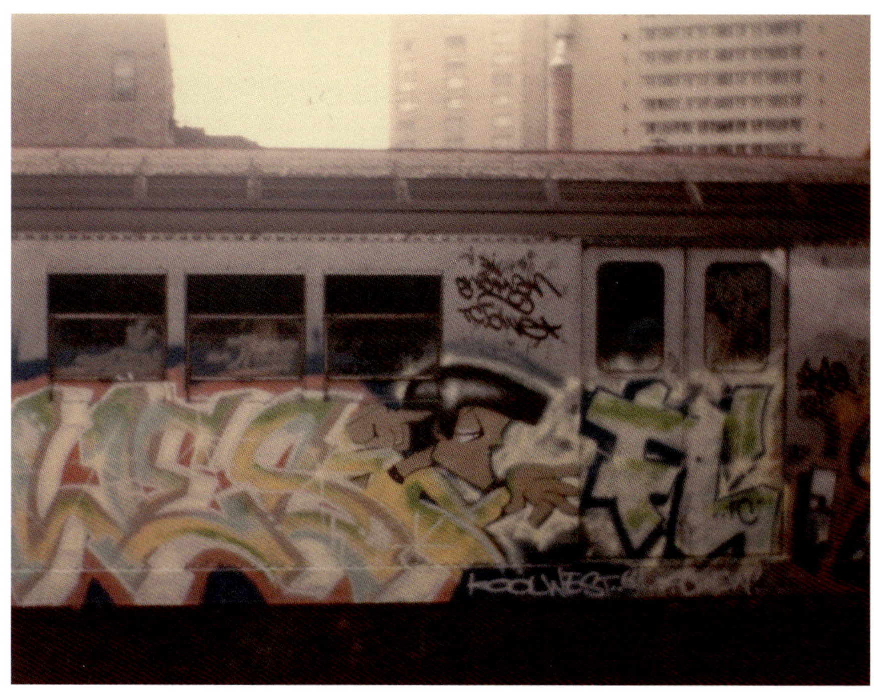

West FC, 1985

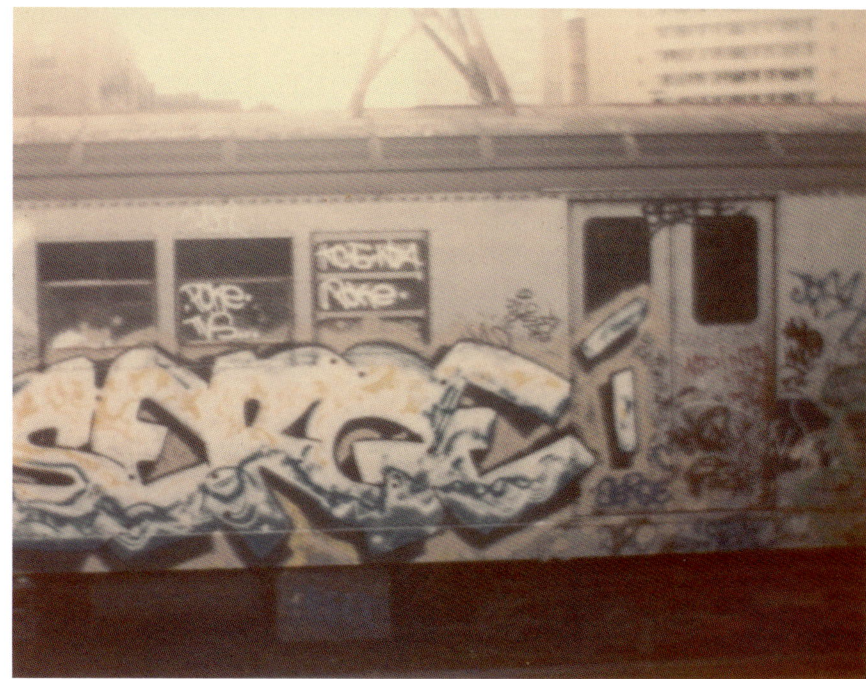

Serge FC, 1985

Westone, 1985

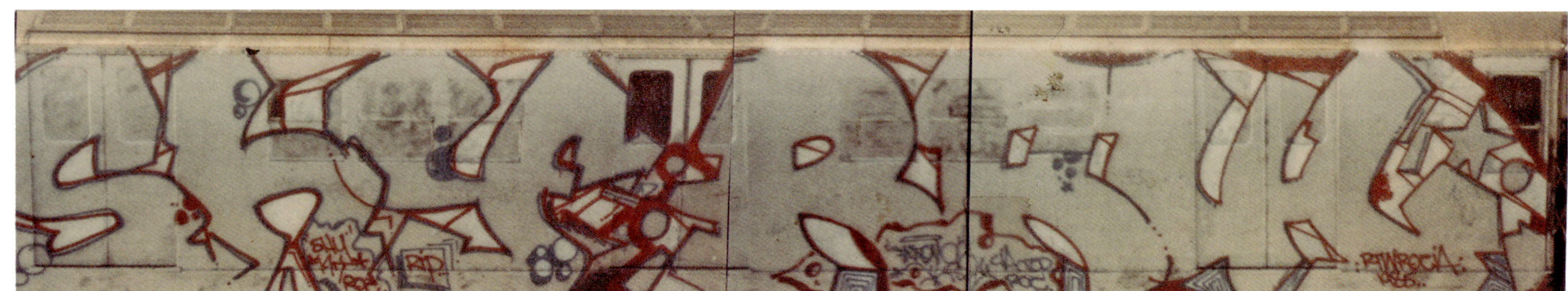

Shy, Raul, 1985

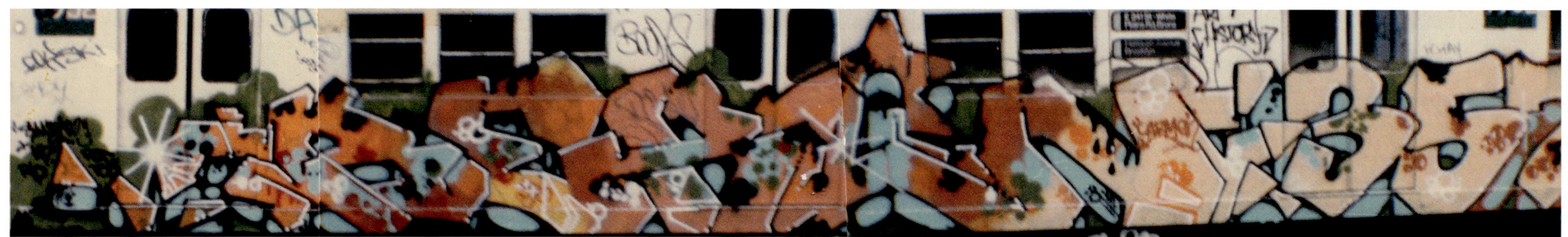

Berlin357, 1985

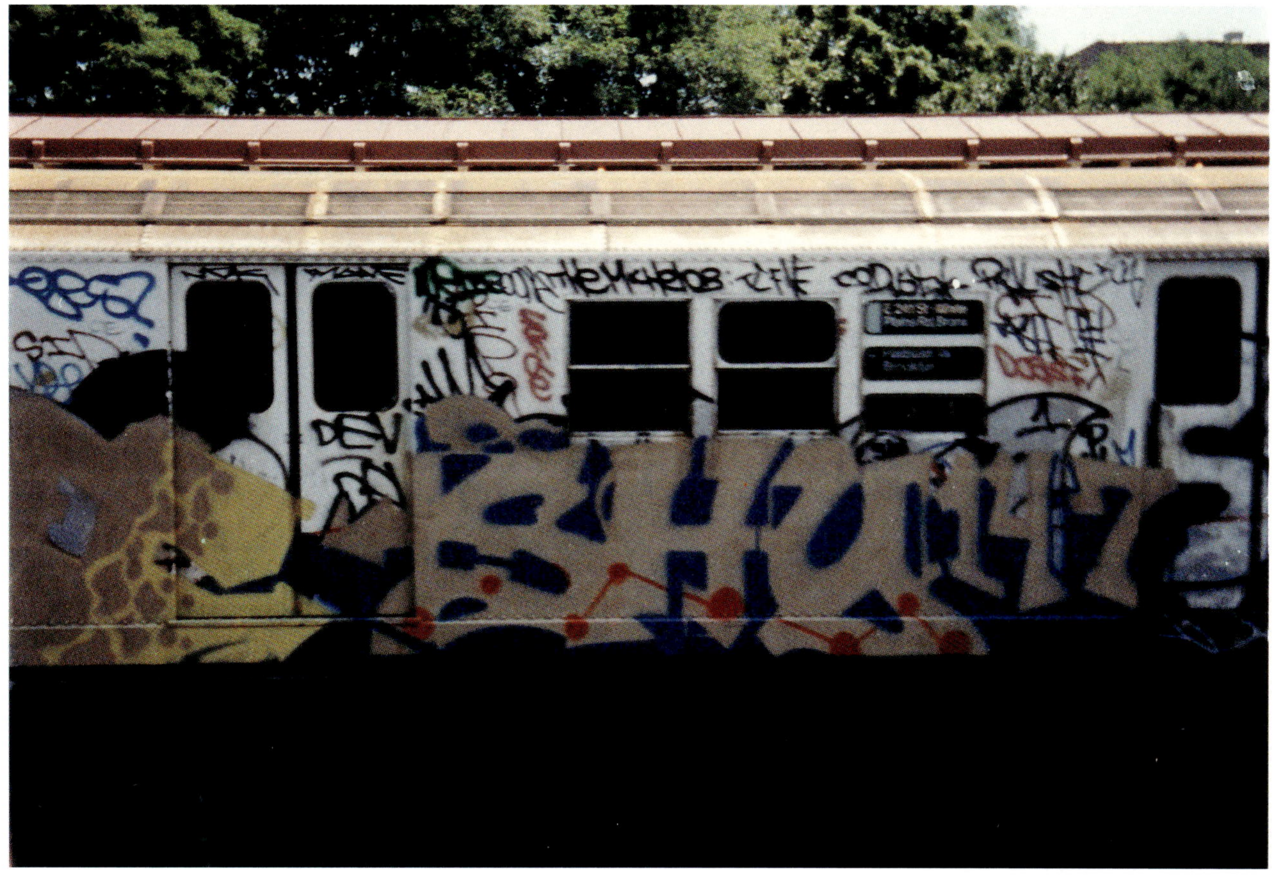

Shy (unfinished)

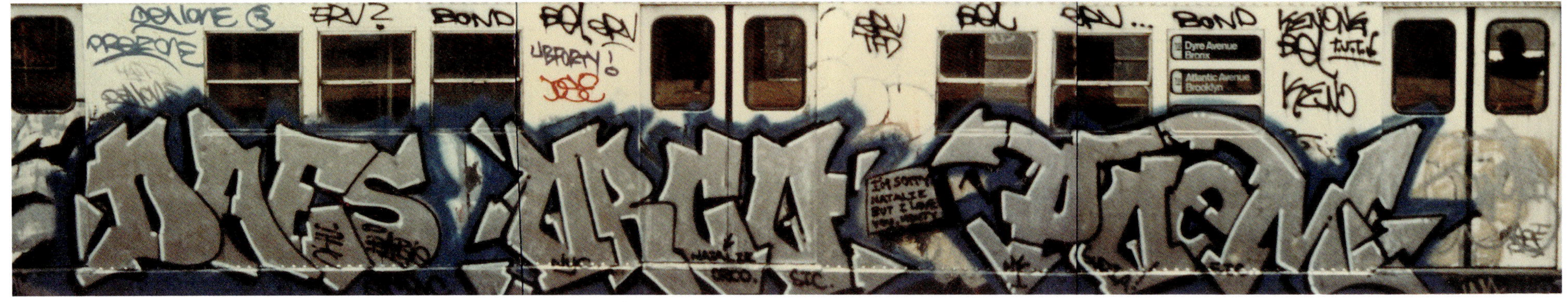

Daes, Orco, Poem, 1985

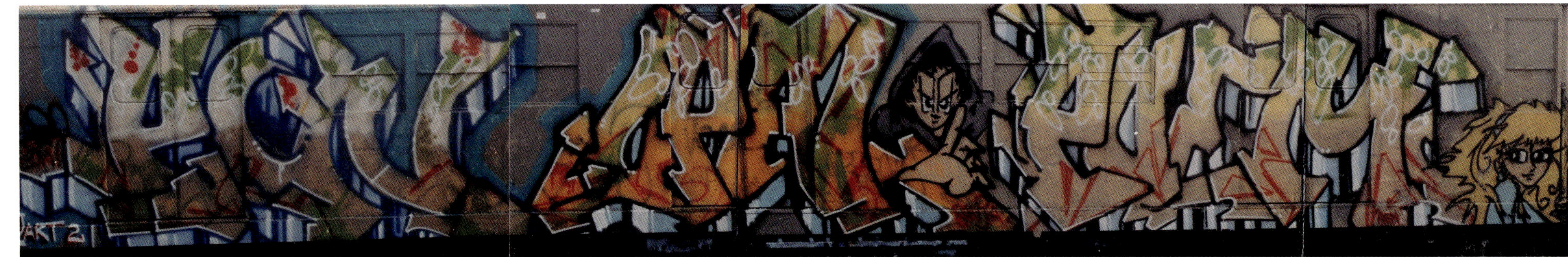

Eon, Opal, Poem (part 2), 1985

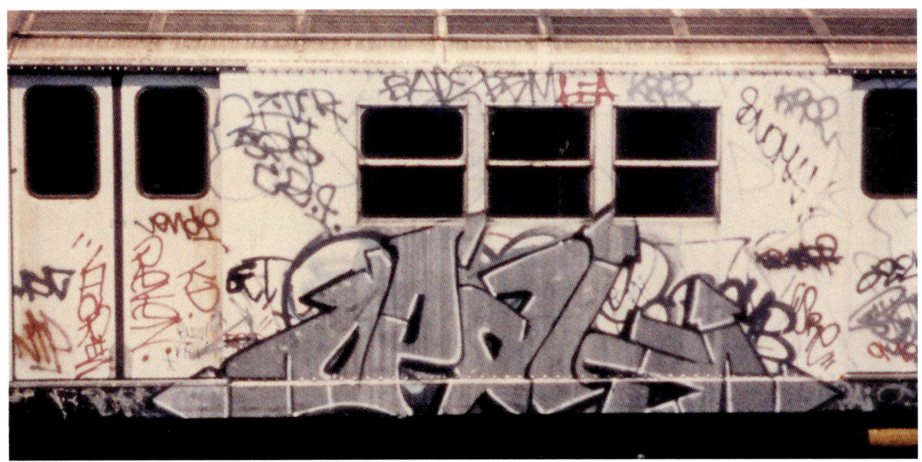

Opal

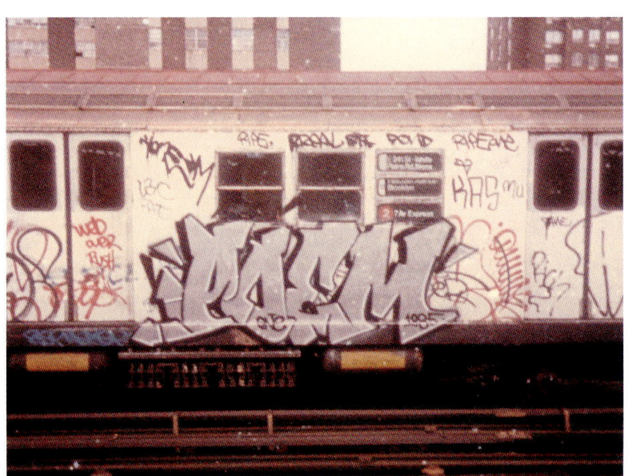

Poem, 1985

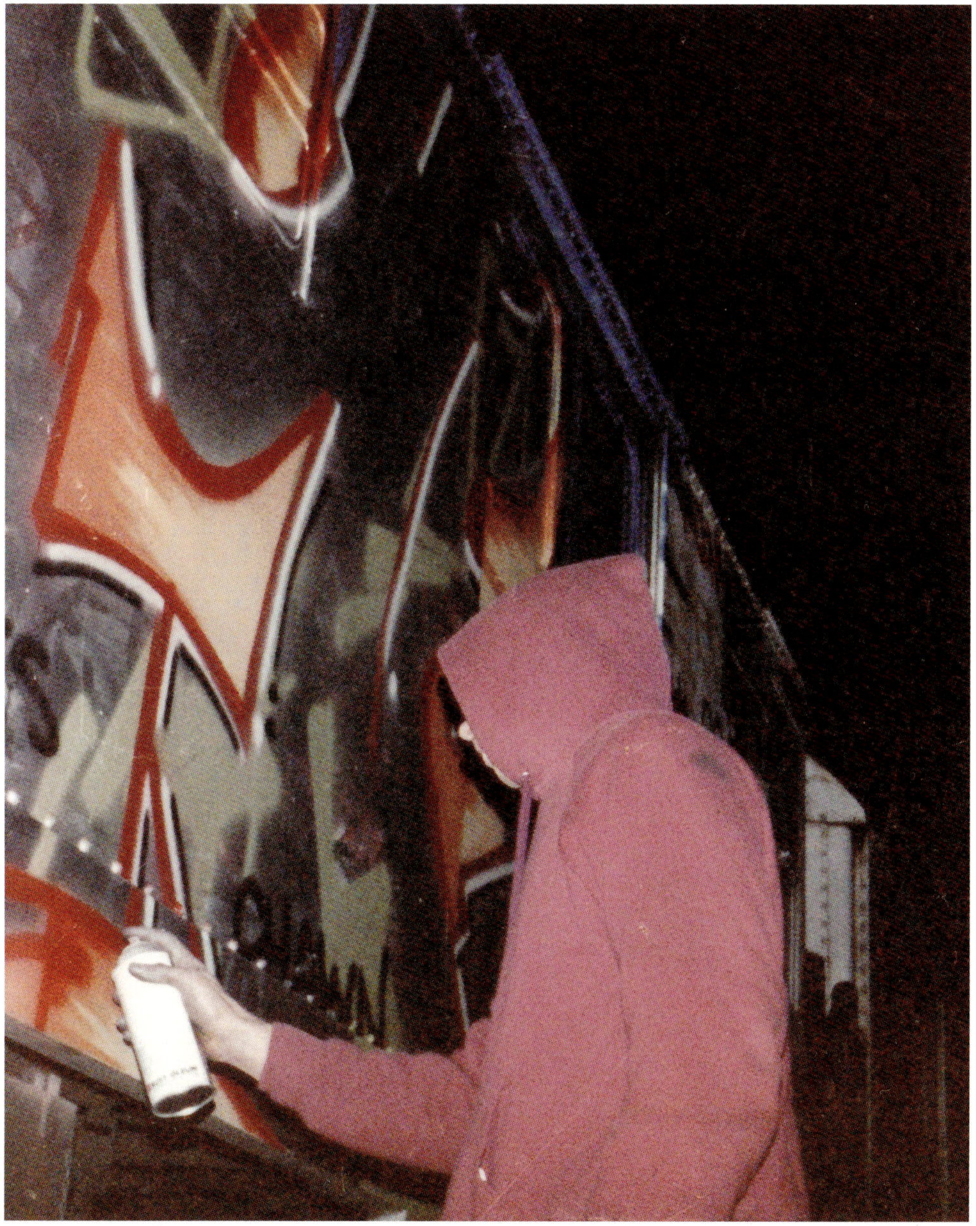

Poem, Baychester layup, 1985 (Photo courtesy of SEEN UA)

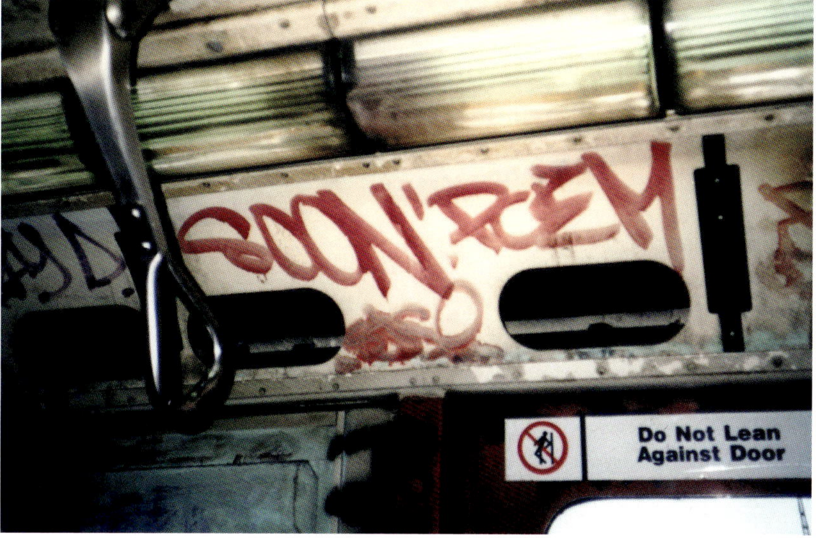

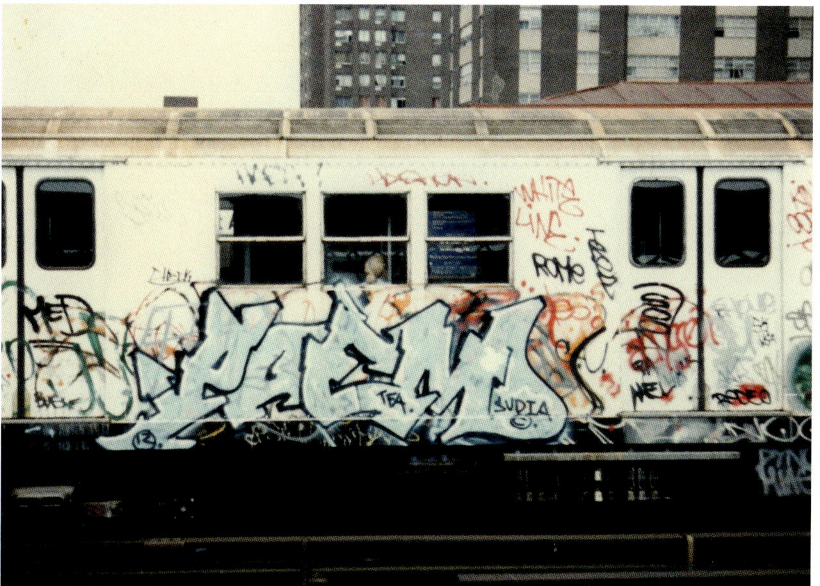

Poem

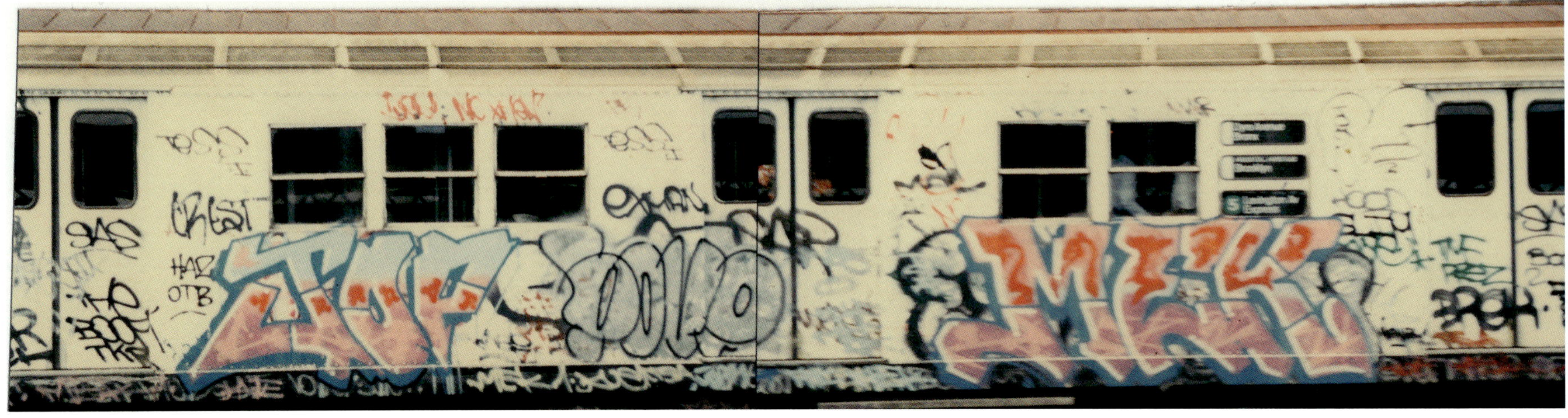

Jop, Mek

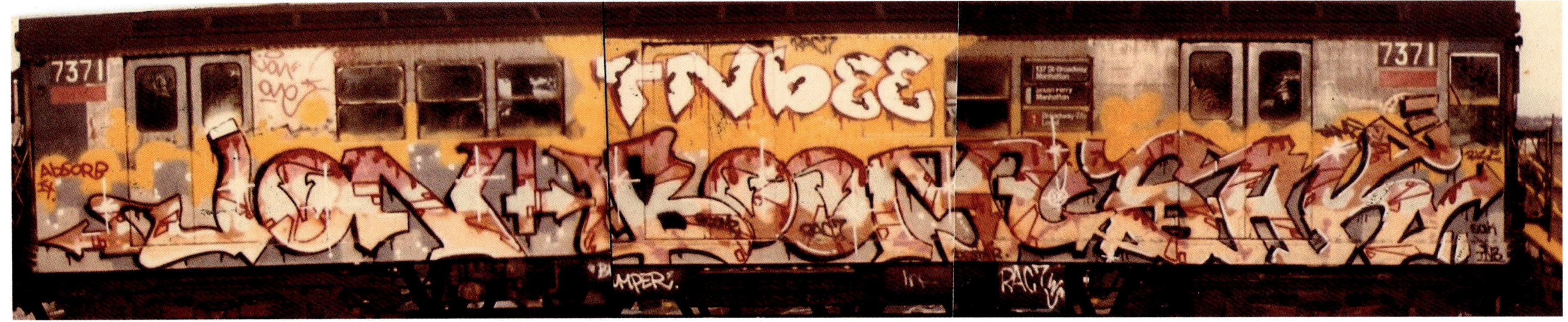

Jon, Boom, Sak (Photo courtesy of Sak MBT)

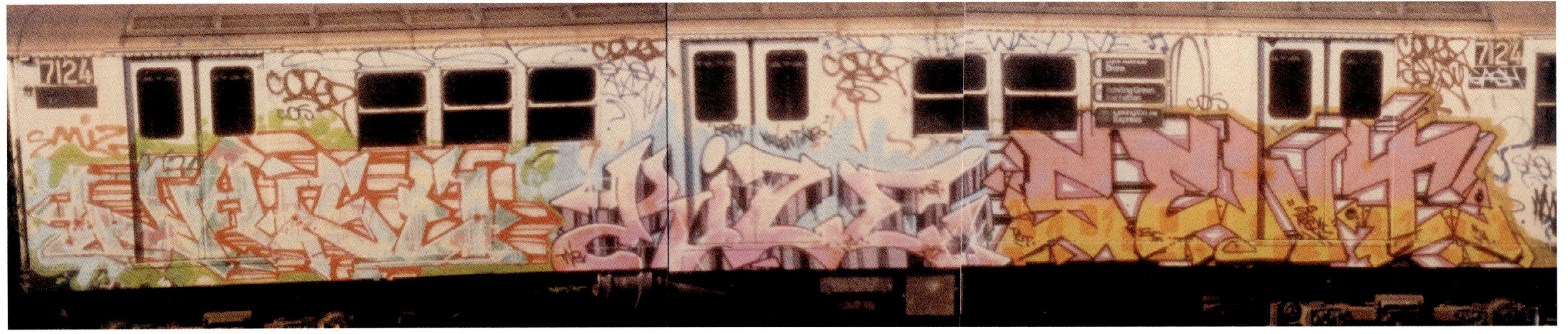

Jase, Rize, Sent, 1985

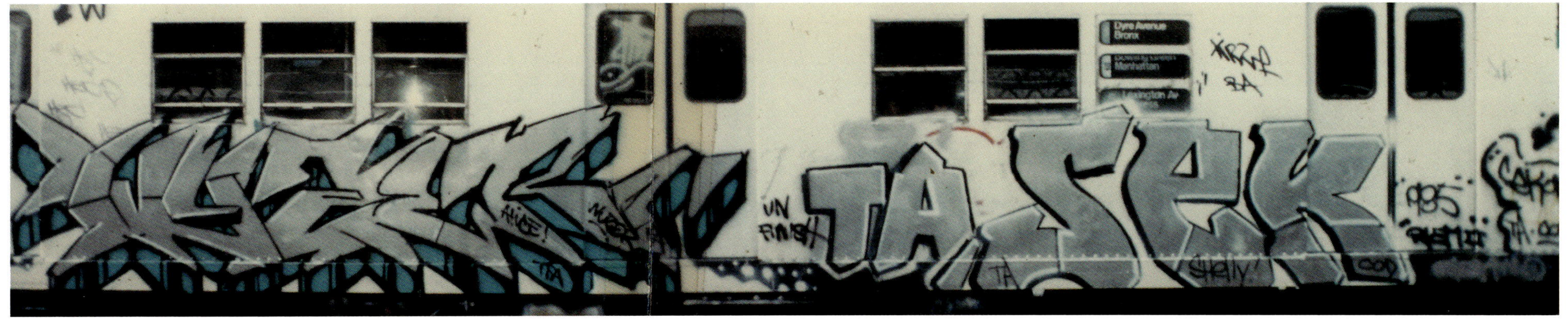

Wuzer, Sek, 1985

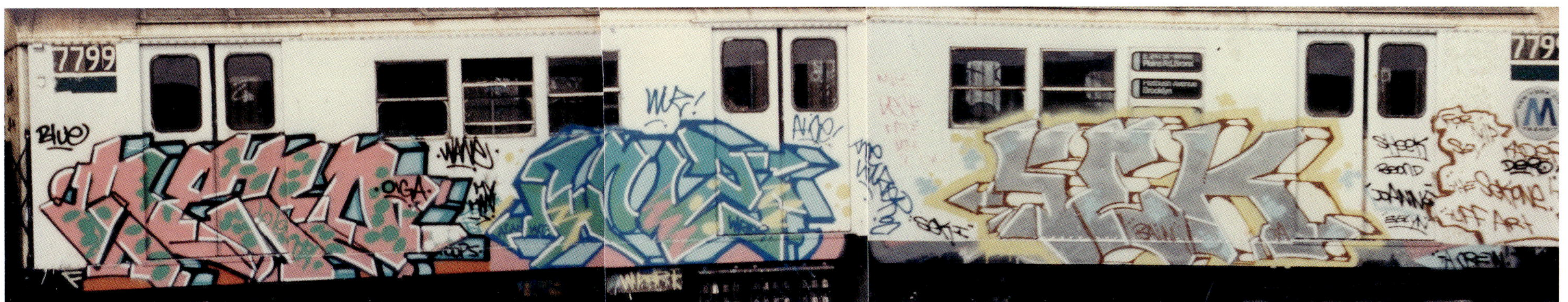

Dero, Wuz, Sek

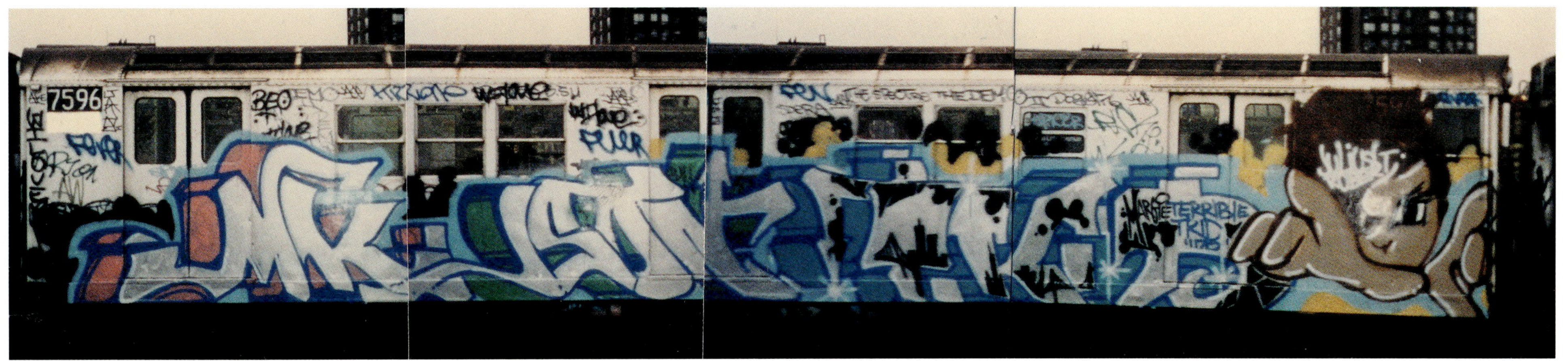

Mk, Json, Tkid, 1985

The last car is where writers (or any other shady characters) can be found. As Rac7 and I entered, T La Rock 's "It's Yours!" was blasting as blunts were being passed around with zero concern for New York's finest. I declined the offer as I wanted to stay sharp for the evening. My adrenaline started pumping once we reached the 180th train station—I knew it was only a few stops until we got off at the Baychester Avenue station. You can always tell a graffiti writer by the way he looks out the window, surveying what's laid up, what isn't, are the lights on?, etc. Other than myself, the only other scrawny little white guy in the car was Poem, he was definitely scopin'. Trustworthy, we told him of our plans to meet up with Tkid and others. Apparently he was due to meet us as well. Rac and I got off first. Poem stayed on to get his paint if I remember correctly. We entered through an already cut hole in the barbed wire. The wind hit us like razor blades. This was gonna be a tough one. We navigated our way through rusted barbed wire and old tires. You can easily break an ankle on all types of fuckin' shit, you know, emergency room stuff. Rac and I started our pieces on the outside lane so as to get some height from the third rail. About two hours later we see Tkid170, 2Draw, Raz, Seen, Poem, Eon, Mkay, and Cavs emerge from the dark as they entered Baychester layups. My adrenaline was pumping on overtime. You have to understand that I was painting with Giants! Guys I always looked up to, and here I was pulling out cars with them. I truly had to step my game up. In the center lanes Poem and Eon was rocking their signature top-to-bottoms. Tkid, Mkay, and Seen (Psycho123) was on the same car doing window-downs. 2Draw, Cavster, and Raz on the car to the left. Soon as Raz cracked his outline he decided not to finish. It was way too cold and luckily for him the MTA kept the heat and lights on. Everyone kept their paint in the train to keep the paint from freezing. We had one car door open to make it accessible to grab the paint and keep warm. It was so cold that night that Seen threw in the towel by doing a throw-up over his piece. He did redeem himself by doing many throw-ups. Tkid finished his piece and wrote in his piece, "In the fuckin' cold my Ts are bold." This was a milestone for me as a Broadway kid coming to the east Bronx to burn with the best. It was a night I'll never forget.

—Omni

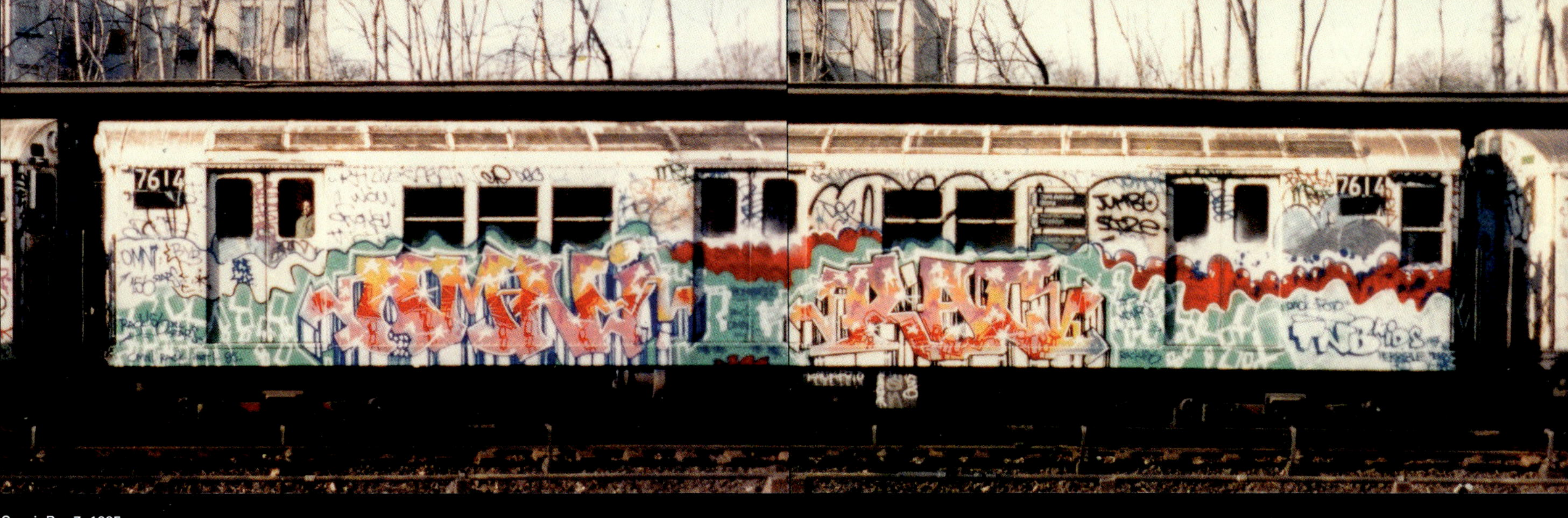

Omni, Rac7, 1985

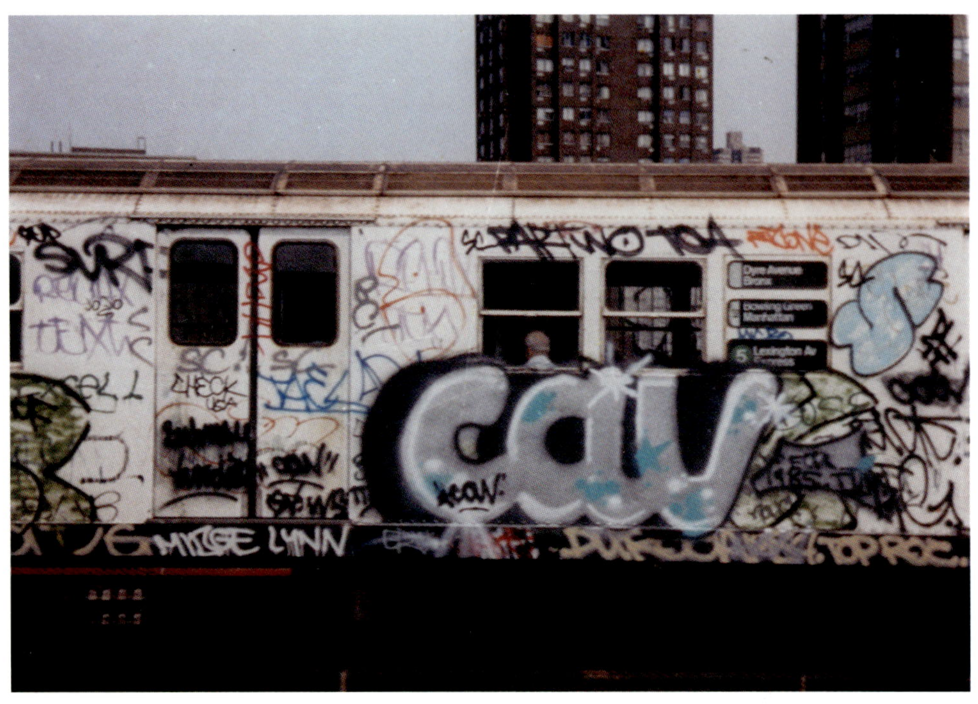

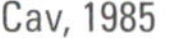

Cav, 1985

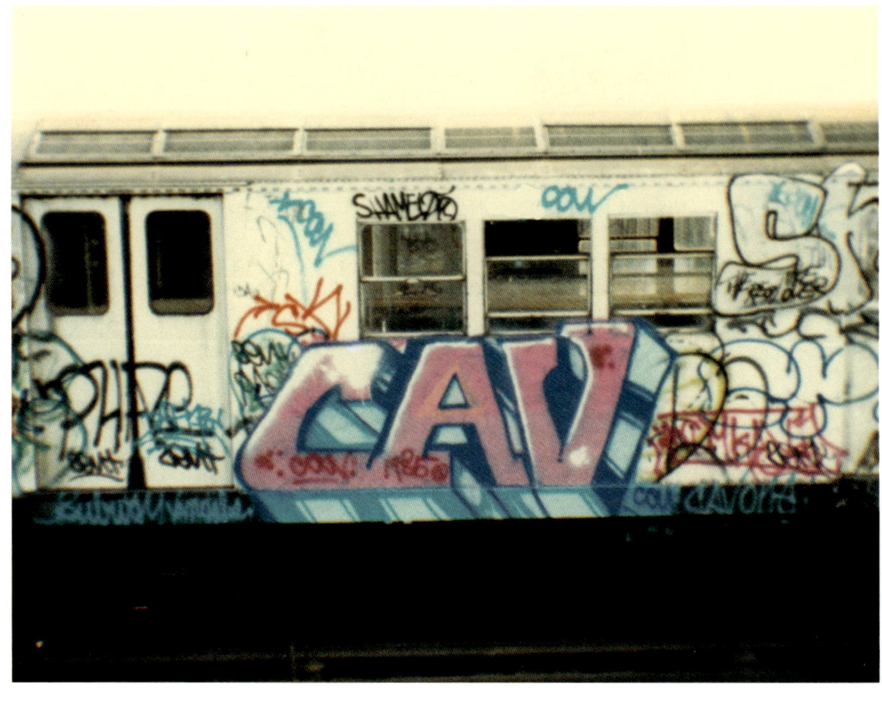

Cav, 1985

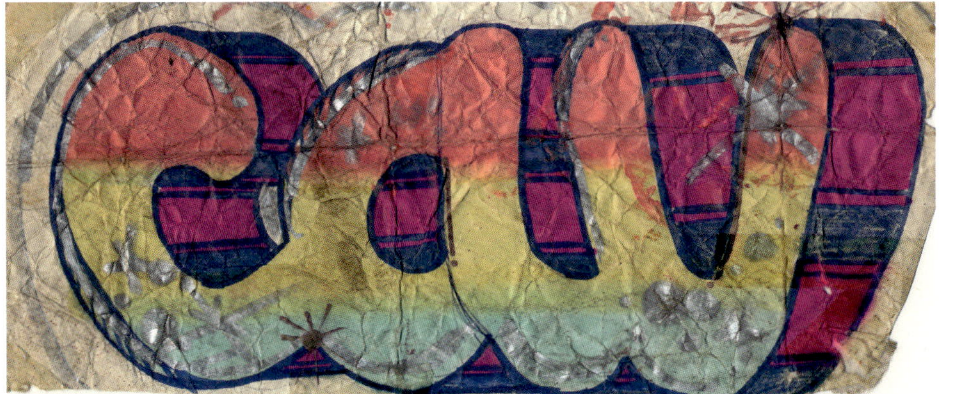

Original outline

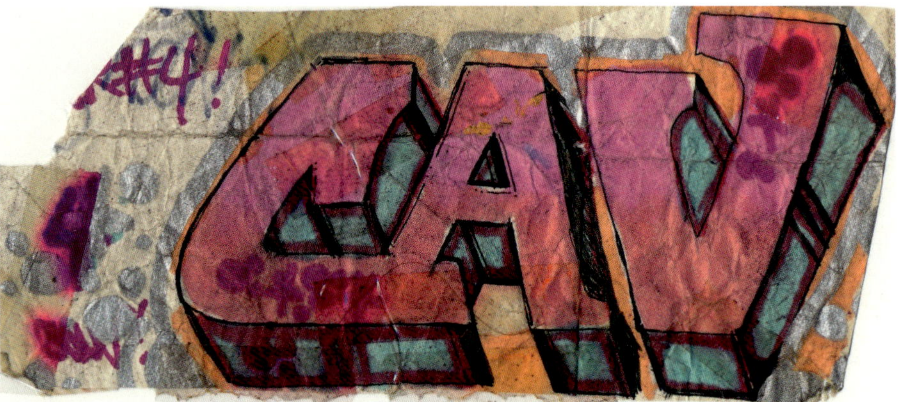

Original outline

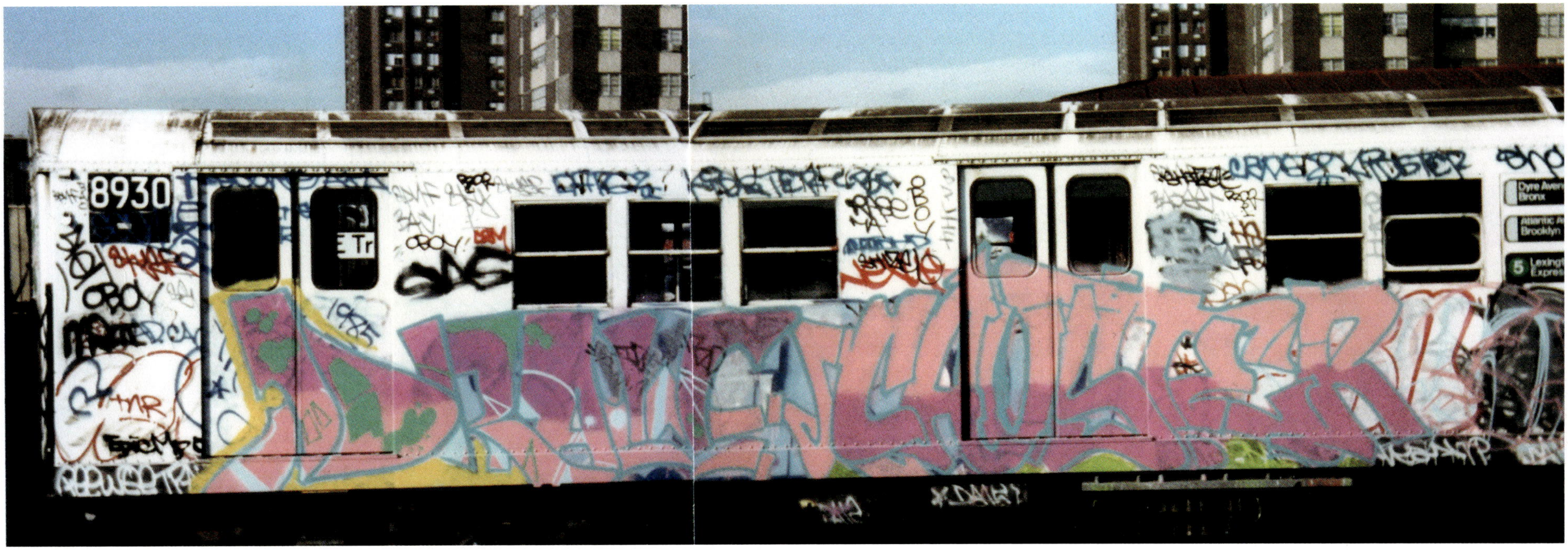

2Draw, Cavster, 1985

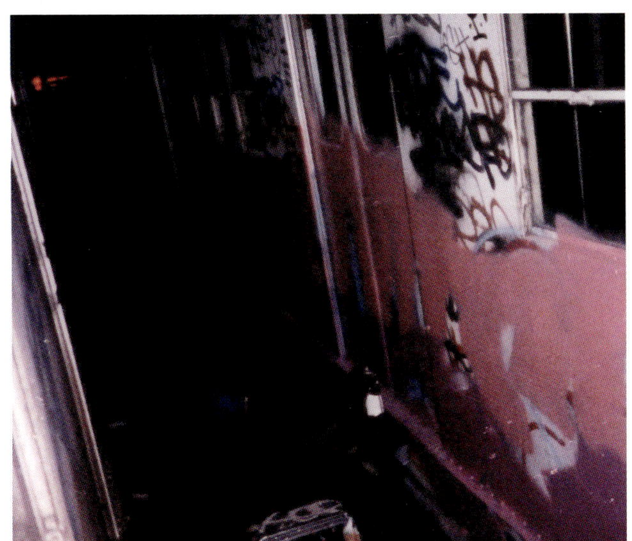

Cavster, Baychester layup, 1985

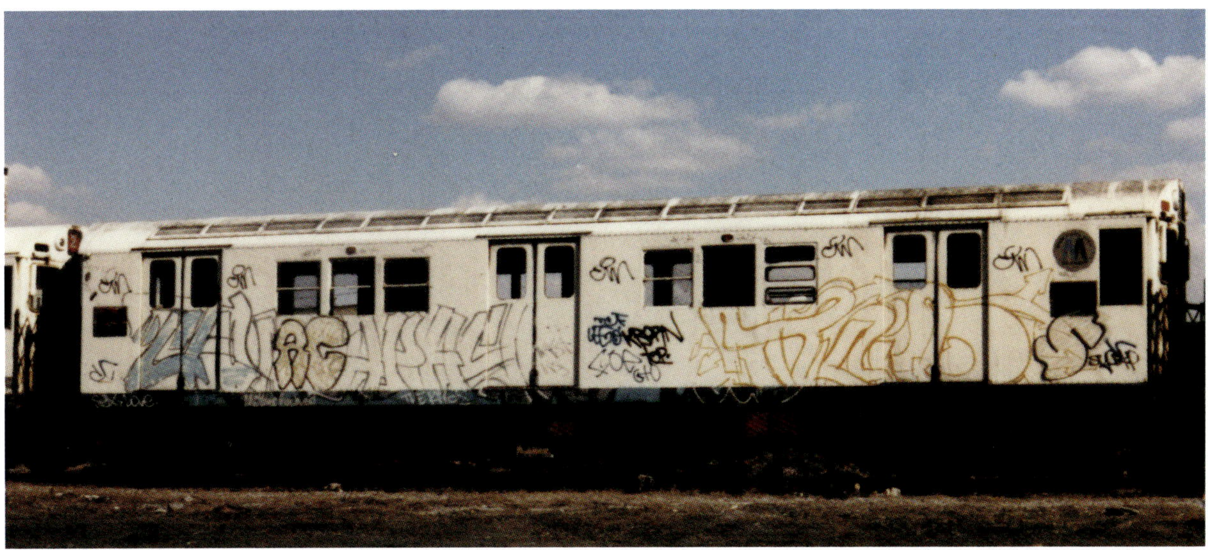

Cav, Apache (Seen UA), Tkid (unfinished), 1985

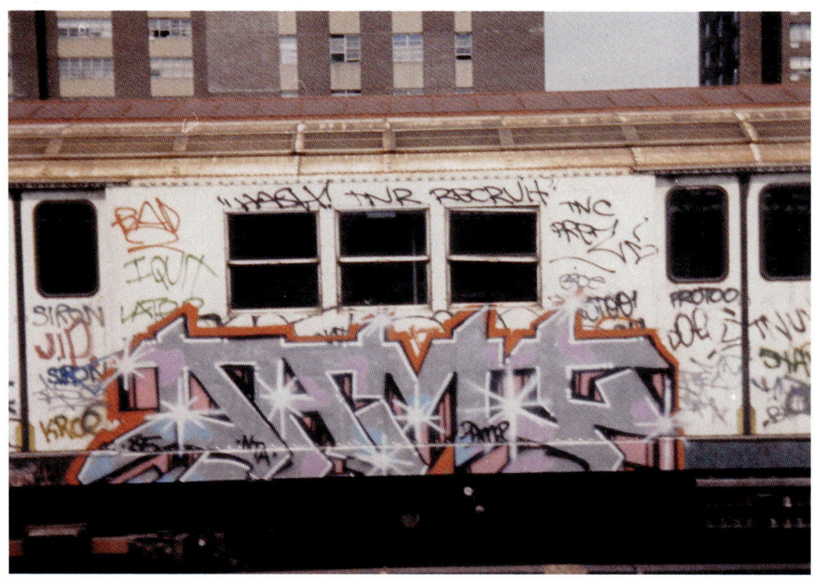

Damp, 1985

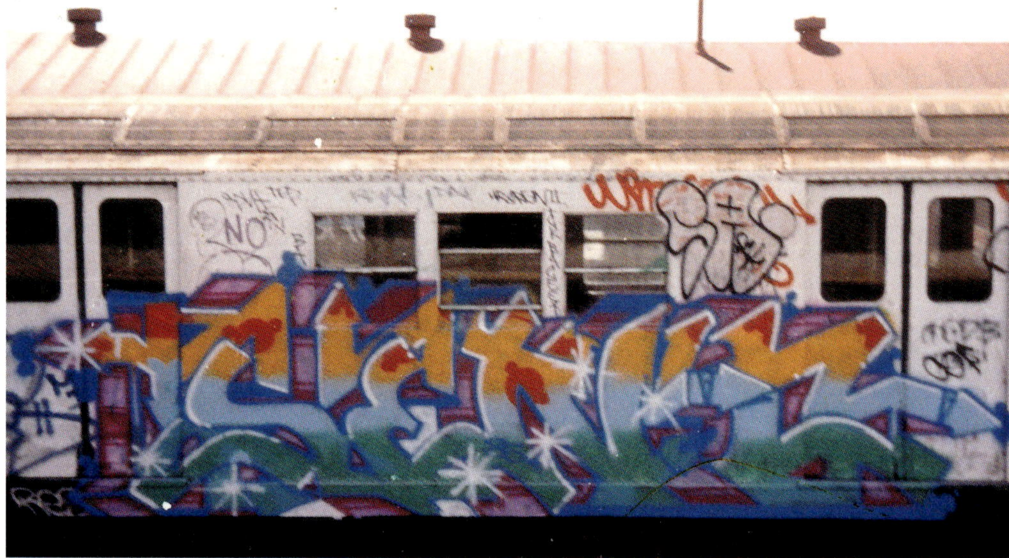

Sent, 1985

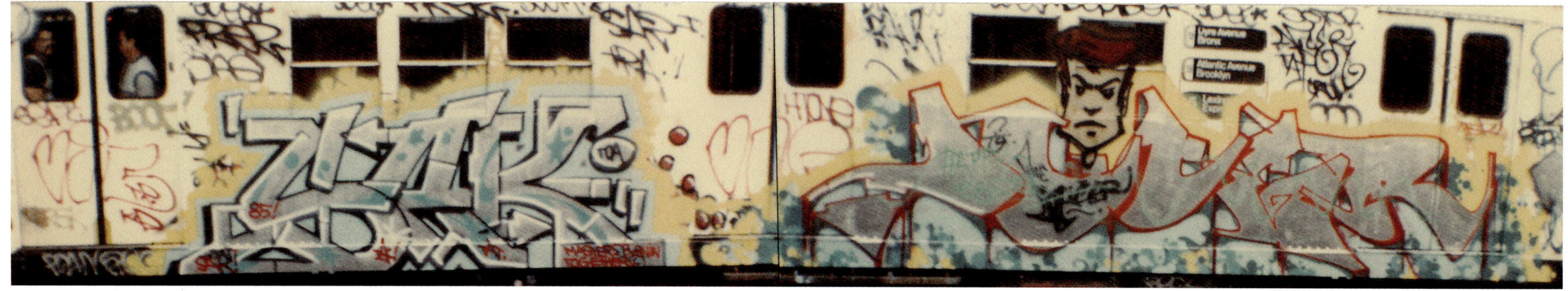

Sak, Nicer, 1985

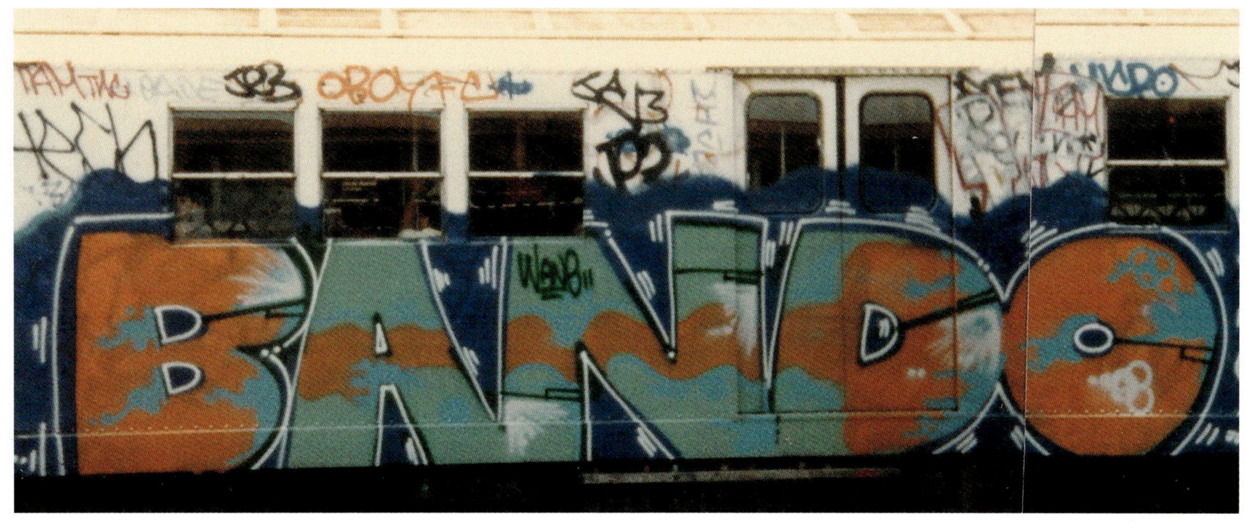

Bando by Jon1

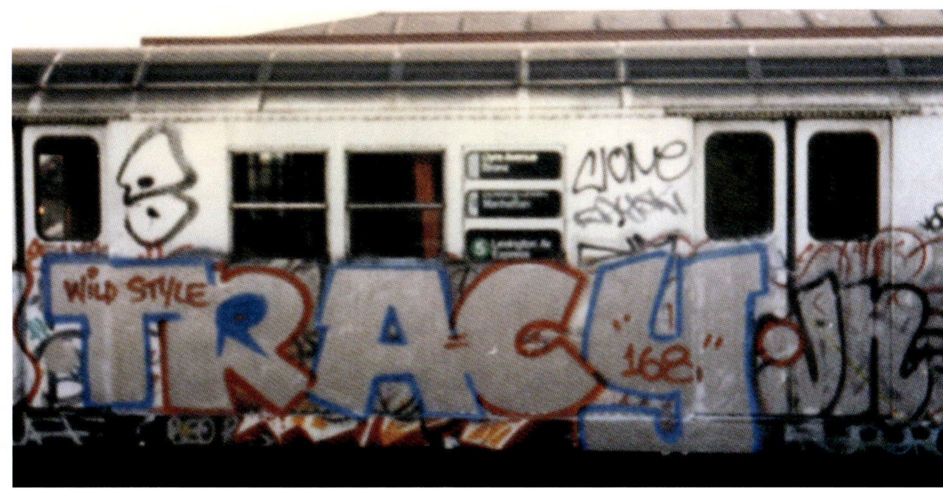

Tracy168

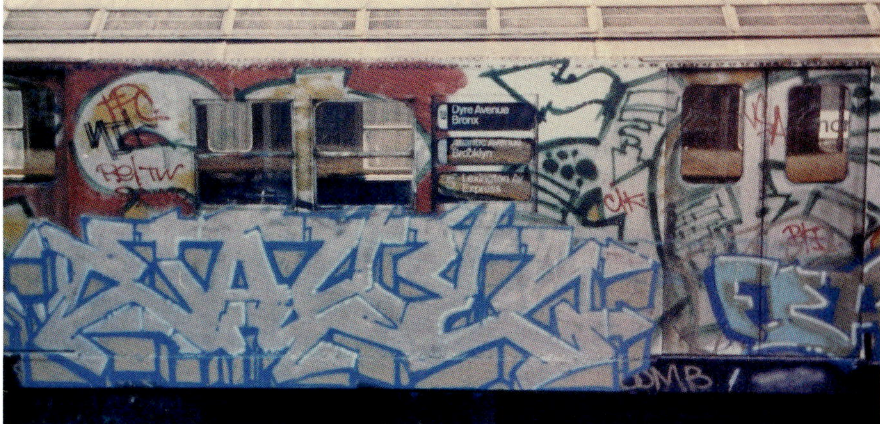

Jase FBA

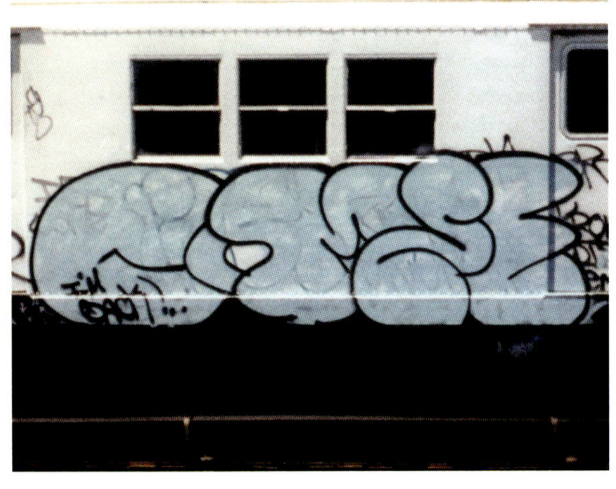

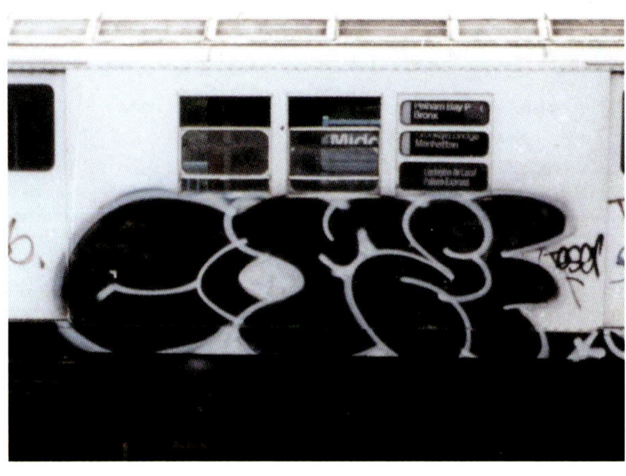

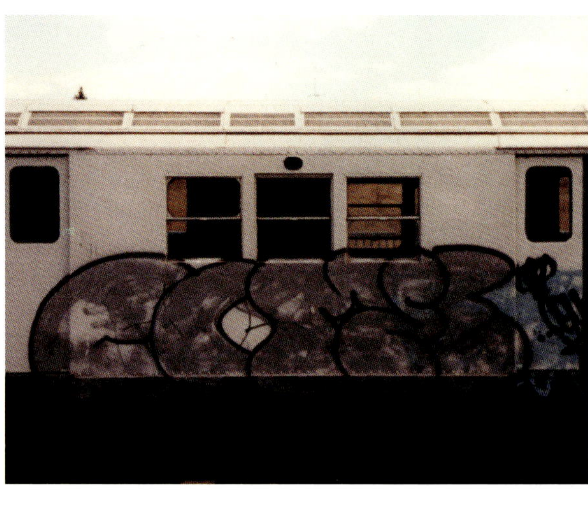

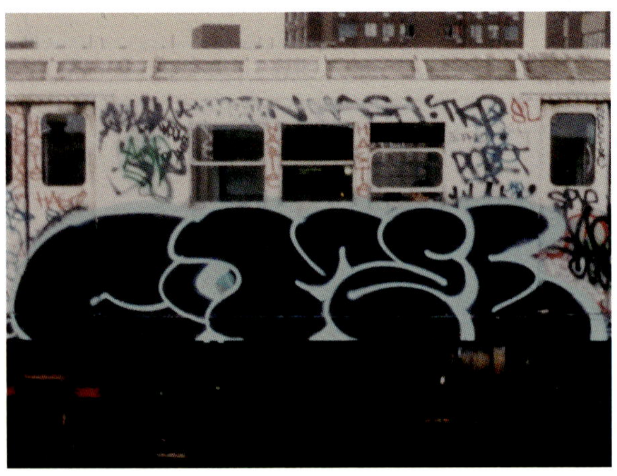

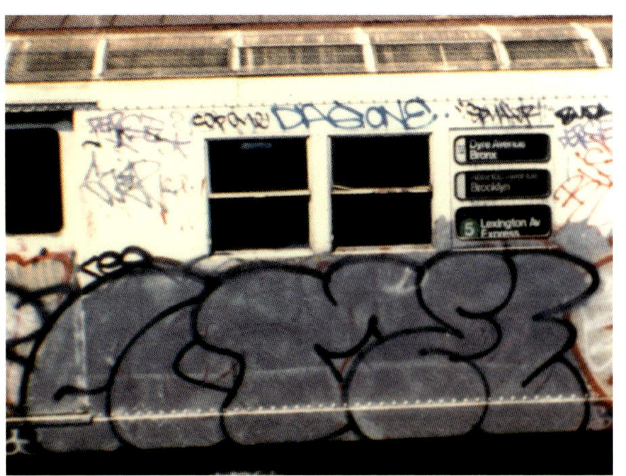
Dyre Avenue
Bronx
Brooklyn
5
Lexington Av

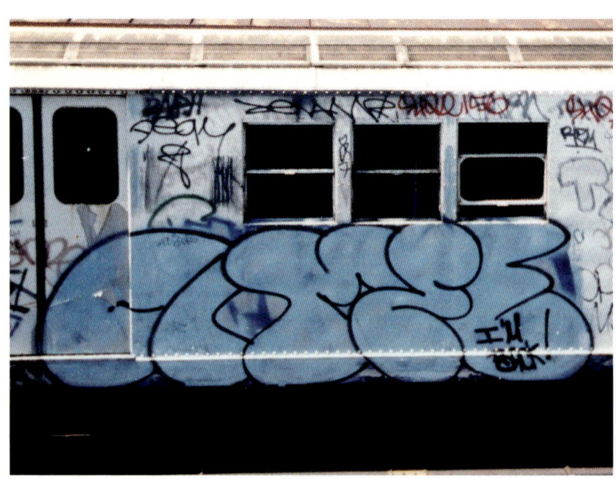

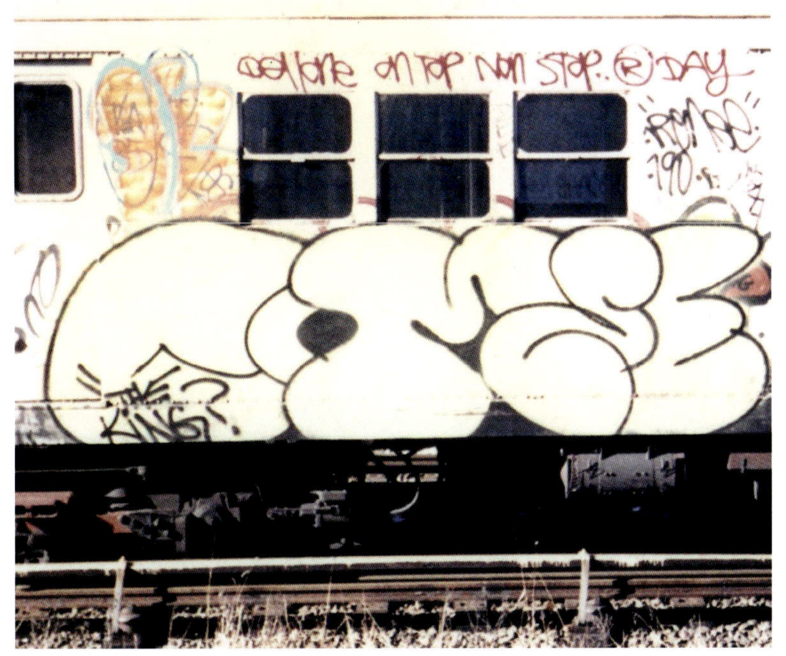

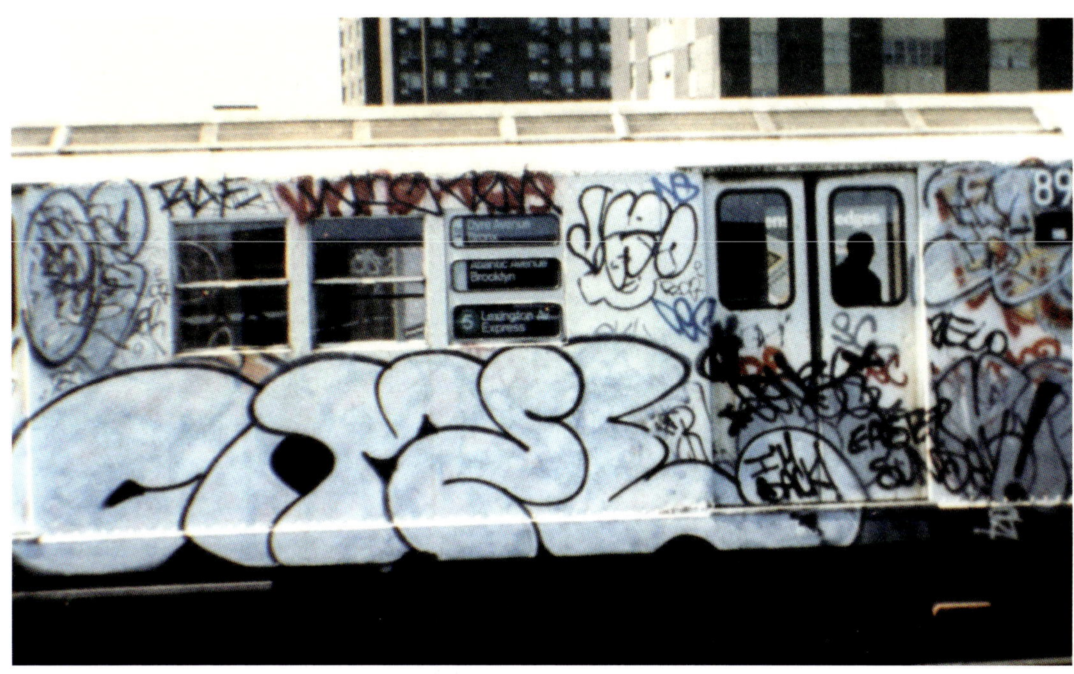

Comet, Easter Sunday, 1986

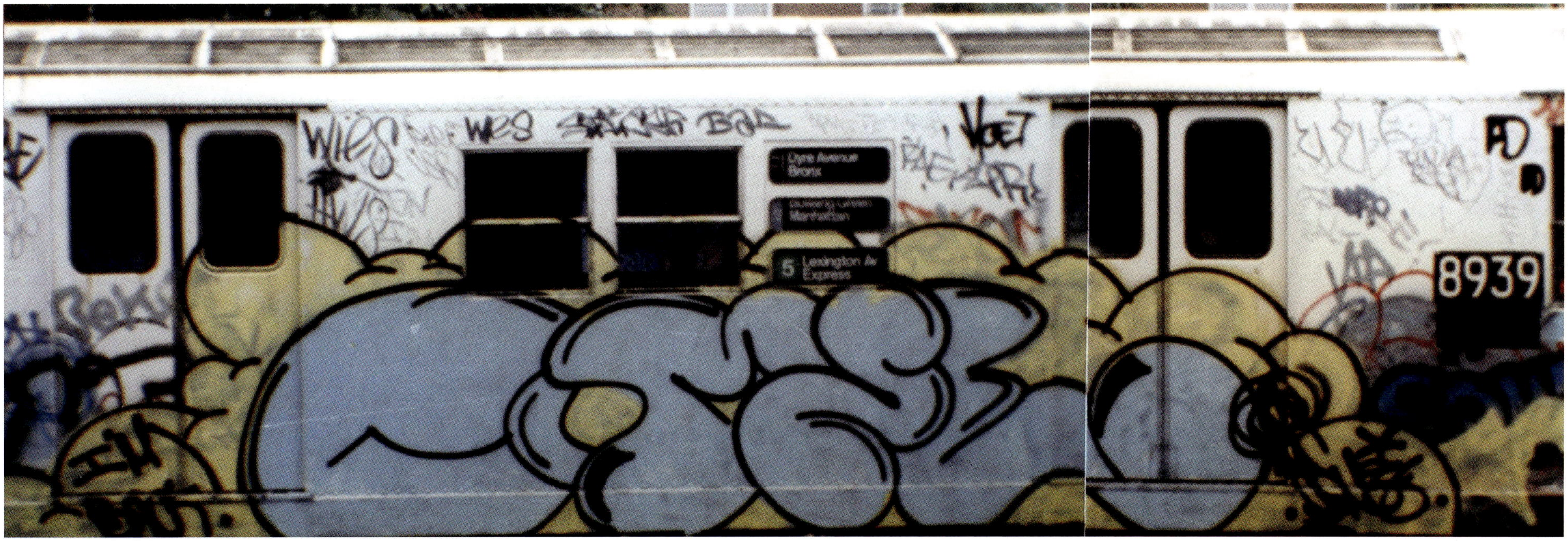

Comet, I'm Back, 1986

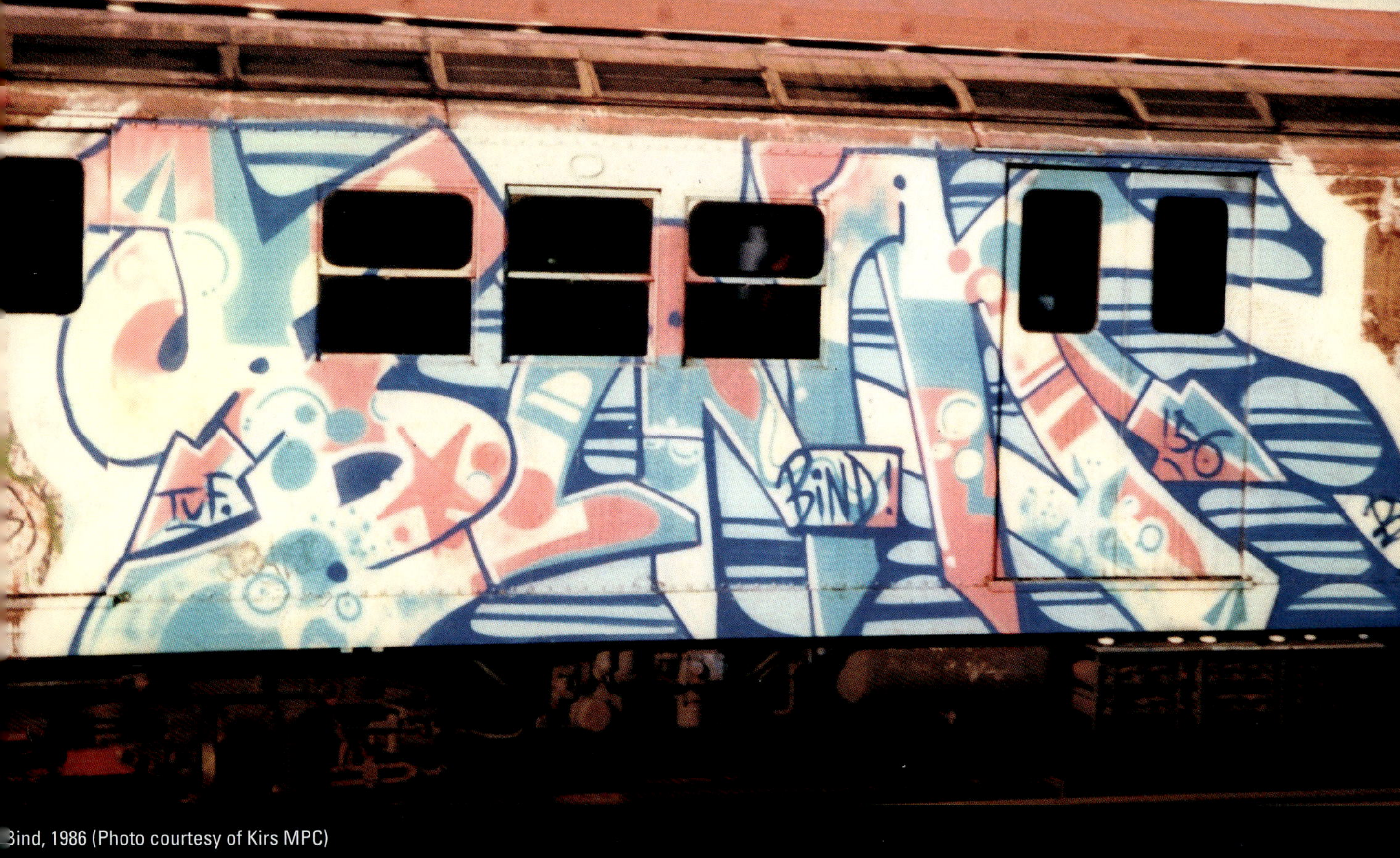

Bind, 1986 (Photo courtesy of Kirs MPC)

Good times in the #1 tunnel with Jon1, Weber, and Staf. I'm an East Side dude, so I never saw this run and never even had a picture until about thirty years later when Kirs MPC hit me up with this one.

–Bind

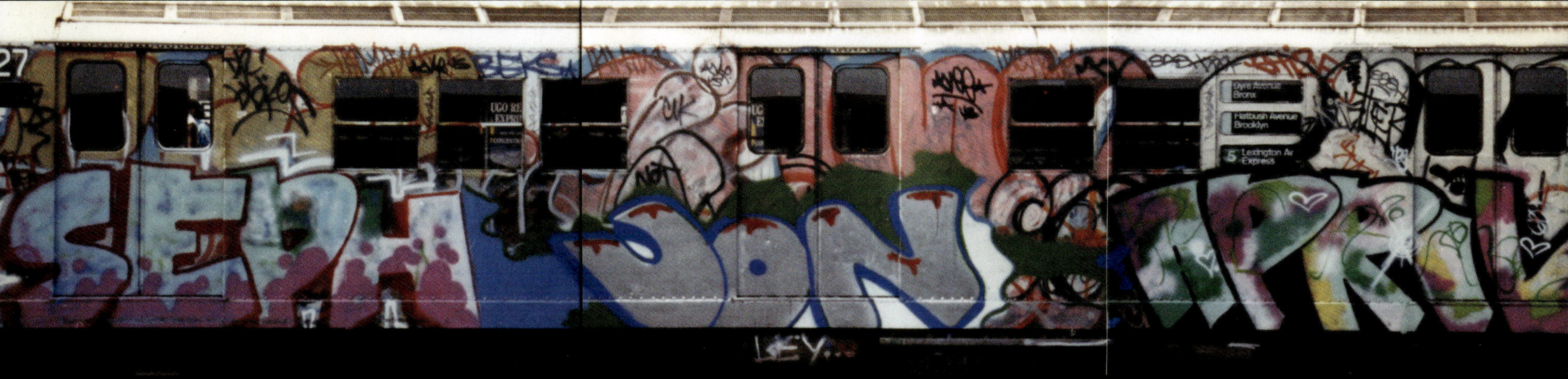

Seph, Jon, April, 1986

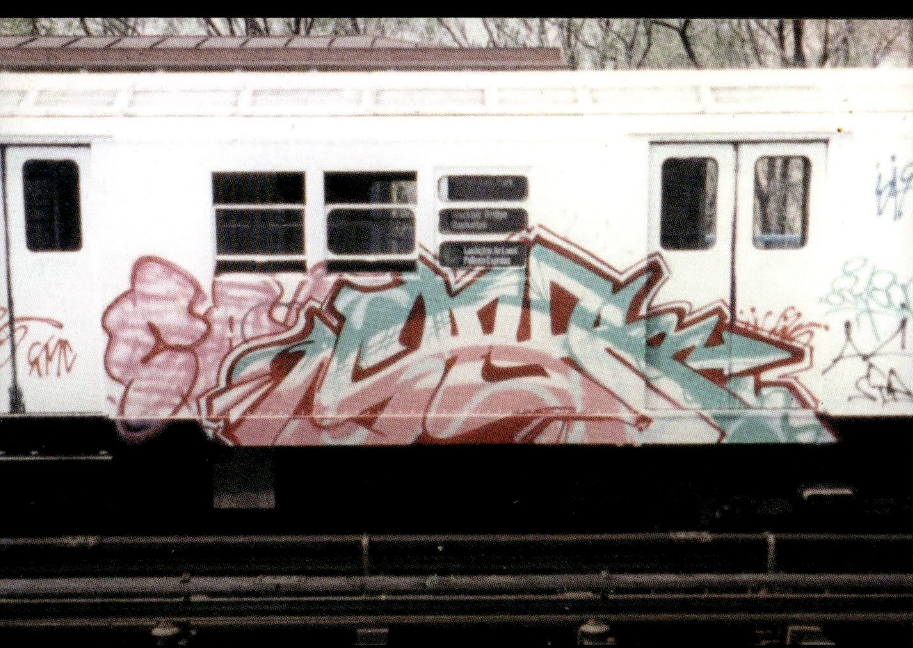

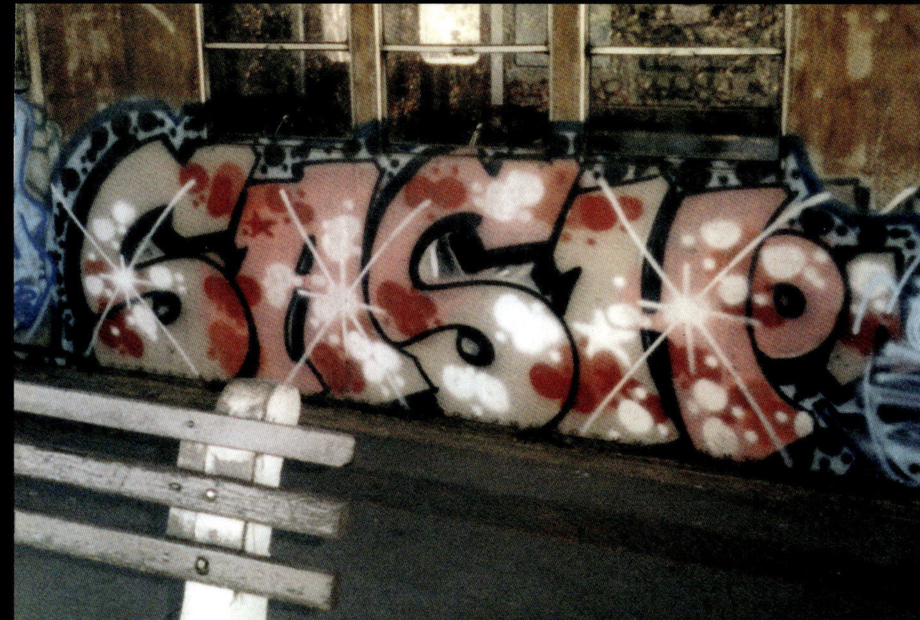

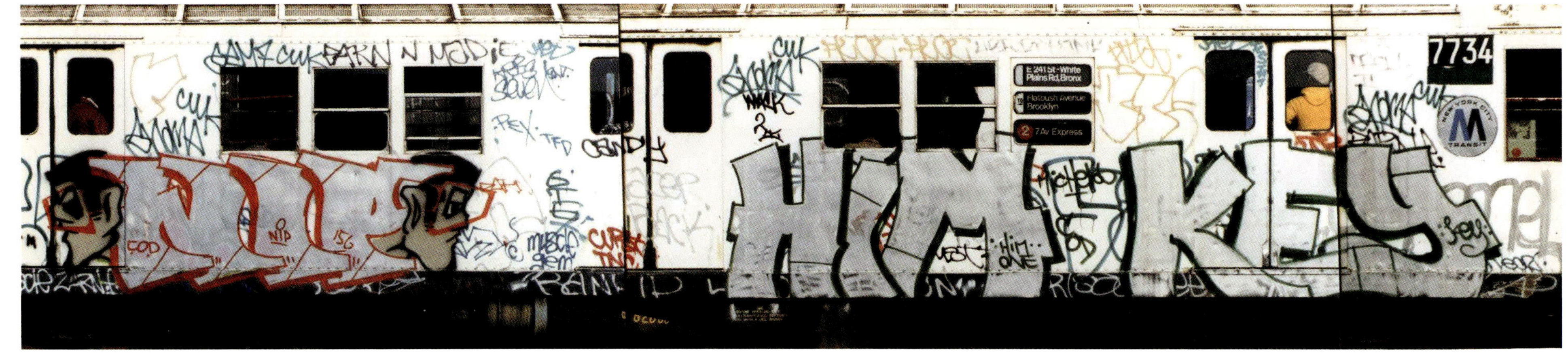

Nip, Him, Key

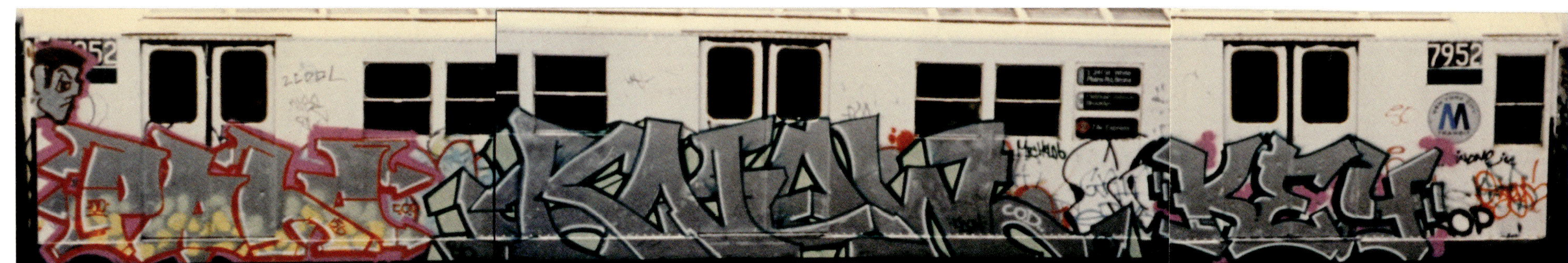

Polo, Know, Key, 1986

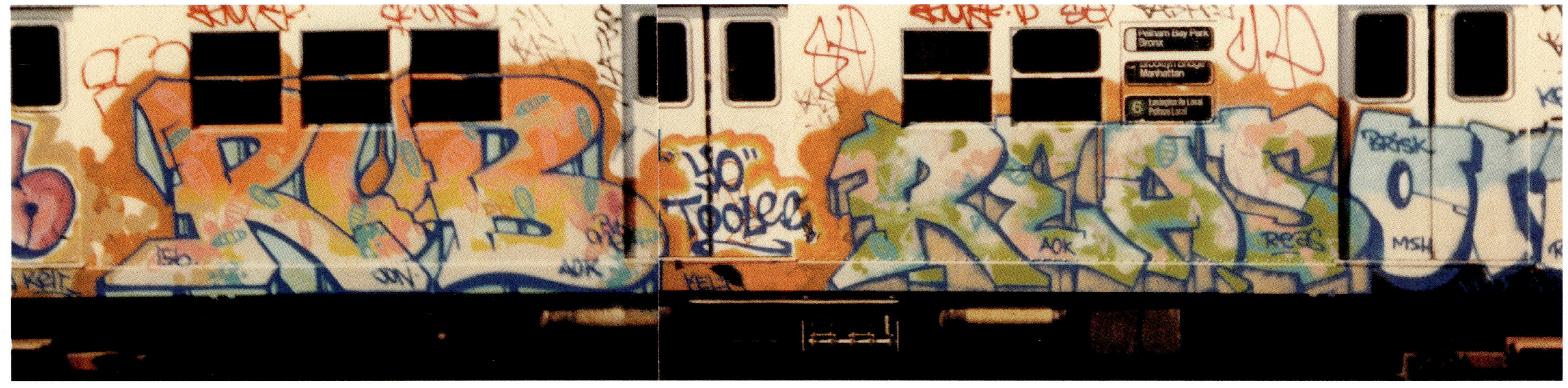

Rub, Reas, 1986

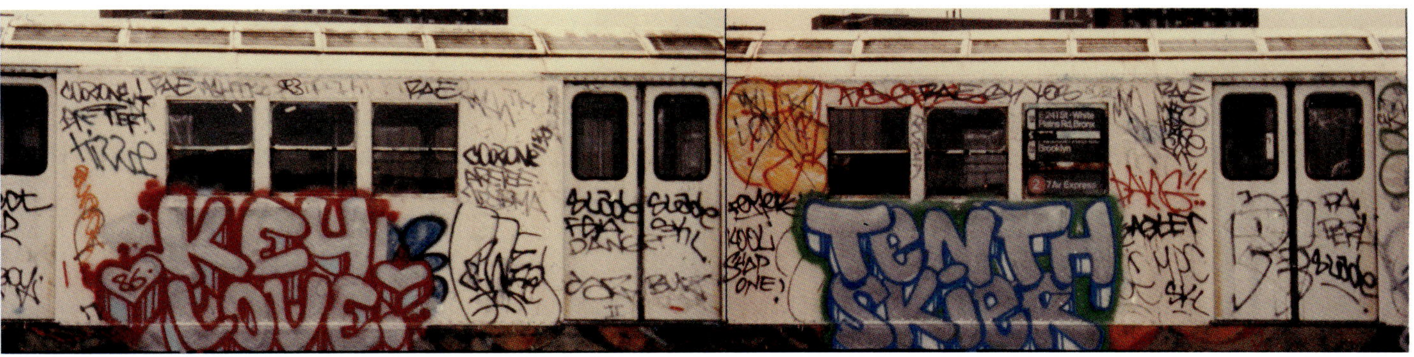

Keylove, Tenthskier, 1986

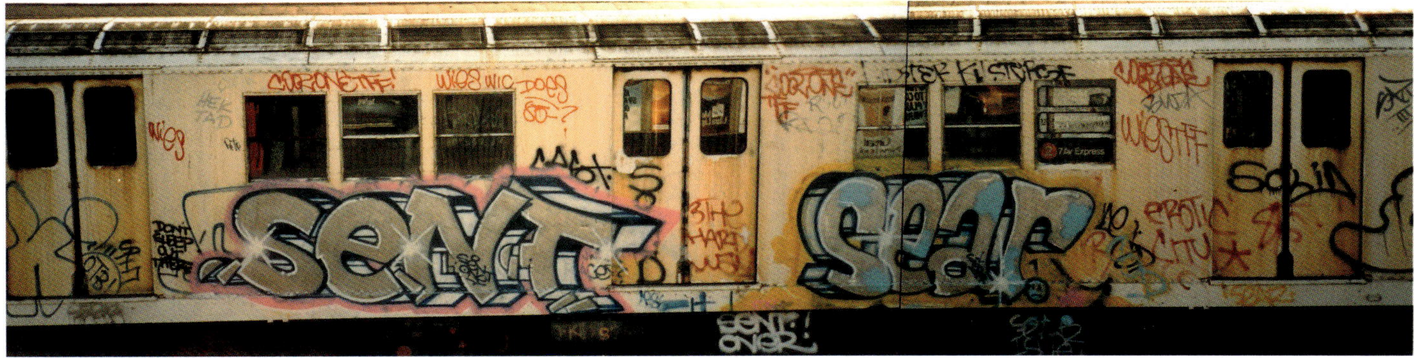

Sent, Sear, 1986

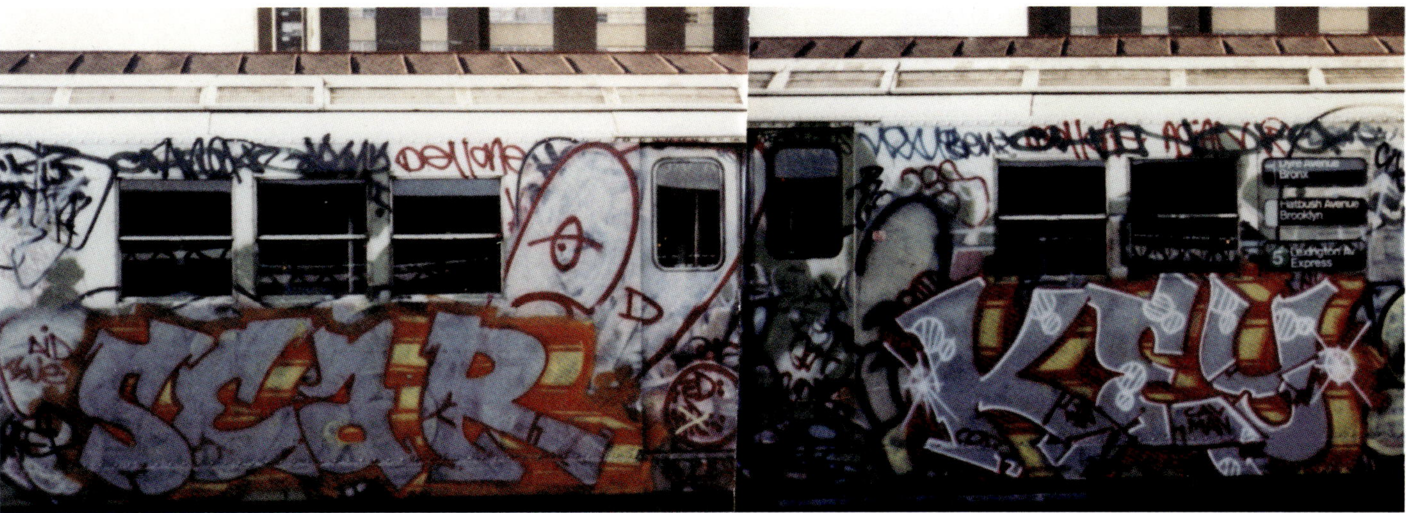

Sear, Key, 1986

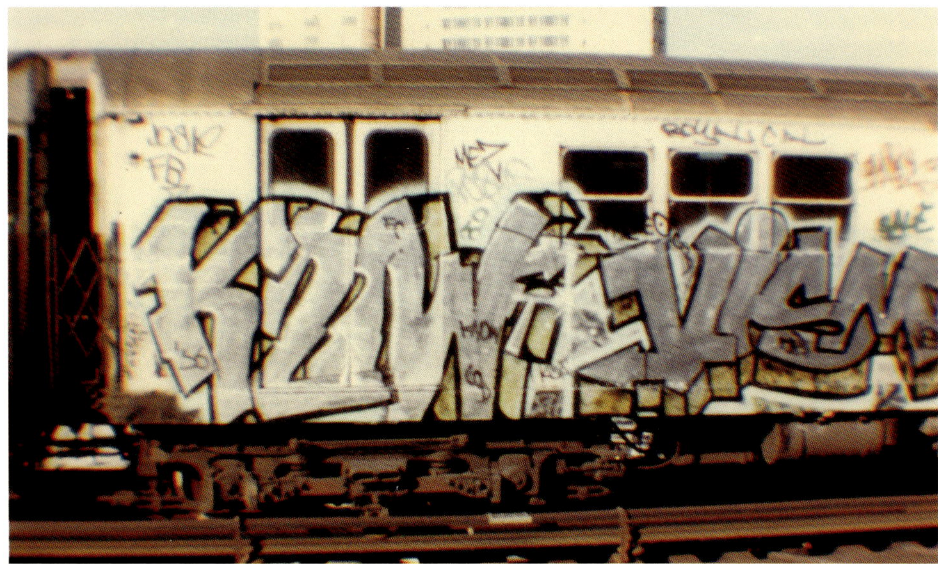

Know, Vism, 1986

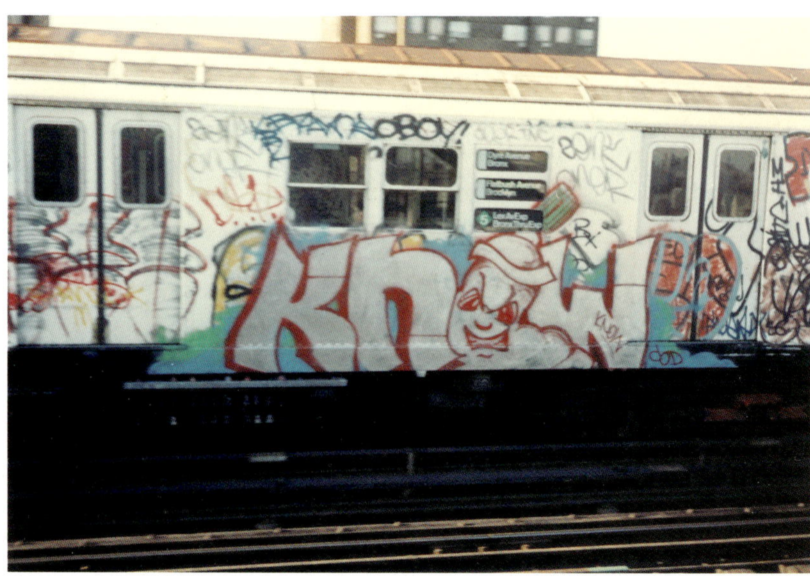

Know COD

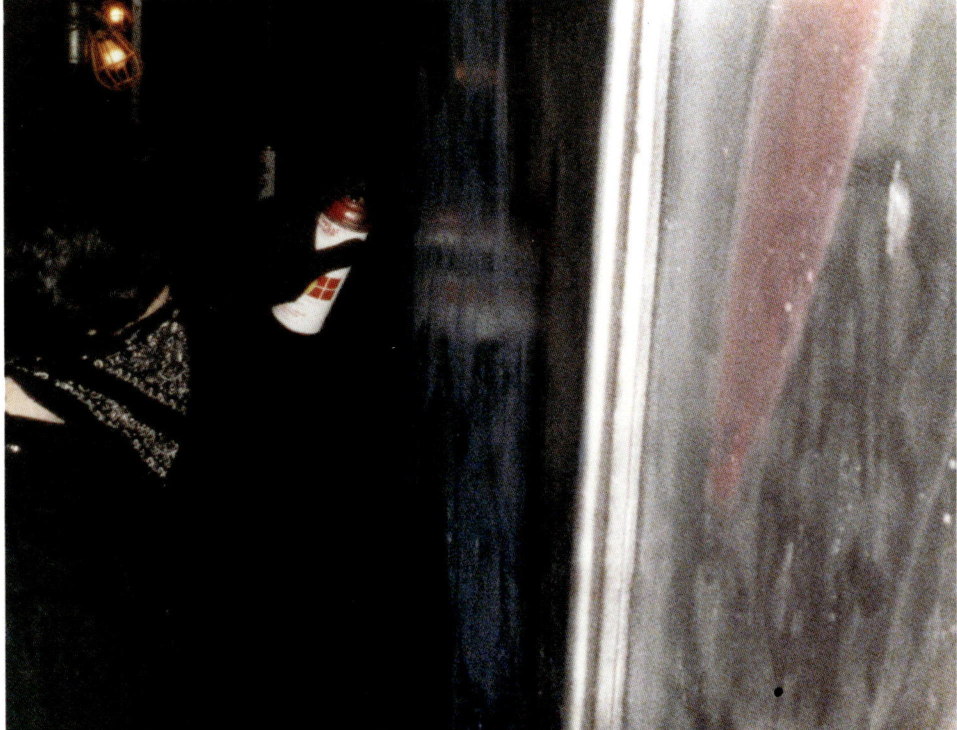

Key painting in the 145th Street 1 Tunnel, 1986

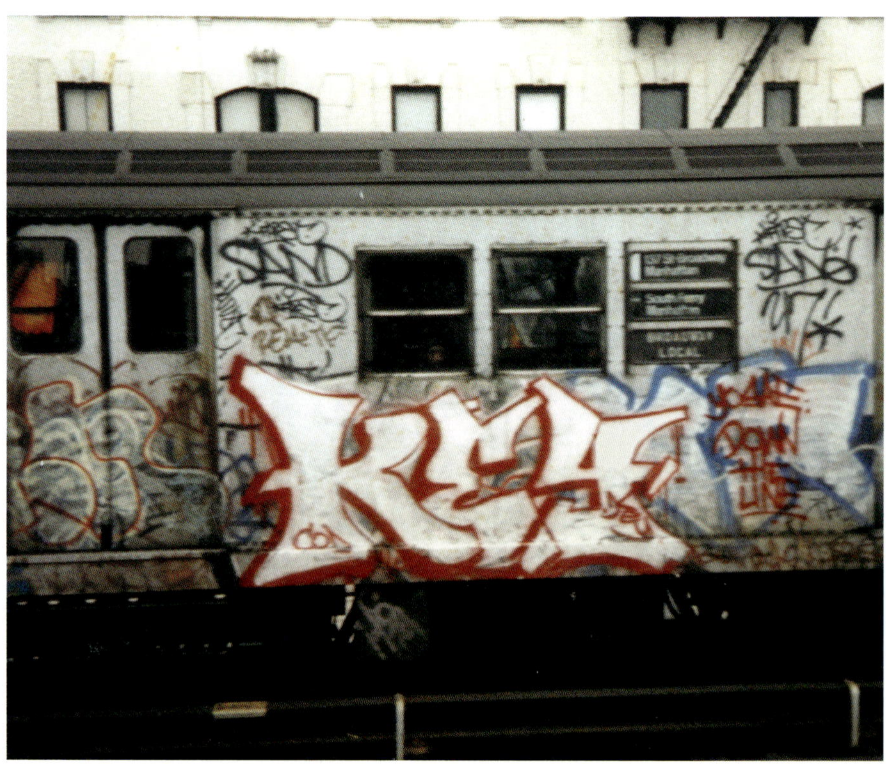

Key on Broadway (1 line), 1986

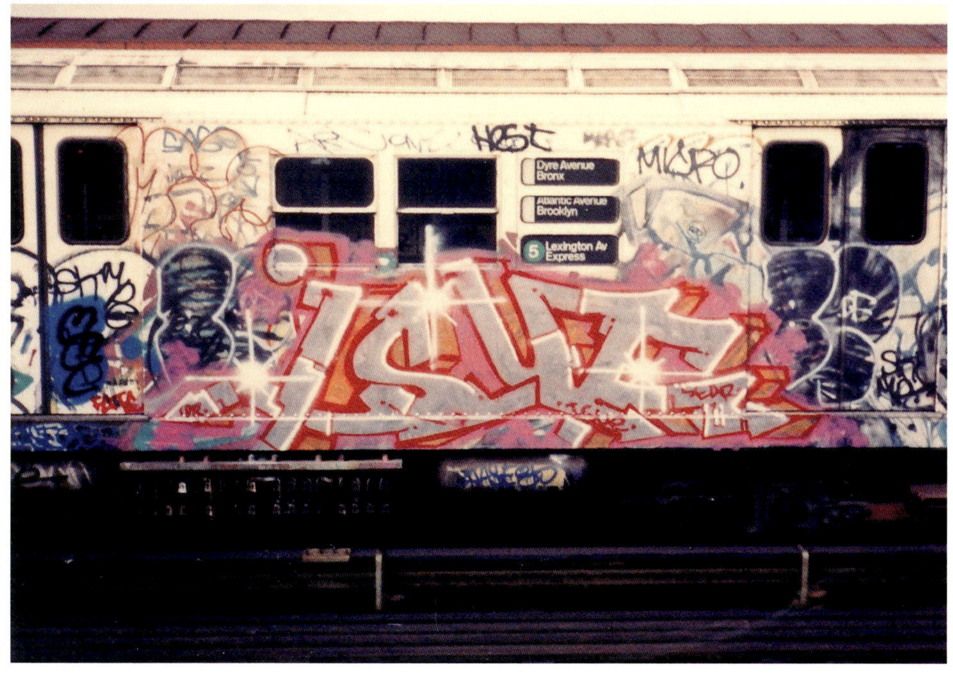

Isue

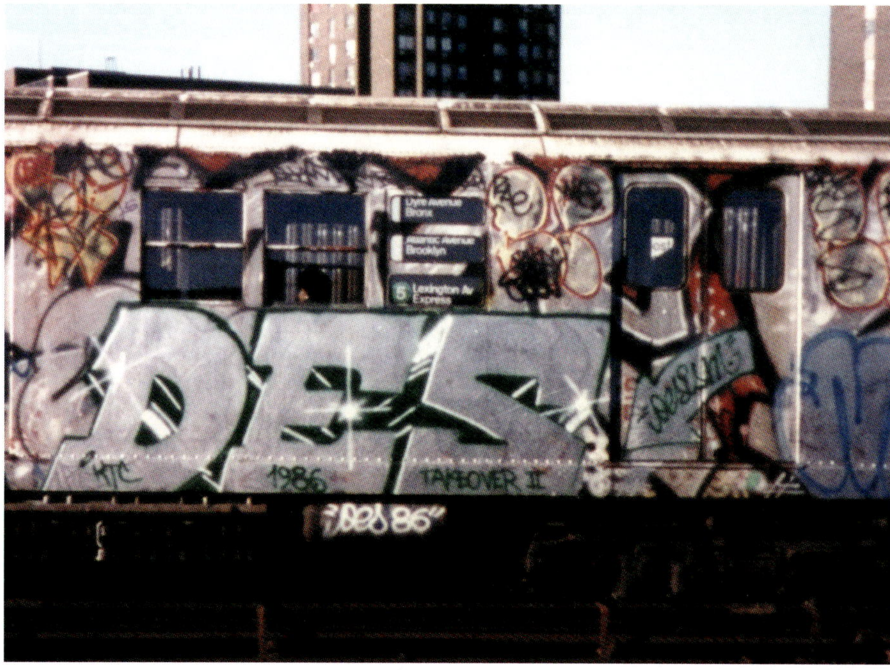

Des KTC, 1986

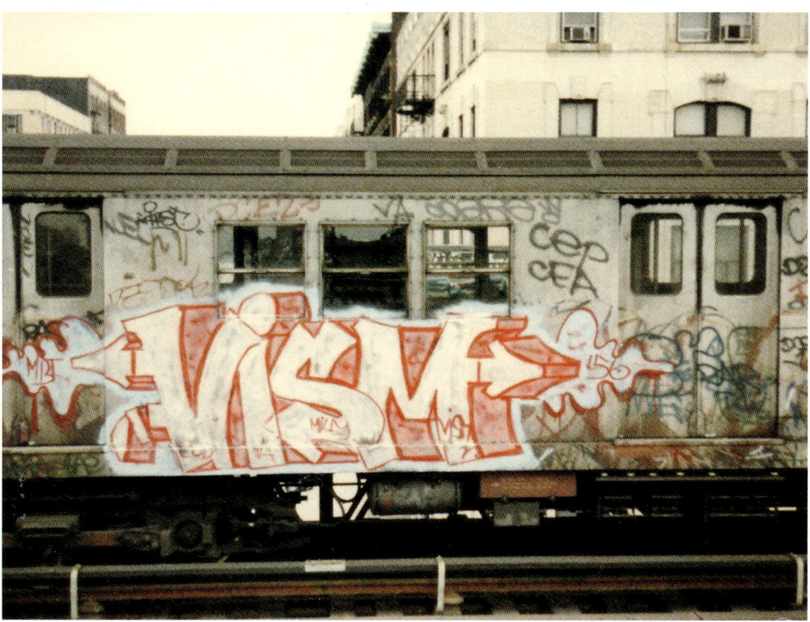

Vism, 1986

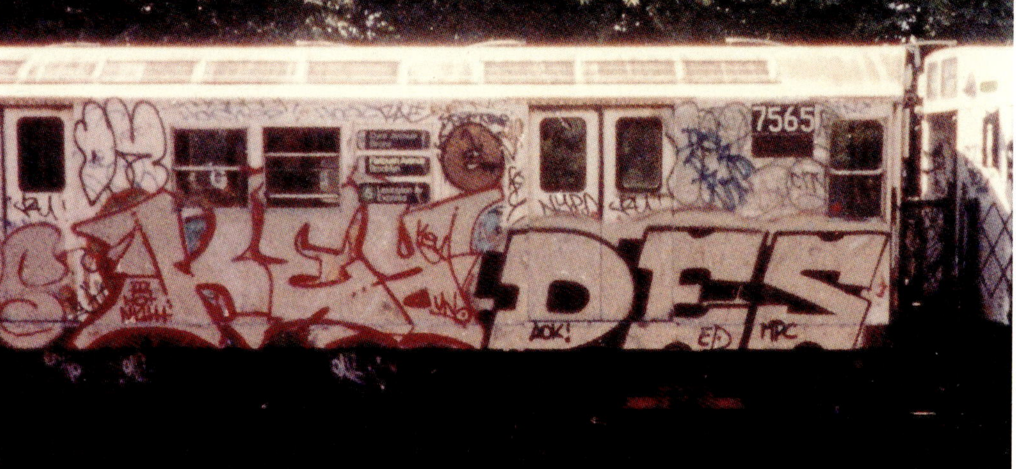

Key, Des, 1986

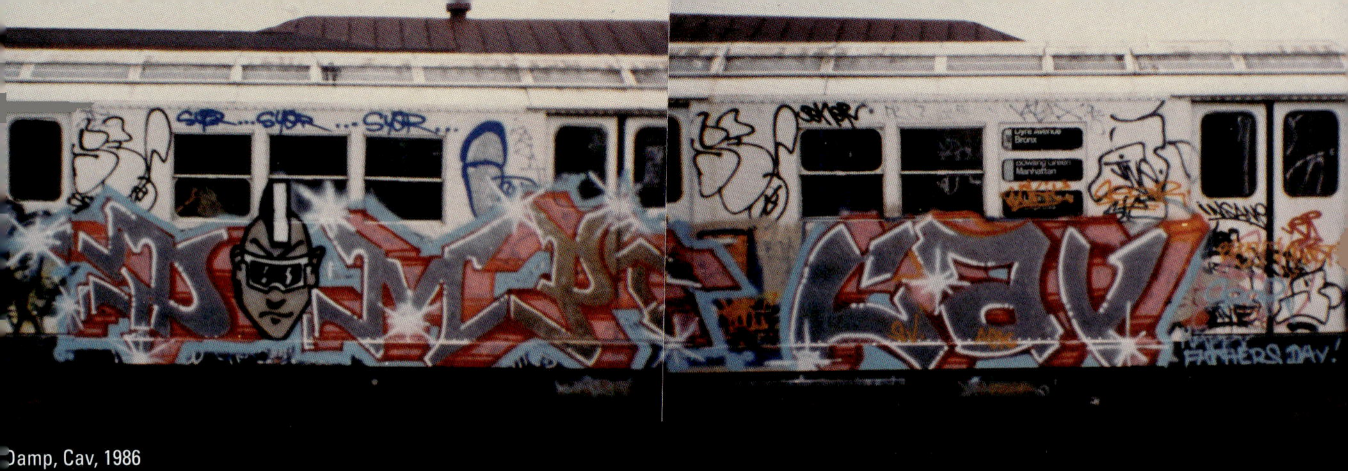

Damp, Cav, 1986

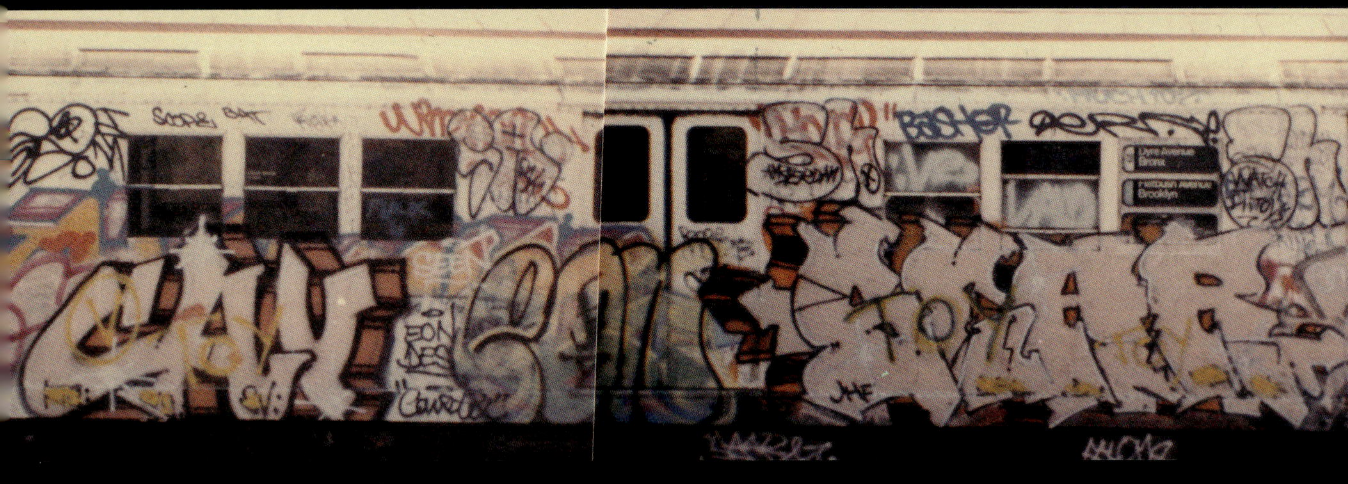

Cav, Sear (crossed out by the Vandal Squad), 1986

In the morning, I went back to Baychester to get flicks of the Cav, Sear. I was standing by the hole looking up to the trains, and to my surprise I see two dudes crossing out our pieces. I had to get a better look to see who they were and sure enough it was the Vandal Squad. As I watched in disbelief, they were dogging our pieces with their Vs. After being toyed out, I noticed that Vism's piece was also crossed out. The Vandal Squad wrote "Never hit the road toy" over Vism's piece. They even put their Vs over my throw-ups. Sometimes I wondered if writers were doing the same thing. When writing your name on the trains, you win some and you lose some just to get fame. That's the name of the game!

–Cavs

Damp, 1986

Dyre Avenue
Bronx
Atlantic Avenue
Brooklyn
5 Lexington Av
Express

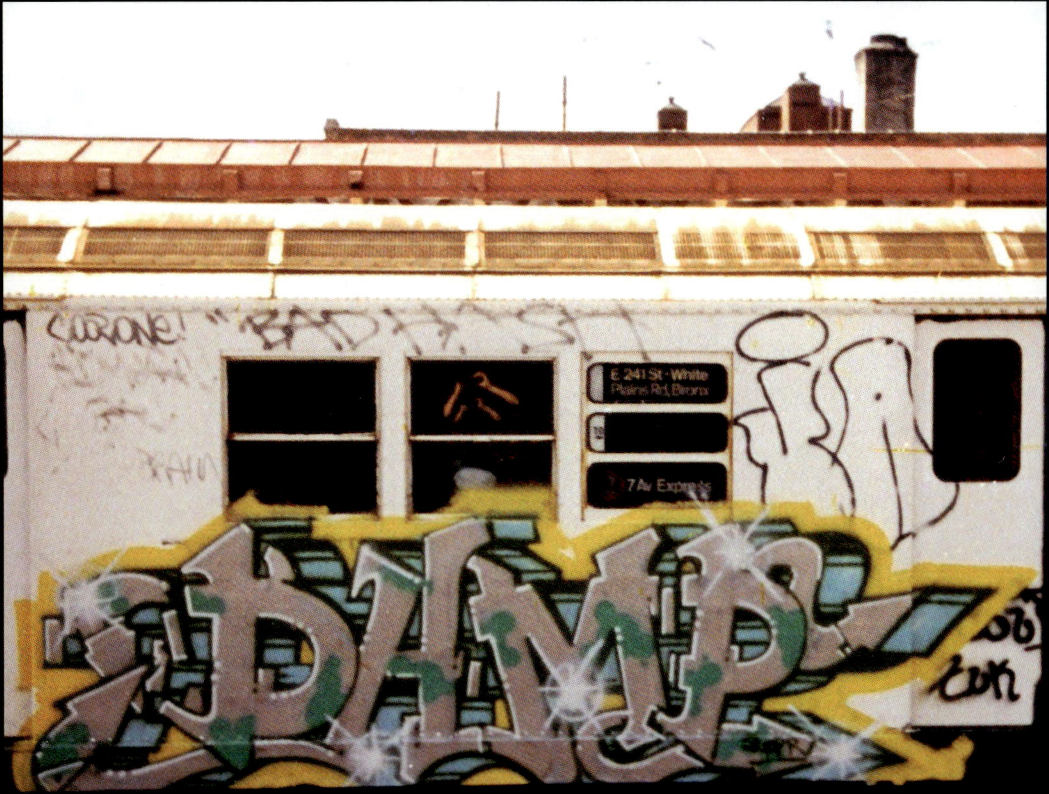

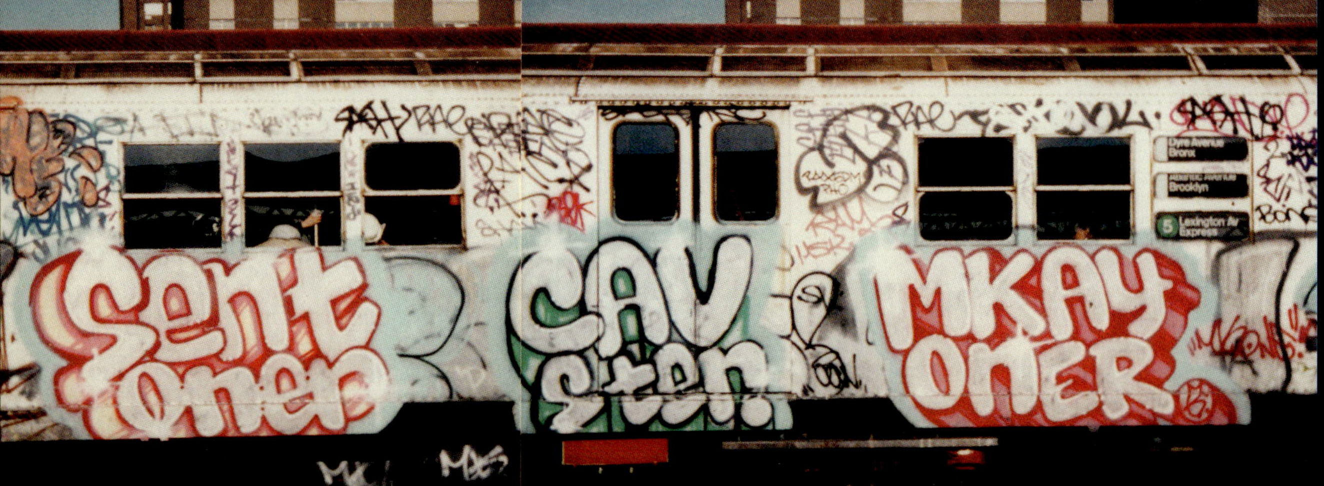

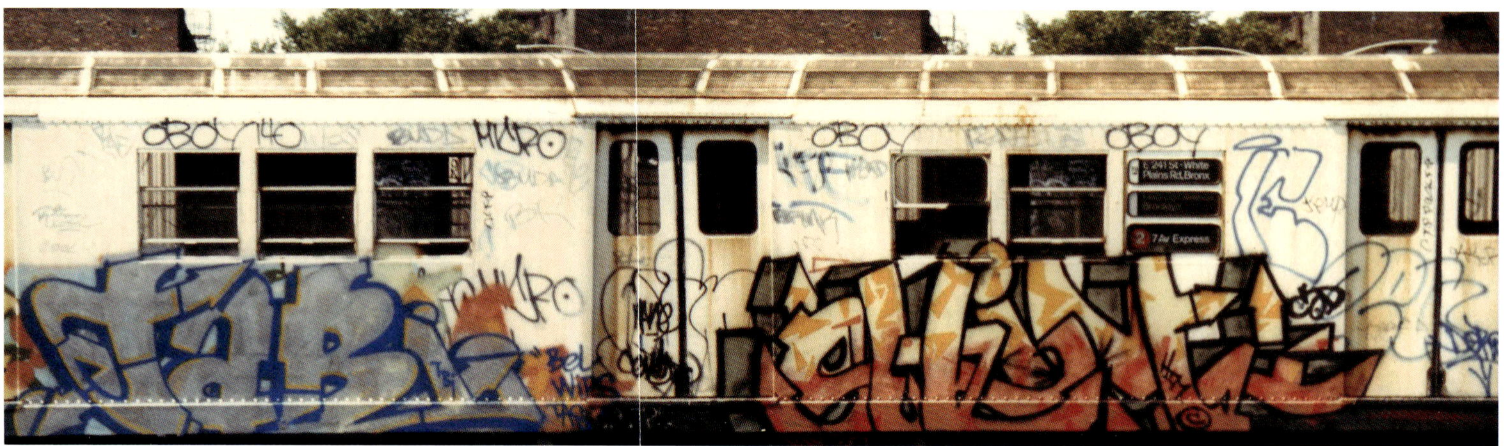

Tab, Him, 1986

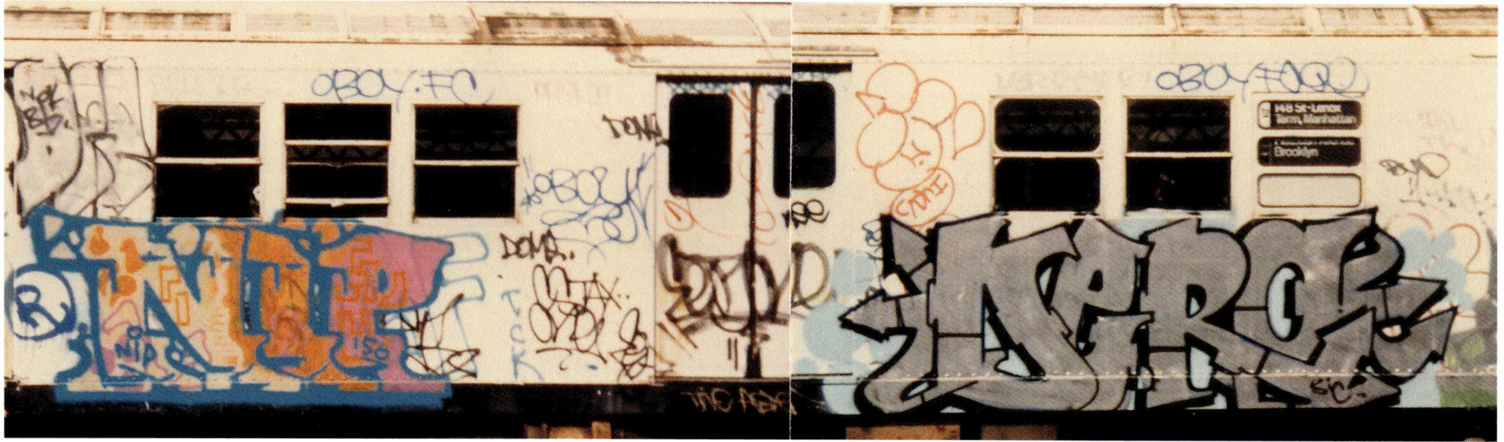

Nip, Dero, 1986

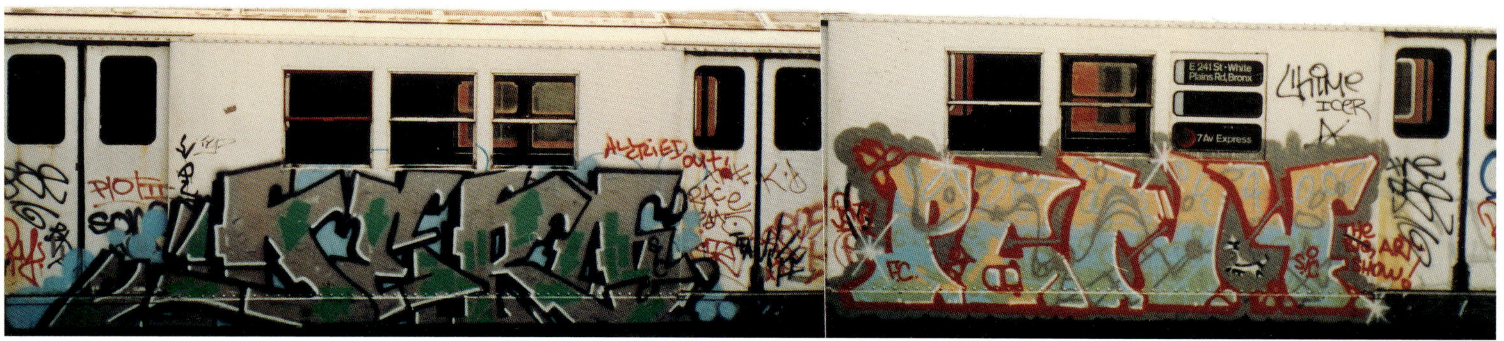

Dero, Pony, 1986

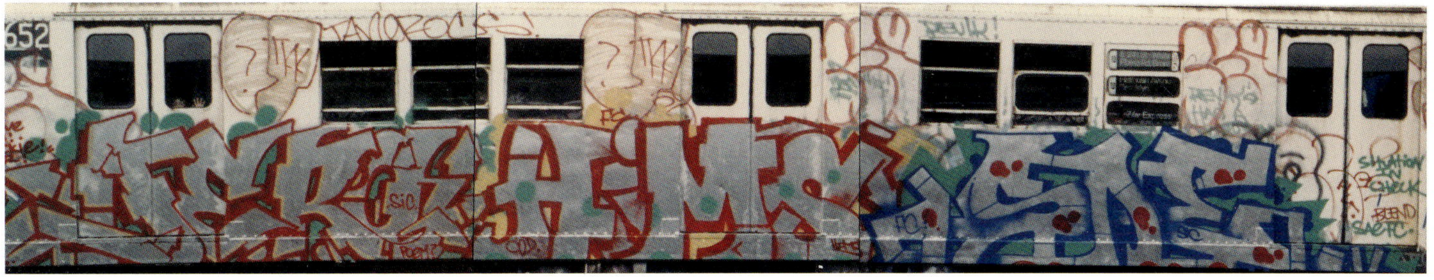

Dero, Hims, Sae, 1986

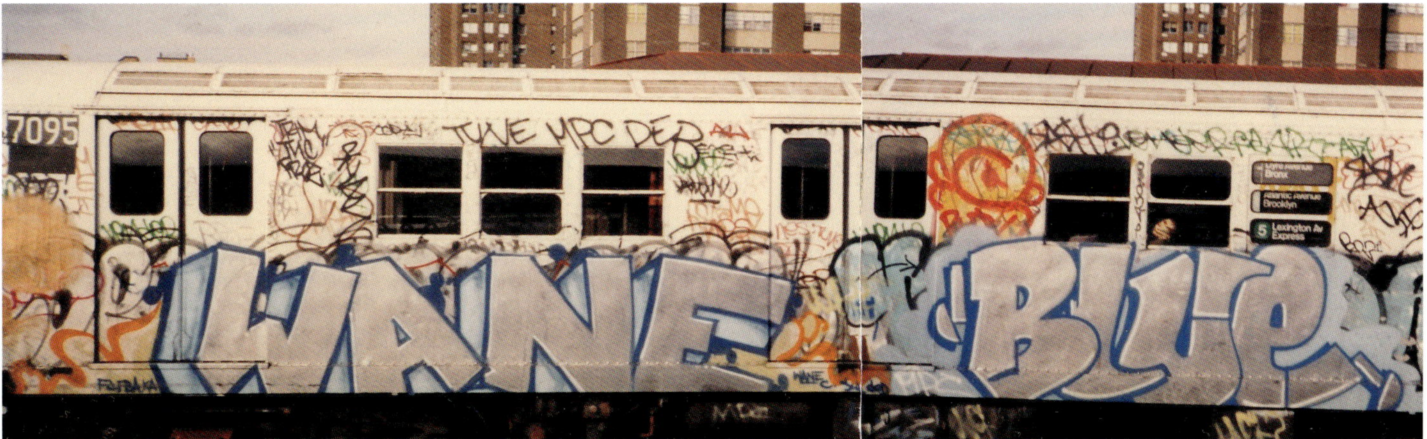

Wane, Blue

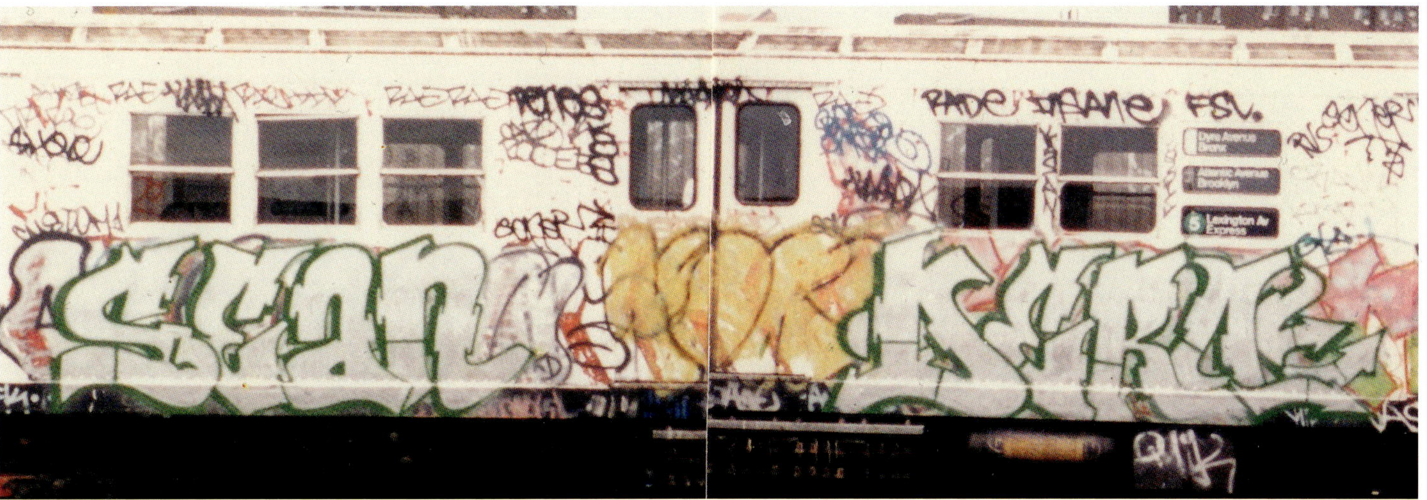

Sean, Dero

I remember the first time I ever did a train. It was 1983 or '84 and I was on the ride of my life. We were headed to 183rd Street to hit the layup on the 4s. A Dez, Dero, Dust car, I was blown away! The truth is, I had no business on that car, those guys were established icons and I was just in fantasyland. Strange as it may seem, it was the end of the line for those Kings and the trains were transitioning. The trains, as they had known them, were gone and in came the White Elephants. At this time, I was kind of feeling like it may be the end for me, too. The feeling was that graff was about to be effectively eradicated but Mr. Blue had other plans.

I was living near Allerton Avenue at the time and a whole bunch of awesome things happened for me that changed the course of my life. I met four of the most influential people of my life, beginning with a gem of an individual named Roland Allen, whom I met in '84 and was known to the graff world as Rolieo. He was a great help to me and strangely enough we met on the basketball courts on Bronx Park East, near where I lived. Overhearing him talking about Blade and the trains, I told him I knew Dez and he started introducing me to the local talent. First was Dien, who was quite established himself, then came Kemt, who was on the rise. Lastly came my good friend for over thirty years, John Edwards, known to the graff world as Poem. Rolieo was done with trains but we did quite a few walls. At this point, I wasn't quite there yet with the paint control, so he helped me a great deal with control. He put me up on the dry look fat caps, the different paint brands to use, schooled me on which colors were watery, and things that were essential to know moving forward. He was really a big help to me and very few people knew this. My first walls with established artists were with Rolieo and Kemt.

As time passed, I started to spend more time with my cousin in Harlem and that's when I met Vulcan. He was another super talented, down to earth individual who gave me the courage to forge ahead. I remember my first Dero piece, that I actually liked, was in the Hall of Fame, where I painted in the corner of a destroyed Zero piece. Of course it wasn't very good, but I was proud of it and it gave me confidence to go out and move ahead. Vulcan helped me fix up the outline. Shortly after this is when I did my next two trains. Dez took me to Zerega, on the 6 line, and I did a window-down off the station and he did a top-to-bottom. I wasn't as tall as he was and definitely did not feel the control or confidence to do a top-to-bottom, so that answers that question! Next up, another window-down on the 6 line with my homie from school, Wuzer. I really didn't like that piece at all but I guess for a five-can piece it wasn't too terrible. At this point, I was determined to make changes and get things right. I believe the time was '85 and I was doing pieces in Harlem with my man Brian, who was down with Kings Arrive, an established crew from the 4 line. He was cool with Delta2, Dar, and Part and lived near the Hall of Fame, so we would hang and do pieces here and there. He also hooked me up with a few commission jobs for a local bar and a grocery store.

Shortly thereafter, I started to hang out on Mapes Avenue in the Bronx and here's where it all went crazy! I started doing airbrush tee shirts on Tremont Avenue, right across the street from Mapes, and met a girl. This was the defining moment of my entire existence as far as I'm concerned. I was crazy about this young lady and had she not totally screwed my head up, I probably would have never been heard of. I returned home to Allerton, reconnected with Poem, who I had met in Columbus High School and it was off to the races. I was so broken up about this young lady I went haywire on the trains. Poem was my fuel and helped me a great deal as I defined my style. Funny thing is, he hooked up with a woman soon after that and disappeared from the trains. In comes a little local kid named Wane, who I also met through Rolieo and then I went into full assault on the 2s and 5s. Wane actually put me on to the 238th Street layups, as they were nice and quiet. At that point, we then pretty much set up shop all over the White Plains layups from Bronx Park East to 238th Street. That was the time of my life! All I did, day in and day out, was paint. If I wasn't in the layups on White Plains Road, I was sharpening my skills under the bridge at 238th Street. Now I had it all on lock! I reconnected with Vulcan, who introduced me to the Godfather of style, Phase2. Seen Tc5 came home from college, and I was on top of the world. I cannot exactly say how many trains I did because I don't have pics of them all. However, I don't think anyone would argue that from '85 to '87 there was not a 2 or 5 train that didn't have one or even two Dero pieces on them. Getting back to the four most influential people as far as my graff existence is concerned, had I not met them when I did, I probably would never have been heard of . . . they are Rolieo, Dez, Vulcan, and Poem. To add one more, as far as schooling with styles and history, that would be Phase2. Thanks Cavs and my man, Key, as well, for letting me make 238th Street my home for all those years . . . . Peace.

—Dero

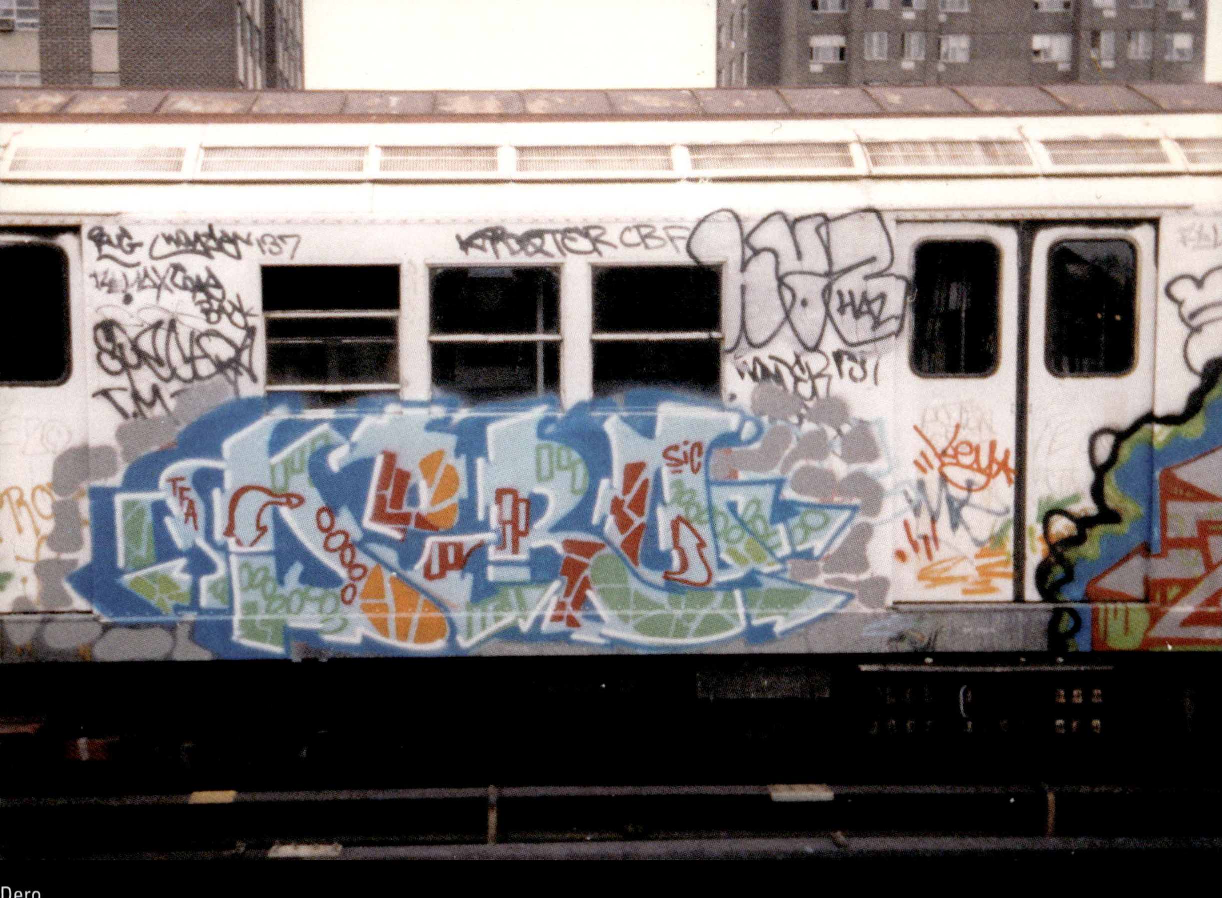

Dero

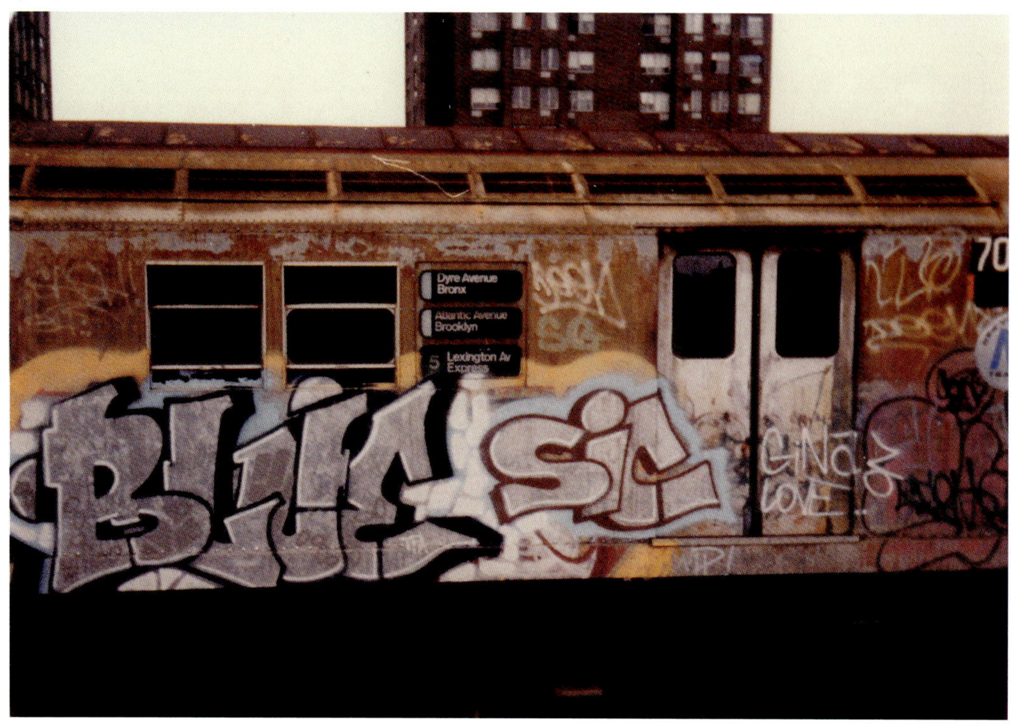

Blue SIC

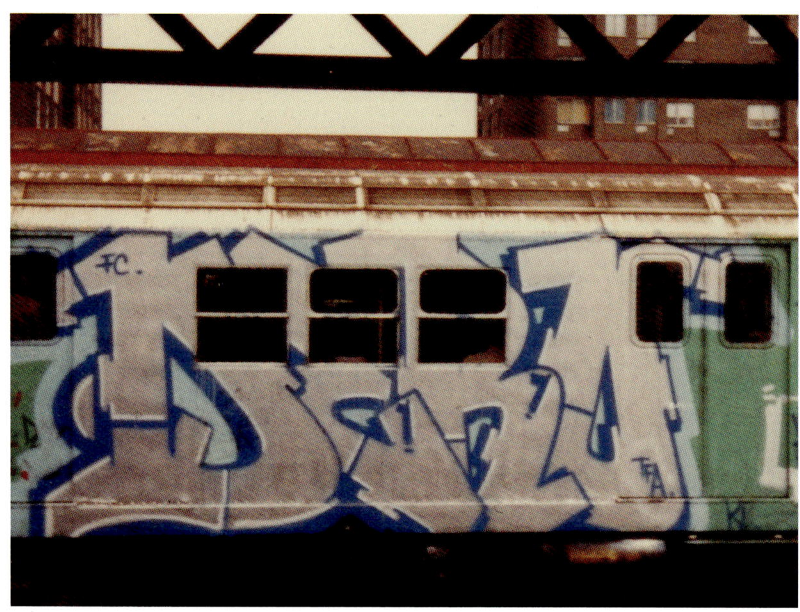

Dero

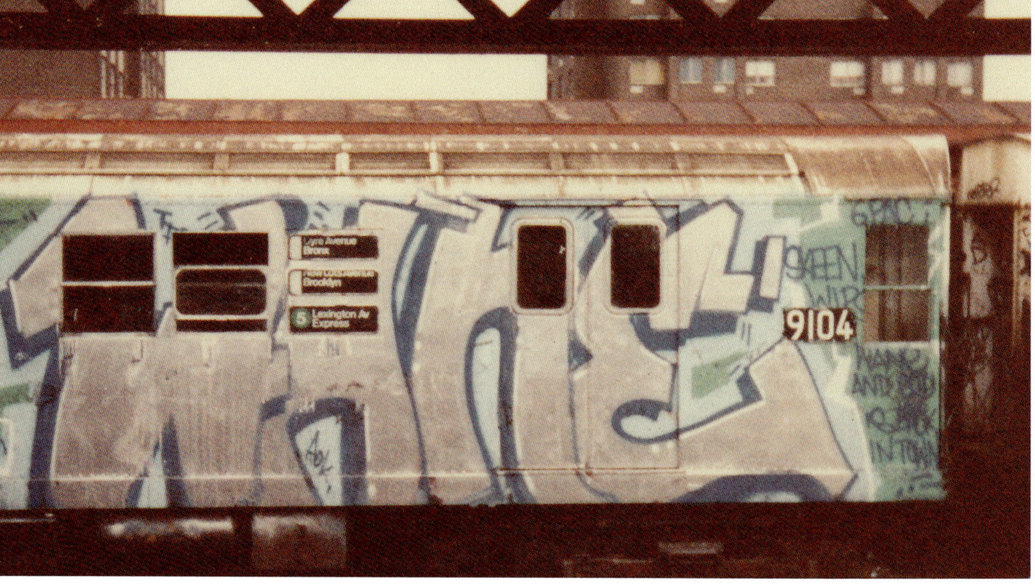

Wane

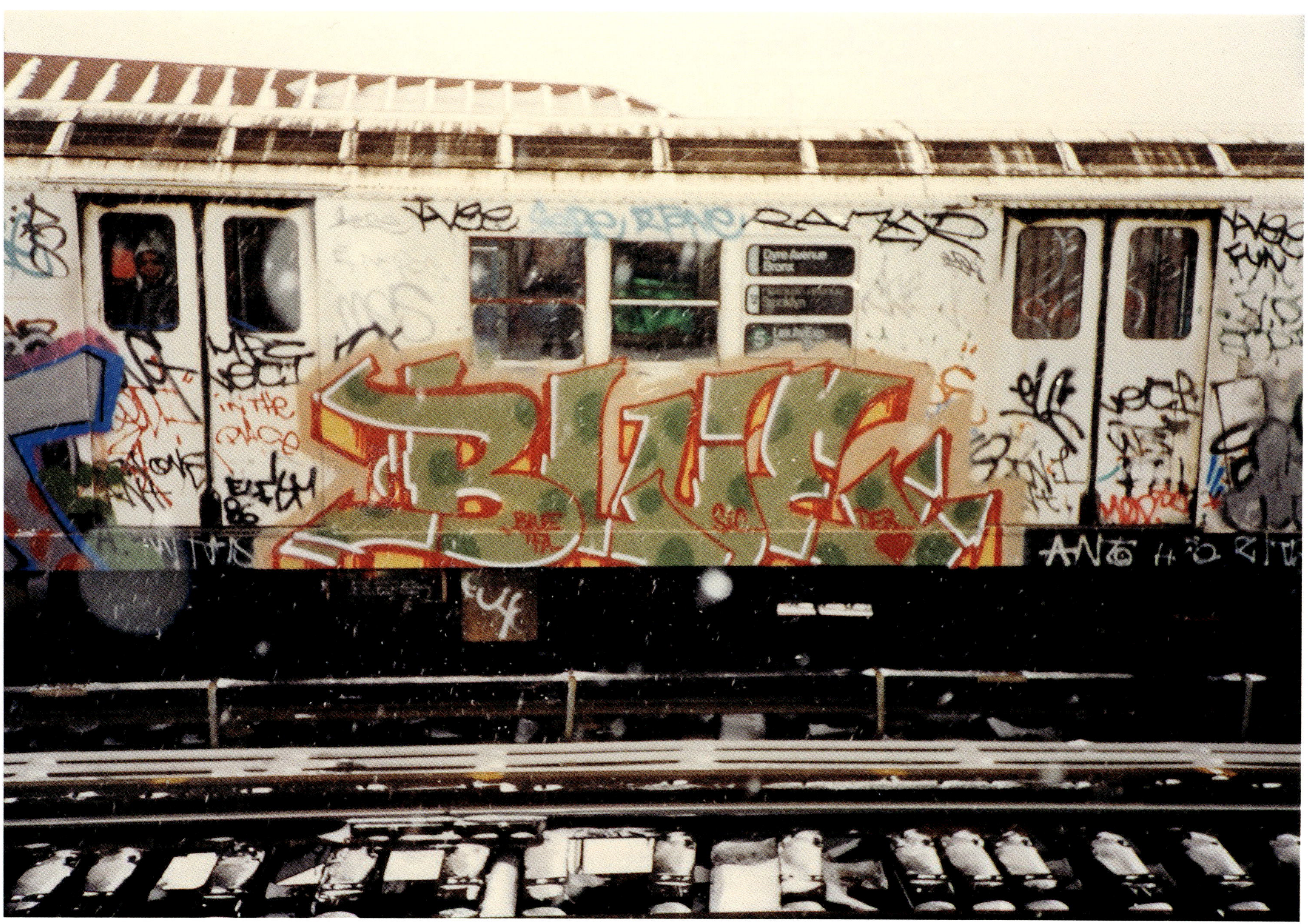

Blue, 1987

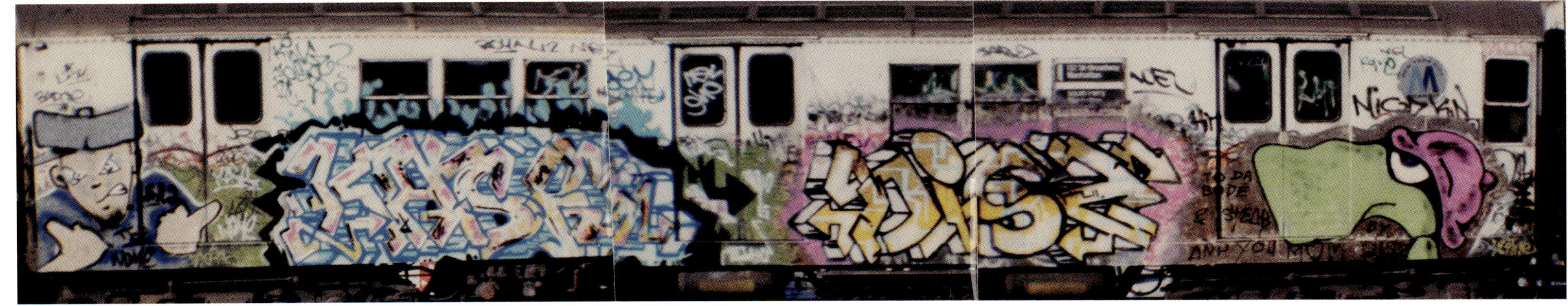

Kase2, Disz, 1986

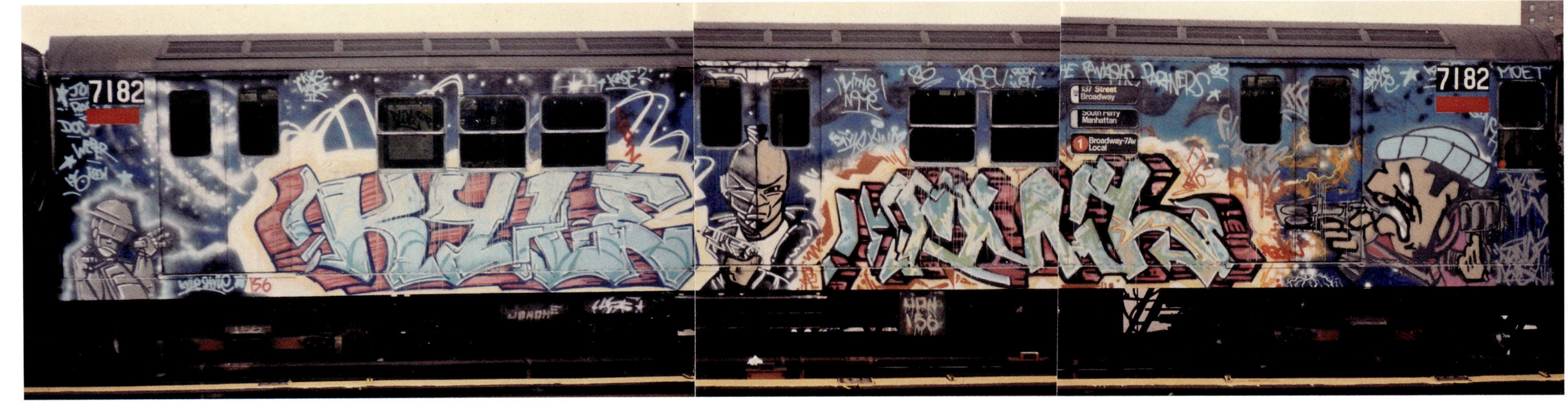

Kyle, Much (Case2), 1986

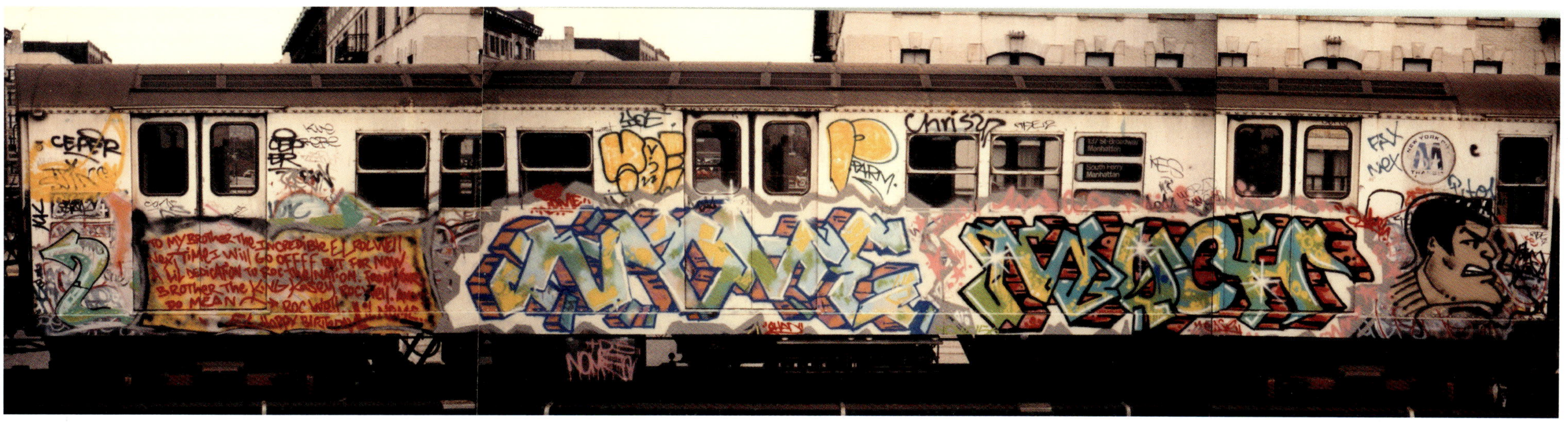

Nome, Much

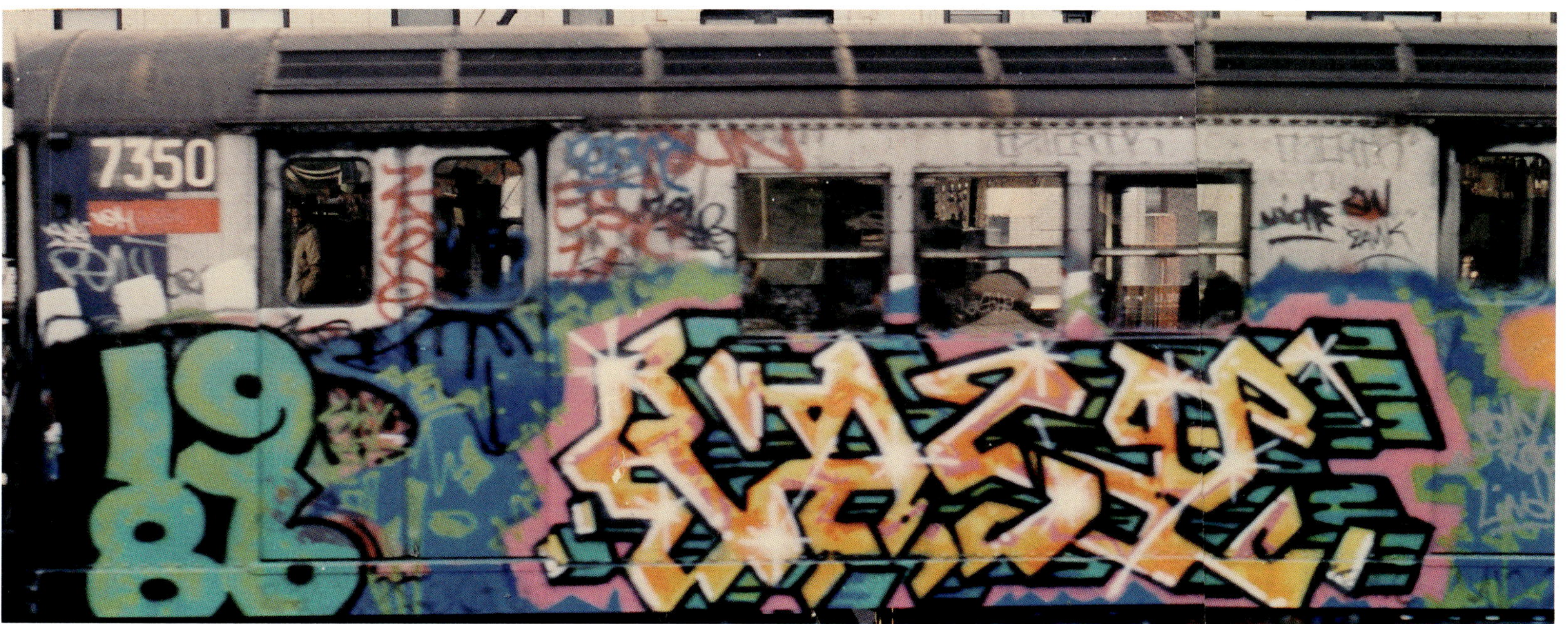

Case2 TFP, 1986

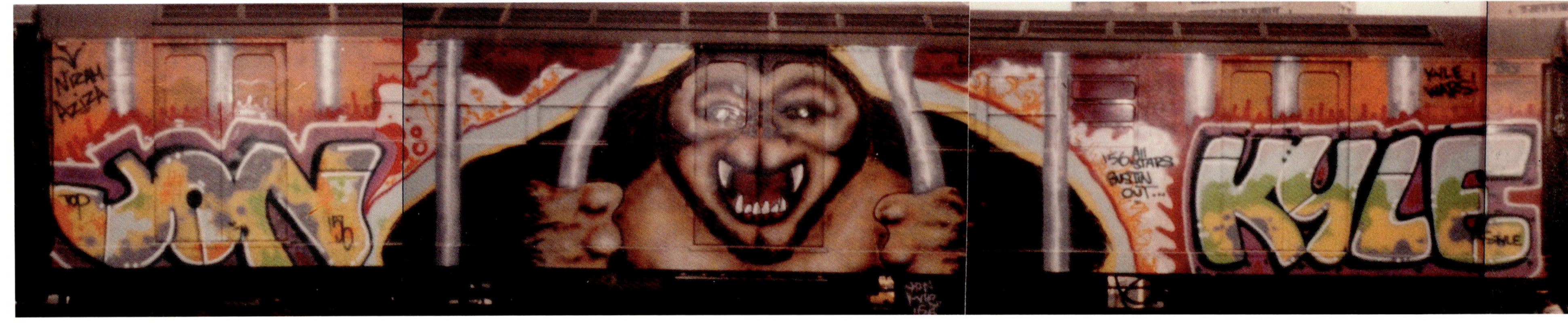

Jon, Kyle

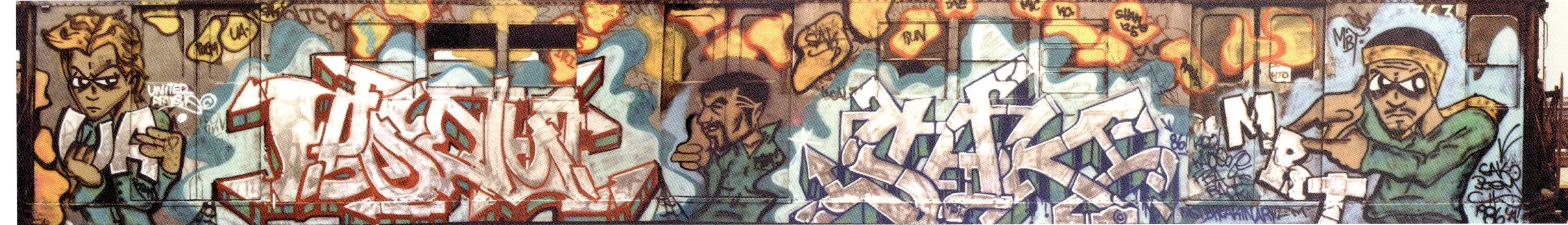

Poem, Sak, 1986

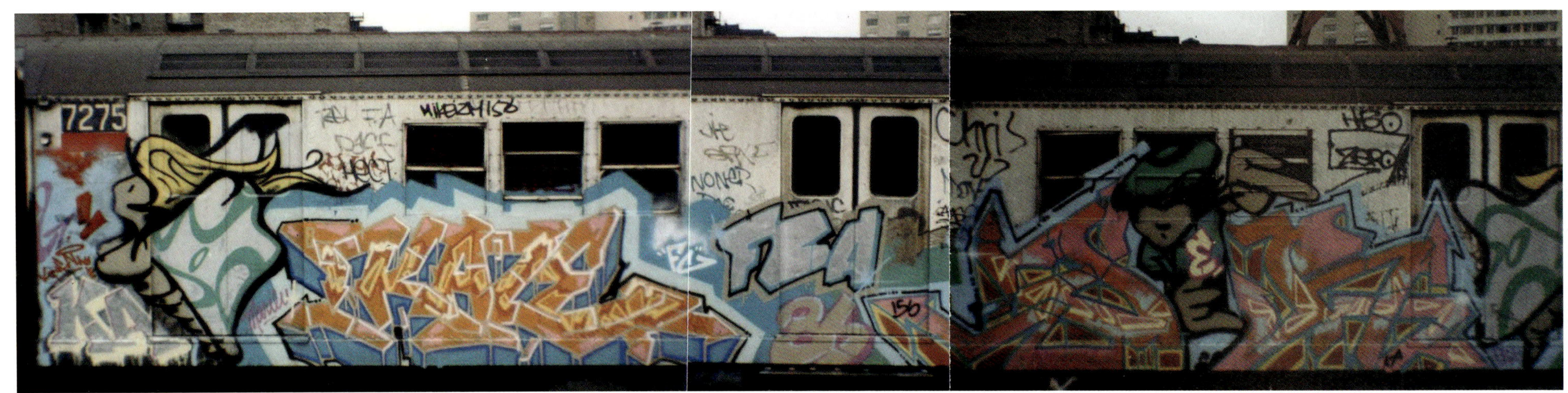

Kaze, Serve, 1986

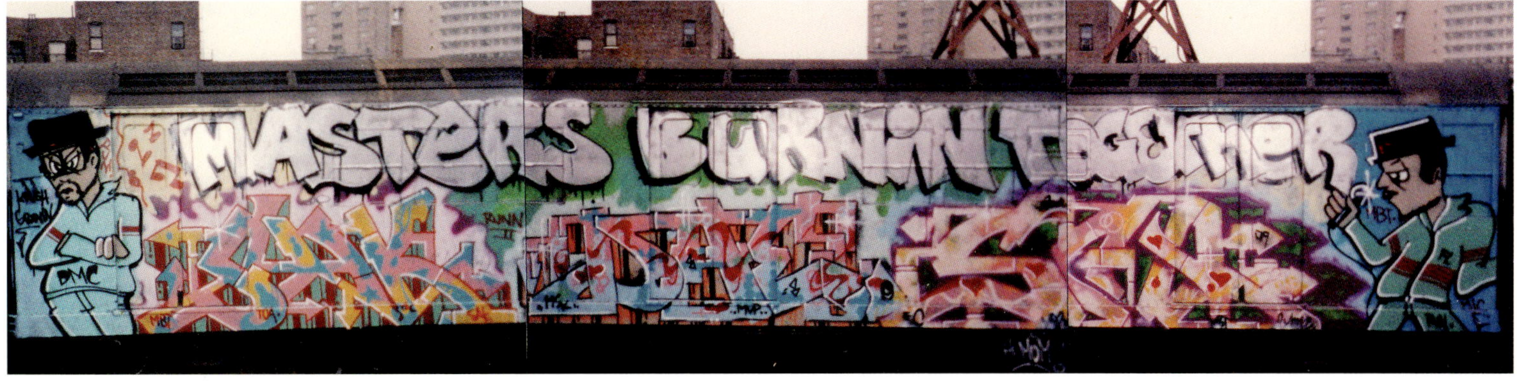

Sak, Dae, Sae, 1986

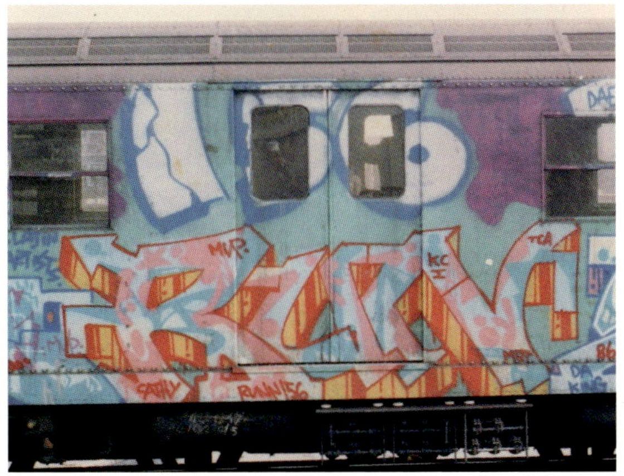

Run, 1986 (Photo courtesy of Sak MBT)

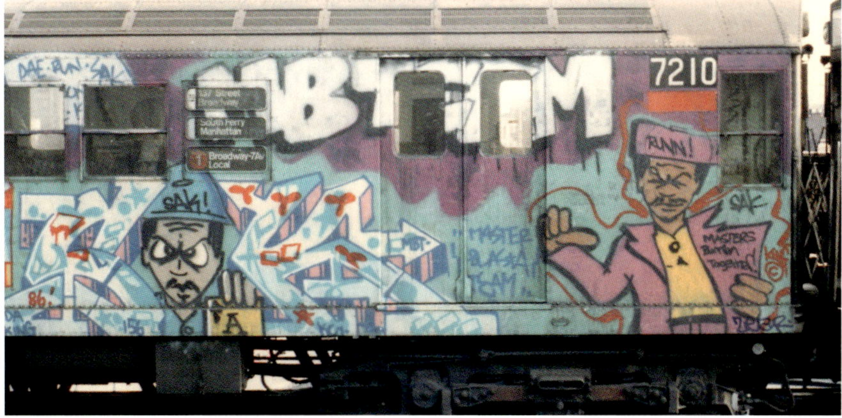

Sak, 1986 (Photo courtesy of Sak MBT)

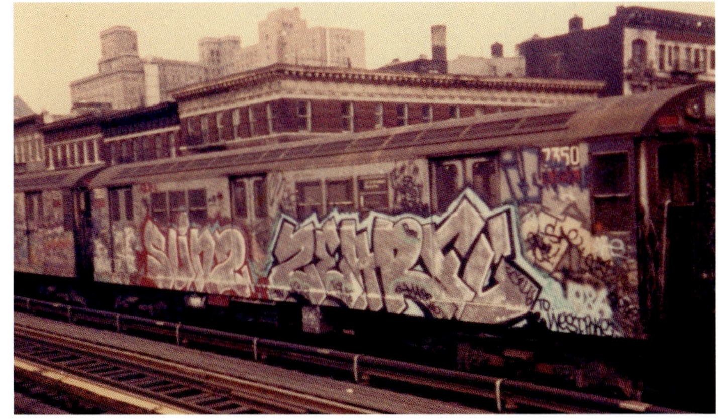

Slin2, Zear FC, 1986

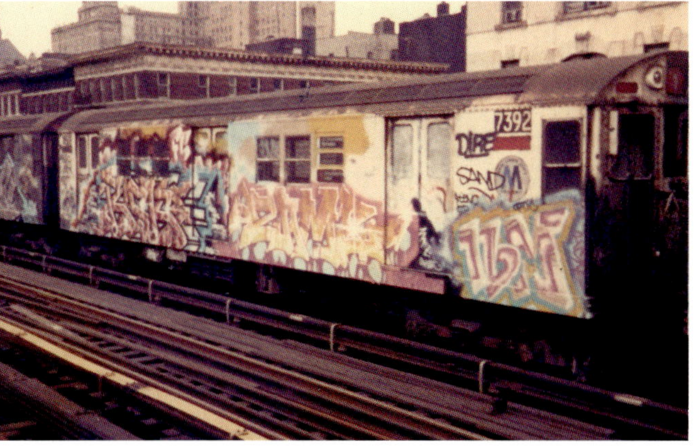

Risk, Zame, 1986

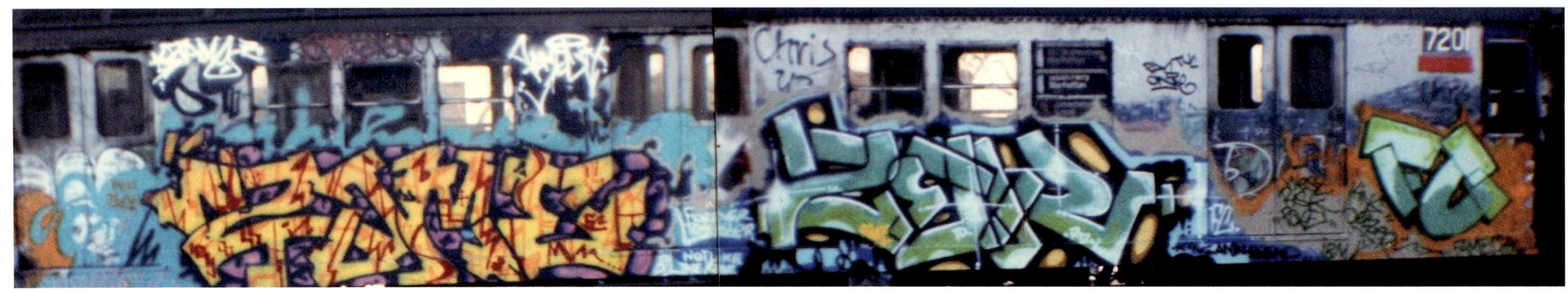

Zame, Zear

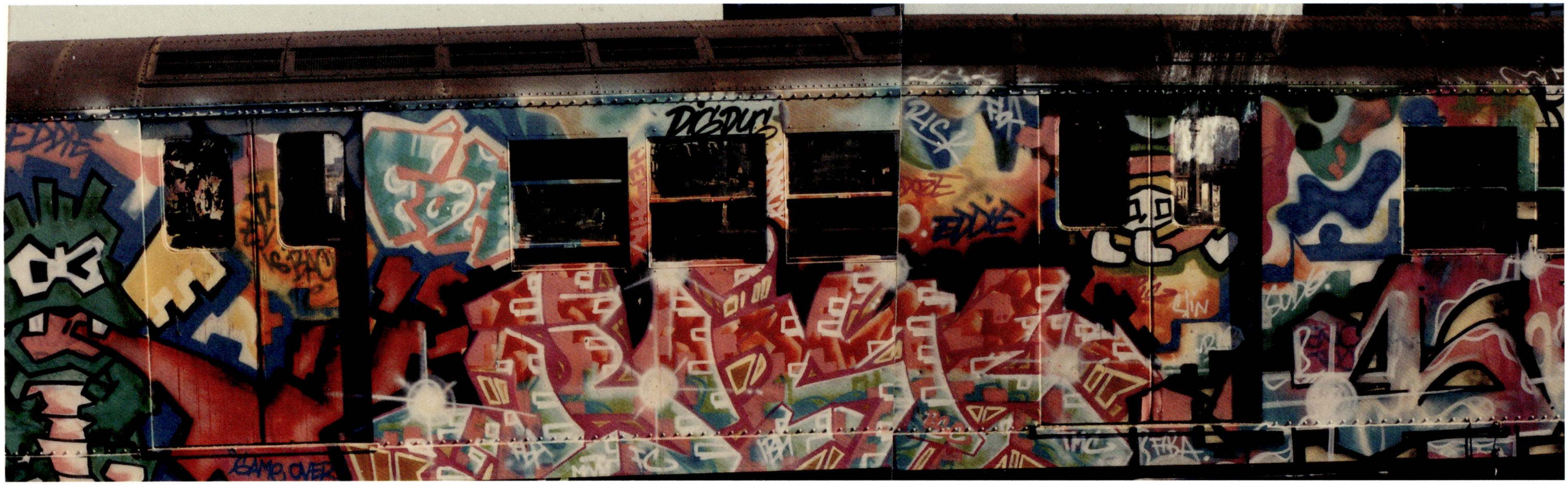

Risk

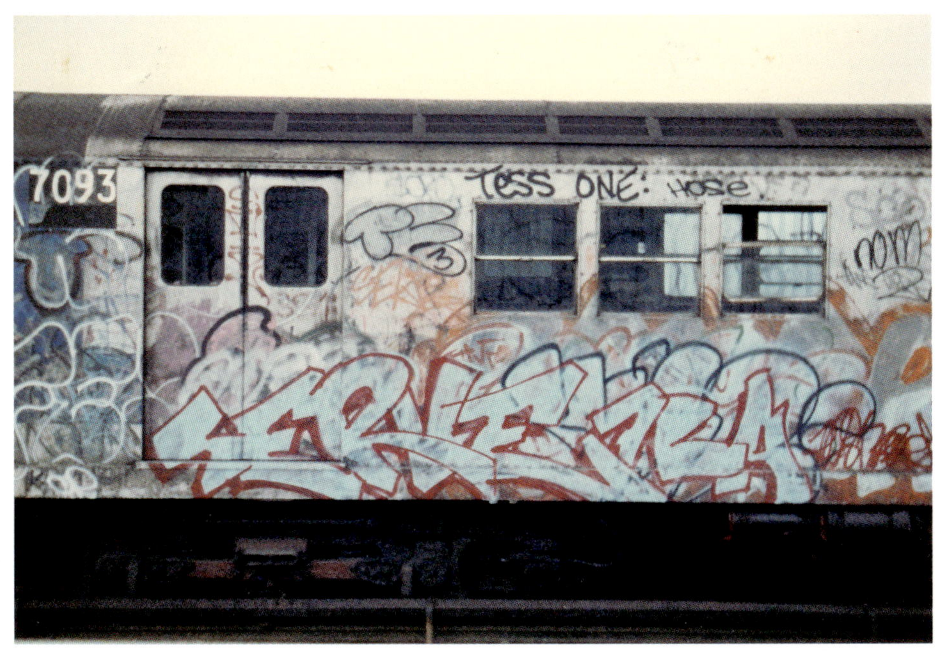

Serve FBA

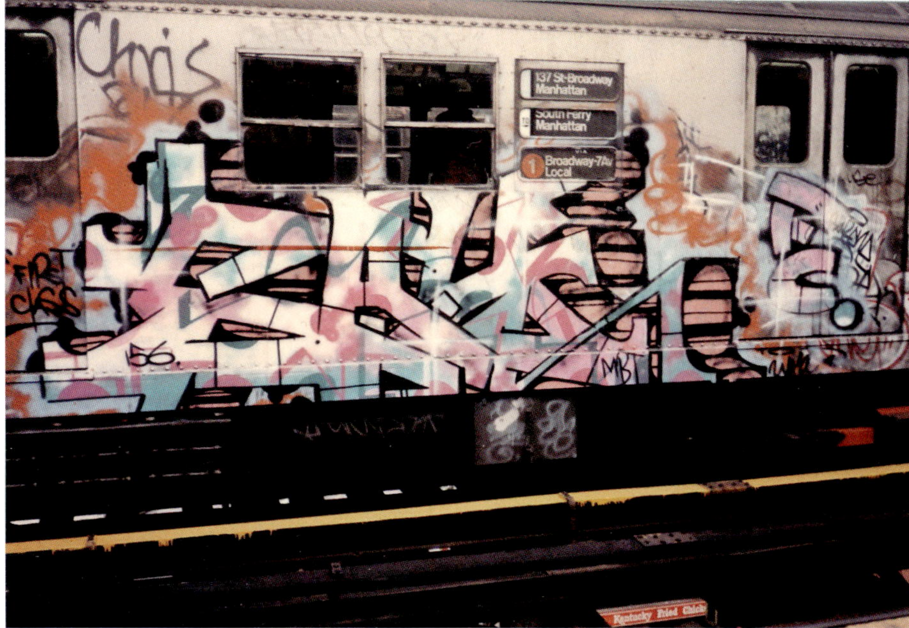

Say

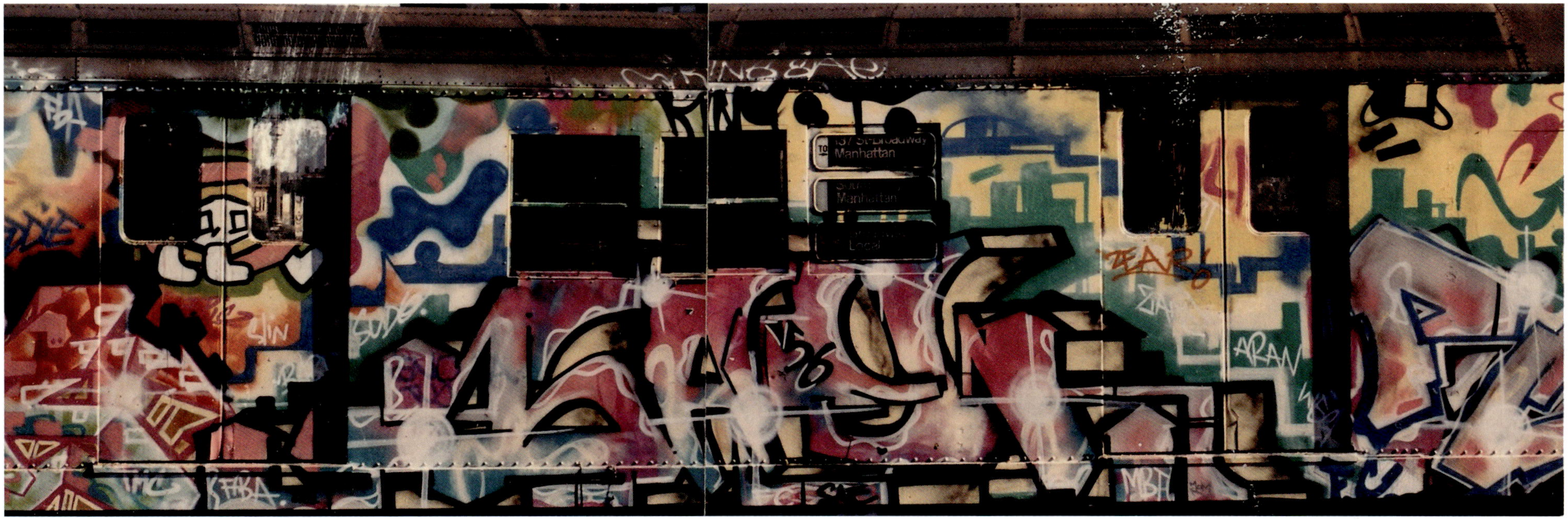

Say

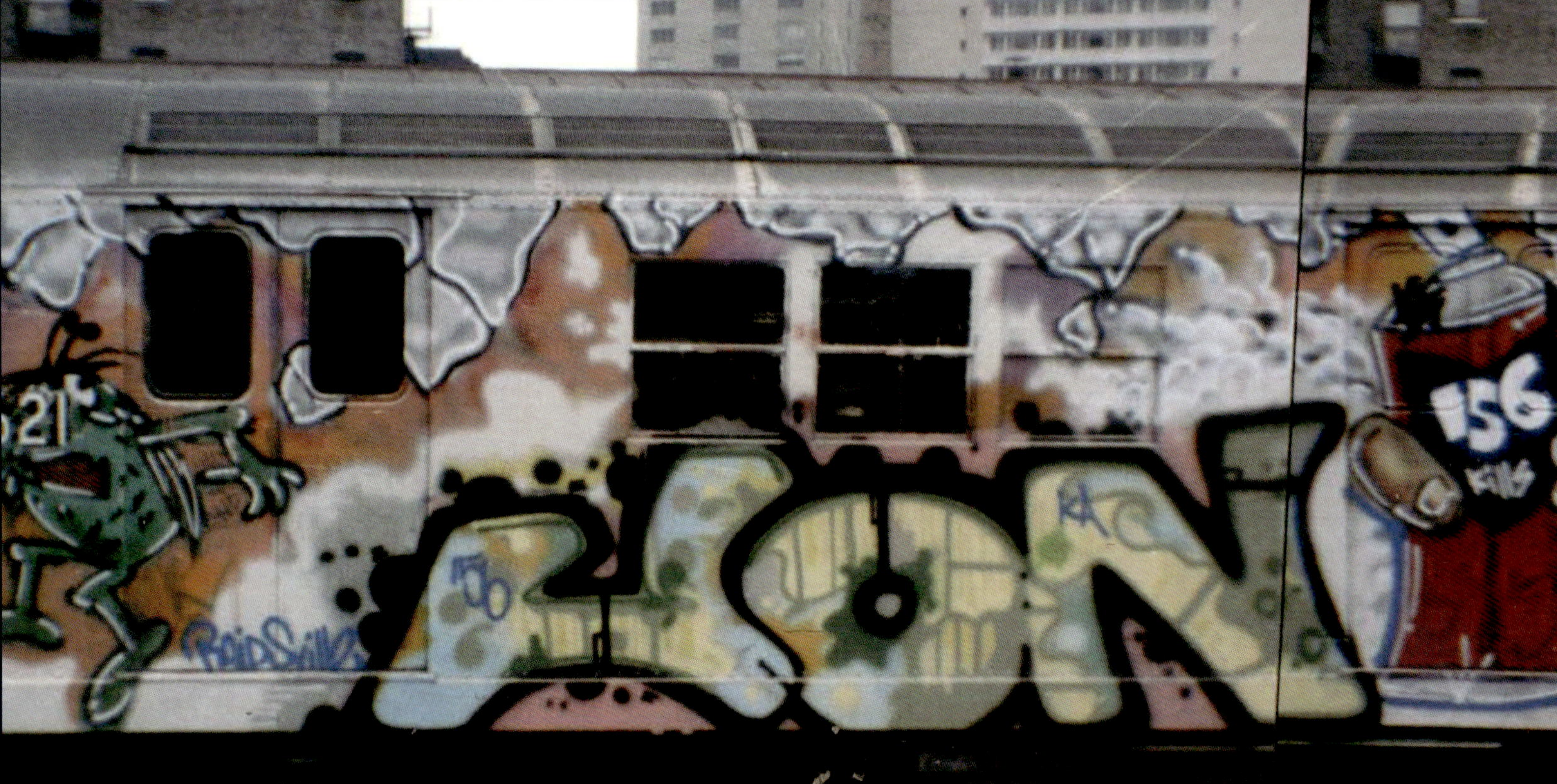

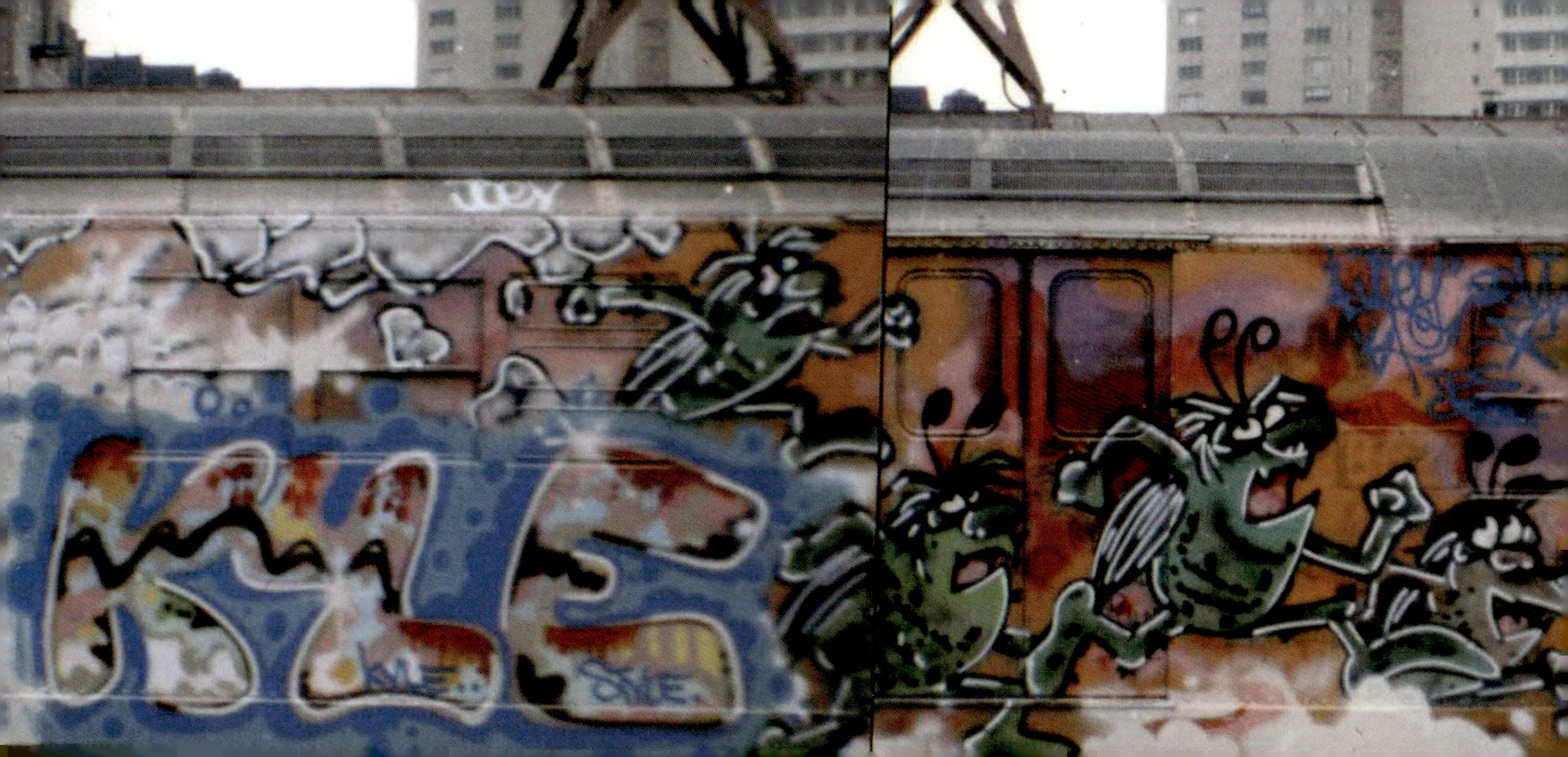

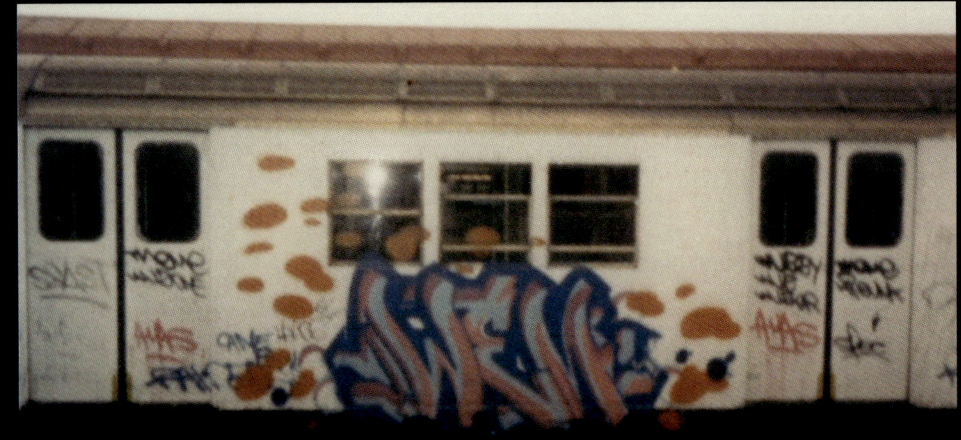

Wen, 1984

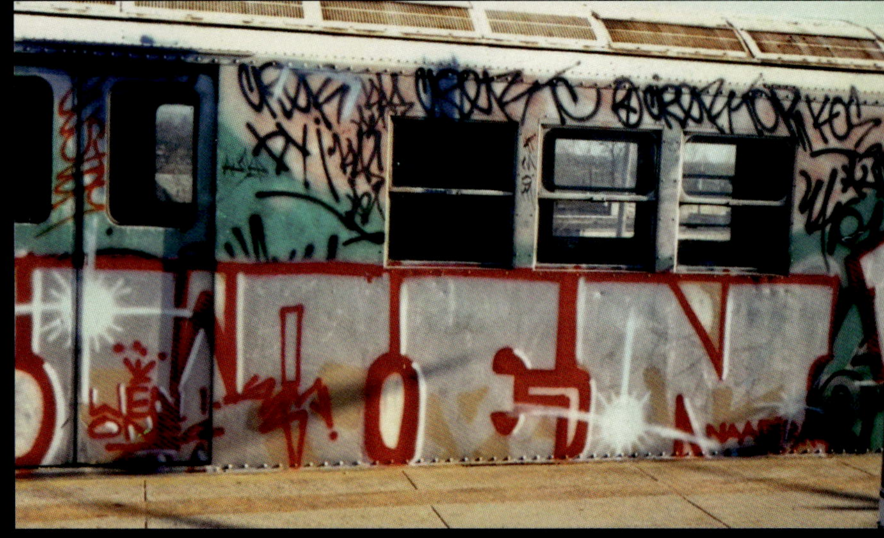

Wen, 1986 (Photo courtesy of Kirs MPC)

The days of painting trains to me were similar to any culture or movement that had harsh and humbling moments. Friendships where formed that have lasted more than thirty years—from the Bronx to around the world. I am always grateful for that and enjoy my life as a writer. Of course I had no clue that this would be what it is today. It's amazing. Live hard and bomb harder. Peace.

–Wen

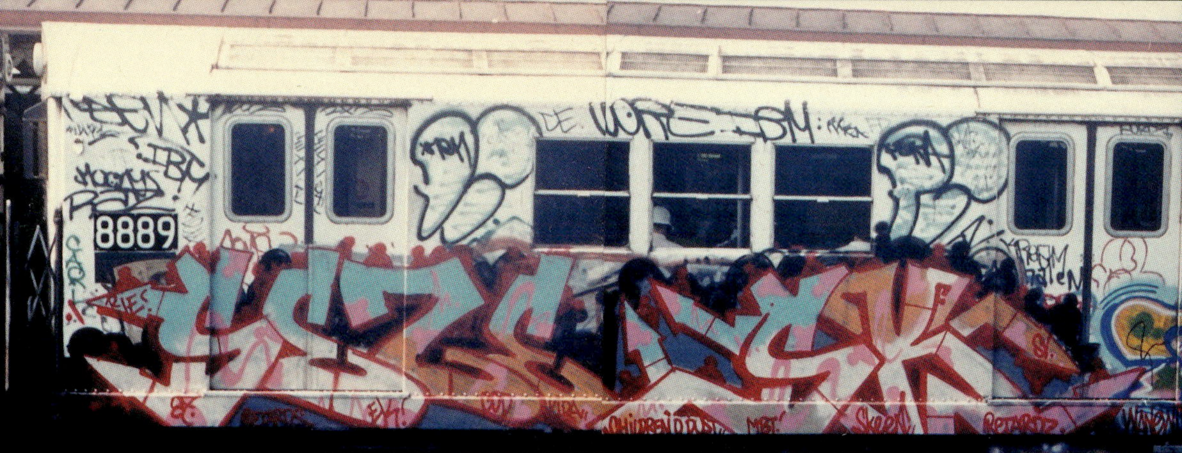

Seze, Skeen COD

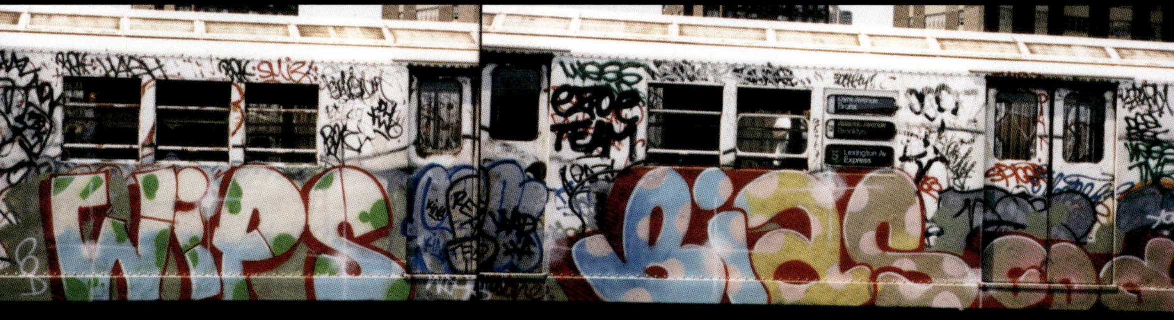

Wips, Bias COD

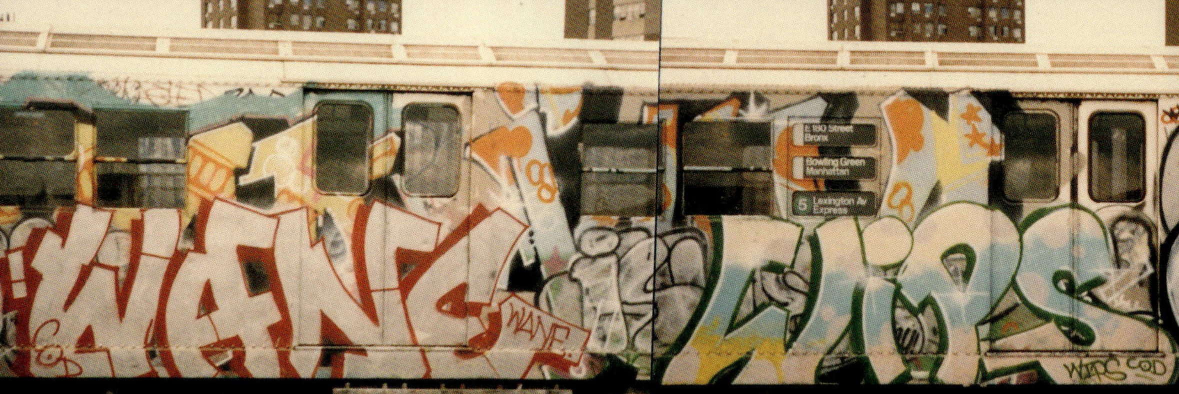

E 180 Street
Bronx
Bowling Green
Manhattan
5 Lexington Av
Express

Sho, Zoo

8909

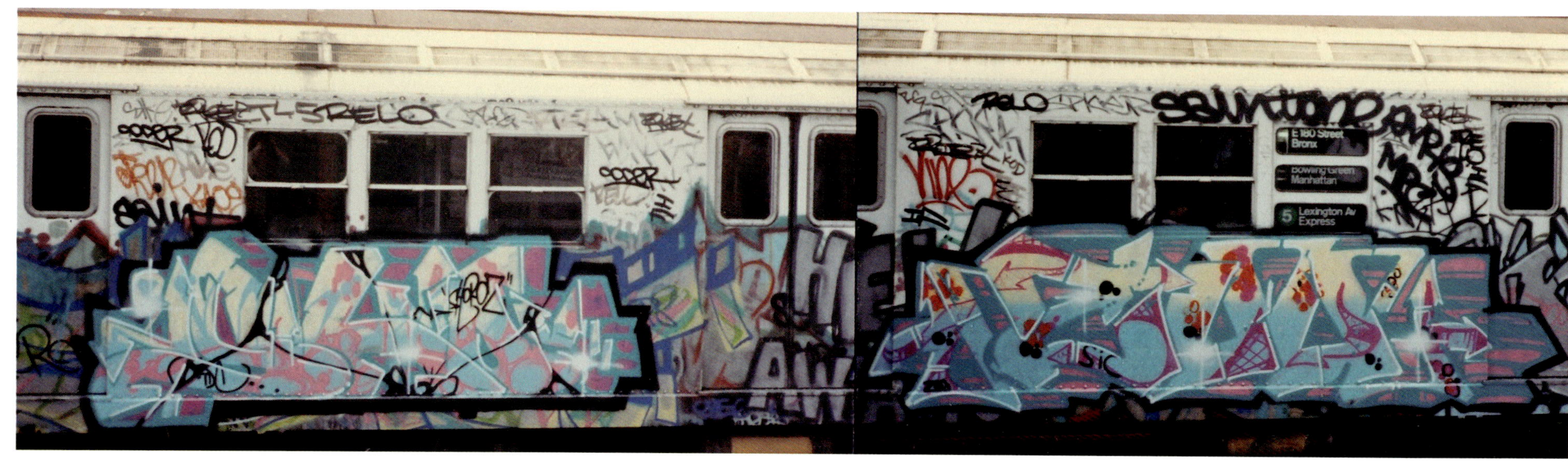

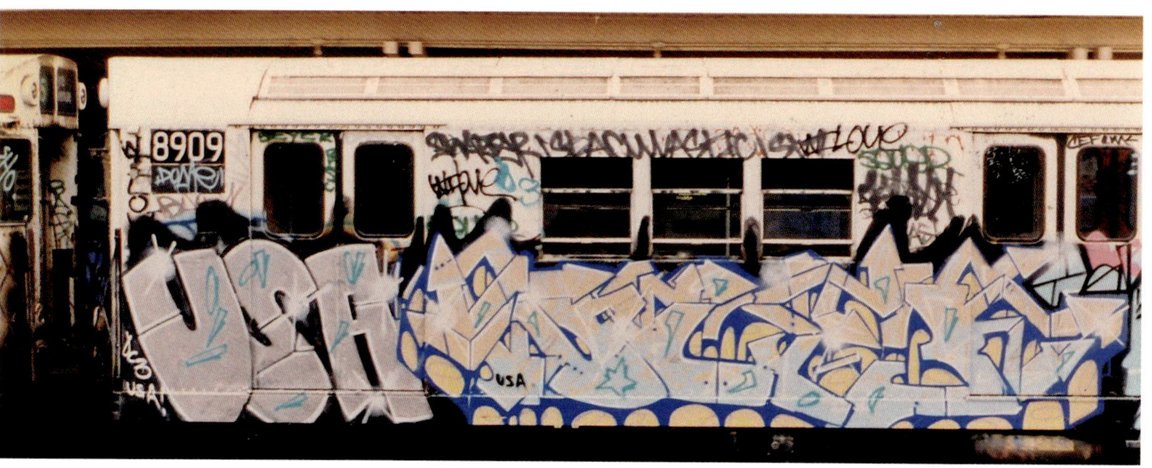

Dc3

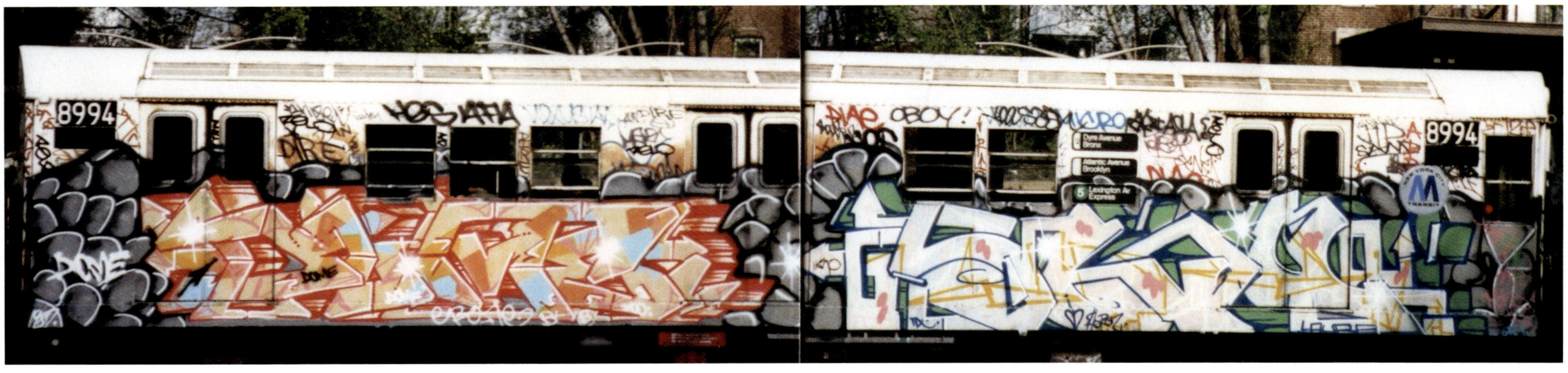

Dome, Sho, 1987

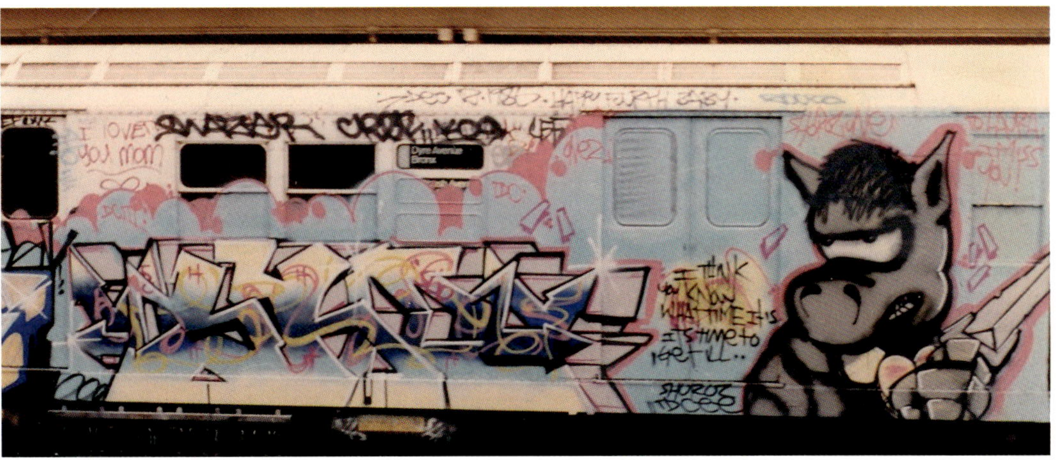

Sho

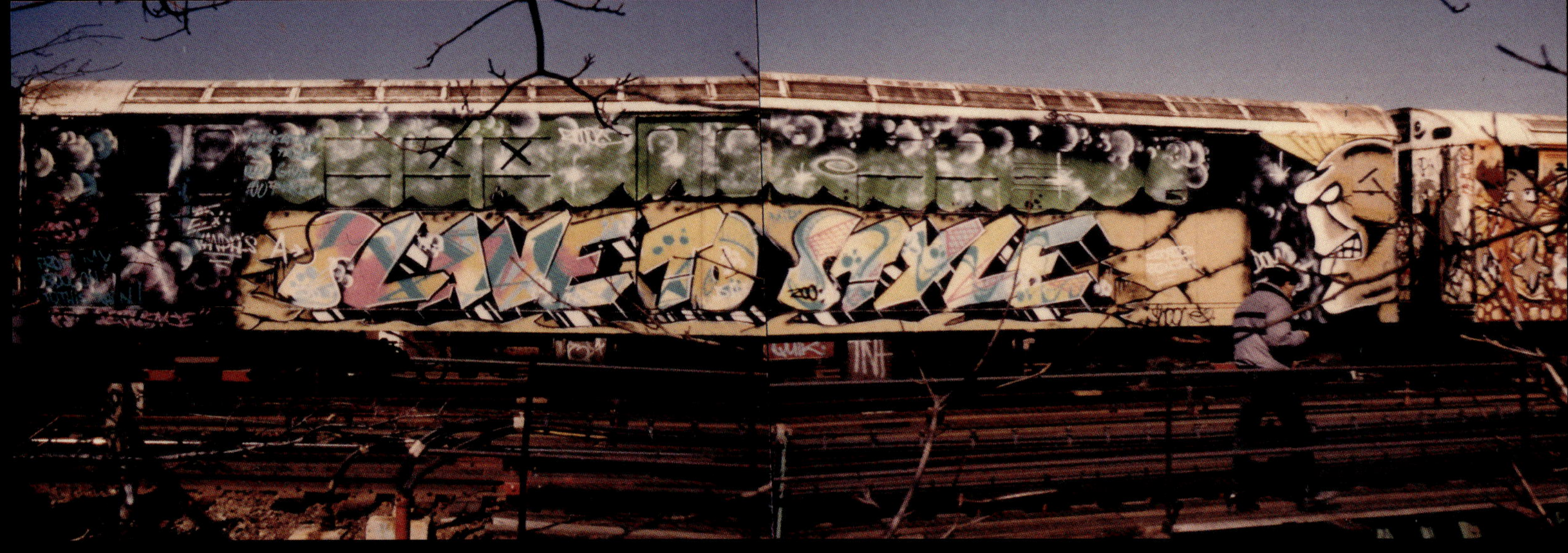

Slave to Style by Dome, 1987 (Photo courtesy of SENTO)

I consider this train to be my magnum opus. At the time I was at the height of my career and I wanted to paint a train with a statement. The story behind this train started in a black book of mine that Vulcan did a master piece in. It was a two-pager Vulcan burner with thick gloss and glitter and on the bottom of the page he drew an alien character throwing a crown into space, with a caption that read, "I don't need a crown." Next to that was a tag that said, "Slave To Style." That one statement caught my attention. So, I decided to paint a whole train with "Slave to Style." I did it in the Bronx at a place called the Esplanade tunnels. I painted for eight hours—it was daylight by the time I finished and there were a few writers sitting on top of trains watching me paint. At that point I knew I had done something great that would go down in history. In the forty years of subway writing, only a hand full of writers did cars like this, and I'm proud to be in that elite group of writers.

–Dome

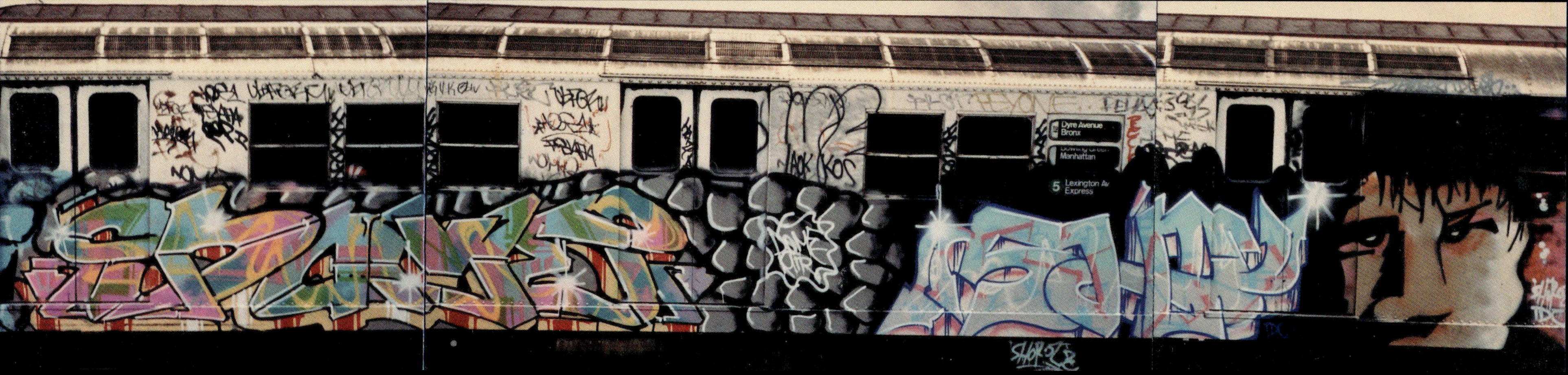
Dyre Avenue
Bronx
Manhattan
5 Lexington Av
Express

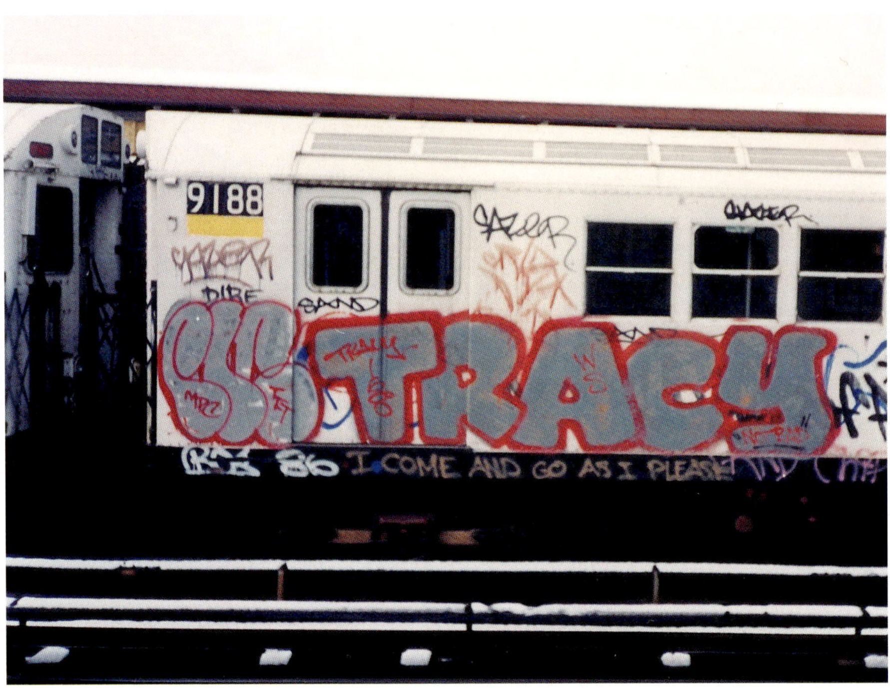

Tracy168

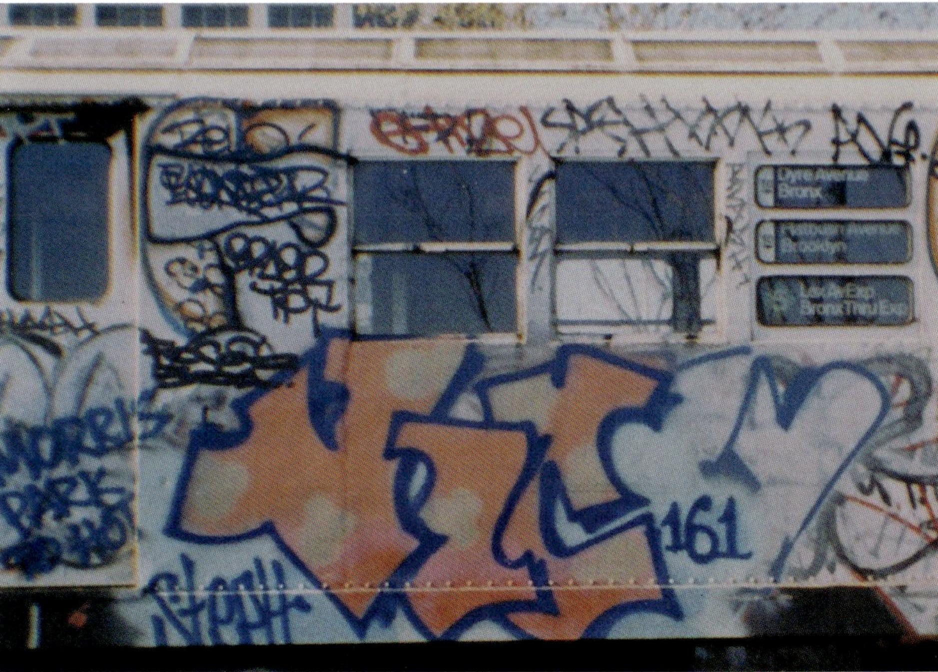

Vic161

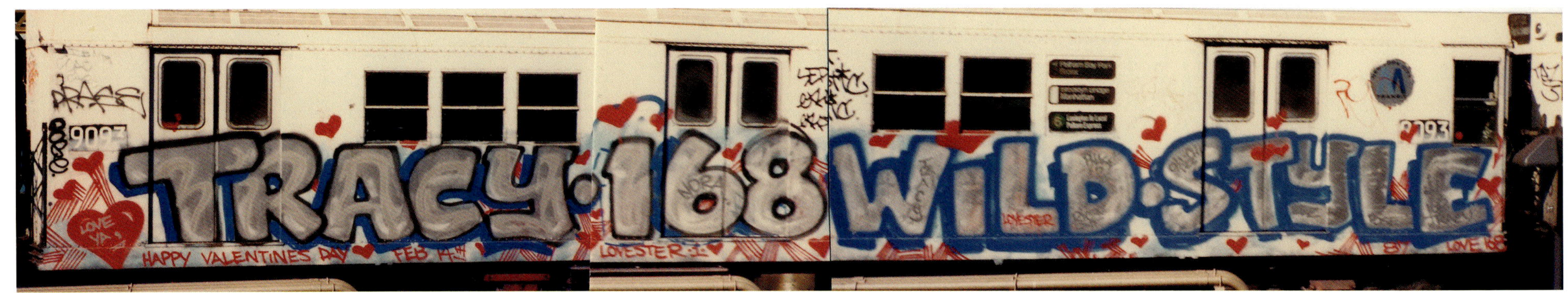

Tracy168 Wild Style, 1987

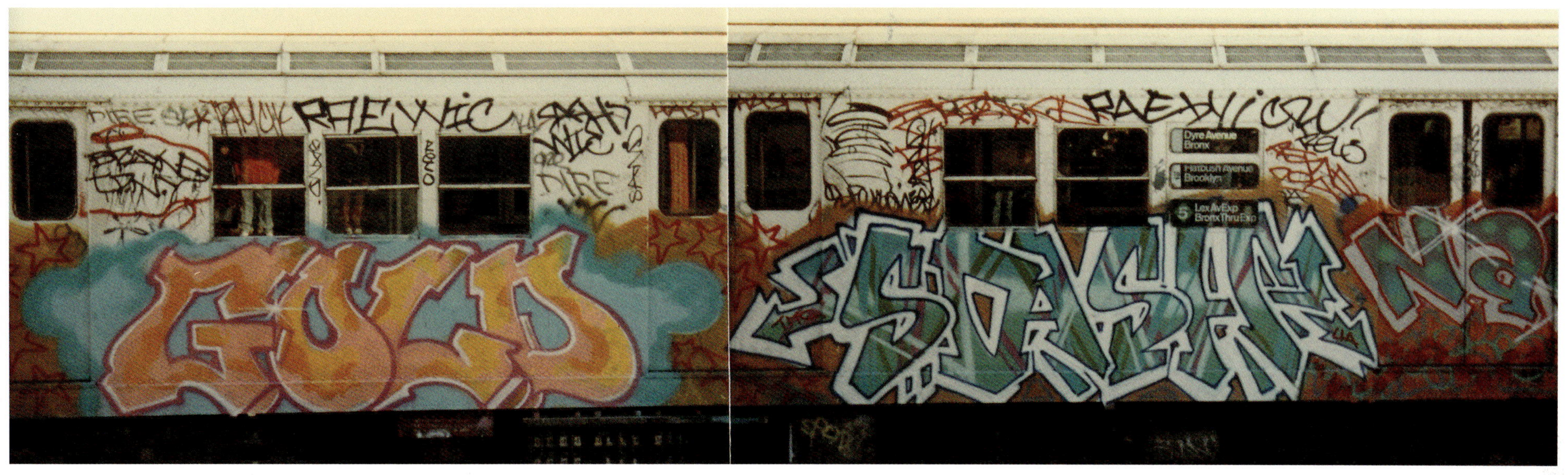

Gold, Stash2

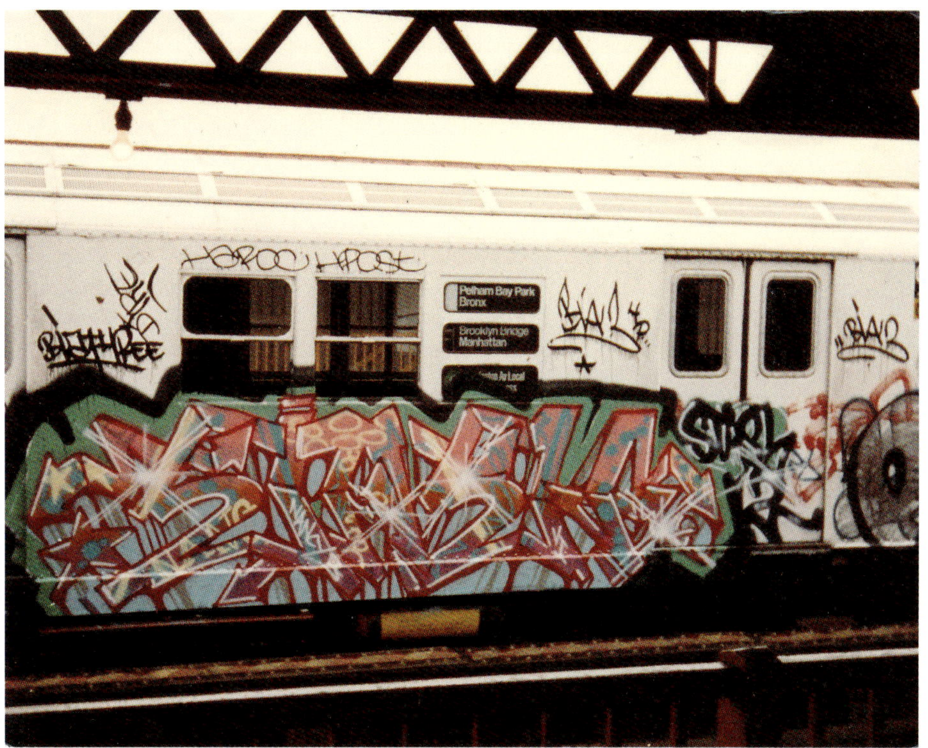

Stash2

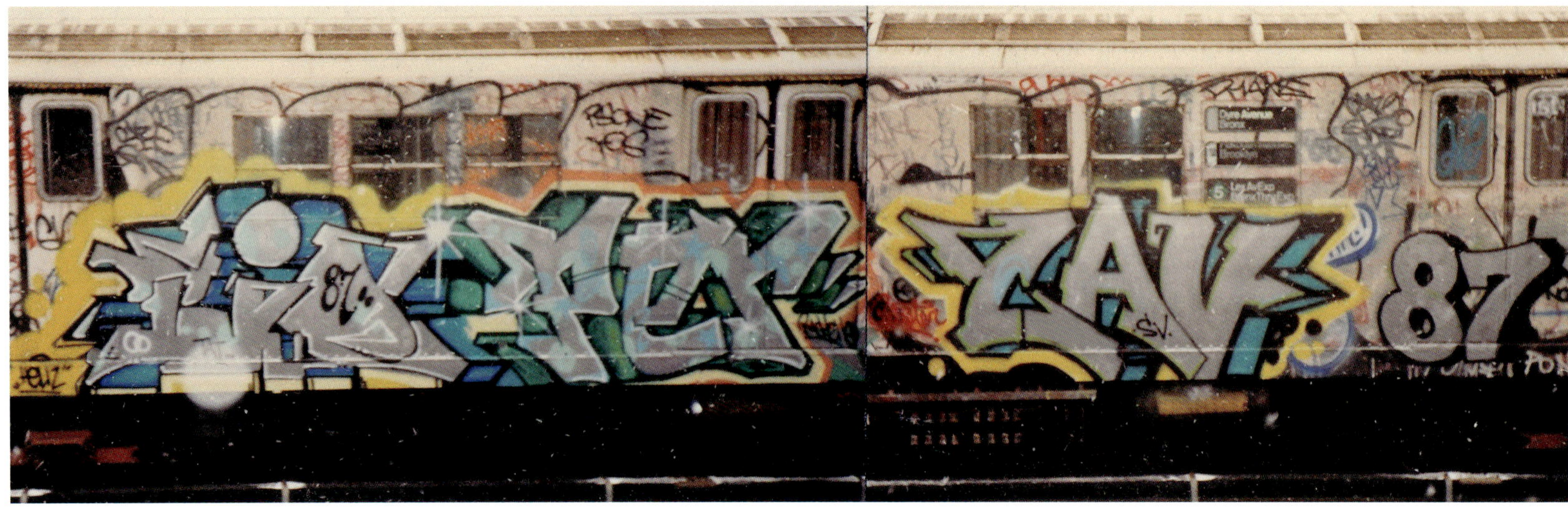

Bio, Per, Cav, 1987

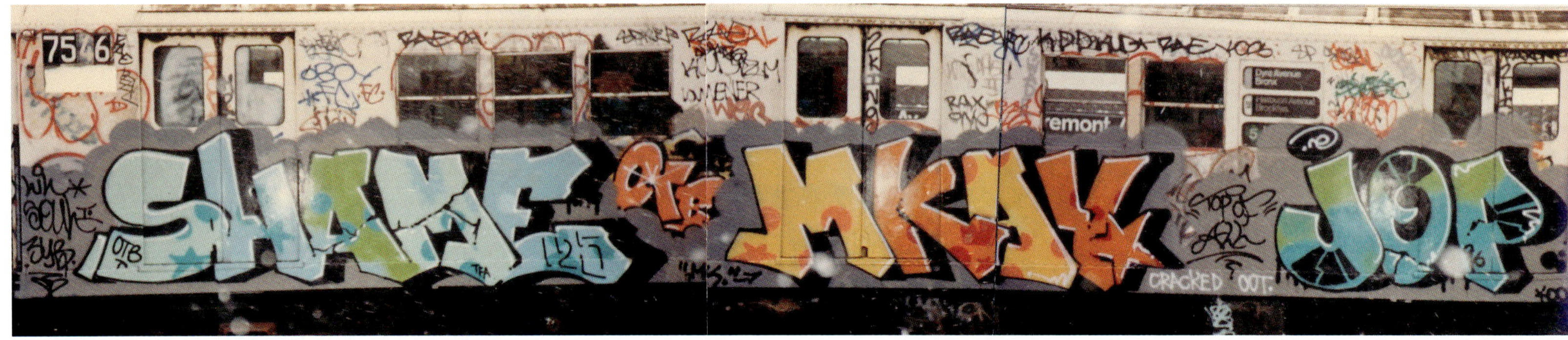

Shame125, Mkay, Jop, 1987

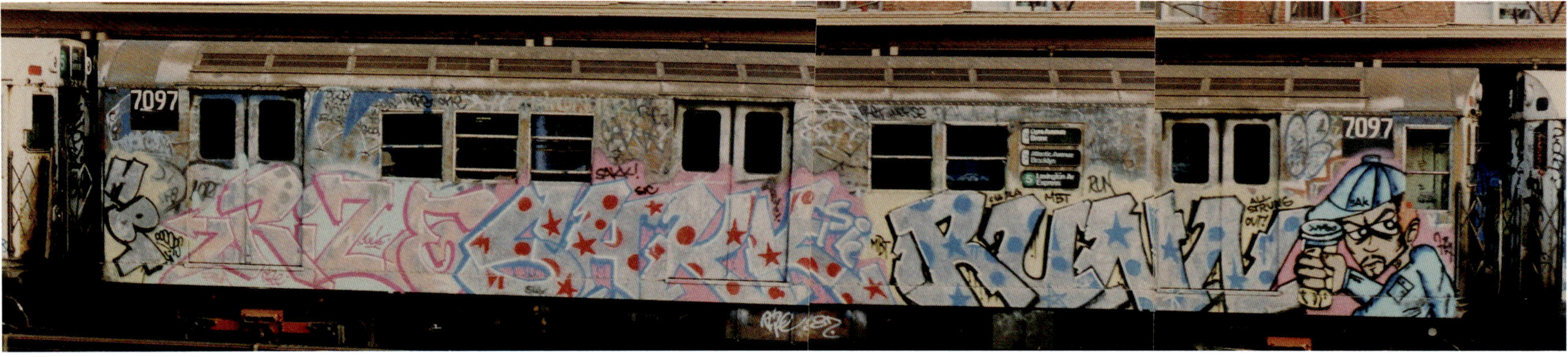

Rize, Sakk, Runn, 1987

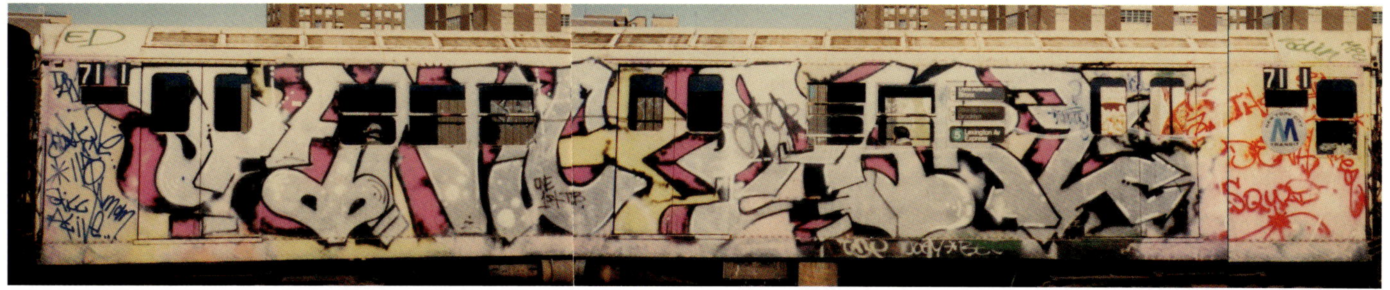
Panic, Part, 1987

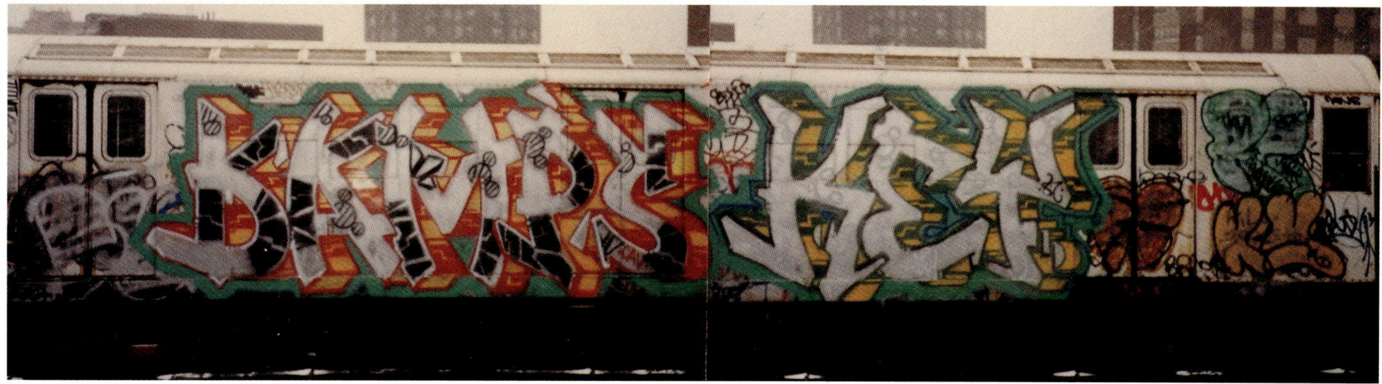
Damps, Key, 1987

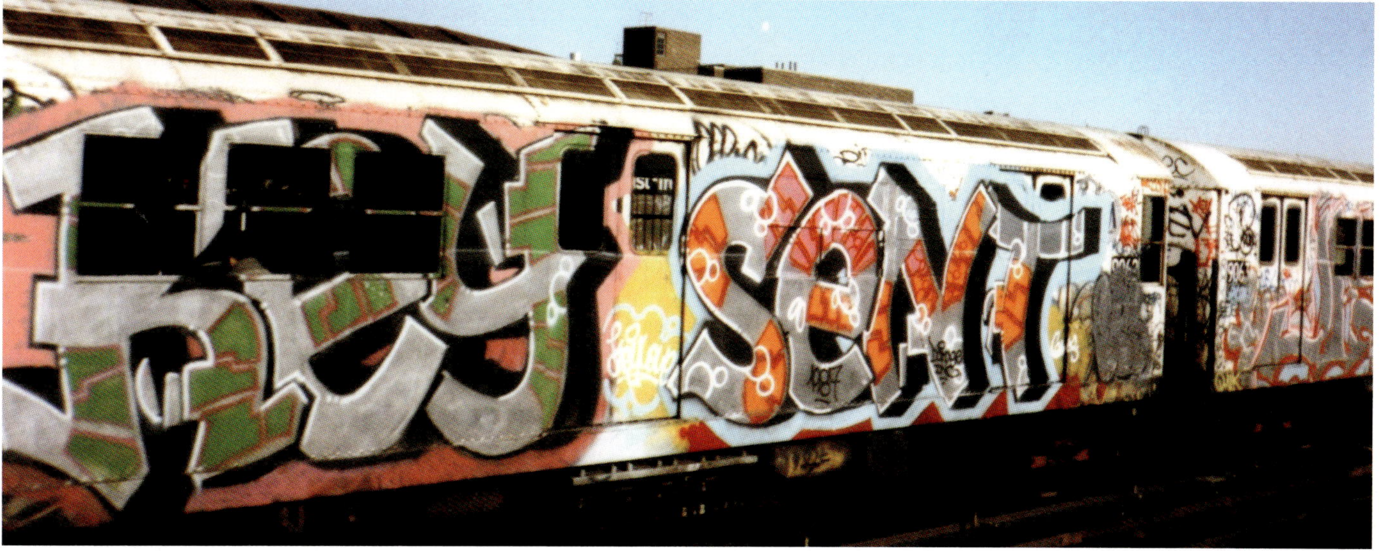
Key, Sent, 1987

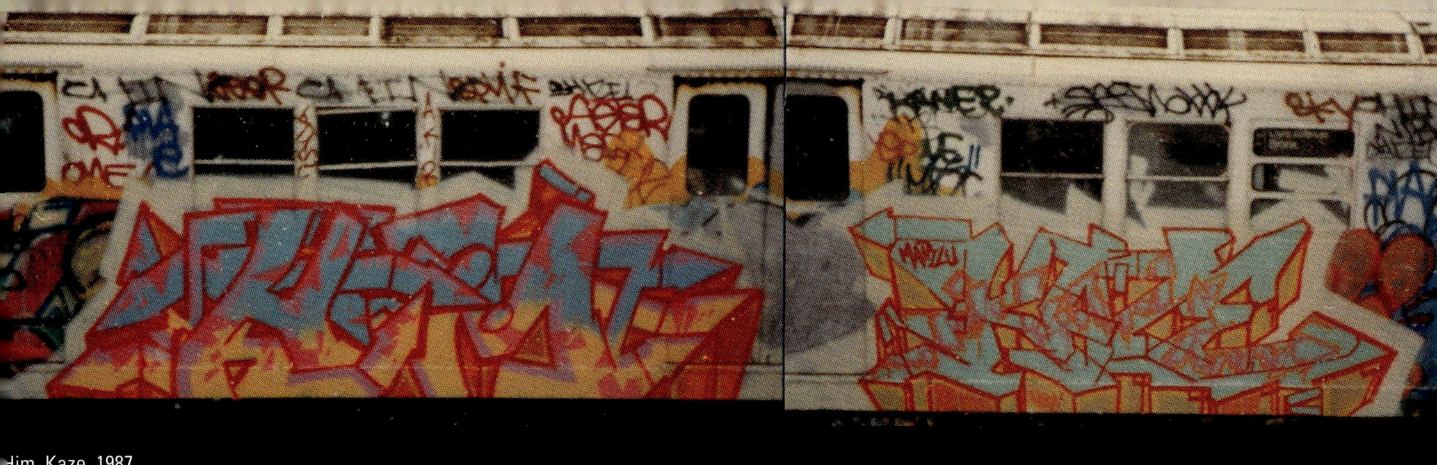

Him, Kaze, 1987

Wane called me to see if I was down to paint. The spot was like the 1 tunnel. We started talking about what colors we had . . . so we both had almond to rock for the background. Then we talked about an outline color, and since I already had an outline ready, the rest was history. We hooked up at 11 PM. Went down there around 12. It all was cool until the conductor and motorman came in to put the train in service at 5 AM. That's why I wasn't able to finish the FC in the middle. It was a great night with my brother Wane FC.

–Kaze

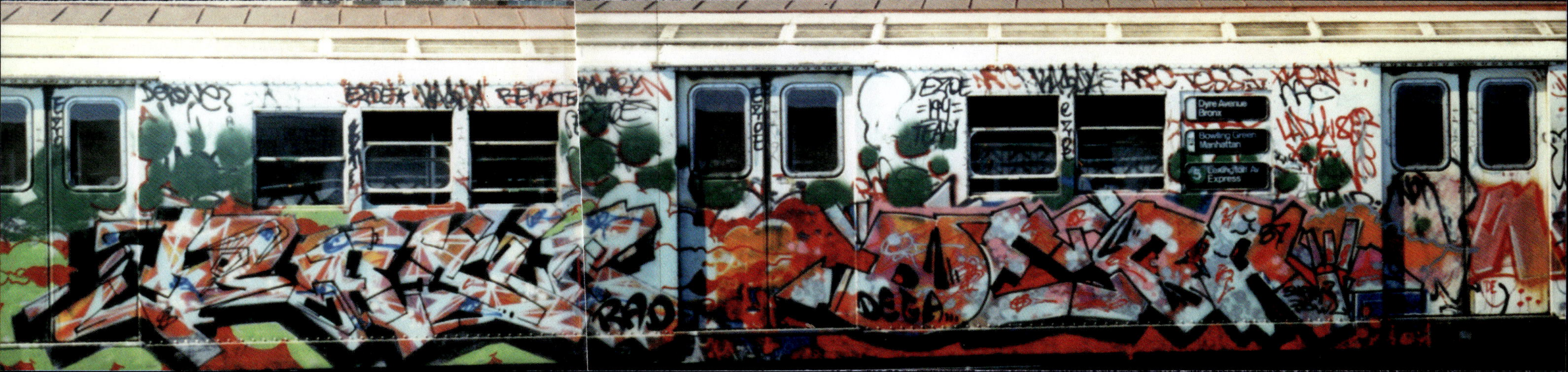

Radio, Dega, 1987

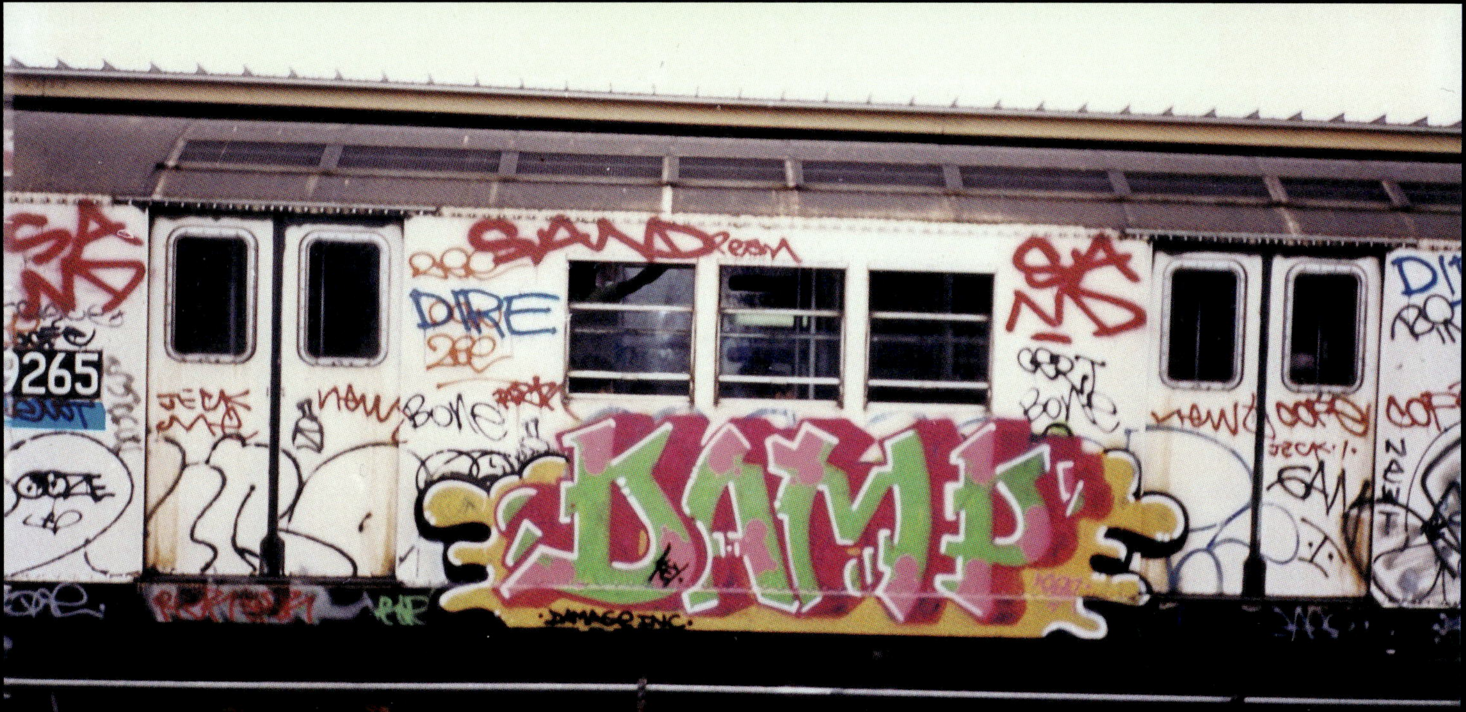

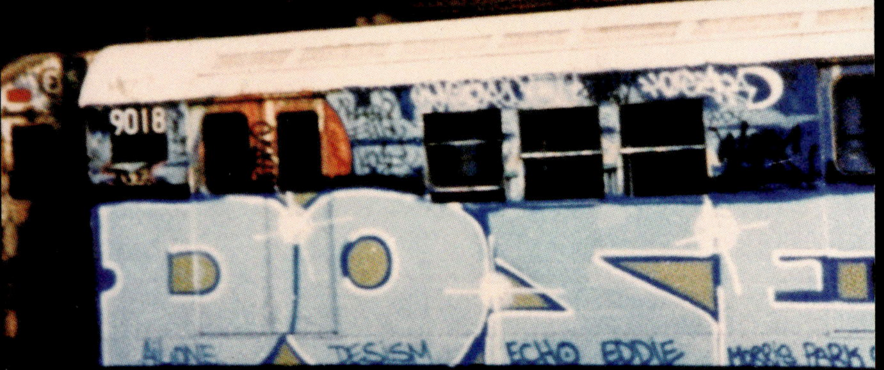

Dose MPC

Dee, Kasa, 1987

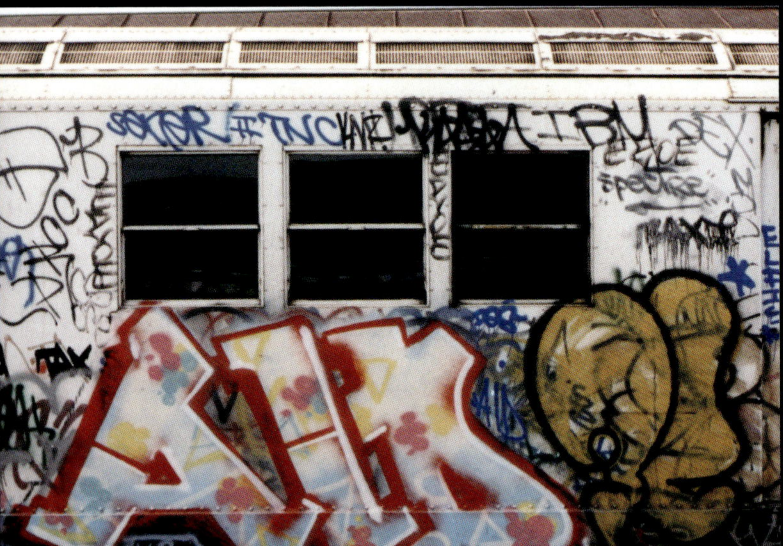

Aid, 1987

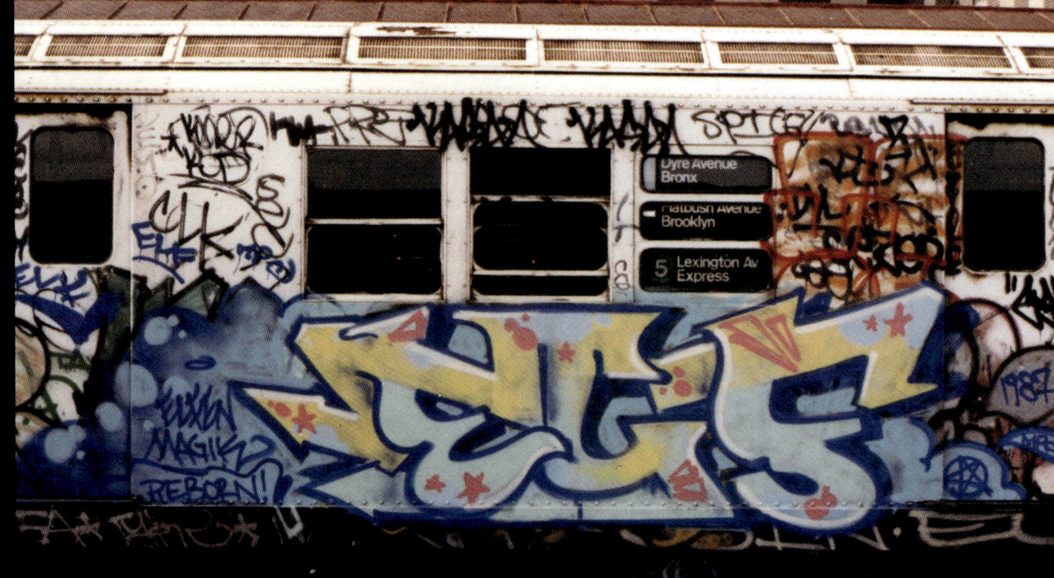

Elf, 1987

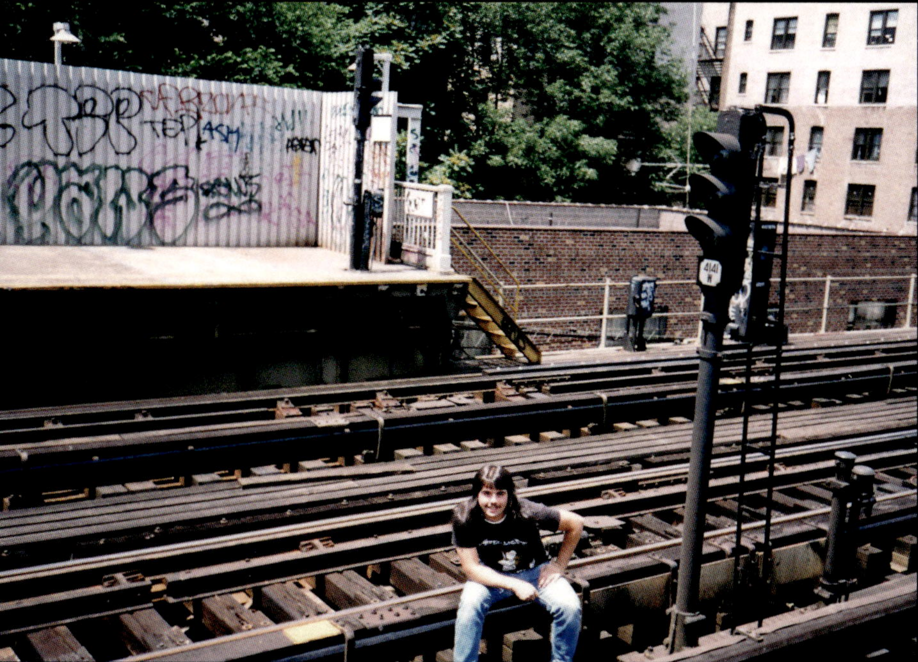

Kirs, Bronx Park East Train Station

I started writing in 1984, and in 1985 I bought my first Kodak Disc camera. At that point I realized I wanted to take pictures of everything I did as well as the 2s and 5 lines in the Bronx. From 1986 to this day I have been close friends with Cavs and Key. In 1988 we started hanging out with Ket and Cole. In those days, the photo missions were insane. Venturing from one end of the city to the other.

–Kirs

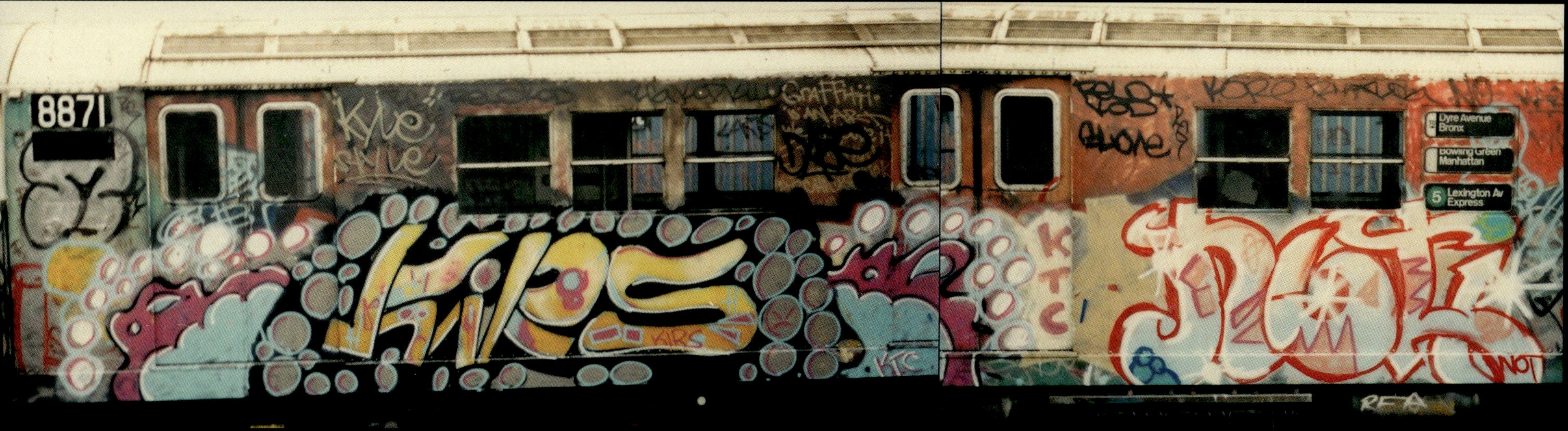

Kirs, Not KTC (Photo courtesy of Kirs MPC)

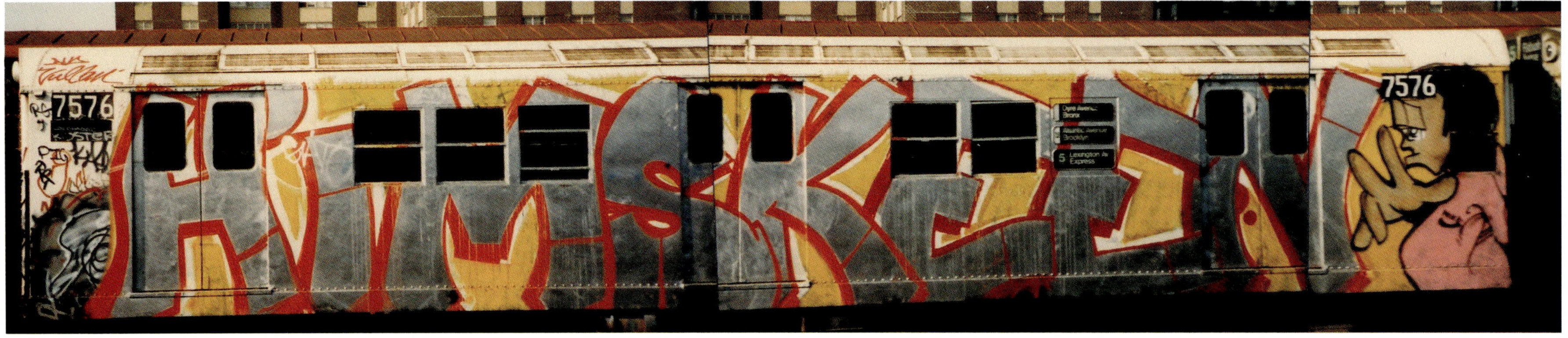

Him, Skeen

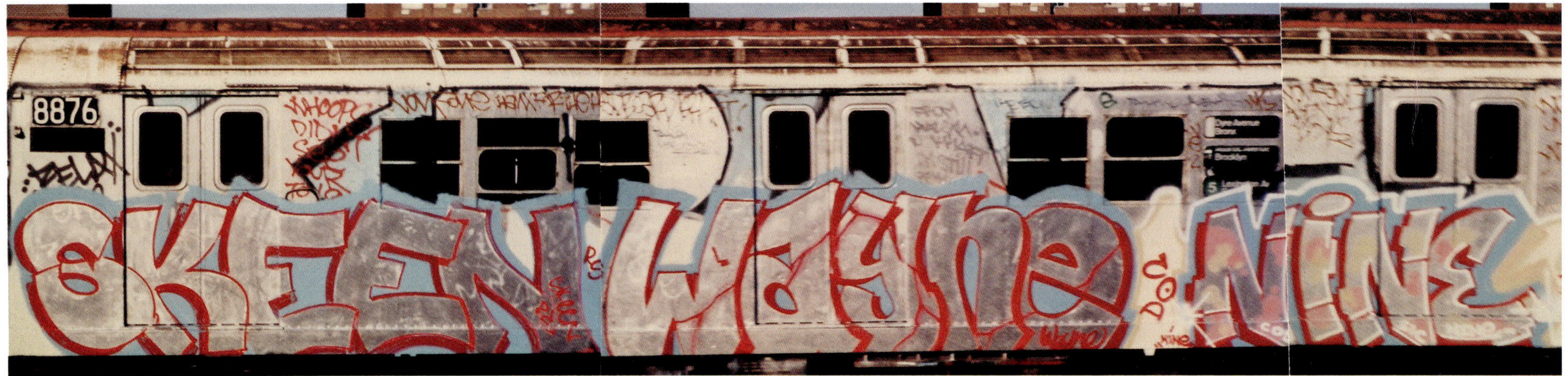

Skeen, Wayne, Nine COD

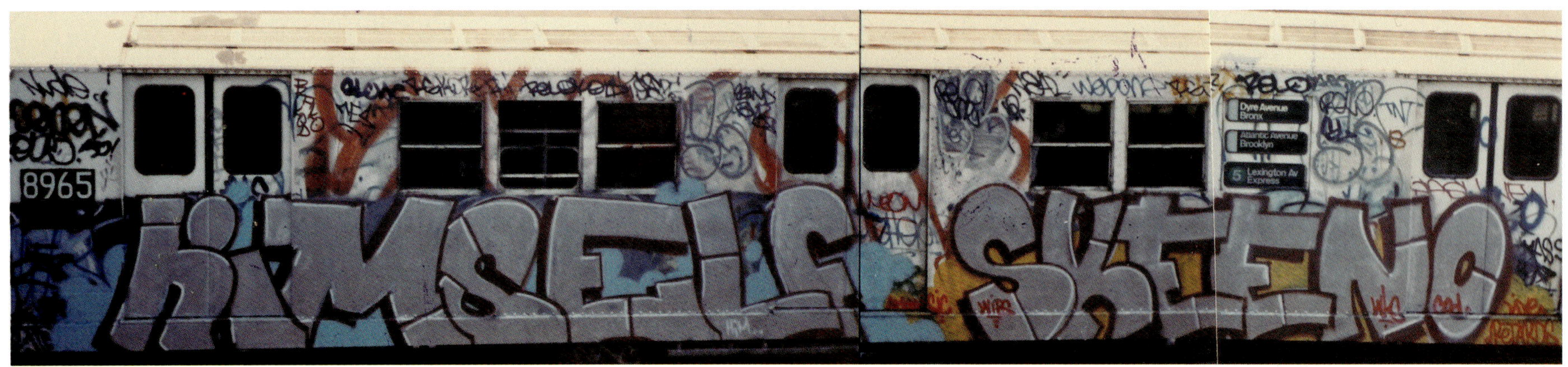

Himself, Skeeno

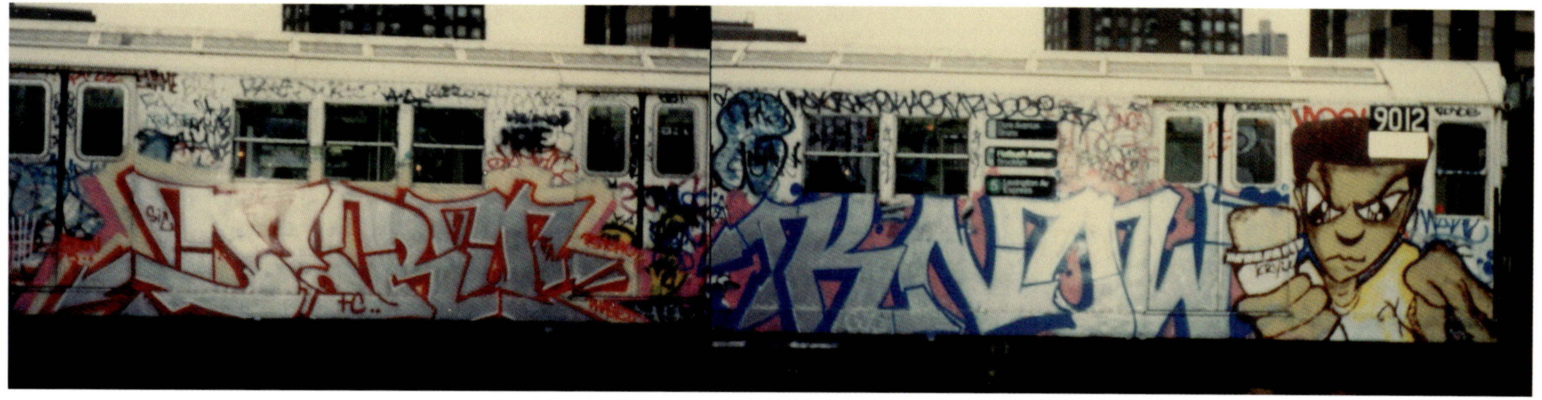

Dero, Know

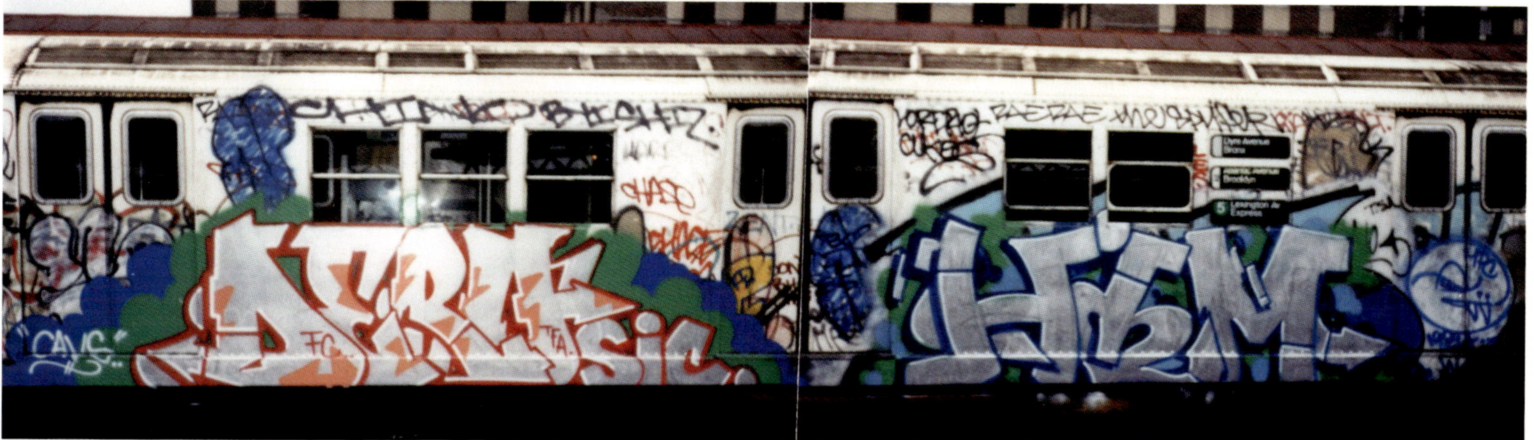

Dero SIC, Him

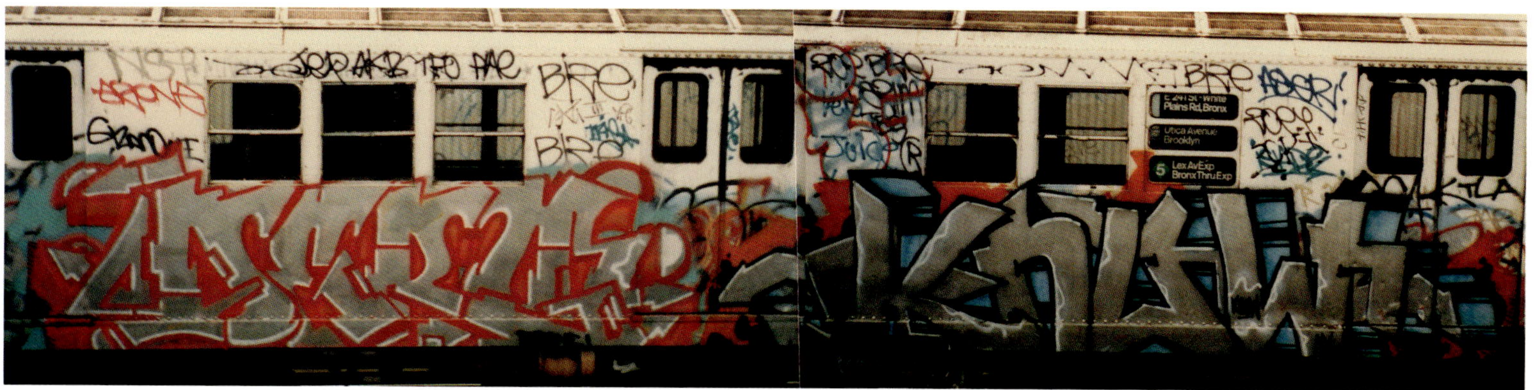

Dero, Know

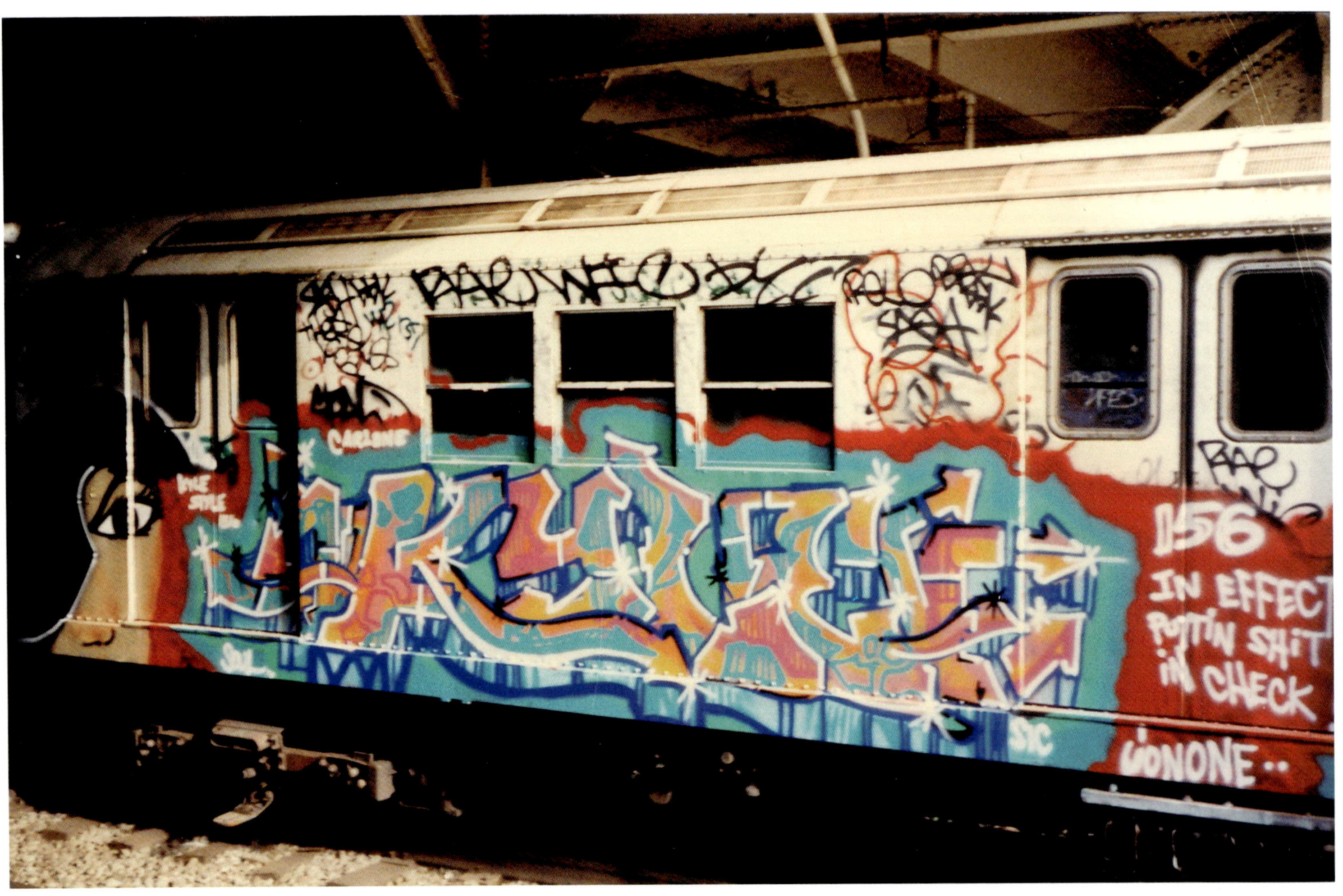

Kyle (Photo courtesy of Kirs MPC)

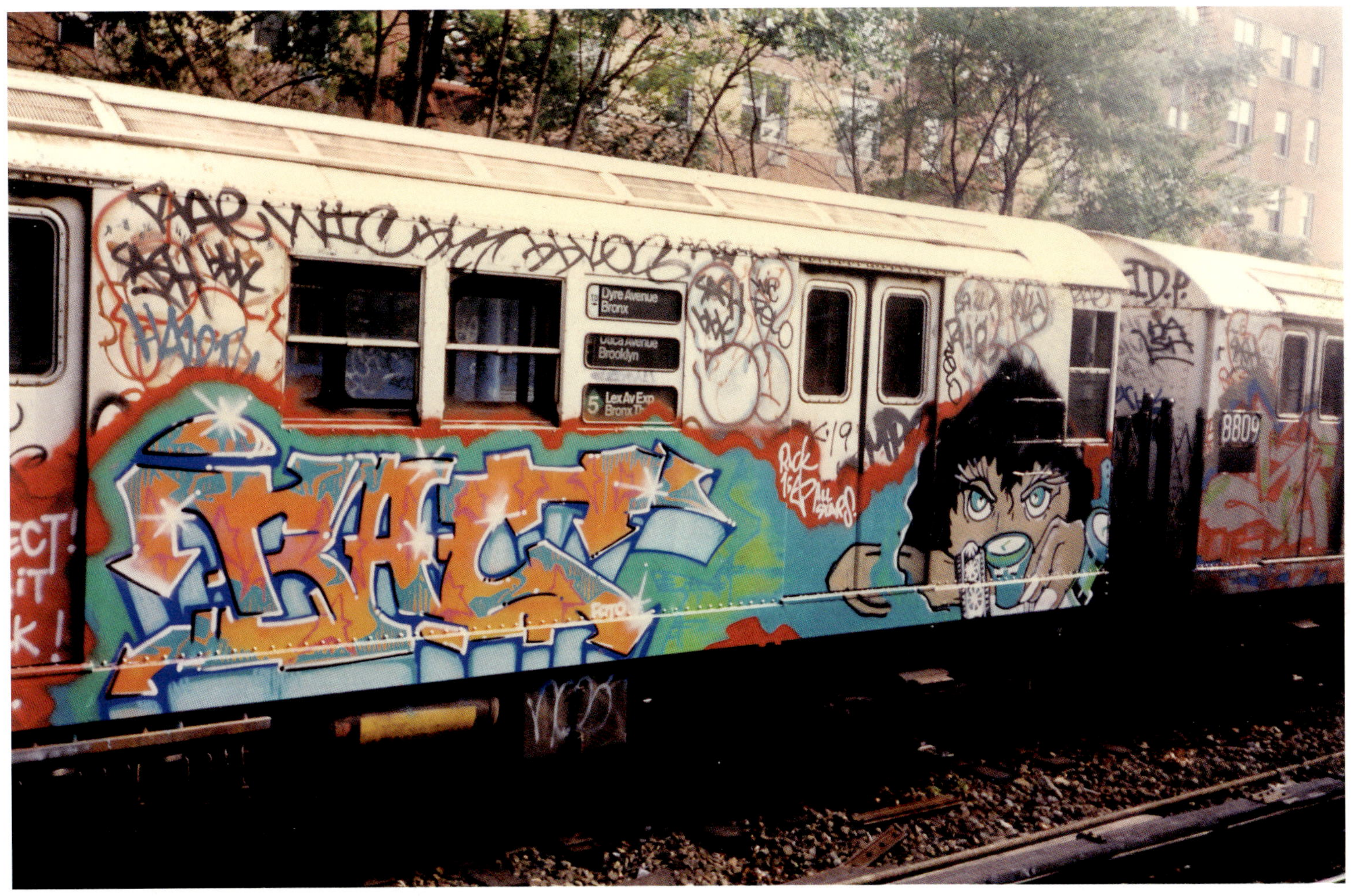

Rac7 (Photo courtesy of Kirs MPC)

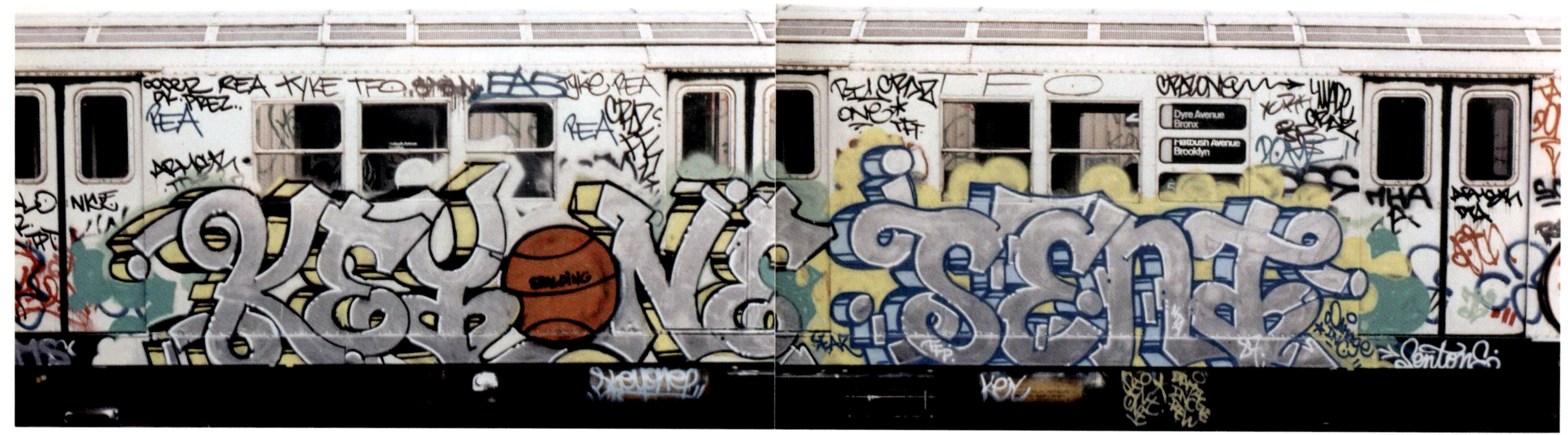

Coach Keyone, Sent, 1987

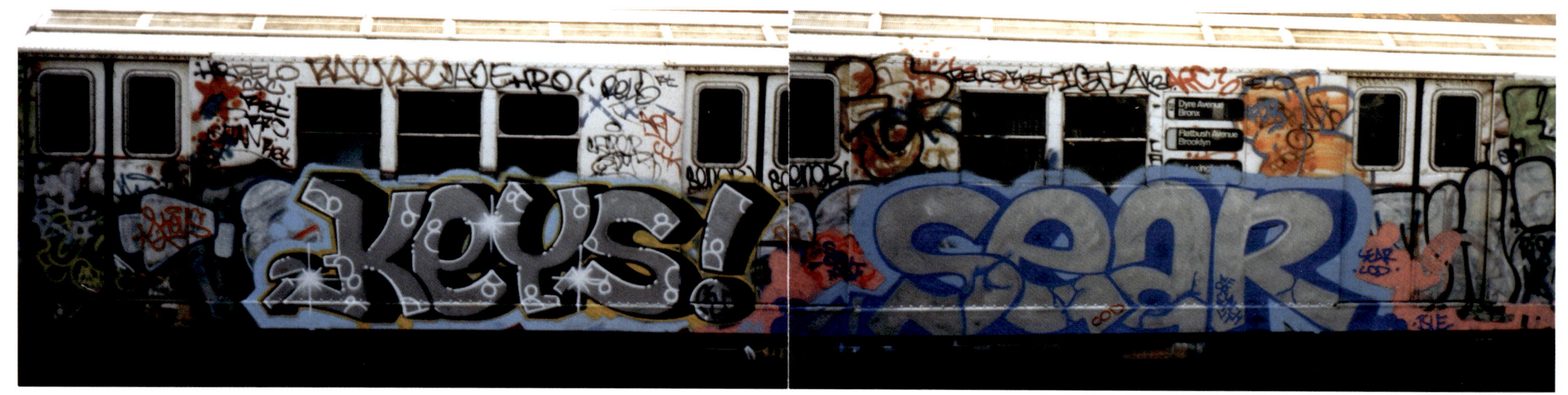

Keys, Sear, 1987

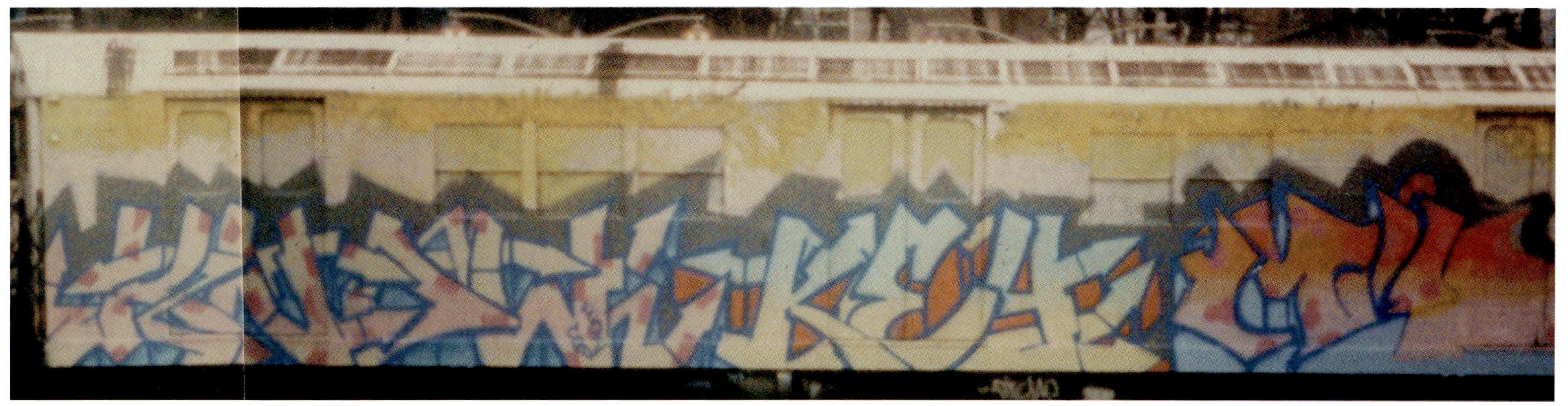

Know, Key, Milo

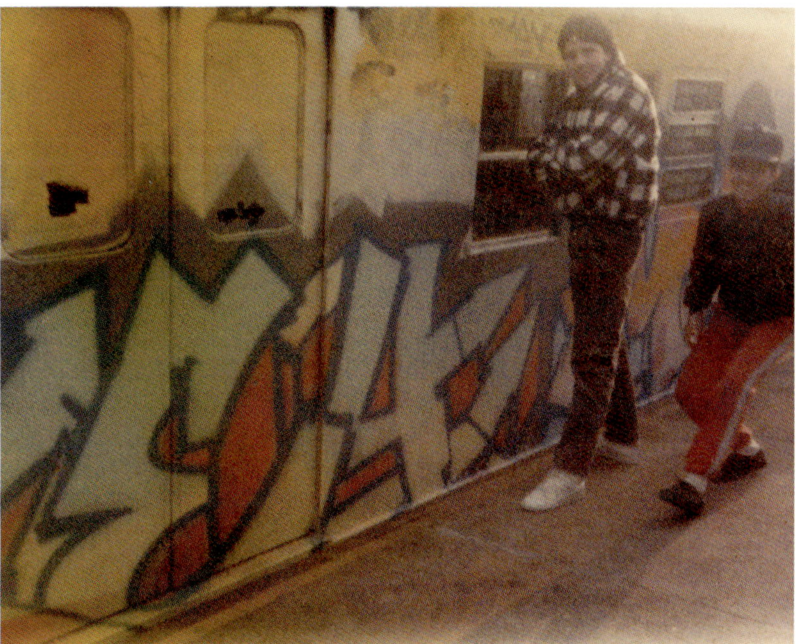

Key in front of his car

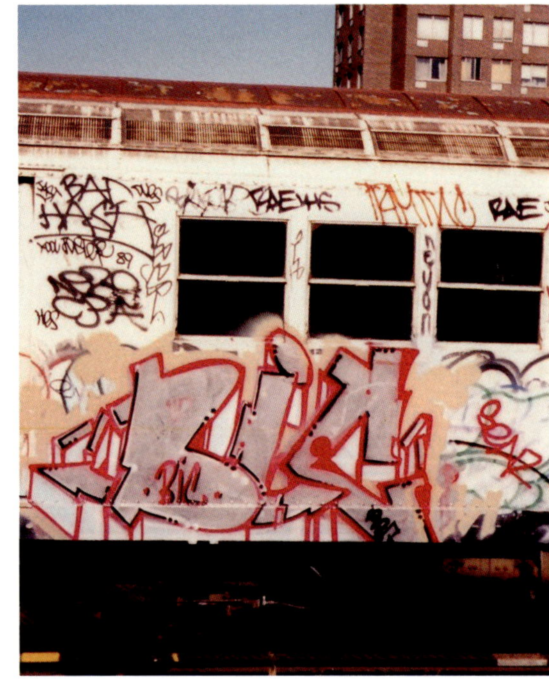

Bic, a.k.a. Sear, 1987

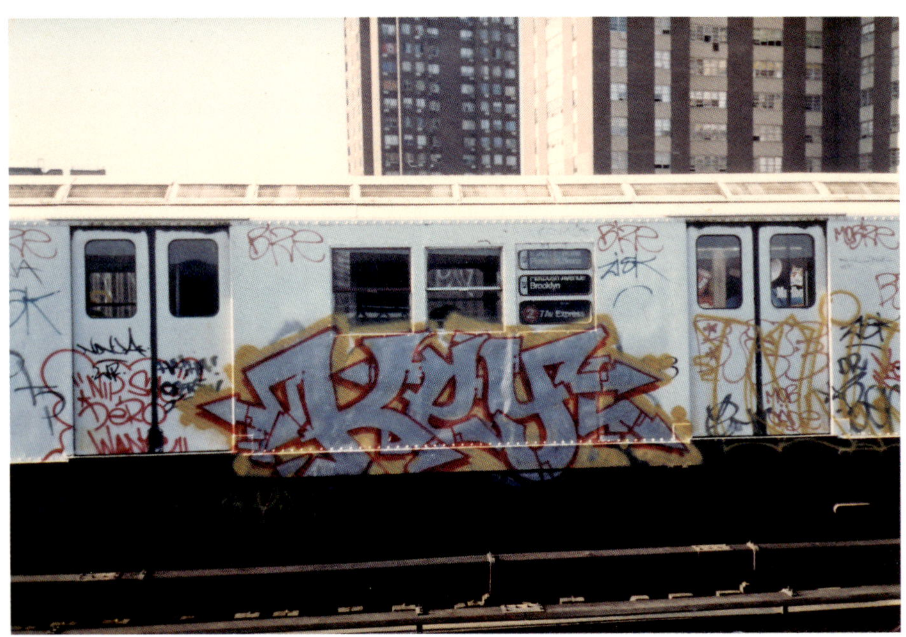

Key, 1986

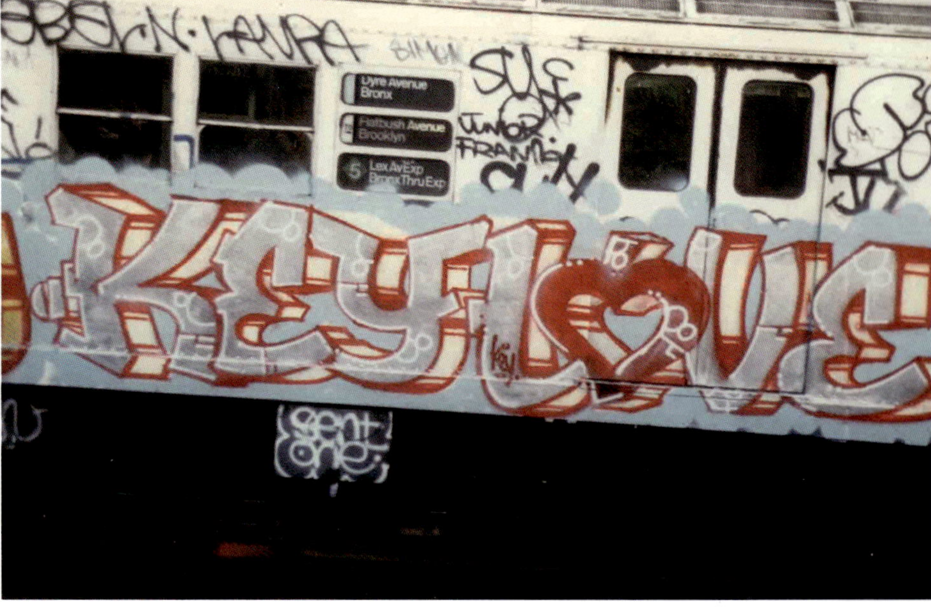

Keylove, 1987

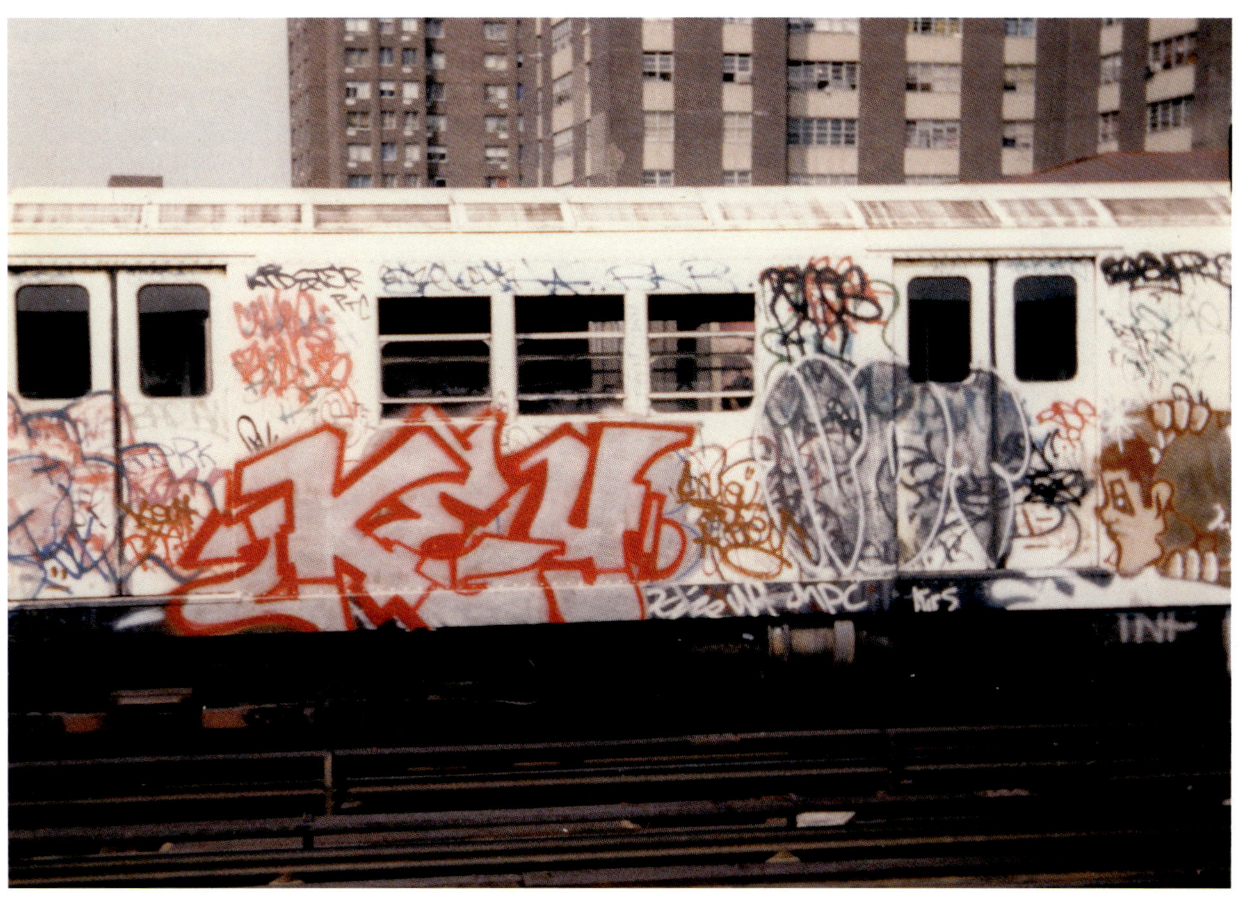

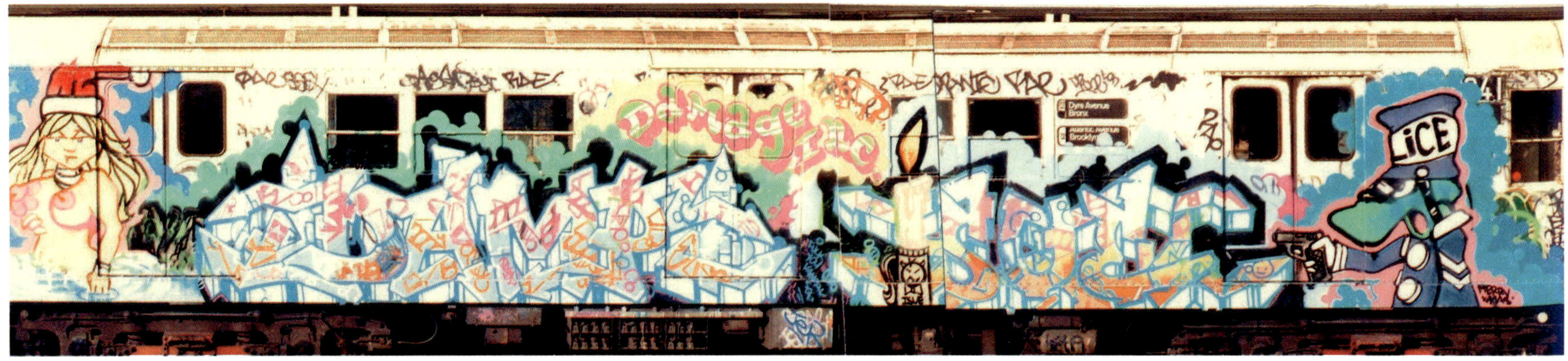

Damp, Isue, 1987

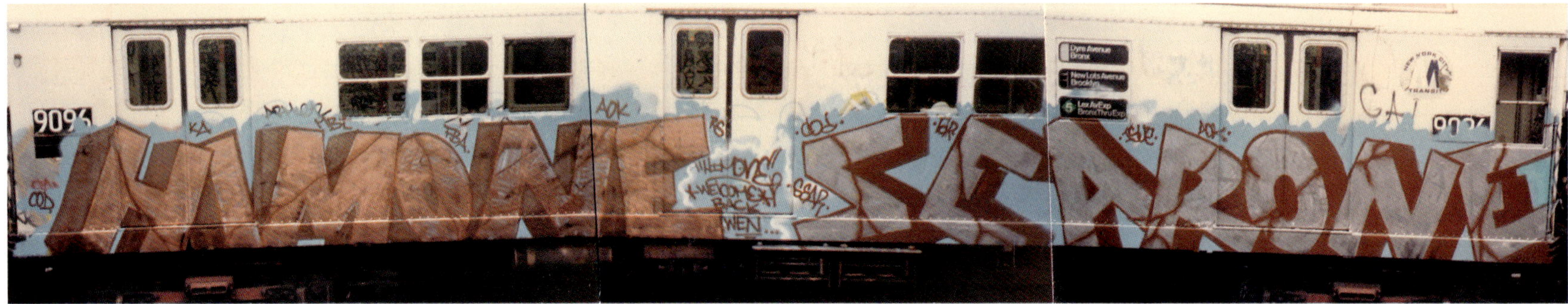

Himone, Searone

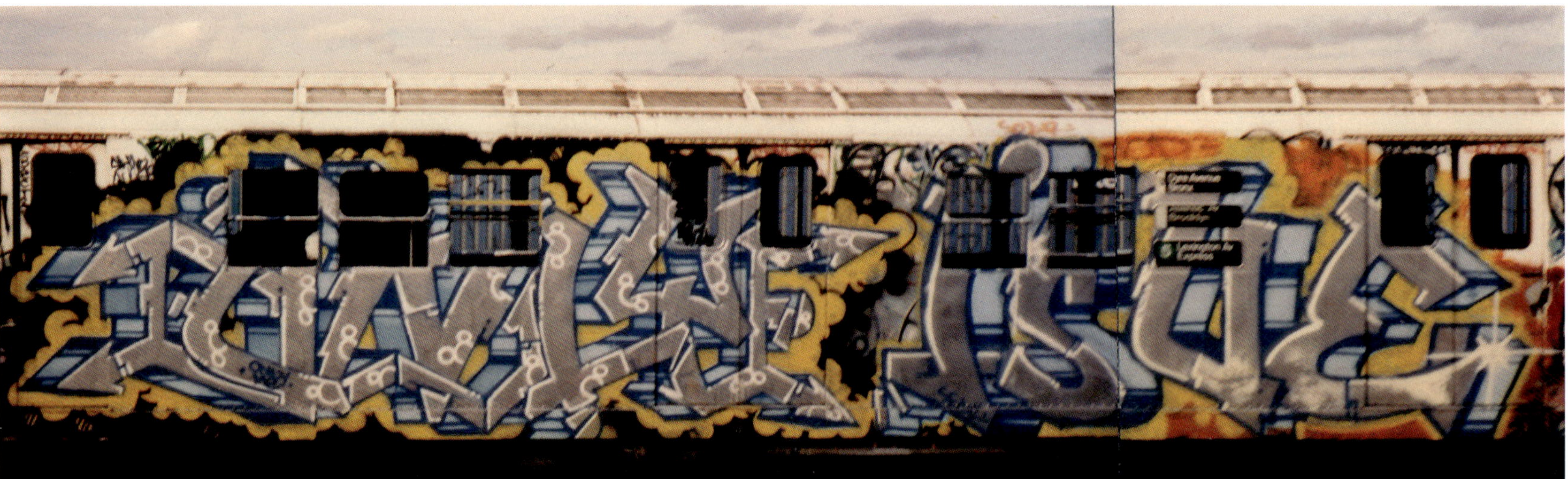

Only, Isue

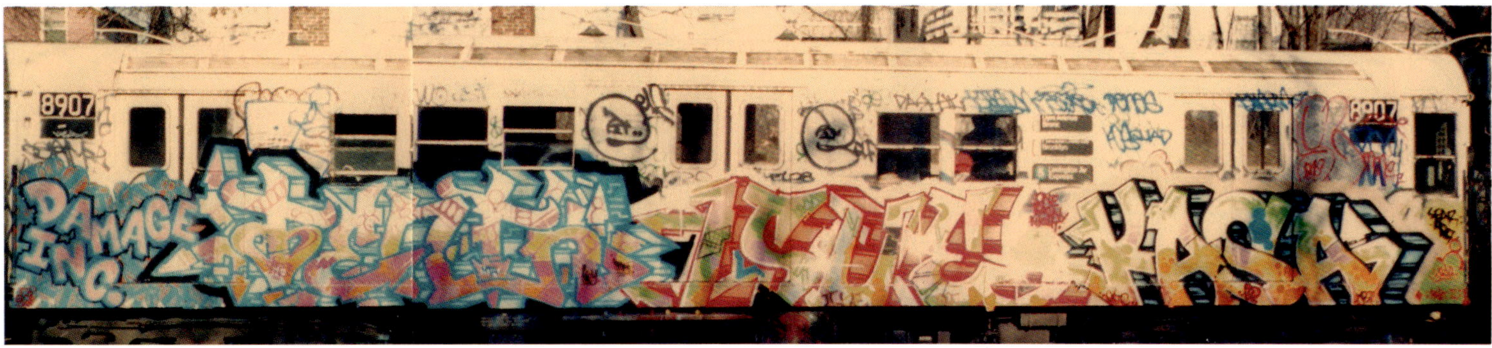

Tenth, Isue, Kasa, 1987

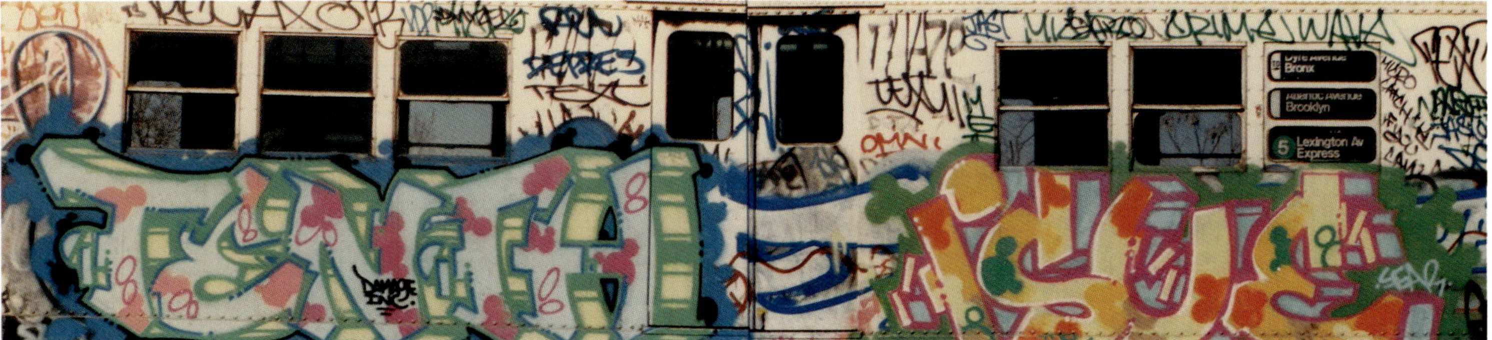

Tenth, Isue

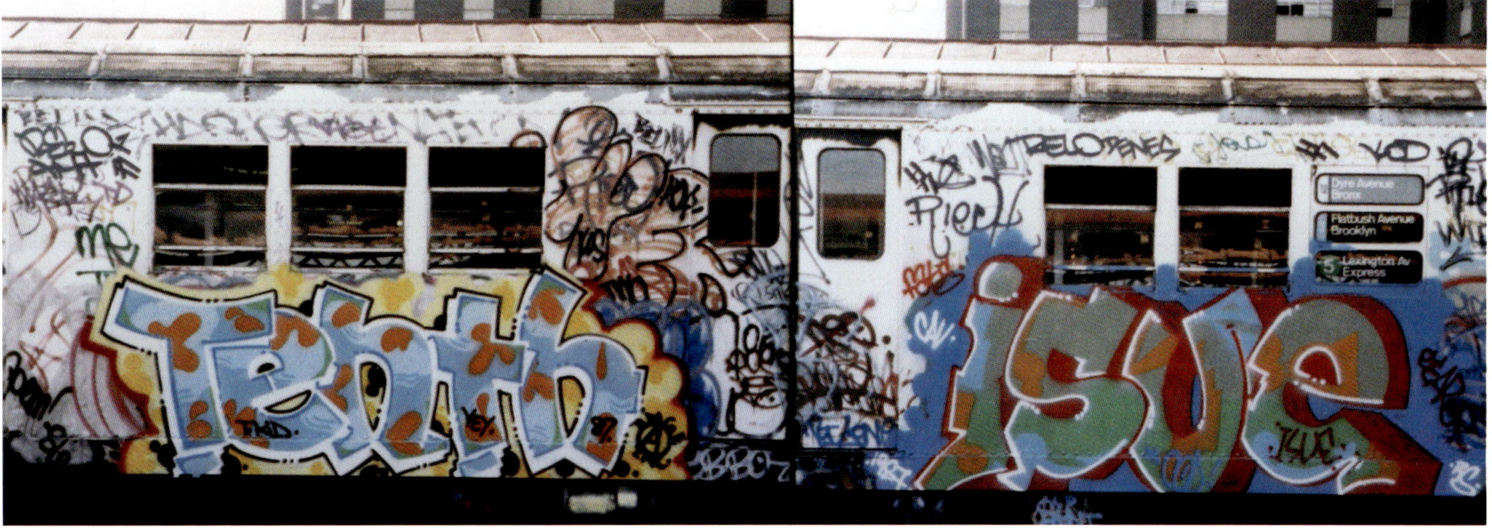

Tenth, Isue, 1987

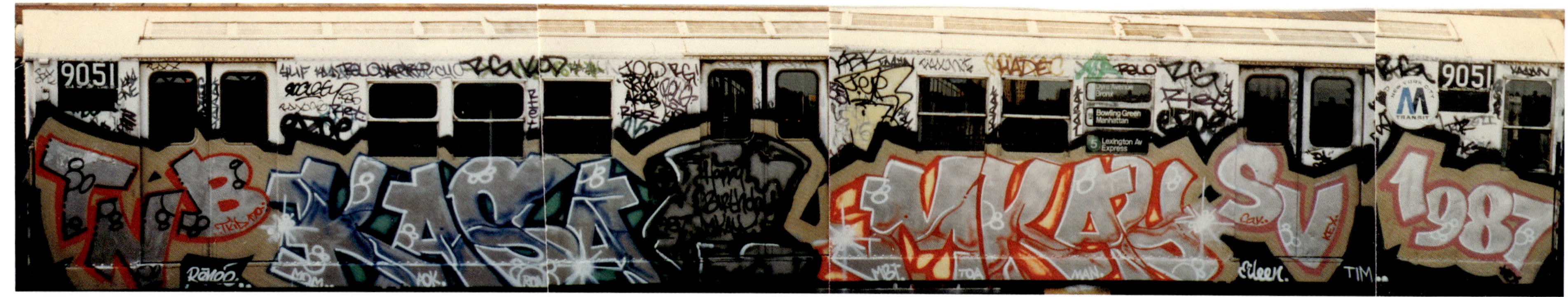

Kasa, Mkay, 1987

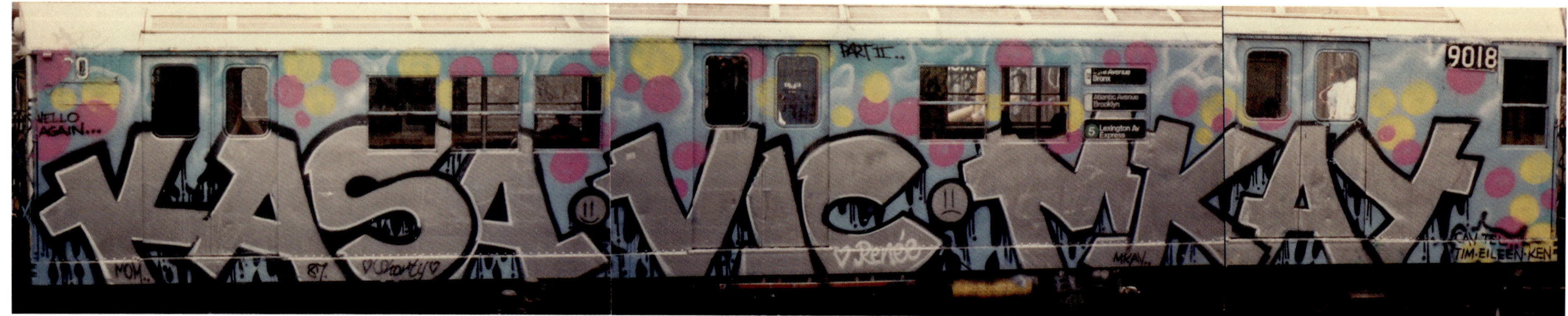

Kasa, Vic, Mkay, 1987

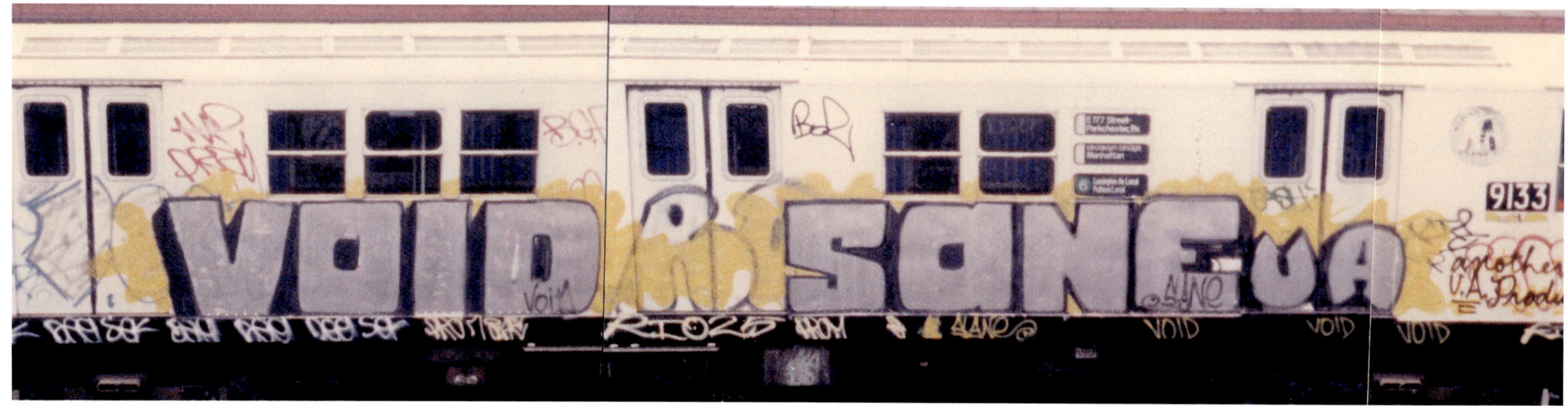

Void, Sane UA

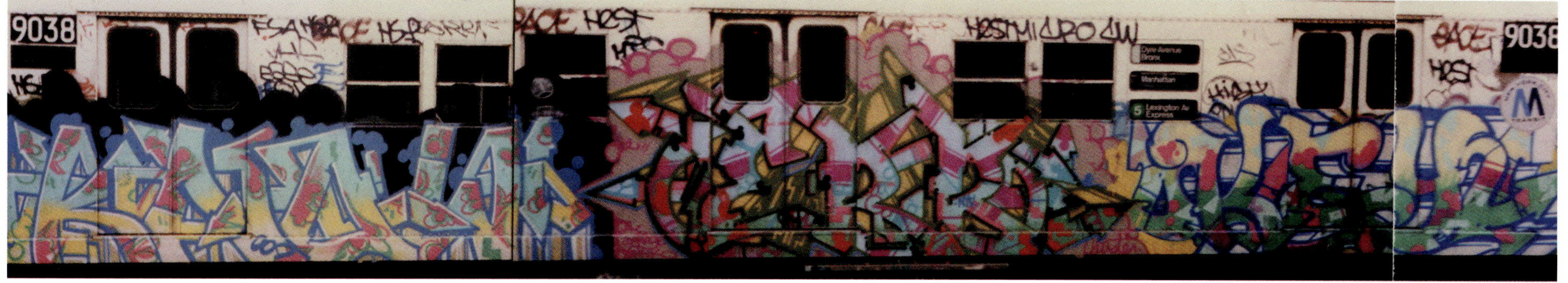

Know, Erb, Key

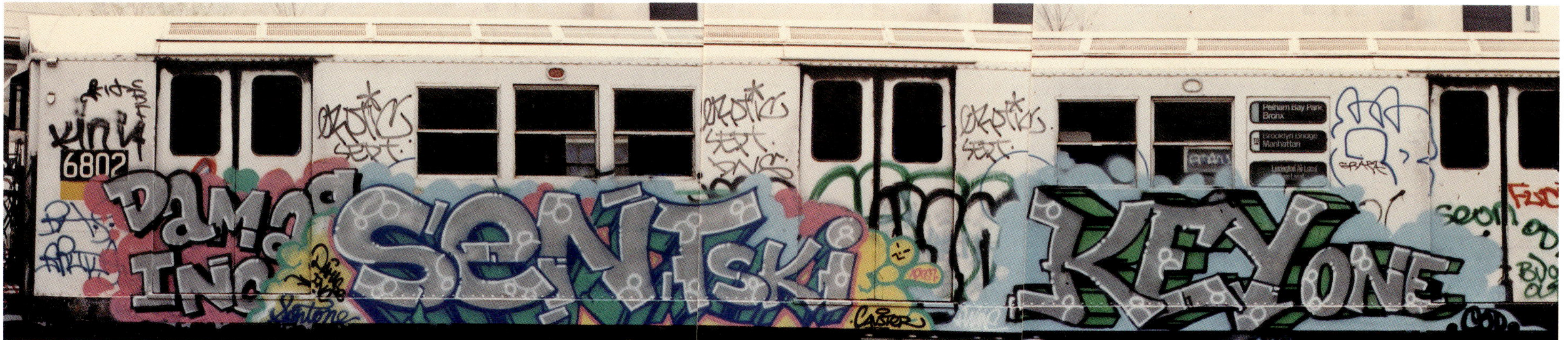

Sentski, Keyone, 1987

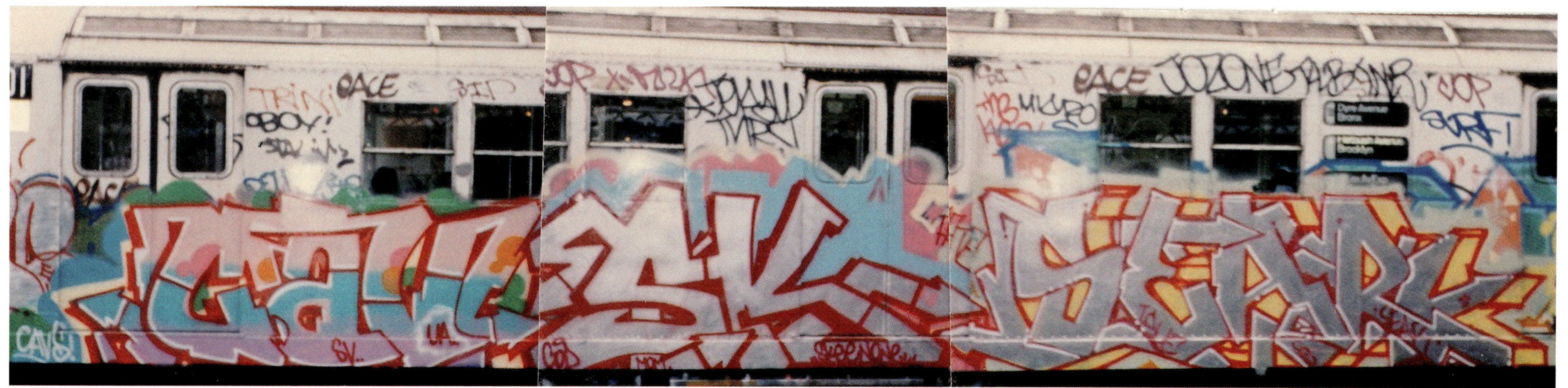

Cav by Dero, Skeen, Sear, 1987

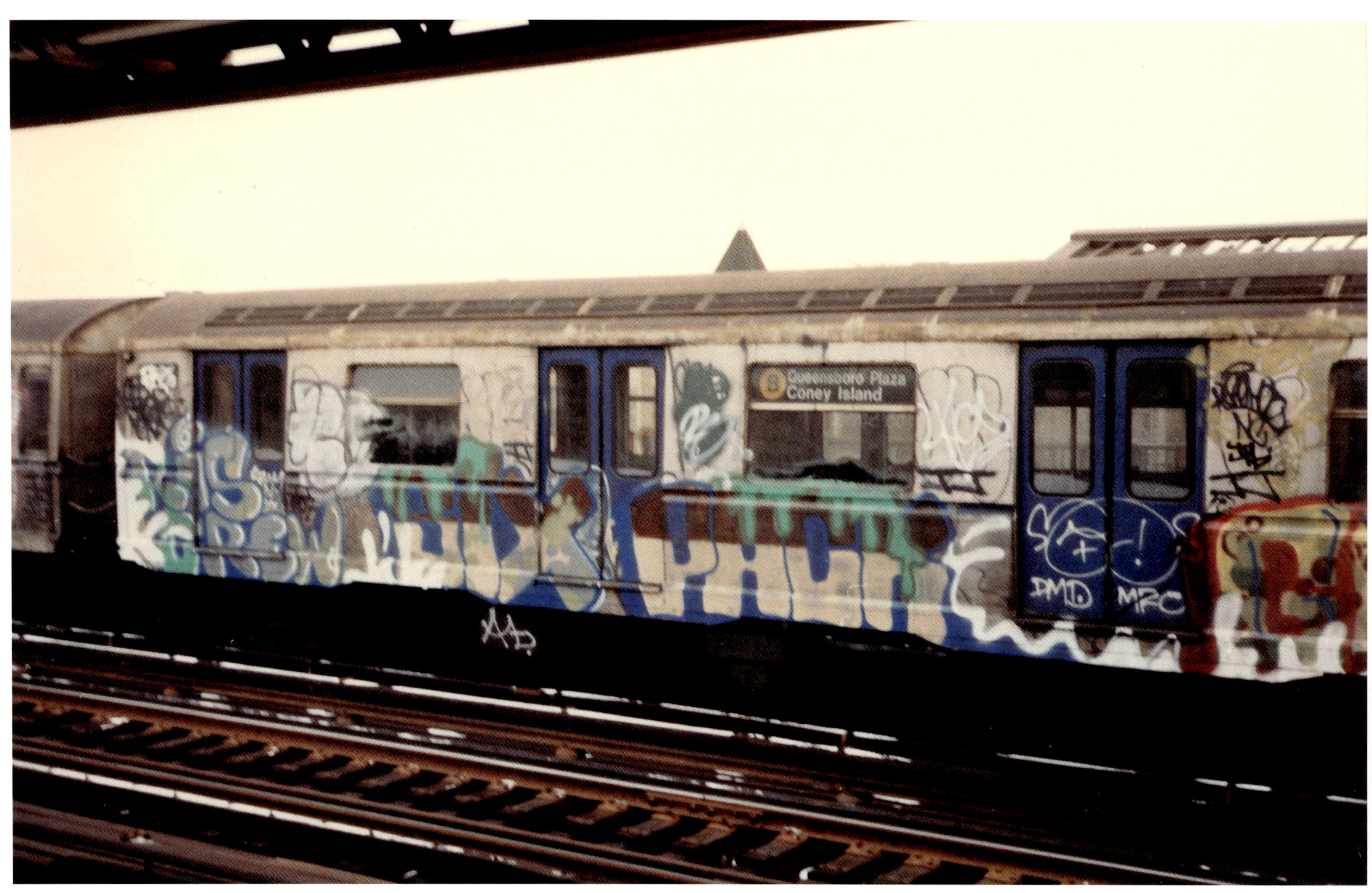

Six Pack RIS Crew (Photo courtesy of Kirs MPC)

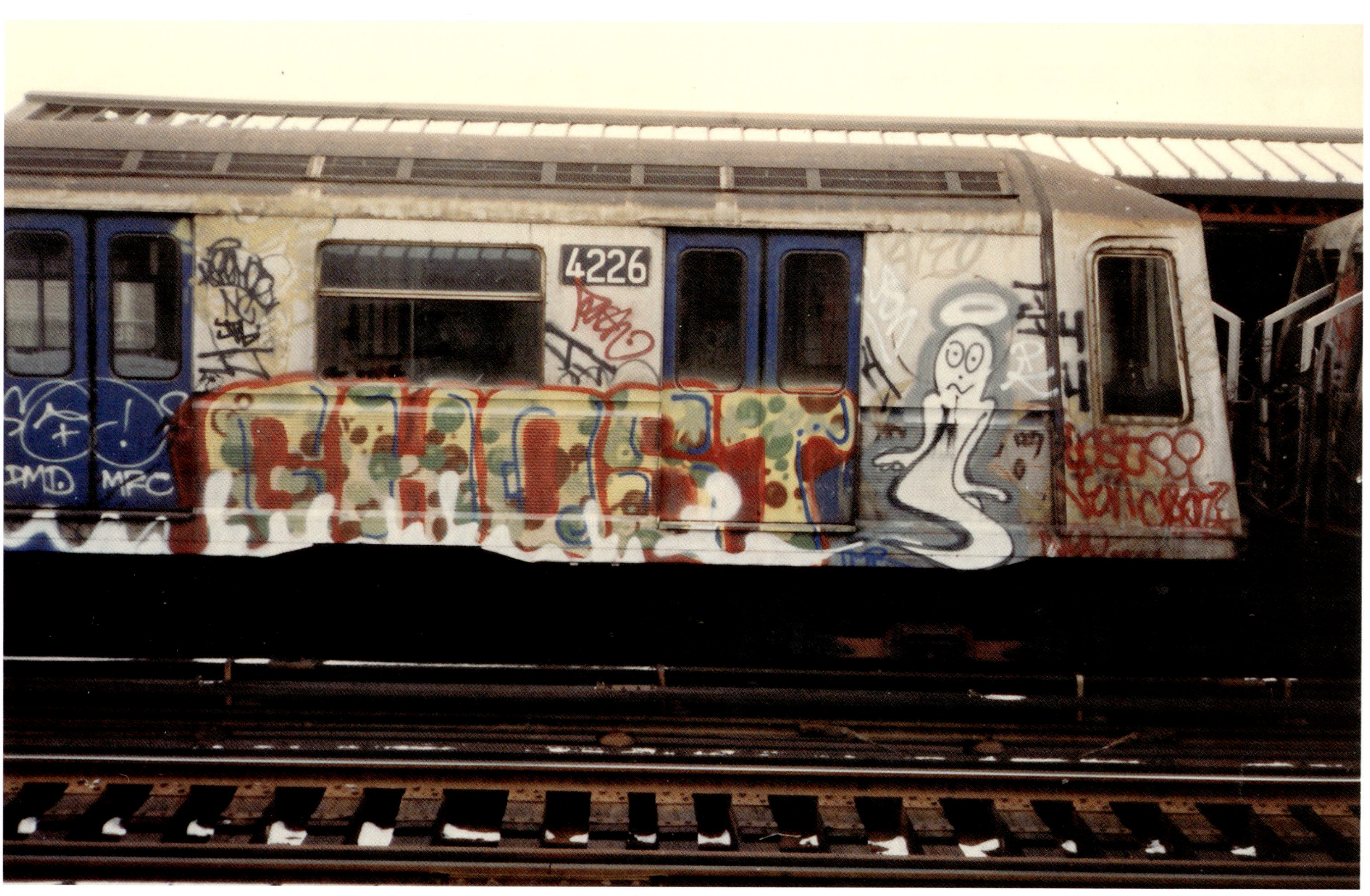

Ghost (Photo courtesy of Kirs MPC)

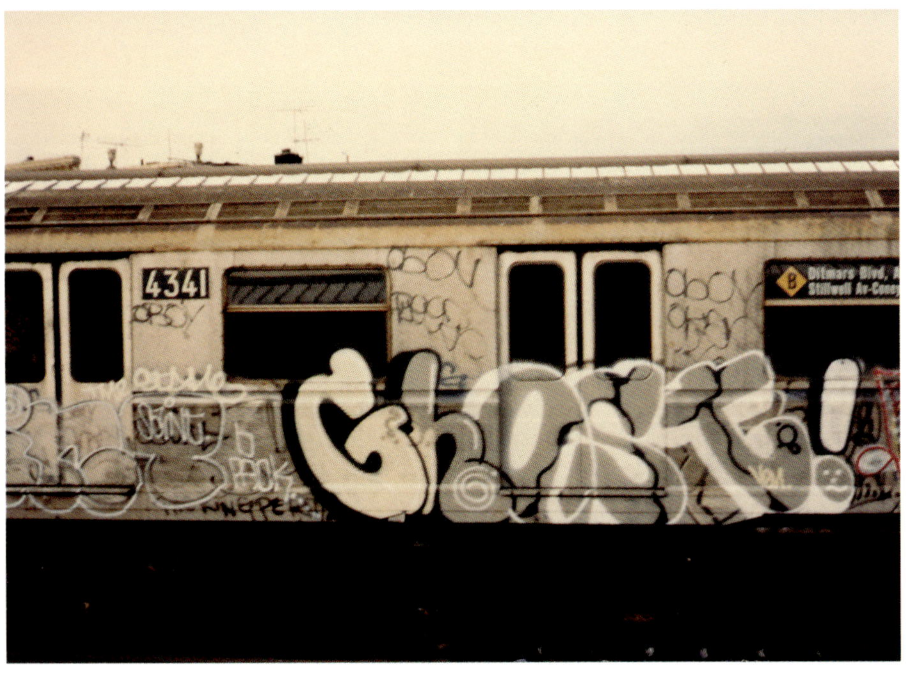

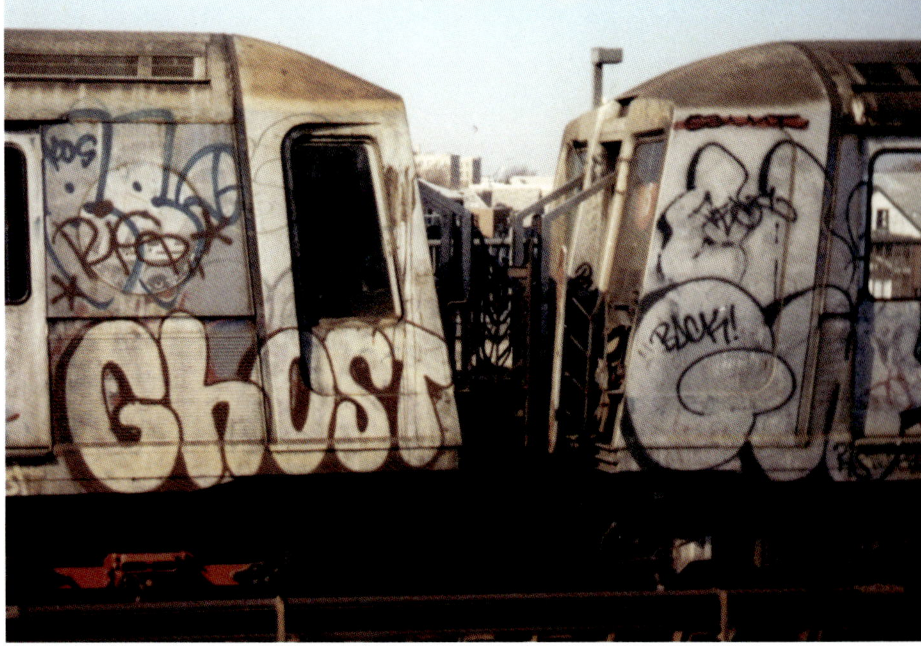

Ghost

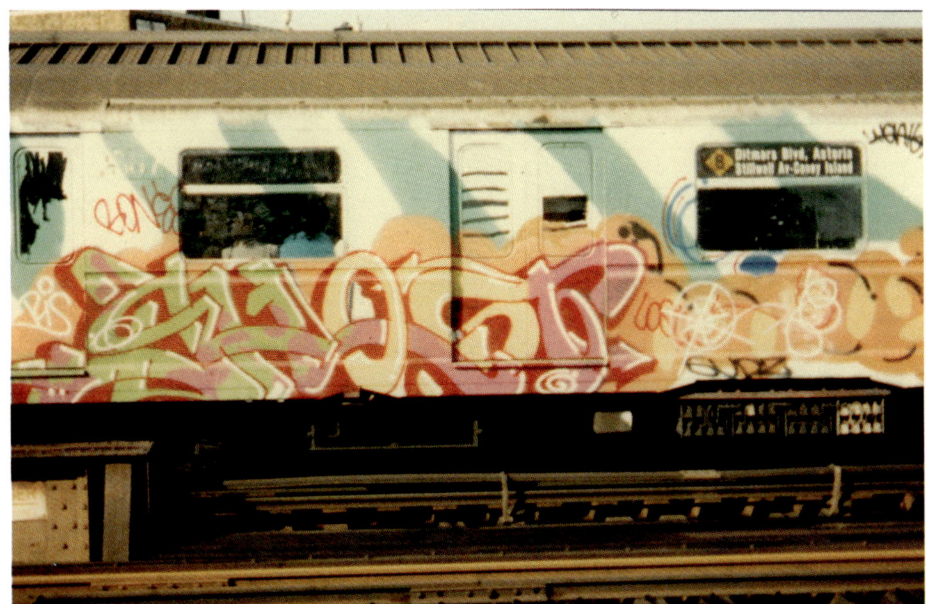

Ghost RIS

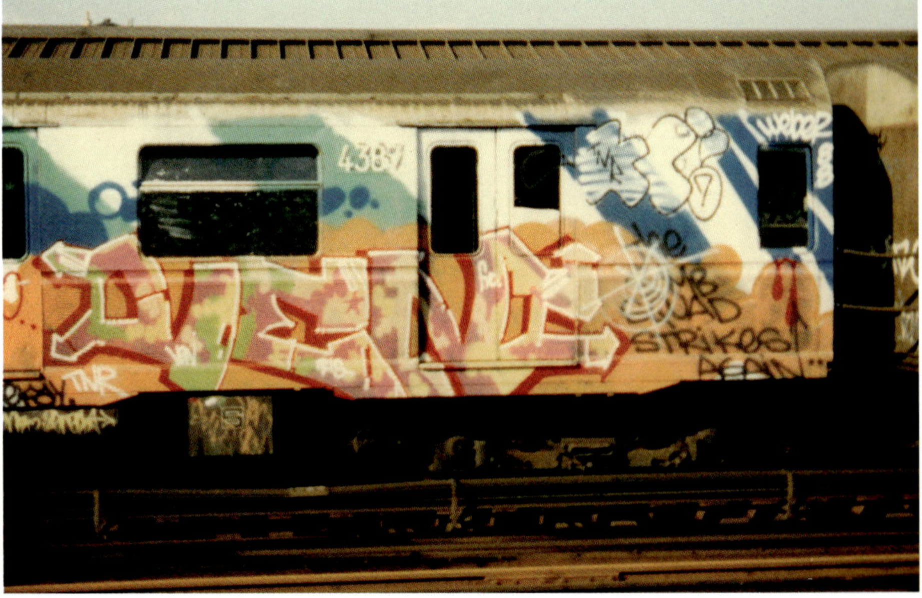

Ven

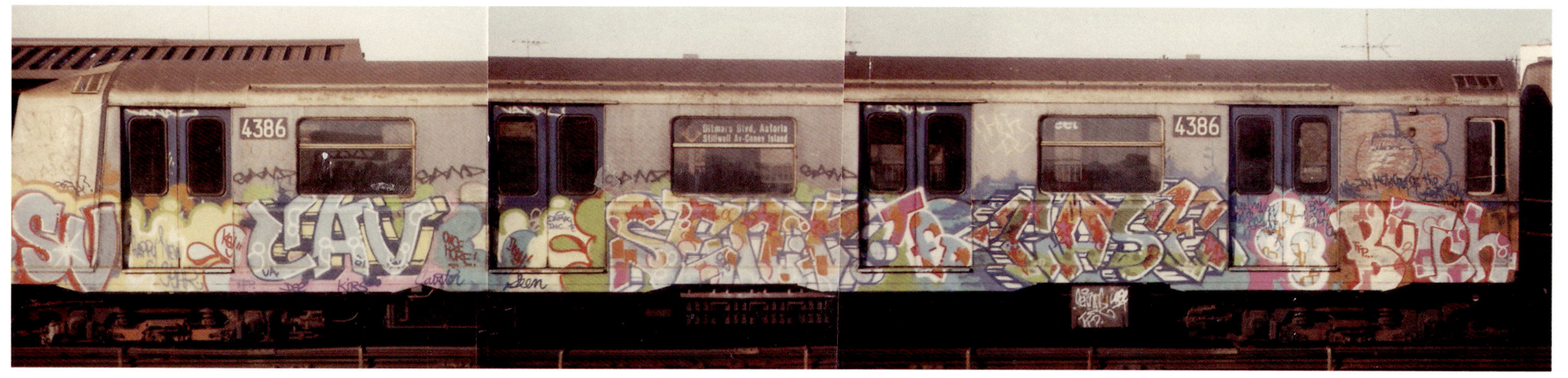

Cav, Sent, Case2, December, 1987

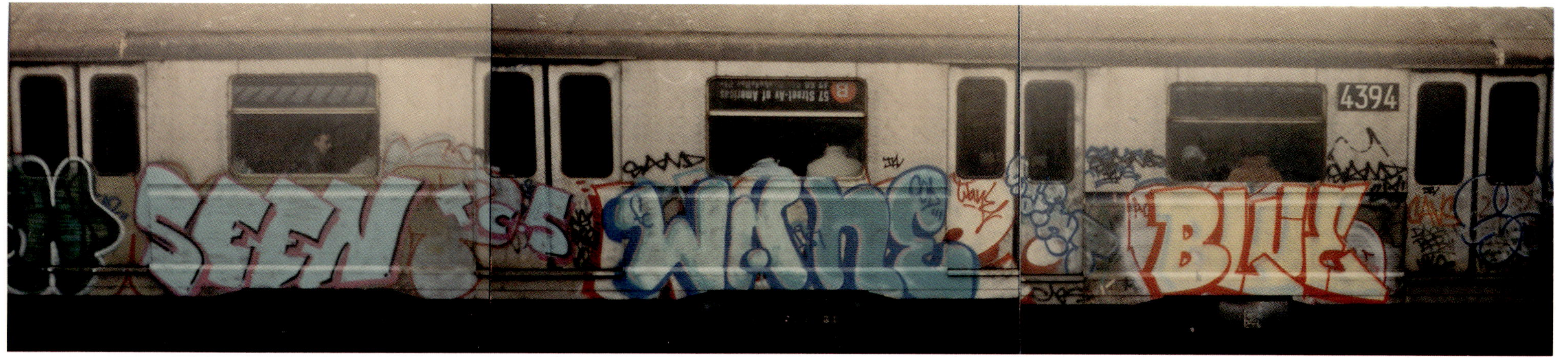

Seen TC5, Wane, Blue

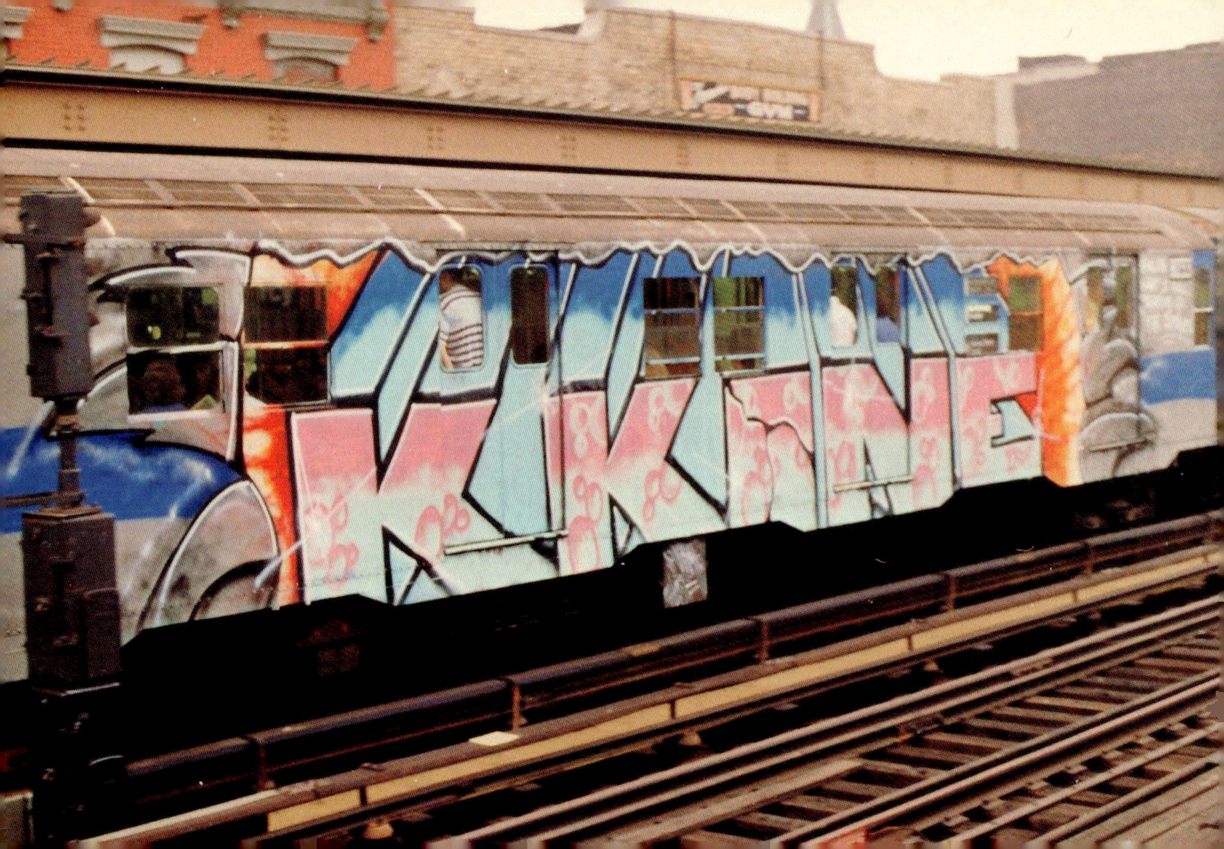

I always wanted to do cars that made people look in awe, like I did when I was benching at Times Square and would see all these new pieces rolling in around 1984–86. I studied the *Subway Art* book along with the pictures I took to see what other people did and how they did it. I was always impressed with people whose pieces looked perfect and even their background was filled in perfectly solid like Sento, West, and Seen UA. The writers who inspired me the most are: Tkid170, Bio, Mack, Cem2, Sak, Shame125, Arab, Raz, Dome, West, Sento, Lace357, Kaze, Serve, Sade, Dune, Flite, and Jon1. There are too many to name but mostly the people in the crews who were doing whole cars with characters, like TAT, FBA, FC, IBM, 156.

–KKONE

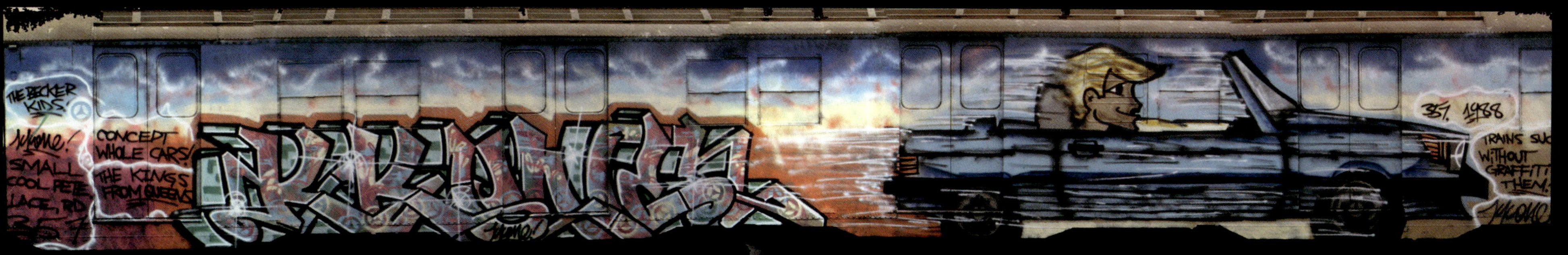

KKONE, 1988 (Photo courtesy of KKONE)

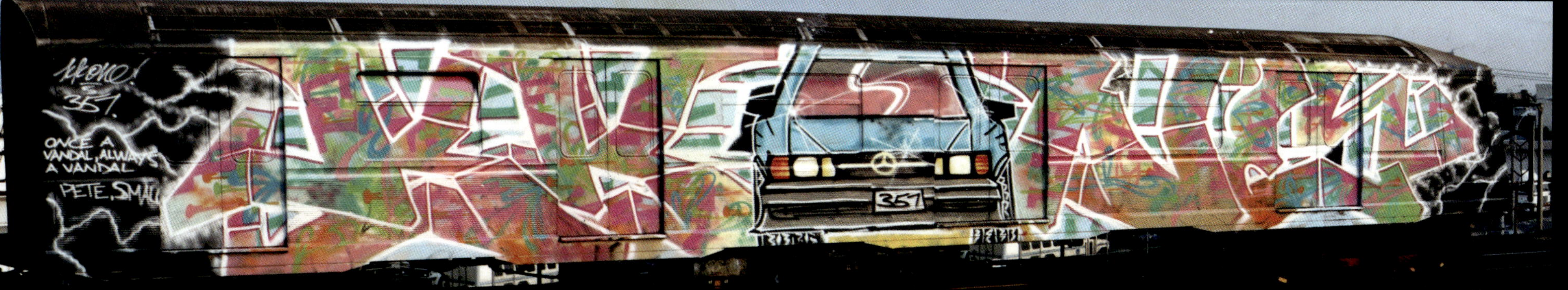

(Photo courtesy of KKONE)

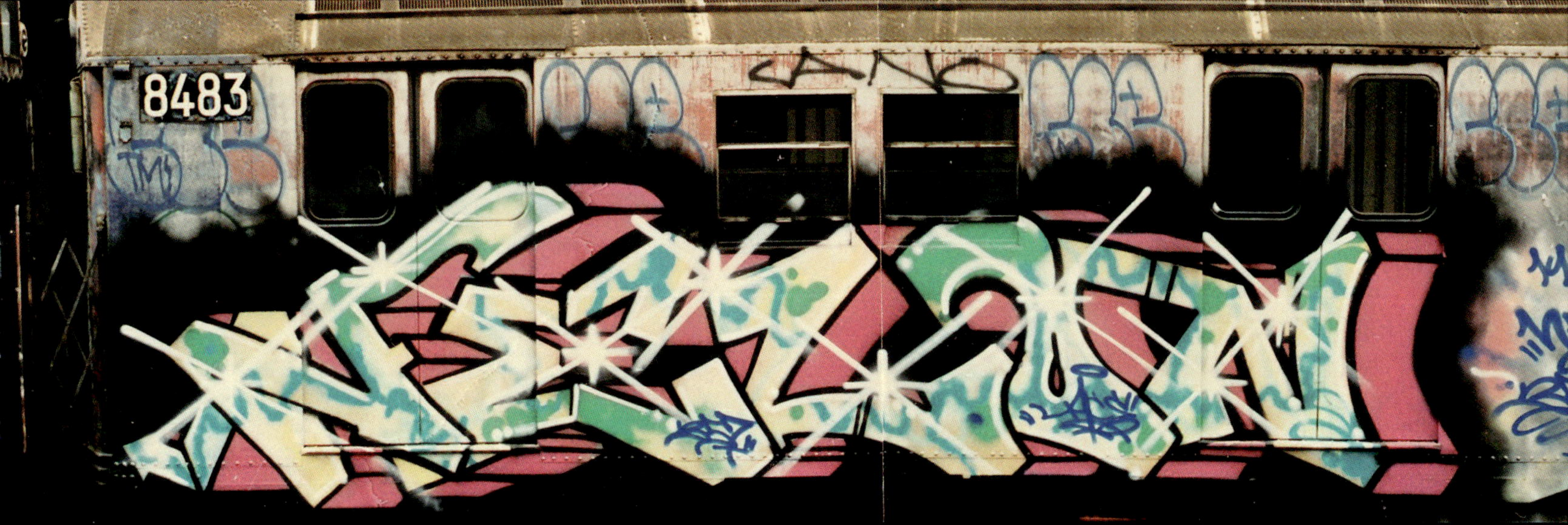

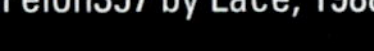

Felon357 by Lace, 1988

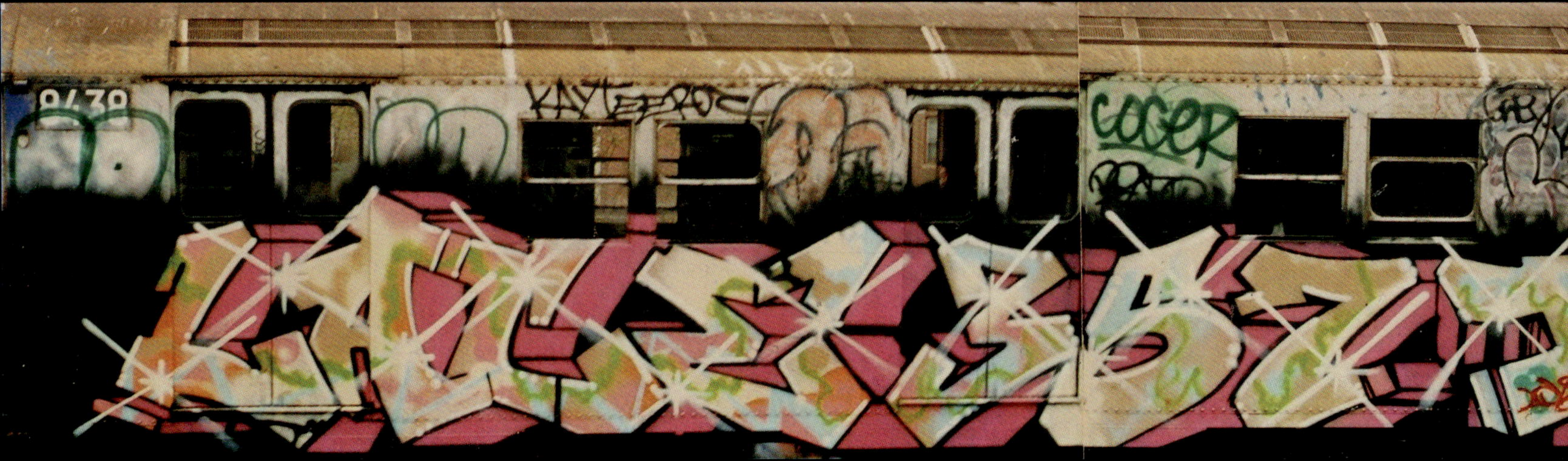

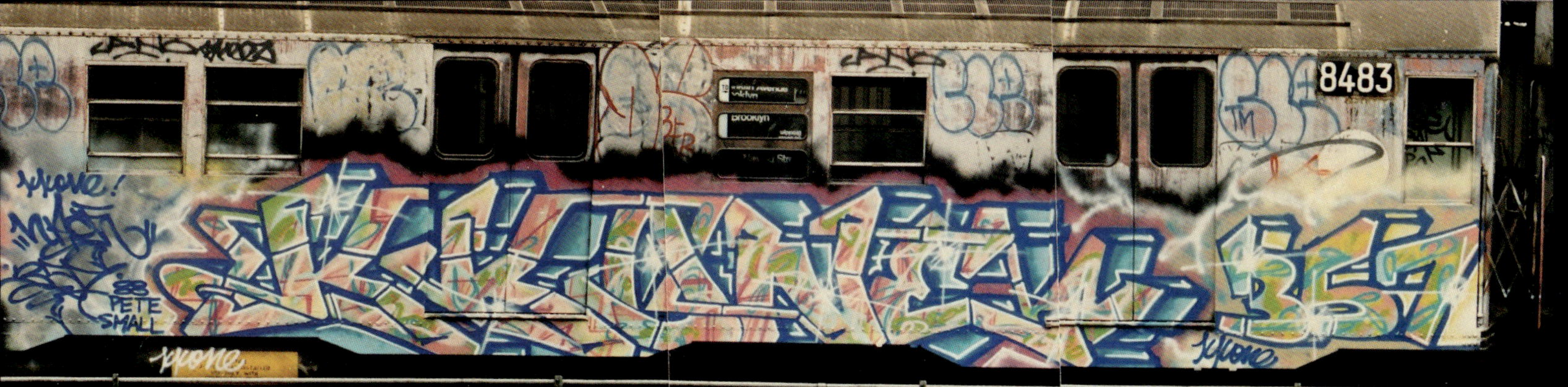

KKONE357, 1988

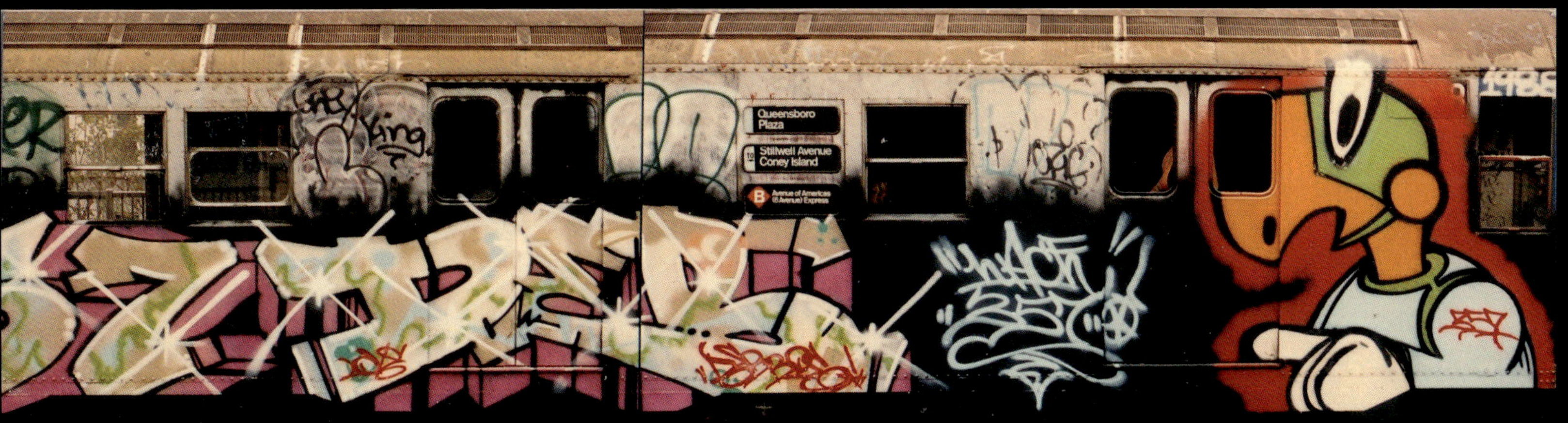

Deb

The first time I hit the Central Park layup I knew it was special. It was a well lit space for top-to-bottoms or window-downs. At first it was real quiet, you could be in there for hours doing whole cars, whatever. There were no police raids and almost no work bums. After a while it got real crazy in there. Writers were showing up from all over the city. I remember one night I did a head count, thirty-seven writers all hitting just two lanes. For most of us it was one big long retirement party.

–Lace357

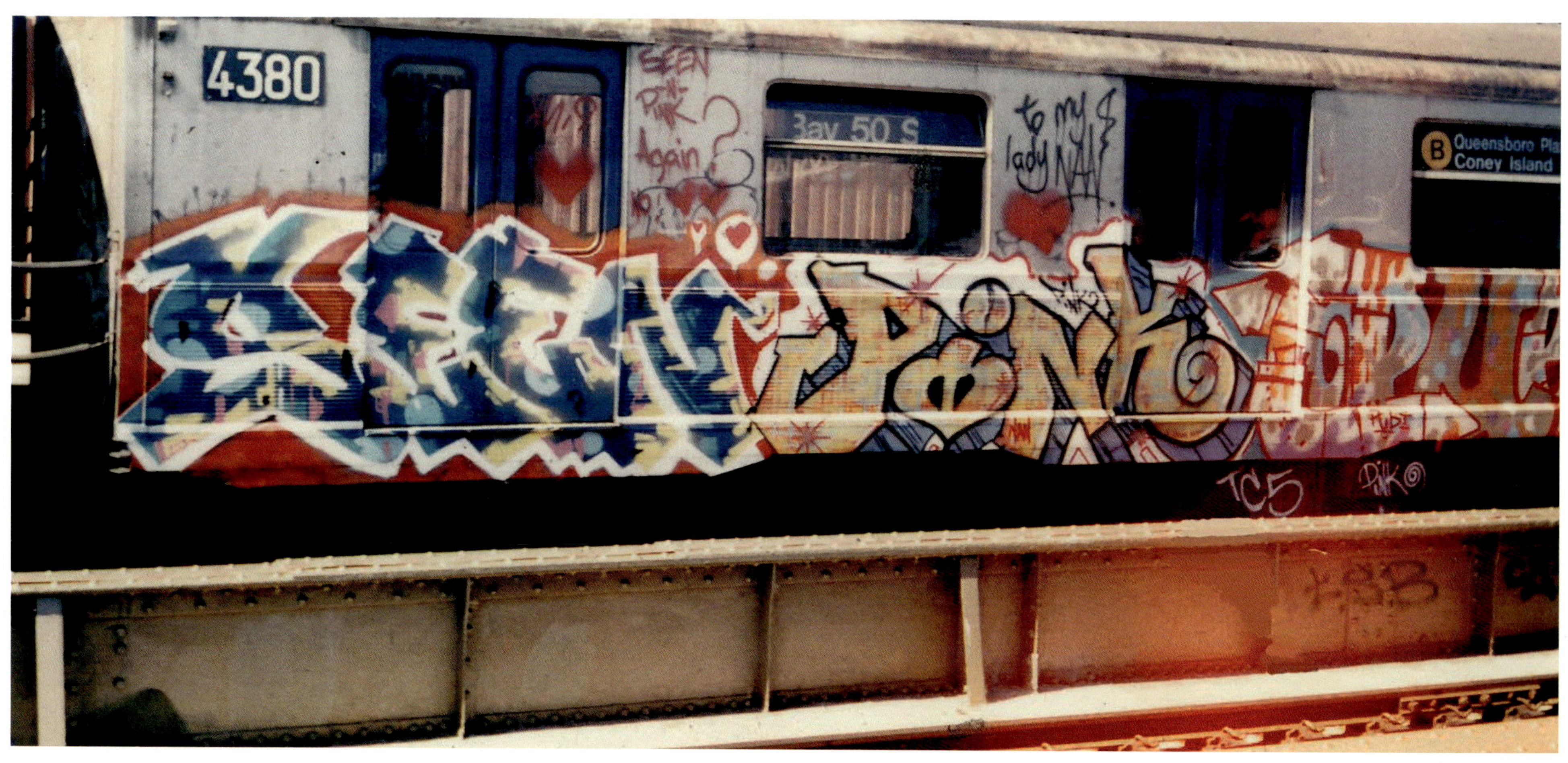

Seen TC5, Lady Pink (Photo courtesy of GKAY)

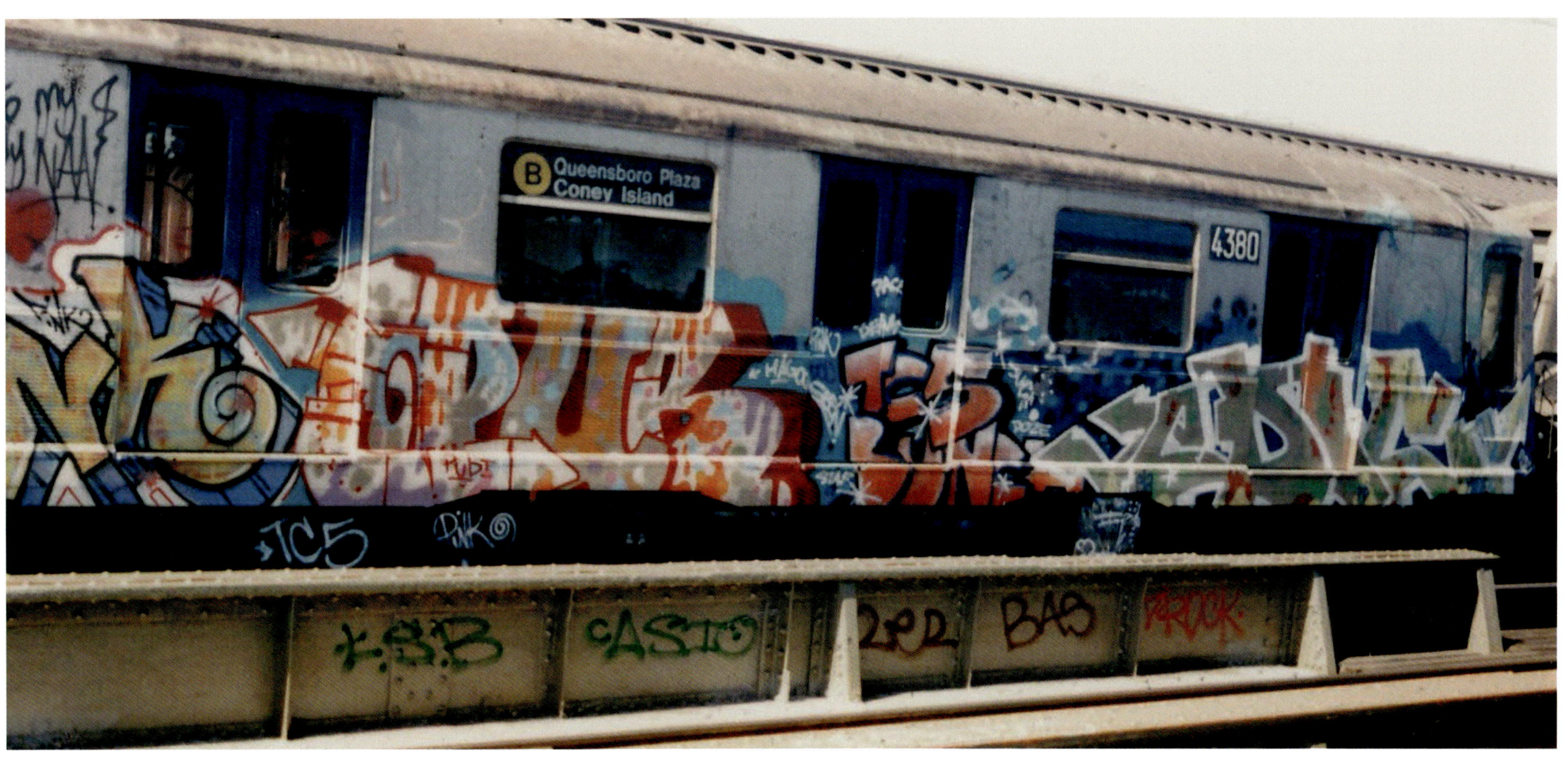

Pub, Doc (Photo courtesy of GKAY)

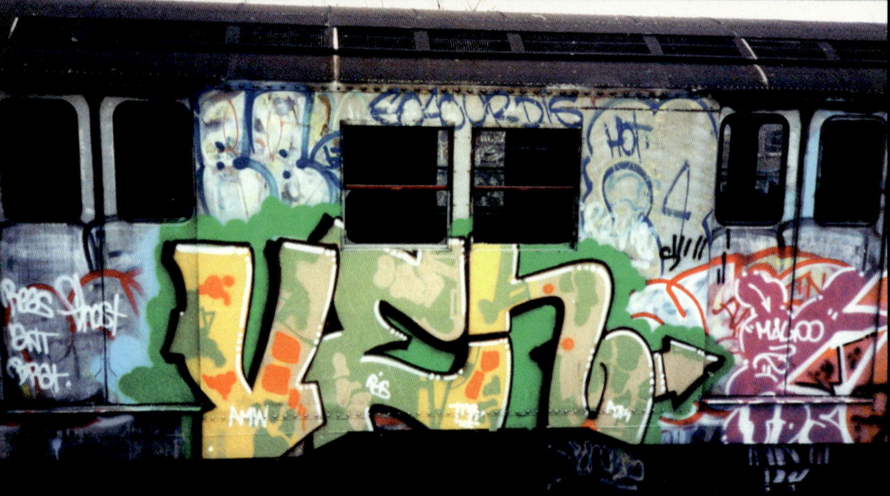

Ven

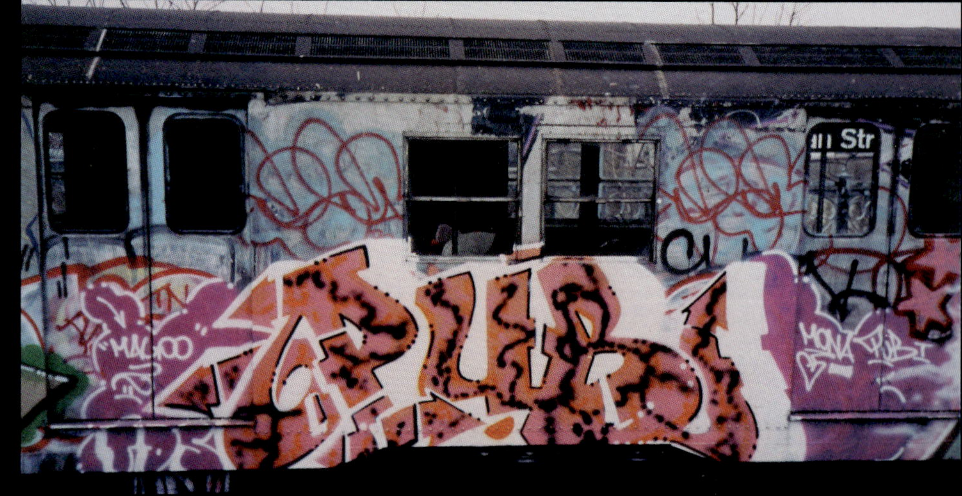

Pub

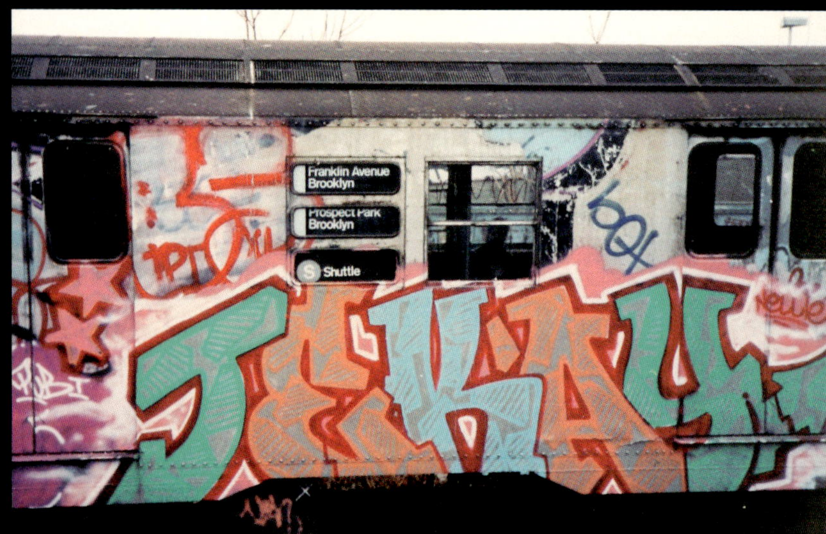

Tekay

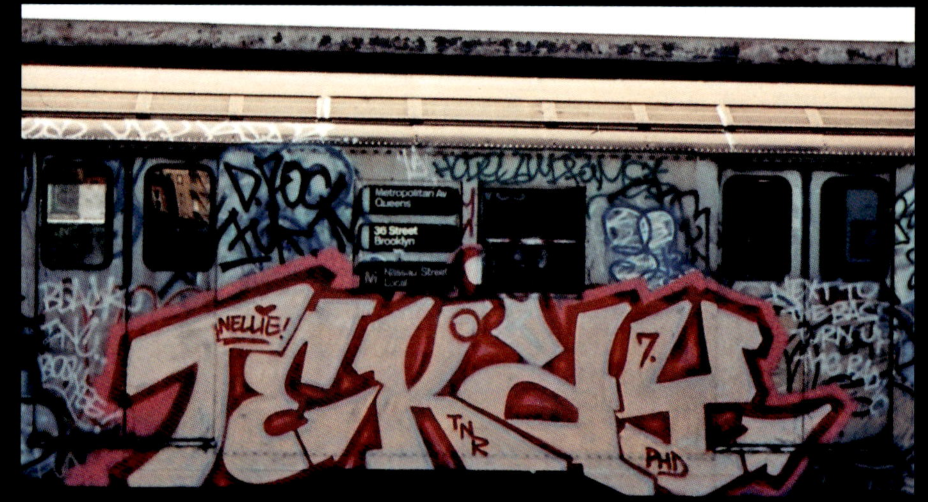

Tekay TNR

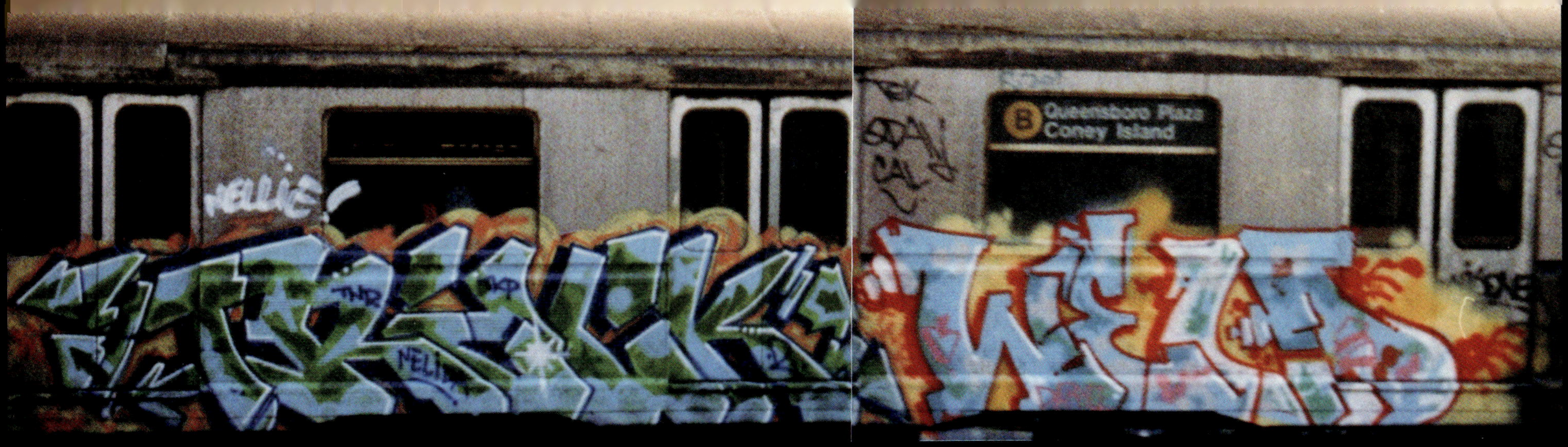

Track2, Weld

I go by the name of Tekay, a.k.a. Track2. I am the prez of The Nations Respected (TNR). I started writing in 1979. I've always been an all-city writer. My favorite spot to paint was the Franklyn Avenue shuttle in Flatbush, Brooklyn. It was down the street from my crib and the trains got split up and went to other lines twice a week.

–Tekay

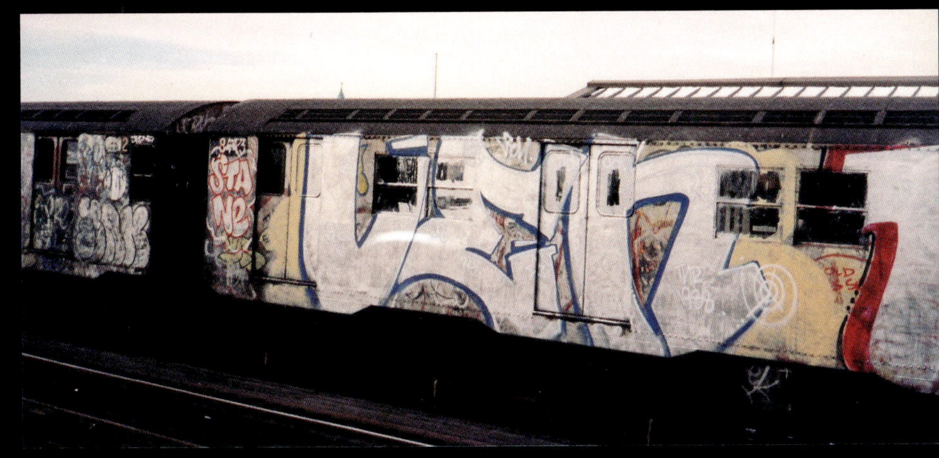

Ven, 1988

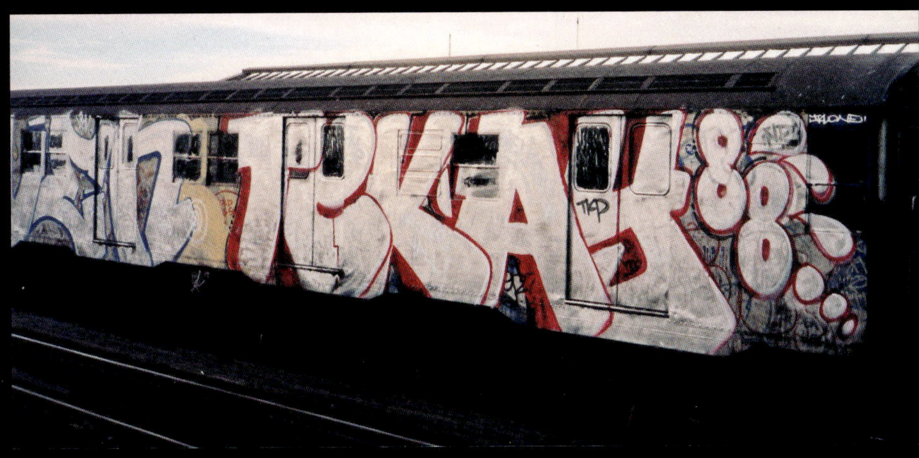

Tekay, 1988

Did you ever wake up and say to yourself, "What a great day to go to a train yard!"? No? Well, I have. Racking paint, getting Jiffs, and taking long train rides to your destination. That is until you realize some bus routes are much quicker! So now what? You're by the yard of choice. Let the theme music start playing in your head. Boom, bash, bam, pop. Open a can and there's your name. This process continues for quite some time throughout the MTA playground.

–Neo-one

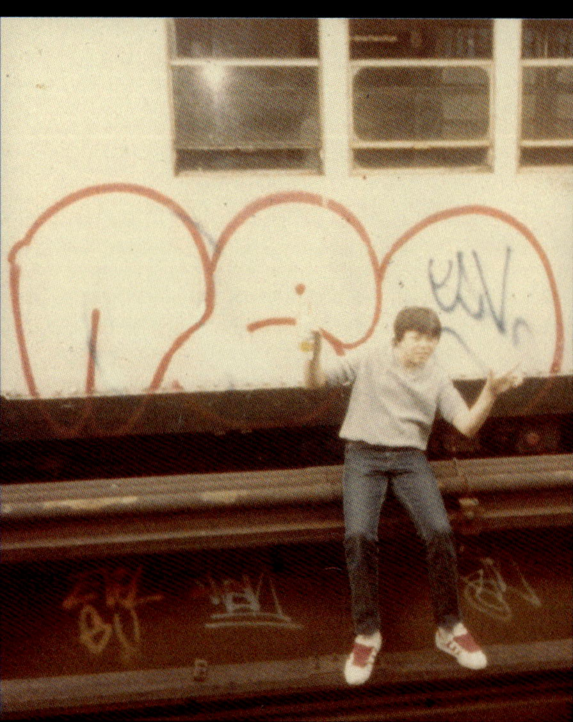

Cav tags up in a Neo throw-up

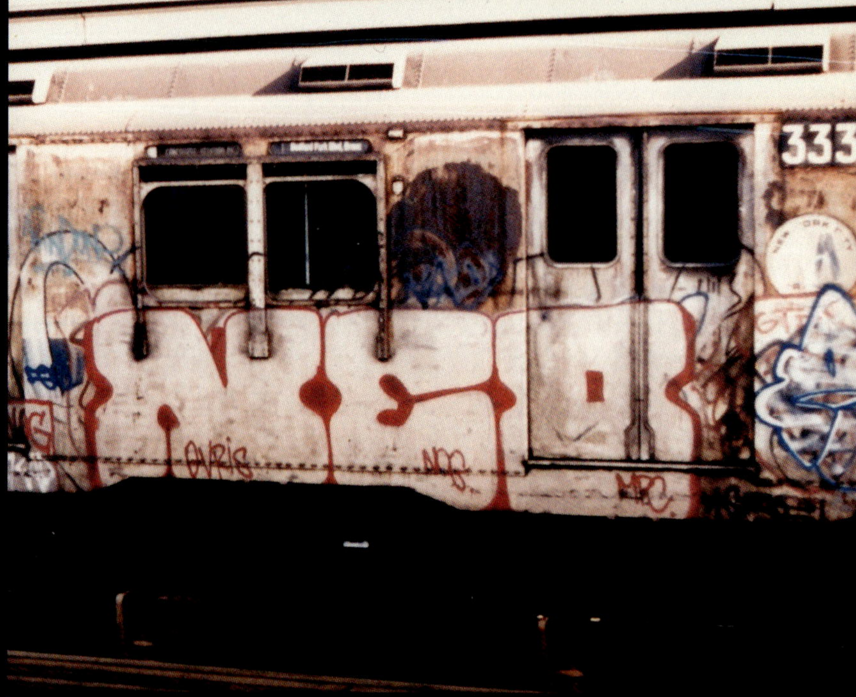

Neo

1986 was an amazing year for Trash/NYHC music and the inspiration for me to take hold of a spray can! The bands included The Crumbsuckers, Celtic Frost, SamHain, Underdog, Leeway, and Slayer. Also there was Agnostic Front's second LP, *Cause for Alarm,* and The Cro Mags' *The Age of Quarrel* (demo only!). And last but not least, Voivod! It was the artwork of their drummer, Away, that lit a fuse and ignited the emotions of a vandal in me. Also, Sean Taggart's album and flyer art was reaching out to my inner mind, telling me to put it on trains and walls. I felt I was in a race with myself. I needed to get my name across and fast. SMOG!! Everything about it spells vandalism. Nothing hip hop or stylish about it. Boy, did I hate hip hop. All of it, from the gazelles to the Adidas. Breakdancing, you say? How about breaking windows. I had a lot of aggression then. Teen angst? Maybe rageing hate! I wanted to be a Storm Trooper of Destruction in the graffiti world. I wanted to be the anti Wild Style. A platform for my music to show. Feelings I couldn't get from just seeing these bands. I needed to paint it, kind of like Caine 1's (RIP) *Welcome to Hell!* To hell and back! I say! Each of my O faces showed it—my ever changing moods. Thank you to Quik RTW and O.E for inspiration. Thank heavens I met like minded people like Roar, K-PRO (Iron Gang crew, ROT crew, Reign of Terror), who jump started me into a life of crime. Then later on Fayde MPC, Chino BYI, my Brothers (RIS crew), Ghost, Reas, Ven, Dutch (RIP), Neo, Storm, DM, EA, JA, and the mighty Cavs who showed me so much. I'm eternally grateful to all.

–Smog ROT

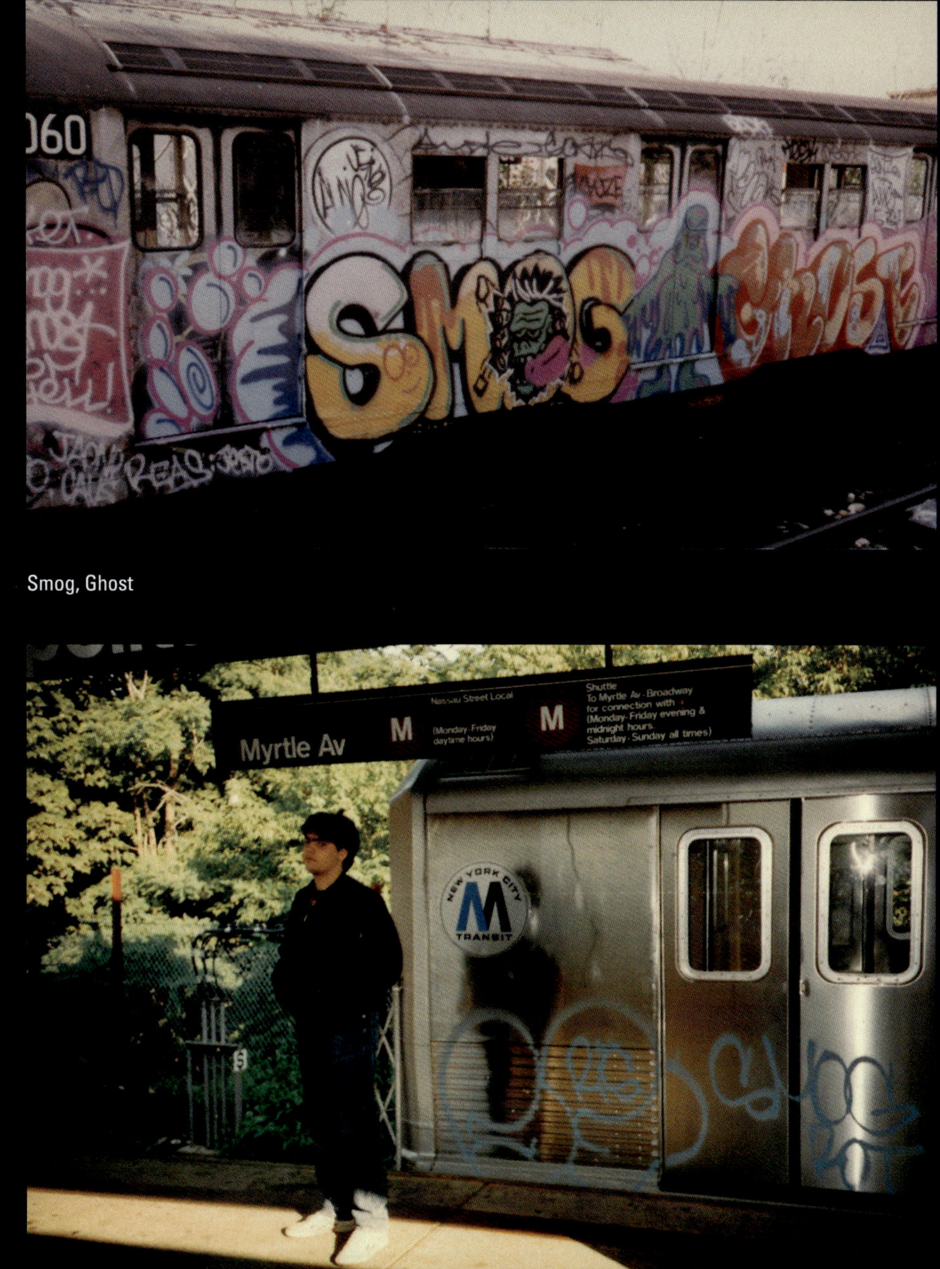

Smog, Ghost

Clean and mean, Smog one, RIS Crew, Queens

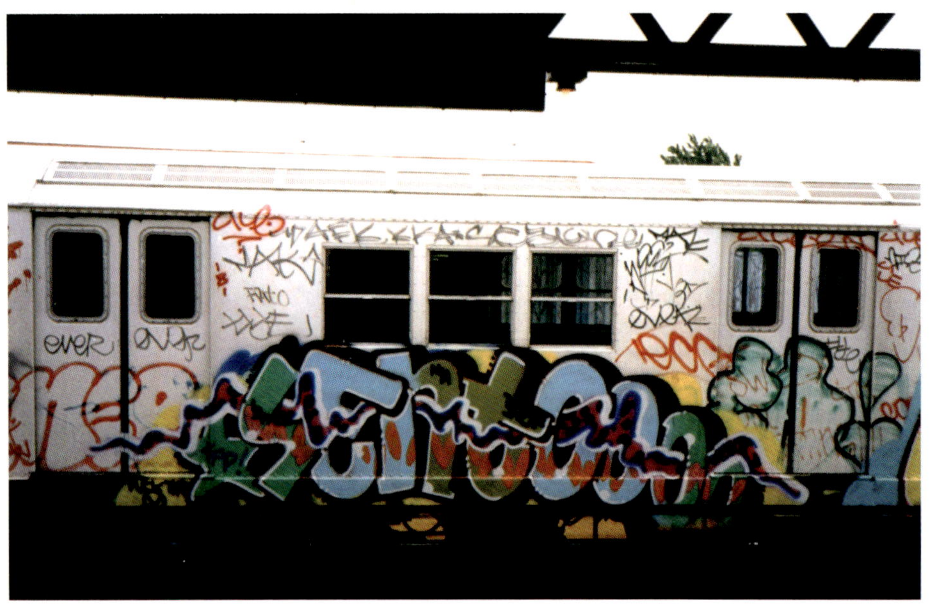

Sento, 1988

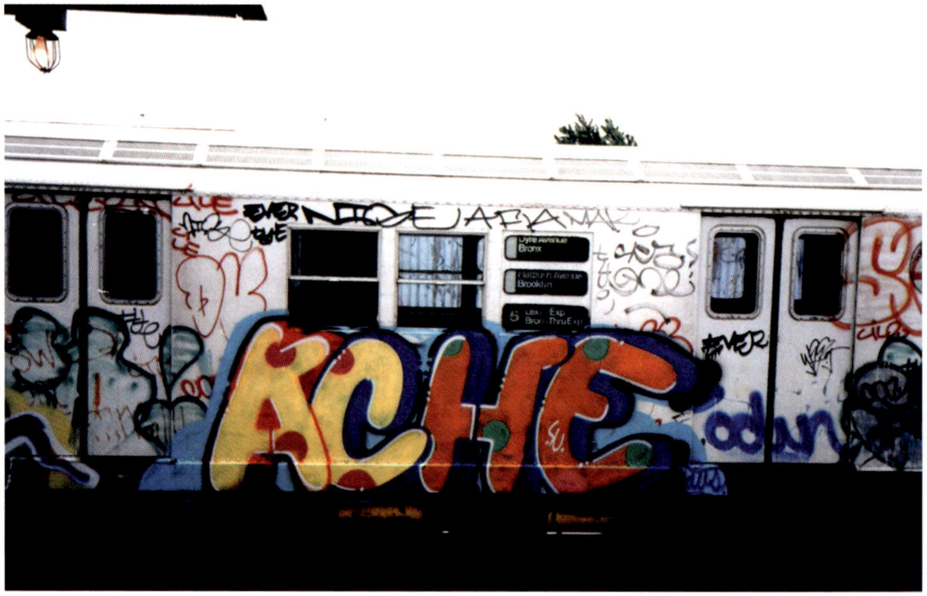

Ache, 1988

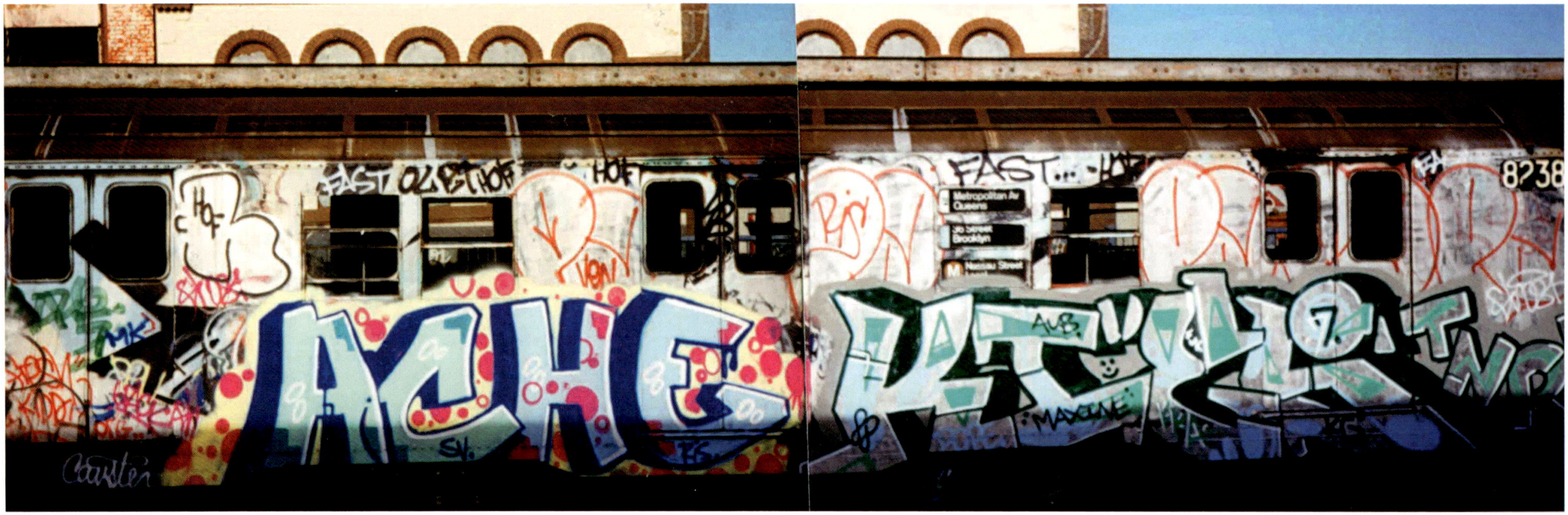

Ache, Kies, 1988

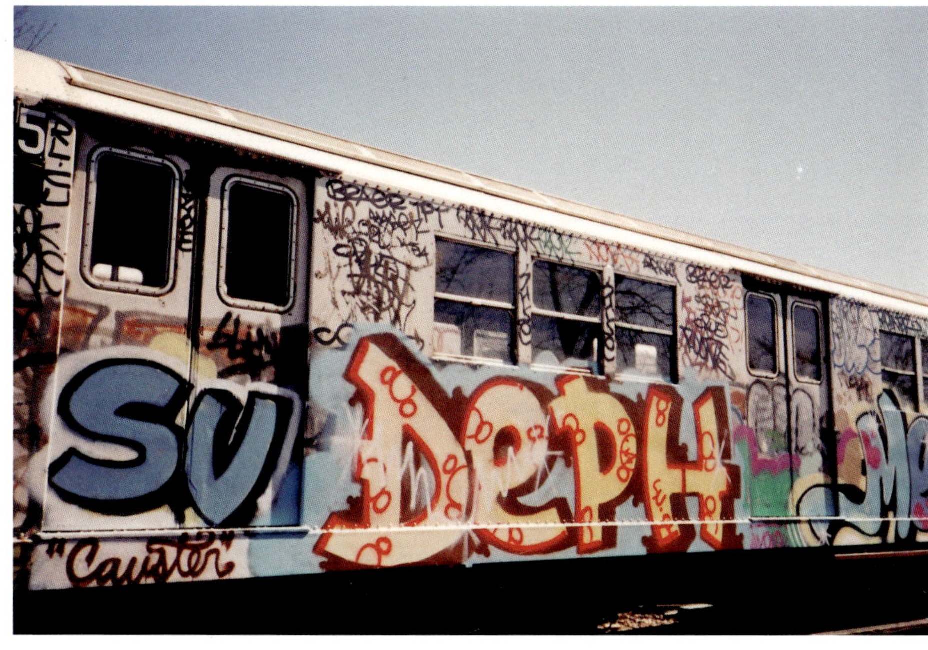

Deph SV, 1988

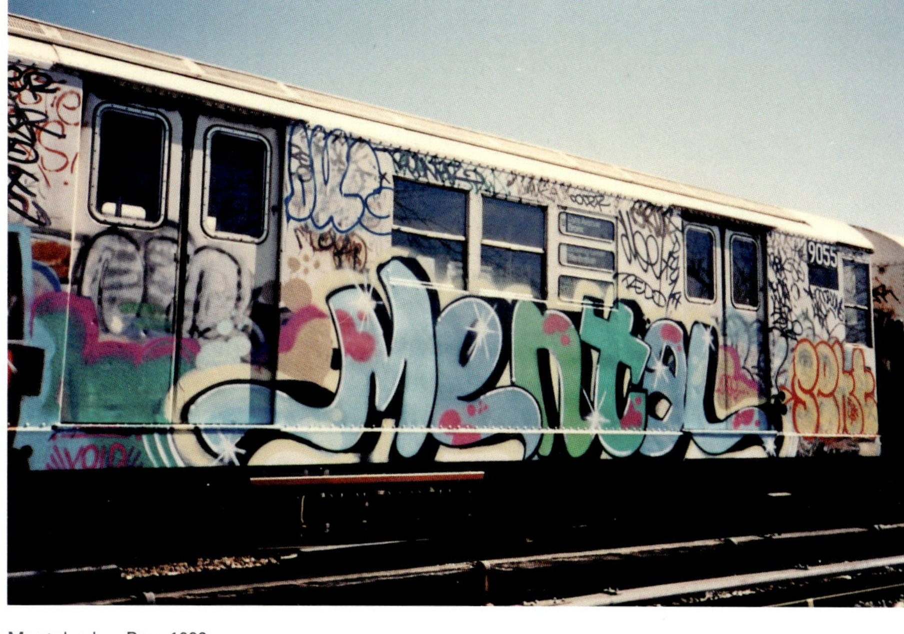

Mental, a.k.a. Dee, 1988

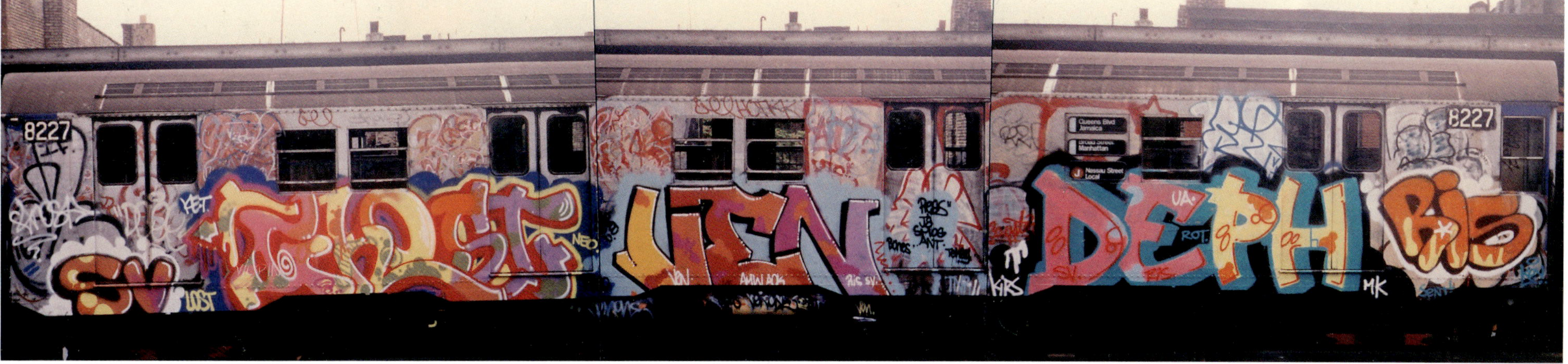

Ghost, Ven, Deph, 1988

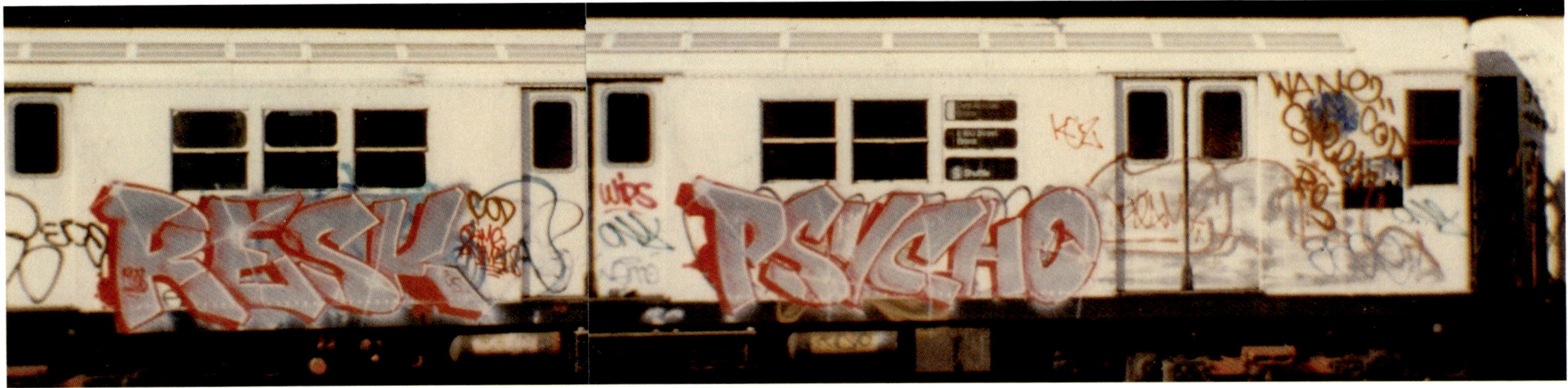

Resk, Psycho IBM, 1988

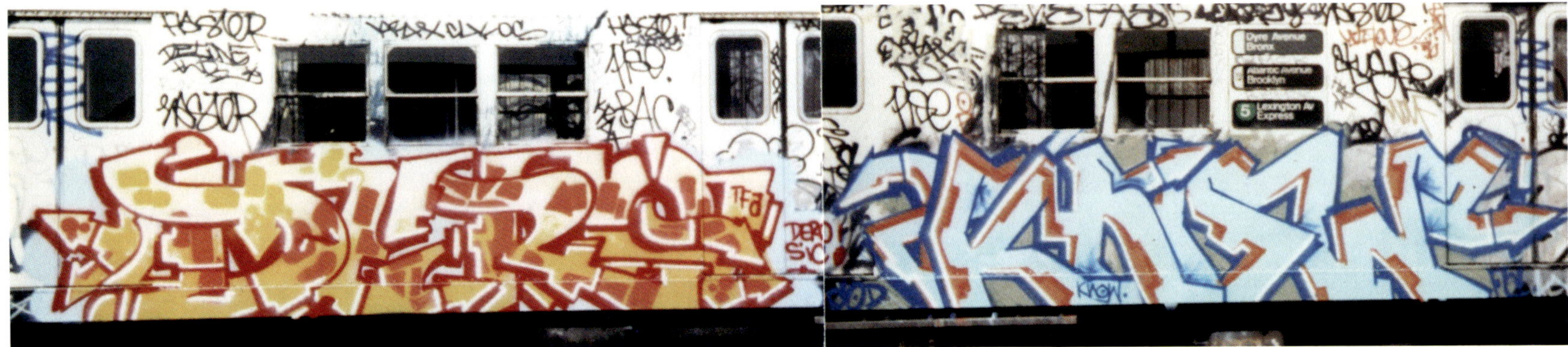

Dero, Know

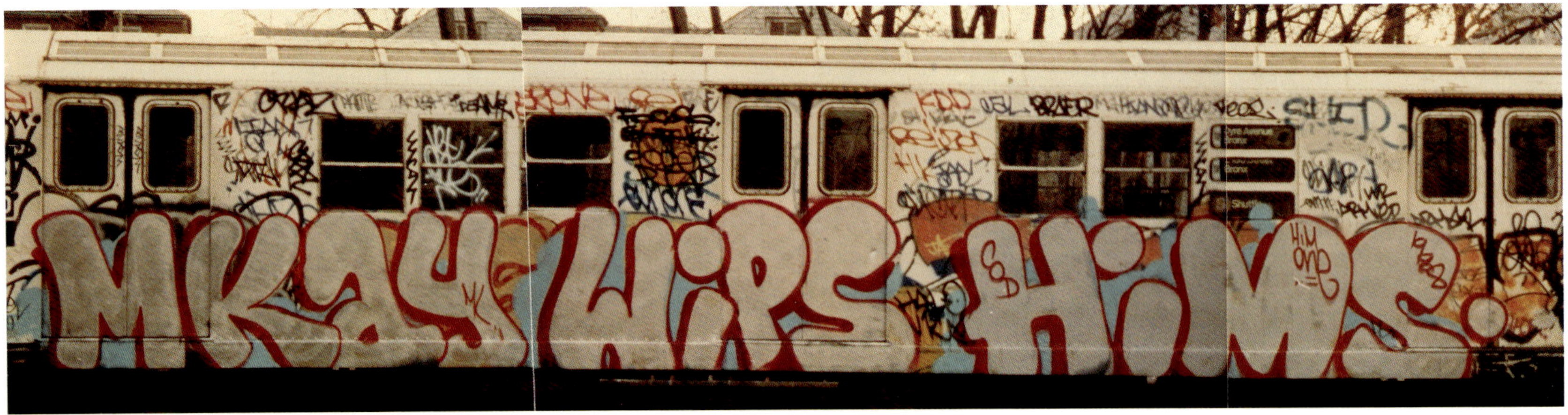

Mkay, Wips, Hims, 1988

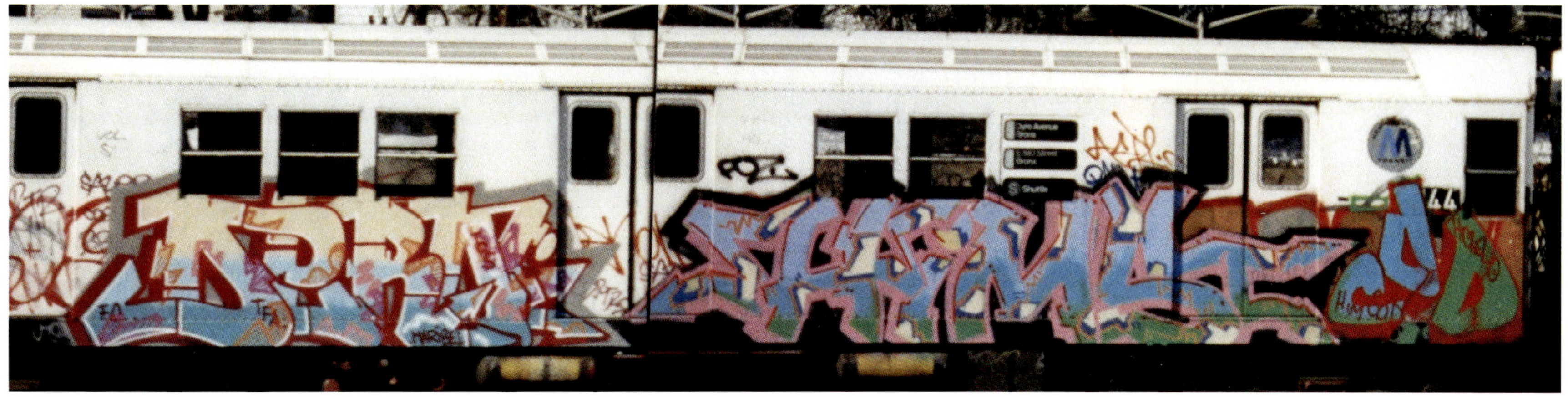
Dero, Hims COD

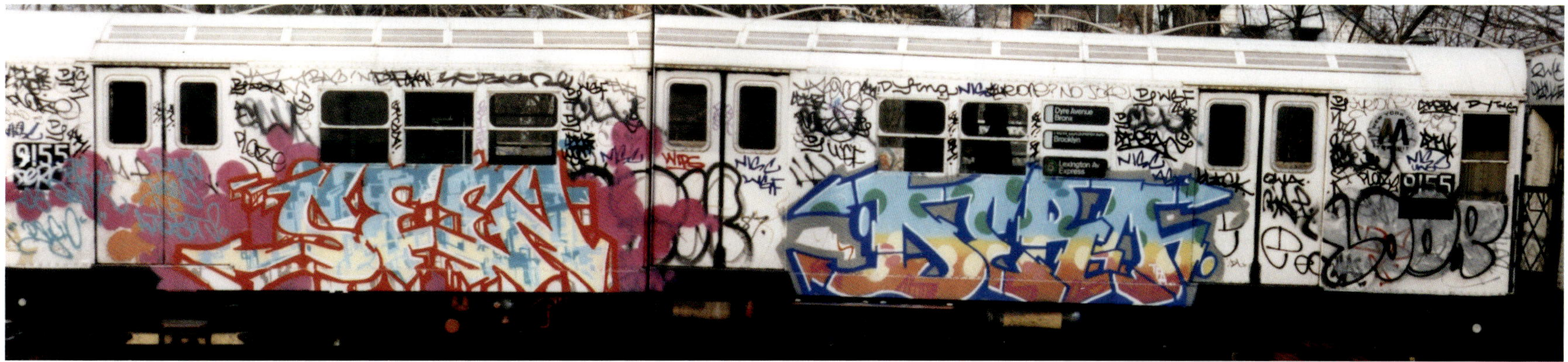
Seen TC5, Dero

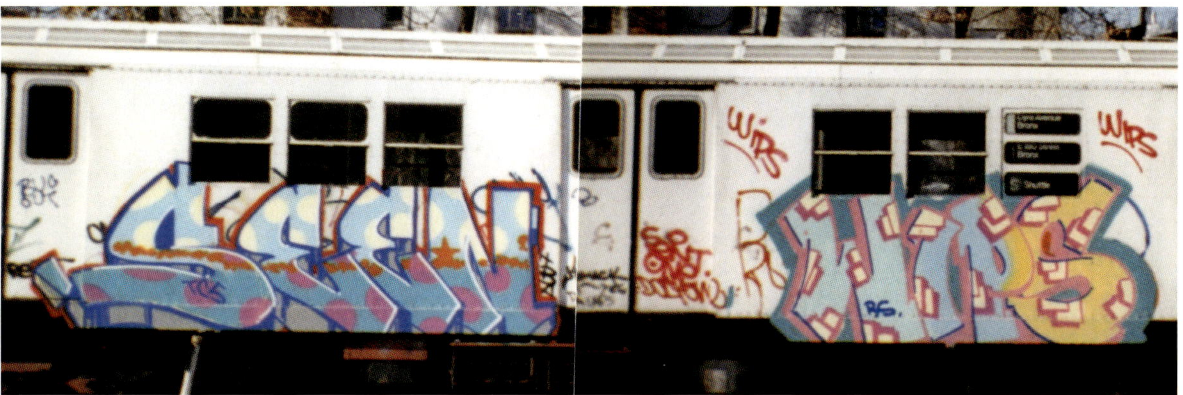
Seen TC5, Wips

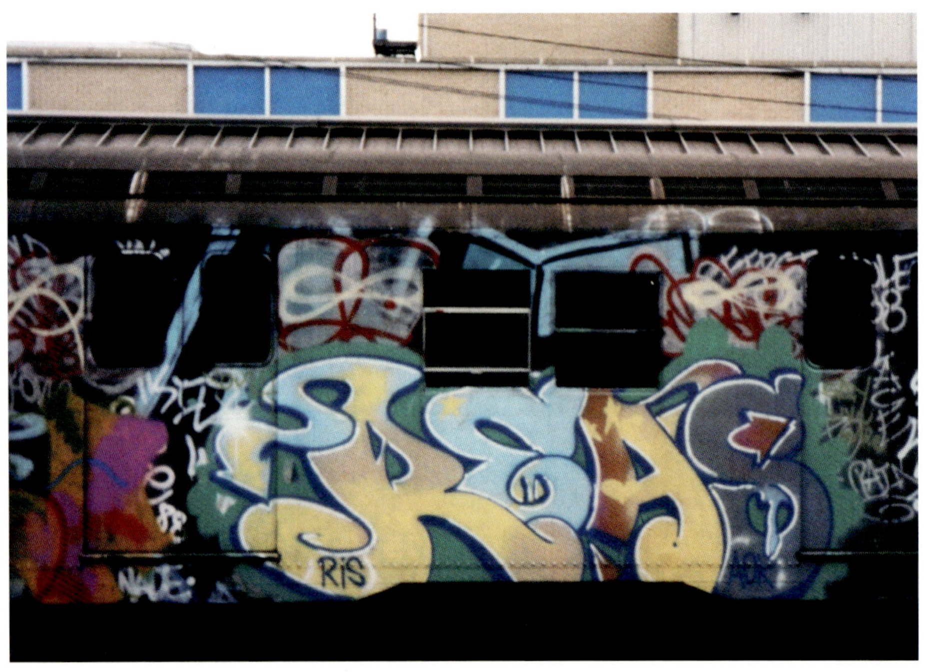

Reas AOK

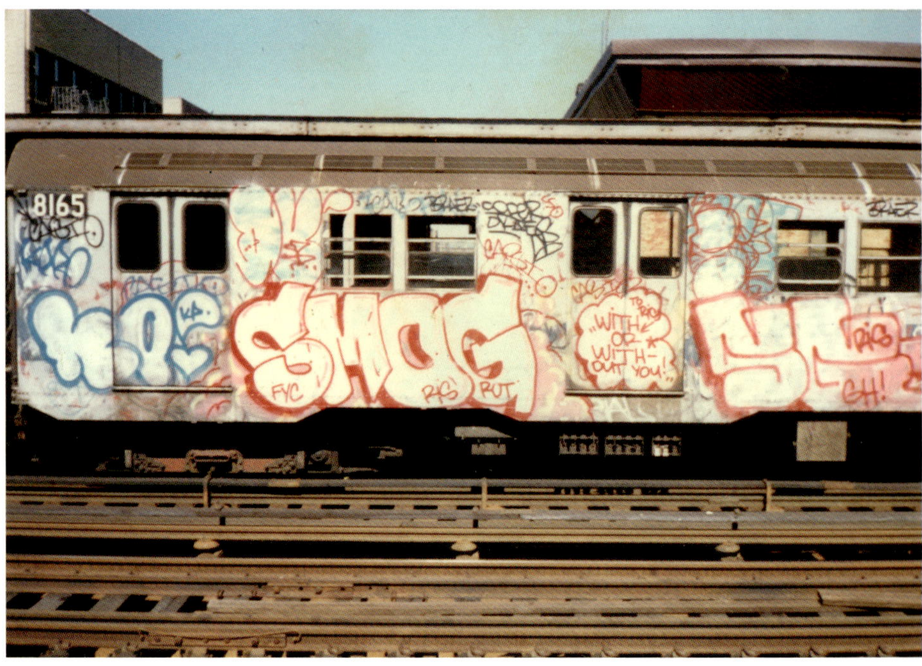

Kpro, Smog

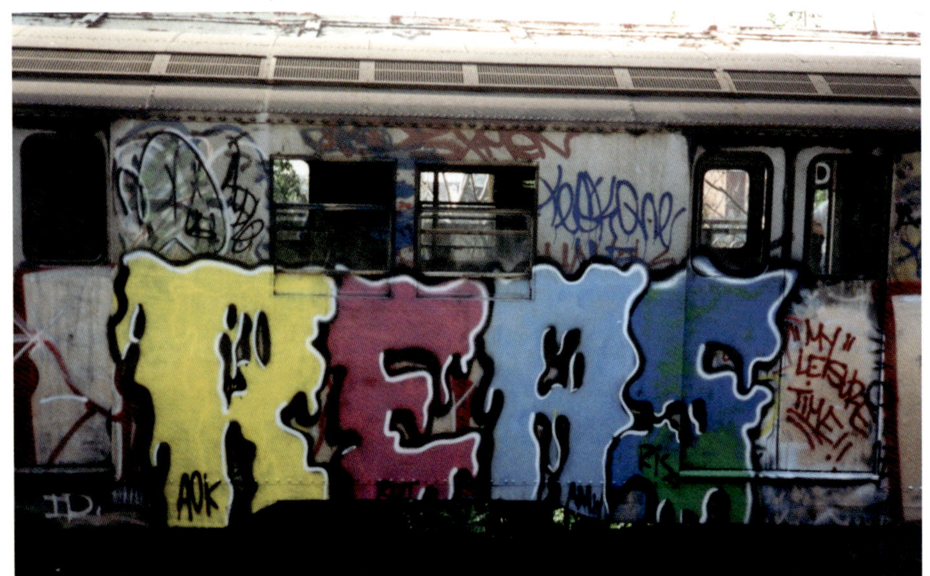

Reas

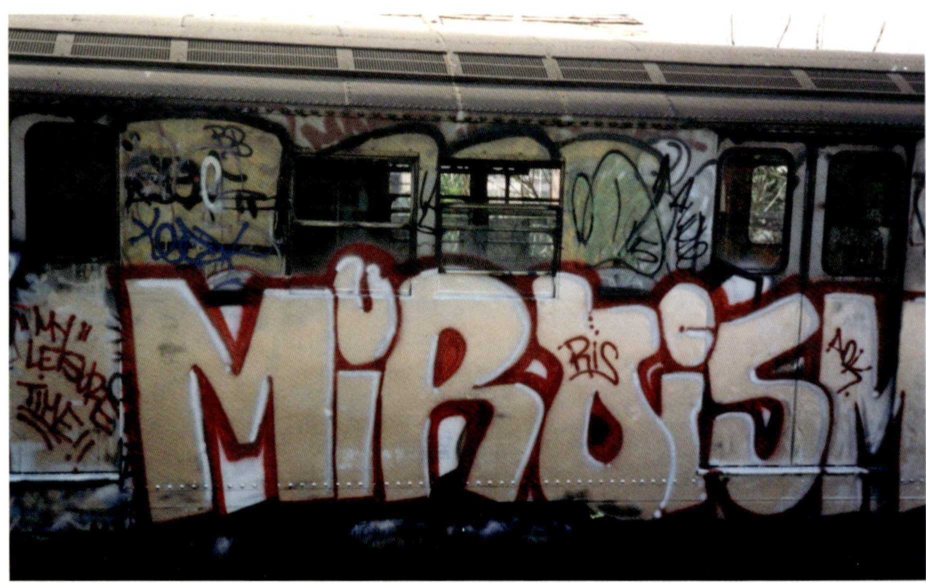

Miroism

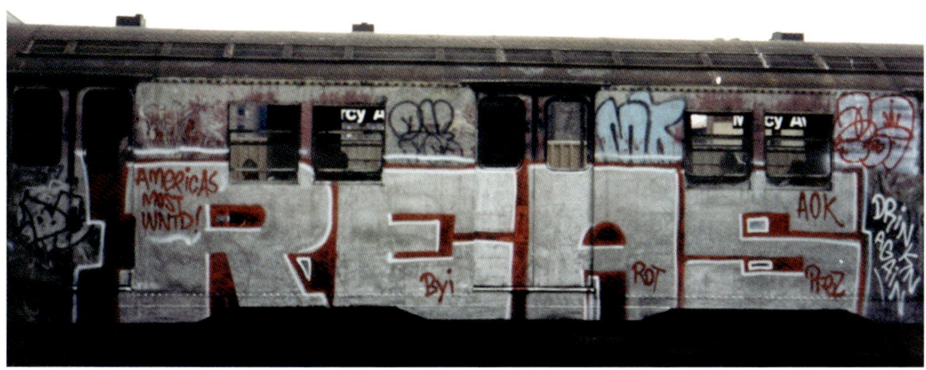

Reas

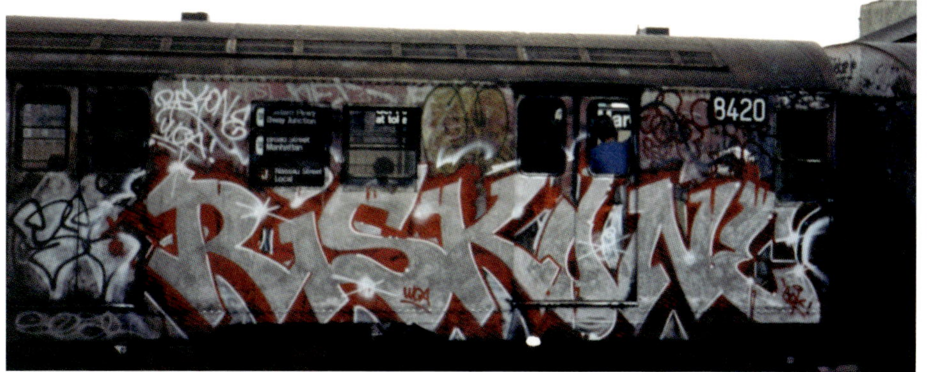

Riskone WCA

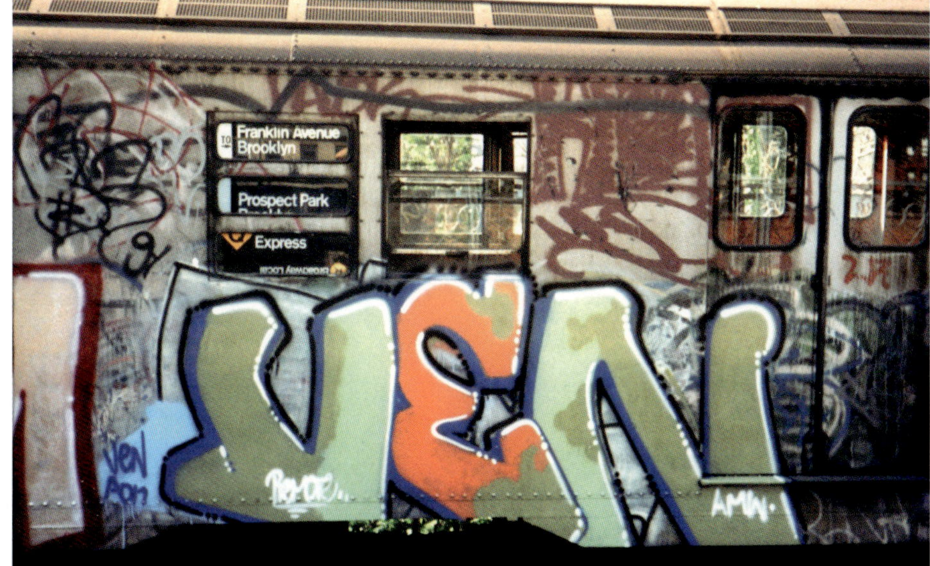

Ven

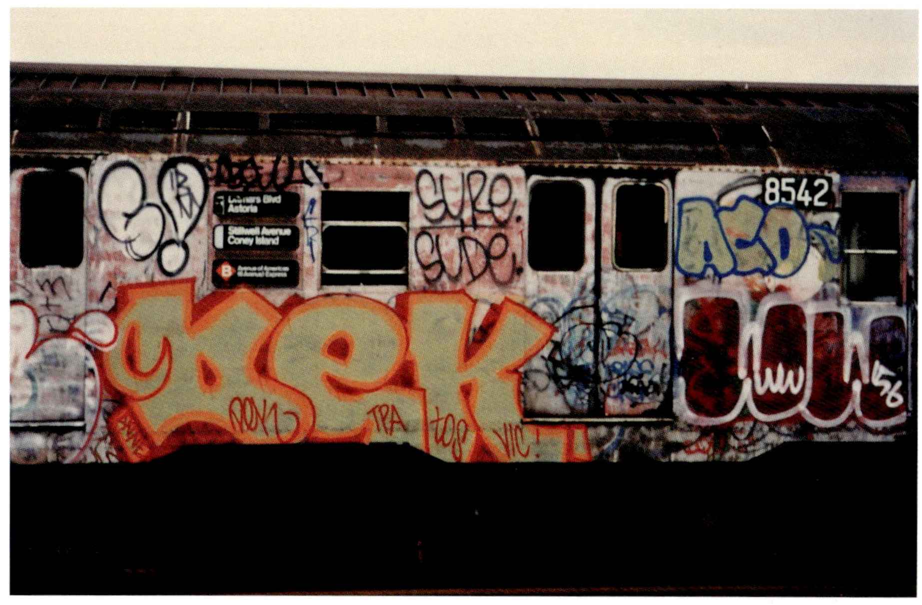

Dek

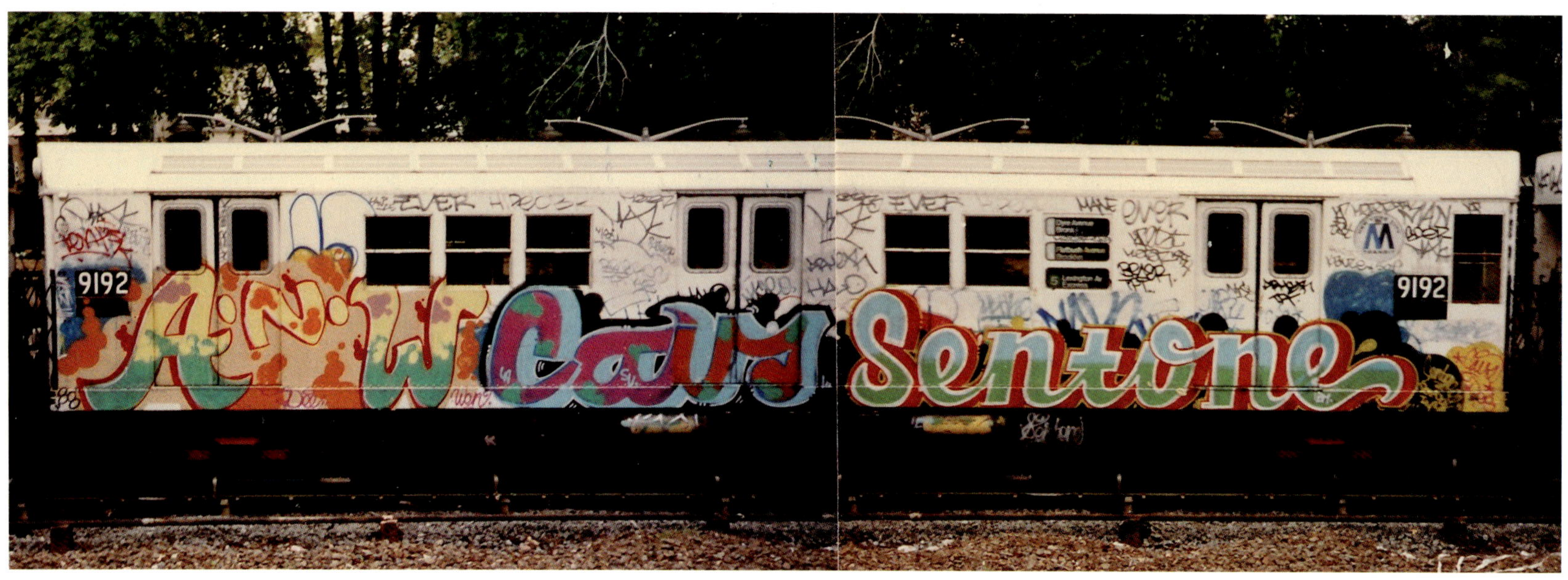

A-n-W by Dee, Cavs, Sentone

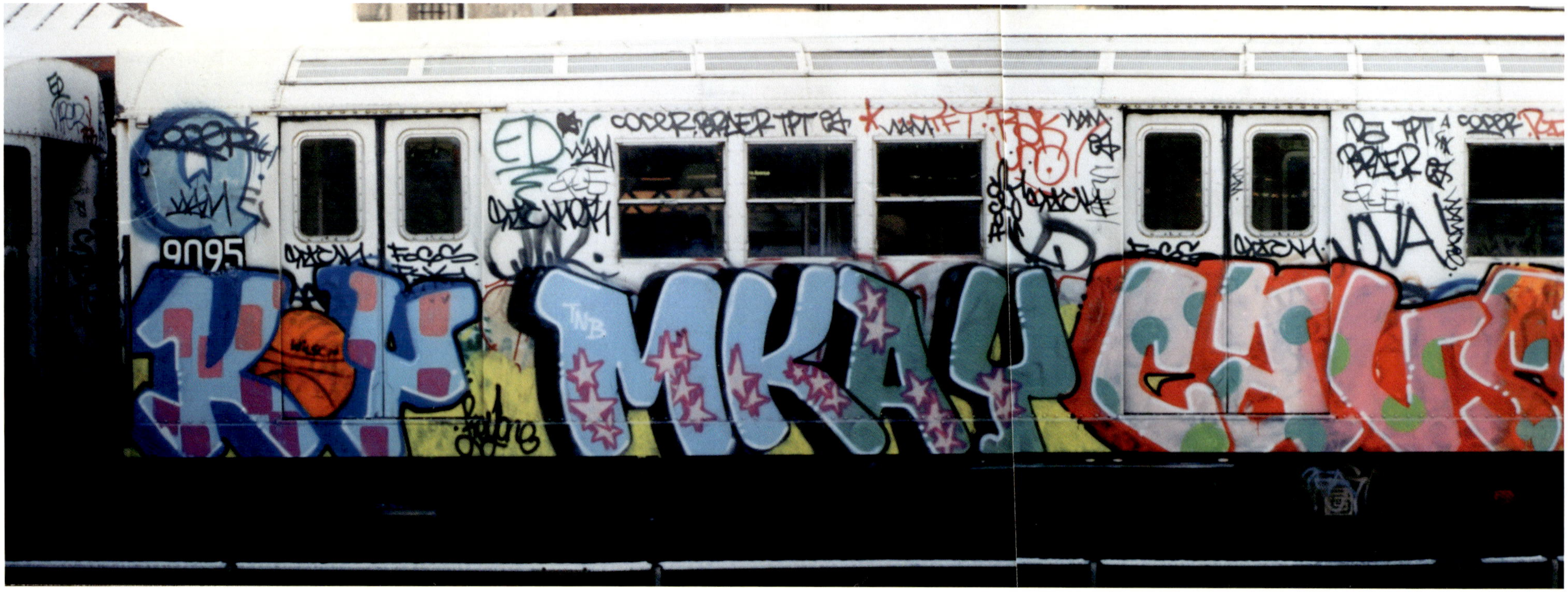

Key, Mkay, Cavs

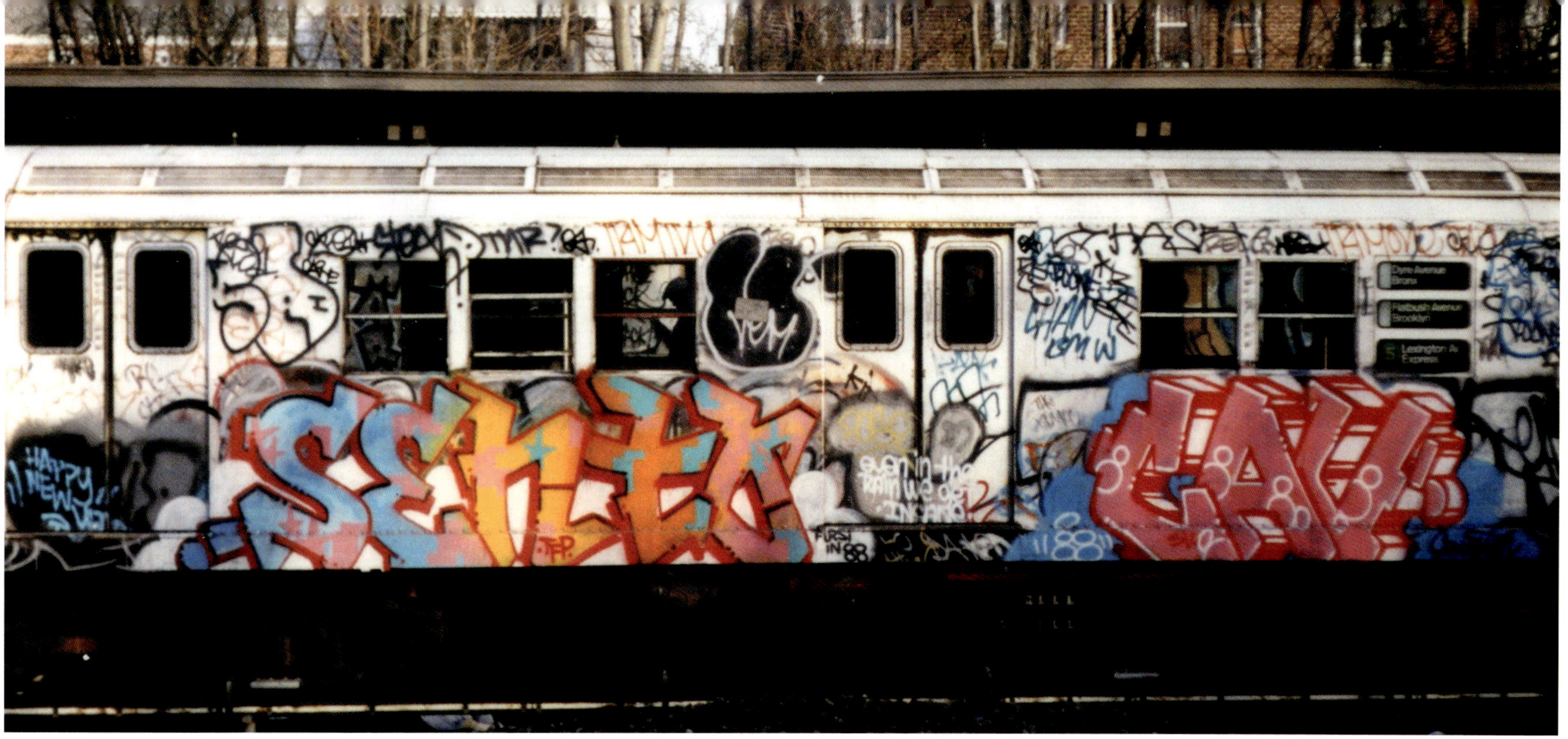

Sento, Cav, 1988

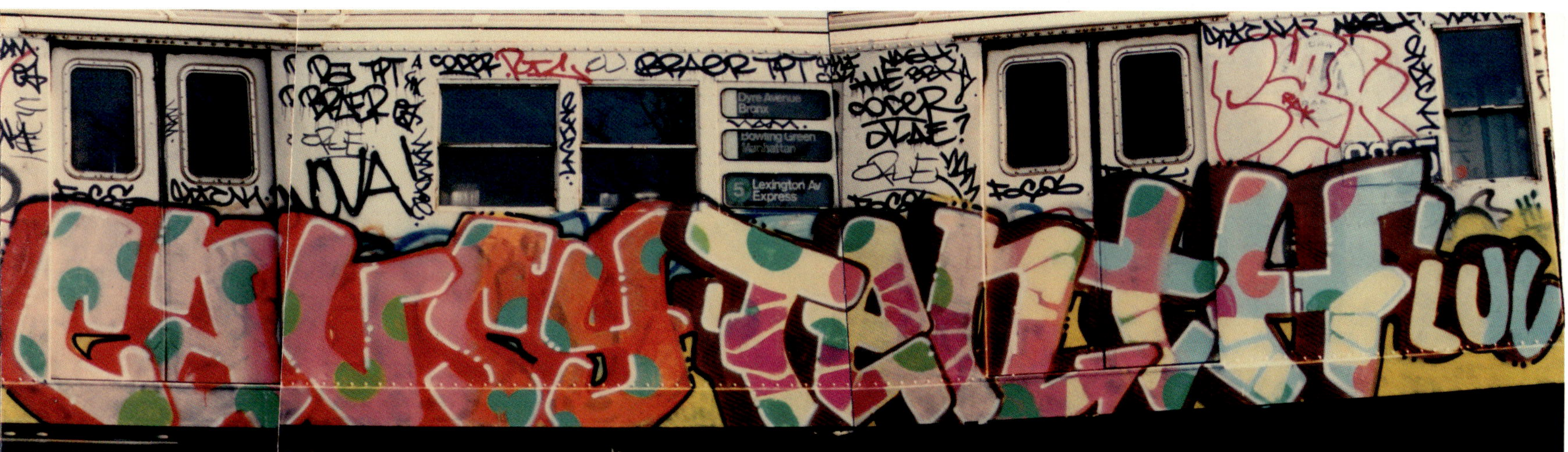

Tenth'Luv

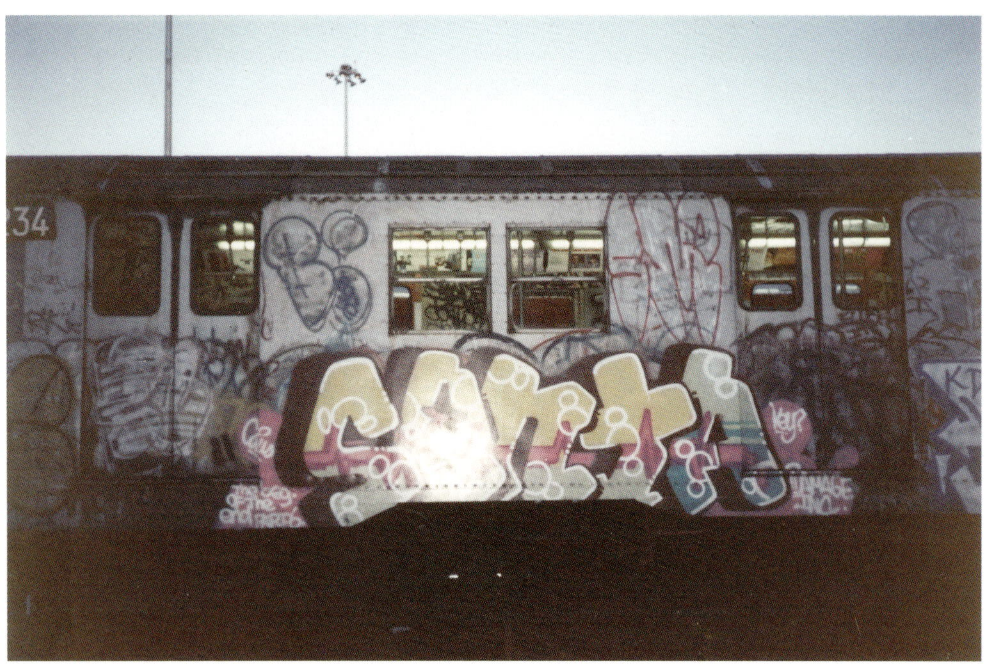

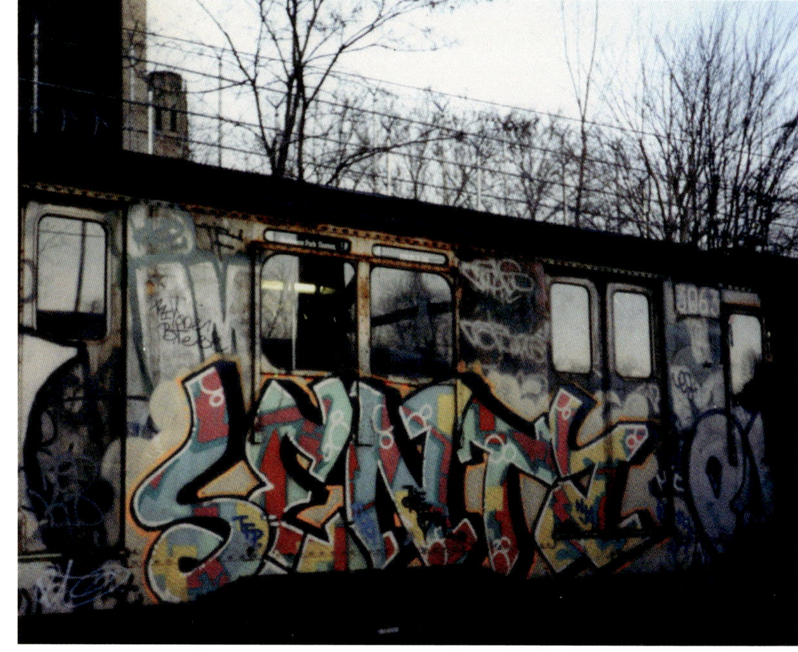

Senta, D Yard at dawn

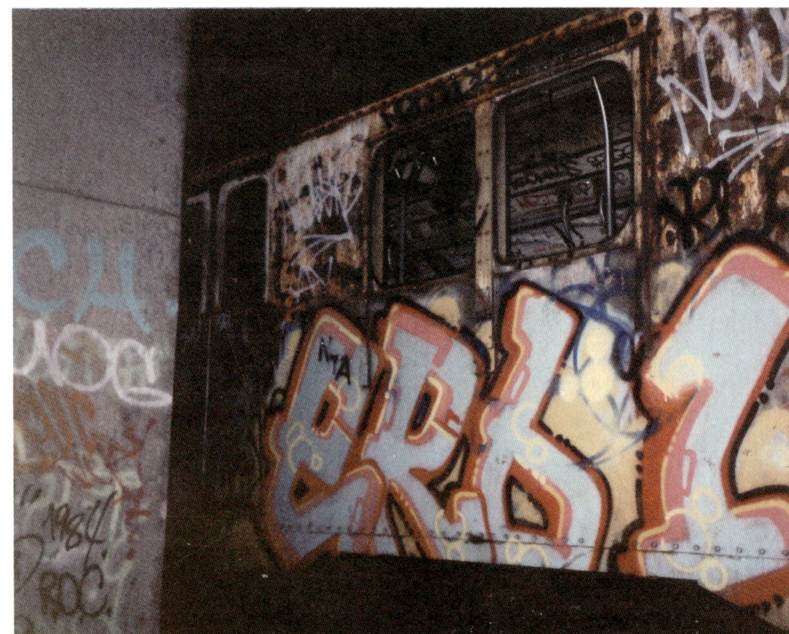

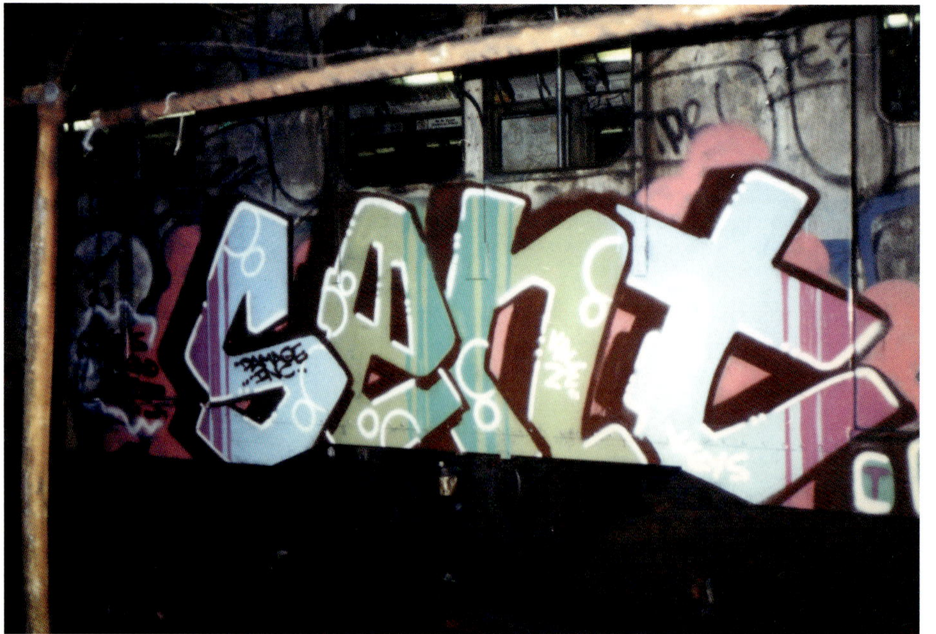

Erb, Pitkin Yard

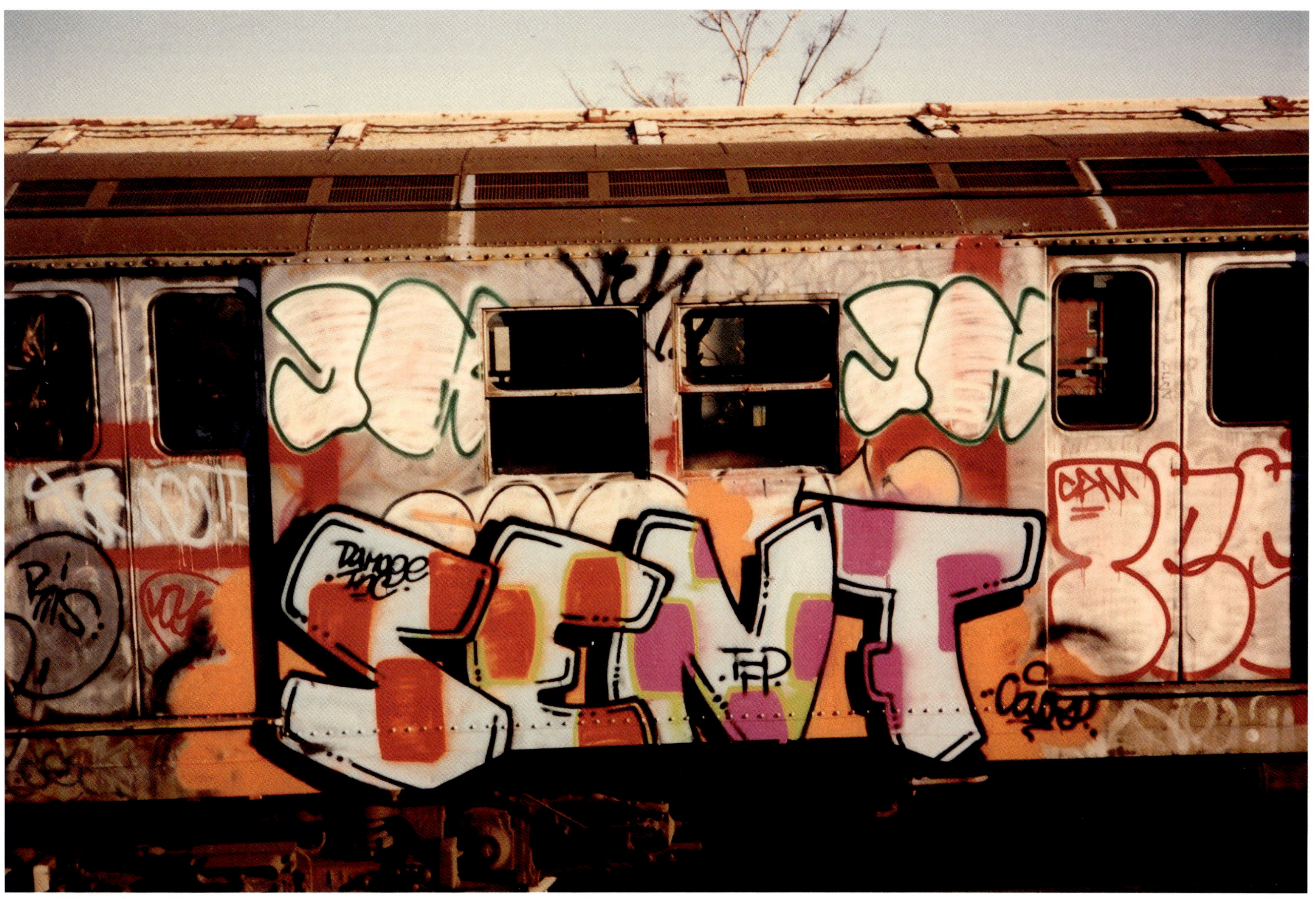

Sent TFP

Sunday 10 AM-ish. Central Park was where we gathered. Rich folks walking their dollar dogs with their million dollar snoots snickering at us. We of the dark camoed-out gear with the backpacks full of spray cans, pockets of fat caps, and clean line Niagara's that were soaked and cleaned the night before. The back pocket. Never a wallet, that shit was in the sock in the shoe on the bottom of the foot positioned just right in case a chase accrued. That pocket gear spot had an up-all-night, sketched out outline on lined school notebook paper. The more faded the blue lines the better. All pockets, every gear spot had a function and you were aware where they all were, including the hammer and shank, just in case. The hatch opened. Like a Central Park magic trick. Right there by the benches in the 70s, the streets that is, if my memory serves me correctly. Eyes peering out: "It's good!" We all had taken turns at some point to be the one to go to the station. Hop was aware of everything that moved on the platform, particularly the Vandal Squad, or even the boys in blue. Once you knew you had none of those eyes on you, then boom, end of station, down the stairs, on the tracks, trooping, eyes adjust (Sento and I used to talk about the adjusting eyes in the dark and a thousand times a thousand such topics, with the elements of the art of scoping out). After a long walk down the tracks, passing rats, and homeless with heroin tracks, and screeching trains with electrical flames that sear the scape like a drape, and up some stairs near a hidden platform. There in the sweet distance, the sound of idling laid-up trains for the weekend. Inside a hidden subterranean grotto under Central Park. These were the letter lines and the crew that I rolled with were Bronx IRT dudes. So we liked the letter lines, but before walking down into this hidden treasure, there was one last thing to do. Up another flight, and another flight, and another. Several stories up old soot-thick fledging stairs to a crack of light and a handle and a twist. The hatch opens, and opened up to a sidewalk level view of Central Park, with the horns and the city and the towers up south of us. All alive and vibrant. A whistle from your homeboys to signal that all is good on the outside. Their spot scoped and secure and we disappear, pre-NY fear as the rich city folks look and sneer. On that day I did an Isue not a Sear with a Damp (Sento) whole car. I believe we did the first whole train on the letter lines that day. Not on an IRT, that had been done many many suns before this day of Sunday fun. Whole car art. Mission done.

–Sear

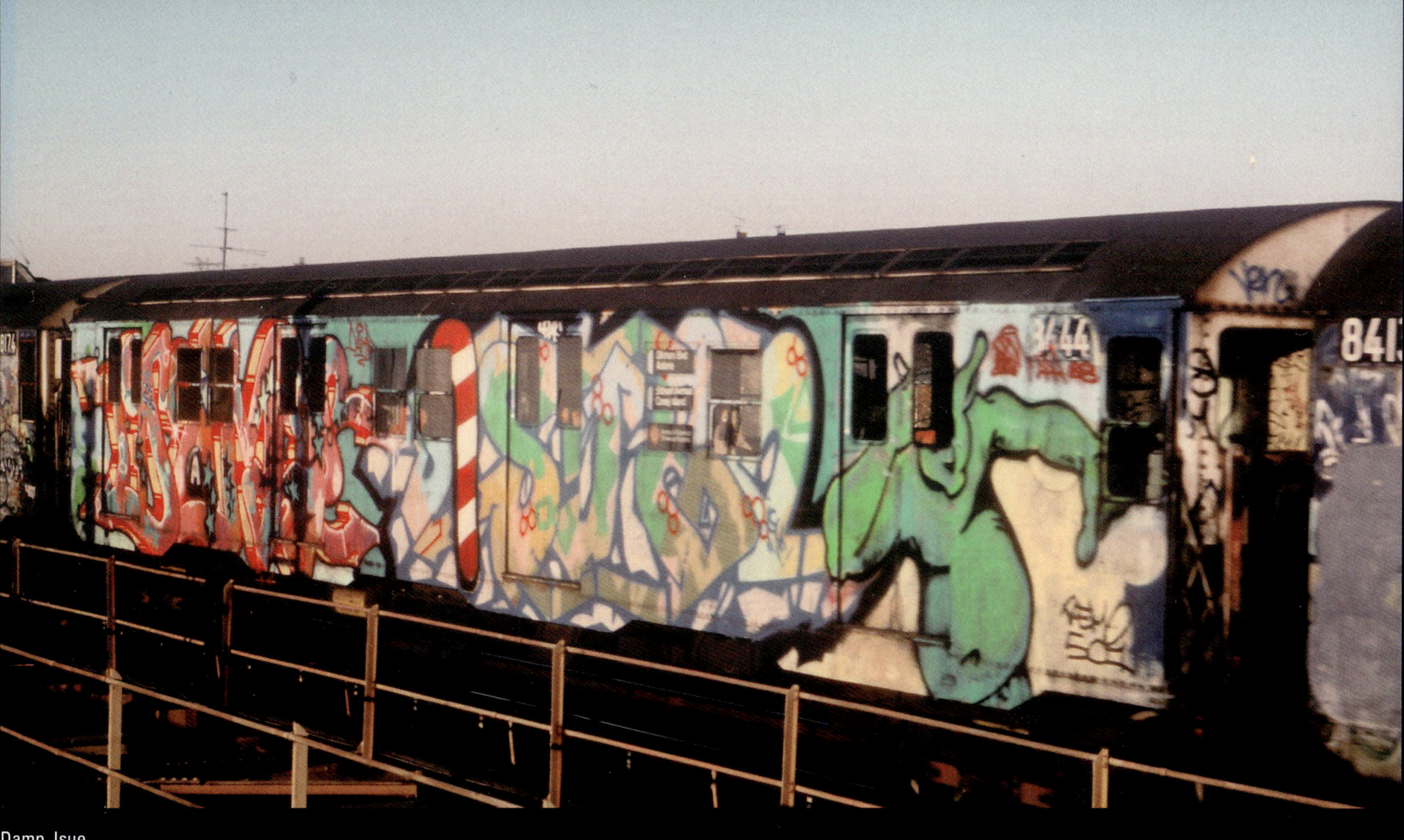

Damp, Isue

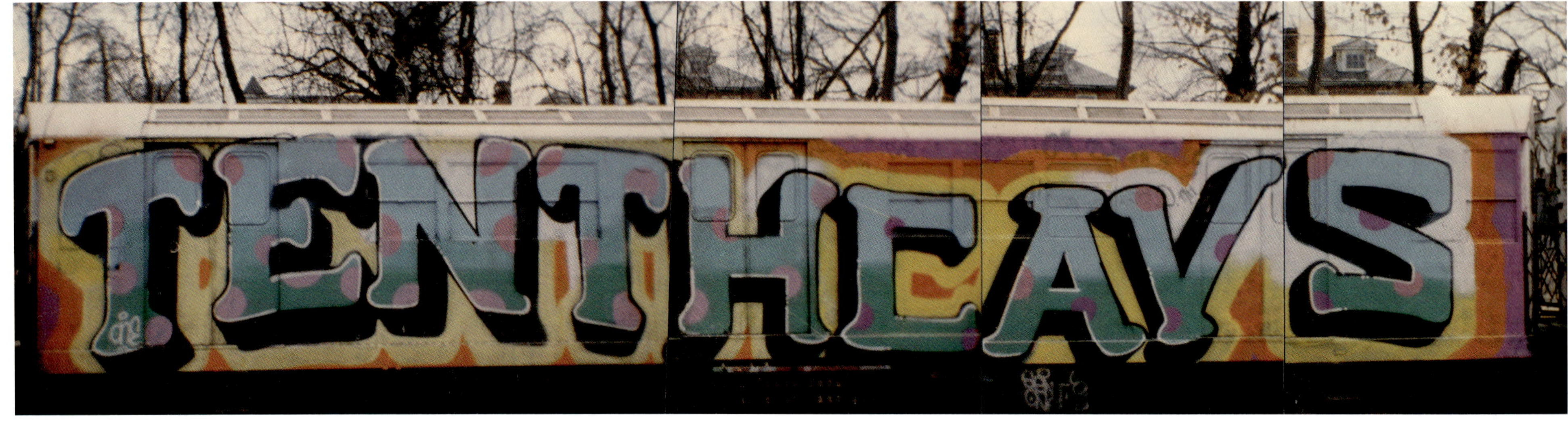

Tenth, Cavs, 1988

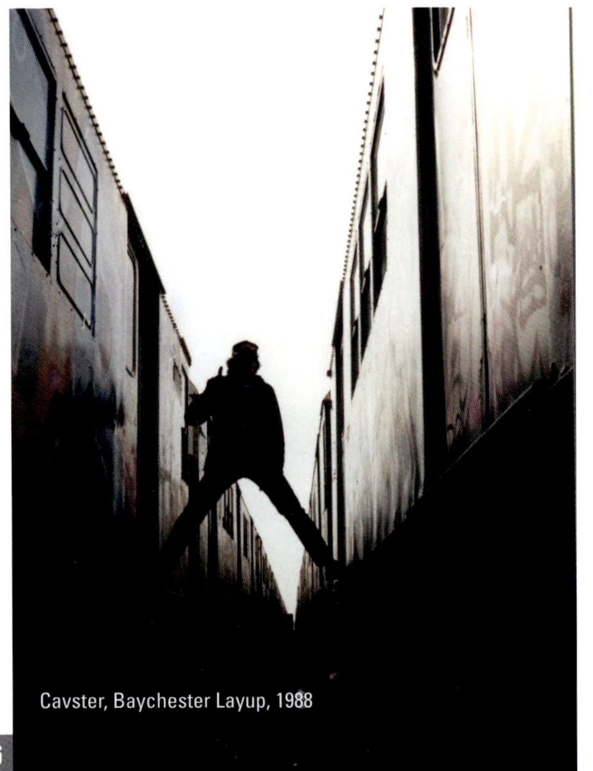

Cavster, Baychester Layup, 1988

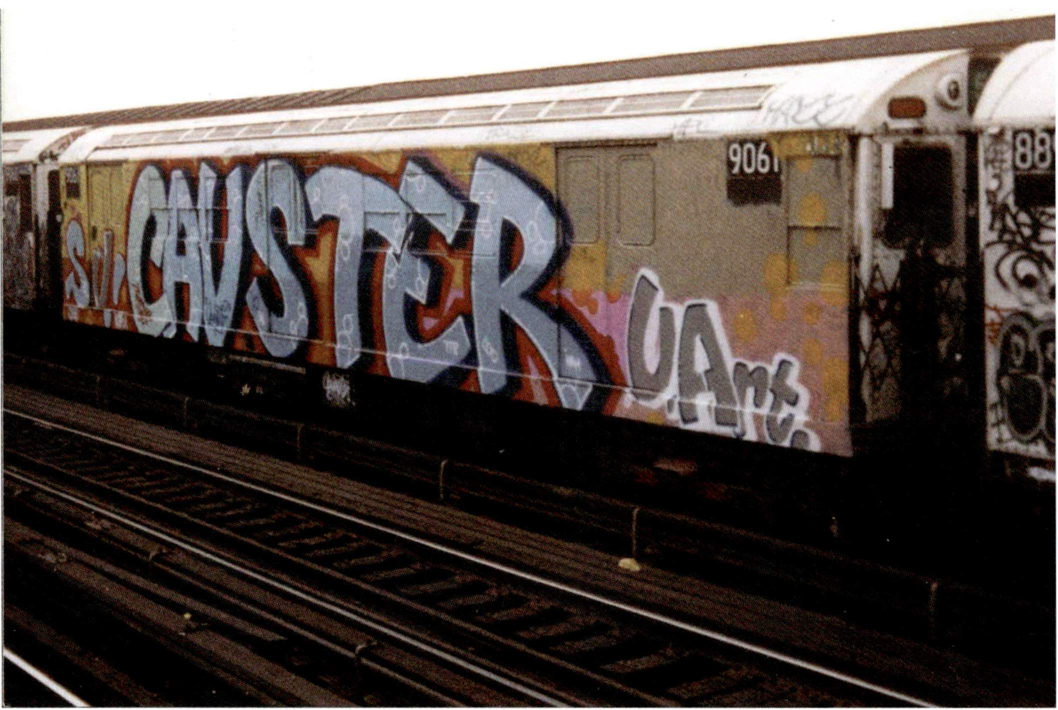

Cavster

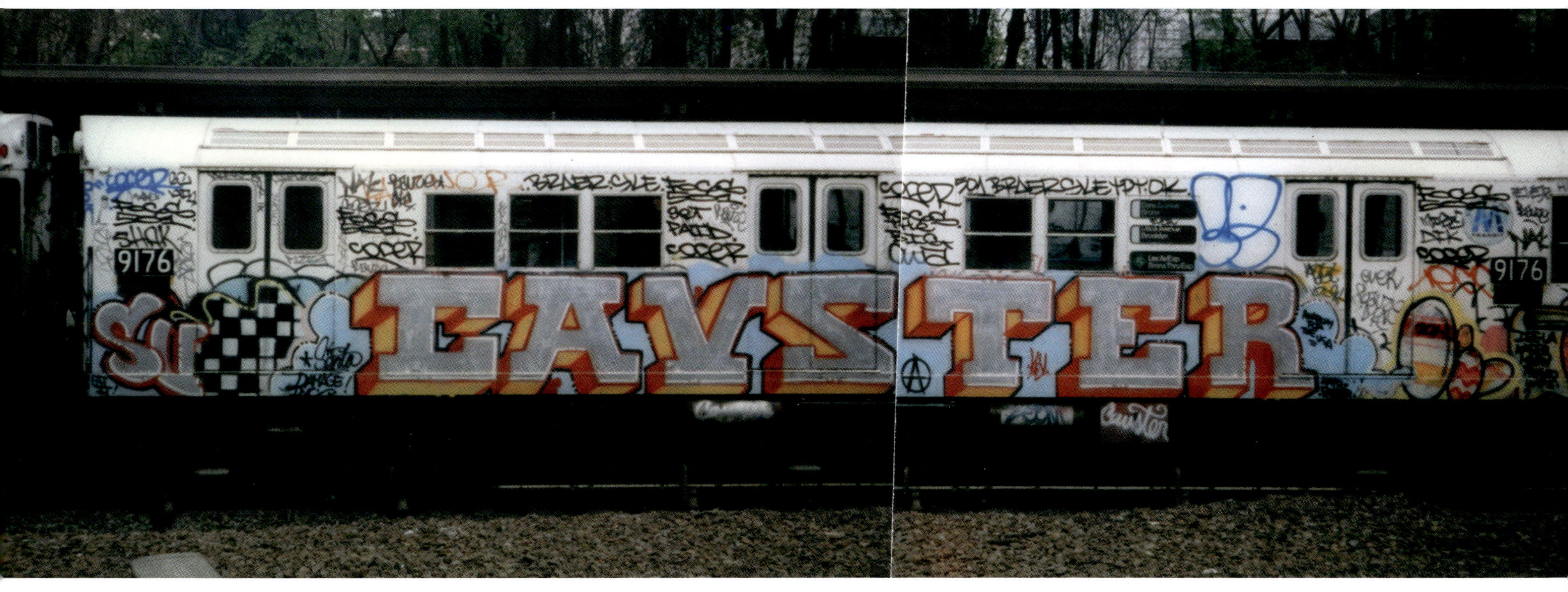

Cavster SV, 1988

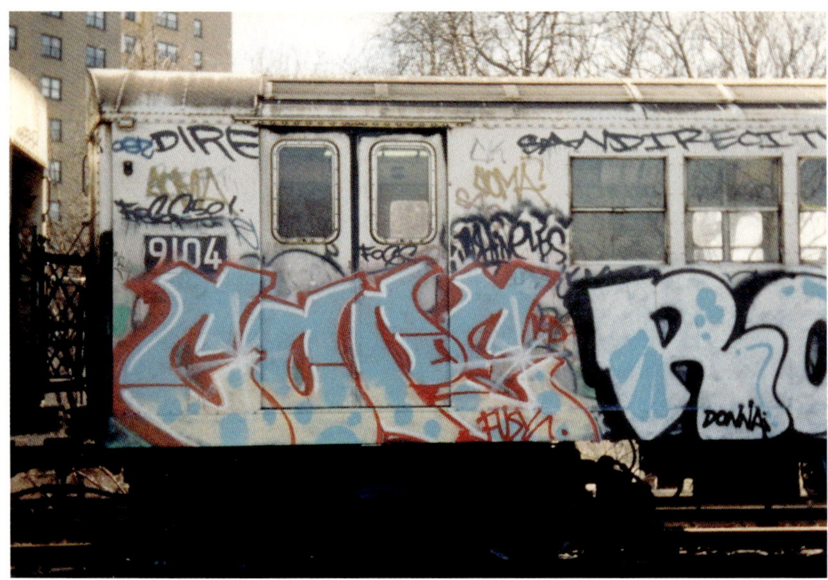

Cope2

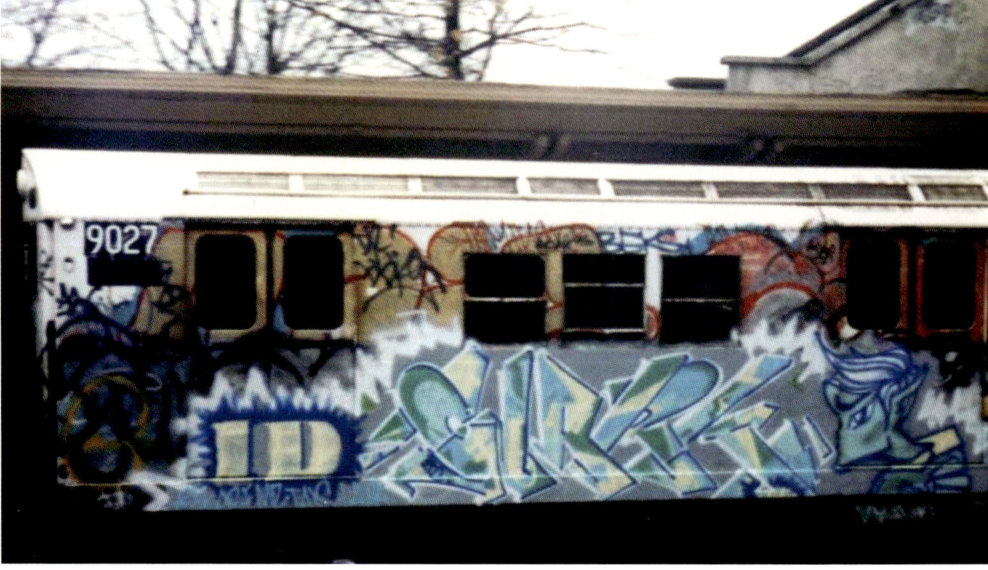

Clark ID (Photo courtesy of Kirs MPC)

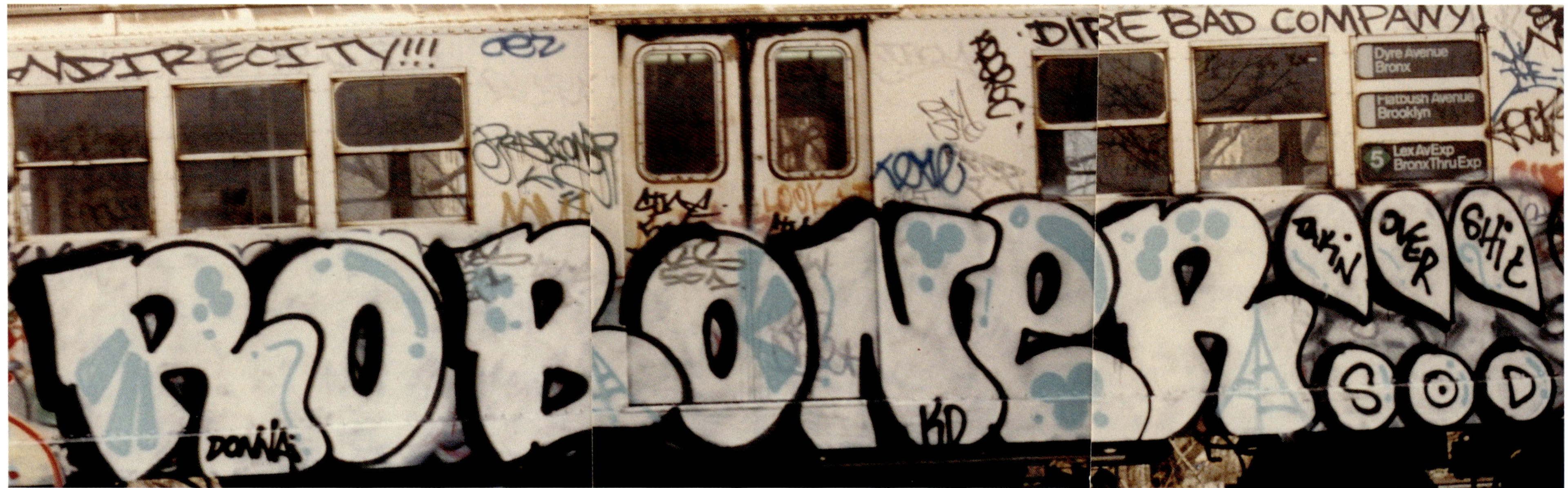

Roboner SOD (Photo courtesy of ROB SOD)

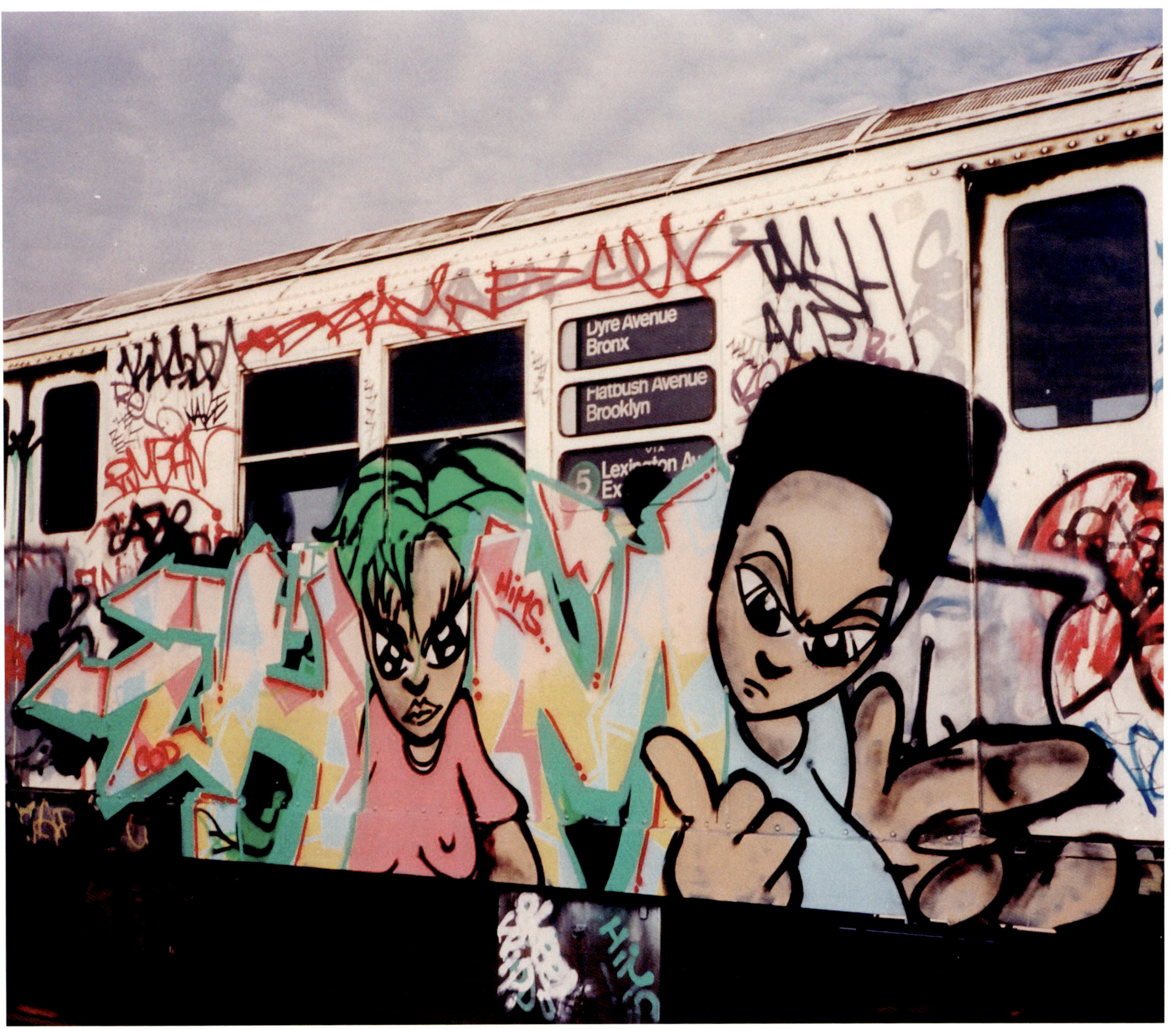
Dyre Avenue
Bronx
Flatbush Avenue
Brooklyn
5

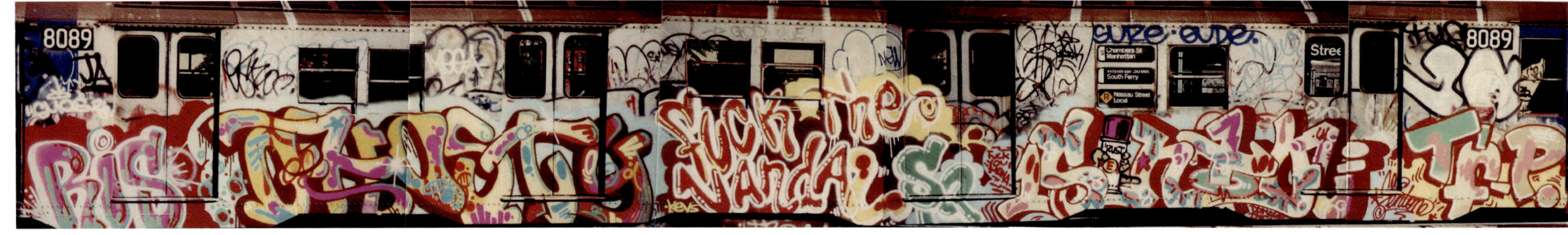

Ghosty, Sento

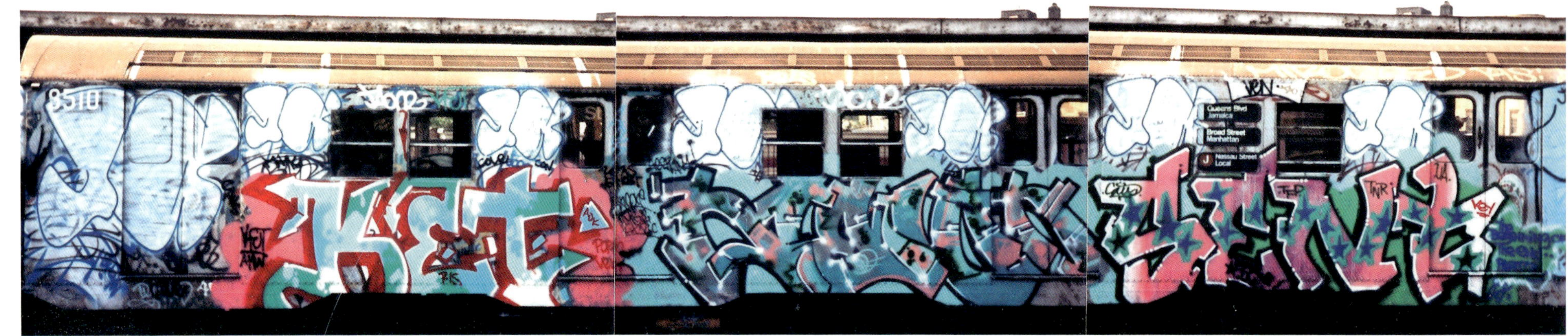

Ket, Neon, Sent

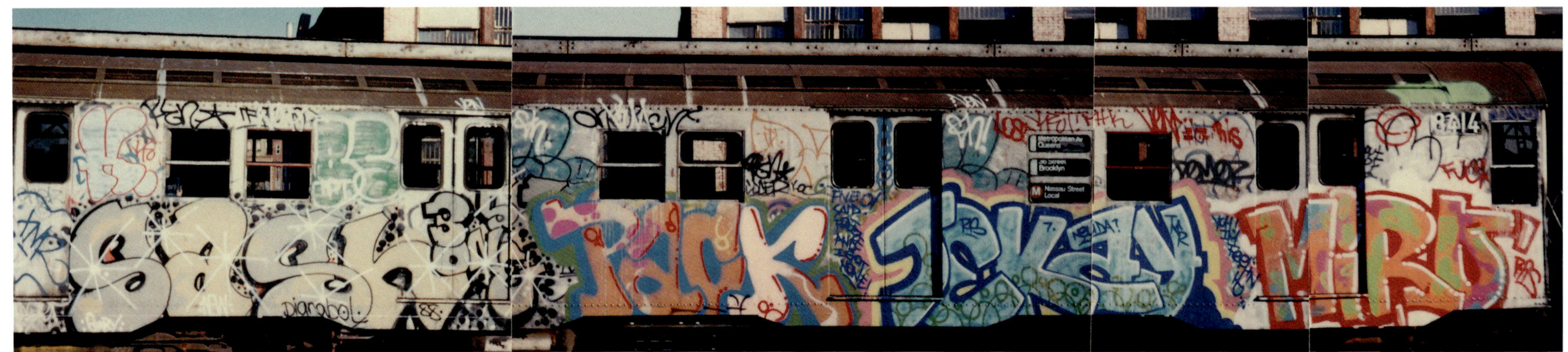

Sash, Pack, Tekay, Miro, 1988

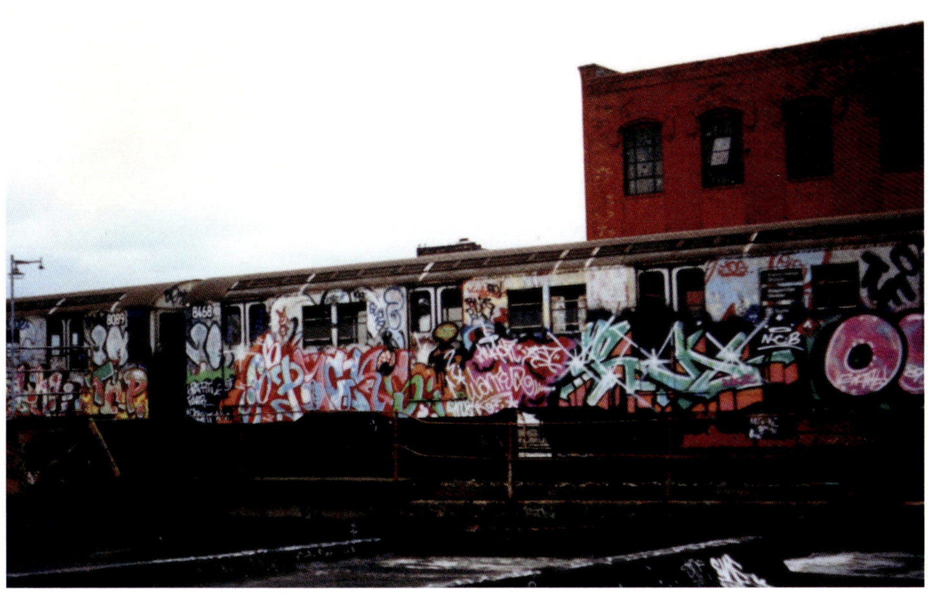

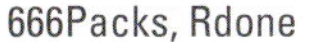
666Packs, Rdone

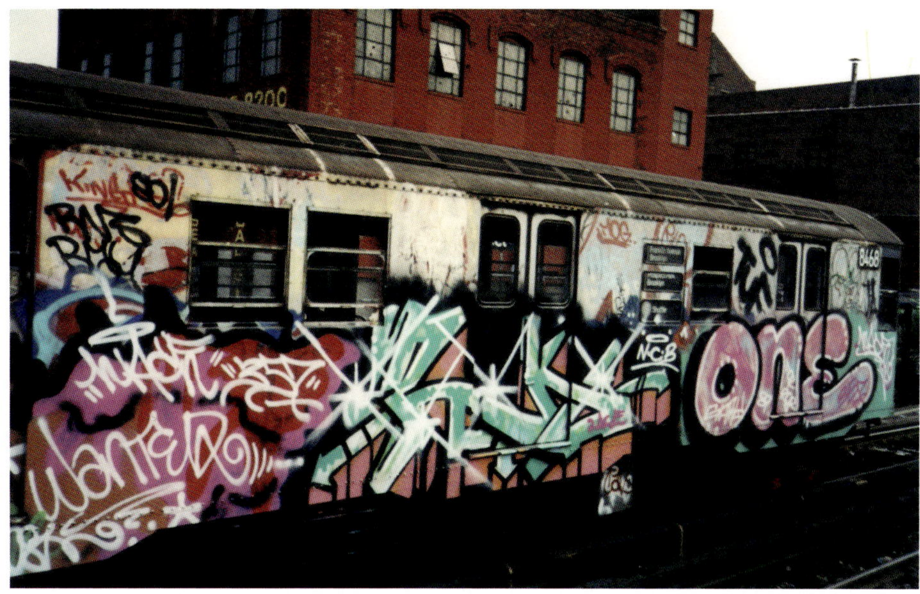

Rdone by Lace357

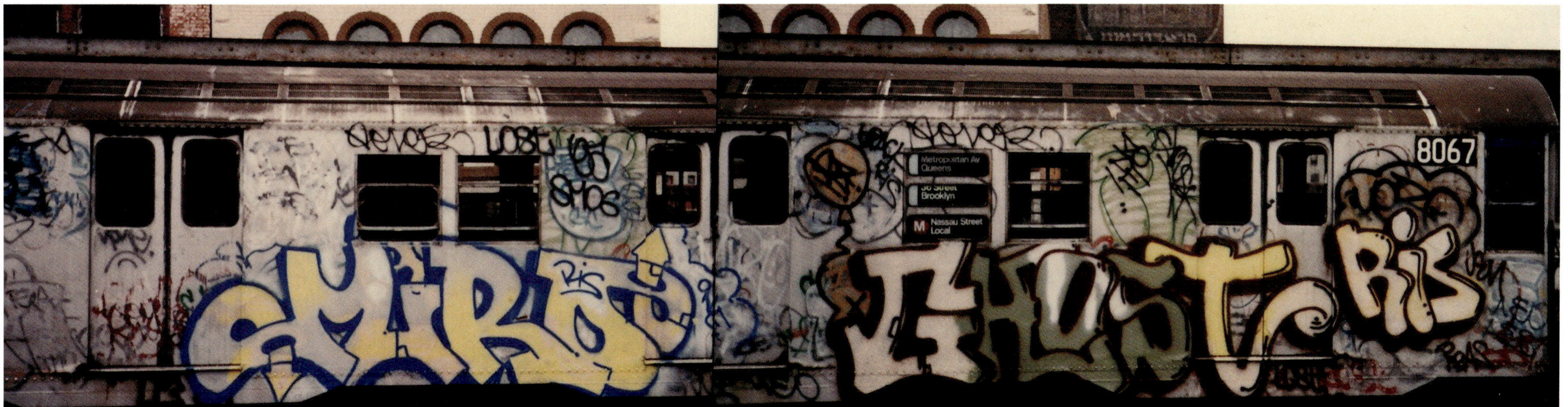

Miro, Ghost RIS

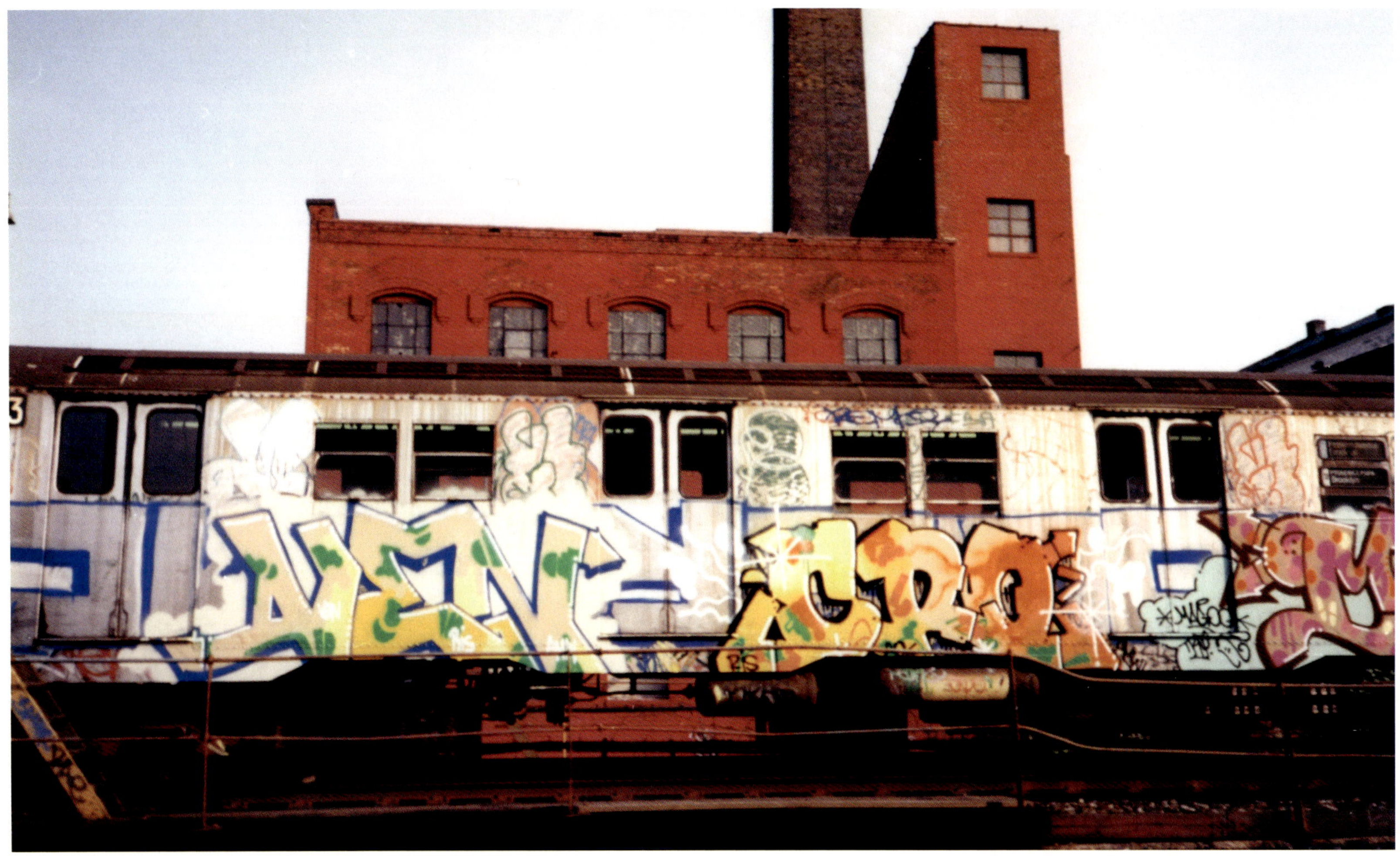

Ven, Cro

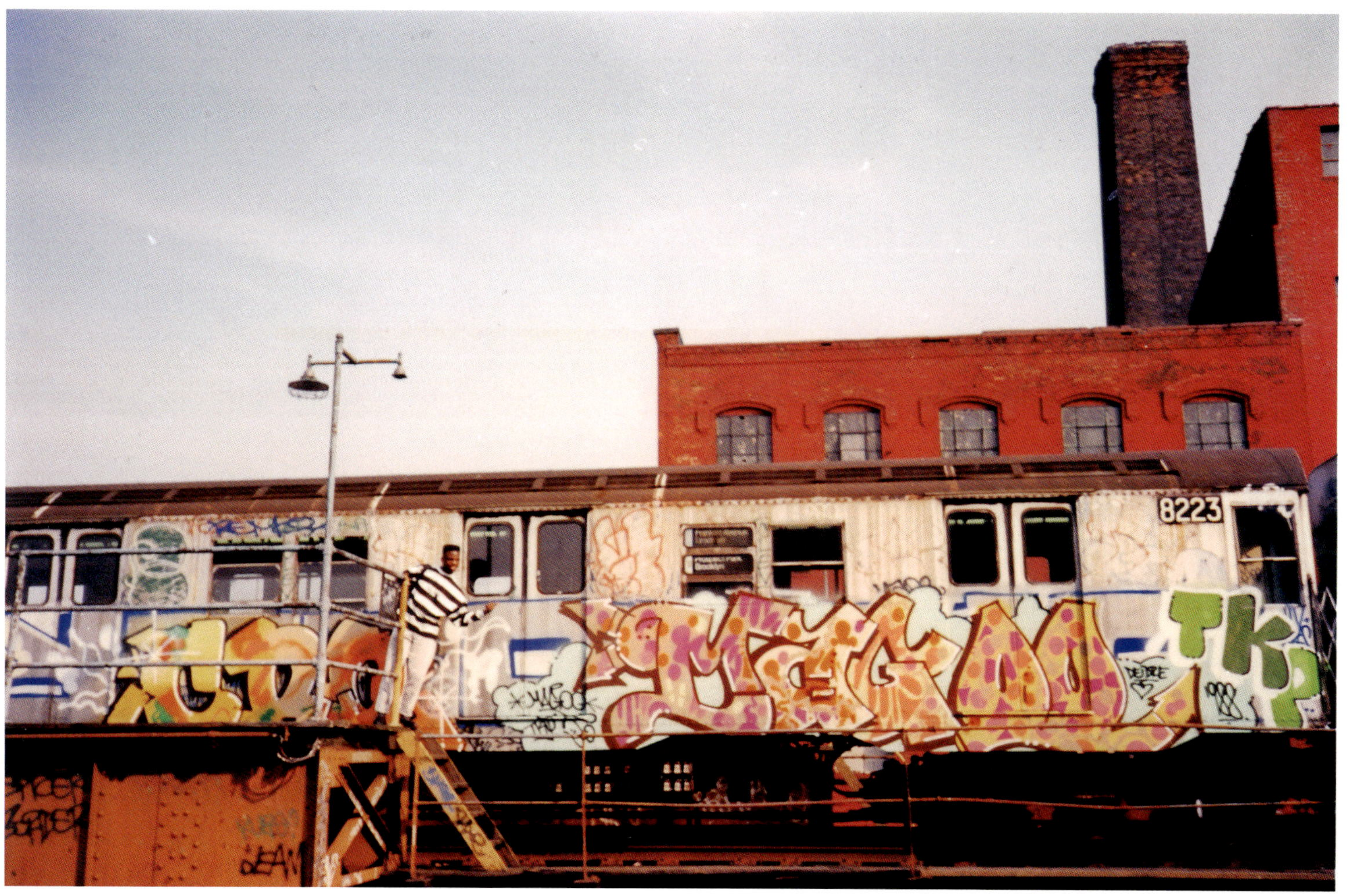

Magoo TKP, 1988

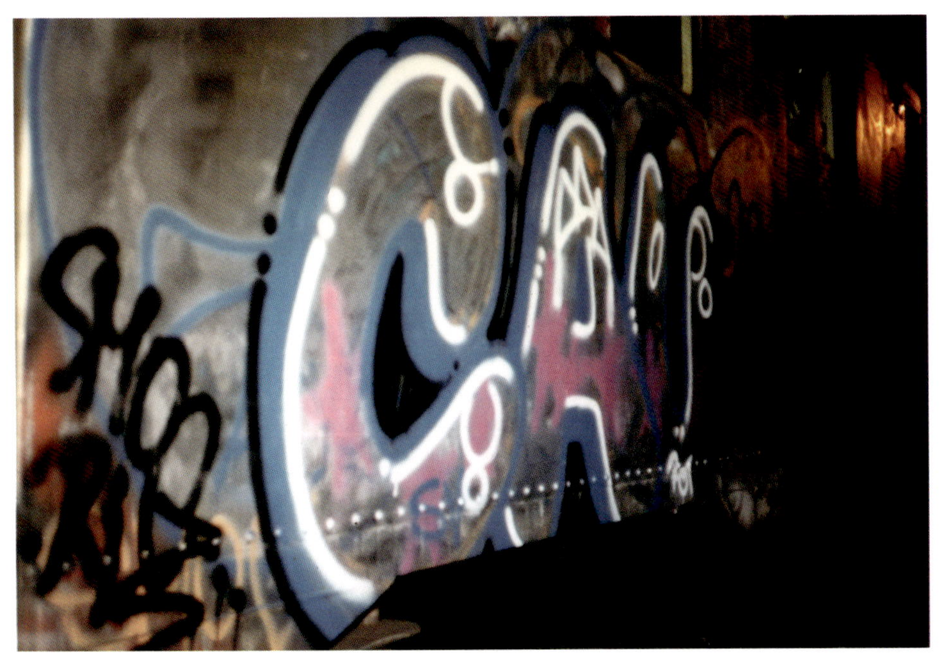

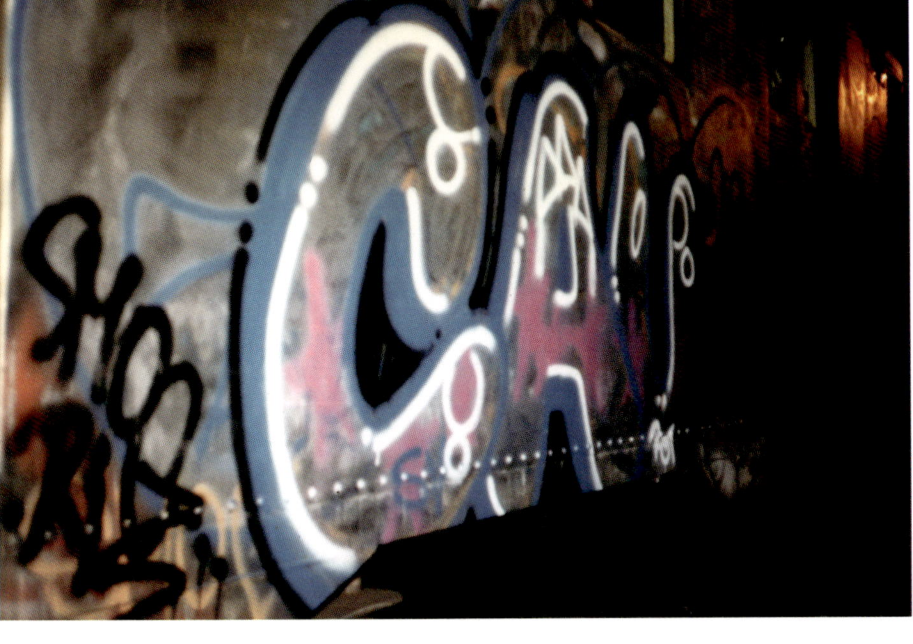

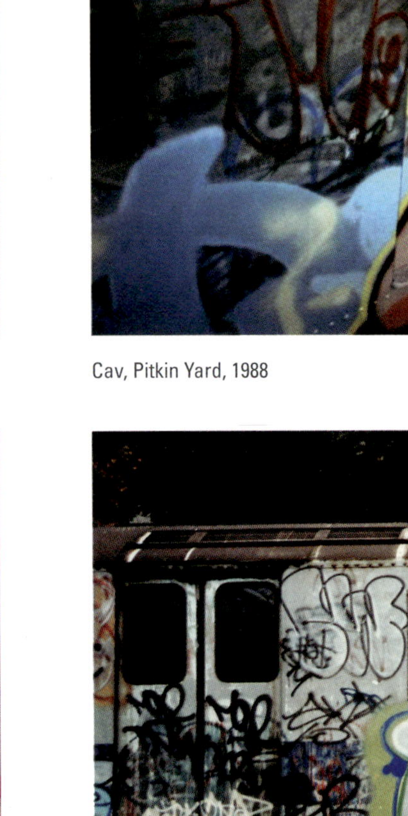

Cav, Pitkin Yard, 1988

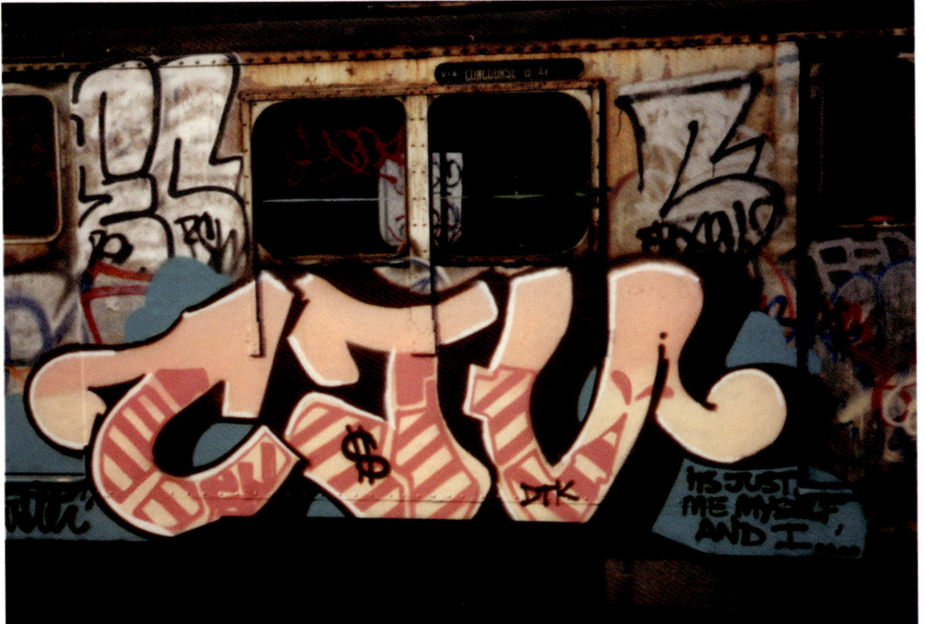

Cav, 1989

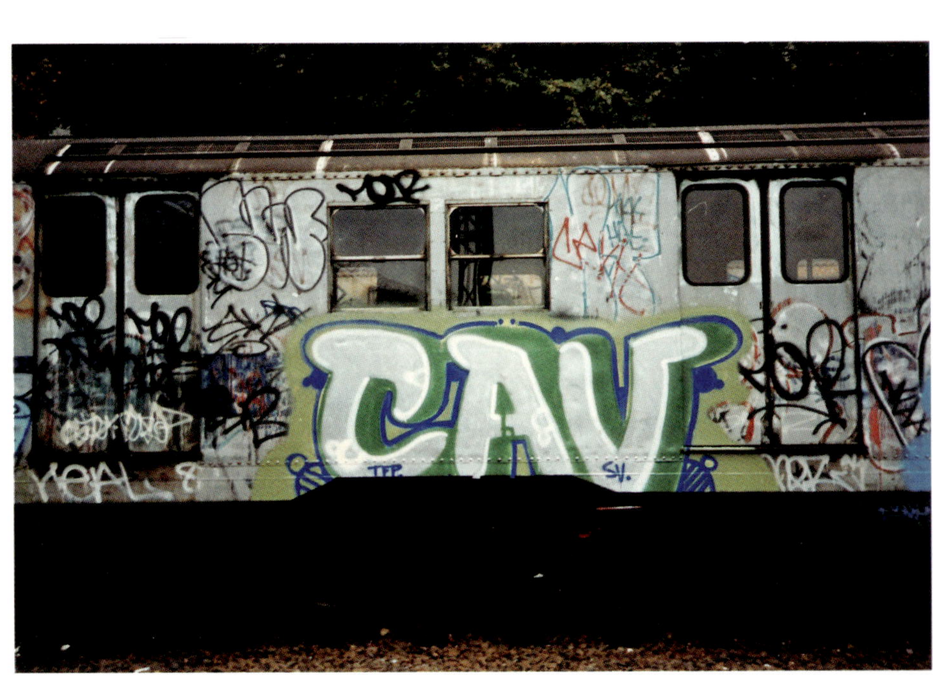

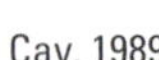

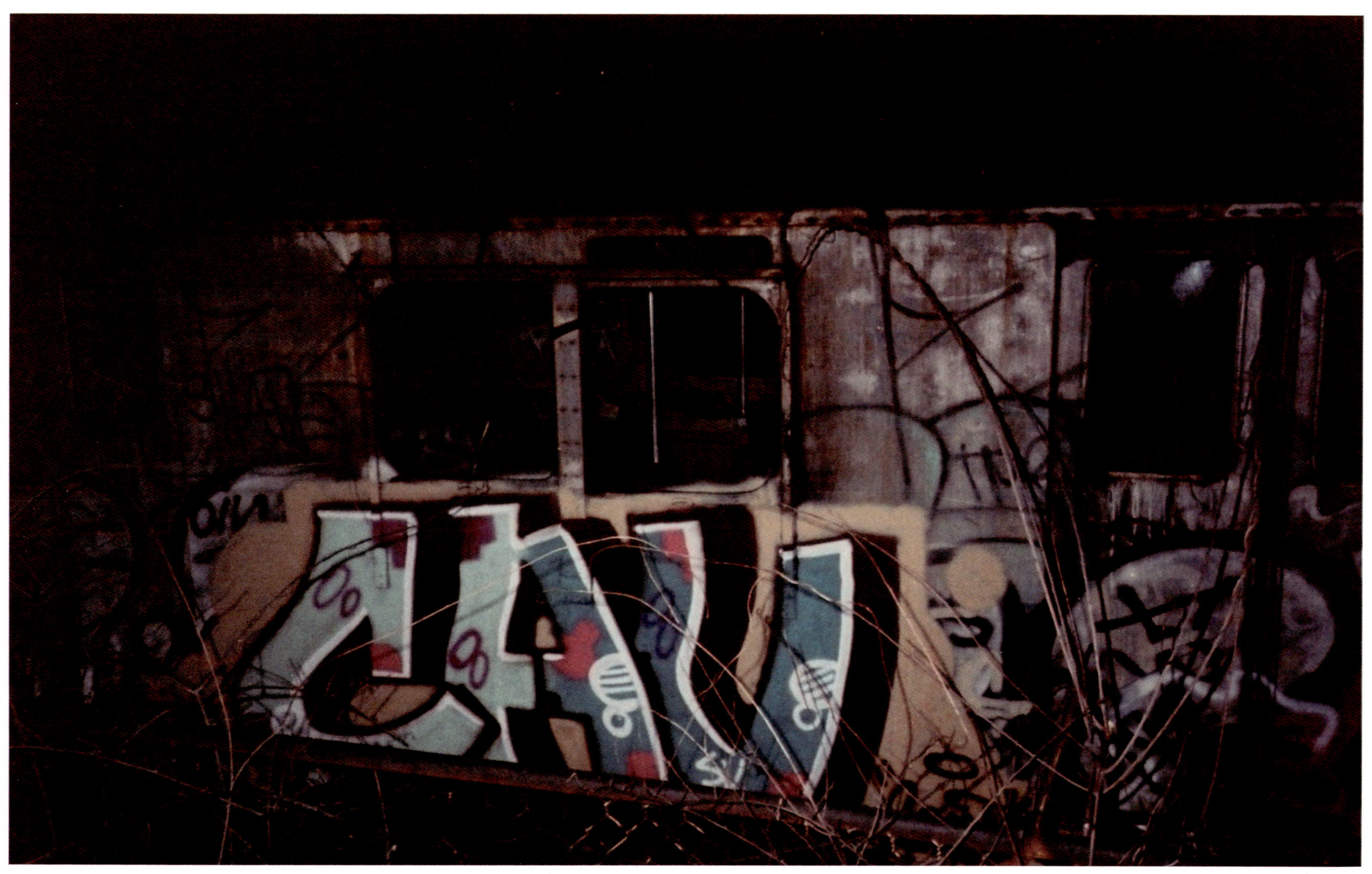

Cav, D Yard, 1988

I saw a Damp, Neon whole car a long time ago but I remember it like it was yesterday because it was so weird. They did this during the mid-day layup at 121st Street. I ran into Ket on his way to work earlier in the day and he told me what they did and that they got raided soon as they finished. Rush hour was about to start and this was the best time to bench on the subways because the trains would be running back to back. After seeing Ket briefly for a minute and knowing what was up, I went directly to Hewes Street train station to try and catch pictures of it. Since it was only hours old and done during the mid-day layup, the windows wouldn't be buffed either. I was psyched! I didn't know exactly what they did, but Ket was so amped when I ran into him. I knew it would be worth it whatever it was. After a few trains I saw a brand new window-down Sent, Neon end-to-end and thought maybe that was what they did. The little voice inside told me there was more and I should wait, and at least there would be something on the other side of that train. I knew Sent sometimes did 10th throw-ups on the other side of his pieces. The return trip from Hewes Street (where I was) to the last stop was about ninety minutes. When it finally came back I could see the paint shining from about three stations away. When it pulled in I was blown away. Damp, Neon, full whole-car with characters and the whole nine. I caught the flicks, but back then there was no convenient digital LED screen on the cameras. So I wanted to be sure I had good flicks. I had some time on my hands so I was gonna wait for it to make another round trip, so I could catch it again. However, on the very next train that pulled in the station, Sgt. Steve Mona of the Vandal Squad steps off the train. Even though I'm just benching and this was way before national security legislation and anti-terrorism laws, I still didn't even want this dude in my space, but it was too late. I had my camera out and he knew what I was up to. He approached and instead of busting my chops, he was all excited. "Did you just see that whole-car?" He asked, and I just played dumb. This dude goes on and says, "We just watched them from behind the fence do that whole thing, but the pieces were so fresh that we didn't want to interrupt them and wanted to wait until they finished to raid them." I knew he wasn't lying either because he told me that he saw Ket filling in the background and part of Sent's letters. He was really excited about it. I didn't know what to think. He was talking like a writer and everything. Then he said today was his mother's birthday and Neon wrote "Happy Birthday Mom" and that he was going to give the photos to his mom for her birthday. By then, the next train came and he got on and left just like that. What he didn't tell me, but I found out later from Ket, is that when the three of them got to the platform, they tried to nab them. Ket and Sent immediately jetted and got away, but Neon got caught. You know your shit is fresh when even the Vandal Squad waits for you to finish to try and raid you. I think that was the last whole-car ever done on a bombed train.

–Coal

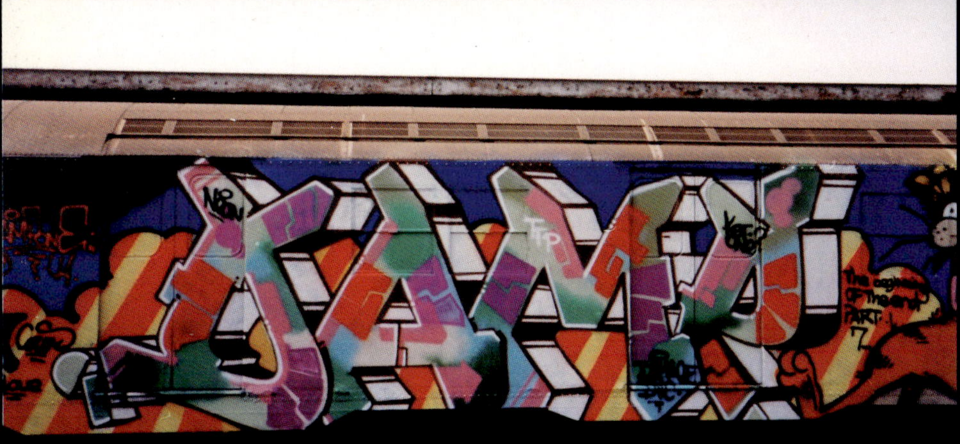

Damp

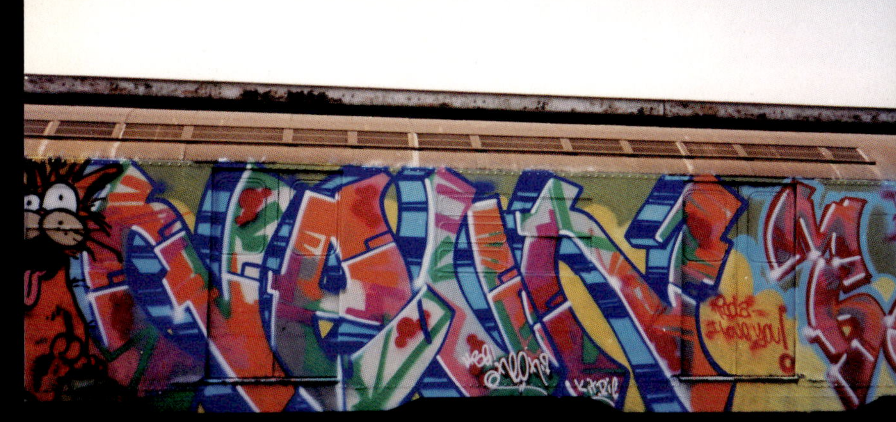

Neon

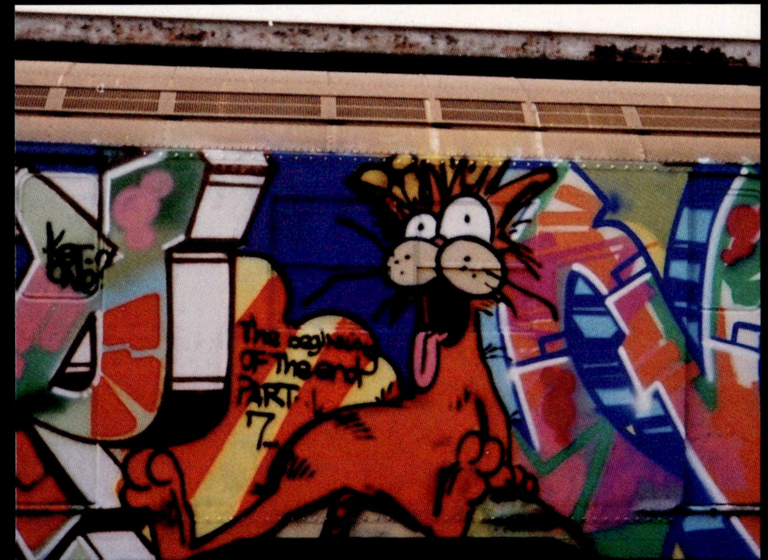

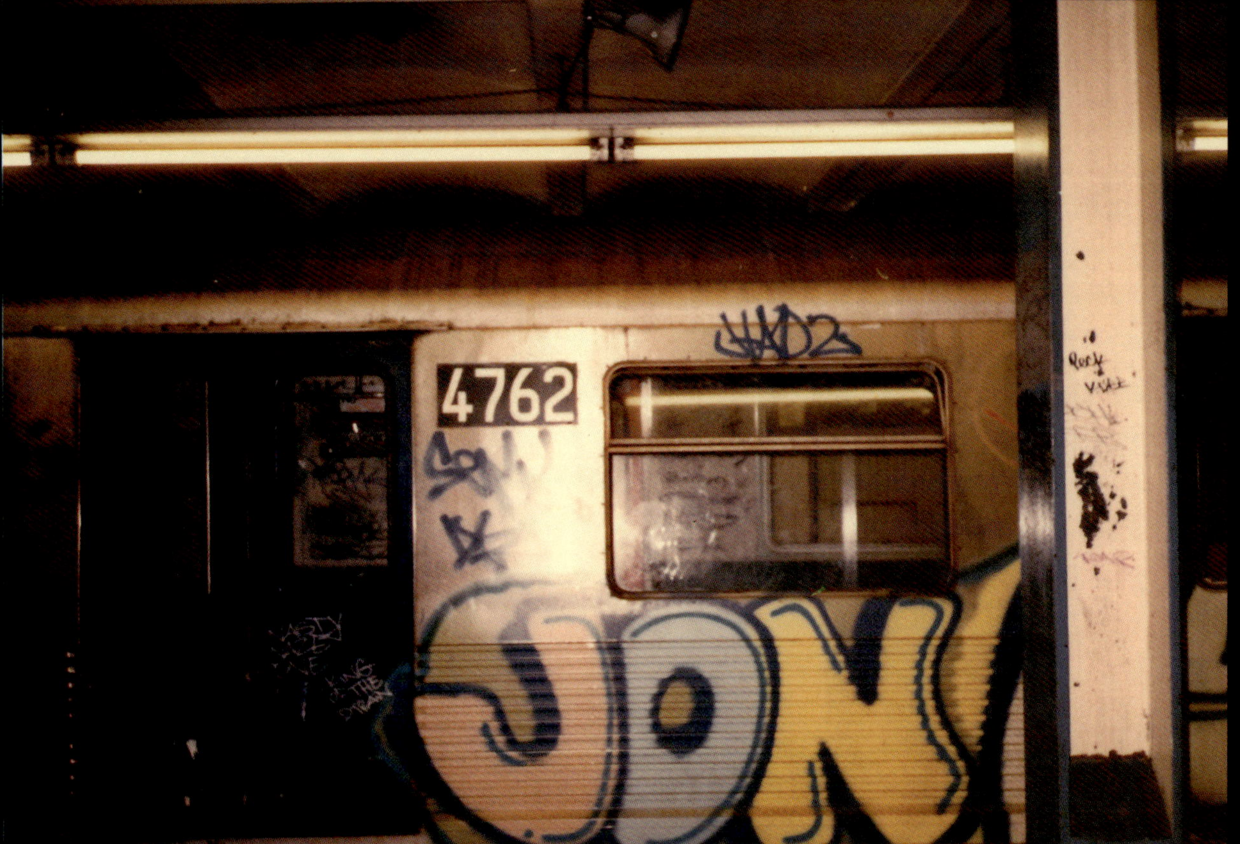
4762

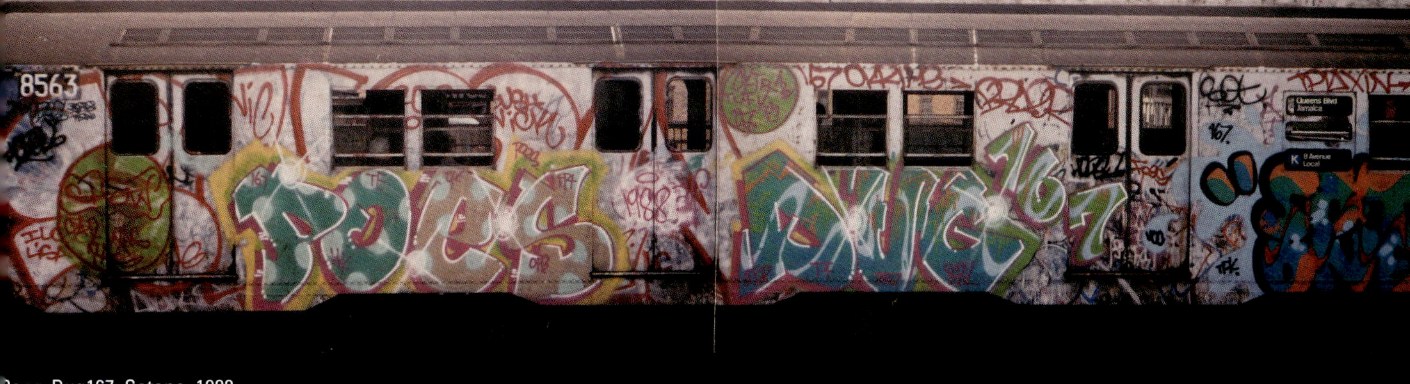

Poes, Dug167, Sotone, 1988

This car was done in 1988 in the L yard in Canarsie, Brooklyn. Sot was my homeboy from back in the days. Dug we just met a few months earlier. At the time Dug was killing it on the CC line with Nash. They were going strong and started scoping out the Js. We linked up and I brought them out to 121st layup. That was still kind of a secret spot for a while, but it wouldn't be much longer. Just before the summer of 1988, word got out about 121st and a lot of toys started hitting it and it was getting burnt. Me and Pema, a.k.a. WWone, were going to the L yard in Canarsie a lot since 1986 and no one was going there at all those last few years, so we kind of kept it secret. We didn't take anybody there. It was a sweet place that everyone thought was out of commission as far as hitting. Once 121st was getting burnt, we decided to let a few of our other friends in on it since graff was nearing the end anyway (or so it seemed). In the summer of '88, Dug, Sot, Trap, Dine, and a few others were coming out to the L yard with us. This was one of the cars we did there.

–Poes one

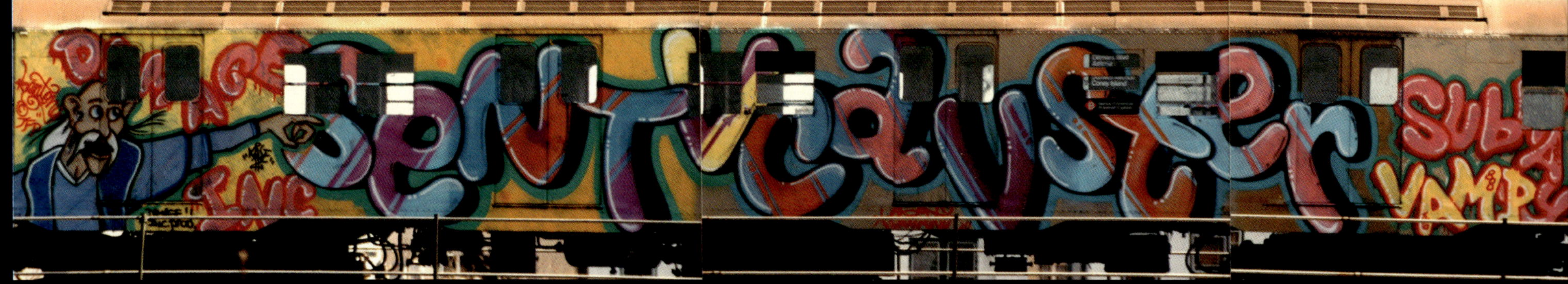

Senta, Cavster, 1988

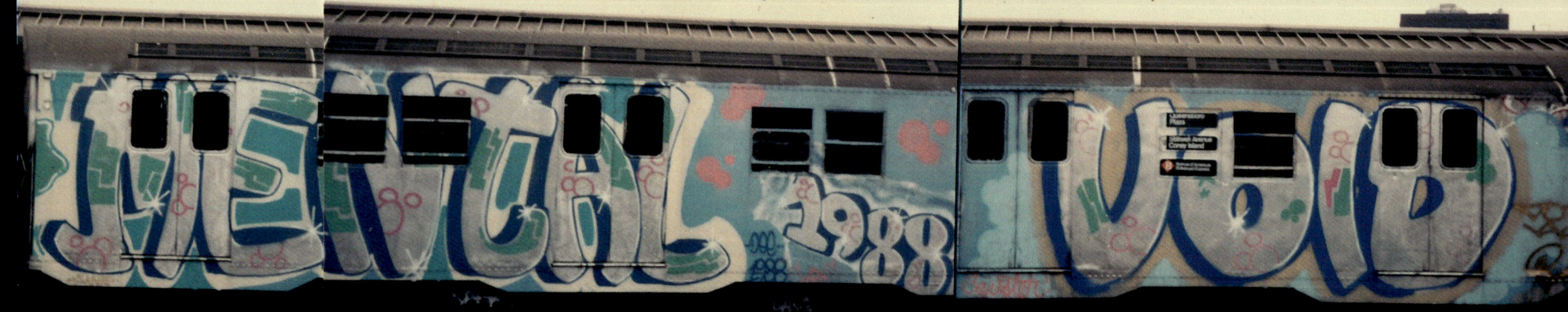

Mental, Void, 1988

At work on a Sunday, I received a call from my friend Dee. He asked if I was down to do some painting. I had just got pinched while bombing the 5 line. I wasn't sure about going until he told me where it was. B line tunnel layup under Central Park. My answer was, "Hell Yes!" When Dee came to pick me up he said we had to meet up with Cavs and Sento. Then we made our way to the city and headed for Central Park. This was all new to me since I was used to yards and layups. There was a hatch in Central Park not too far from 59th Street. Once the hatch was opened, we jumped down to a beam that led to the stairs. When we made it to the tracks we had a short troop to the trains. After scoping it out, Sento turned off the lights in the trains. Cavs and Sento placed several empty spray cans on the walkway to serve as a booby trap. If we were going to get raided, we would know about it ahead of time. On the platform side of the layup, Cavs and Sento were working on a whole-car and Dee was rocking a Mental top-to-bottom. I was sketching a Void outline on the other side of the train. I was halfway done when Dee came up on me and asked, "What are you doing?" I told him a color panel piece. He showed me his piece and said I should rock a top-to-bottom on the same car and make it a whole-car. So when the train pulled out on Monday morning the end results were two top-to-bottom whole-cars. That was the last train I ever painted and it couldn't have been any better to paint with some of the best in the game.

–Void

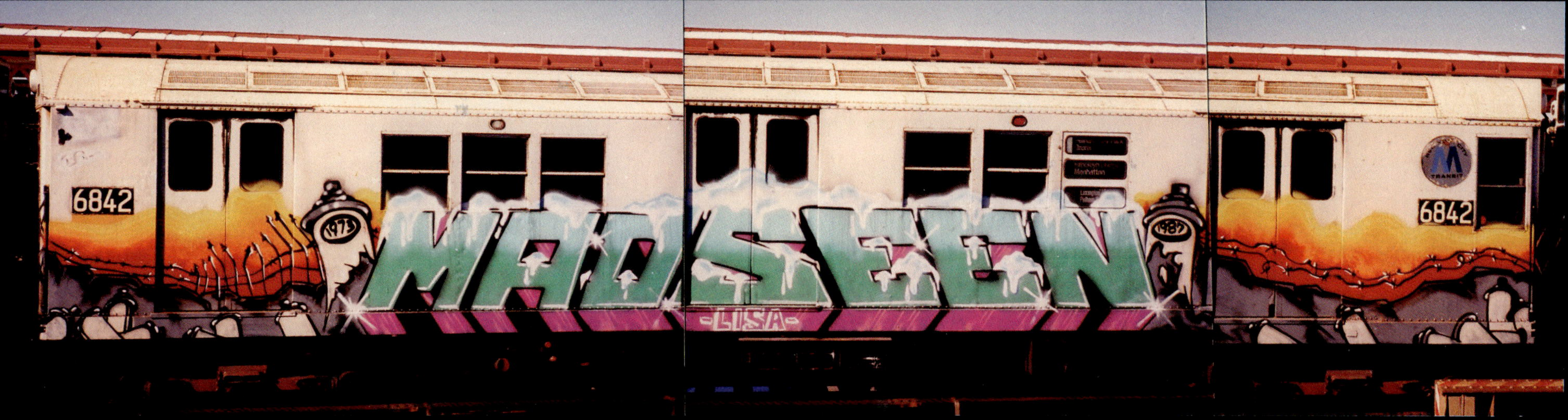

Madseen

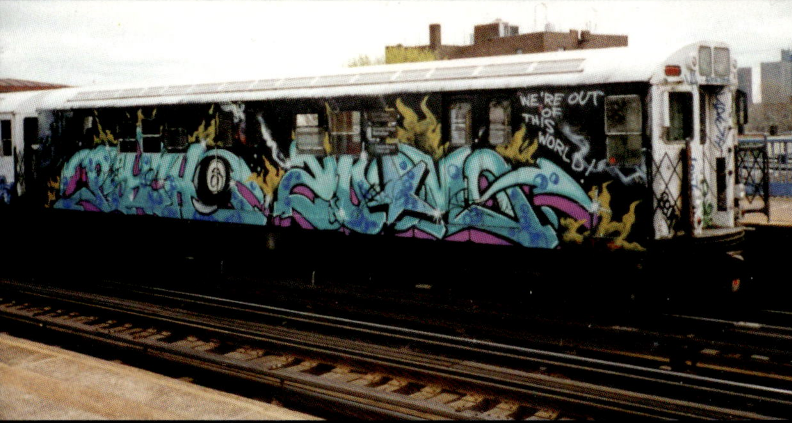

Psycho123, Zoom

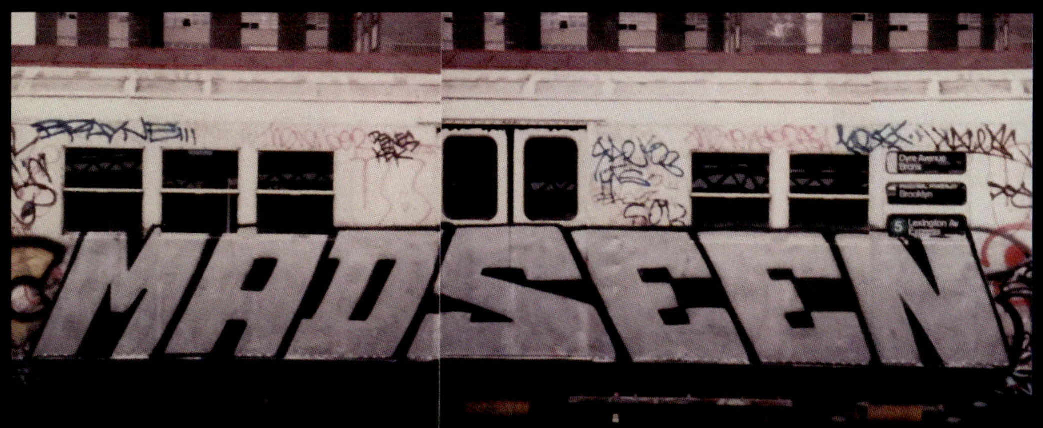

Madseen

I went to the end of the bombed train era, down to the last train, which was April of 1989, and then still hit clean trains after.

–Seen UA

I remember going to the Hall of Fame for the first time in the early '80s. I didn't have my own camera so I borrowed my mom's 126 camera. I think it was a Kodak and it had cartridge-type film that you don't see anymore. If you wanted to take flash pictures you had to put in a little bulb in a slot on the front left of the camera. Once you took a flash you had to replace the bulb if you wanted to do it again. It didn't take great pictures but it was all I had till I was able to get a 110 camera of my own. I have those flicks somewhere, I think. By 1983–84, I realized that a lot of pros were using 35mm SLRs to take really good flicks, so I went downtown and got my first 35mm camera. It was some Russian brand that I don't recall right now, but it introduced me to the workings of the aperture, f-stops, background, foreground, and pushing the ISO on the film. That camera was sturdy and I had it for years until I got a Japanese SLR, I think it was a Ricoh and that's the one I used to catch most of my work from about 1986 well into the 90s. I remember I had to convince Cavs to give up the disc camera and move on to 35mm in the mid '80s. He gave me some dough and I picked him up a 35mm and his flicks looked much better after that. We were benching one day on the 6 line and some other writers came later and we talked for a bit. While we waited they began doing tags on the station with markers. Anyway, there were DTs on the opposite platform and they saw this and snuck up on those kids and slammed them up against the wall while one of those cats ran down the tracks and got away. Just in time too, cause the train was coming down the track on his heels. One of my favorite spots was Baychester layup. Even though I got raided there quite a bit, I knew it well enough to figure out what to do if shit got hot. Another spot that was okay sometimes was Esplanade tunnels. I didn't like it so much because I felt the cops could trap you in there if they caught you sleeping. One time Sear and I were doing a Christmas car with some Bode characters. We were maybe three-quarters done and I put away my sketchbooks and extra cans in a hidden spot and only left the essential cans out to finish the pieces. To make a long story short, I heard something to my left and about a car away was a DT coming right at us. Sear and I dropped everything and squeezed into the train right behind us, practically stepping all over ourselves to climb up on top of the train. We looked down and he was staring right at us shouting the same old nonsense all cops say, "Come down from there, there is nowhere to go, we have you surrounded, don't make me chase you or else, blah-blah." We ran on top of the trains for thirty to forty cars till we ran out of train and jumped down onto the tracks and disappeared into Morris Park. Later on we saw the car running and the cops had crossed it out and we were pissed. I ran into it when I went to do another piece and was able to fix it up and even fill in the windows again. I missed catching it with windows and I had to finish again when I saw it later on down the line. That piece was a lot of work!!!

–Sento

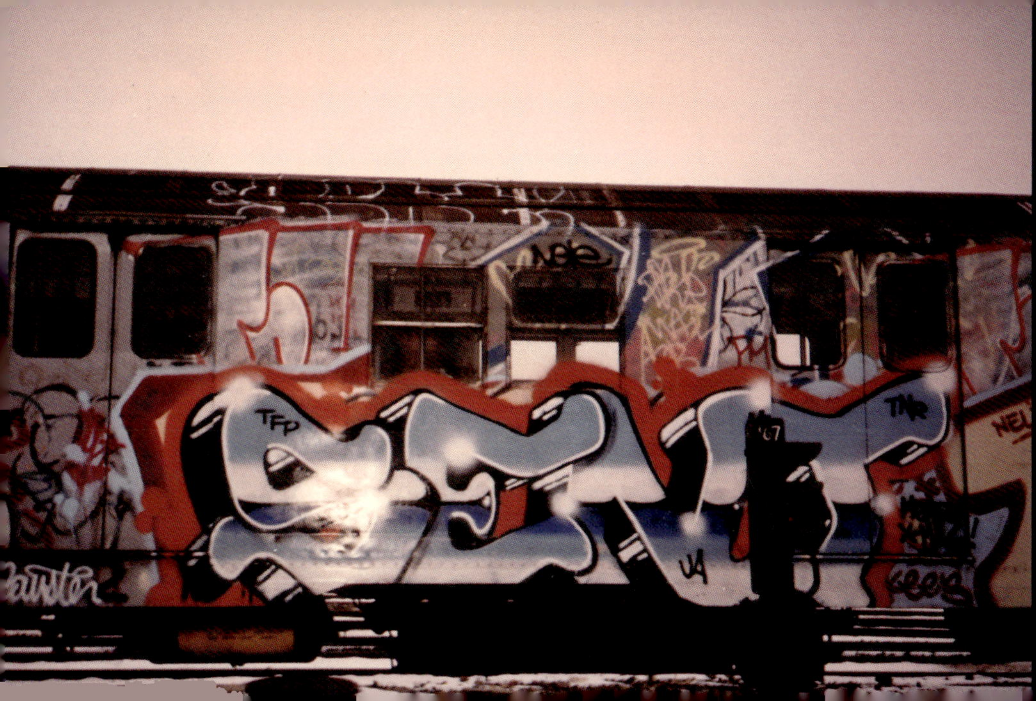

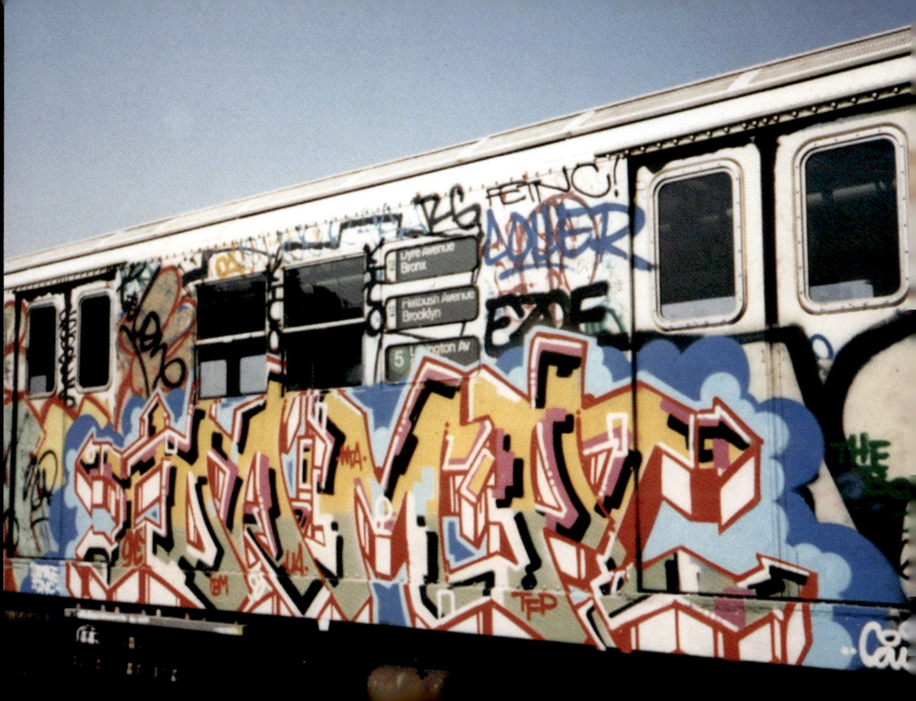
Dyre Avenue
Bronx
Flatbush Avenue
Brooklyn

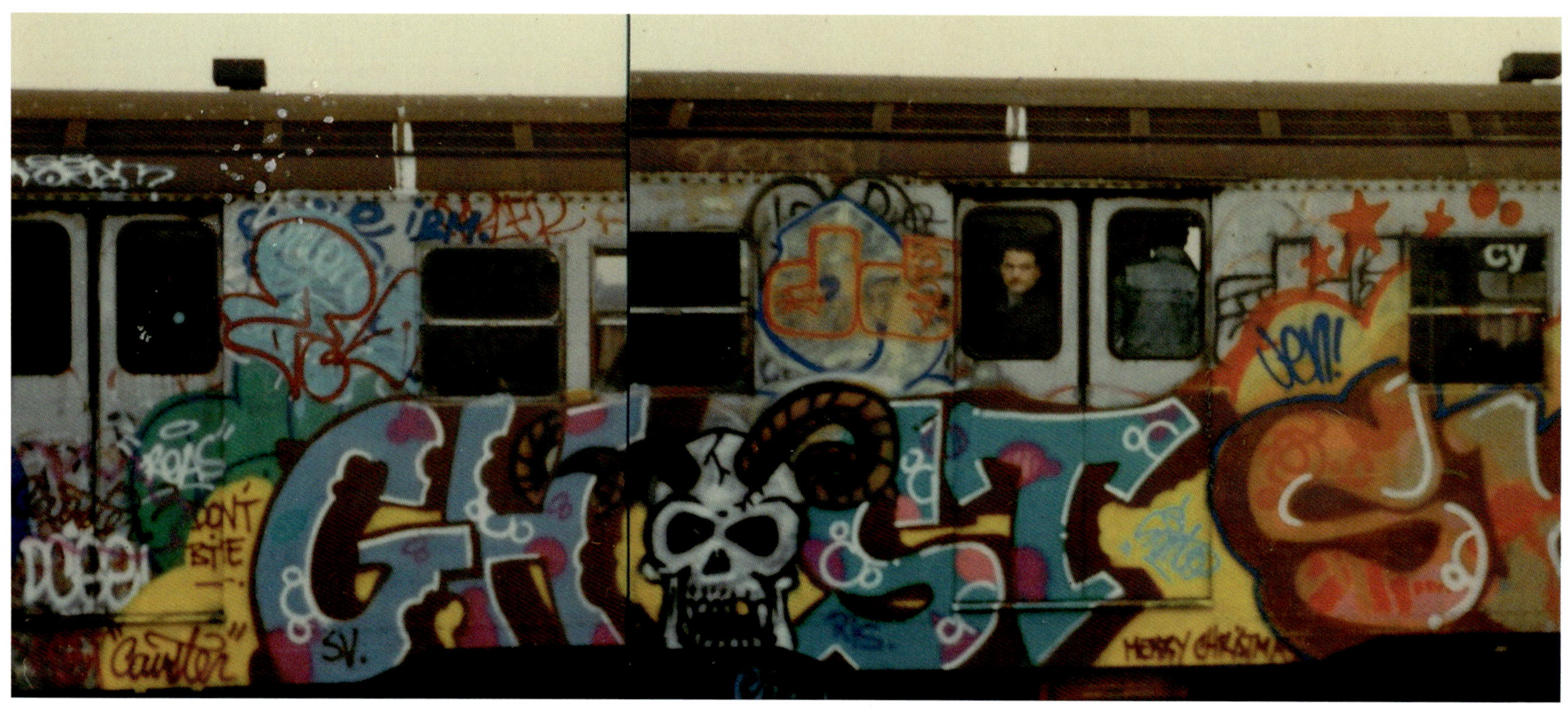

Ghost by Sento and Cavs ("Shithead159" by Ghost and Reas on the right side of the car), 1989

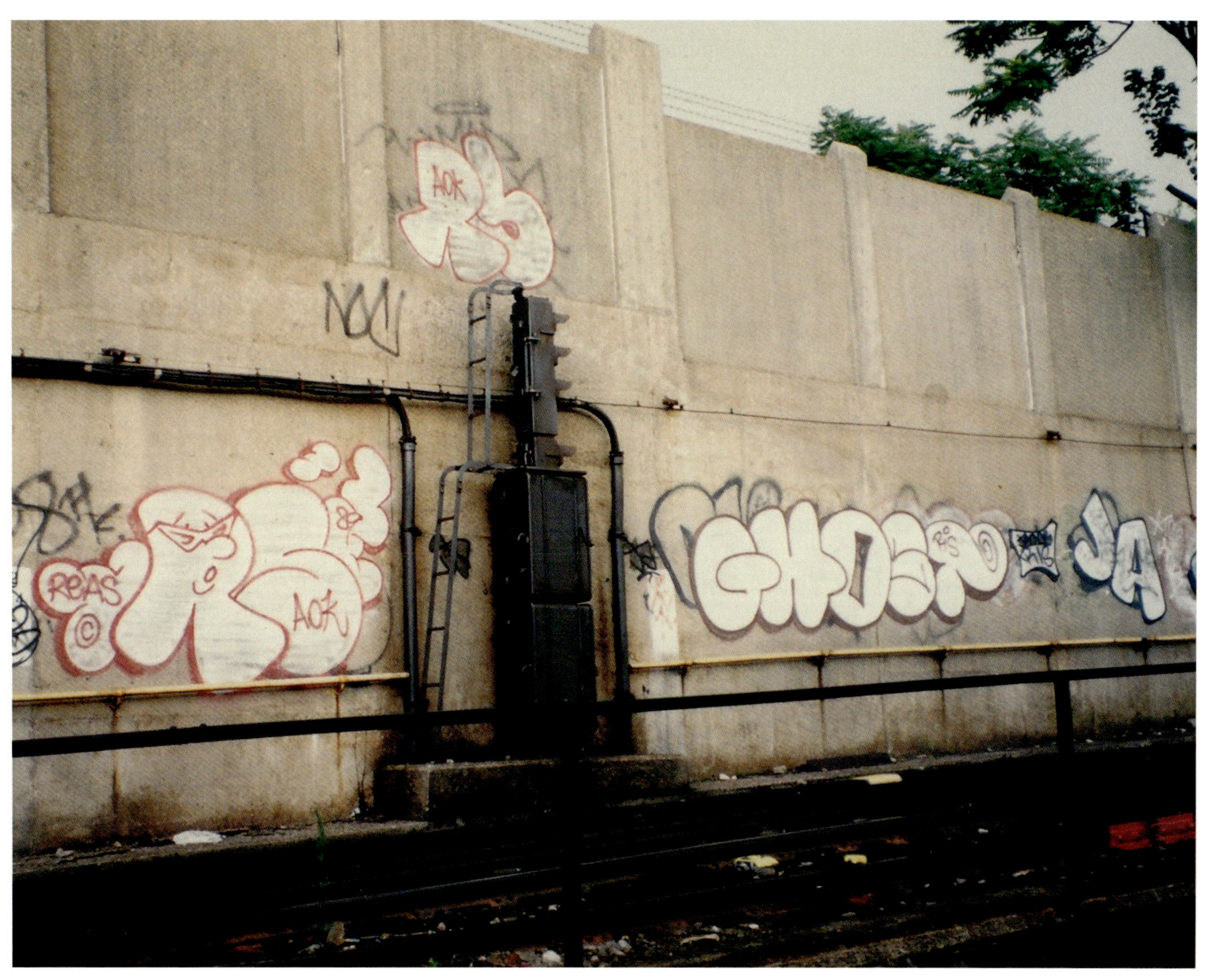
AOK
REAS
AOK

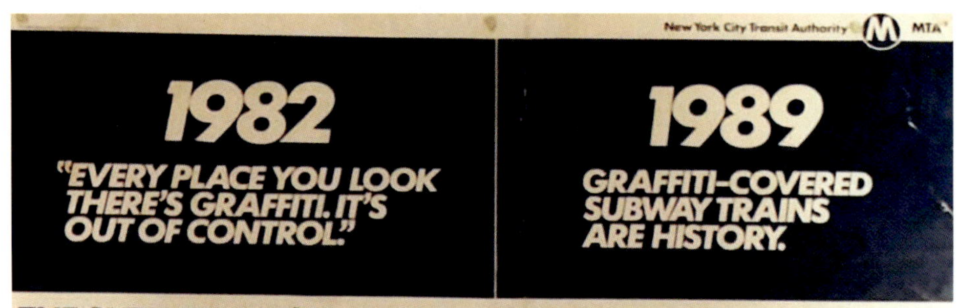
New York City Transit Authority
MTA
1982
"EVERY PLACE YOU LOOK THERE'S GRAFFITI. IT'S OUT OF CONTROL."
1989
GRAFFITI-COVERED SUBWAY TRAINS ARE HISTORY.
THE SUBWAY. WE'RE COMING BACK. SO YOU COME BACK.

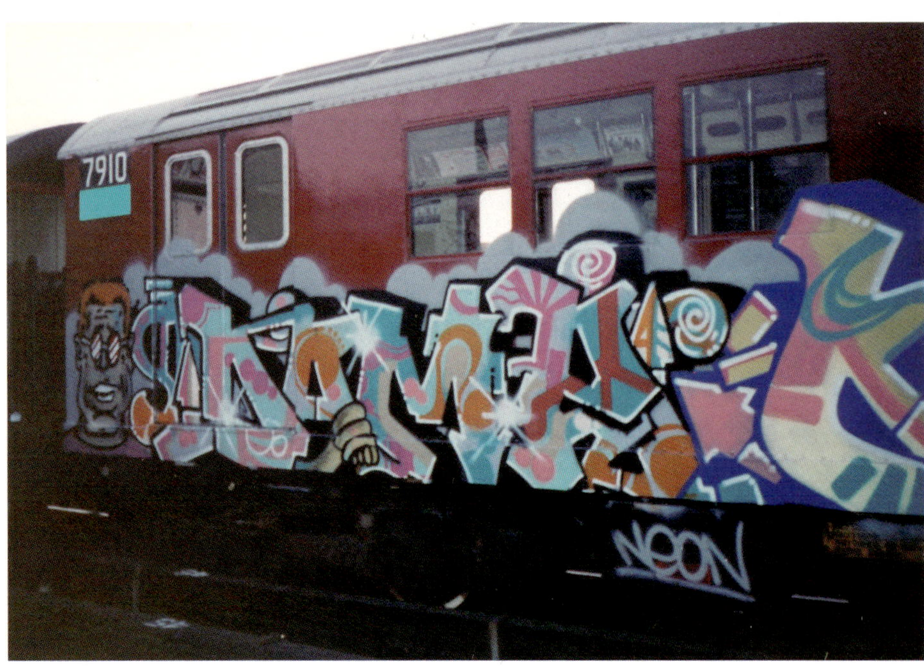
7910
NEON

Damp, 1989

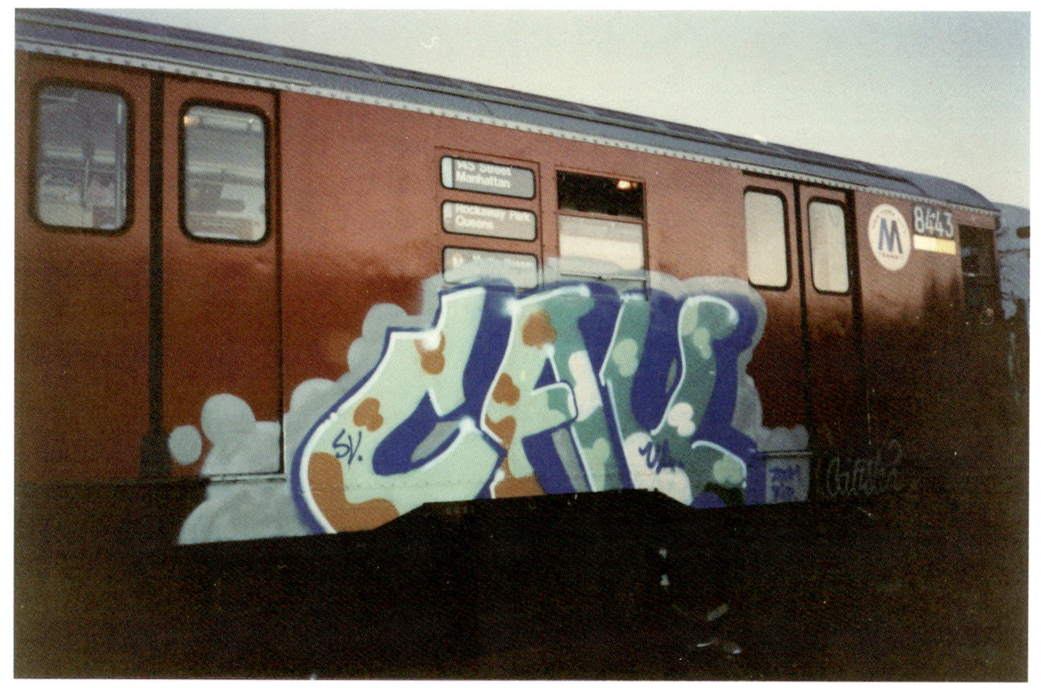

Cav (Ghost Yard), 1989

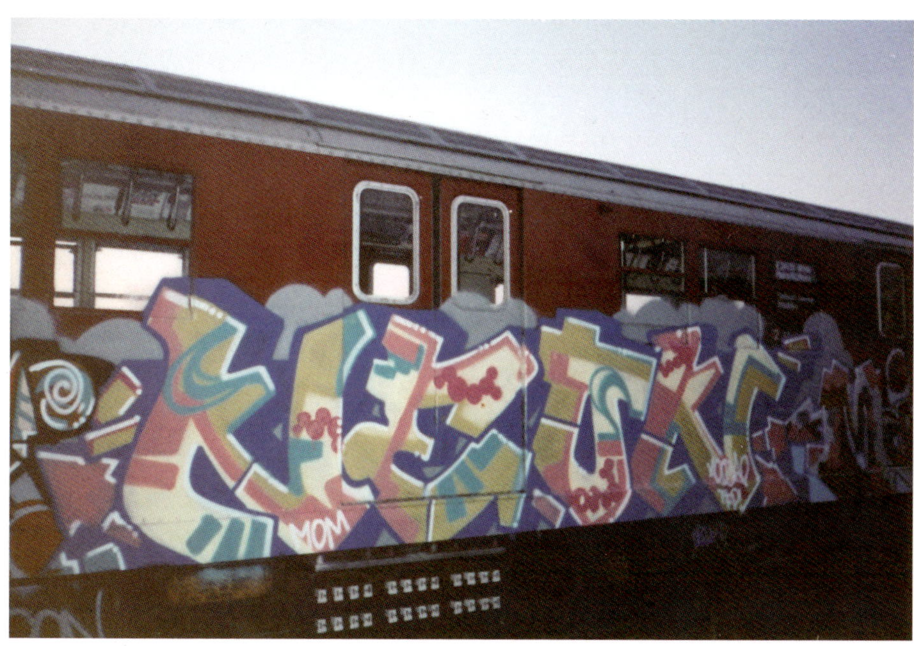

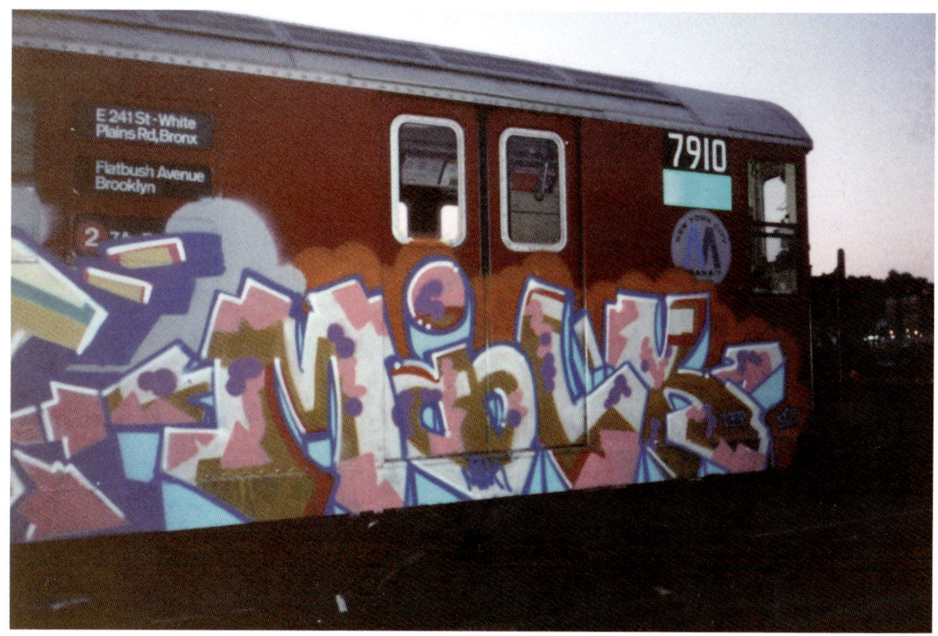

Neon, 1989

Milk, 1989

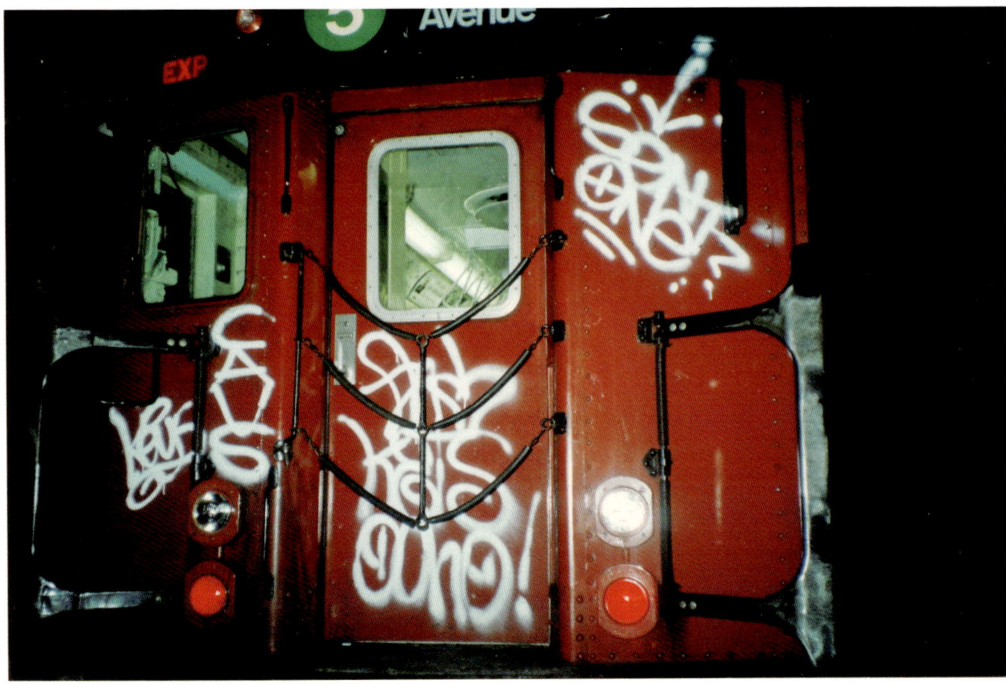

Dyre Avenue

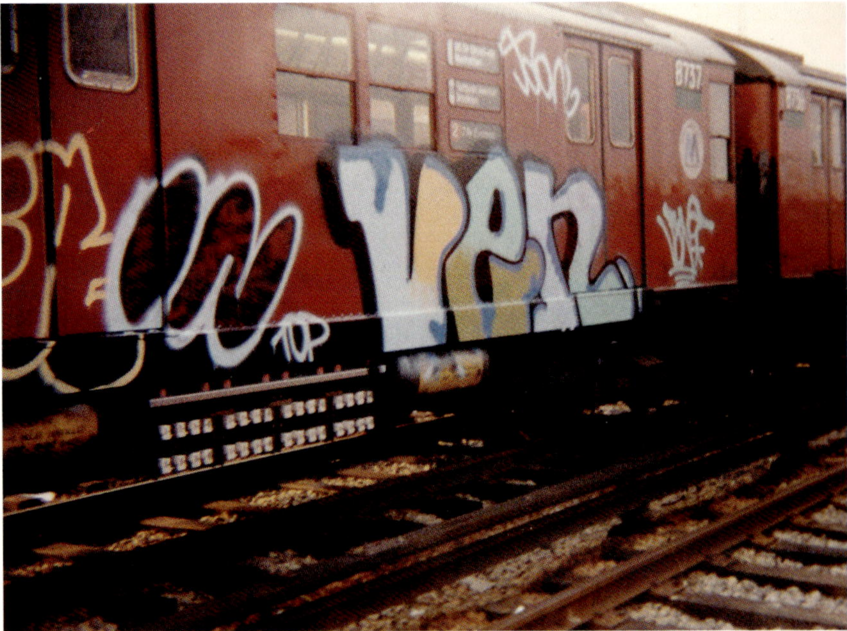

Ven, 2 Yard (241st)

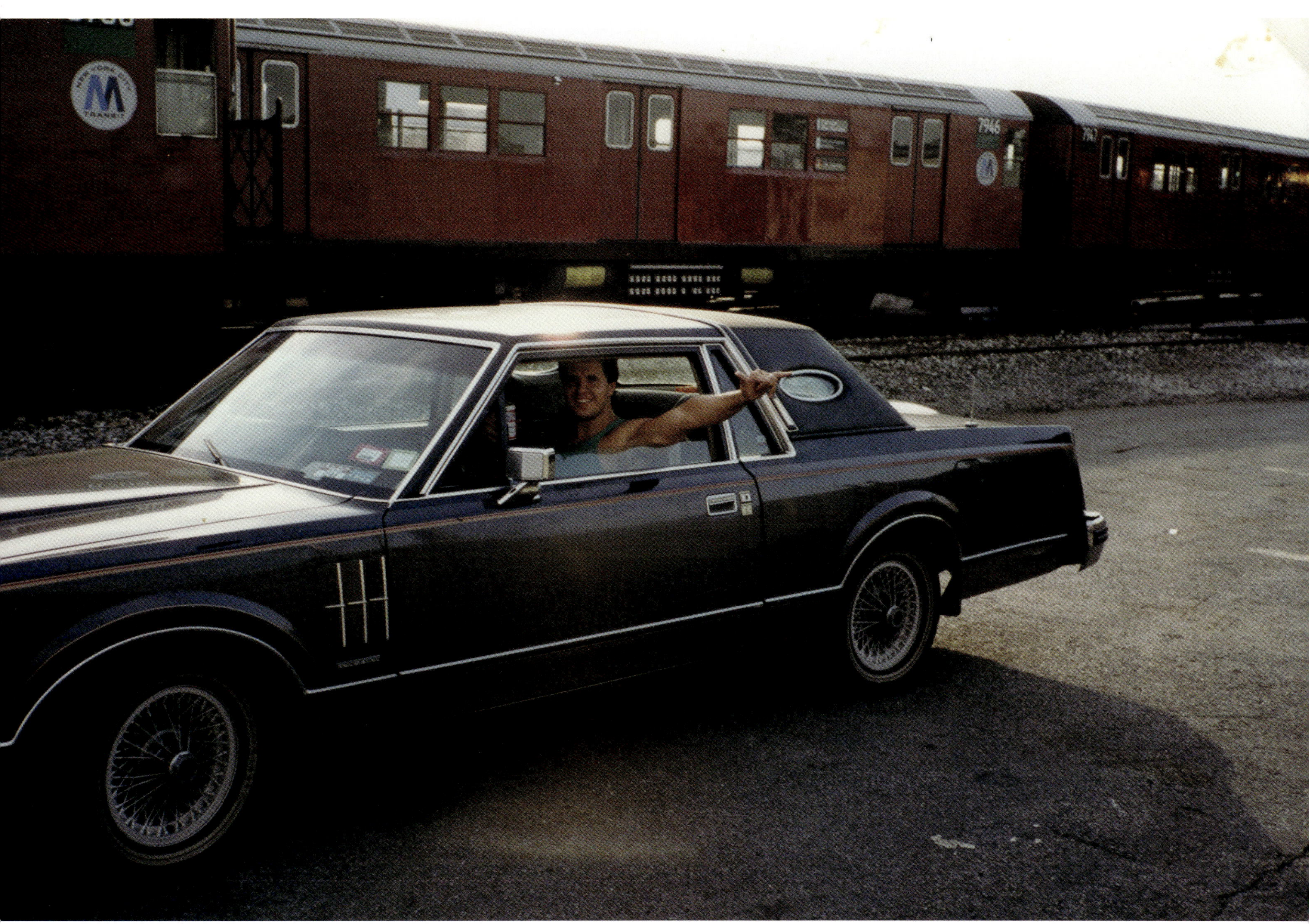

Sar in the 2 Yard (241st) (Photo courtesy of SAR TMB)

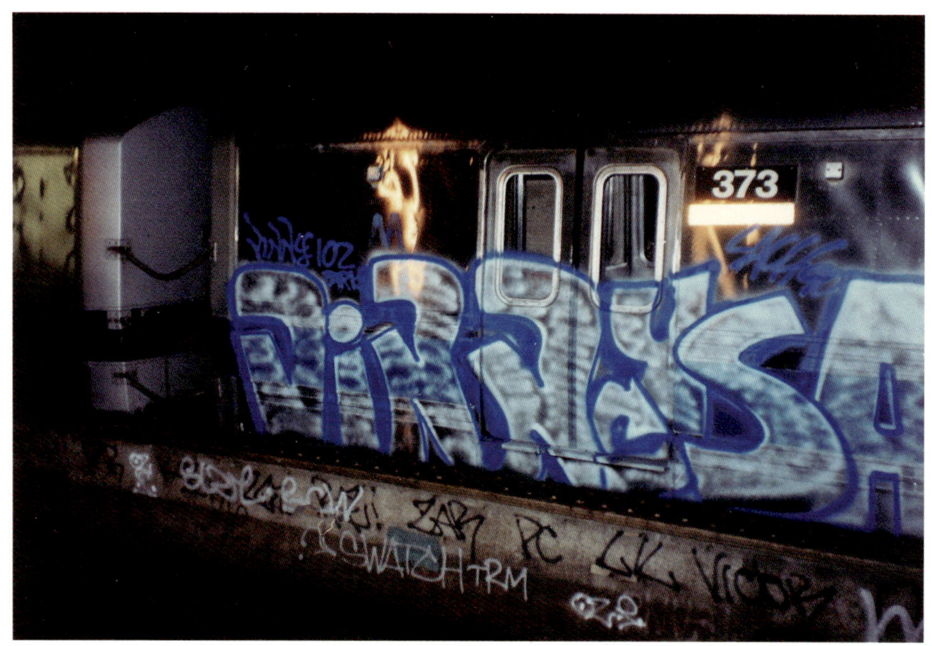

Vinny by Sach

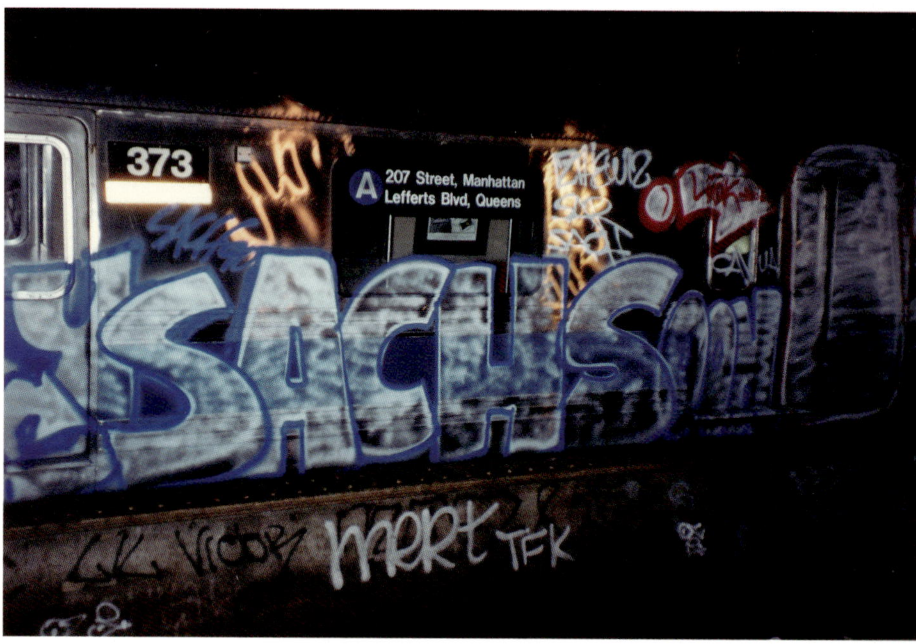

Sachsoon

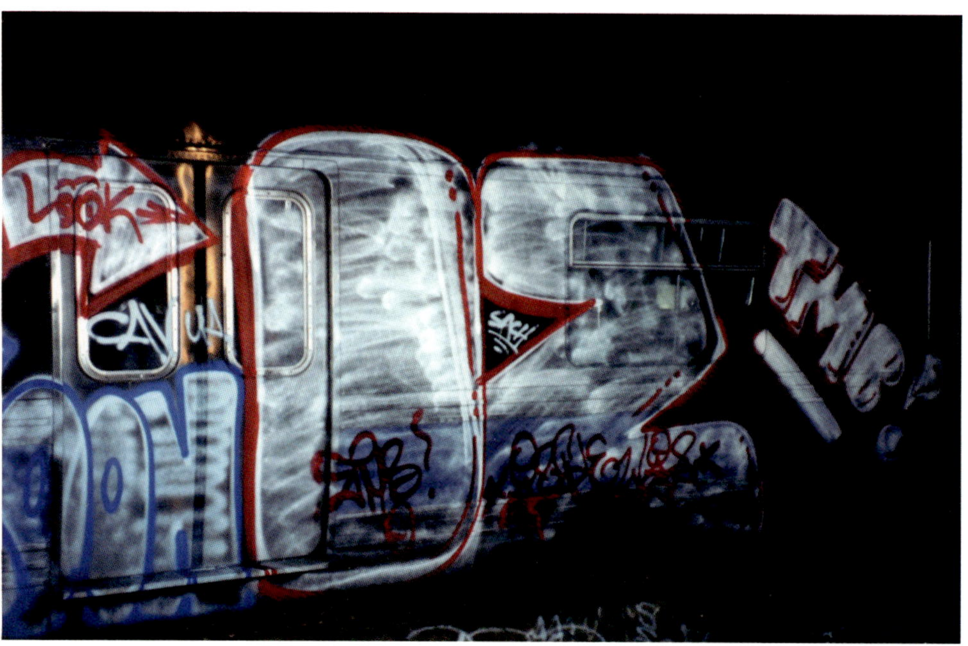

IZ TMB

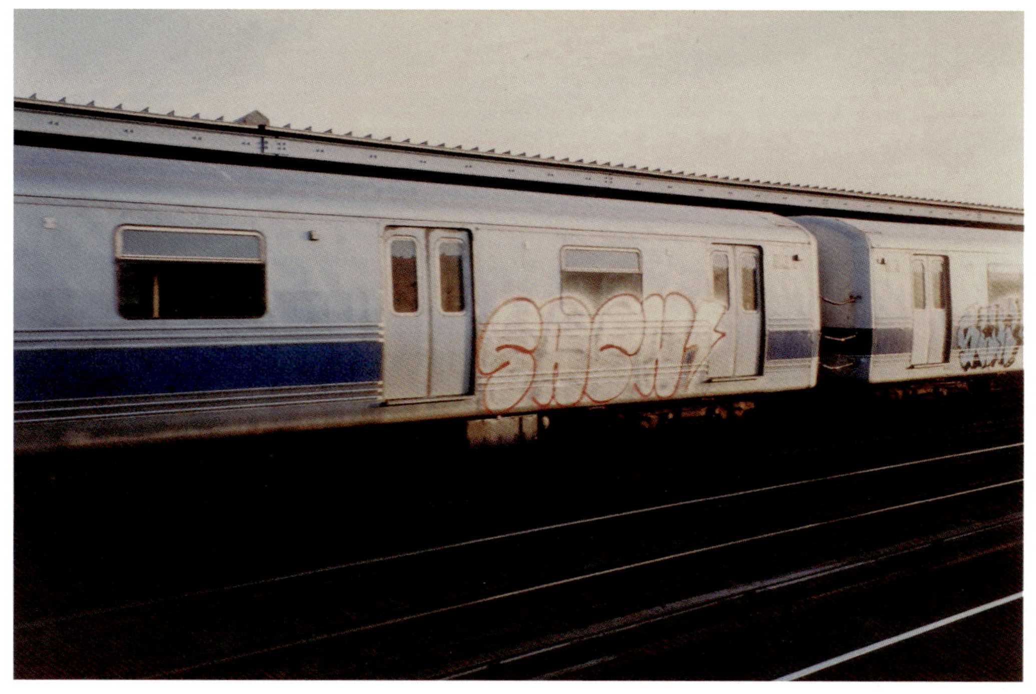

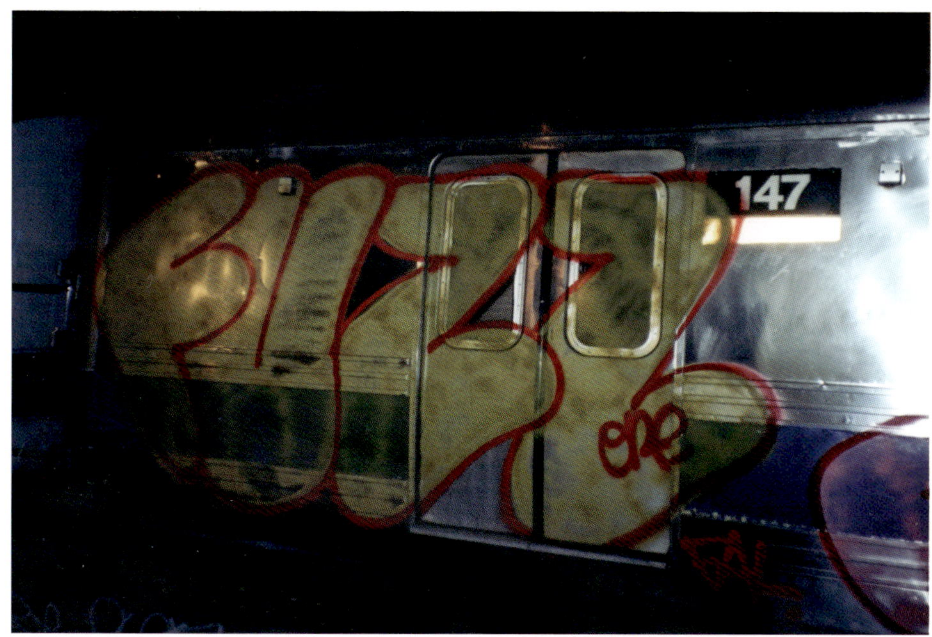

Fuzz FAL

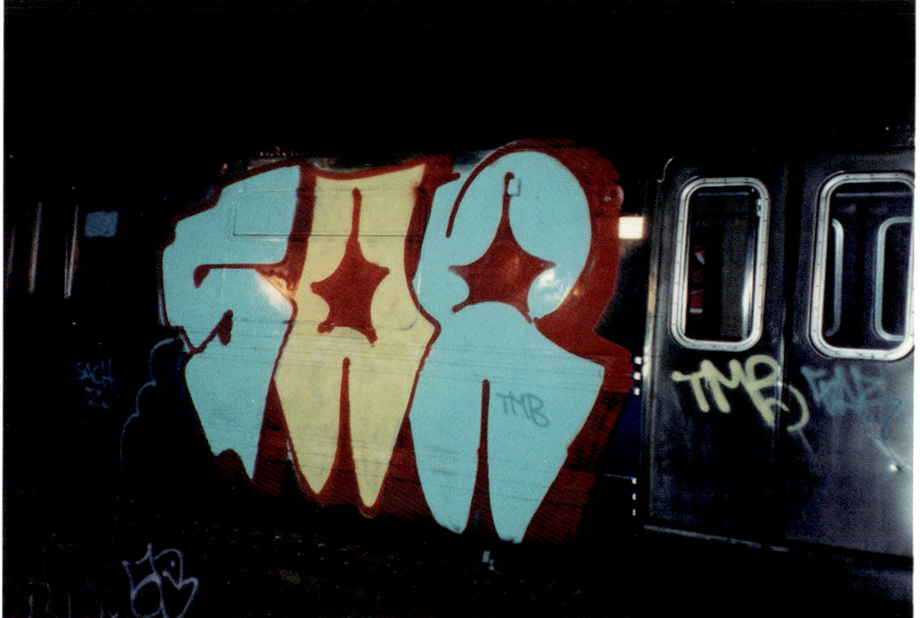

Sar TMB

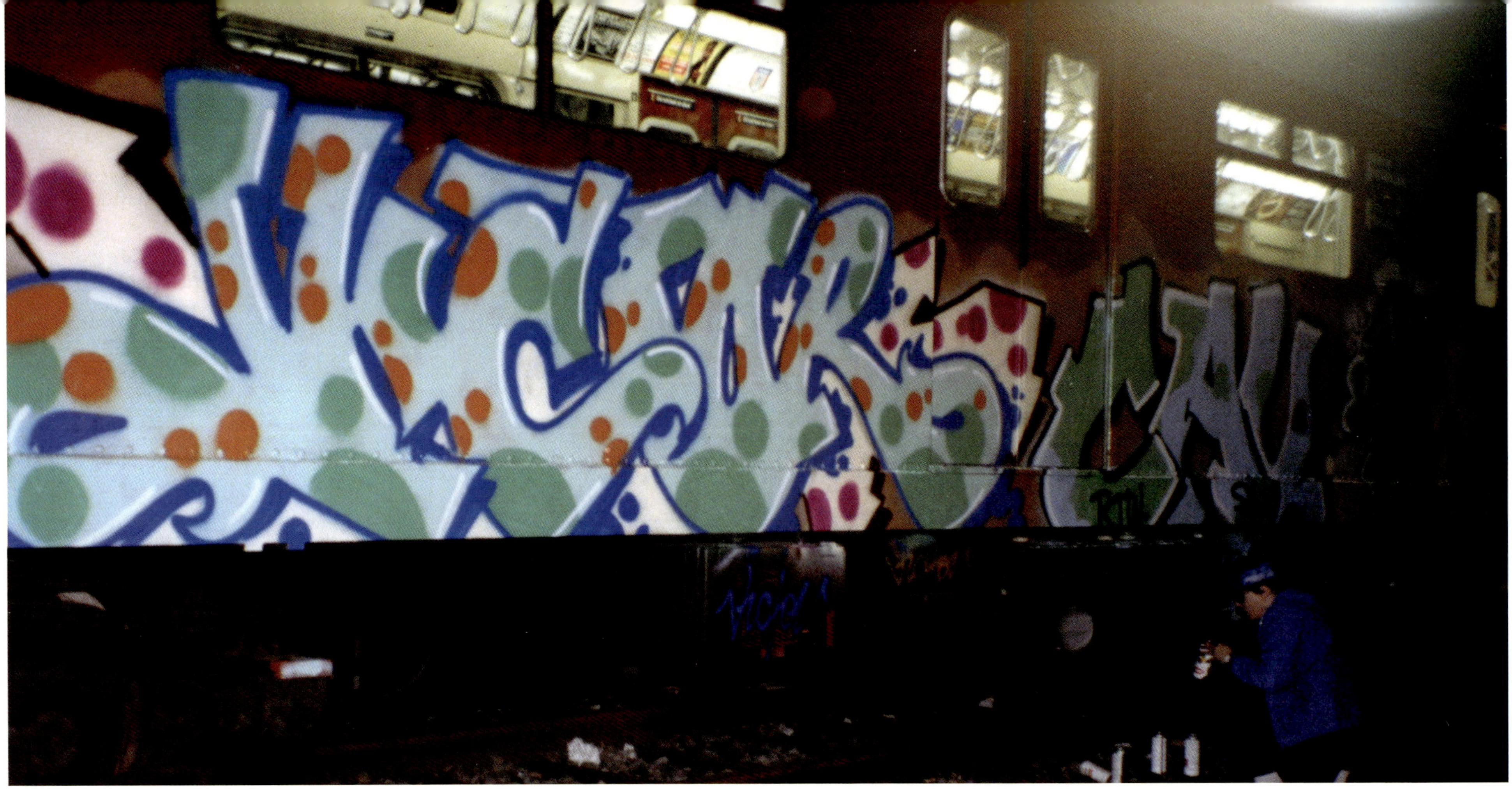

Victor, Cav, Sar (7 Yard), 1990 (Photo courtesy of SAR TMB)

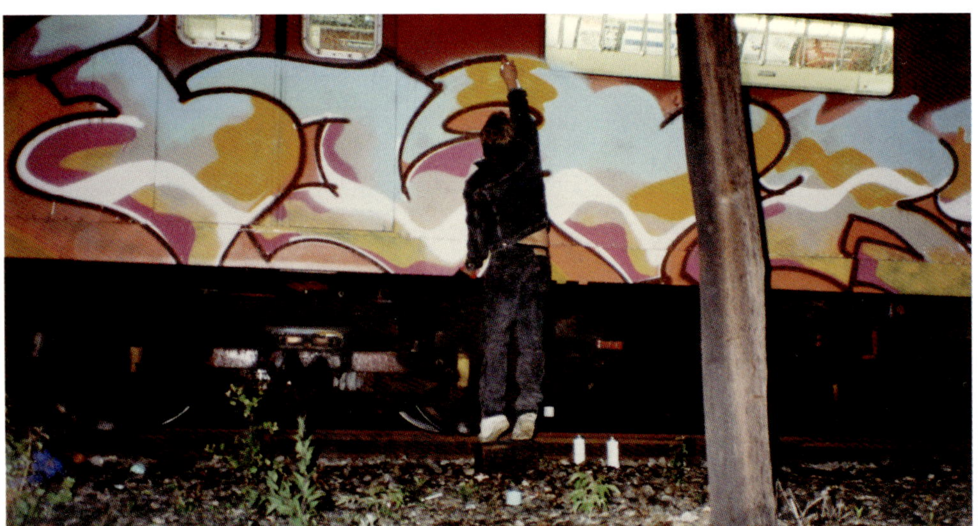

(Photo courtesy of SAR TMB)

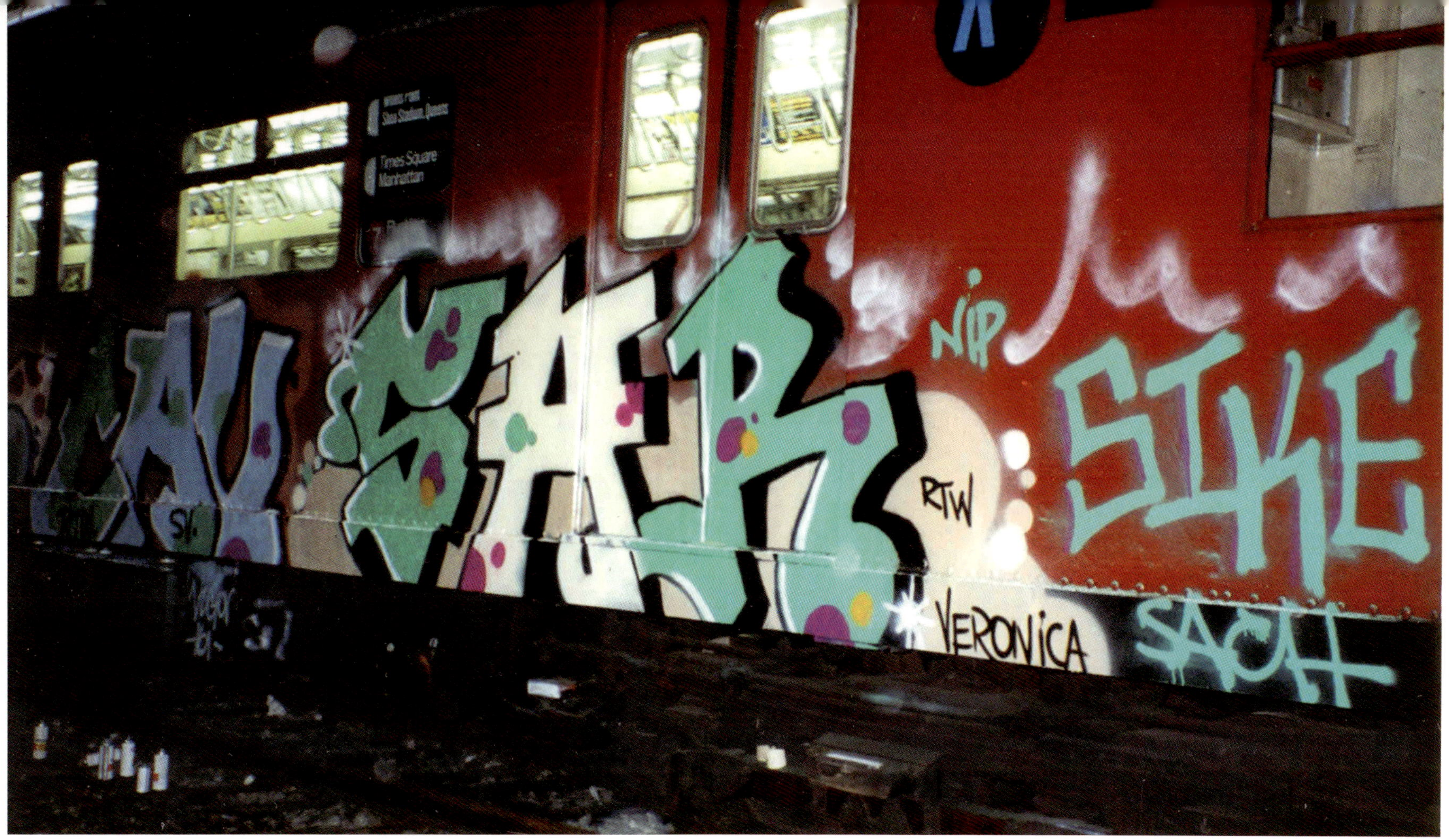

(Photo courtesy of SAR TMB)

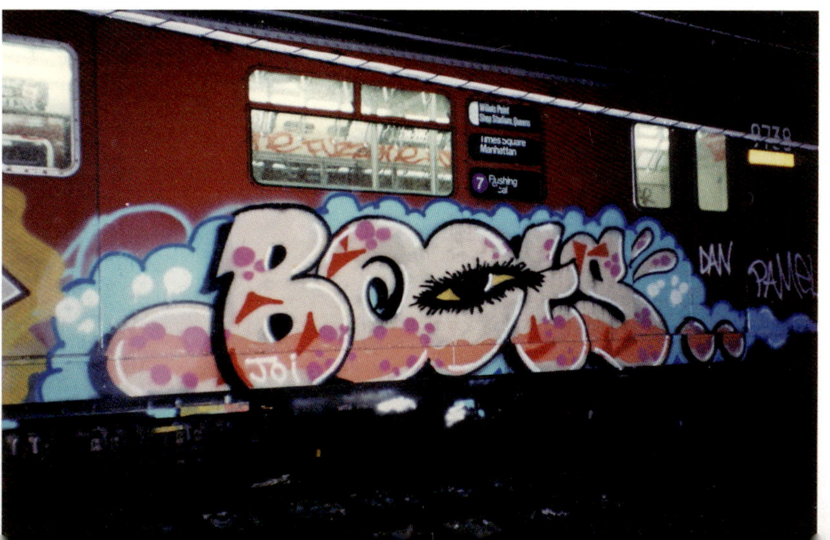

Boots119, 1990

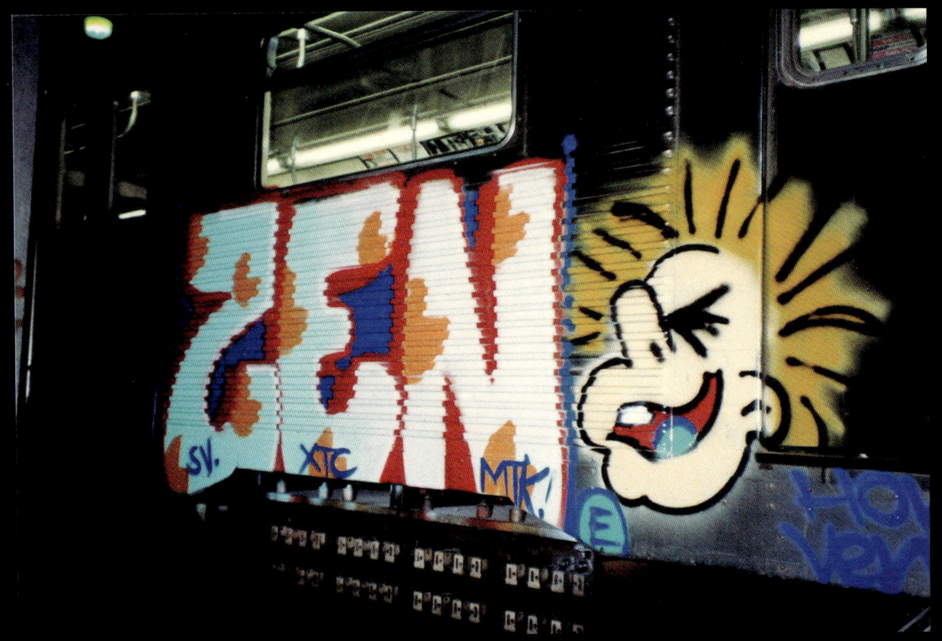

Zeno, Pitkin Yard

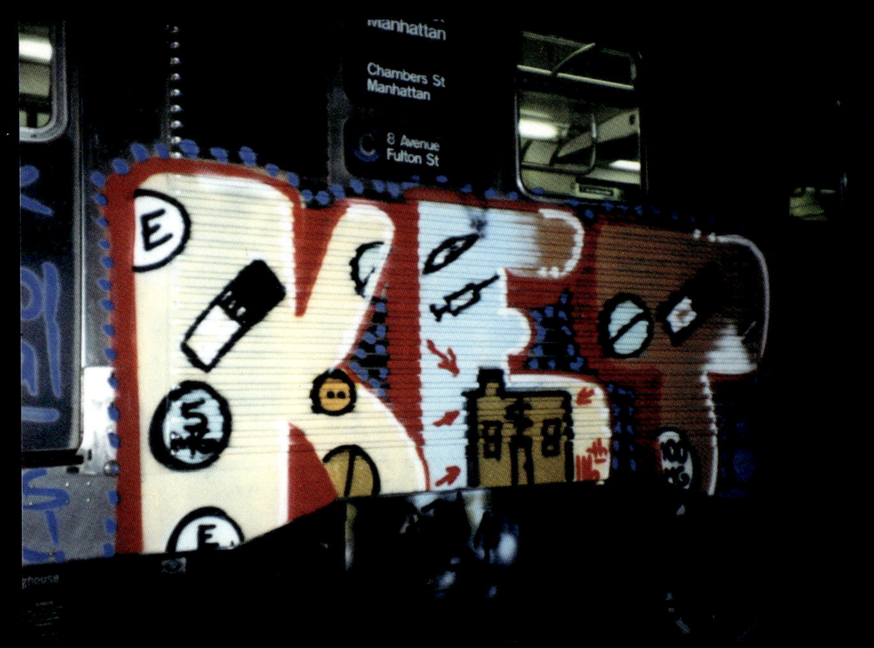

Ket, Pitkin Yard

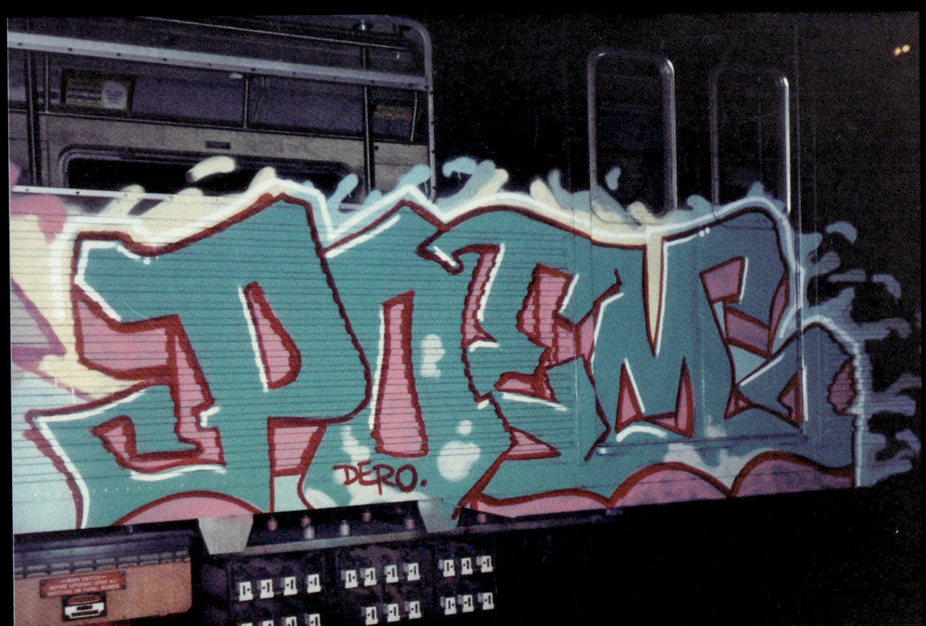

Poem (Photo courtesy of Poem)

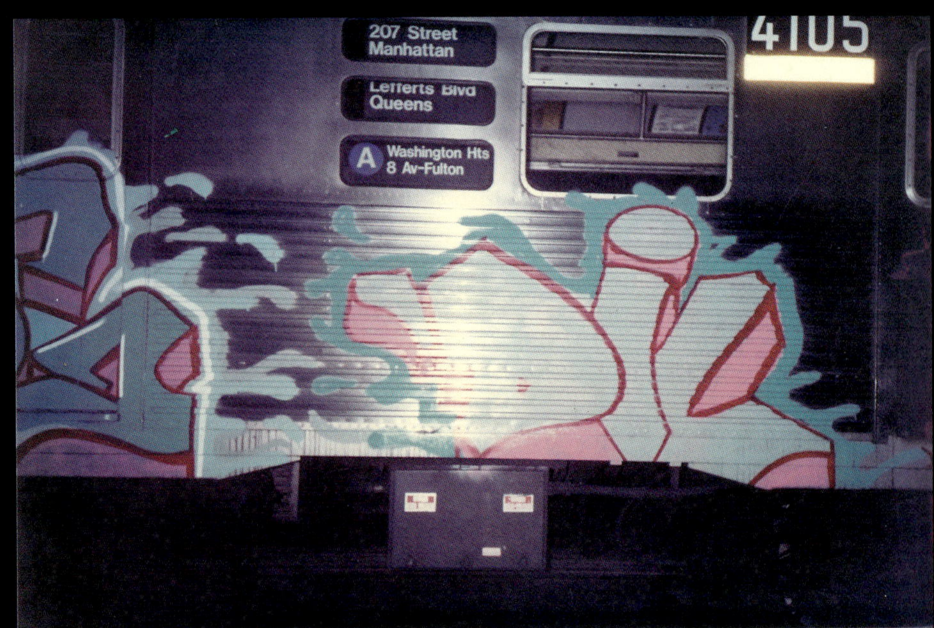

Dil (Photo courtesy of Poem)

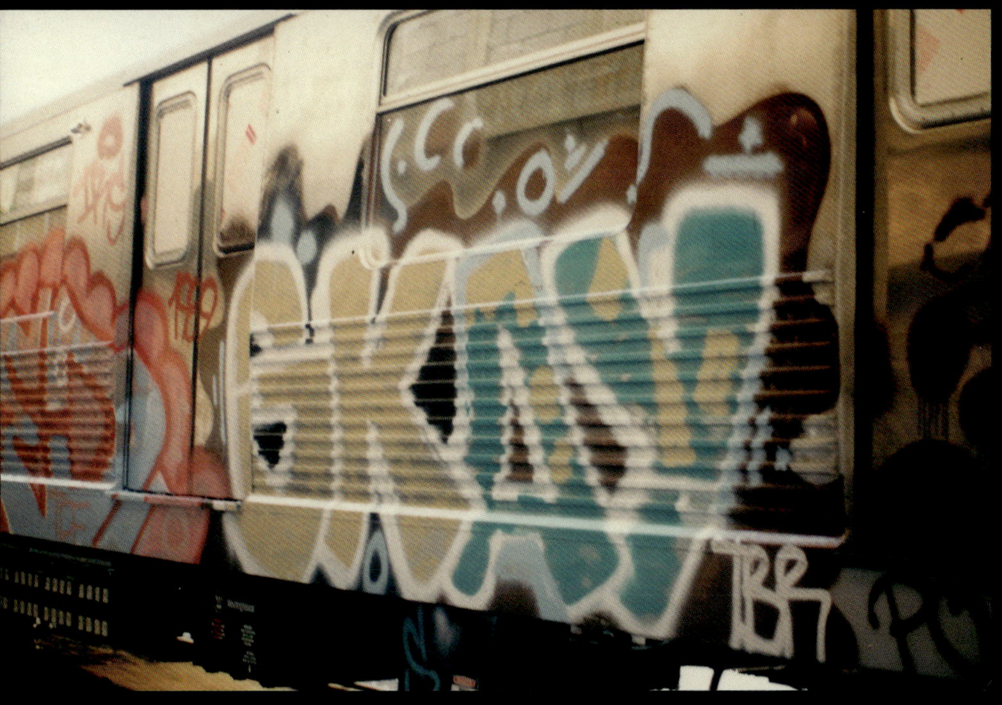

Gkay (Sed missing) (Photo courtesy of Gkay)

Back then RIS and AOK were the most famous crews for bombing clean trains because they did so much. Under the radar though were a lot of others that bombed the clean trains. They weren't known because ninety-nine percent of the time it didn't run. So, no one really knew that it was being done in the first place. I mostly hit them with my boys Sed and Base but on occasion with Cav and Ket as well. Even some old RTW and TMB guys came back. Also, Sach, Sar, the legendary Iz the Wiz, and, for a shorter time, Min. Also Fuzz FAL and Sent TFP got down killing various train lines. It was a blast!

–Gkay

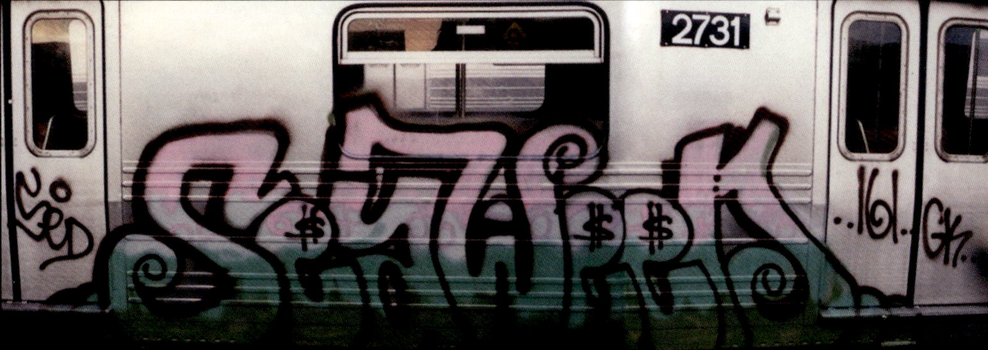

Seaweed by Sed (Photo courtesy of Gkay)

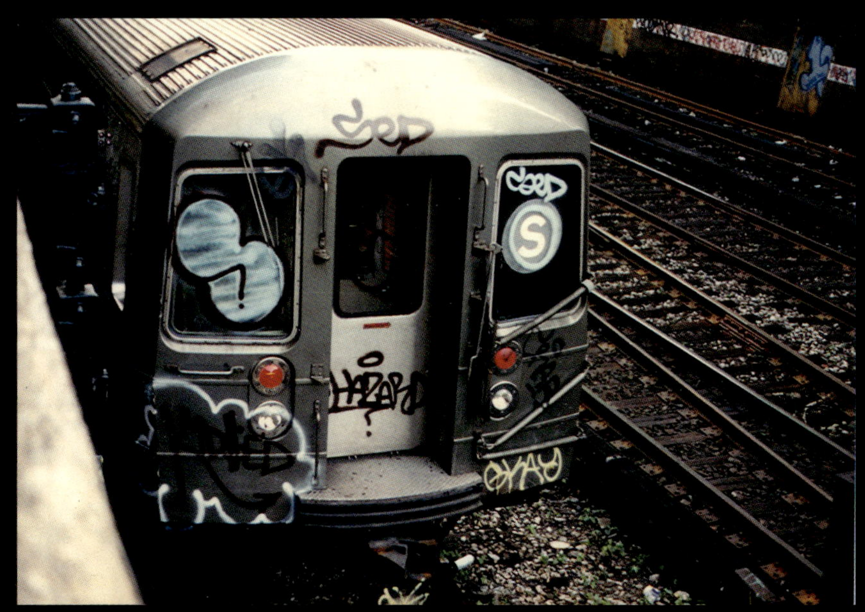

(Photo courtesy of Gkay)

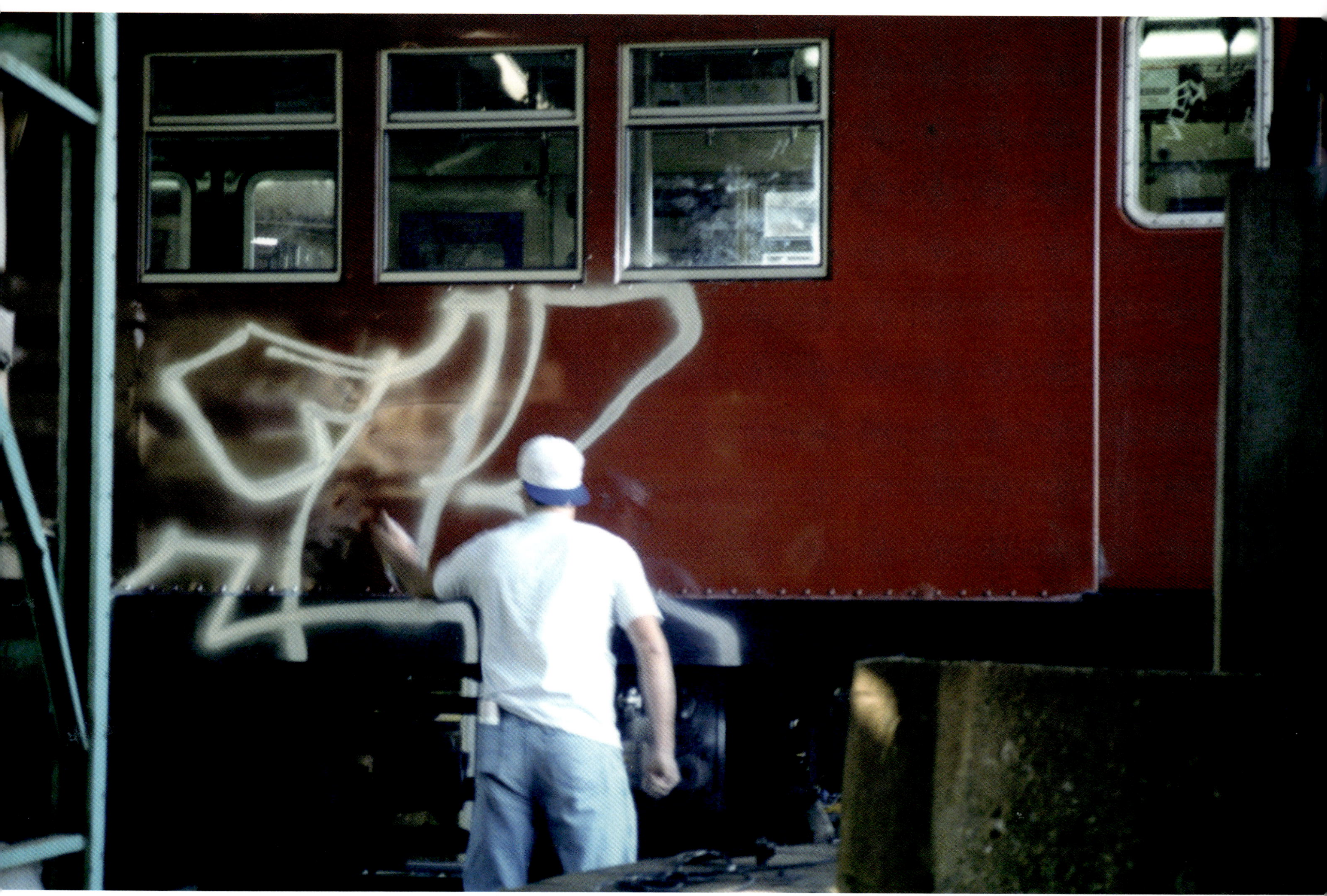

Key in the 2 Yard (241st)

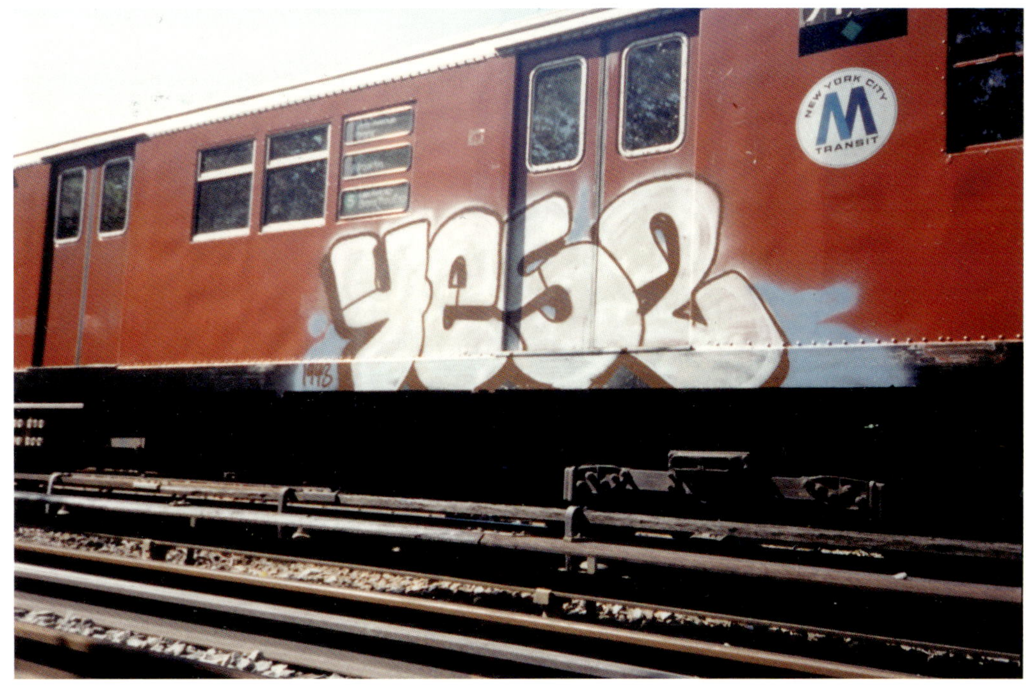

Yes2 (Photo courtesy of Yes2)

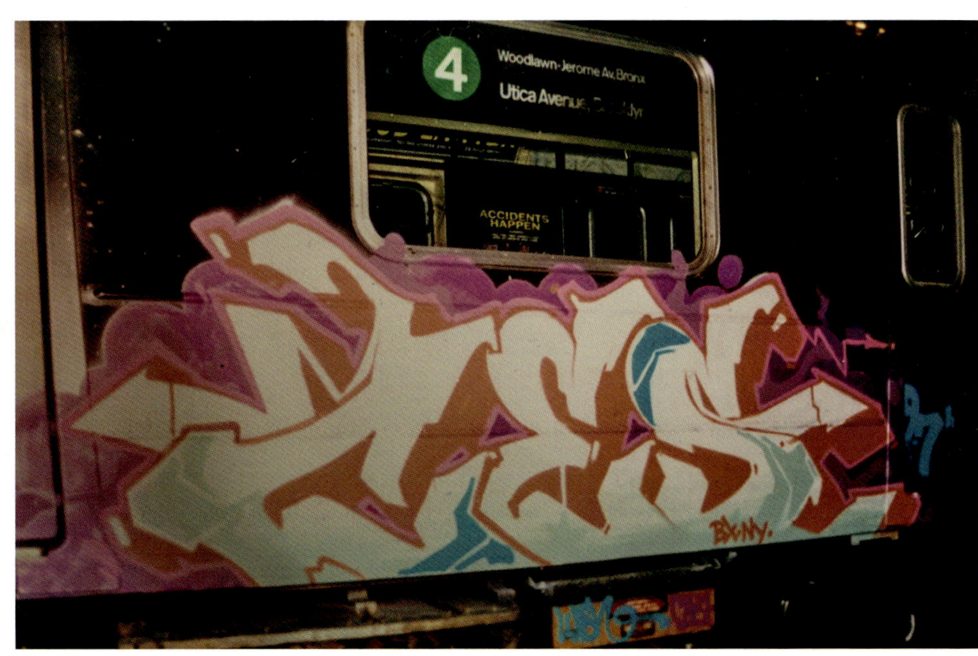

Ces (Photo courtesy of Ces)

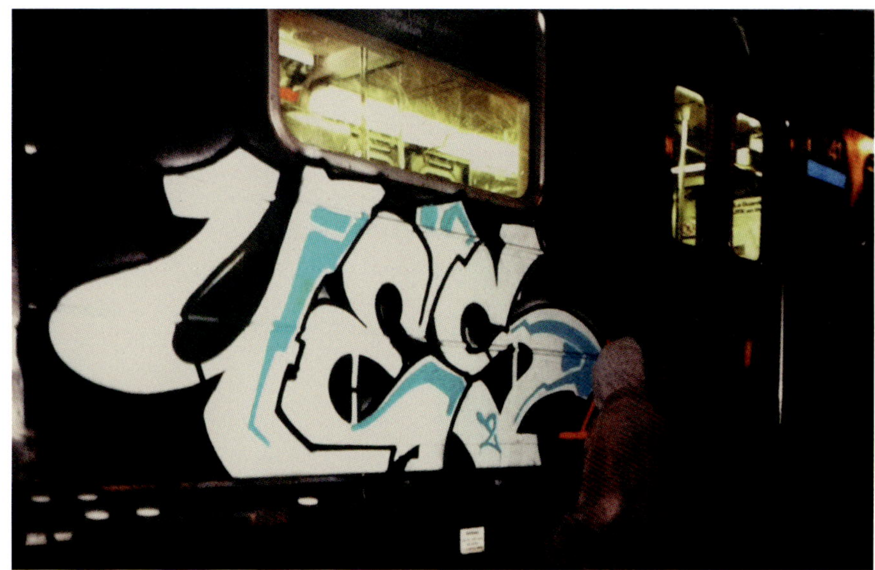

(Photo courtesy of Yes2)

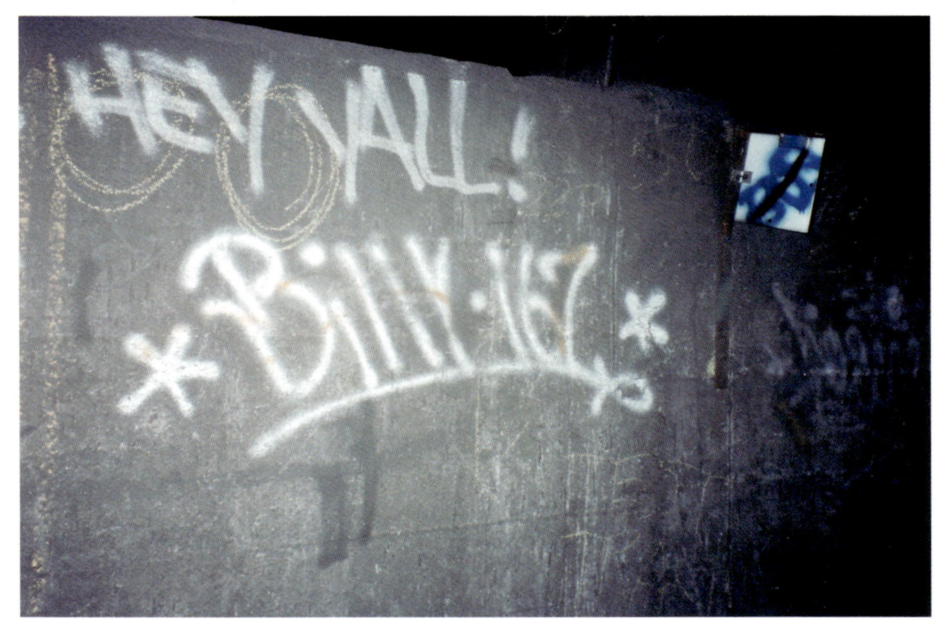

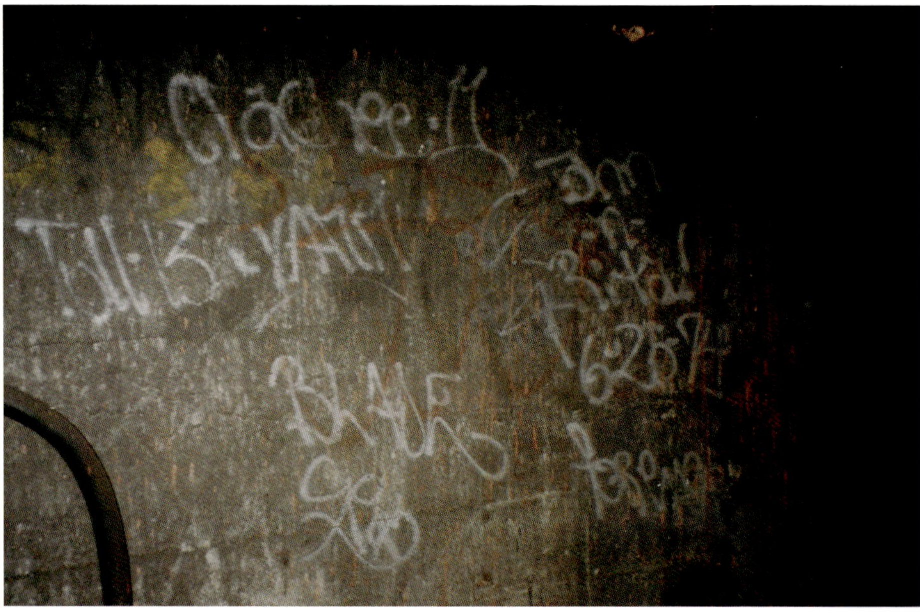

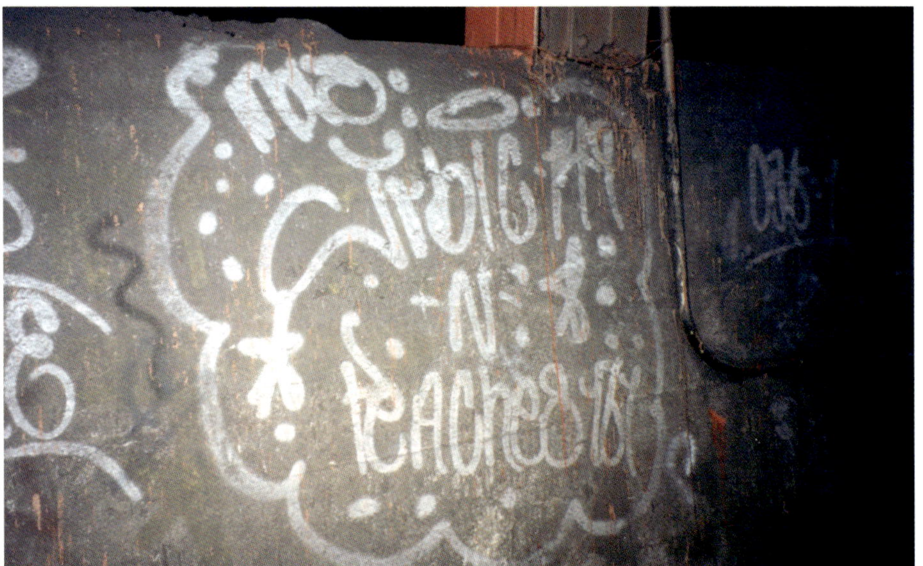

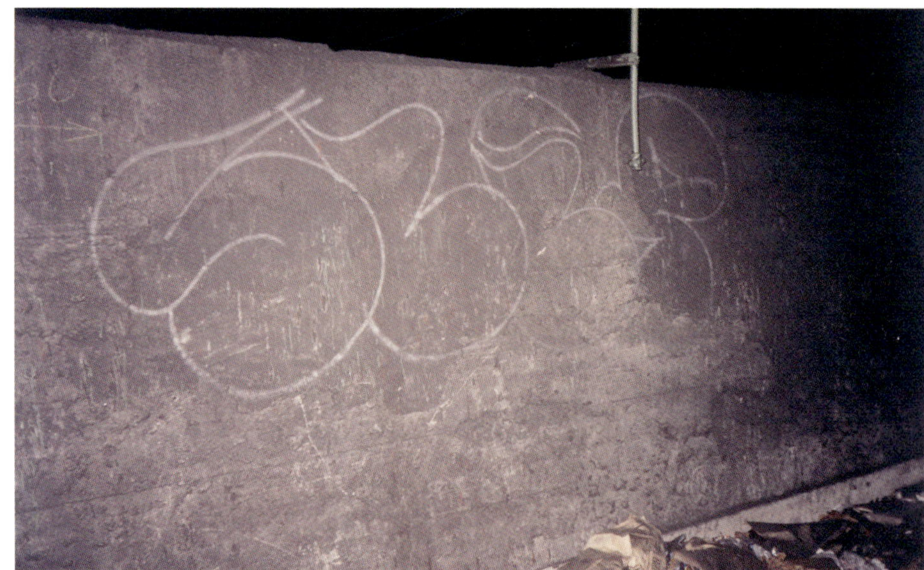

Esplanade Tunnels

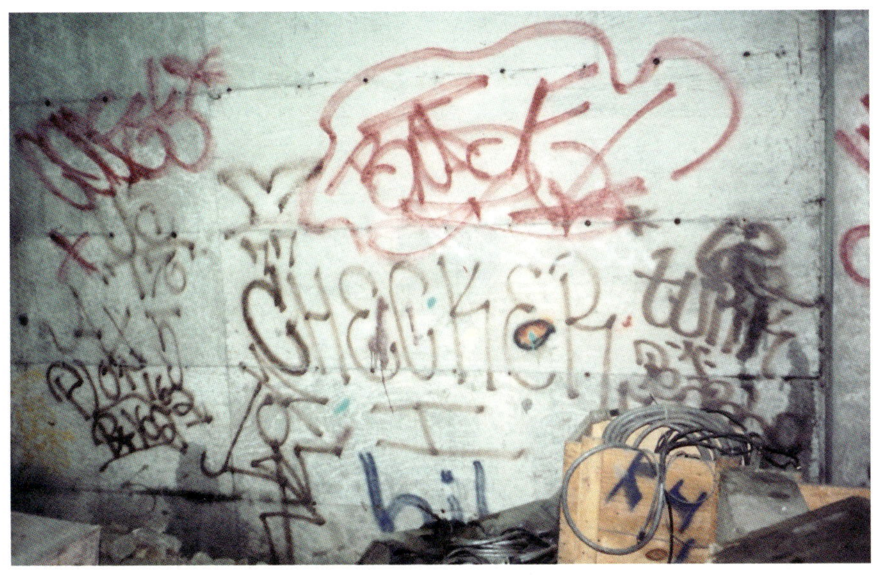

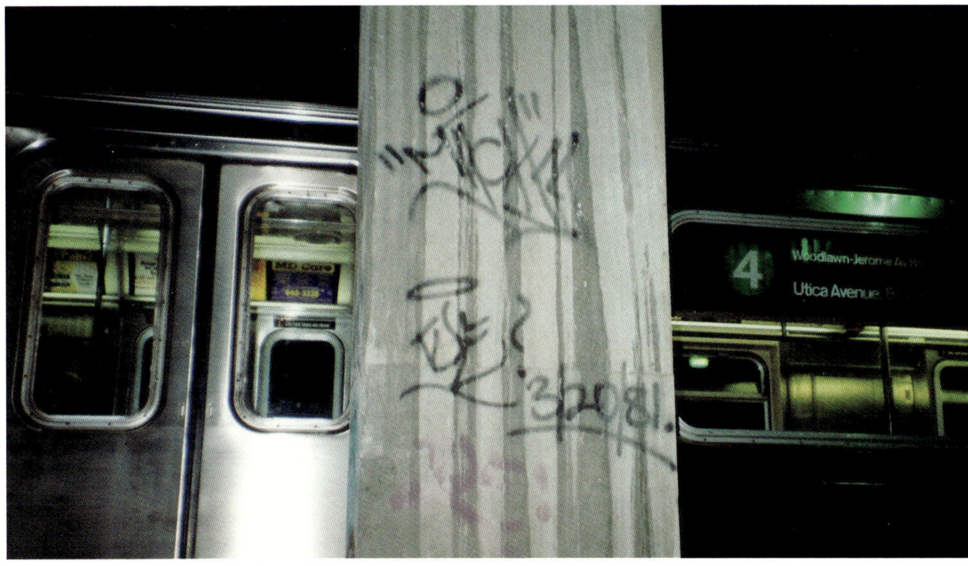

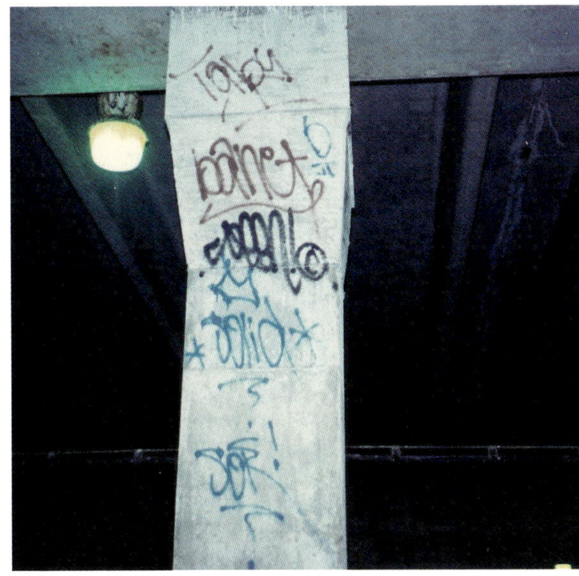

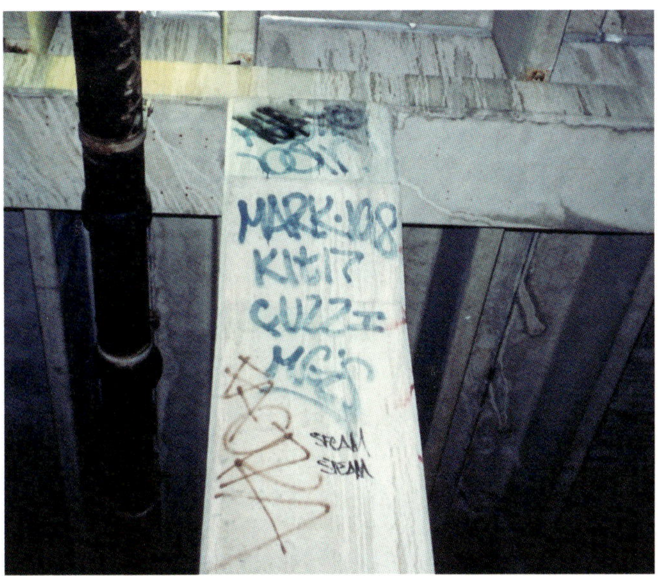

Tracy Towers (4 Yard)

I met Freedom one evening and he put me down with AW (Acid Writers). That night I hit 110 cars, elevated ones, and AW was up everywhere. I was a bit of a loner for a while. You get more done that way, and then I started hanging with other writers for a couple years branching out to Brooklyn and Queens. Then, during the spring of 1984, I was going to the 1 Tunnels solo four times a week—Monday through Thursday like clockwork—realizing I could get more done with no heat on my own. I was in and out of the 1 Tunnel hitting every car inside and out—a hundred cars in about ninety minutes. Then I just stopped cold to start a family.

–Chris217 AW

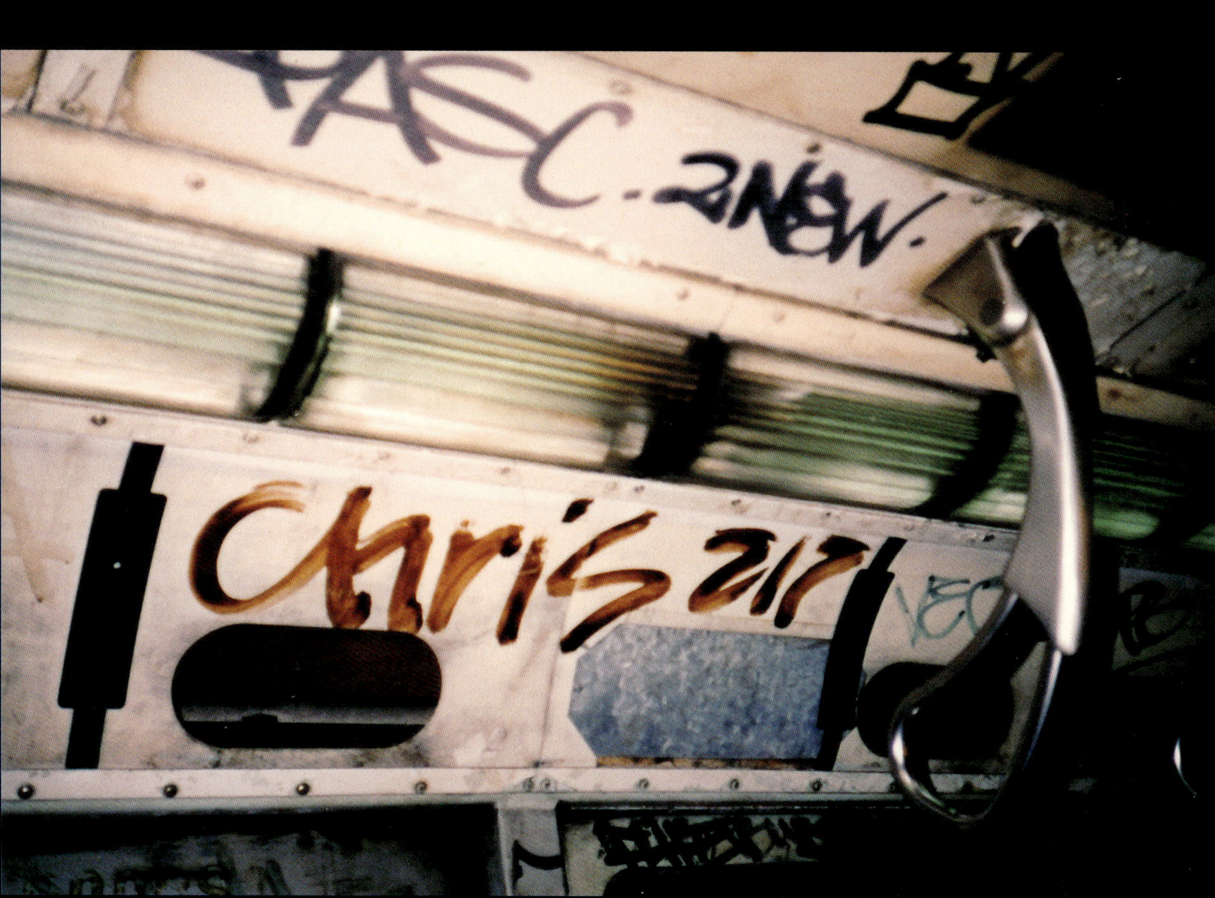

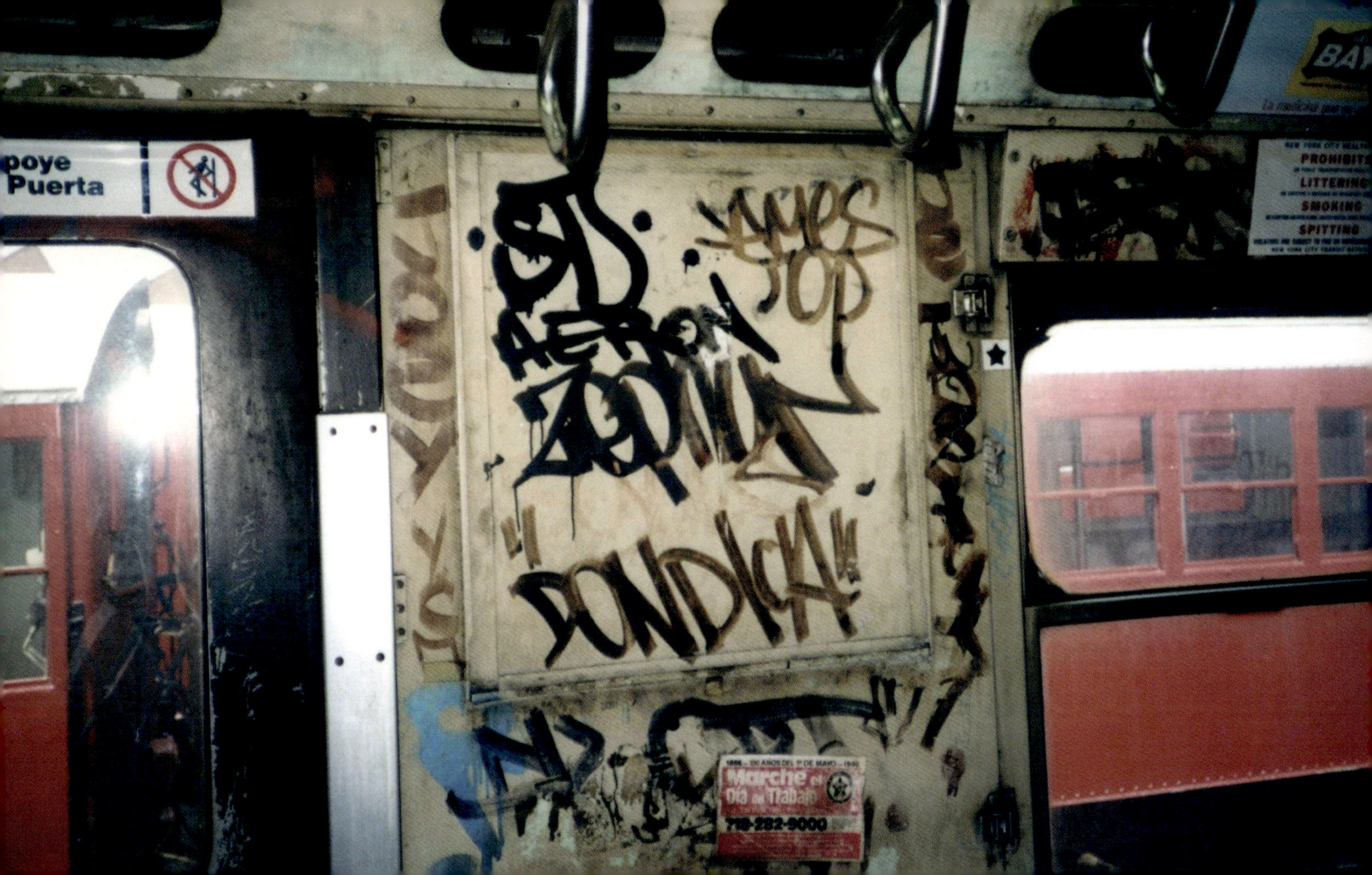
poye
Puerta
PROHIBITS
LITTERING
SMOKING
SPITTING
718-282-9000

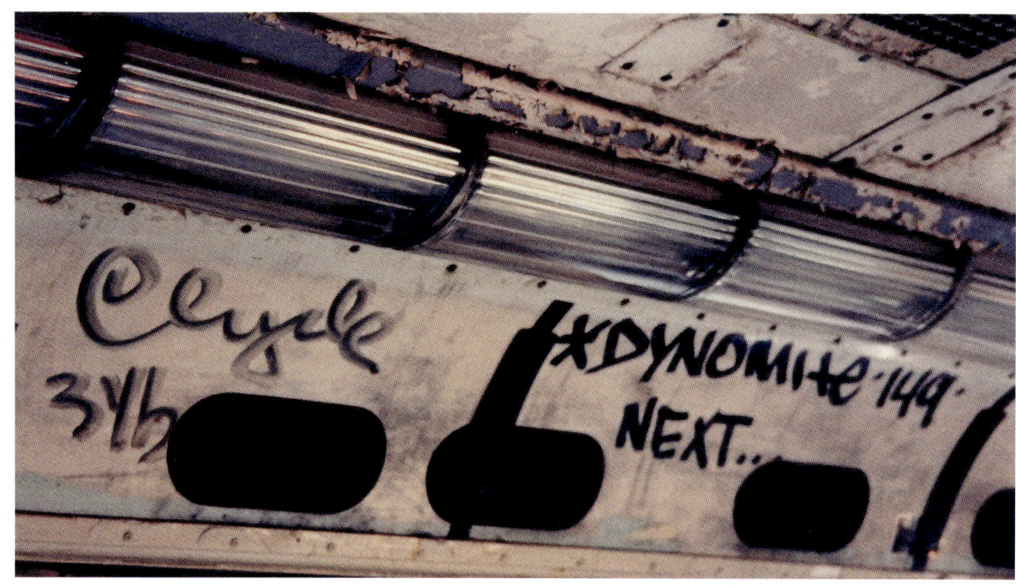
Clyde
DYNOMITE 149
NEXT...

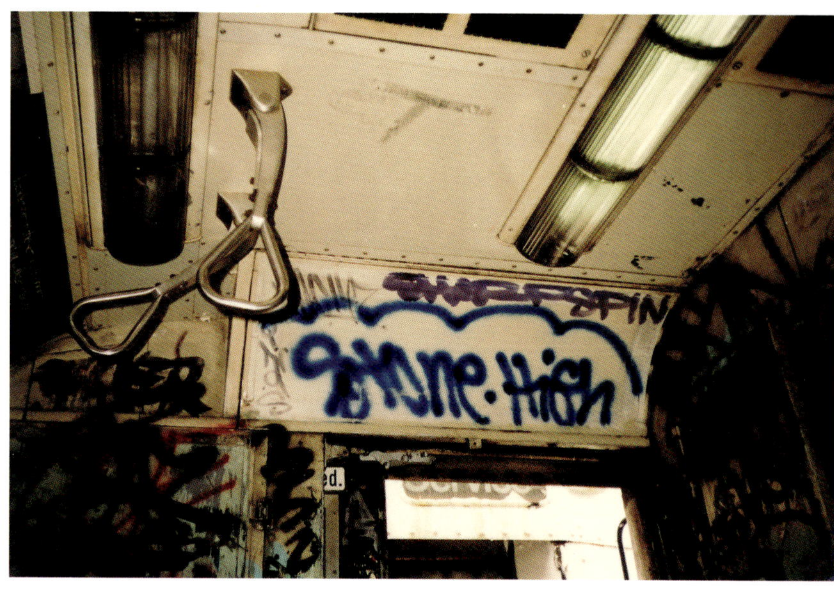

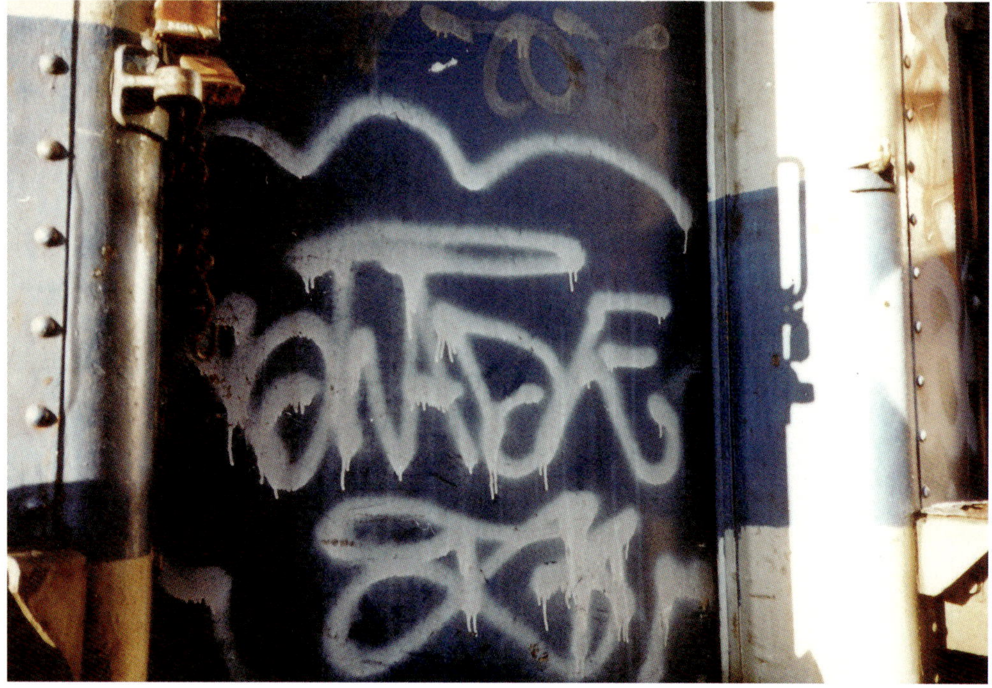

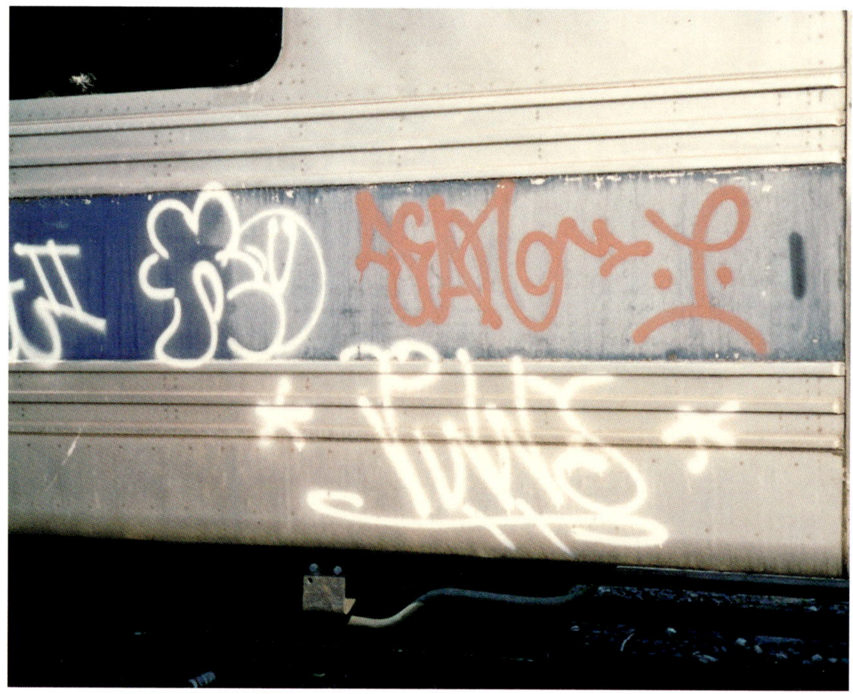

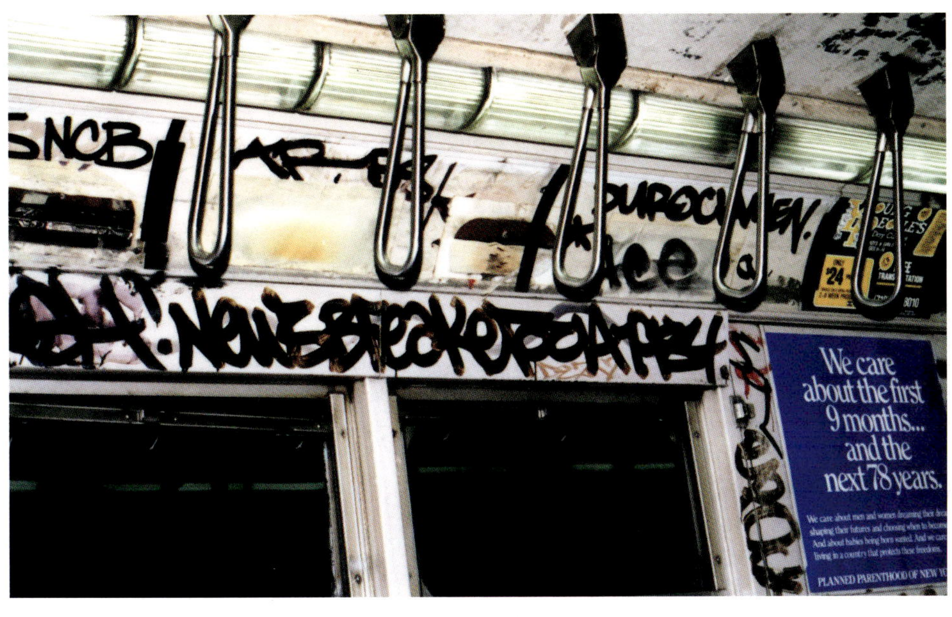
We care
about the first
9 months...
and the
next 78 years.

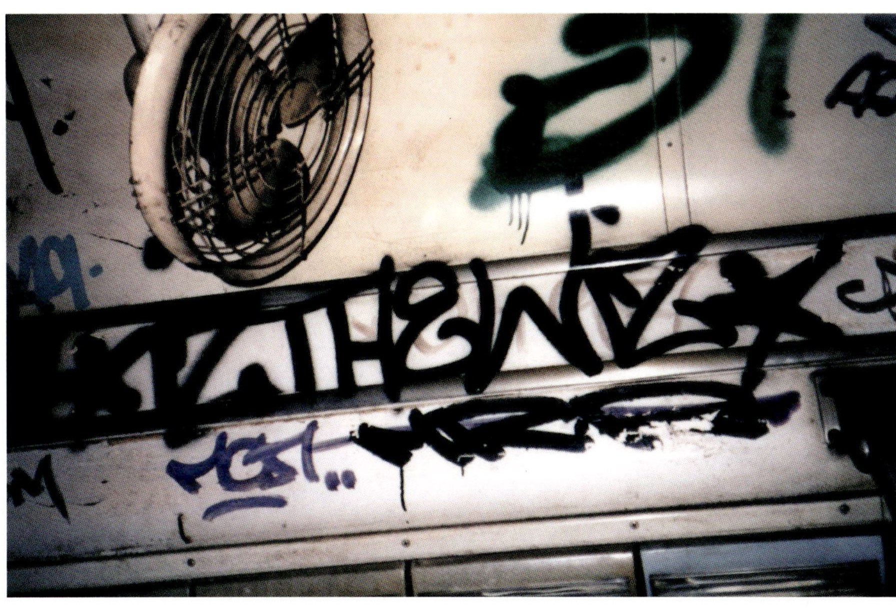

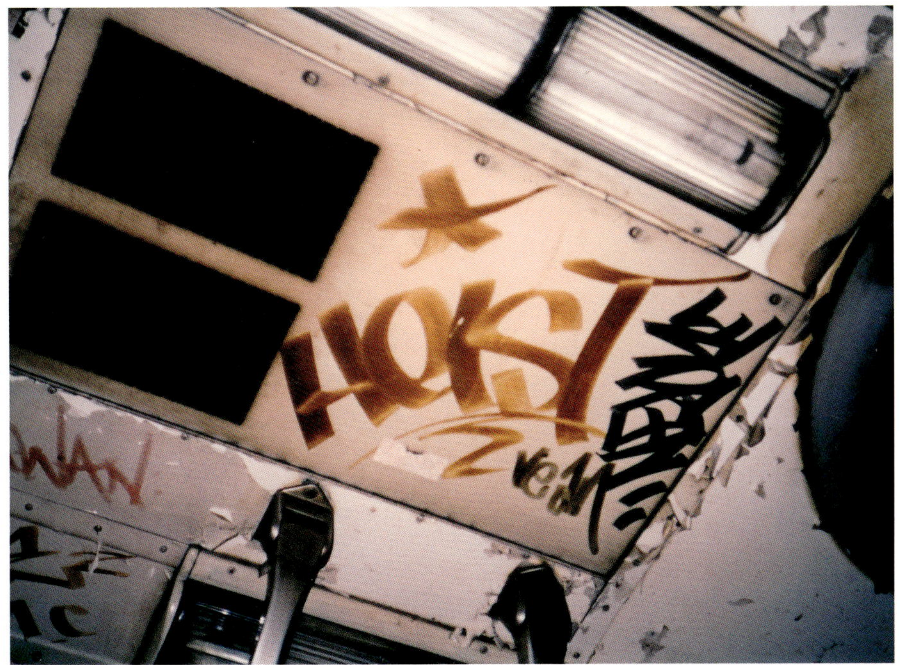

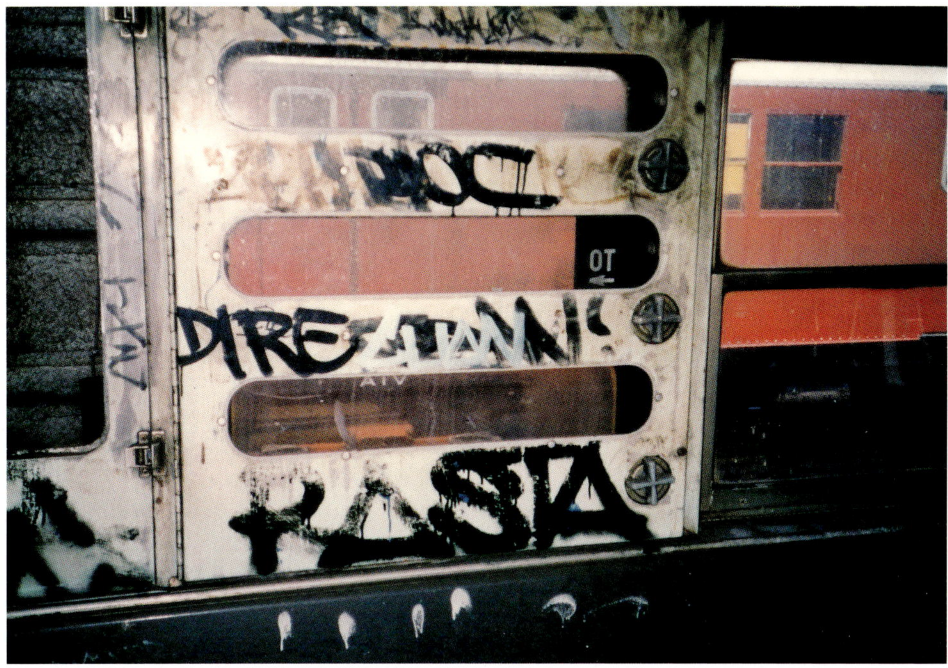

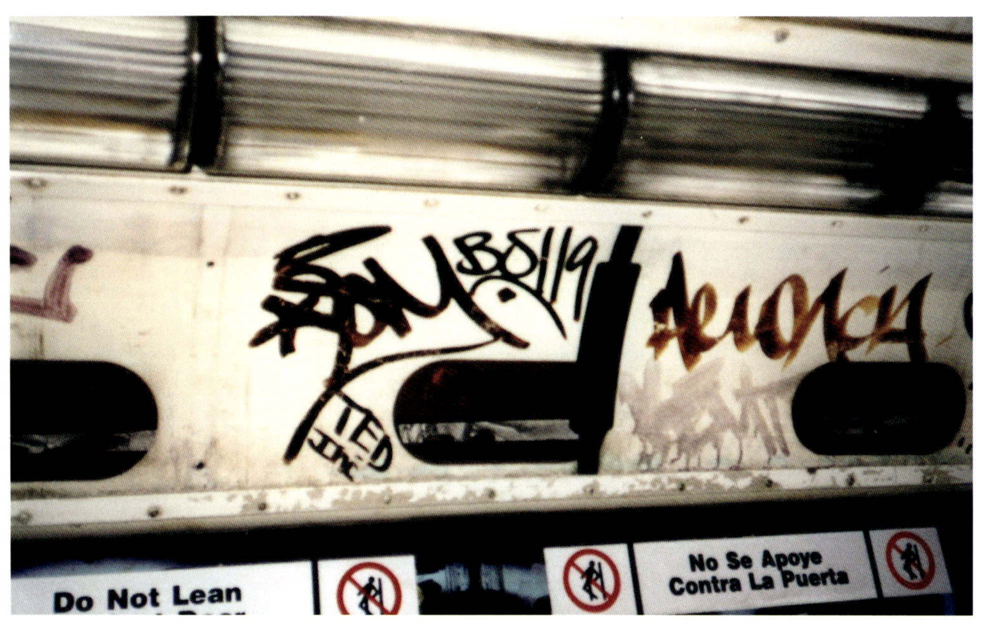
Do Not Lean
No Se Apoye
Contra La Puerta

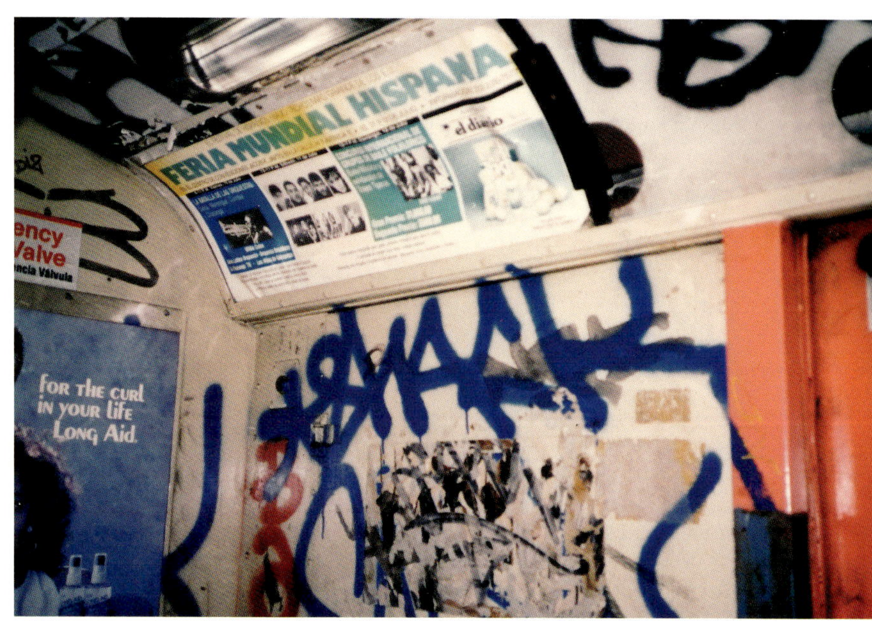
FERIA MUNDIAL HISPANA
el diario
For the curl
in your life
Long Aid.

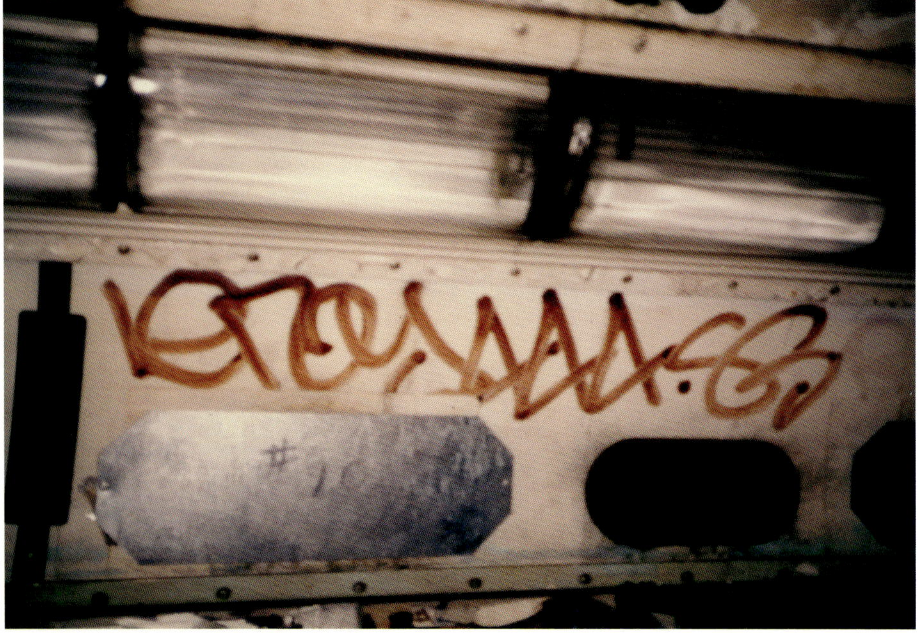

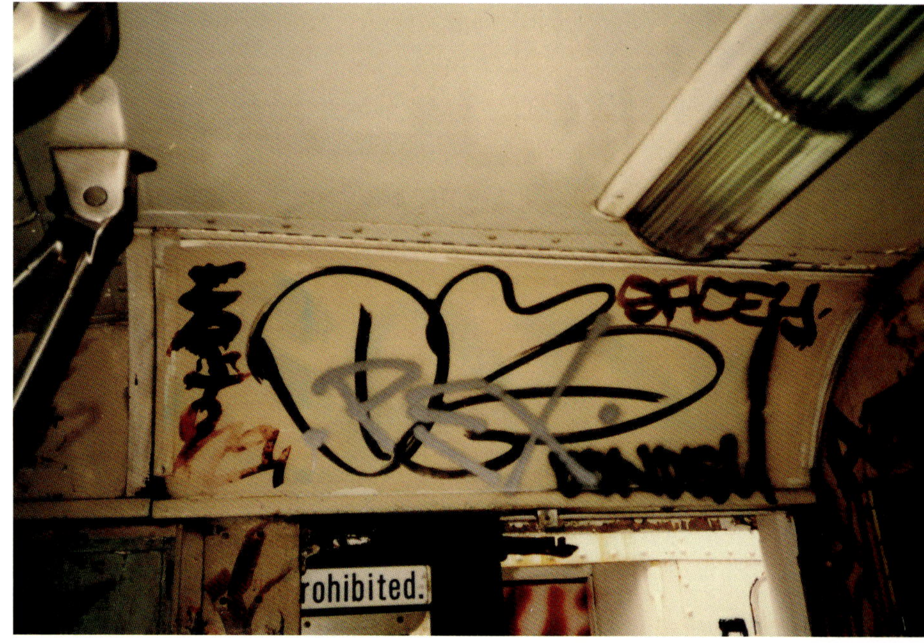

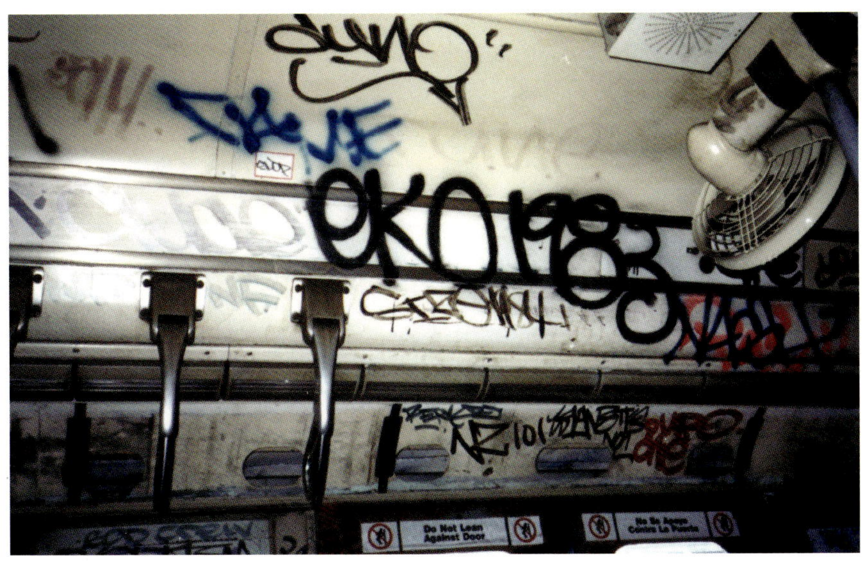
Do Not Lean Against Door

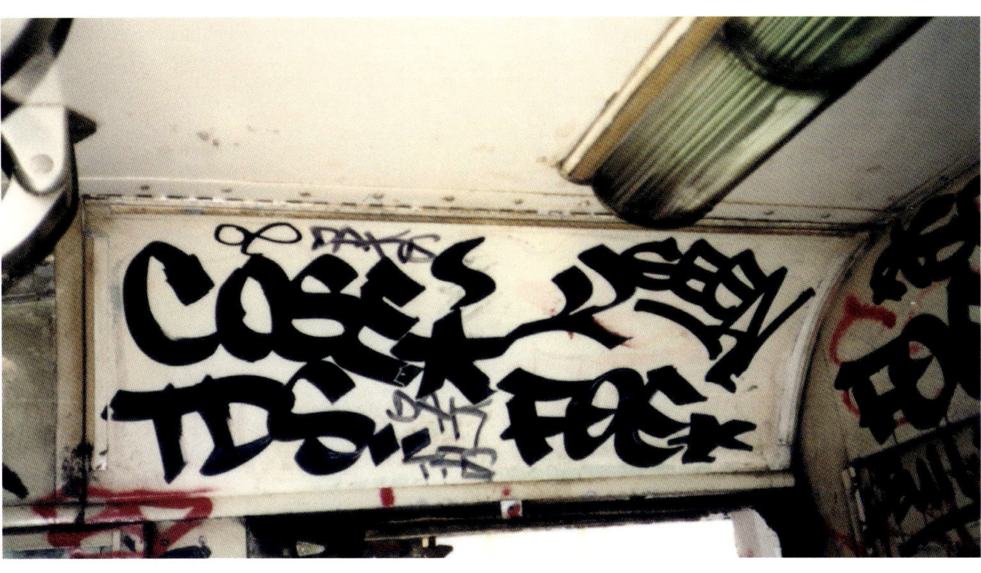
COSE
TDS

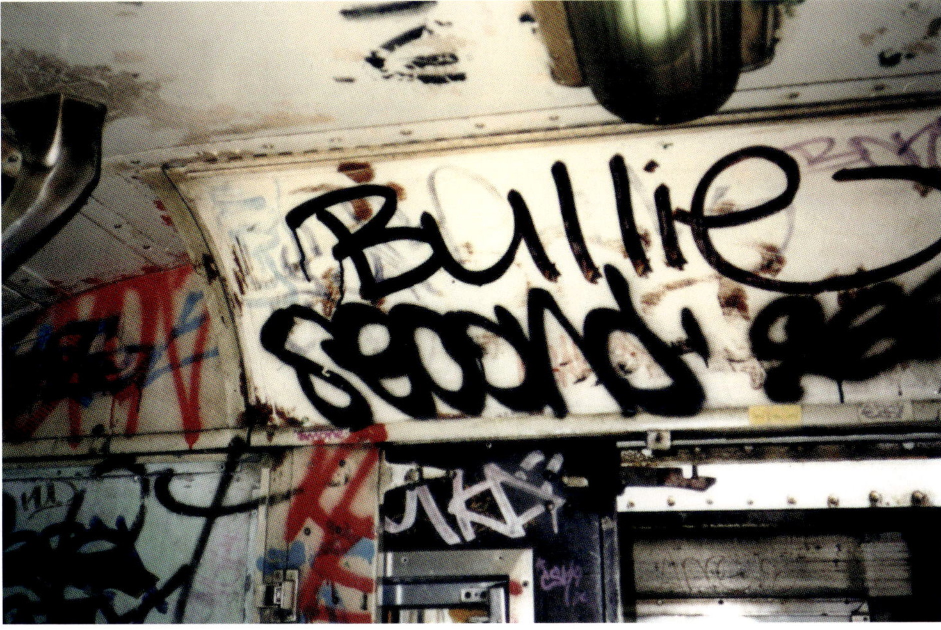
Bullie
second

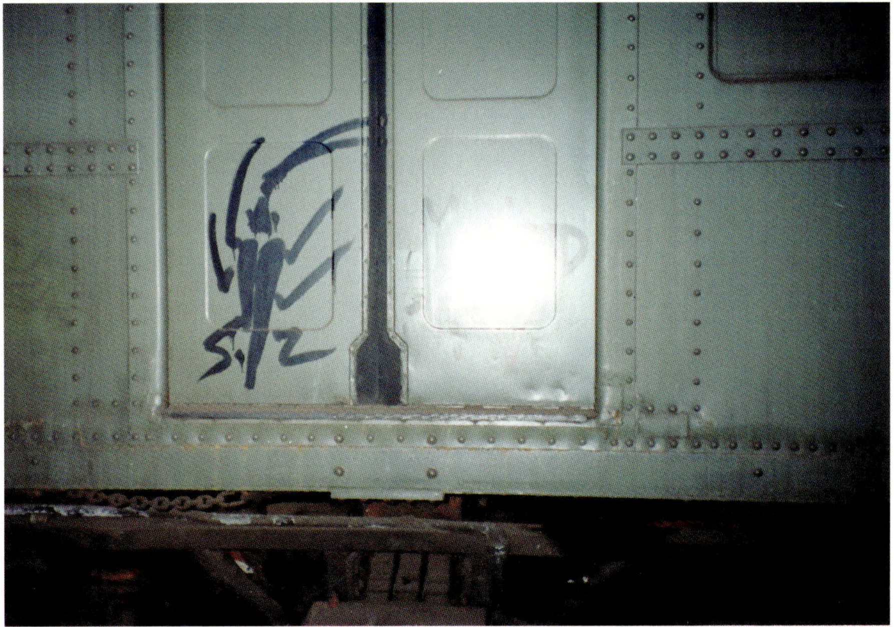

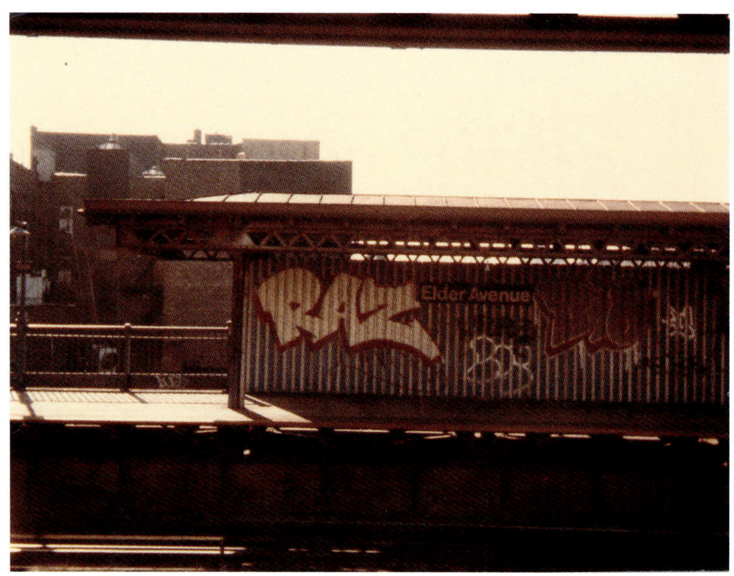
Elder Avenue

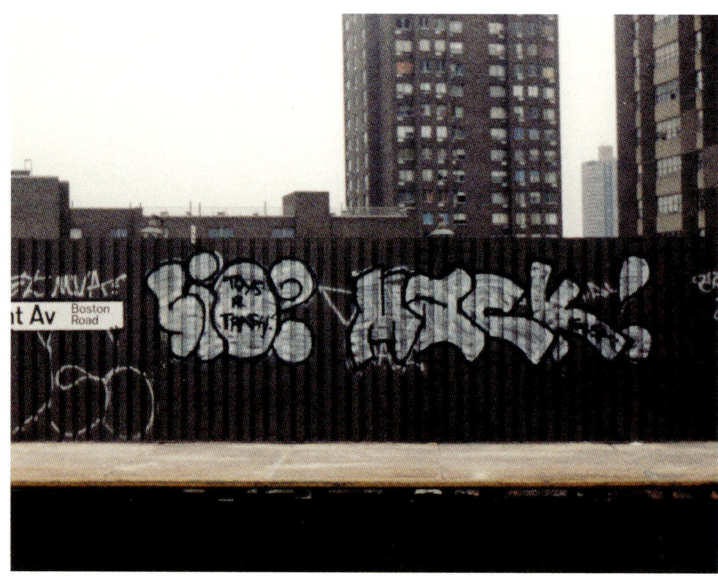
nt Av
Boston
Road

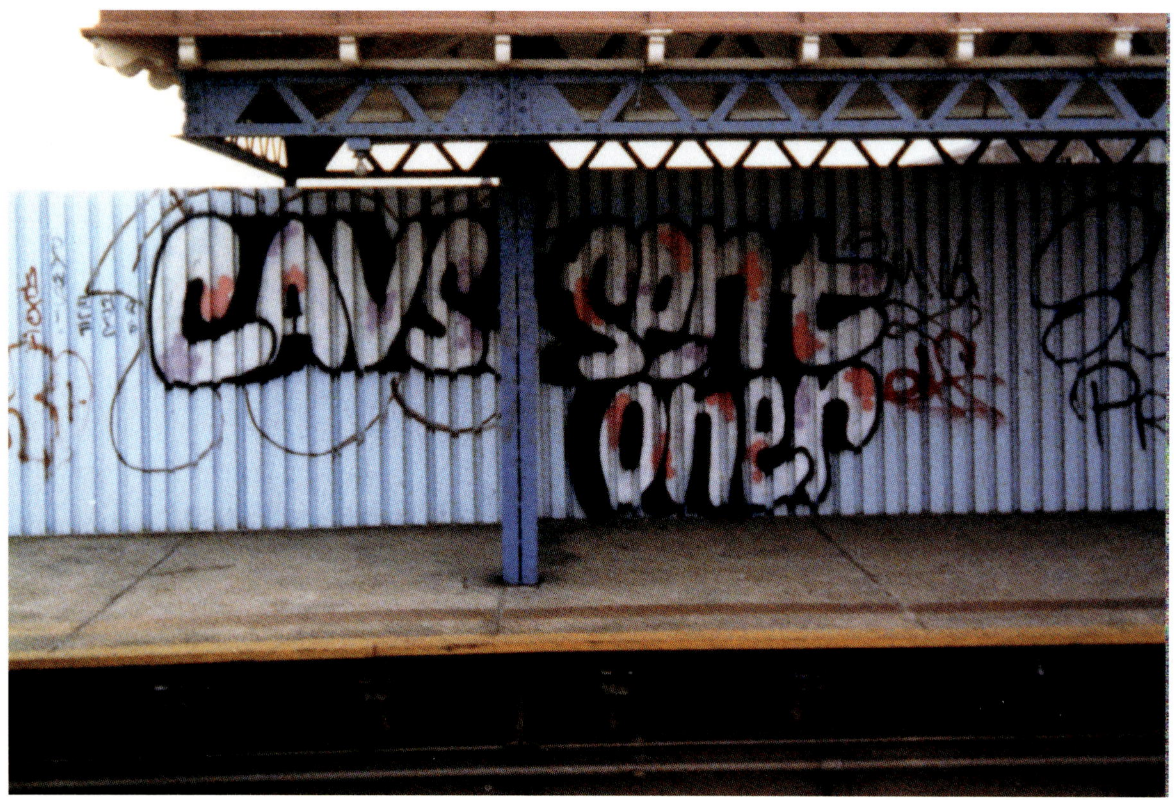

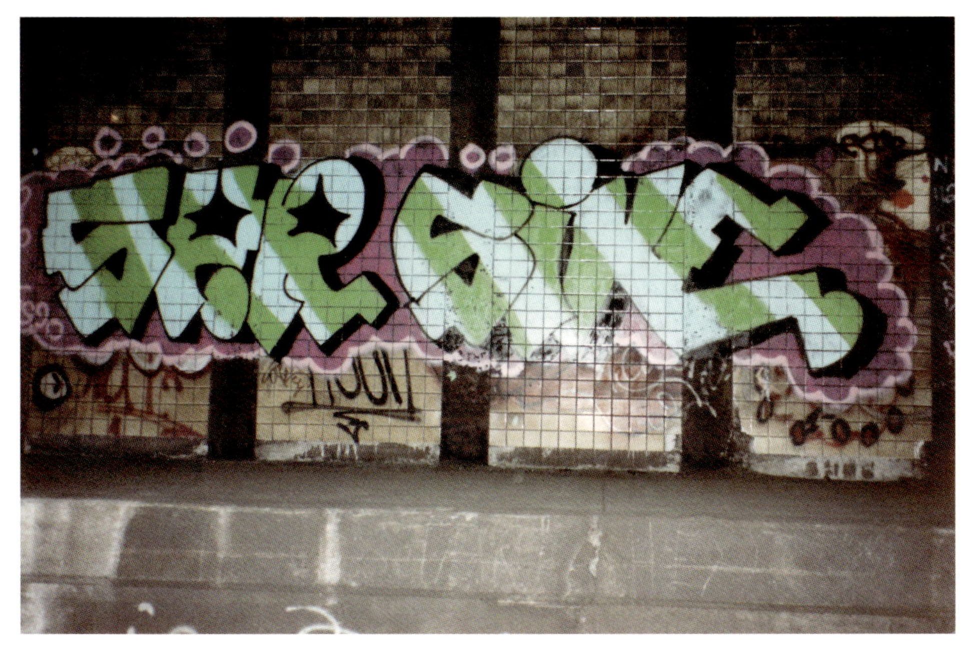

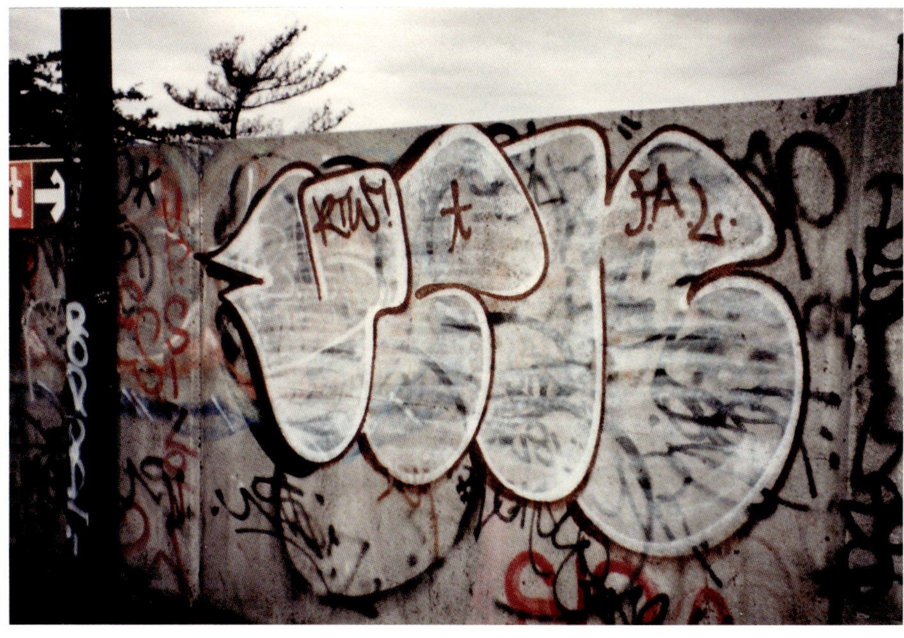

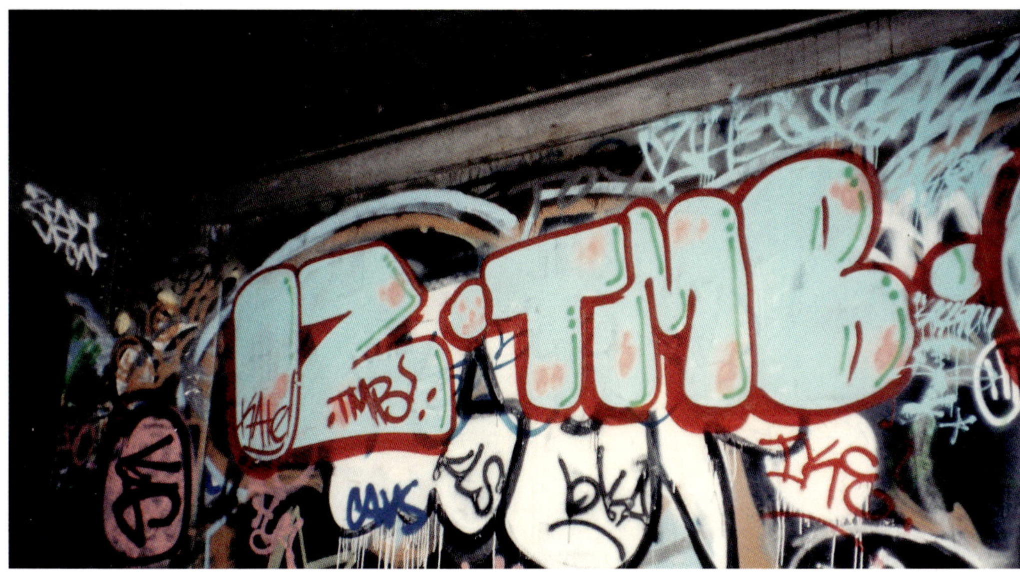

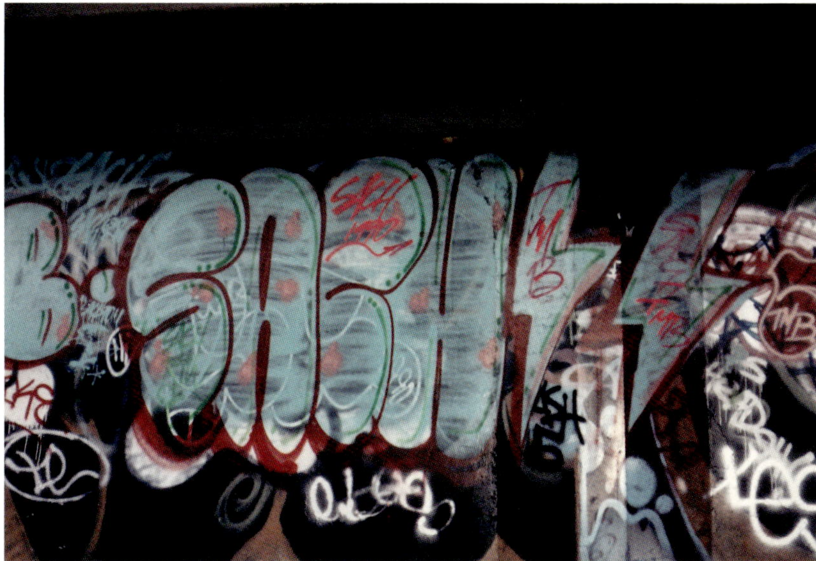

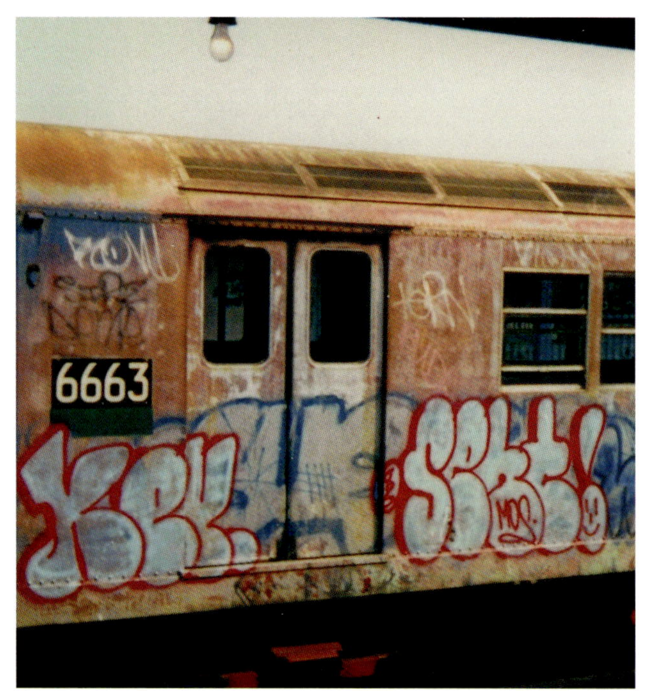
6663

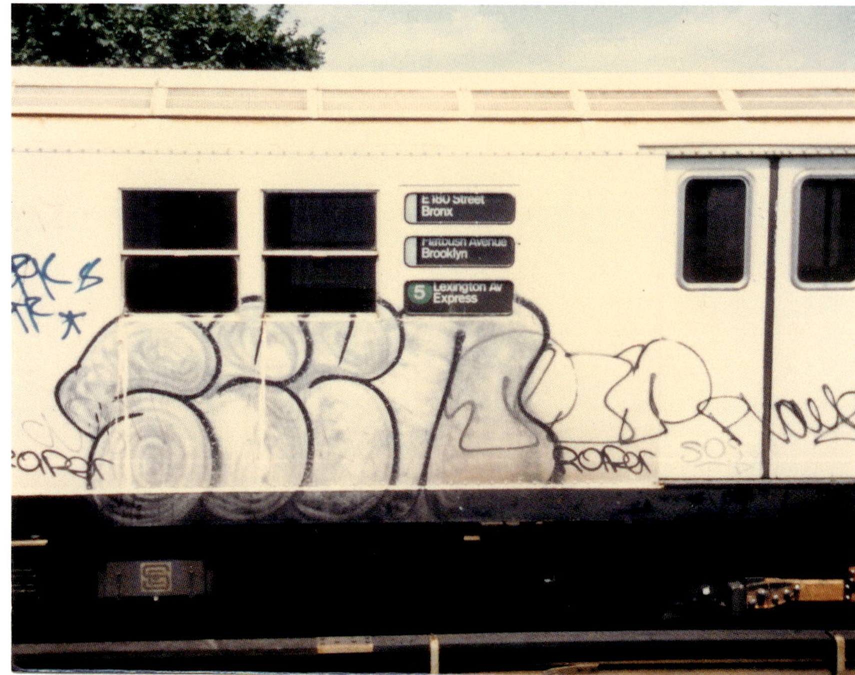
E 180 Street
Bronx
Flatbush Avenue
Brooklyn
5 Lexington Av
Express

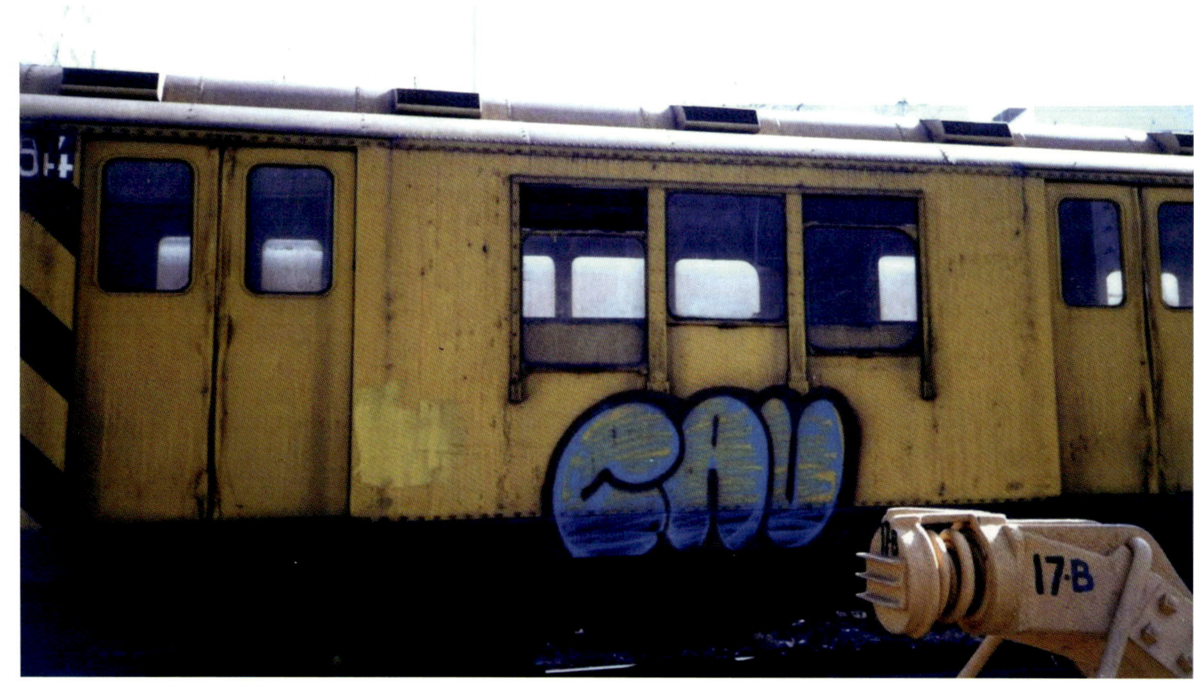
17-B

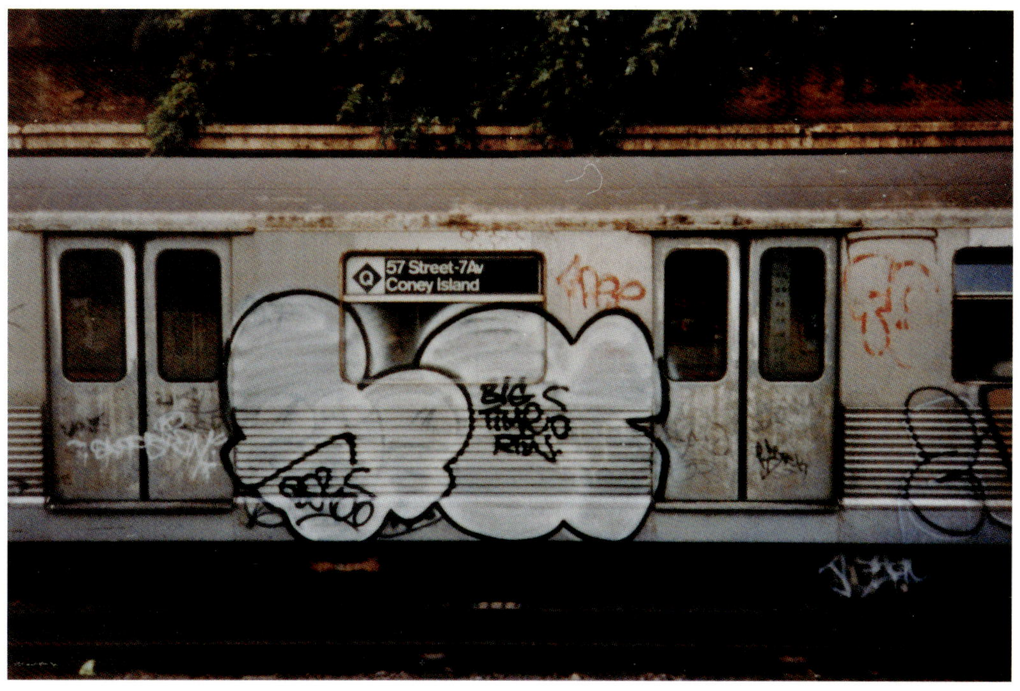

(Photo courtesy of Ven AOK)

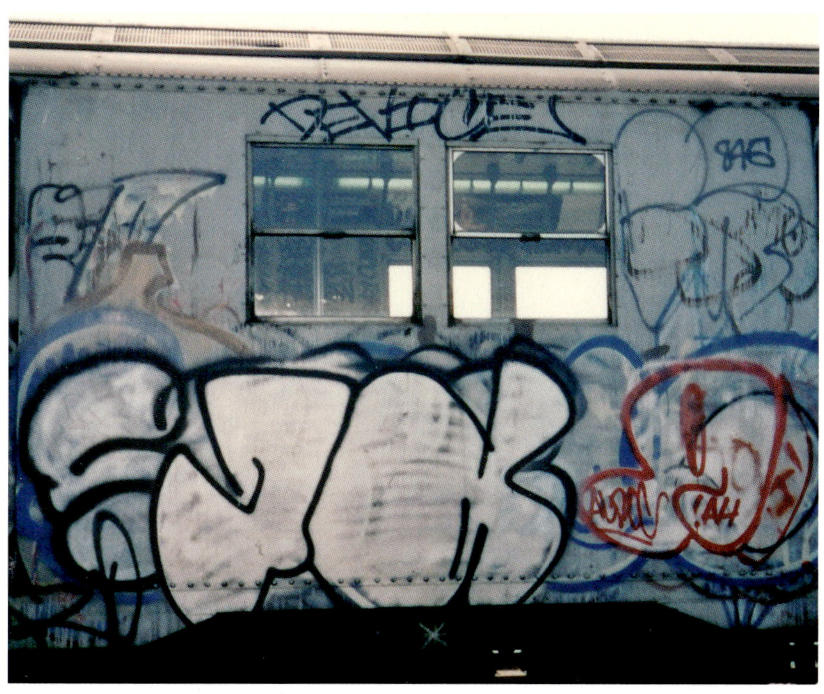

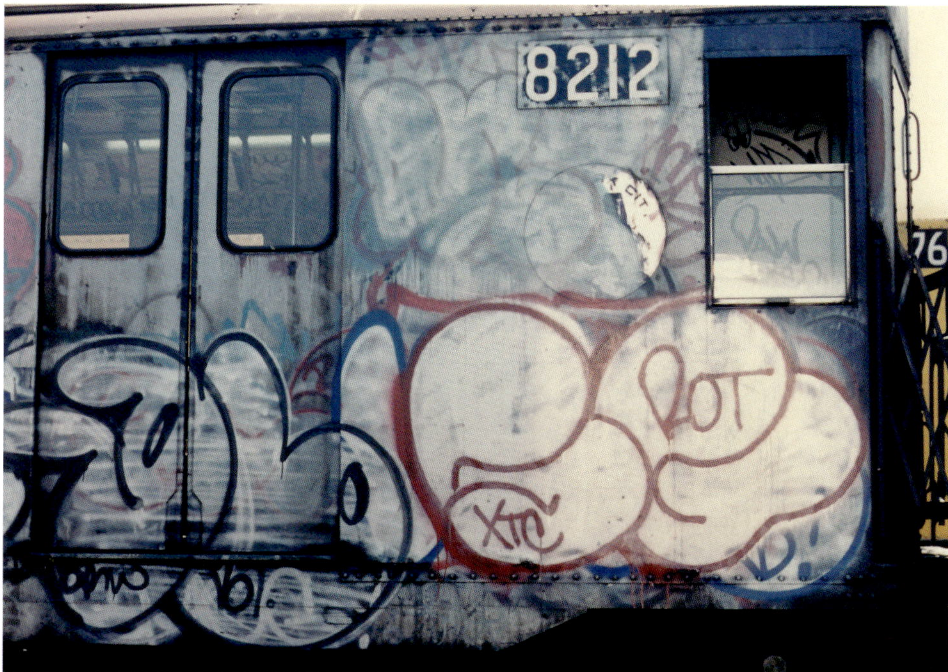

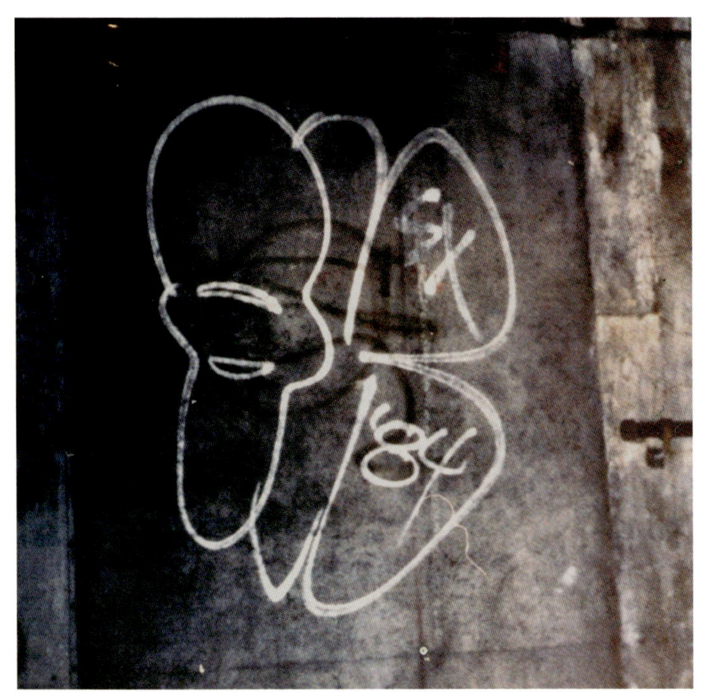
84

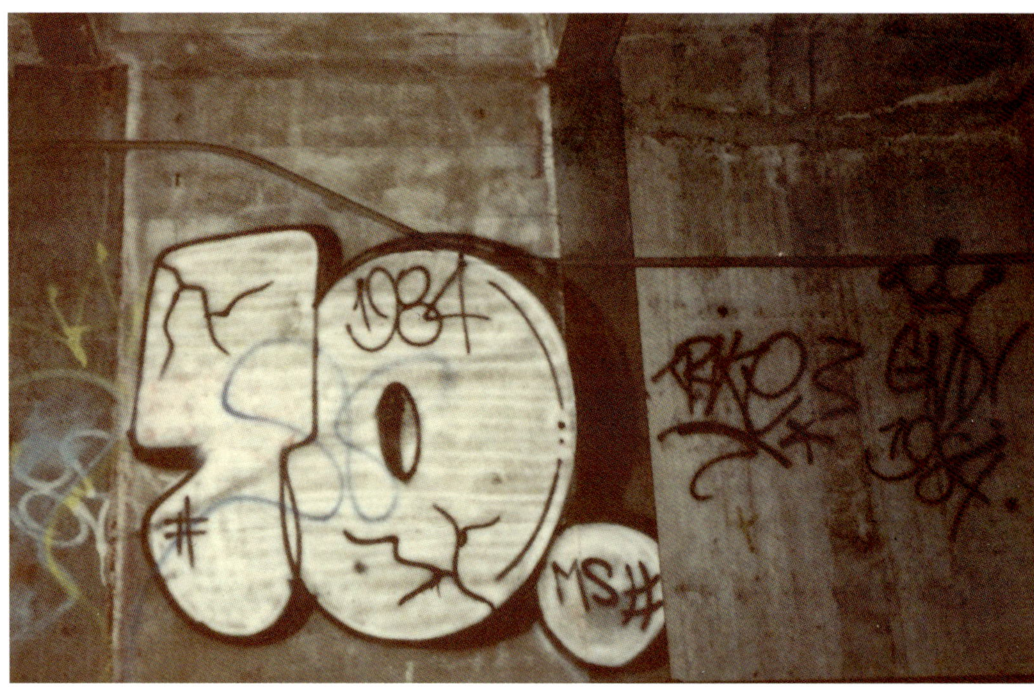
1984
MS

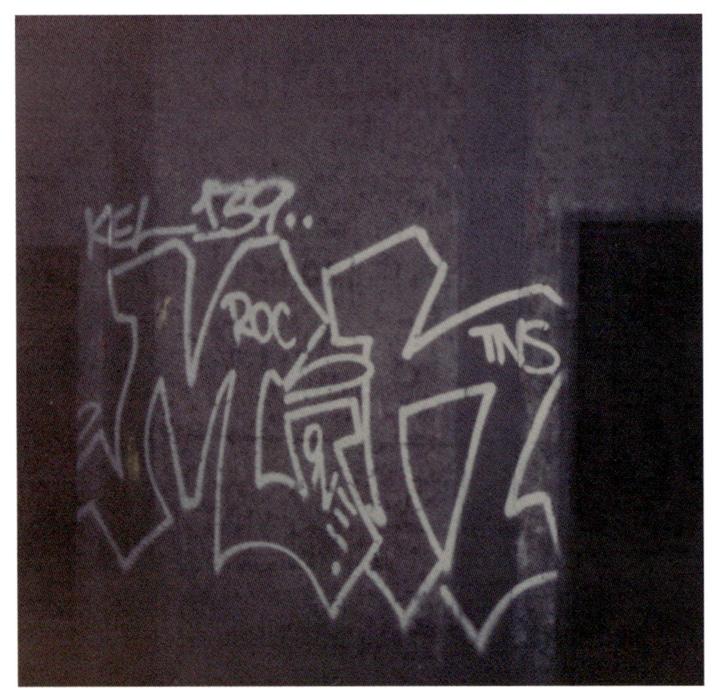
ROC
TNS

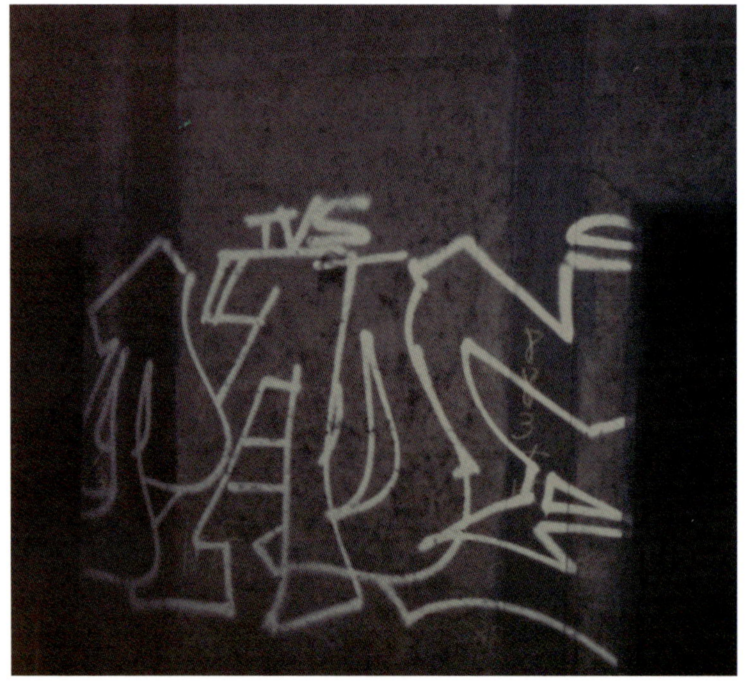
TVS

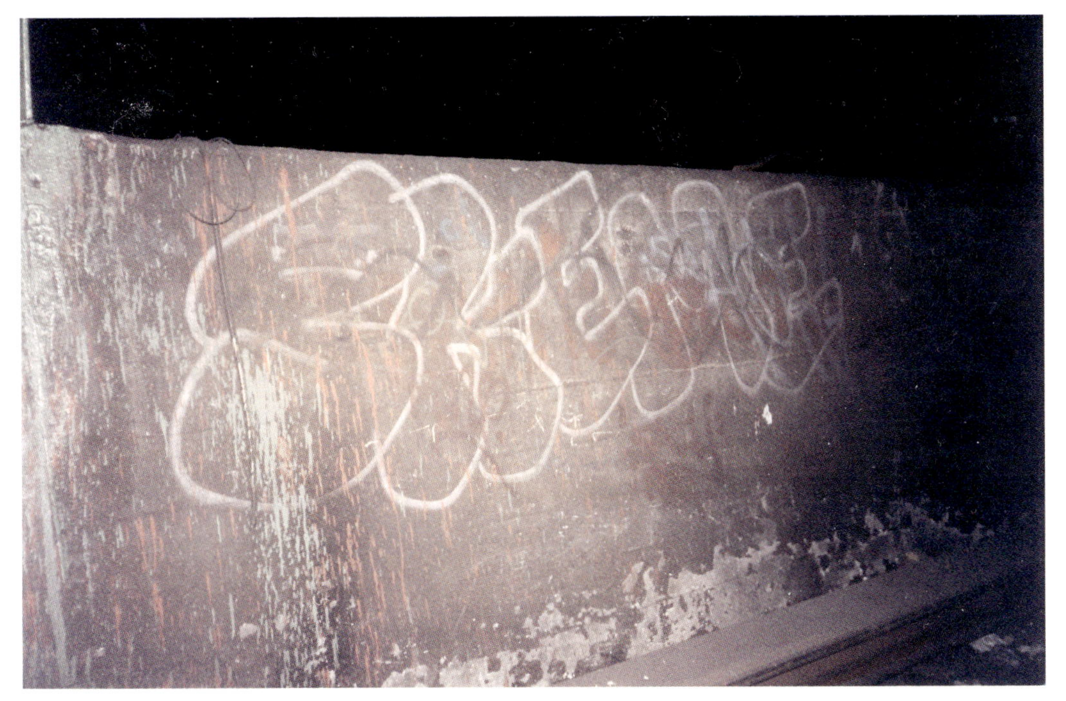

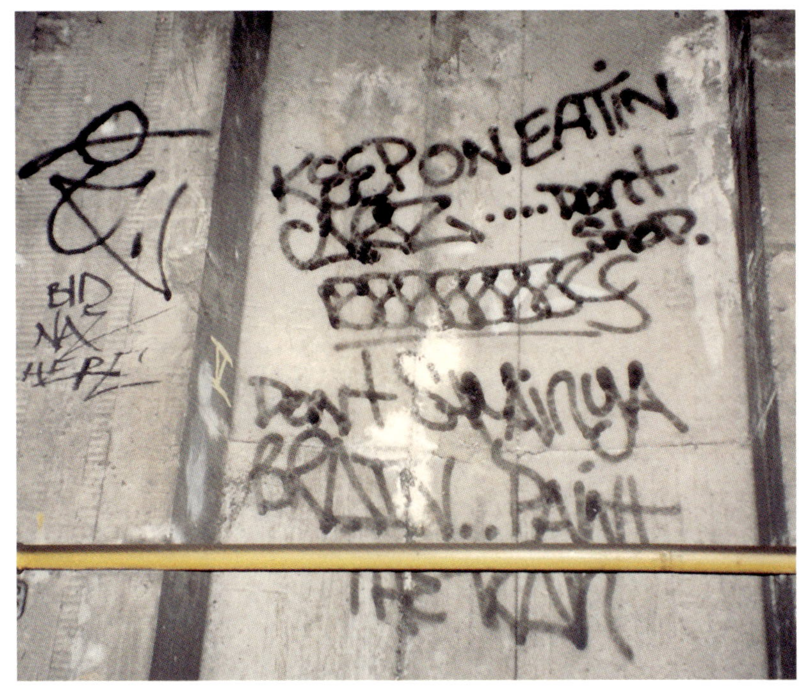
KEEP ON EATIN
...Don't stop.

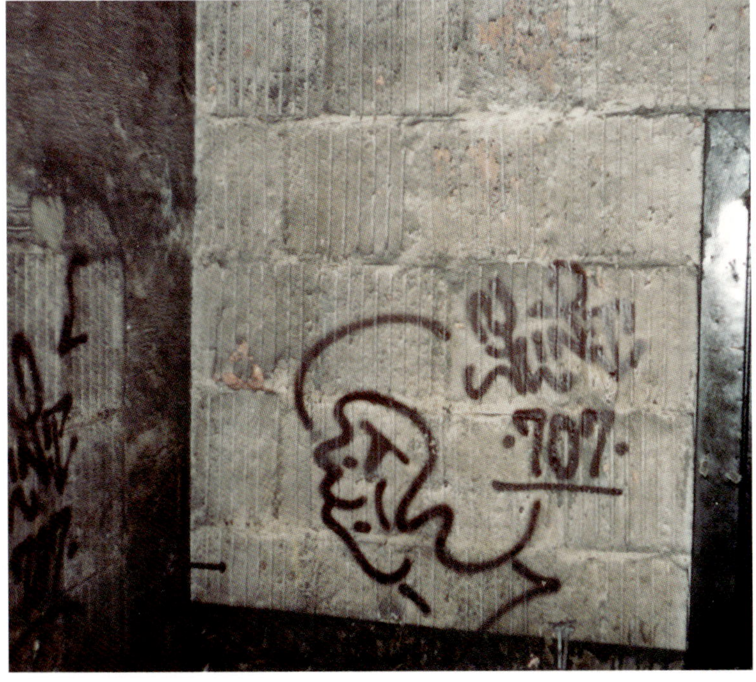
707

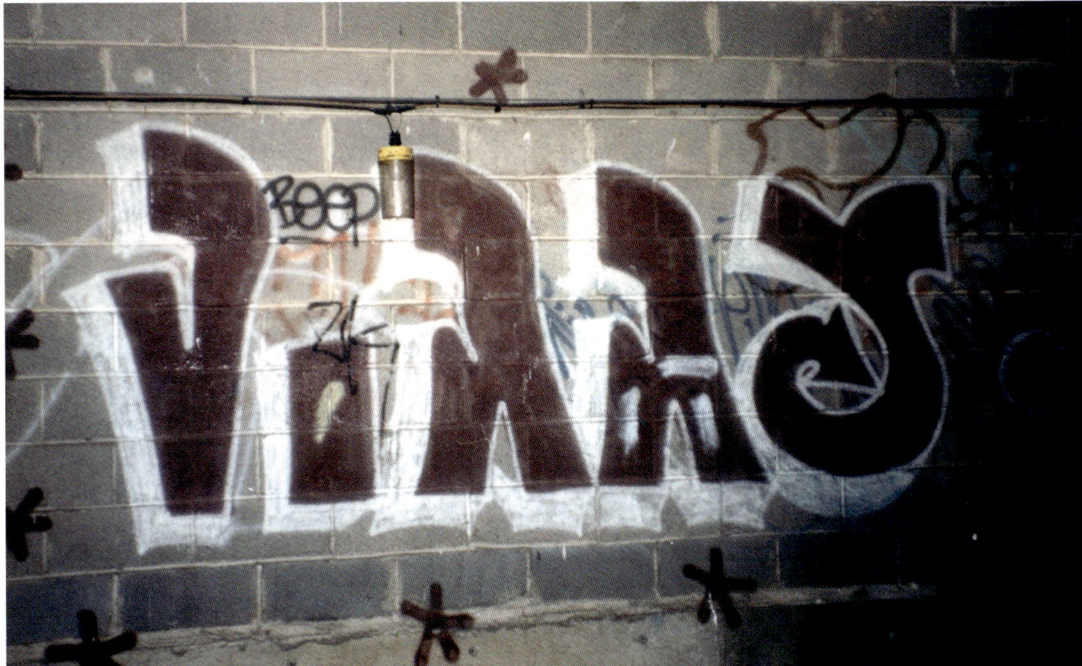

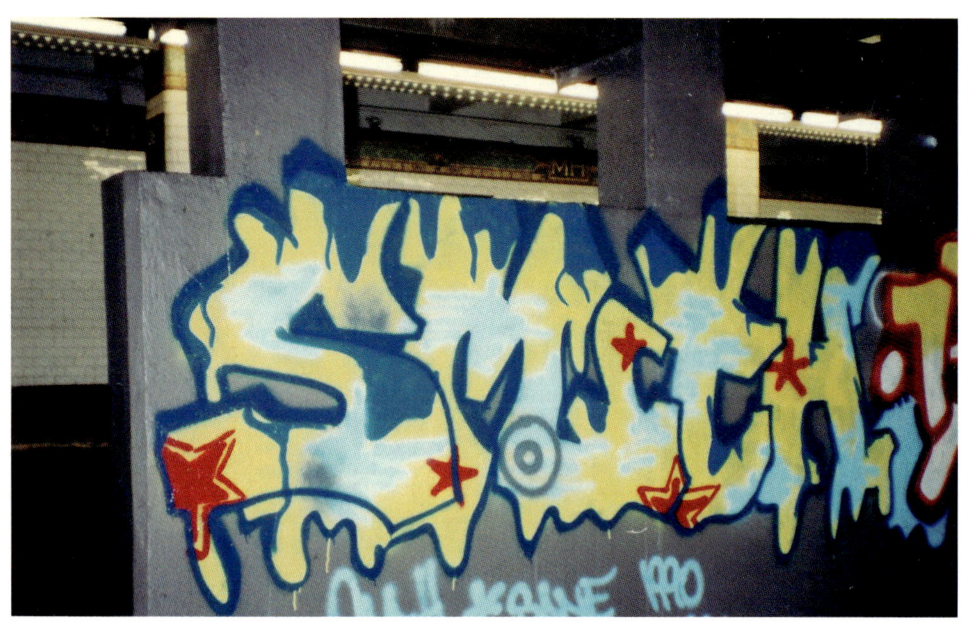

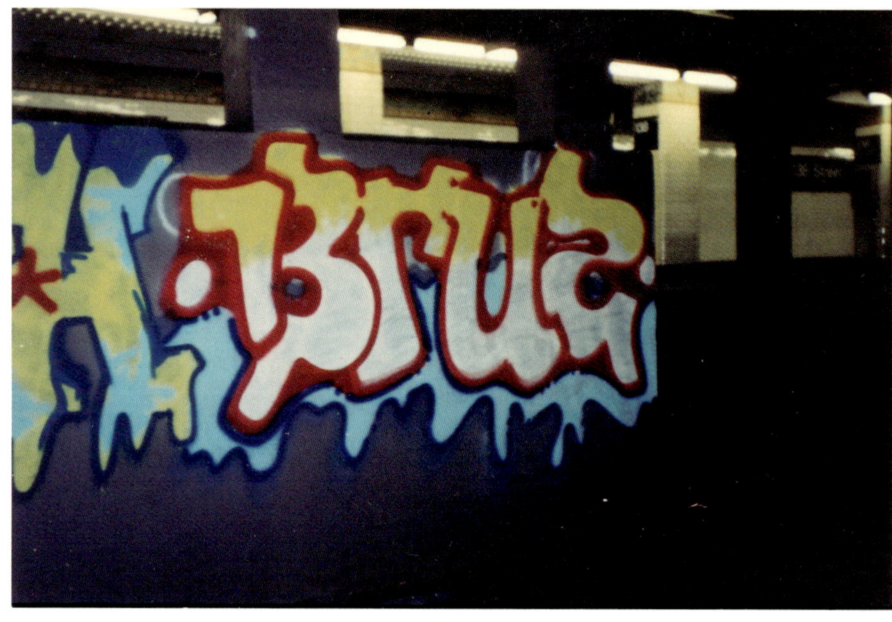

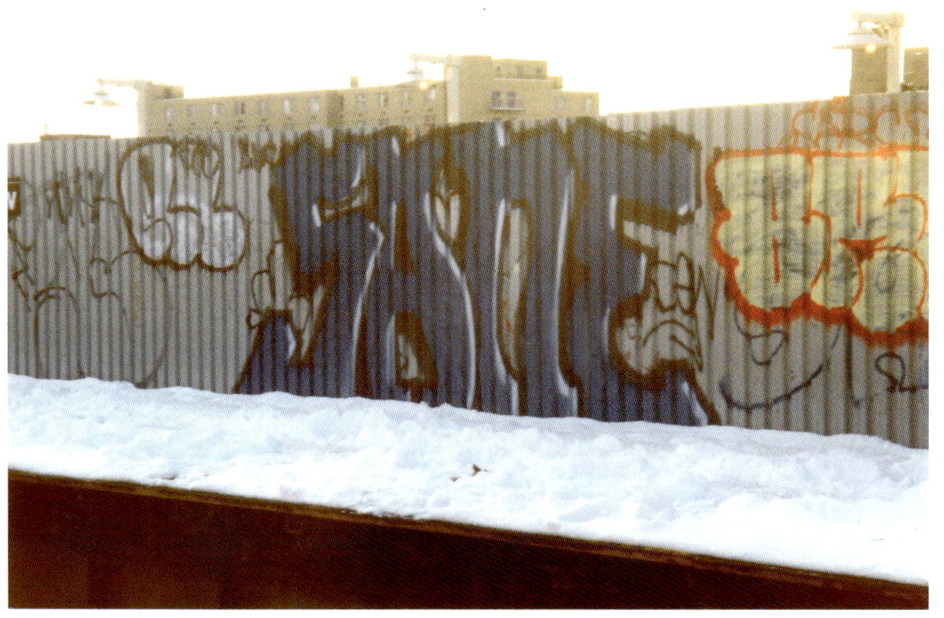

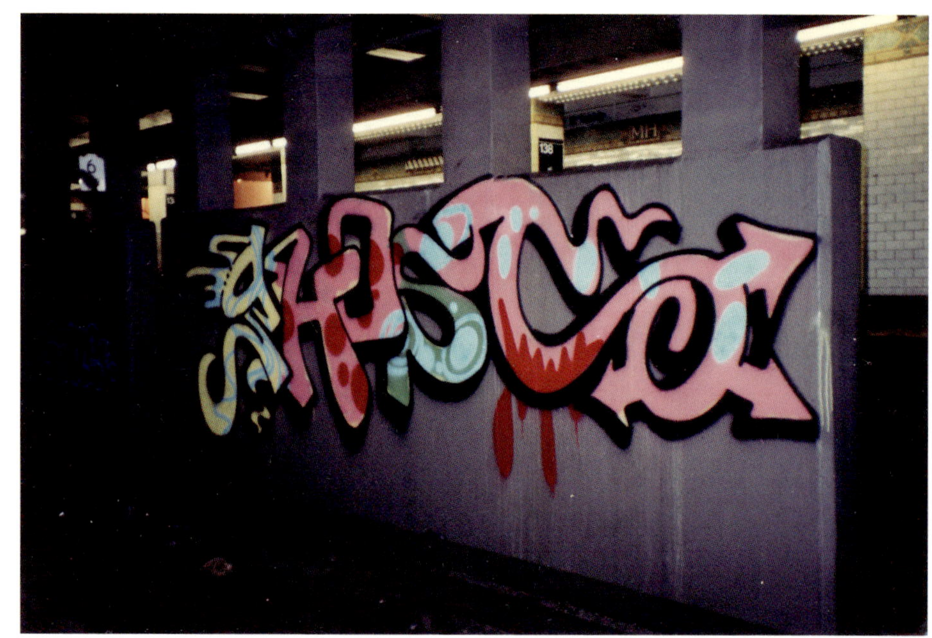

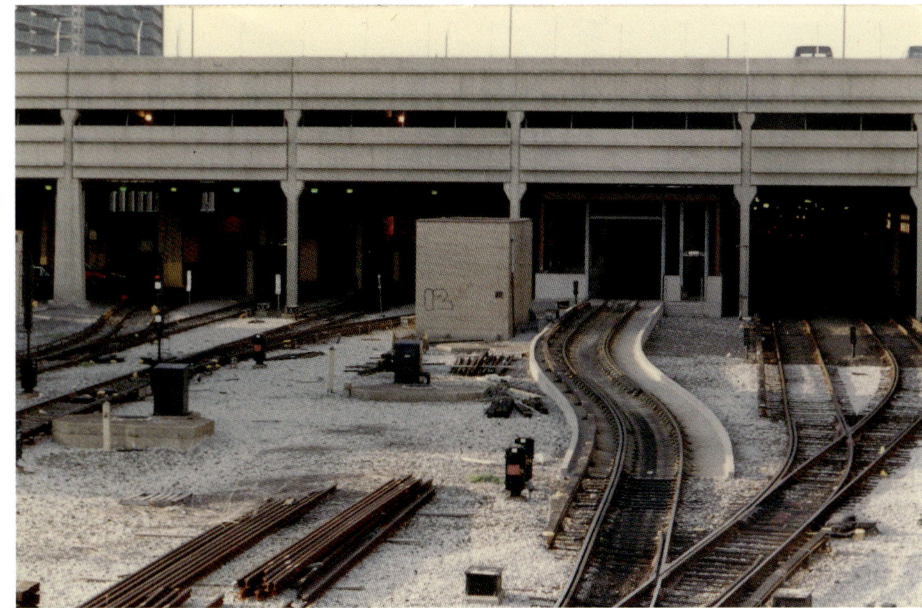

Pitkin Yard

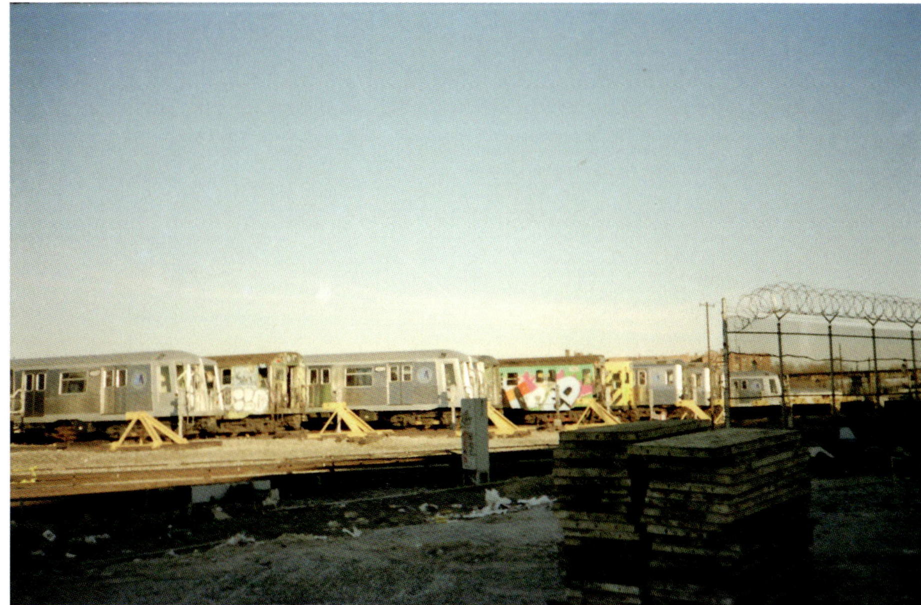

Coney Island Yard

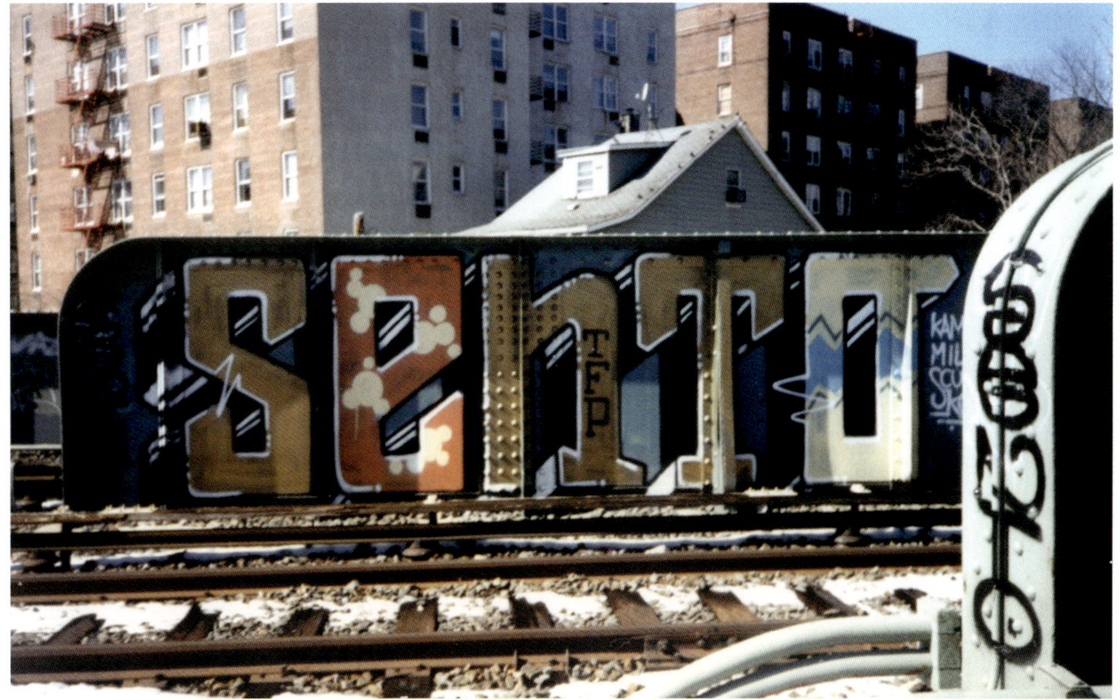

Esplanade stick outs

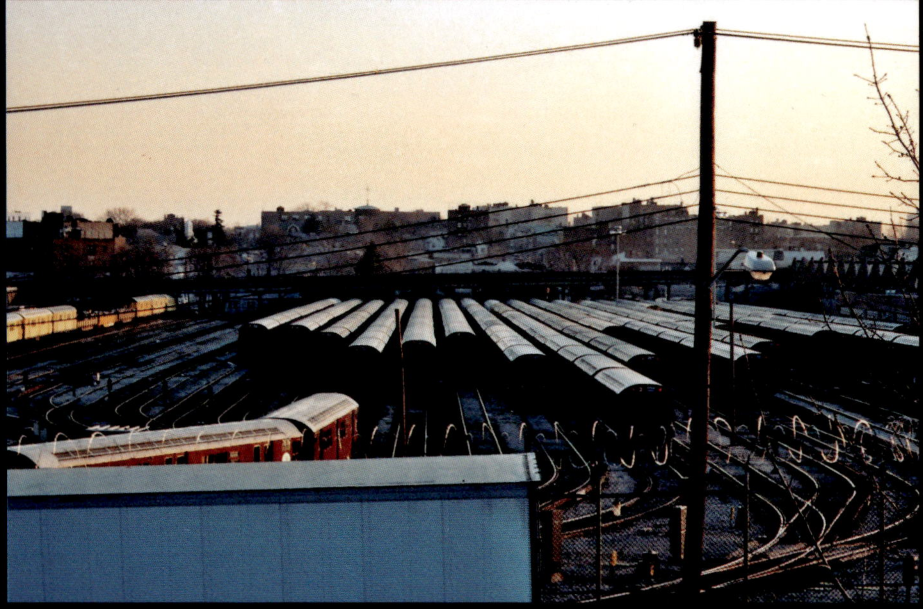
2 Yard (241st)

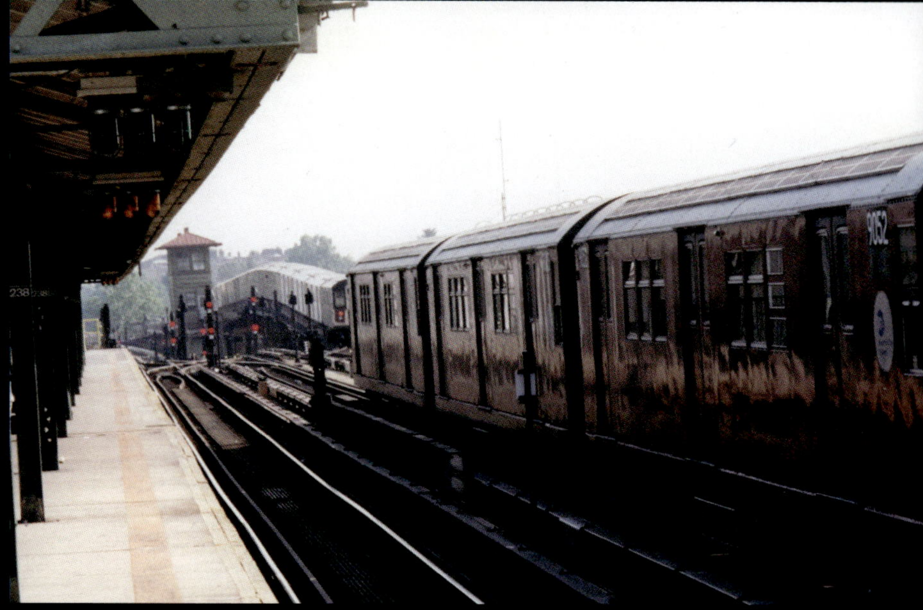

East 238th Street Train Station

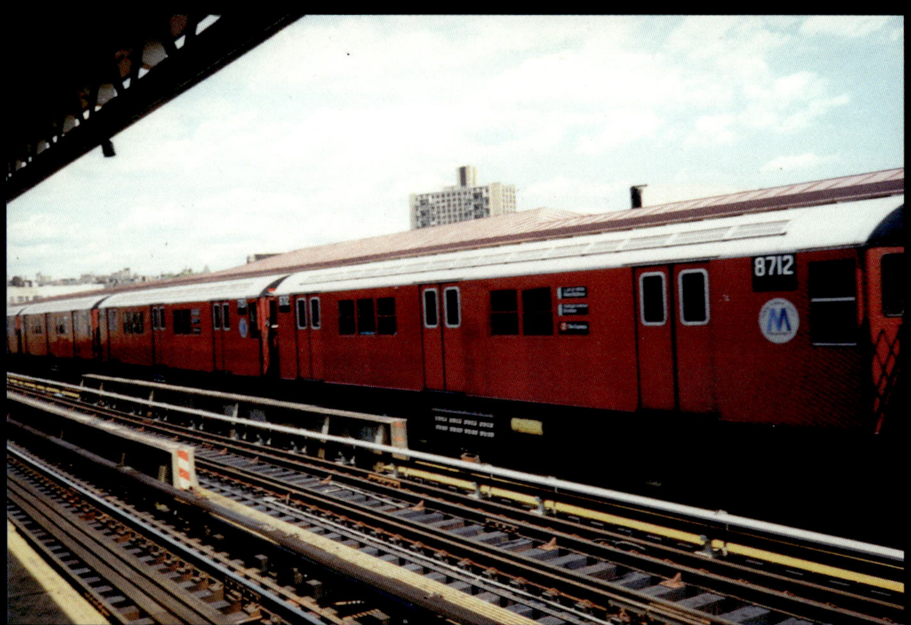

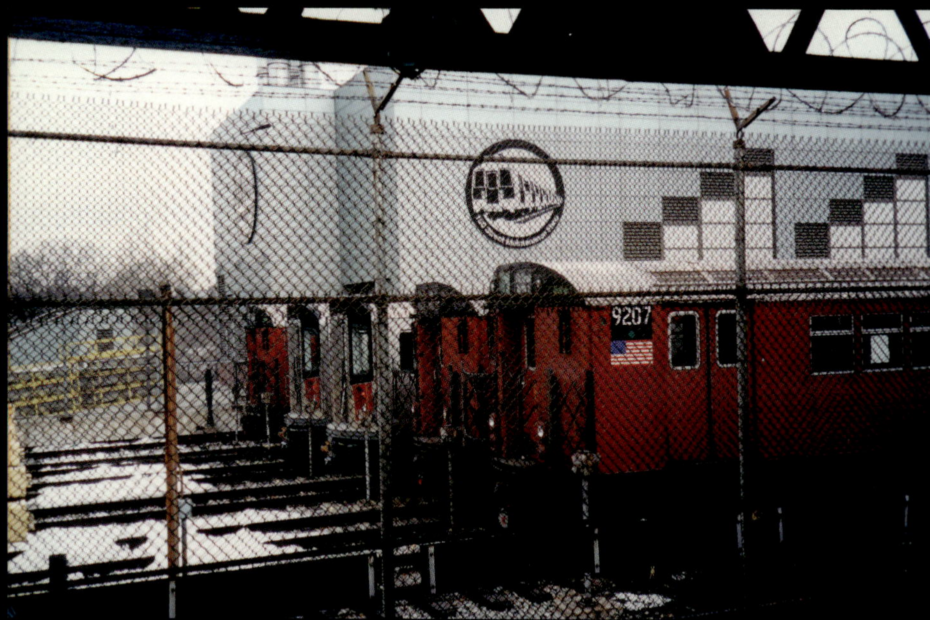

180th Yard

Redbird is the name given to 1,410 New York City Subway cars of the following types: R26, R28, R29, R33 Main Line (ML), R33 World's Fair (WF), R36 ML, and R36 WF. These cars were painted deep red to combat graffiti, which had become a major problem in the 1970s and 1980s. The deep red color was referred to as Gunn Red or ″Broad Street Red″ in honor of its originator David L. Gunn, the former SEPTA General Manager who became President of the New York City Transit Authority during this period. Initially entering service in various colors, these cars received the new paint scheme between 1984 and 1989. Sixteen R17s were also given this paint scheme in 1985–86, but were retired by 1988, well before the name ″Redbird″ caught on.

Most Redbirds were phased out from 2001 to 2003 and replaced by the new R142 and R142A cars. The final trip made by a train consisting of Redbirds was made on November 3, 2003 on the 7 line. 1,292 Redbirds have been sunk at sea off the coasts of Delaware (Redbird Reef), Georgia, New Jersey, South Carolina, and Virginia as artificial reefs to promote marine life, to serve as a barrier and to enhance recreational scuba diving by Weeks Marine Inc. An episode of *CSI: NY* titled "The Deep" used these cars as part of the story line, and even featured well-replicated underwater shots of mock ups of the cars. However, the show places them in New York City's East River. (Excerpted from Wikipedia)

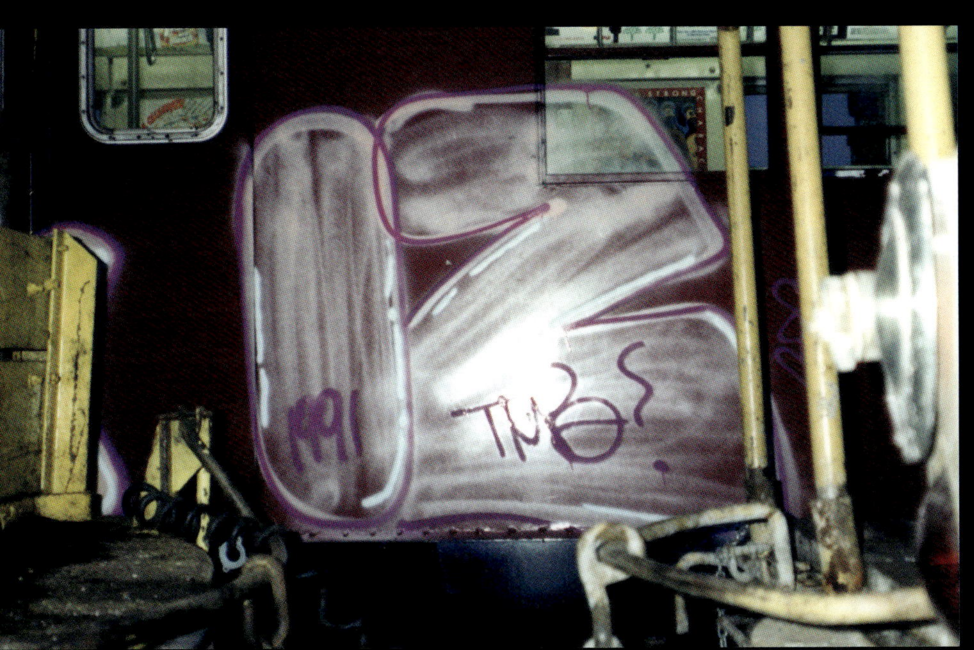

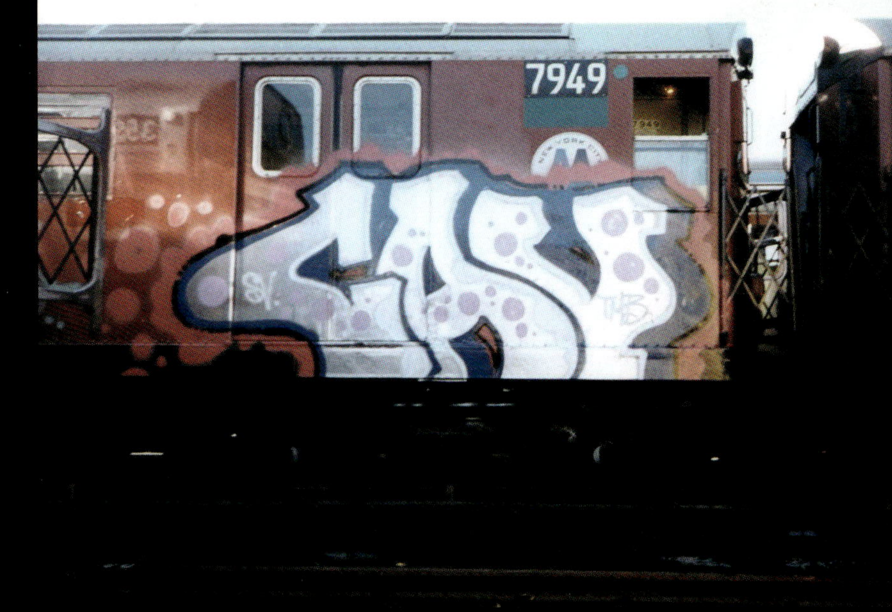

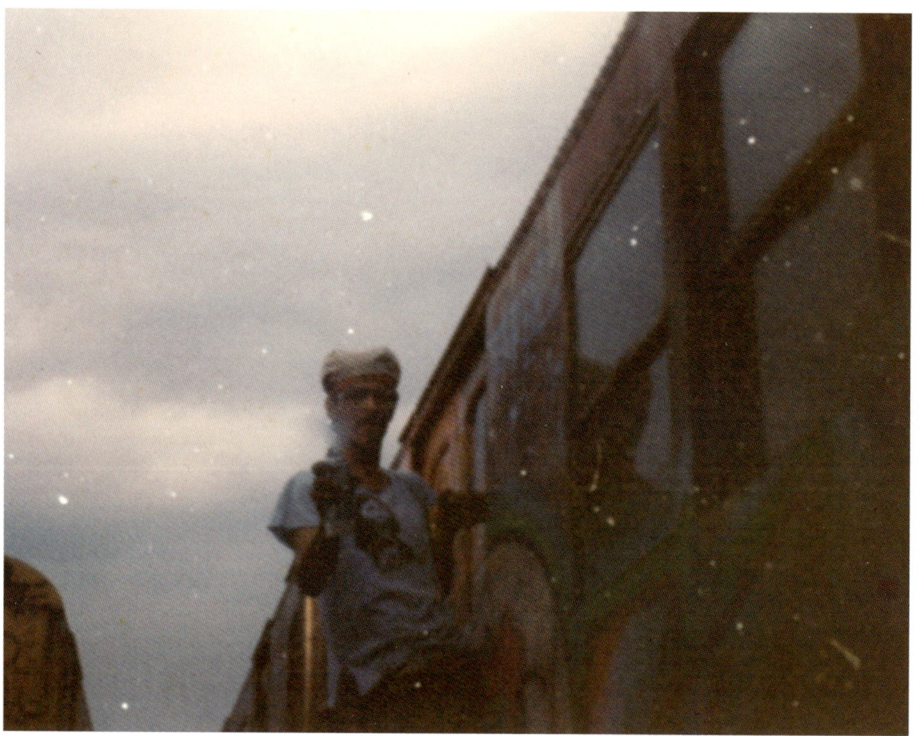

Tkid170th in the Ghost Yard, 1984

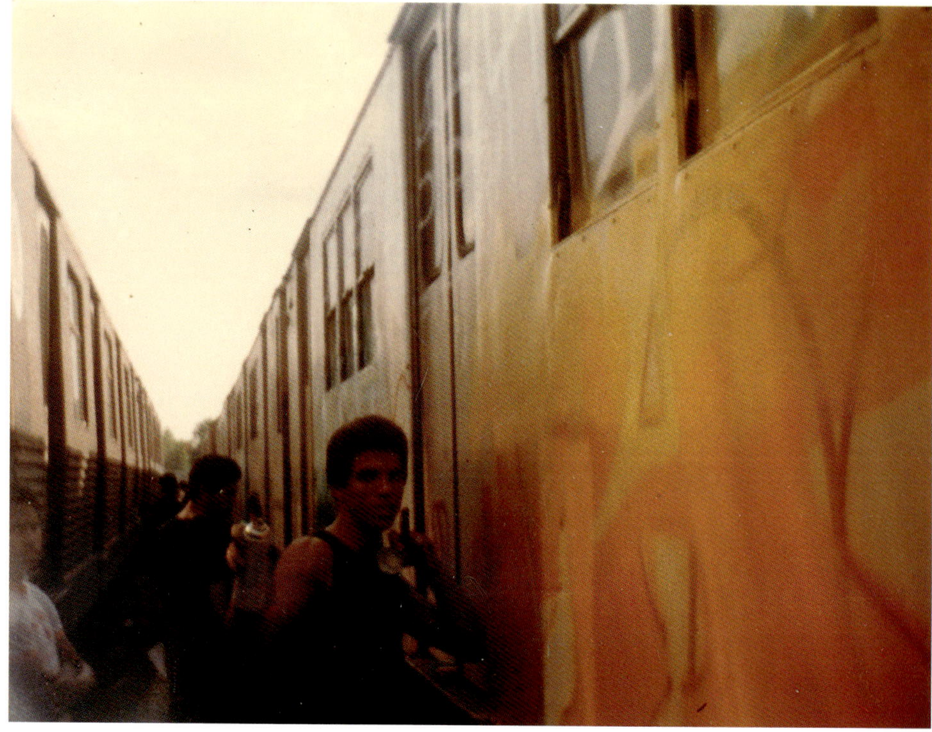

Mack in the Ghost Yard, 1984

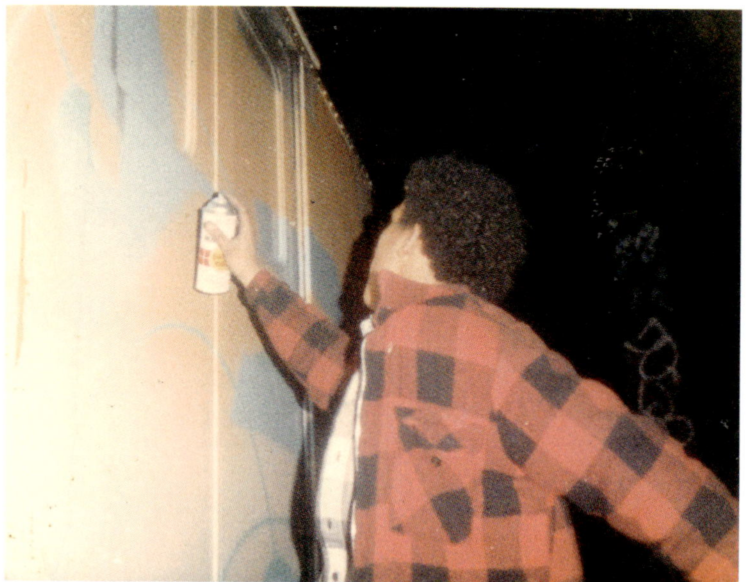

Raz, Esplanade Tunnels, 1985

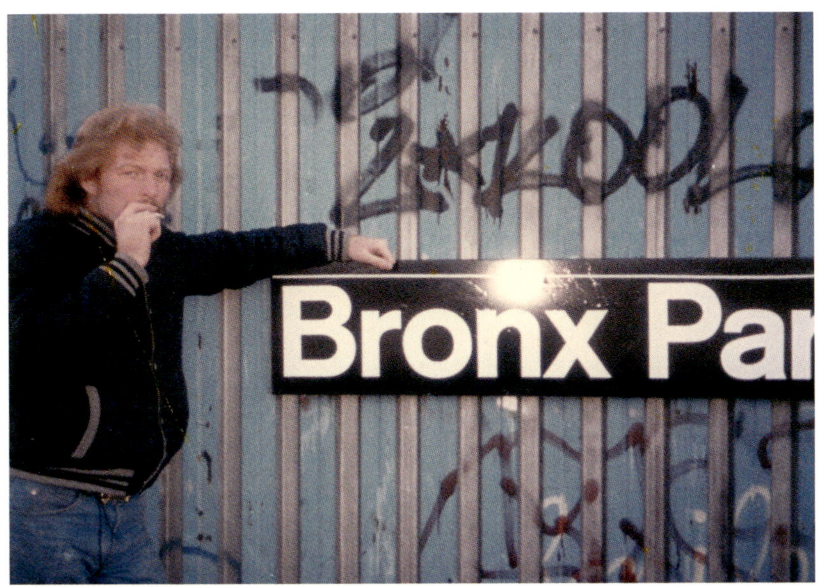

Cap MPC (Bronx Park East Train Station), 1984

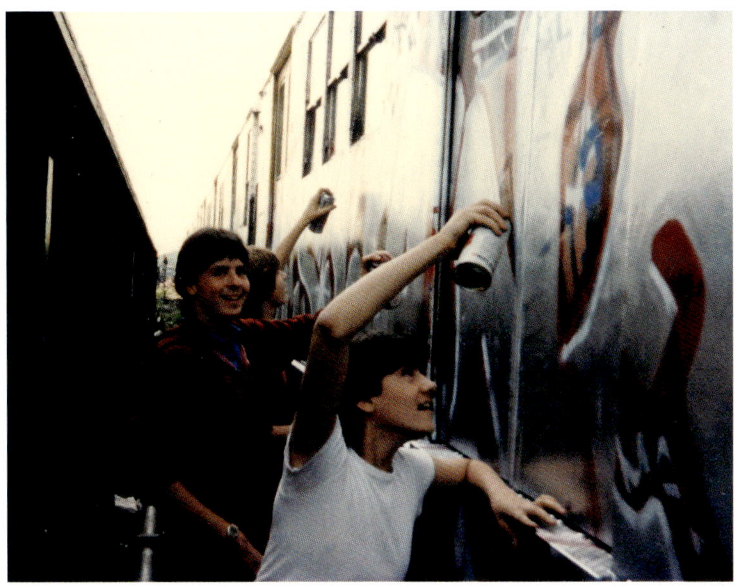
Echo, Key, and Paws (Esplanade stick outs), 1986

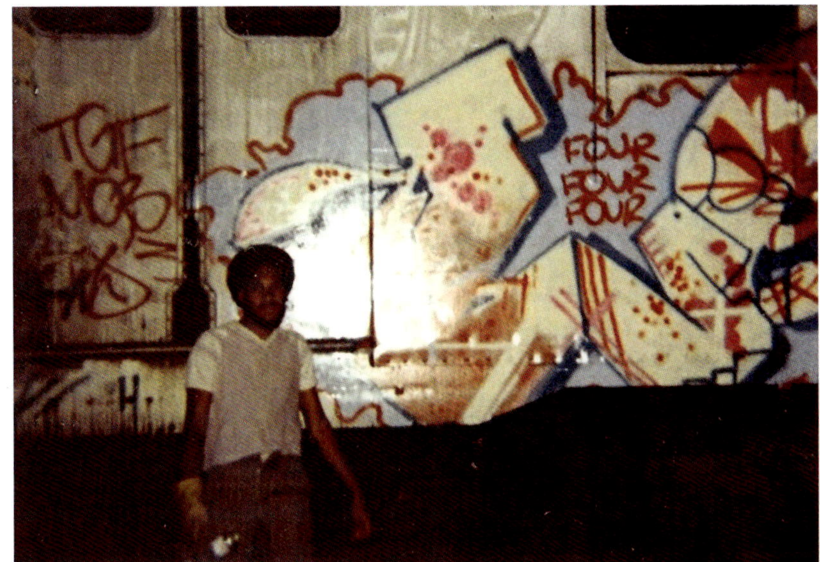

LM4

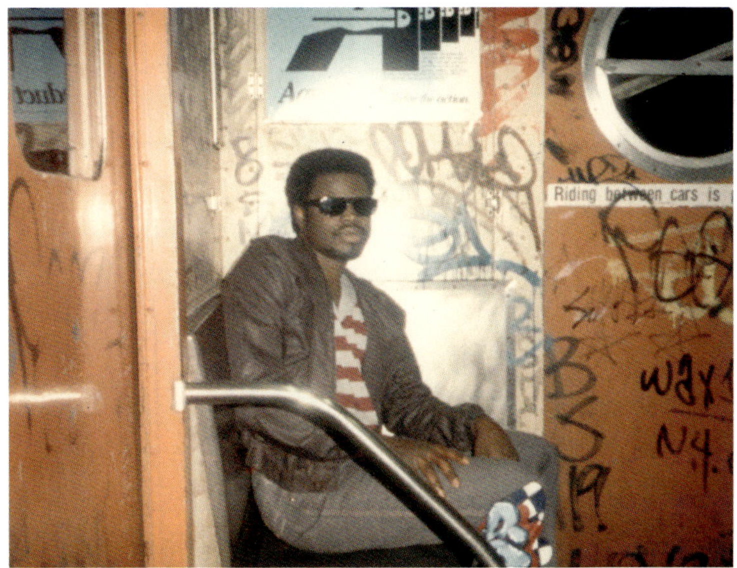
Chain3

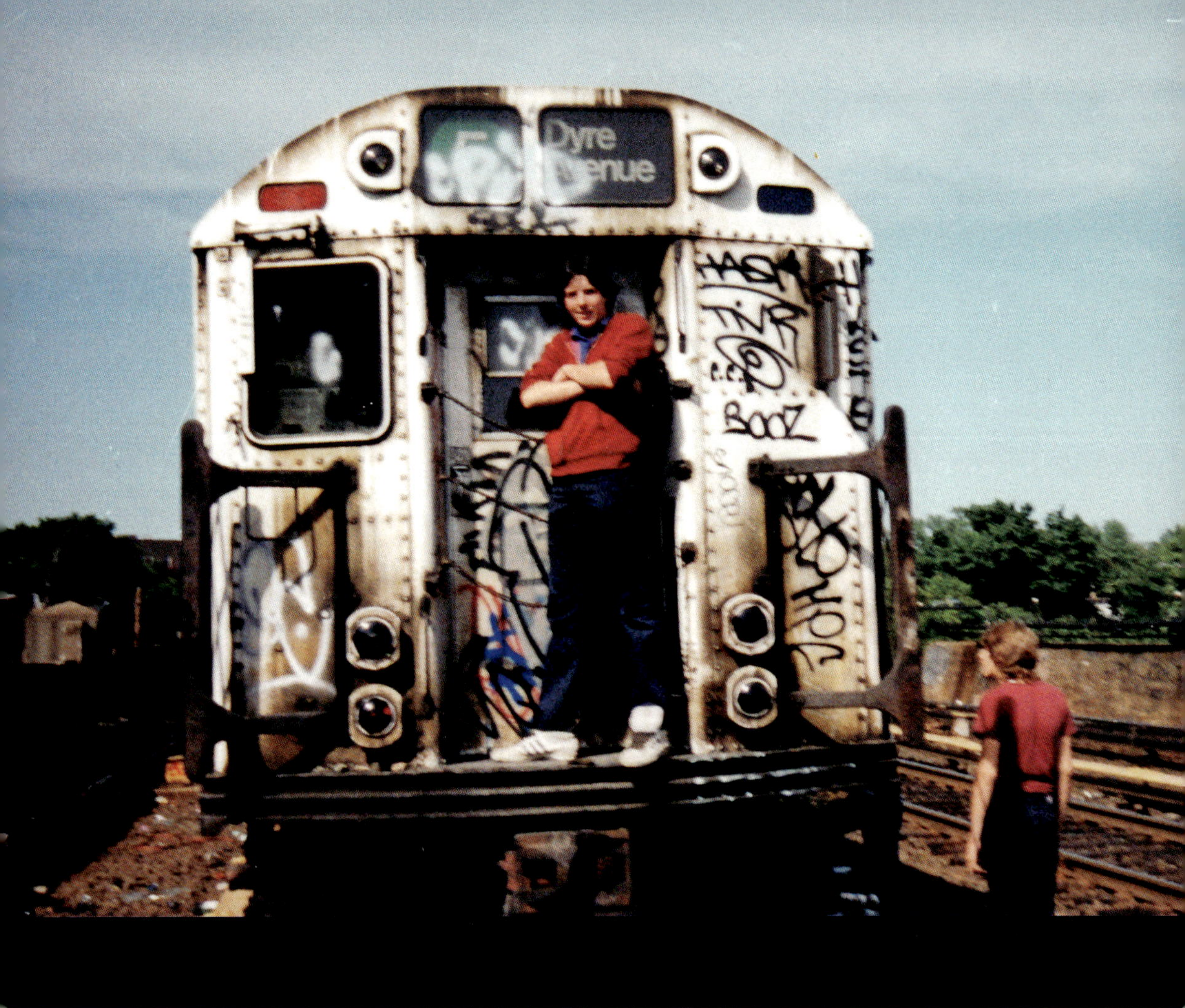

PHOTO CONTRIBUTORS:

Ozzie TGF, Ter3, Martha Cooper, Rolieo, Lace357, Tod Lange, Poes, Paul Iovino, Sento, Sak MBT, Seen UA, Kirs, Kkone, Gkay, Rob SOD, Sar TMB, Ven AOK, Poem, Yes2, and Ces

SPECIAL THANKS:

Henry Chalfant, Ozzie TGF, Mr.Edd, Cap MPC, Pove GU, Min RTW, Rolieo, Web, Med, Sak MBT, Lee TF5, Raz, Mack, Part TDS, Dez TFA, BG183, Bio, Sharp, Omni, Bind, Dero, Wen, Dome, Kaze, Kirs, Kkone, Lace357, Tekay, Neo, Smog ROT, Sear, Coal, Void, Poes, Seen UA, Sento, Gkay, and Chris217 AW

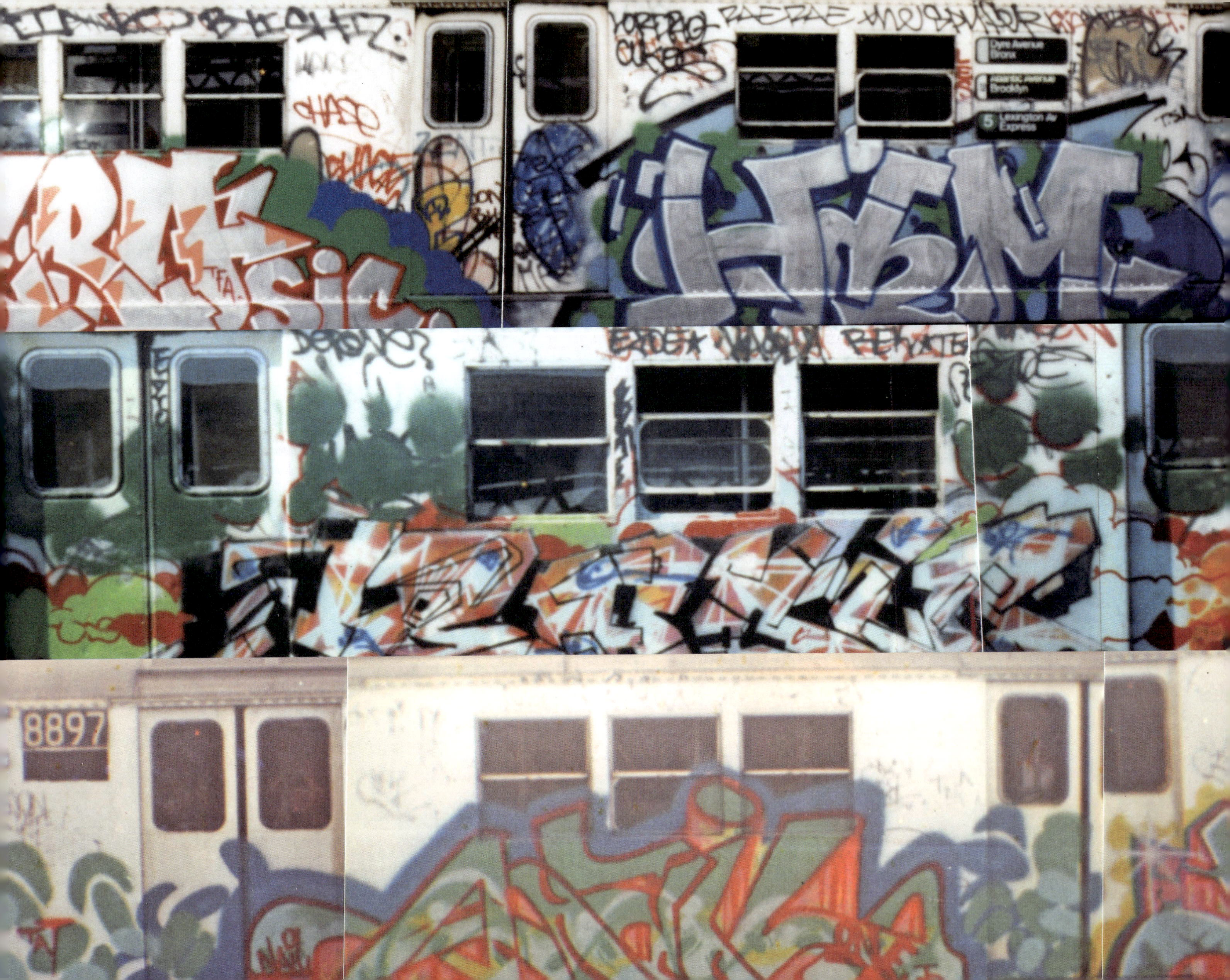
Dyre Avenue
Bronx
Atlantic Avenue
Brooklyn
5 Lexington Av
Express
8897